Press and Speech under Assault

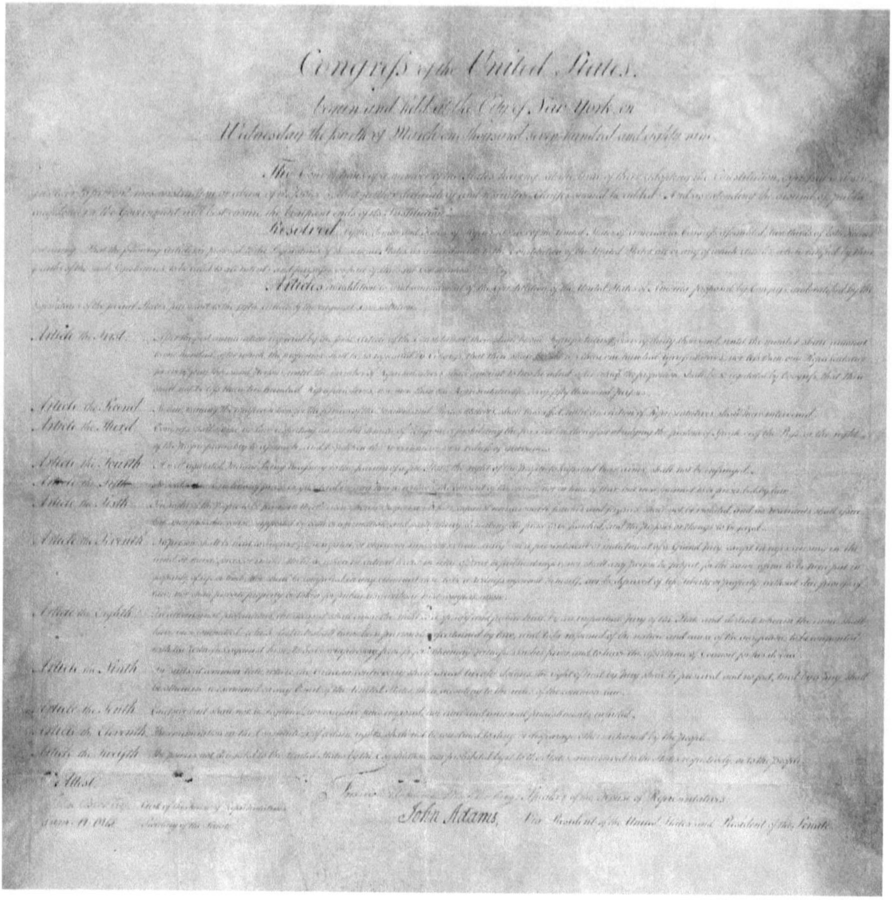

Congress of the United States,
begun and held at the City of New York, on
Wednesday the fourth of March one thousand seven hundred and eighty nine.

Resolved

Articles

John Adams,

Figure 0.0 United States Bill of Rights (engrossed version, 25 Sept. 1789). (Courtesy of National Archives.)

Press and Speech under Assault

The Early Supreme Court Justices, the Sedition Act of 1798, and the Campaign against Dissent

WENDELL BIRD

OXFORD
UNIVERSITY PRESS

OXFORD
UNIVERSITY PRESS

Oxford University Press is a department of the University of Oxford.
It furthers the University's objective of excellence in research, scholarship,
and education by publishing worldwide. Oxford is a registered trademark
of Oxford University Press in the UK and in certain other countries

Published in the United States of America by Oxford University Press
198 Madison Avenue, New York, NY 10016, United States of America

Library of Congress Cataloging-in-Publication Data
Bird, Wendell R., author.
Press and speech under assault : the early Supreme Court justices and the Sedition
Act of 1798 / by Wendell Bird.
p. cm.
ISBN 978–0–19–046162–1 (pbk. : alk. paper) — ISBN 978–0–19–046163–8 (ebook)
1. United States. Sedition Act of 1798. 2. Seditious libel—Law and legislation—United States.
—History—18th century. 3. Freedom of expression—United States.
—History—18th century. 4. Alien and Sedition laws, 1798. I. Title.
KF9397.A3281798B57 2016
345.73'0231—dc23
2015025447

To Julie
with Love

CONTENTS

PREFACE

> Almost any morning you open your daily paper you can see where some person somewhere in the world is on trial or has just been convicted of supposed disloyalty to a new group controlling the government. . . .
>
> —Justice Hugo Black, United States Supreme Court[1]

What do these recent news headlines have in common, other than being from a single month?[2]

Venezuela's Maduro Would Free Lopez if U.S. Freed Puerto Rican (4 Jan. 2015)

Bangladesh Clamps Down on Opposition Amid Violent Clashes (9 Jan. 2015)

Saudi Arabia Increases Jail Sentence for Human Rights Lawyer (13 Jan. 2015)

Turkish Court Bans Websites Publishing Charlie Hebdo Cover (14 Jan. 2015)

China 'Has the Power' to Introduce Tough Security Laws in Hong Kong (20 Jan. 2015)

South Korea Supreme Court Upholds Sedition Ruling Against Ex-MP (22 Jan. 2015)

Egypt Appeals Court Orders Retrial in Case of Al Jazeera Journalists (1 Jan. 2015)

U.S. Rebukes Saudis for Sentencing Blogger to 1,000 Lashes (8 Jan. 2015)

Cuba Frees Political Prisoners in U.S. Deal (9 Jan. 2015)

German Man Arrested on Terror Charges (10 Jan. 2015)

Cartoonist Says India's Condemnation of Paris Attacks Is Hypocritical (12 Jan. 2015)

Bangladesh Files Sedition Charges Against Opposition Leader (12 Jan. 2015)

[1] Hugo L. Black, *The Bill of Rights*, 35 N.Y.U.L. Rev. 865, 880 (1960).

[2] The first six appeared in the *New York Times*, and the rest in the *Wall Street Journal*.

South Korea Arrests Government Critic Suspected of Breaking National Security Law (13 Jan. 2015)

Asia's Political Cartoonists at Risk (13 Jan. 2015)

French Comedian Faces Trial Over Online Comments (14 Jan. 2015)

Former South Korean Lawmaker's Treason Conviction Upheld (22 Jan. 2015)

Exploiting Terrorism as a Pretext for Repression (27 Jan. 2015)

Criminal Speech? The Weibo Posts That Could Send Chinese Lawyer Pu Zhiqiang to Prison (28 Jan. 2015)

These and other articles, appearing nearly daily somewhere in the world, involve the "crime" of criticizing government or governmental officials—seditious libel or seditious words. Most Americans—including most American lawyers—are surprised to learn that this is a crime in most other countries, including those reported on in the headlines above, and that it was a crime in the United States until 1964 or later.

Seditious libel finally was treated as unenforceable, though not necessarily unconstitutional, in the United States in 1964 because of the First Amendment's protection of freedoms of speech and press. Before, it posed a high barrier to full exercise of freedoms of speech and press, as the Sedition Act crisis showed during 1798–1801. When the First Amendment was written in 1789 and ratified during 1789–1791, Blackstone's *Commentaries on the Laws of England* and many individuals claimed that freedoms of press and speech only meant freedom from licensing, not freedom from prosecution for seditious libel. Many scholars have asserted that the First Amendment freedoms meant nothing more than that.

What was the prevailing view on the breadth of freedoms of press and speech in 1789–1791? What were the views of the early Supreme Court justices on the scope of the First Amendment, around 1789 and when some of them held court during prosecutions under the Sedition Act of 1798? How broad are that Amendment's protections of press and speech? That is the subject of this book.

ACKNOWLEDGMENTS

I am deeply indebted to a number of people for their assistance with this book, though I alone bear responsibility for errors.

Profound gratitude is owed particularly to Dr. Michael R. T. Macnair, professor of law at University of Oxford, who supervised my D. Phil. thesis in legal history and provided invaluable guidance peppered with vital comments. My deepest thanks also are extended to the examiners, Dr. Joshua Getzler, also a professor of law at Oxford, and Dr. Michael Lobban, professor of legal history at London School of Economics. The Bodleian Libraries at Oxford were ever helpful, particularly the Law, Vere Harmsworth, and History Faculty Libraries and the Radcliffe Camera, along with the All Souls and Oriel College Libraries.

Emory University School of Law has graciously enabled me to continue research as a Visiting Scholar. The libraries at Emory have provided assistance far beyond the call of duty.

Many undergraduate and law school professors have provided critical training, though not necessarily sharing my views, including particularly Dr. Samuel T. McSeveney in history at Vanderbilt University, and Dr. Kermit L. Hall, then there; and Professor Charles M. Gray, then at Yale Law School.

A number of manuscript collections and libraries have been very helpful in my quests to read all surviving letters, essays, opinions, and other papers and writings of all of the first twelve justices of the Supreme Court, and to review all the court files for the prosecutions under the Sedition Act. My deep gratitude is expressed to the archive staffs of Library of Congress' Manuscript Division, National Archives (the national office and many regions), New York Public Library's Manuscripts and Archives Division, Duke University's Perkins Library Special Collections, Harvard Law School Library, Mount Vernon Library, North Carolina State Archives' Manuscript Department, Rutgers University's Special Collections, South Carolina Historical Society, and University of North Carolina's Southern Historical Collection Manuscripts Department; as well as to the archive staffs of College of Charleston Library, Charleston Library Society, Haverford College's Magill Library, Historical

Society of Pennsylvania, Massachusetts Historical Society, Maryland Historical Society, Maryland State Archives, New Jersey Historical Society, Peabody Essex Museum, Swarthmore College's Friends Historical Library, South Carolina Department of Archives and History, Tennessee State Library and Archives, University of South Carolina's South Caroliniana Library, Yale University Library's Manuscripts and Archives, and others too numerous to mention; and also to the compilers at Columbia University Library of the Papers of John Jay.

A number of individuals have helped me in locating and copying archival records. My appreciation is great for Laura Ruttum at the New York Public Library's Manuscripts and Archives Division, Vincent McGrath at the Tennessee State Library and Archives, Andrew Pierce in Massachusetts, Risher Fairey in South Carolina, and others at the various other archives.

Material from the *Documentary History of the Supreme Court* is reprinted with agreement from the publisher, Columbia University Press. Insert the following text as new paragraph after last line:

Illustrations on the cover are from the following sources: Chief Justice John Jay portrait by Gilbert Stuart 1794 (courtesy of National Gallery of Art); Chief Justice Oliver Ellsworth portrait by John Trumbull 1792 (courtesy of Yale University Art Gallery); Chief Justice John Rutledge portrait by John Trumbull 1791 (courtesy of Yale University Art Gallery); Justice William Cushing portrait by James Sharples 1797 (courtesy of Independence National Historic Park); Justice James Wilson watercolor on ivory by Jean Pierre Henri Elouis 1792 (courtesy of Smithsonian American Art Museum/Art Resource); Justice John Blair portrait by Charles Willson Peale (courtesy of United States Supreme Court); Justice James Iredell portrait (courtesy of James Iredell Historic Association); Justice Thomas Johnson portrait (detail) by Raymond Chard 1926 (courtesy of Collection of Maryland State Archives); Justice William Paterson portrait by James Sharples ante 1811 (courtesy of Princeton University Art Museum/Art Resource); Justice Samuel Chase portrait by John Wesley Jarvis 1811 (courtesy of National Portrait Gallery, Smithsonian Institution/Art Resource); Justice Bushrod Washington portrait by unidentified artist (courtesy of United States Supreme Court); Justice Alfred Moore portrait (courtesy of United States Supreme Court).

INTRODUCTION

> "Rights" obviously lay at the heart of the Anglo-American controversy: the rights of Englishmen, the rights of mankind, chartered rights.
>
> —Bernard Bailyn[1]

Sir William Blackstone summarized the common law of freedoms of press and speech, in his *Commentaries*, and the common law provided that those freedoms meant only liberty from prior restraints on publishing, and not liberty from criminal punishment after publishing such things as criticism of government. The Framers of the Constitution adopted that narrow view and opposed a Bill of Rights, and no one at the time questioned that criticism of government was criminalized as seditious libel.[2] The early Supreme Court justices, because they were all Federalists, said nothing about freedoms of press and speech before the 1798 crisis, being indifferent or hostile. Those justices and Federalists generally followed the narrow Blackstone definition and unanimously supported the Sedition Act of 1798. The Sedition Act was enforced by fourteen prosecutions (in addition to three prosecutions under federal common law for seditious libel). The Virginia and Kentucky Resolutions opposing the Sedition Act were opposed by all the other states, and were unable to attract any other state's support.

That is a major part of the typical textbook history of the First Amendment, the early Supreme Court, and the Federalists in the 1790s. *And that is all false.*

To the contrary, Blackstone did not summarize the English common law liberty of press and speech when he wrote in 1769—instead he created a new restrictive doctrine that was only adopted into the English common law the *next* year, in 1770. He acknowledged that there were other views besides his restrictive doctrine. In fact, long before 1769, some saw freedoms of press and speech as protections from not just prior

[1] Bernard Bailyn, Ideological Origins of the American Revolution 307 (enl. ed., HUP, Cambridge 1992).

[2] Defined as "the intentional publication of a writing that 'scandalized' the government, that is, tended to bring it into disesteem." Green 40; *accord* Hamburger 725–26, 762; OCSC 765. A list of abbreviated titles is at the end of this book.

restraints but from subsequent punishments such as seditious libel prosecution. The early Supreme Court justices were not indifferent, much less antagonistic—instead they were all supportive toward freedoms of press and speech before the Sedition Act of 1798 (which criminalized seditious libel, particularly criticism of government and its officials). The Federalist Party did not unanimously support the Sedition Act—instead a significant minority opposed it. The Federalist justices of the early Supreme Court did not uniformly find that Act constitutional—instead they divided over the question. There were not just fourteen prosecutions under the Sedition Act—there were eleven additional cases prosecuting sixteen more defendants for seditious writings and words, and eleven additional cases prosecuting eighty-three more defendants for seditious combinations and conspiracies, in addition to several attempted indictments and several instructions to prosecute. The other states did not all reject the Virginia and Kentucky Resolutions and their condemnation of the Sedition Act—only half did while some supported the resolutions, some deadlocked, and some chose not to take positions.

That is the subject of this book. It is a new examination of what freedoms of press and speech meant in the common law in 1769–1770, when Blackstone published his fourth volume and Lord Chief Justice Mansfield adopted his narrow doctrine, and through 1789–1791, when the First Amendment was ratified. It is a first discussion of the unexplored terrain of what the twelve pre-Marshall justices of the Supreme Court believed those freedoms meant before the crisis of 1798. It is the first close scrutiny of how three justices dealt with the First Amendment and the Sedition Act of 1798 during trials under it, and the first analysis of what the remaining nine early justices thought about that epochal First Amendment controversy. It is the first corroboration of an unrecognized half of the Sedition Act prosecutions. And it is a revisionist evaluation of how an overlooked minority of the Federalists opposed the Sedition Act, including an unrecognized half of the early justices; and how an unrecognized minority of states joined with Virginia and Kentucky to oppose the Sedition Act on the basis of the First Amendment. This is far from a defense of the Federalist Party, but it is an effort to set the record straight.

The book looks at four phases of the meaning of freedoms of press and speech before and in the early Supreme Court. (1) Blackstone claimed to give a summary of the common law meaning of those freedoms, and his was a very narrow meaning, simply freedom from prior restraint (primarily from a license requirement) and not also freedom from subsequent punishment (such as arrest and further prosecution for the publication or speech). In stating that definition, Blackstone chose the narrowest of the many definitions in popular usage, and chose one that had never appeared in an English common law decision, though Lord Chief Justice Mansfield obligingly inserted it into common law the next year. Blackstone and Mansfield also claimed an ancient common law basis for a framework for prosecuting seditious libel that greatly assisted government prosecutors. That, too, misdescribed the English common law. (2) The pre-Marshall justices of the Supreme Court expressed strong commitments to freedoms of press and speech, before the crisis of 1798, and discussed them in expansive terms without in any case adopting the constrictive Blackstone-Mansfield definition or framework before that crisis period. (3) Those early justices divided almost evenly over the constitutionality of the Sedition Act and over the Blackstone-Mansfield definition during 1798–1801, and the Federalist Party divided as well, as did the other states in considering the Virginia and Kentucky Resolutions. (4) The justices who adopted the Blackstone-Mansfield definition presided over more than twice as many Sedition Act cases as have been confirmed before now, and some justices were more involved than has been believed.

All four of those phases raise challenges to existing histories and constitutional law accounts. (1) In most accounts addressing the issue, the Blackstone-Mansfield definition is accepted as an accurate summary of the English common law on point, and as a result freedoms of press and speech are treated by many as having a very narrow meaning in 1789–1791 of only freedom from licensing and not also freedom from subsequent punishment. Thus, many claim that the First Amendment was a weak safeguard of press and speech, and did not protect criticism of government or officials or protect against its prosecution as seditious libel. (2) In existing publications, the early justices are uniformly treated as saying nothing, or nothing worth noting, about freedoms of press and speech in the years before 1798. (3) All those early justices are also uniformly treated as supporting the Blackstone-Mansfield definition and framework and the Sedition Act during 1798–1801, and the Federalist Party is similarly treated as monolithically supportive, while the other states are described as unanimously opposed to the Virginia and Kentucky Resolutions. (4) The Sedition Act prosecutions are everywhere described as fourteen or fifteen prosecutions, along with three other federal prosecutions under common law. These points in existing literature could not be further from fact, historically and constitutionally.

Understandings of Freedoms of Press and Speech—The Blackstone-Mansfield Definition and Opposing Views

William Blackstone claimed to summarize the English common law definition, when his *Commentaries* stated in 1769 that English "liberty of the press is indeed essential to the nature of a free state: but this consists in laying no *previous* restraints upon publications, and not in freedom from censure for criminal matter when published."[3] His and Lord Mansfield's support for unique rules for prosecuting seditious libel, compared to the rules for prosecuting other crimes, was also described by them as fidelity to ancient common law.

In fact, that definition of liberties of press and speech was not to be found in the English common law in 1769, when Blackstone published his purported summary of

[3] 4 Sir William Blackstone, Commentaries on the Laws of England 151 (CP, Oxford 1765–69) (4 vols.).

the common law meaning, and it only was inserted into English common law a year later by Mansfield. The Blackstone-Mansfield definition amounted to their adoption of the narrowest of the various definitions of freedoms of press and speech that were advocated at the time. And when Mansfield described the unique rules for seditious libel as part of the ancient common law, he deliberately started his history in the middle of 1688, in order to ignore a contrary decision earlier that same year, and left out the most significant decision of the 1750s as well, in order to fabricate unanimity in the prior ninety-six years, before stretching that to antiquity. Both the Blackstone-Mansfield definition and those jurists' framework for seditious libel were perceived by many as efforts by English judges to suppress dissent including America's patriot movement, and to facilitate convictions in criminal trials of dissidents.

Blackstone acknowledged that there were other views of liberties of press and speech, when he wrote that liberty of press "properly understood" was not violated by prosecuting seditious libels.[4] Other views abounded in England and in America.[5] Because of that, both scholars and judges through the years have divided between the Blackstone-Mansfield definition and more expansive definitions of freedoms of press and speech. Those believing that the Blackstone-Mansfield definition dominated the late eighteenth century have, like Philip Kurland, concluded that the First Amendment was proposed "against this background of accepted law," that "writers and the courts treated the notion of freedom of the press as the right not to have expressions censored before publication," and not as a protection against subsequent prosecution.[6] Those believing that expansive

[4] *Id.*

[5] Wendell Bird, *Liberties of Press and Speech: "Evidence Does Not Exist To Contradict the . . . Blackstonian Sense" in Late Eighteenth-Century England?*, 36 Oxford J. of Legal Studies __ (forthcoming 2016); Wendell Bird, Freedoms of Press and Speech in the First Decade of the U.S. Supreme Court 100–43 (2012) (unpublished D.Phil. thesis in legal history, University of Oxford).

[6] Philip D. Kurland, *The Original Understanding of the Freedom of the Press Provision of the First Amendment*, 55 Miss. L.J. 225, 234, 236, 237, 246 (1985). *E.g.*, 2 Paul A. Freund et al., Constitutional Law: Cases and Other Problems 1545 (2d ed., Little Brown, Boston 1961); Leonard W. Levy, Legacy of Suppression: Freedom of Speech and Press in Early American History vii, ix, x, 176–248 (HUP, Cambridge 1960); Creation 63; Jerome L. Merin, *Libel and the Supreme Court*, 11 Wm. & Mary L. Rev. 371, 375, 376, 377–78, 379 (1969); Walter Berns, *Freedom of the Press and the Alien and Sedition Acts: A Reappraisal*, 1970 Sup. Ct. Rev. 109; Walter Berns, The First Amendment and the Future of American Democracy 84 (Basic Books, New York 1976); Leonard W. Levy, Emergence of a Free Press xi–xii, 170–72 (OUP, New York 1985); Hamburger 745–46 n.261; John P. Reid, 1 Constitutional History of the American Revolution: The Authority of Rights 4 (UWP, Madison 1986); Michael T. Gibson, *The Supreme Court and Freedom of Expression from 1791 to 1917*, 55 Fordham L. Rev. 263, 327, 331 (1986); Stanley C. Brubaker, *Original Intent and Freedom of Speech and Press*, in The Bill of Rights: Original Meaning and Current Understanding 82, 83 (Eugene W. Hickok ed., UPV, Charlottesville 1991); Federalism 700 & n.25; David P. Currie, The Constitution in Congress: The First Congress, 1789–1801, at 261 & n.198 (UChiP, Chicago 1994); Walt Brown, John Adams and the American Press 32–34 (McFarland, Jefferson 1995); William R. Casto, *Oliver Ellsworth*, 1996 J. Sup. Ct. History 73; Norman L. Rosenberg, *Seditious Libel*, OCSC 765, 766; James P. Martin, *When Repression Is Democratic and*

definitions prevailed, like Jeffery Smith, have asserted that the Framers chose broad language to protect freedoms of press and speech, and chose not to adopt the English common law of seditious libel.[7]

Figure 0.1 Initial Justices of the United States Supreme Court (Cushing, Jay, Blair, and Wilson, without Rutledge or Iredell). Engraving by unknown artist. Drawing by Irwin Smith. (Courtesy of Historical and Special Collections, of Harvard Law School Library.)

Constitutional: The Federalist Theory of Representation and the Sedition Act of 1798, 66 U. Chi. L. Rev. 117, 125–26 nn.14–15 (1999); Michael I. Meyerson, *The Neglected History of the Prior Restraint Doctrine*, 34 Ind. L. Rev. 295, 311–13, 320 & n.178, 321–22 (2001); Richard D. Brown, *The Shifting Freedoms of the Press in the Eighteenth Century*, in The Colonial Book in the Atlantic World 366, 375 (Hugh Amory & David D. Hall eds., CUP, Cambridge 2000); William Cohen, The First Amendment: Constitutional Protection of Expression and Conscience 5 (Foundation Press, New York 2003); Eric Barendt, Freedom of Speech 163–64 & n.47 (OUP, New York 2005); Richard Labunski, James Madison and the Struggle for the Bill of Rights 258 & n.16 (OUP, New York 2006); Russell L. Weaver & Donald E. Lively, Understanding the First Amendment 6, 4 (2d ed., Lexis-Nexis, Newark 2006); Empire 258; Repressive Jurisprudence 5–9, 52–71; *see* Merrill Jensen, *Review*, 75 Harv. L. Rev. 456, 458 (1961).

[7] Jeffery A. Smith, Printers and Press Freedom: The Ideology of Early American Journalism 31–73 (OUP, Oxford 1988). *E.g.*, David A. Anderson, *The Origins of the Press Clause*, 30 UCLA L. Rev. 455 (1983). Other examples are in Chapter 3.

The early Supreme Court justices faced that same divergence, between the Blackstone-Mansfield definition of liberties of press and speech and much broader definitions, as they formed their views of freedoms of press and speech between 1775 and 1798, and then as some of them modified their views after enactment of the Sedition Act of 1798. These contexts, the history of freedoms of press and speech and the Blackstone-Mansfield definition and framework, are discussed in Chapters 1–3.

The Early Supreme Court Justices and the First Amendment before the Battles

The early Supreme Court, consisting of the six initial justices and their six successors,[8] served during the Court's formative decade, the 1790s, from the appointment of most initial justices in September 1789, soon after ratification of the Constitution, until the appointment of Chief Justice John Marshall in January 1801. Though the first twelve justices were appointed by Presidents George Washington and John Adams, their names are mostly not widely known. The six initial justices were John Jay of New York, John Rutledge of South Carolina, William Cushing of Massachusetts, James Wilson of Pennsylvania, John Blair of Virginia, and James Iredell of North Carolina. (The Court's earliest session is depicted in Figure 0.1.) The six successor justices, as Rutledge, Jay, and Blair resigned and then as Wilson and Iredell died, were Thomas Johnson of Maryland (who also resigned), William Paterson of New Jersey, Samuel Chase of Maryland, Oliver Ellsworth of Connecticut, Bushrod Washington of Virginia, and Alfred Moore of North Carolina. These early justices, and their dates of service, are listed in the table at the end of this chapter.

The early justices stand so much in the shadow of John Marshall that otherwise outstanding books and articles sometimes get their names wrong (James Iredell is variously called Samuel Iredell and Thomas Iredell),[9] move them to other states (Rutledge is described as of Virginia, and Moore is described as of Georgia),[10] or replace them with nonexistent justices ("Justice Richard Peters" and "Justice Timothy Pickering").[11]

[8] As conventionally counted. OCSC 965, 972; 1 JUSTICES xv.

[9] IRVING BRANT, THE BILL OF RIGHTS: ITS ORIGIN AND MEANING 230, 246 (Bobbs-Merrill, Indianapolis 1965).

[10] Saikrishna B. Prakash & John C. Yoo, *The Origins of Judicial Review*, 70 U. CHI. L. REV. 887, 944 n.226 (2003); Herbert A. Johnson, *The Constitutional Thought of William Johnson*, 89 S.C. HIST. MAG. 132, 134 (1988).

[11] JOHN C. MILLER, CRISIS IN FREEDOM 65, 66, 94, 137, 197, 198 (Little, Brown, Boston 1952); ADAMS FEDERALISTS 155; Charles Kerr, *The Thirty Years' War on the Supreme Court*, 17 VA. L. REV. 629, 633 (1931).

However, President Washington saw the initial appointments as critical to the new republic, and sought "to select the fittest characters to expound the laws and dispense justice." He believed that "the first organization of the federal judiciary is essential to the happiness of our country, and to the stability of our political system," and deemed the Supreme Court to be "the key-stone of our political fabric."[12] Consequently, most initial justices were or had been chief justices of their states' highest courts,[13] and half drafted their state constitutions.[14] The initial and successor justices together included two signers of the Declaration of Independence,[15] six participants in the Constitutional Convention (of whom four signed the Constitution),[16] four leaders in state ratification conventions,[17] and two leaders in congressional adoption of the Bill of Rights.[18]

These early justices' views of freedoms of press and speech, though fairly well developed before the 1798 battles, have been all but ignored in period histories, in their biographies, and in Supreme Court histories.[19]

In fact, not one early justice adopted the Blackstone-Mansfield definition or framework for freedom of press and seditious libel before 1798. Instead, all expressed broad and unrestricted views of freedoms of press and speech before that date (except one whose papers are largely unpreserved). The early justices' views of those freedoms before 1798 are the subject of Chapters 4–5.

[12] George Washington to Robert Harrison (28 Sept.1789), 4 WASHINGTON PAPERS-PRESIDENTIAL 98–99; George Washington to John Jay (5 Oct.1789), 4 *id.* 137. *Accord* George Washington to Thomas Johnson (28 Sept.1789), 4 *id.* 103; George Washington to Edmund Randolph (28 Sept.1789), 4 *id.* 106, 107; George Washington to John Rutledge (29 Sept.1789), 4 *id.* 114–15.

[13] Jay, Rutledge, Cushing, and Blair. Wilson briefly had been a judge on the Continental Congress' committee of appeals and court of appeals, and Iredell briefly had been a trial judge.

[14] Jay and Rutledge, and later Wilson.

[15] Wilson and Chase, as well as Rutledge's brother. 5 JCC 515. They were two of the only six signers of both the Declaration and the Constitution.

[16] Rutledge, Wilson, Blair, Paterson, Chase, and Ellsworth (though the latter two did not sign the Constitution). 33 JCC 500; James Madison to Thomas Jefferson (6 June 1787), 24 LETTERS OF DELEGATES 303.

[17] Jay, Cushing, Wilson, and Iredell.

[18] Paterson and Ellsworth. 4 DHFFC 8–9; COMPLETE BILL OF RIGHTS-SOURCES 88, 89.

[19] *E.g.*, no mention of their views in BERNARD SCHWARTZ, A HISTORY OF THE SUPREME COURT 1–31 (OUP, New York 1993); 1 DAVID P. CURRIE, THE CONSTITUTION IN THE SUPREME COURT: THE FIRST HUNDRED YEARS, 1789–1888, at 1–58 (UChiP, Chicago 1985); CHARLES G. HAINES, THE ROLE OF THE SUPREME COURT IN AMERICAN GOVERNMENT AND POLITICS, 1789–1835, at 7–159 (UCalP, Berkeley 1944); Charles Warren, *The First Decade of the Supreme Court of the United States*, 7 U. CHI. L. REV. 631 (1940); John D. Cushing, A Revolutionary Conservative: The Public Life of William Cushing, 1732–1810, at 328 (1959) (unpublished Ph.D. dissertation, Clark University) (no mention; "there is nothing to indicate what, if anything, Cushing contributed . . . as a circuit judge," and "little of significance" in Supreme Court sessions); *cf.* WILLIAM G. BROWN, THE LIFE OF OLIVER ELLSWORTH 200 (Macmillan, New York 1905) (single sentence).

The Early Supreme Court Justices, the Sedition Act of 1798, and Prosecutions of the Minority Party

The Sedition Act flatly made it a crime to "write, print, utter or publish any false and malicious writing against the government[,]. . . congress, or the president, with intent . . . to bring them . . . into contempt, or disrepute; or to excite against them . . . the hatred of the good people of the United States."[20] Its words were not technical, ambiguous, or easily misunderstood. Three successor justices are known to have presided over Sedition Act prosecutions, and upheld the constitutionality of the Act. A fourth wrote a letter supporting it.

Beyond cursory references to that,[21] the early justices' views of freedoms of press and speech during the 1798–1801 storm have also been all but ignored. The First Amendment reasoning of the three known to have presided over prosecutions has not been adequately described or assessed. The other nine justices have been lumped together as part of a Federalist Party unanimously supporting the Sedition Act and its constitutionality, in statements such as that "[n]ot a single Federalist in the United States opposed the constitutionality of the Sedition Act"[22] (and only Marshall opposed its expedience). An equally common

[20] Sedition Act of 1798, 1 Stat. 596 [ch.74] (expired Mar.1801).

[21] James M. Smith, Freedom's Fetters: The Alien and Sedition Laws and American Civil Liberties 232, 233, 234, 321–22, 326–27, 347–48, 354, 379, 381 (CorUP, Ithaca 1956) (mentions three justices excluding any First Amendment argument, without their analysis); John C. Miller, Crisis in Freedom: The Alien and Sedition Acts 129, 218 (Little, Brown, Boston 1952) (same for two justices); *see* Charles Slack, Liberty's First Crisis: Adams, Jefferson, and the Misfits Who Saved Free Speech 130 (Atlantic Monthly Press New York 2015) (same for two justices); Phillip L. Blumberg, Repressive Jurisprudence in the Early American Republic: The First Amendment and the Legacy of English Law 144–45 (CUP, Cambridge 2010) (same for three justices). Some do not even acknowledge that any justice discussed the First Amendment. *E.g.*, 1 Melvin I. Urofsky & Paul Finkelman, A March of Liberty: A Constitutional History of the United States 204 (3d ed., OUP, New York 2011) ("none of the Federalist judges paid any attention" to arguments that the Sedition Act was unconstitutional).

[22] *E.g.*, Freedom's Fetters 155; *accord* Repressive Jurisprudence 92–99; Perilous Times 36, 39, 43; R. Kent Newmyer, *Dusting Off Samuel Chase*, 20 Reviews in American Hist. 486, 487 (1992); Levy 280; Stephen B. Presser & Becky B. Hurley, *Saving God's Republic: The Jurisprudence of Samuel Chase*, 1984 U. Ill. L. Rev. 771, 778; David A. Anderson, *The Origins of the Press Clause*, 30 UCLA L. Rev. 455, 517 (1983); David L. Annis, Mr. Bushrod Washington, Supreme Court Justice on the Marshall Court 88 (1974) (unpublished Ph.D. dissertation, Notre Dame University); Donald H. Stewart, The Opposition Press of the Federalist Period 470 (SUNYP, Albany 1969); 3 Dumas Malone, Jefferson and His Time 389 (Little Brown, Boston 1962); Brant, *supra* note 9, at 259; John C. Miller, The Federalist Era, 1789–1801, at 232–33, 240, 241 (Harper, New York 1960); Noble E. Cunningham, The Jeffersonian Republicans 126 (UNCP, Chapel Hill 1957); Adams Federalists 163; Crisis 182, 22.

approach has been to aggregate the early justices as a faceless "Federalist judiciary" that supported the Sedition Act.[23] Nearly as common has been simply to ignore their individual views, while stressing that unanimity of Federalist support of the Sedition Act and its constitutionality, whether in histories of the Act,[24] in justices' biographies,[25] or in Supreme Court histories;[26] or even to transform sitting justices into opponents[27] and remaining justices into

[23] *E.g.*, Michael Kent Curtis, *The Fraying Fabric of Freedom: Crisis and Criminal Law in Struggles for Democracy and Freedom of Expression*, 44 TEX. TECH L. REV. 95, 99 (2011); Jude M. Pfister, Constitutional Development in the United States Supreme Court During the 1790s, at 133, 149, 150–51 (2007) (LL.D. thesis, Drew University); Arthur E. Wilmarth, *Elusive Foundation: John Marshall, James Wilson, and the Problem of Reconciling Popular Sovereignty and Natural Law Jurisprudence in the New Federal Republic*, 72 GEO. WASH. L. REV. 113, 186 n.435 (2003); James P. Martin, *When Repression Is Democratic and Constitutional: The Federalist Theory of Representation and the Sedition Act of 1798*, 66 U. CHI. L. REV. 117, 125 n.14, 175 (1999); Charles F. Hobson, *Book Review*, 40 AM. J. LEGAL HISTORY 508, 508–09 (1996); 1 CURRIE, *supra* note 19, at 161, 177, 260; Philip D. Kurland, *The Original Understanding of the Freedom of Press Provision of the First Amendment*, 55 MISS. L.J. 225, 239 n.44, 240, 247 (1985); SAVING 778; BRANT, *supra* note 9, at 71 ("all" justices supported), 308; MILLER, *supra* note 21, at 241 ("to a man"); Charles Kerr, *The Thirty Years' War on the Supreme Court*, 17 VA. L. REV. 629, 636 (1931); Thomas F. Carroll, *Freedom of Speech and of the Press in the Federalist Period: The Sedition Act*, 18 MICH. L. REV. 615, 634 (1920).

[24] *E.g.*, discussions of the Act and prosecutions without justices' reasoning on constitutionality, in 1 HISTORY OF SUPREME COURT 633–51; SUSAN DUNN, JEFFERSON'S SECOND REVOLUTION 101–20 (Houghton Mifflin, Boston 2004); David Jenkins, *The Sedition Act of 1798 and the Incorporation of Seditious Libel into First Amendment Jurisprudence*, 45 AM. J. LEGAL HISTORY 154, 164–83, 188–97 (2001); Mark A. Smith, Crisis, Unity, and Partisanship: The Road to the Sedition Act 310–63 (1998) (unpublished Ph.D. dissertation, University of Virginia); NORMAN L. ROSENBERG, PROTECTING THE BEST MAN: AN INTERPRETIVE HISTORY OF THE LAW OF LIBEL 79–100 (UNCP, Chapel Hill 1986); Daniel N. Hoffman, *Contempt of the United States*, 25 AM. J. LEGAL HISTORY 343, 353–60 (1981); Walter Berns, *Freedom of the Press and the Alien and Sedition Laws: A Reappraisal*, [1970] SUP. CT. REV. 109, 111–35; William L. Richter, Federalism and Civil Liberties: A Reappraisal of the Alien and Sedition Act Controversy of 1798, at 37–82 (1963) (unpublished M.A. thesis, University of Chicago); Thomas F. Carroll, *Freedom of Speech and of the Press in the Federalist Period: The Sedition Act*, 18 MICH. L. REV. 615, 627–48 (1920).

[25] *E.g.*, WILLIS P. WHICHARD, JUSTICE JAMES IREDELL 113 (CAP, Durham 2000) (half-page); RUTLEDGE 259–78; WILSON 30–31; JAMES HAW ET AL., STORMY PATRIOT: THE LIFE OF SAMUEL CHASE 194–99, 202–07 (MHS, Baltimore 1980) (in brief Sedition Act discussion, no mention of First Amendment or press-speech); JOHN E. O'CONNOR, WILLIAM PATERSON: LAWYER AND STATESMAN, 1745–1806, at 245–49 (RUP, Rutgers 1979) (same); David L. Annis, Mr. Bushrod Washington 88–94 (1974) (unpublished Ph.D. dissertation, Notre Dame University) (same); Nettie S. Herndon, James Iredell 291 (1944) (unpublished Ph.D. dissertation, Duke University) (5 sentences, same); JOHN JAY 416–18; JOHNSON 492–510.

[26] WARREN 191; 1 HISTORY OF SUPREME COURT 637, 645, 656; like JUSTICES and OCSC.

[27] WILLIAM G. BROWN, THE LIFE OF OLIVER ELLSWORTH 265–66 (Macmillan, New York 1905) (denying supported constitutionality); Leonard B. Rosenberg, *William Paterson: New Jersey's Nation-Maker*, 85 N.J. HISTORY 7, 32 (1967) ("never challenged the constitutionality").

supporters[28] of the Act.[29] These early justices' analysis of the Sedition Act and of freedoms of press and speech is a significant, though understudied and generally misunderstood, part of constitutional history.[30]

That silence on the remaining justices' views is largely because existing literature unconsciously follows a syllogism—a false one. (1) All Federalists, or all Federalist judges, supported the constitutionality of the Sedition Act (including Marshall, though he alone opposed the expedience of the Act).[31] (2) All early justices were Federalists. (3) Thus, all early justices viewed the Sedition Act as constitutional.

In fact, the first premise is demonstrably false. Even when the Sedition Act was approved in the House of Representatives by a 44–41 vote, at least four Federalists were among the negative votes. As the Act was reconsidered for extension or repeal, at least fourteen other committed Federalists and transitional Federalists voted against the Act. The Federalists' upcoming vice presidential candidate of 1800, and presidential candidate of 1804 and 1808, Charles Cotesworth Pinckney, opposed the Sedition Act as unconstitutional, in private correspondence. The former Federalist attorney general and secretary of state, Edmund Randolph, opposed the Act as unconstitutional (he had recently converted to Republicanism). The incoming Federalist secretary of state, John Marshall, opposed the Act and voted against its extension as inexpedient though

[28] *E.g.*, David Jenkins, *The Sedition Act of 1798 and the Incorporation of Seditious Libel into First Amendment Jurisprudence*, 45 Am. J. Legal History 154, 168–69 (2001) ("Wilson apparently had no reservations about the constitutionality of federal seditious libel prosecutions," based on a *pre*-First Amendment statement about the *state* constitution (which Wilson later modified) which he contrasted with the *federal* Constitution); Anderson 504–505 n.285 (Wilson); Levy-Liberty 29 & n.30 (Wilson); Leonard W. Levy, Legacy of Suppression 201 (BP-HUP, Cambridge 1960) (Wilson); DeAlva S. Alexander, Political History of the State of New York 85, 92 (Friedman, Port Washington 1969) (Jay, no citation); Morton Borden, The Federalism of James A. Bayard 38 (ColumUP, New York 1955) (same). Others misdescribe Wilson, one of America's most outspoken critics of Blackstone, as holding a "Blackstonian view." Open Press 111, 113; *e.g.*, Jenkins, *supra* note 28, at 168–69; Hamburger 746 n.261; Andrew Lenner, *A Tale of Two Constitutions: Nationalism in the Federalist Era*, 40 Am. J. Legal History 72, 77 (1996); Leonard W. Levy, The Legacy *Reexamined*, 37 Stan. L. Rev. 767, 787 (1985).

[29] Or to limit admission of support of the Sedition Act to a single footnote. John D. Cushing, A Revolutionary Conservative: The Public Life of William Cushing, 1732–1810, at 334 (1959) (unpublished Ph.D. dissertation, Clark University).

[30] This book does not address the significance of original meaning or intentions, subjects about which much ink has been spilled. *E.g.*, Thomas I. Emerson, *Colonial Intentions and Current Realities of the First Amendment*, 125 U. Pa. L. Rev. 737, 739 (1977). All sides of the debate give it some level of significance.

[31] *E.g.*, Freedom's Fetters 155; *accord* Anderson 517; Levy 280; Crisis 182, 22; Adams Federalists 163; Repressive Jurisprudence 92–99; Bushrod Washington 88.

not as unconstitutional. A number of other Federalist politicians questioned the constitutionality of the Sedition Act or otherwise opposed it, some remaining as Federalists and some transitioning out of the Federalist fold, as discussed at the beginning of Chapter 8. Hence, it is simply not true that all Federalists supported the Sedition Act. Nor is it true that the challenges to the Act's constitutionality in the Virginia and Kentucky Resolutions, written by Madison and Jefferson, were not supported by any other state,[32] or that "no other states followed" in concluding that "the Alien and Sedition Acts violated the First Amendment,"[33] as is ubiquitously asserted. Instead, two unacknowledged states supported those two states' resolutions, two saw deadlock of their two legislative chambers, and two others chose not to oppose or support, as discussed at the end of Chapter 6.[34]

The second premise is technically correct—all early justices were Federalists—but is still misleading. Federalists were not monolithic, but divided, sometimes quite acrimoniously, into High Federalists, Adams Federalists, and other moderate Federalists who gradually left the party. Recognizing this opens the possibility that Federalists divided not just on negotiation with France, and on Adams's reelection, but on the Sedition Act.

The conclusion of the syllogism is false as well. Five of the six nonsitting justices (as of late 1798), including Alfred Moore who later replaced James Iredell, appear to have viewed the Sedition Act as a violation of freedoms of press and speech.

However, the sitting justices, excluding Alfred Moore, defended the Sedition Act as consistent with the First Amendment based on their newfound belief in the Blackstone-Mansfield definition and framework for freedom of press and of seditious libel, which they also applied to freedom of speech, limiting those to the narrow freedoms recognized by English common law. The views of the six sitting justices, and of the six nonsitting justices, about the Sedition Act and about the First Amendment in that period are the subject of Chapters 6–8.

Those sitting justices who presided over Sedition Act trials, and the other sitting justices who defended the Sedition Act, did so on circuit courts. The Supreme

[32] *E.g.*, Repressive Jurisprudence 88; Empire 270; Reclaiming 75; 3 DHSC 238; Securing 223; Opposition 474; Crisis 171.

[33] Richard Labunski, James Madison and the Struggle for the Bill of Rights 257 (OUP, New York 2006); *e.g.*, Larry D. Kramer, *Putting the Politics Back into the Political Safeguards of Federalism*, 100 Colum. L. Rev. 215, 275 (2000); Federalism 720; Crisis 172 n.30; Jay 1089; Contemporary Opinion 235, 237 (whose discussion is mistaken); Ethelbert D. Warfield, The Kentucky Resolutions of 1798: An Historical Study 114–15 (Putnam, New York 1894).

[34] And in Wendell Bird, *Reassessing Responses to the Virginia and Kentucky Resolutions: New Evidence from the Tennessee and Georgia Resolutions and from Other States*, 35 J. Early Republic 519 (2015).

Court in its first decade (and its first century) did not rule corporately on the constitutionality of the Sedition Act or on other First Amendment issues. That did not diminish the threat the assault posed to freedoms of press and speech.

The Unrecognized Additional Prosecutions under the Sedition Act of 1798

Scholarly discussions of the implementation of the Sedition Act describe fourteen or fifteen prosecutions under it, and three more under common law.[35] A suspicion has persisted that there were more prosecutions, but no more have been confirmed in federal court records or prosecutor records, except two very brief acknowledgments of the prosecution of Dr. Samuel Shaw.[36]

In fact, it is now possible to confirm twenty-two additional cases under the Sedition Act, prosecuting sixteen more defendants for seditious writings and words and prosecuting eighty-three defendants for seditious combinations and conspiracies. Additionally, there were three attempted indictments that grand juries rejected, and six prosecutorial instructions to bring Sedition Act charges.

These additional confirmed cases expand the role of the three justices who presided over Sedition Act trials, changing who presided over the most proceedings. They also add a fourth justice to those who presided over Sedition Act trials, and show a fifth justice to have been responsible for presiding over three indictments. They show that the Adams administration's attack on the Republican press and opposition was more than twice as broad as has been recognized, and that a significant minority of Sedition Act prosecutions were directed at seditious speech rather than seditious publications. These additional confirmed cases are the subject of Chapter 7.

The Significance of the Early Justices' Views and the Sedition Act Battles

Why do the Sedition Act, and the early justices' views of it and the First Amendment, matter? The Sedition Act controversy was the first major debate on the meaning of the First Amendment, and the early justices were the first federal judges

35 The books, chapters, articles, and other discussions of these fourteen and three prosecutions are cited at the beginning of Chapter 7.

36 1 History of Supreme Court 638 n.107 (one sentence); Repressive Jurisprudence 139–40 (half page without "any details of the case").

to interpret freedoms of press and speech, and the only Supreme Court justices to do so for nearly a century. Their opinions stimulated further development of the Jeffersonian-Madisonian theories of freedoms of press and speech, as well as congressional and public debate about those freedoms. The Sedition Act and its defense by sitting justices illuminated fundamental philosophical cleavages between the first American political parties, as they were still coalescing, and contributed greatly to national victory by the Republican Party and to eclipse of the Federalist Party. That fight was the largest-scale expression of dissent yet in the new American republic, and cemented political parties as permanent features of American politics. The Republican victory of 1800 brought the first transfer of power over the federal government, and began the longest period of one party's dominance in this country's history. The Sedition Act stood through that period as a monument to the decline and approaching death of the Federalist Party, and to the most repressive federal action toward press and speech during the 1790s or for nearly a century.

More broadly, the Sedition Act controversy showed two distinctive forms of republicanism, as the revolutionary generation and the postrevolutionary generation grappled with what republicanism meant beyond rejection of a king and adoption of representative government. The clash of those two forms of republicanism, in establishing revolutionary states and then in establishing the federal government, brought the adoption of state declarations of rights and the federal Bill of Rights, addressing what rights individuals retained and did not surrender to government, including the right to dissent from the administration and its measures.

How could America, and the Supreme Court justices, divide less than a decade after the First Amendment was adopted in 1789 and ratified in 1789–1791, on the meaning of freedoms of press and speech and whether the Sedition Act of 1798 violated them? The common response, that the Sedition Act was enacted and enforced by Federalists, with the assumption that Federalists gladly violated or ignored the First Amendment, is insufficient, because those who became the Federalist Party had generally supported the First Amendment when it was adopted in 1789 (and had generally based their opposition in 1787 on its superfluity rather than objection to the particular rights enshrined). Further, the early justices of the Supreme Court held a broad view of freedoms of press and speech before 1798. The cultural context of a new fragile government that stood or collapsed with popular confidence in its officials' characters was certainly important,[37] but that does not explain the divergence of the early justices. During 1798–1801, their

[37] Joanne B. Freeman, *Explaining the Unexplainable: The Cultural Context of the Sedition Act*, in THE DEMOCRATIC EXPERIMENT 20, 27–31, 41 (Meg Jacobs et al. eds., PUP, Princeton 2003).

division into support of the Sedition Act by most sitting justices, and apparent opposition by most nonsitting justices, came from something more philosophical and historical, as did those sitting justices' change to more constrictive views of freedoms of press and speech. The primary reasons for the justices' division appear to be their opposing positions on several connected issues: the extent of rights to dissent, the Blackstone-Mansfield definition of freedom of press or a more liberal approach, the legal status of the common law of seditious libel, the effect of new state and federal constitutions on that doctrine and on seditious libel, and the strength of each justice's commitment to freedoms of press and speech or to the law of seditious libel.

This book, by addressing the pre-Marshall justices' views of the First Amendment and of its first major test, over the Sedition Act of 1798, fills a gap in the outstanding existing histories—of the 1790s by Elkins and McKitrick and by Wood,[38] of the Federalists (but not the Supreme Court) by Fischer, Kerber, and Ben-Atar and Oberg,[39] of the Supreme Court in that decade by Goebel, Casto, Gerber, and others,[40] of its documents by Marcus,[41] of the Bill of Rights by Schwartz and Cogan,[42] and of freedoms of press and speech by Siebert, Rabban, and others.[43]

[38] Stanley Elkins & Eric McKitrick, The Age of Federalism (OUP, New York 1993); Gordon S. Wood, Empire of Liberty: A History of the Early Republic, 1789–1815 (OUP, Oxford 2009).

[39] David Hackett Fischer, The Revolution of American Conservatism: The Federalist Party in the Era of Jeffersonian Democracy xvi–xviii (Harper & Row, New York 1965); Linda K. Kerber, Federalists in Dissent: Imagery and Ideology in Jeffersonian America xii (CorUP, Ithaca 1970); Federalists Reconsidered 1, 6–7, 96 (Doron Ben-Atar & Barbara B. Oberg eds., UPV, Charlottesville 1998).

[40] Julius Goebel, History of the Supreme Court of the United States Vol.1—Antecedents and Beginnings to 1801 (Macmillan, New York 1971); William R. Casto, The Supreme Court in the Early Republic: The Chief Justiceships of John Jay and Oliver Ellsworth (USCP, Columbia 1995); Seriatim: The Supreme Court before John Marshall (Scott D. Gerber ed., NYUP, New York 1998).

[41] The Documentary History of the Supreme Court of the United States, 1789–1800 (Maeva Marcus ed., ColUP, New York 1985–2007) (8 vols).

[42] Bernard Schwartz, The Bill of Rights: A Documentary History (Chelsea House, New York 1971); Neil H. Cogan, The Complete Bill of Rights: The Drafts, Debates, Sources, and Origins (2nd ed., OUP, New York 2015).

[43] Fred S. Siebert, Freedom of the Press in England, 1476–1776 (UIP, Urbana 1952); Leonard W. Levy, Emergence of a Free Press (OUP, New York 1985) (other than the relentless Blackstonian argument); David M. Rabban, Free Speech in Its Forgotten Years (CUP, New York 1997); David A. Anderson, *The Origins of the Press Clause,* 30 UCLA L. Rev. 455 (1983). The definition of the press is debated in Eugene Volokh, *Freedom for the Press as an Industry, or for the Press as a Technology?,* 160 U. Pa. L. Rev. 459 (2012); Sonja R. West, *Press Exceptionalism,* 127 Harv. L. Rev. 2434 (2014).

The following chapters fill in the story. Chapter 1 discusses the background of developing freedoms of press and speech in the seventeenth and eighteenth centuries. Chapters 2 and 3 address the crime of seditious libel, and challenge the claim that the Blackstone-Mansfield definition accurately summarized the English common law of freedoms of press and speech, noting instead that Mansfield first introduced that definition into the English common law *after* Blackstone's summary. They also challenge the claim that the Blackstone-Mansfield framework for seditious libel prosecution was an ancient part of the common law. Chapters 4 and 5 discuss the views of the first twelve justices about liberties of press and speech, before 1798, and question the general assumptions that they opposed or disregarded freedoms of press and speech before that time, and that they embraced the Blackstone-Mansfield definition or framework before that time. Chapters 6 and 8 consider the views of those justices on the Sedition Act of 1798, and the trials some presided over during 1798–1800, which were the center of a concerted campaign to eliminate the opposition press and the opposition party. Those chapters challenge the prevailing view that they and the Federalist Party uniformly supported the Sedition Act (that "not a single Federalist questioned the constitutionality of the Sedition Law"), and that they uniformly adopted the Blackstone-Mansfield definition. In between, Chapter 7 addresses the possibility that there were additional Sedition Act prosecutions, and in finding corroboration of twenty-two additional cases and other attempted cases, changes the long-standing canon of fourteen or fifteen prosecutions along with three additional common law prosecutions.[44]

[44] A word about terminology: To avoid confusion, throughout "England" will be used unless the entire United Kingdom is meant, and "America" will refer to the English mainland colonies before 1776 and to the United States after 1776. The "patriots" and "loyalists" will refer to pre-revolutionary and revolutionary parties, "federalists" and "anti-federalists" to those supporting and opposing the federal Constitution, and "Federalists" and "Republicans" to the emerging political parties of the 1790s. The "early Supreme Court" will refer to the Court of the 1790s, until John Marshall became chief justice in early 1801, and the "initial justices" and "successor justices" to the two rough halves of those dozen justices (listed in the table).

A word about style: In quotations, original spelling is retained but capitalization is modified for consistency; all emphasis is original unless indicated. American legal publication style is used throughout, from *The Bluebook: A Uniform System of Citation*.

Table 0.1 **The Supreme Court Justices Before John Marshall**

THE EARLY JUSTICES (1789–1800)

INITIAL JUSTICES	*Appointed*	*Resigned or Died*	*Discussed at Pages*
John Jay (C. J.)	24 Sept. 1789	29 June 1795	117, 410
John Rutledge	24 Sept. 1789	5 Mar. 1791	134, 424
(briefly C. J. until rejected)	1 July 1795	15 Dec. 1795	
William Cushing	24 Sept. 1789	13 Sept. 1810	148, 309, 452
James Wilson	24 Sept. 1789	21 Aug. 1798	162, 435
John Blair	24 Sept. 1789	25 Oct. 1795	182, 444
James Iredell	8 Feb. 1790	20 Oct. 1799	191, 311

(Robert Harrison was the initial justice, who upon not taking office was replaced by James Iredell)

SUCCESSOR JUSTICES			
Thomas Johnson	5 Aug. 1791	16 Jan. 1793	204, 446
William Paterson	27 Feb. 1793,		
	4 Mar. 1793	9 Sept. 1806	211, 268
Samuel Chase	26 Jan. 1796	19 June 1811	218, 285
Oliver Ellsworth (C. J.)	3 Mar. 1796	15 Dec. 1800	232, 317
Bushrod Washington	29 Sept. 1798	26 Nov. 1829	240, 302
Alfred Moore	4 Dec. 1799	26 Jan. 1804	245, 448

THE SEDITION ACT JUSTICES (1798–1801)

SITTING JUSTICES (AS OF SEPTEMBER 1798)			
William Cushing	24 Sept. 1789	13 Sept. 1810	148, 309, 452
James Iredell	8 Feb. 1790	20 Oct. 1799	191, 311
William Paterson	27 Feb. 1793,		
	4 Mar. 1793	9 Sept. 1806	211, 268
Samuel Chase	26 Jan. 1796	19 June 1811	218, 285
Oliver Ellsworth (C. J.)	3 Mar. 1796	15 Dec. 1800	232, 317
Bushrod Washington	29 Sept. 1798	26 Nov. 1829	240, 302

NONSITTING JUSTICES (AS OF SEPTEMBER 1798)			
John Jay (C.J.)	24 Sept. 1789	29 June 1795	117, 410
John Rutledge	24 Sept. 1789	5 Mar. 1791	134, 424
(briefly C.J. until rejected)	1 July 1795	15 Dec. 1795	
James Wilson	24 Sept. 1789	21 Aug. 1798	162, 435
John Blair	24 Sept. 1789	25 Oct. 1795	182, 444
Thomas Johnson	5 Aug. 1791	16 Jan. 1793	204, 446
Alfred Moore	4 Dec. 1799	26 Jan. 1804	245, 448

Source: OCSC 965; 1 DHSC 9–10, 13, 19, 23, 28, 49–50, 52–53, 56–57, 59, 64–66, 68, 72–78, 80, 89–91, 96, 98–100, 112–13, 120–21, 123, 132–35, 140–41. There often were many months between the appointment and commission date and the oath of office.

ABBREVIATIONS

Books

The following are the most commonly used abbreviations; others are listed after Chapter 9:

Annals	Debates and Proceedings in the Congress of the United States . . . Annals of the Congress of the United States (Gales & Seaton, Washington 1834–1856) (42 vols.)
Blackstone's Commentaries	Sir William Blackstone, Commentaries on the Laws of England (Clarendon Press, Oxford 1765–1769) (4 vols.)
DHRC	The Documentary History of the Ratification of the Constitution (Merrill Jensen et al. eds., State Historical Society of Wisconsin, Madison 1976–) (23 vols. thus far)
DHSC	The Documentary History of the Supreme Court of the United States, 1789–1800 (Maeva Marcus ed., Columbia University Press, New York 1985–2007) (8 vols.)
Elliot's Debates	The Debates in the Several State Conventions on the Adoption of the Federal Constitution (Jonathan Elliot ed., J. B. Lippincott, Philadelphia 1836) (5 vols.)
Essays-Constitution	Essays on the Constitution of the United States, Published During Its Discussion by the People, 1787–1788 (Paul L. Ford ed., Historical Printing Club, Brooklyn 1892)

Farrand's Records	The Records of the Federal Convention of 1787 (Max Farrand ed., rev. ed. Yale University Press, New Haven 1940) (4 vols.)
Federal-State Constitutions	Federal and State Constitutions, Colonial Charters, and Other Organic Laws (Francis N. Thorpe ed., Government Printing Office, Washington 1909) (7 vols.)
Iredell Correspondence	Life and Correspondence of James Iredell (Griffith J. McRee ed., Appleton, New York 1857–1858) (2 vols.)
Iredell Papers	The Papers of James Iredell, Vols. 1–2 (Don Higginbotham ed., North Carolina Department of Archives & History, Raleigh 1976) The Papers of James Iredell, Vol. 3 (Donna Kelly & Lang Baradell eds., North Carolina Office of Archives & History, Raleigh 2003)
Jay Correspondence	The Correspondence and Public Papers of John Jay (Henry P. Johnson ed., Putnam's Sons, New York 1890–1893) (4 vols.)
Jay Papers	Papers of John Jay (Columbia University Libraries [10,000 documents]) <http://www.columbia.edu/cu/lweb/digital/jay/>
Jay-Peace	John Jay, The Winning of the Peace: Unpublished Papers, 1780–1784 (Richard B. Morris ed., Harper & Row, New York 1980)
Jay-Revolutionary	John Jay, The Making of a Revolutionary: Unpublished Papers, 1745–1780 (Richard B. Morris ed., Harper & Row, New York 1975)
Journals of Assembly-S.C.	Journals of the Commons House of Assembly, 1760–1775 (South Carolina Department of Archives and History, Columbia) [manuscript]
Levy	Leonard W. Levy, Emergence of a Free Press (Oxford University Press, New York 1985, repr. 1987)
Paterson Correspondence	William Paterson, Correspondence and Other Papers, 1766–1804 (Rutgers University, New Brunswick, Special Collections, Ac.888)
Paterson Essays	William Paterson, Essays on Politics and Government (1789–1793) (Rutgers University, New Brunswick, Special Collections, in Writings and Correspondence, Ac.0.963)

PICKERING PAPERS	Timothy Pickering Papers (Massachusetts Historical Society, Boston, 69 reels)
WHARTON'S STATE TRIALS	FRANCIS WHARTON, STATE TRIALS OF THE UNITED STATES DURING THE ADMINISTRATIONS OF WASHINGTON AND ADAMS (Carey & Hart, Philadelphia 1849)
WILSON WORKS	COLLECTED WORKS OF JAMES WILSON (Kermit L. Hall & Mark D. Hall eds., Liberty Fund, Indianapolis 2006) (2 vols.)
WILSON WRITINGS	Life and Writings of James Wilson (Burton A. Konkle ed., Friends Historical Library, Swarthmore College) (6 vols., unpublished ms.)

Cases and Publications

In addition to abbreviations in cases and publications following the standard legal style book, *Uniform System of Citation*, the following are used:

App.	Appendix
C.P.	Court of Common Pleas
Exch.	Court of Exchequer
H.C.	House of Commons
H.L.	House of Lords
K.B.	Court of King's Bench
n.d.	no date given
n.p.	no publisher given
s.c.	same case
s.v.	sub verbum
ser.	series

Manuscripts

CCL	College of Charleston Library, Charleston
CLS	Charleston Library Society, Charleston
DU	Duke University (Perkins Library), Special Collections, Durham
HC	Haverford College (Magill Library), Haverford
HLS	Harvard Law School Library, Cambridge
HSP	Historical Society of Pennsylvania, Philadelphia
LC	Library of Congress, Manuscript Division, Washington

MHS	Massachusetts Historical Society, Boston
MdHS	Maryland Historical Society, Baltimore
MSA	Maryland State Archives, Annapolis
MVL	Mount Vernon Library, Mount Vernon
NA	National Archives, Washington
NCSA	North Carolina State Archives, Manuscript Dept., Raleigh
NJHS	New Jersey Historical Society, Newark
NYPL	New York Public Library, Manuscripts and Archives Division
PEM	Peabody Essex Museum, Phillips Library, Salem
RU	Rutgers University, Special Collections, New Brunswick
SC	Swarthmore College, Friends Historical Library, Swarthmore
SCDAH	South Carolina Department of Archives and History, Columbia
SCHS	South Carolina Historical Society, Charleston
SCL	South Caroliniana Library, University of South Carolina, Columbia
UNC-SHC	University of North Carolina, Manuscripts Department (Southern Historical Collection), Chapel Hill
YUL	Yale University Library, Manuscripts & Archives, New Haven

Publishers

AHA	American Historical Association
BP-HUP	Belknap Press, Harvard University Press
BUP	Boston University Press
CAP	Carolina Academic Press
CAUP	Colorado Associated University Press
CP	Clarendon Press
CUP	Cambridge University Press
ColUP	Columbia University Press
CorUP	Cornell University Press
DUP	Duke University Press
FDUP	Fairleigh Dickinson University Press
GPC	Genealogical Publishing Co.
GPO	United States Government Printing Office
HCSC	Historical Commission of South Carolina
HP	Hambledon Press, London
HSP	Historical Society of Pennsylvania
HUP	Harvard University Press
JHUP	Johns Hopkins University Press
LB	Little, Brown, Boston

LF	Liberty Fund, Indianapolis
LSUP	Louisiana State University Press
MHS	Massachusetts Historical Society
MUP	Manchester University Press
NCDAH	North Carolina Dept. of Archives & History
NJHC	New Jersey Historical Commission
NJHS	New Jersey Historical Society
NYHS	New York Historical Society
OhUP	Ohio University Press
OUP	Oxford University Press
PHMC	Pennsylvania Historical and Museum Cm.
PSUP	Pennsylvania State University Press
PUP	Princeton University Press, Princeton
RHS	Royal Historical Society
RUP	Rutgers University Press
SCP	Saint Catherine Press
SHSW	State Historical Society of Wisconsin
SUNYP	State University of New York Press
SUP	Stanford University Press
THC	Tennessee Historical Commission
UCP	University of California Press
UChiP	University of Chicago Press
UCSB	University of California Santa Barbara
UDP	University of Delaware Press
UGP	University of Georgia Press
UIP	University of Illinois Press
UKP	University of Kentucky Press
UMP	University of Massachusetts Press
UMoP	University of Missouri Press
UNCP	University of North Carolina Press
UNP	University of Nebraska Press
UPK	University Press of Kentucky
UPKan	University Press of Kansas
UPP	University of Pennsylvania Press
UPitP	University of Pittsburgh Press
UPV	University Press of Virginia
URP	University of Rochester Press
USCP	University of South Carolina Press
UTP	University of Tennessee Press
UWP	University of Wisconsin Press
YUP	Yale University Press

1

The Right to Dissent, and the Growth of Freedoms of Press and Speech in the Eighteenth Century

> Nothing but opinions circulated through the medium of a paper, produced the American struggle for liberty.... Had those illustrious worthies who maintained our cause been intimidated from publishing their sentiments under ... prosecutions as a libeller, there is no doubt we should have sunk to the lowest class of slaves.
>
> —Philadelphia Newspaper (1782)[1]

Most Americans, and even most historians and legal scholars, are unaware that in England at the beginning of the seventeenth century, as emigration to America began, opposition to the King or Parliament was sedition if not treason, printing of books and pamphlets and newspapers was only legal if the text was approved by licensors, and criticism of government or officials could be criminally prosecuted as seditious libel or seditious words. Most people are also unaware that a century later, at the beginning of the eighteenth century, in both England and America, criticism of the administration or its officers could still be criminally prosecuted as seditious libel or seditious words, dissent was only tolerated to an undefined degree, and press and speech were merely tolerated and had no real legal protection. As the eighteenth century progressed, freedoms of press and speech were increasingly discussed, in England and America, and those discussions reached a crescendo as the colonial disputes of the prerevolutionary decade provoked thought about rights, and as English judges claimed to define the common law rights in very narrow terms. Advocates of the colonies' rights were threatened with prosecution for sedition or treason, and revolutionary leaders knew that if

[1] Junius Wilkes, *For the Chronicle of Freedom*, INDEPENDENT GAZETTEER (Philadelphia), 9 Nov. 1782, at 2.

they lost they likely would be hanged. For the first time in history, written protections for freedoms of press and speech appeared as the American Revolution prompted new state declarations of rights, and later as the ratification debates over the Constitution brought a federal Bill of Rights.

Figure 1.1 John Wilkes and his counsel. Painting by Richard Houston 1769. (Courtesy of, and copyright, National Portrait Gallery, London.)

The Developing Freedoms of Press and Speech in Eighteenth-Century England

In eighteenth-century England, Hoppit says that "[f]reedom of speech, of worship, and of the press were all celebrated as never before."[2] Dickinson finds general agreement on freedom of press, "liberty of conscience, [and] freedom of expression."[3] Voltaire believed that "liberty has . . . been established" in England.[4] But was that all true? Some dissent indeed had come to be tolerated,[5] but, outside of freedom of petition and speech in Parliament, expression was not secured as a right, and dissent could be punished as a crime.

[2] 7 Oxford History 6. A list of abbreviated titles is at the end of this book.

[3] Dickinson-Politics 5, 169; *id.* at 198 (Whigs).

[4] Voltaire, *On Parliament*, in Letters on England 44, 45 (Leonard Tancock trans., Penguin Books, Harmondsworth 1980); *accord* 7 Oxford History 7 (misquoting).

[5] 7 Oxford History 9; 8 *id.* at 289.

Toleration of Dissenting Press and Speech at the Beginning of the Eighteenth Century

The American revolutionaries who framed the state declarations of rights and constitutions in 1776, and after, did so in the context of English rights and English debates about those rights.[6] So did those who framed and ratified the Bill of Rights in 1789–1791. They looked to English history for guidance in protecting against absolutism, by subjecting governments to rule of law and constitutional restraint,[7] and by protecting rights. They demanded written constitutions and used unrestricted language because so many believed English rights were inadequately protected and were frustrated by limitations.[8] It was in this English context that early Supreme Court justices developed their views on press and speech, and addressed the first cases raising First Amendment challenges[9] (which were cases involving the Sedition Act of 1798).

The mere toleration of press and speech that existed at the beginning of the eighteenth century was the result of tortuous change in the seventeenth century, which served as a reference point for all sides in colonial debates, constitutional period discussions, and Sedition Act debates. The major events are only briefly summarized here, since they have been well discussed elsewhere.[10]

The Tudor kings and queens, beginning with Henry VIII, censored the press by Star Chamber[11] and Privy Council regulation.[12] The Star Chamber decree of 1586[13] became the core regulation as it strengthened requirements for prior approval for printing and prohibited sedition.[14] As the Stuarts inherited the throne, James I required strict compliance with that decree,[15] and he and Charles I added

[6] Which was their dominant heritage in the late eighteenth century. IDEOLOGICAL ORIGINS 66; MICHAEL J. BRADDICK, STATE FORMATION IN EARLY MODERN ENGLAND, c.1550–1700, at 337 n.1 (CUP, Cambridge 2000).

[7] IDEOLOGICAL ORIGINS 182, 184; FEDERALIST No.5, at 24 (Jay).

[8] CREATION 261, 266, 268, 268–87; IDEOLOGICAL ORIGINS 175, 182.

[9] Sitting on circuit courts (Chapter 6).

[10] FREDRICK S. SIEBERT, FREEDOM OF THE PRESS IN ENGLAND, at 107–302 (UIP, Urbana 1952); HAMBURGER 674–91.

[11] Star-Chamber Ordinance (29 June 1566), SELECT STATUTES 168; 1 KEMP 16; *accord* CLEGG-CAROLINE 18, 27; LAMBERT 13.

[12] Order of Privy Council Requiring All Books to Be Licensed before Publication (8 Sept. 1570), 5 ARBER lxxvi; *accord* CLEGG-CAROLINE 18; 5 OXFORD HISTORY 411–14.

[13] Which was "the basis of all licensing" is disputed. *E.g.*, LAMBERT 15, 11–12; CLEGG-CAROLINE 23.

[14] Star-Chamber Ordinance (23 June 1586), SELECT STATUTES 169, 169; KEMP 107; *accord* LAMBERT 13–14; CLEGG-CAROLINE 29; TESSA WATT, CHEAP PRINT AND POPULAR PIETY, 1550–1640, at 44 (CUP, Cambridge 1991).

[15] A Proclamation against the Disorderly Printing, Uttering and Dispersing of Books, Pamphlets, &c. (23 June 1622), SELECT STATUTES 394; *accord* CLEGG-CAROLINE 14.

new proclamations censoring the press,[16] prohibiting "intermeddl[ing] by penne or speech, with causes of state,"[17] and restricting speech in other ways.[18]

The Star Chamber under Charles I sought to increase control of the press and speech, as Archbishop William Laud "argued that political dissidence expressed in words or writing amounted to treason,"[19] and launched six show prosecutions[20] along with many others.[21] The Star Chamber decree of 1637 prohibited printing "any seditious, scismaticall, or offensive bookes or pamphlets, to the scandall of Religion, or the Church, or the Government, or Governours of the Church or State," and prohibited printing even innocuous books or pamphlets without prior licensing by censors.[22]

Parliament, when it was finally summoned in 1640 after eleven years of Charles I's personal rule and of Star Chamber prosecutions such as the show prosecutions,

[16] A Proclamation against the Disorderly Printing, Uttering, and Dispersing of Bookes, Pamphlets, &c (25 Sept. 1623), 1 STUART PROCLAMATIONS 583; A Proclamation against Seditious, Popish and Puritanicall Bookes and Pamphlets (15 Aug.1624), 1 *id.* at 599; Proclamation (14 June 1626), 2 *id.* at 90, 92; SELECT STATUTES 395; Proclamation (27 Feb.1639), 2 STUART PROCLAMATIONS 662, 665; Proclamation (30 Mar.1640), 2 *id.* at 703, 704; *accord* CLEGG-CAROLINE 15; HALLER 49–50, 232.

[17] A Proclamation against Excesse of Lavish and Licentious Speech of Matters of State (24 Dec. 1620), 1 STUART PROCLAMATIONS 495, 495; *accord* A Proclamation against Excesse of Lavish and Licentious Speech of Matters of State (26 July 1621), 1 *id.* at 519; CLEGG-CAROLINE 14–15.

[18] CONSTITUTIONAL DOCUMENTS OF THE REIGN OF JAMES I 287 (J.R. Tanner ed., CUP, Cambridge 1952); *accord* COLCLOUGH 77–119; BROOKS 144, 153–55.

[19] BROOKS 179; 1 KEMP 307.

[20] Proceedings in the Star-Chamber against Dr. Alexander Leighton, 3 State Trials 383 (Star Chamber 1630); Proceedings against Wm. Prynn, 3 State Trials 561 (Star Chamber 1632–33); Proceedings in the Star-Chamber against Dr. John Bastwick, Mr. Henry Burton, and William Prynn, 3 State Trials 711 (Star Chamber 1637); Trial of John Lilburn and John Wharton, 3 State Trials 1315 (Star Chamber 1637); accord BROOKS 179–80, 217–18; MICHAEL R. WATTS, THE DISSENTERS: FROM THE REFORMATION TO THE FRENCH REVOLUTION 66–68 (CP, Oxford 1978); HALLER 232–33, 219–25, 253–59, 259–61.

[21] BROOKS 178–79 (satire 1627); CRESSY 16 (Alexander Gill 1628); RICHARD BURT, LICENSED BY AUTHORITY: BEN JONSON AND THE DISCOURSES OF CENSORSHIP 89 (CorUP, Ithaca 1993) (Christopher Malloy 1629); Proceedings against Mr. Richard Chambers, 3 State Trials 374 (Star Chamber 1629); Proceedings in the Star-Chamber against the Earl of Bedford et al., 3 State Trials 387 (Star Chamber 1630); Proceedings in the Star-Chamber against Henry Sherfield, 3 State Trials 519 (Star Chamber 1632); Proceedings in the Star-Chamber against Dr. John Williams, 3 State Trials 770 (Star Chamber 1637); *accord* BROOKS 180, 188–89; CRESSY 186–87 (William Pickering 1638); KEVIN SHARPE, THE PERSONAL RULE OF CHARLES I 676 (YUP, New Haven 1992) (Walter Long, David Foulis); JULIAN DAVIES, THE CAROLINE CAPTIVITY OF THE CHURCH 126–71 (CP, Oxford 1992); HALLER 20, 230, 262–64.

[22] A DECREE OF STARRE-CHAMBER, CONCERNING PRINTING (Robert Barker, London 1637); A Decree of Starre-Chamber, Concerning Printing §I (11 July 1637), 4 ARBER 528; 1 KEMP 346; *accord* SHARPE, *supra* note 21, at 649–50; LAMBERT 22–23.

abolished the Star Chamber in mid-1641,[23] and with it the decree on censorship (which was "a revolution within the revolution").[24] However, Parliament reinstated censorship just two years later, and renewed it after various lapses through the Interregnum.[25]

The conflict between Parliament and Charles I escalated into the English Civil War. As they discussed conditions for restoring Charles I to rule, Army debates during 1647–1649 touched on expression, in Putney[26] and Whitehall.[27] Freedom of speech appeared in the army's proposals and responses,[28] which were debated at Putney, and was touched upon in the officers' version of an Agreement of the People,[29] which resulted from debates at Whitehall (though their focus was freedom of religion). Freedom of press was practiced though not preached in the debates.[30]

The Restoration reign of Charles II, seeking to rebuild society on earlier Stuart lines,[31] immediately issued proclamations suppressing several books and

[23] An Act for the Regulating of the Privy Council, and for Taking Away the Court Commonly Called the Star-Chamber (5 July 1641), 17 Car 1 c10 §3; 7 STATUTES 338; THE CONSTITUTIONAL DOCUMENTS OF THE PURITAN REVOLUTION, 1625–60, at 179 (Samuel R. Gardiner ed., OUP, Oxford 1906); *accord* AYLMER 18.

[24] DAVID CRESSY, ENGLAND ON EDGE: CRISIS AND REVOLUTION, 1640–42, at 292 (OUP, Oxford 2006); *see id.* at 292–302.

[25] 2 KEMP 72 (1643), 183 (1647), 233 (1649), 345 (1653), 424 (1655).

[26] *Putney Debates*, ARMY DEBATES 1–124, 438–55; *accord* MICHAEL MENDLE, PUTNEY DEBATES OF 1647 (CUP, Cambridge 2001).

[27] *Whitehall Debates*, ARMY DEBATES 125–78, 456–73; *accord* AUSTIN WOOLRYCH, SOLDIERS AND STATESMEN: THE GENERAL COUNCIL OF THE ARMY AND ITS DEBATES, 1647–1648 (CP, Oxford 1987); J.C. Davis, *Religion and the Struggle for Freedom in the English Revolution*, 35 HISTORICAL J. 507 (1992).

[28] *The Heads of the Proposals* (1 Aug.1647), ARMY DEBATES 422, 423, 424; [Edward Sexby], *The Case of the Army Truly Stated* (15 Oct.1647), *id.* at 429, 434; *An Agreement of the People* (3 Nov.1647), *id.* at 443, 444; *accord* WOOLRYCH, *supra* note 27, at 160–65, 207–09, 279; MARK A. KISHLANSKY, THE RISE OF THE NEW MODEL ARMY 272, 288 (CUP, Cambridge 1979); VALLANCE 159.

[29] *Agreement of the People* (15 Jan.1649), CONSTITUTIONAL DOCUMENTS, *supra* note 23, at 359, 369; [Henry Ireton], *A Remonstrance of Fairfax and the Council of Officers* (16 Nov.1648), ARMY DEBATES 456, 463; *contra* John Lilburne, *A Plea for Common Right and Freedom* (28 Dec.1648), *id.* at 472; *accord* AYLMER 155; VALLANCE 170.

[30] Most petitions and statements appeared as handbills. *E.g.*, Notes, THE LEVELLER TRACTS, 1647–1653, at 51, 64, 88, 135, 147, 156 (William Haller & Godfrey Davies eds., ColUP, New York 1944); *The Case of the Army Stated*, ARMY DEBATES 2; *A Declaration of the Engagements, Remonstrances, Representations . . . of the Army*, *id.* at 45 & n.1; *accord* Michael Mendle, *Putney's Pronouns*, in PUTNEY DEBATES, *supra* note 26, at 125, 127–30.

[31] PAUL SEAWARD, THE CAVALIER PARLIAMENT AND THE RECONSTRUCTION OF THE OLD REGIME, 1661–1667, at 16–17, 34, 162–95 (CUP, Cambridge 1989); JOHN MILLER, CHARLES II, at 56–57 (Weidenfeld & Nicholson, London 1991); ZUCKERT 99.

unlicensed newsbooks,[32] prosecuted "seditious pamphlet[s],"[33] and enforced warrants to search for unauthorized publications.[34] Parliament's first act during the Restoration criminalized words as high treason, a year later.[35] The Licensing Act of 1662[36] soon followed, patterned on the Star Chamber's Decree of 1637, and when it lapsed in 1679,[37] proclamations from Charles II took its place until it was reenacted.[38] During Charles II's and James II's reigns "a greater number of individuals fell [a]foul of the law, and were punished more severely for their actions, than had ever previously been the case."[39]

England's Revolution of 1688 brought relief, but the Bill of Rights of the next year provided no protection for freedom of press, and little protection for nonparliamentary speech. When the Licensing Act finally lapsed in May 1695,[40] the press

[32] 1 TUDOR-STUART PROCLAMATIONS 389 (13 Aug.1660, no.3239), 391 (25 Sept.1660, no.3258); *accord* GREAVES 208, 212; JOAD RAYMOND, PAMPHLETS AND PAMPHLETEERING IN EARLY MODERN BRITAIN 328–82 (CUP, Cambridge 2003); RONALD HUTTON, THE RESTORATION: A POLITICAL AND RELIGIOUS HISTORY OF ENGLAND AND WALES, 1658–1667, at 156 (CP, Oxford 1985); AYLMER 109; PETER FRASER, THE INTELLIGENCE OF THE SECRETARIES OF STATE AND THEIR MONOPOLY OF LICENSED NEWS, 1660–1688 at 35 (CUP, Cambridge 1956); JAMES SUTHERLAND, THE RESTORATION NEWSPAPER AND ITS DEVELOPMENT vii (CUP, Cambridge 1986).

[33] Proceedings upon an Impeachment against William Drake, 5 State Trials 1363 (H.C. 1660); *accord* GREAVES 210–11, 216–25.

[34] Lois G. Schwoerer, *Liberty of the Press and Public Opinion: 1660–1695*, in LIBERTY SECURED? BRITAIN BEFORE AND AFTER 1688, at 199, 201 (J.R. Jones ed., SUP, Stanford 1992); GREAVES 216.

[35] Act for Safety and Preservation of His Majesty's Person and Government against Treasonable and Seditious Practices and Attempts (1661), 13 Car 2, stat 1, c1; 8 EHD 63–64 §1, 64 §2.

[36] Act for Preventing the Frequent Abuses in Printing Seditious Treasonable and Unlicensed Books and Pamphlets and for Regulating Printing and Printing Presses (1662), 13–14 Car 2 c33; 8 EHD 67; *accord* Michael Treadwell, *The Stationers and the Printing Act at the End of the Seventeenth Century*, in 4 CHB 755, 755–65; CHRISTOPHER HILL, THE CENTURY OF REVOLUTION, 1603–1714, at 213–14 (2d ed. Nelson, Walton-on-Thames 1980); HAROLD WEBER, PAPER BULLETS: PRINT AND KINGSHIP UNDER CHARLES II, at 152–53 (UKP, Lexington 1996).

[37] JONATHAN SCOTT, ENGLAND'S TROUBLES: SEVENTEENTH-CENTURY ENGLISH POLITICAL INSTABILITY IN EUROPEAN CONTEXT 183 (CUP, Cambridge 2000); Timothy Crist, *Government Control of the Press after the Expiration of the Printing Act in 1679*, 5 PUBLISHING HIST. 49, 49–50 (1979); SUTHERLAND, *supra* note 32, at vii.

[38] 1 TUDOR-STUART PROCLAMATIONS 424 (24 July 1668, no.3516), 431 (12 June 1672, no.3570), 435 (2 May 1674, no.3595), 439 (29 Dec.1675, no.3622), 439 (8 Jan.1676, no.3625), 448 (31 Oct.1679, no.3699), 450 (12 May 1680, no.3715); *accord* DOROTHY AUCHTER, DICTIONARY OF LITERARY AND DRAMATIC CENSORSHIP IN TUDOR AND STUART ENGLAND 382 (Greenwood, Westport 2001).

[39] Jason McElligott, *"A Couple of Hundred Squabbling Small Tradesmen"?*, in NEWS NETWORKS IN SEVENTEENTH-CENTURY BRITAIN AND EUROPE 85, 98 (Joad Raymond ed., Routledge, London 2006); *accord* SIEBERT, *supra* note 10, at 243; WEBER, *supra* note 36, at 158.

[40] Schwoerer, *supra* note 34, at 230; 4 CHB 770.

gained toleration, but freedom of press remained unsecured, as threats of seditious libel prosecution continued.[41] Religious dissent similarly gained only toleration.[42]

Calls for Freedom of Press

Within weeks of the lapse of press licensing in 1695, England's single official newspaper was joined by many alternatives in London[43] and in the provinces,[44] and its bookshops brimmed with books, pamphlets, and other works.[45] Periodicals soon arose and multiplied.[46]

The following decades rang with calls for freedom of the press. Initial ones were responses to unsuccessful efforts to reinstitute licensing during 1695–1705, when there were thirteen parliamentary efforts for reinstatement,[47] and to Tory attempts to introduce censorship under cover of a copyright bill[48] and to tax printed items during 1705–1714.[49] But cries for freedom of press after 1714[50] cannot be explained as reactions to proposed regulation. Instead, they are best

[41] 1 TUDOR-STUART PROCLAMATIONS 506 (23 Jan.1698, no.4242), 509 (29 Jan.1700, no.4271); *accord* HAMBURGER 724–25, 726–34.

[42] Act for Exempting Their Majesties' Protestant Subjects Dissenting from the Church of England from the Penalties of Certain Laws (May 1689), 1 W&M c18; 8 EHD 400.

[43] 5 THOMAS B. MACAULAY, THE HISTORY OF ENGLAND FROM THE ACCESSION OF JAMES THE SECOND 2540–42 (Charles H. Firth ed., MacMillan, London 1913–15); *accord* Michael Harris, *London Newspapers*, in 5 CHB 413, 417–18; R.B. Walker, *The Newspaper Press in the Reign of William III*, 17 HISTORICAL J. 691, 699–701 (1974).

[44] C.Y. Ferdinand, *Newspapers and the Sale of Books in the Provinces*, in 5 CHB 434, 437; 7 OXFORD HISTORY 178; BREWER-PARTY 142–43.

[45] 7 OXFORD HISTORY 9, 11, 178; 8 *id.* 90–99, though the claim of an "explosion of . . . books," 7 *id.* at 178, does not match the actual stable level for 1695–1700, 4 CHB 784, and for 1703–1743, Michael F. Suarez, *Towards a Bibliometric Analysis of the Surviving Record, 1701–1800*, in 5 CHB 39, 43. *Accord* DICKINSON-POLITICS 7, 205, 206; BREWER-PARTY 138.

[46] James Tierney, *Periodicals and the Trade, 1695–1780*, in 5 CHB 479; 7 OXFORD HISTORY 443–45.

[47] 9 CALENDAR-WILLIAM 80 (9–11 Feb.1698), 151 (17–18 Mar.1698); RONAN DEAZLEY, ON THE ORIGIN OF THE RIGHT TO COPY: CHARTING THE MOVEMENT OF COPYRIGHT LAW IN EIGHTEENTH-CENTURY BRITAIN (1695–1775) 2, 7–29 (Hart Pub., Oxford 2004); LAURENCE HANSON, GOVERNMENT AND THE PRESS, 1695–1763, at 8–10 (OUP, London 1936 repr. 1967).

[48] DEAZLEY, *supra* note 47, at 33–36; 4 KEMP 178; FAILED LEGISLATION, 1660–1800: EXTRACTED FROM THE COMMONS AND LORDS JOURNALS 258 (Julian Hoppit ed., Hambledon, London 1997).

[49] Mark Rose, *Copyright, Authors and Censorship*, in 5 CHB 118, 129; Act for Laying Several Duties upon All Sope and Paper . . . and upon Certain Printed Papers (1711), 10 Anne c19 [sometimes listed c18]; 4 KEMP 200.

[50] *E.g.*, AN EPISTLE TO EUSTACE BUDGELL 13 (John Hughs, London 1734); THE INDEPENDANT [*sic*] BRITON: OR, FREE THOUGHTS . . . AS TO SECURING THE LIBERTY OF THE PRESS 12, 14, 50–51 (T. Cooper, London 1742); A LETTER TO THE REVEREND DR. ZACHARY PEARCE (M. Cooper, London 1743) (subtitled "Observations as to the Danger of the Press, and the Necessity of Preserving its Freedom"); [HORACE WALPOLE], A LETTER TO THE WHIGS 7 (M. Cooper, London 1747); *accord* Marie Peters, *Historians and the Eighteenth Century English Press*, 34 AUSTRALIAN J. OF POLITICS & HIST. 37 (1988).

explained as alarm about the lack of legal security for the press, and about the threat of arrests and further prosecutions for seditious libel.

The Whigs parried taxes on newspapers and pamphlets by sponsoring newspapers and writers, which the Tories matched.[51] That lent some institutional protection to the press.[52] Political parties, both Whig-Tory and Country-Court,[53] owed their emergence and existence in part to ability to print and speak in defense or opposition to the administration's principles and measures.[54] Dissenting thought poured forth from radical Whigs, religious minorities, and various radicals.[55]

However, the English press remained under the shadow of arrest, and possible prosecution, for seditious libel, as the cases of John Wilkes and of Junius's publishers show. Freedom of press was claimed but lacked legal protection;[56] like freedom of religion for non-Anglicans, it was claimed but was merely tolerated. Many said there was a right to liberty of press, or there should be, but Blackstone asserted that it was only liberty from "*previous* restraints upon publications, and not freedom from censure for criminal matter when published."[57]

Cries Against Seditious Libel and Seditious Words as Restraints on Freedoms of Press and Speech

The threat of seditious libel prosecution was a fact of English life throughout the eighteenth century.[58] Following the example of William III, Anne, the month of

[51] DICKINSON-POLITICS 204; JEREMY BLACK, THE ENGLISH PRESS IN THE EIGHTEENTH CENTURY 140, 146–51 (UPP, Philadelphia 1987); 8 OXFORD HISTORY 47.

[52] Gordon S. Adam, The Press and Its Liberty: Myth and Ideology in Eighteenth-Century Politics 4–5, 15–16 (1978) (unpublished Ph.D. thesis, Queen's University (Kingston)).

[53] DICKINSON 122–23, 2–4, 6–7, 57–90 (Whigs), 13–56 (Tories), 163–92 (Country), 121–62 (Court); IDEOLOGICAL ORIGINS 45–52; CREATION 14–15; REED BROWNING, POLITICAL AND CONSTITUTIONAL IDEAS OF THE COURT WHIGS 175–209 (LSUP, Baton Rouge 1982); DAVID HUME, *Of the Parties of Great Britain* (1742), in ESSAYS MORAL, POLITICAL AND LITERARY 63, 63–64 (OUP, Oxford 1963).

[54] DICKINSON 122–23, 169, 6–7; DICKINSON-POLITICS 2–3; KENYON 35–169; BREWER-PARTY 30, 39–40, 267–69. However, some have argued that ideology merely masked pursuit of power, SIR LEWIS NAMIER, THE STRUCTURE OF POLITICS AT THE ACCESSION OF GEORGE III 156–57, 171–72 (2d ed. Macmillan, London 1973), an argument that others have challenged. HERBERT BUTTERFIELD, GEORGE III AND THE HISTORIANS 191–299, esp. 219–20 (Collins, London 1957); W.A. SPECK, TORY AND WHIG: THE STRUGGLE IN THE CONSTITUENCIES, 1701–1715, at 111–14 (Macmillan, London 1970); LINDA COLLEY, IN DEFIANCE OF OLIGARCHY: THE TORY PARTY, 1714–60, at 290–91, 177–262 (CUP, Cambridge 1982); FRANK O'GORMAN, THE RISE OF PARTY IN ENGLAND: THE ROCKINGHAM WHIGS, 1760–82, at 476, 472 (Allen & Unwin, London 1975).

[55] ROBBINS 152–368; ENGLISH SOCIETY 277–348.

[56] HARRIS-NEWSPAPERS 153.

[57] 4 BLACKSTONE'S COMMENTARIES 151 (emphasis in original).

[58] *E.g.*, 15 State Trials 715 (1712); 15 *id.* at 1323 (1719), 17 *id.* at 626 (1731), 18 *id.* at 1203 (1752); *accord* 7 OXFORD HISTORY 181 (Defoe 1703); Case of Robert Clare, Printer (1705–06), 4 KEMP 118; *see* 12 State Trials 1207 (1689–90).

her accession to the throne, issued a proclamation prohibiting seditious libel,[59] and called for legislation against "false and scandalous libels,"[60] in order to punish the "unprecedented" "volume of Whig polemic against the government."[61] Parliament censured particular books in 1704, 1705, 1710, and 1720,[62] and royal proclamations sought out authors of others in 1700, 1704, 1705, and 1714.[63] There were numerous seditious libel prosecutions, which are described in the next chapter.

The most contentious prosecution for seditious libel and seditious speech[64] before 1763 was directed at Dr. Henry Sacheverell for his political sermon in St. Paul's Cathedral in 1709, the twentieth anniversary of William III's landing. Sacheverell "preach[ed] fire and brimstone Toryism" and, in demanding civil obedience and condemning resistance any time and anywhere,[65] implied "that the Revolution *had* involved resistance, and was therefore wrong,"[66] which further suggested that William and his successors usurped the crown from James II.[67] The charges were that Sacheverell acted "to create jealousies and divisions among her Majesty's subjects, and to incite them to sedition and rebellion."[68] At the parliamentary trial in 1710,[69] Sacheverell backed down from his apparent position on the Revolution,[70] but the Whig prosecutors also backed down by "modifying the general right of resistance almost out of existence"[71] and by avoiding any

[59] By the Queen, Proclamation, for Restraining the Spreading of False News, and Printing and Publishing of Irreligious and Seditious Papers and Libels (26 Mar.1702), 4 KEMP 107; 1 TUDOR-STUART PROCLAMATIONS 514. It was reissued a year later. 1 *id.* at 518 (25 Feb.1703).

[60] 4 KEMP 194 (Jan.1712).

[61] KENYON 158; *accord* ENGLISH SOCIETY 15; Michael Harris, *London Newspapers*, in 5 CHB 413, 420–22.

[62] 4 CALENDAR-ANNE no.945; ENGLISH SOCIETY 285.

[63] 10 CALENDAR-WILLIAM 364 (11 Mar.1700); 3 CALENDAR-ANNE no.1023 (1704); Proclamation ["The Memorial of the Church of England"] (no.4399) (20 Dec.1705), 1 TUDOR-STUART PROCLAMATIONS 523; Proclamation, for Discovering the Author of a False, Malicious, and Factious Libel, Intituled, The Public Spirit of the Whigs (no.4538) (15 Mar.1714), 1 *id.* at 536.

[64] Articles of Impeachment against Henry Sacheverell (1710), 8 EHD 205, 206 ("preached a sermon," and "afterwards likewise published in print"); Trial of Henry Sacheverell, 15 State Trials 1, 2 (H.L. 1710) (his books were "scandalous and seditious libels"); *accord* GEOFFREY HOLMES, THE TRIAL OF DOCTOR SACHEVERELL 81, 99–100, 101, 154 (Eyre Methuen, London 1973); Mark Rose, *Copyright, Authors and Censorship*, in 5 CHB 118, 128.

[65] 7 OXFORD HISTORY 46.

[66] KENYON 130; HENRY SACHEVERELL, THE PERILS OF FALSE BRETHREN, BOTH IN CHURCH AND STATE (H. King, London 1709).

[67] ROBBINS 77.

[68] KENYON 2; ROBBINS 77; 8 EHD 206–07.

[69] GEOFFREY HOLMES, THE TRIAL OF DOCTOR SACHEVERELL (Eyre Methuen, London 1973); KENYON 128–45.

[70] DICKINSON 49–50.

[71] KENYON 138–39, 141–42; *accord* DICKINSON 78, 79; *contra* ROBBINS 81.

discussion of natural rights.[72] The Whigs snatched defeat from the jaws of victory through irresolution, failing to use the trial to popularize Whig principles, and throwing themselves as well as Sacheverell out of office.[73]

After many such prosecutions early in the century, the government changed its weapon of choice to intimidation by arrest.[74] Seditious libel served as "the most important legal instrument of press control."[75]

The law of seditious libel drew growing criticism during the eighteenth century. The "immensely popular" essayists,[76] *Cato's Letters*, found seditious libel, particularly restriction of criticizing magistrates and policy on "all publick matters," to be irreconcilable with freedom of speech:

> This secret was so well known to the court of King Charles I that his wicked ministry procured a proclamation to forbid the people to talk of Parliaments, which those traitors had laid aside. To assert the undoubted right of the subject, and defend his Majesty's legal prerogative, was called disaffection, and punished as sedition....
>
> ....
>
> The administration of government is nothing else, but the attendance of the trustees of the people upon the interest and affairs of the people. And as it is the part and business of the people, for whose sake alone all publick matters are, or ought to be, transacted, to see whether they be well or ill transacted; so it is the interest, and ought to be the ambition, of all honest magistrates, to have their deeds openly examined, and publickly scanned: Only the wicked governors of men dread what is said of them....[77]

Cato's subsequent letters continued to discuss the danger and ineffectiveness of seditious libel.[78] Though Trenchard and Gordon, the authors,[79] briefly genuflected

[72] ROBBINS 82. The trial before the Lords is reconstructed in Clyve Jones, *Debates in the House of Lords on "The Church in Danger," 1705, and on Dr Sacheverell's Impeachment, 1710*, 19 HISTORICAL J. 759, 762–71 (1976).

[73] KENYON 132, 145; Geoffrey Holmes, *The Sacheverell Riots*, in REBELLION, POPULAR PROTEST, AND THE SOCIAL ORDER IN EARLY MODERN ENGLAND 232 (Paul Slack ed., CUP, Cambridge 1984); 1 TUDOR-STUART PROCLAMATIONS 531.

[74] BLACK, *supra* note 51, at 135–88, esp.136–37; HARRIS-NEWSPAPERS 134–54, esp. 141–46; *e.g.*, A COLLECTION OF POLITICAL AND HUMOROUS LETTERS, POEMS, AND ARTICLES OF NEWS (J. Clark, London 1748) (title page noting printer's arrest).

[75] Mark Rose, *Copyright, Authors and Censorship*, in 5 CHB 118, 128; *accord* DEAZLEY, *supra* note 47, at 5–6.

[76] PRINTERS 25, 29; *accord* PRELUDE 96 n.34; OPEN PRESS 35, 44–47; ZUCKERT xix, 289–319.

[77] 1 CATO'S LETTERS 110–11 (no.15) (4 Feb.1720).

[78] 2 *id.* 712, 713–16 (no.100) (27 Oct.1722), 717, 718–22 (no.101) (3 Nov.1722); 1 *id.* 228 (no.32) (10 June 1721).

[79] 22 ODNB 960; 55 *id.* 307; ZUCKERT xix.

toward a need to punish libel against the government,[80] their other letters showed little obeisance to such punishments, calling libels "an evil arising out of a much greater good," and finding any restriction irreconcilable with freedom and fatal to speech and writing, because "men [lie] upon the watch to stifle liberty, under a pretence of suppressing libels."[81]

Many others, too, criticized seditious libel restraints as inconsistent with freedoms of press and speech, as the century drew on,[82] though many defended seditious libel. By 1769, a wide range of Whigs argued that "the law of libels leaves not the shadow of the liberty of the press,"[83] and raised various objections to it.[84]

However, that criticism had no effect on the English judiciary, whose almost unanimous view was that seditious libels posed mortal danger to government and must be criminally squelched. Lord Chief Justice Raymond had added a new argument in 1731, charging the jury that "the liberty of the press is only a legal liberty, such as the law allows," not a "liberty to print what he pleases."[85] That, of course, when followed, made liberty of the press nothing but a tautology. However, even he did not give the narrow definition that Blackstone later published.

[80] 2 Cato's Letters 717 (no.100), 719–20 (no.101); 1 *id.* 231–32, 234 (no.32).

[81] 1 *id.* 232–33 (n.32); *accord* 2 *id.* 713 (no.100).

[82] Wendell Bird, *Liberties of Press and Speech: "Evidence Does Not Exist To Contradict the . . . Blackstonian Sense" in Late Eighteenth Century England?*, 36 Oxford J. of Legal Studies __ (forthcoming 2016); Wendell Bird, Freedoms of Press and Speech in the First Decade of the U.S. Supreme Court 100–43 (2012) (unpublished D.Phil. thesis in legal history, University of Oxford); *e.g.*, [Baron George Lyttleton], Considerations upon the Present State of Our Affairs 34–35 (2d ed. T. Cooper, London 1739); [Hugh Hume, Earl of Marchmont], A Serious Exhortation to the Electors 16 (T. Cooper, London 1740); The E—of C——f—d's Speech in the H—se of L—ds, against the Bill for Licensing All Dramatic Performances 13 (n.p., Dublin 1739); The Independant Briton: Or, Free Thoughts . . . as to Securing the Liberty of the Press 12, 13, 15, 17 (T. Cooper, London 1742); Gentleman of the Middle-Temple, A Critical Review of the Liberties of British Subjects 113 (R. Watkins, London 1750); see [Lord Bolingbroke], The Doctrine of Innuendo's Discuss'd, or the Liberty of the Press Maintain'd 16, 11 (n.p., London 1731) ("forced constructions upon every paper . . . support unreasonable prosecutions," and will "destroy the liberty of the press").

[83] Edmund Burke, *Speech on Wilkes's Privilege* (23 Jan.1769), in The Writings and Speeches of Edmund Burke 100, 101 (Paul Langford ed., CP, Oxford 1981–2000).

[84] Junius 16–17 & n. (Junius's preface); 3 Burgh 246–66; Joseph Priestley, An Essay on the First Principles of Government; and on the Nature of Political, Civil, and Religious Liberty 173–74 (James Williams, Dublin 1768).

[85] Trial of Mr. Richard Francklin, 17 State Trials 625, 671, 628 (K.B. 1731); The Craftsman (London), 2 Jan.1731 (no.235), 10 EHD 248.

Dissenting Press and Speech, Wilkes, and Junius

Freedoms of press and speech were tested, and advocated, by John Wilkes (depicted in Figure 1.1),[86] in a cause célèbre that brought debate throughout England[87] and America[88] and that spread belief in unrestrained press and speech.[89] Wilkes's newspaper, *The North Briton*, called a speech delivered by the King "the most abandon[]ed instance of ministerial effrontery ever attempted to be imposed on mankind," full of "odious measures."[90] Wilkes was arrested in 1763 under a general warrant for "the authors, printers and publishers of a seditious and treasonable paper, intitled, The North Briton, No. 45."[91] However, he was soon released from prison, when Lord Chief Justice Charles Pratt (later Lord Camden) granted habeas corpus, based on Wilkes's privilege against arrest as a member of Parliament.[92] As Wilkes left court, thousands "escorted Wilkes home to his house" and shouted "Wilkes and Liberty!,"[93] as they would for each ensuing court appearance.[94] Wilkes successfully challenged the general warrant under which he was arrested, as Pratt ruled that such warrants, with "discretionary power given to messengers to search wherever their suspicions may chance to fall," were "totally subversive of the liberty of the subject," and illegal.[95]

The Commons disagreed that Wilkes was within parliamentary privilege, resolving in late 1763 that it "does not extend to the cases of writing and publishing

[86] Case of John Wilkes, 19 State Trials 982 (K.B. 1763); *see generally* GEORGE RUDÉ, WILKES AND LIBERTY (CP, Oxford 1962); PETER D. G. THOMAS, JOHN WILKES: A FRIEND TO LIBERTY (CP, Oxford 1996); ARTHUR H. CASH, JOHN WILKES: THE SCANDALOUS FATHER OF CIVIL LIBERTY (YUP, New Haven 2006); VALLANCE 205–29; 58 ODNB 953. The cynical view of Wilkes is in DICKINSON-POLITICS 224–25; THOMAS 215–20; Jonathan G. Conlin, *High Art and Low Politics: A New Perspective on John Wilkes*, 64 HUNTINGTON LIBRARY Q. 356, 375–78 (2001).

[87] BREWER-PARTY 163–200; *see* DICKINSON 206.

[88] Pauline Maier, *John Wilkes and American Disillusionment with Britain*, 20 WILLIAM & MARY Q. (3d ser.) 373, 373 (1963); *e.g.*, AN AUTHENTICK ACCOUNT OF THE PROCEEDINGS AGAINST JOHN WILKES (n.p., [Boston] 1763).

[89] RUDÉ 109 (some petitions defended freedom of press).

[90] *North Briton* (London, No.45), 23 Apr.1763, reprinted in 10 EHD 252, 252–53; *accord* THOMAS 27–29.

[91] *Warrant* (30 Apr.1763), 10 EHD 256; Case of John Wilkes, 19 State Trials 982, 982 (K.B. 1763); *accord* RUDÉ 22; THOMAS 29–30; ENGLISH SOCIETY 309–11.

[92] Case of John Wilkes, 19 State Trials 982, 990–93 (K.B. 1763); *accord* RUDÉ 26–27; THOMAS 30–31.

[93] RUDÉ 27 (quoting George Onslow); THOMAS 31–32.

[94] RUDÉ 27, 34, 40, 42, 44, 49, 50, 53, 65; THOMAS 45, 47, 76, 83; ARTHUR H. CASH, JOHN WILKES: THE SCANDALOUS FATHER OF CIVIL LIBERTY 257, 266 (YUP, New Haven 2006); *see* DICKINSON 212.

[95] Wilkes v. Wood, 19 State Trials 1153, 1166–67 (C.P. 1763); *accord* RUDÉ 28–30; THOMAS 32–35, 46.

seditious libels," and furthermore that "*North Briton*, No. 45, is a false, scandalous, and seditious libel."[96] Although the majority of the House of Lords concurred, a dissent of seventeen Lords condemned the Commons' decision, warning that seditious libel earlier had been abused by the Star Chamber and the Crown and that it now threatened to undergird "outrageous and vindictive prosecutions" of the press.[97] However, the Commons expelled Wilkes in January 1764.[98]

With parliamentary privilege not applying, Wilkes was charged with seditious libel in February 1764, and when he fled to France, he lost by default and was adjudged an outlaw.[99]

Wilkes returned to England in 1768, was again elected to the Commons, and surrendered himself to prison.[100] That was commemorated by London riots "almost every night" for a month and a half.[101] Lord Chief Justice Mansfield's court sentenced him to twenty-two months in prison and to a fine of £1000, in June 1768.[102] Wilkes published a pamphlet condemning the trial as "Star Chamber proceedings," and stood on freedoms of the English including freedoms of speech and press, which he accused Mansfield of trying to suppress:[103]

> There can be no such thing, my lord, as public liberty, without freedom of speech, which is the right of every man; this sacred privilege is so essential to free governments, that the security of property and freedom of speech always go together....
>
> ... Freedom of speech, my lord, is the great bulwark of liberty, they prosper and die together; the liberty of the press is the terror of traitors and oppressors, and a barrier against them.... [104]

[96] SELECT STATUTES-CASES 302, reprinting 29 JHC 667, 675 (14 Nov.1763, 24 Nov.1763); *accord* RUDÉ 33–34; THOMAS 36–42. Simultaneously Parliament found his "Essay on Women" an obscene libel. RUDÉ 33; ENGLISH SOCIETY 309–10.

[97] 19 State Trials 994–99; SELECT STATUTES-CASES 302, 305, 308, reprinting 30 JHL 426 (29 Nov.1763); *accord* THOMAS 45.

[98] RUDÉ 35; THOMAS 47–54; 1 SIMON MACCOBY, ENGLISH RADICALISM 13–33 (Allen & Unwin, London 1935–61).

[99] Proceedings in the Case of John Wilkes, 19 State Trials 1075 (K.B. 1763–70) (two libels); *accord* RUDÉ 35; THOMAS 54–55. Various printers of No. 45 were also prosecuted and convicted. 2 MANSFIELD MANUSCRIPTS 826, 828.

[100] *Id.* at 1077; *accord* RUDÉ 41, 46–48; THOMAS 70–76, 80, 82.

[101] RUDÉ 45; THOMAS 82–84.

[102] 19 State Trials 1077, 1124, which the Lords affirmed, 19 *id.* at 1136; *accord* RUDÉ 57; THOMAS 80, 82, 85–86, 111, 115.

[103] JOHN WILKES, A LETTER TO THE RIGHT HONOURABLE WILLIAM LORD MANSFIELD 13 (John Wilkes, London 1768).

[104] *Id* 12–13, 24.

The Commons once more expelled Wilkes at the beginning of February 1769,[105] again for seditious libel and obscene libel.[106] Nevertheless, Wilkes was reelected two weeks later, and the Commons the next day disqualified him.[107] Wilkes was again reelected three weeks after that, and was again disqualified the next day.[108] Though the administration's candidate lost to Wilkes by 1043–296 votes, the Commons voided the election and seated the loser.[109] This led to petitions in favor of Wilkes from over half of England's counties and a number of cities,[110] and a dissent by forty-two Lords condemning the Commons' violation of "the fundamental right of election," warning that "the day may come again when freedom of speech may be criminal in that House."[111] The City of London later responded by electing Wilkes Lord Mayor.[112]

The long-running Wilkes affair spurred the growth of radicalism,[113] including formation of the Society of Supporters of the Bill of Rights,[114] "the first radical society" and "the first important extra-parliamentary organization."[115] Wilkite radicals fervently supported freedoms of press and speech.[116] In fact, the "Wilkite phenomenon" was made possible by the press,[117] as was its spread to America.

The border of English freedom of press was also crossed by essays of "Junius," denouncing corruption in Britain's administration, as they were published in 1769 through 1772.[118] The series of essays began and ended with defenses of Wilkes,[119] and in between were scathing toward Mansfield.[120] The government

[105] THOMAS 79, 80, 92–98, citing 32 JHC 178–79 (3 Feb.1769); DICKINSON 211.

[106] Described in Wilkes v. R, Wilm. 322, 324–25, 97 Eng. Rep. 123, 124 (H.L. 1769); 2 MANSFIELD MANUSCRIPTS 825.

[107] SELECT STATUTES-CASES 332–33, reprinting 32 JHC 228–29 (17 Feb.1769); *accord* RUDÉ 67; THOMAS 98–99.

[108] RUDÉ 68; THOMAS 99–101.

[109] SELECT STATUTES-CASES 333, reprinting 32 JHC 451 (8 May 1769); RUDÉ 68, 70; THOMAS 101–03; DICKINSON 211.

[110] RUDÉ 105, 133, 135; *see* THOMAS 103–04; DICKINSON 195.

[111] SELECT STATUTES-CASES 333–36, reprinting JHL (2 Feb.1770).

[112] RUDÉ 170, 191; THOMAS 147–53, 153–54.

[113] RUDÉ 196–98, 106–08, 115, 116, 135, 197; *see* DICKINSON 197–205; DICKINSON-POLITICS 178–80; IAN MCCALMAN, RADICAL UNDERWORLD: PROPHETS, REVOLUTIONARIES AND PORNOGRAPHERS IN LONDON, 1795–1840, at 8–18 (CUP, Cambridge 1988).

[114] RUDÉ 106; THOMAS 109–24.

[115] DICKINSON 210, 213.

[116] DICKINSON 197, 202.

[117] BREWER-PARTY 160, 167; Peter D.G. Thomas, *John Wilkes and the Freedom of the Press (1771)*, 33 BULL. OF INST. OF HISTORICAL RESEARCH 86 (May 1960).

[118] JUNIUS 25, 320; *see* BREWER-PARTY 154–55; THOMAS 126. The probable identity of Junius is summarized in T.H. Bowyer, *Junius, Philip Francis and Parliamentary Reform*, 27 ALBION 397, 397 n.1 (1995).

[119] JUNIUS 25, 342; *accord id.* at 63–67, 86–115, 257–59, 272–77, 292.

[120] JUNIUS 15–18, 302 (no.61) (17 Oct.1771), 320 (no.68) (21 Jan.1772).

launched a frenetic but doomed effort to identify the author,[121] and brought mostly unsuccessful prosecutions of the bookseller, printer, and publisher.[122]

The next major battleground for freedom of press was over the right to publish proceedings of Parliament, which had been long opposed by Parliament as a violation of its privileges.[123] The main battle involved John Millar, a printer, and Brass Crosby, the new Lord Mayor of London, in 1770. The Commons ordered the arrest of Millar and other printers.[124] The Lord Mayor responded by releasing Millar and instead arresting the messenger,[125] in a plan apparently concocted by Wilkes.[126] Parliament found Crosby and others guilty and imprisoned them.[127] Upon his release as Parliament adjourned, Crosby was welcomed with a "salute of twenty-one guns" and "a triumphal procession of fifty-three carriages" accompanied by "loud and universal huzzas."[128] Crosby's position quickly triumphed, and Boswell observed in 1791 that "all parts of the kingdom have a fair, open, and exact report of the actual proceedings of their representatives and legislators."[129]

Nascent Calls for Freedom of Speech

Freedom of speech within Parliament had fared better in the Bill of Rights than freedom of press.[130] However, freedom of speech outside Parliament, except in petitions, remained unprotected by British law.

Freedom of speech had long been claimed or demanded. John Tutchin, two years after his seditious libel trial, wrote that "here we dare speak and write the truth, this is an essential part of our freedom," whereas France's lack of that freedom evinced "vassalage."[131] A 1742 publication, similarly using "freedom in

[121] JUNIUS xvi-xvii.

[122] Trial of John Almon, 20 State Trials 803 (K.B. 1770); Case of Henry Sampson Woodfall, 20 State Trials 895 (K.B. 1770); Trial of John Miller, 20 State Trials 869 (K.B. 1770).

[123] A. Aspinall, *The Reporting and Publishing of the House of Commons' Debates 1771–1834*, in ESSAYS PRESENTED TO SIR LEWIS NAMIER 227, 228 (opposed in 1642, 1695, 1697, 1722, 1728, 1738) (Richard Pares & A.J.P. Taylor eds., Macmillan, London 1956); 10 EHD 178 (1738); 7 CALENDAR-WILLIAM 431, 488 (1696); THOMAS 125.

[124] THOMAS 131–32; RUDÉ 156, 158, along with 7 other newspapers.

[125] 19 *id.* at 1147; *accord* ROBBINS 351, 358; THOMAS 132; RUDÉ 158–59.

[126] THOMAS 125, 128–29; RUDÉ 157.

[127] THOMAS 137; RUDÉ 163.

[128] THOMAS 138; RUDÉ 164.

[129] 1 JAMES BOSWELL, BOSWELL'S LIFE OF JOHNSON 115 (L.F. Powell ed., 2d ed., CP, Oxford 1964); *accord* R v. Wright, (1799) 8 T.R. 293, 296–98, 101 Eng. Rep. 1396, 1398–99 (K.B.) (true reports not prosecutable libels); Peter D.G. Thomas, *The Beginning of Parliamentary Reporting in Newspapers, 1768–1774*, 74 ENG. HISTORICAL REV. 623, 630–33 (1959); RUDÉ 165, though futile parliamentary obstacles remained, THOMAS 139–40.

[130] 1 W&M (sess 2) c2; 8 EHD 122, 123–24; 9 STATUTES 67.

[131] John Tutchin, *Observator* (London), 1706, reprinted in 4 KEMP 309, 310.

speech" synonymously with freedom "of the press," affirmed it to be part of the "right to liberty."[132] An essay in *Commonsense* in 1738 extolled "freedom of inquiry" and "free discussion of all subjects, unrestrained but by equitable laws, which constitutes the very essence of our civil liberty."[133] Horace Walpole wrote that "[l]iberty of speech and liberty of writing are the two instruments by which Englishmen call on one another to defend their common rights."[134] Country Whigs similarly tended to support "free expression and free association."[135] Wilkes saw freedom of speech as a human right and as essential to free government.

Cato's Letters had given the strongest call for unrestrained freedom of speech, so long as it did not injure another. The fifteenth letter opened with that call:

> Without freedom of thought, there can be no such thing as wisdom, and no such thing as public liberty, without freedom of speech: Which is the right of every man, as far as by it he does not hurt or control the right of another; and this is the only check which it ought to suffer, the only bounds which it ought to know.
>
> This sacred privilege is so essential to free government, that the security of property; and the freedom of speech, always go together. . . . [136]

Implicit in "the only bounds which it ought to know" was that speech should not be limited by seditious words doctrines. In essays republished as the *Independent Whig*, Trenchard and Gordon further described why speech is essential to free government through a "right of examining all publick measures and, if they deserve it, of censuring them."[137] Again, an implicit assumption of a right to censure public measures was that such speech should not be punishable as sedition. Gordon later devoted a section to "Freedom of Speech" in essays introducing his translation of *Tacitus*.[138]

[132] The Independant Briton: Or, Free Thoughts . . . as to Securing the Liberty of the Press 11 (T. Cooper, London 1742); *accord* [Thomas Hayter], An Essay on the Liberty of the Press 8 (J. Raymond, London 1755).

[133] *To the Gentlemen, Merchants, Freeholders, and Others* (21 Jan.1738), in Commonsense: or, the Englishman's Journal 349, 350 (J. Purser, London 1738).

[134] 1 Memoirs of the Reign of King George III: Horace Walpole 212 (Derek Jarrett ed., YUP, New Haven 2000).

[135] Dickinson 179–80; Dickinson-Politics 198. *E.g.*, Charles D'Avenant [Davenant], Essays upon Peace at Home, and War Abroad 47 (James Knapton, London 1704); The Livery-Man: or, Plain Thoughts on Publick Affairs 50, 22 (n.p. 1740).

[136] 1 Cato's Letters 110, 110 (no.15) (4 Feb.1720); *accord* 1 *id.* at 111–16; 2 *id.* at 712, 713 (no.100) (27 Oct.1722); 2 *id.* at 717, 721 (no.101) (3 Nov.1722).

[137] Quoted in Robbins 115 & n.62.

[138] 1 Thomas Gordon, The Works of Tacitus 105–06 (Tho. Woodward, London 1728) (Discourse 9, §1), mentioned in Robbins 115 & n.61.

Such radical Whigs were the consistent advocates of free speech, as of free press.[139] One in 1712 recalled that "Republican writers have ever been extolling the benefit of freedom of speech," and that "Whigs have argu'd for allowing the press its full swing."[140] A number of "eighteenth-century Commonwealthmen" advocated protection for freedom of speech.[141] James Burgh in 1775 devoted a chapter of his *Political Disquisitions* to "Of the Liberty of Speech and Writing in Political Subjects."[142]

In addition, the step from advocacy of liberty as "the inherent right of all mankind,"[143] to identification of freedom of speech or freedom of press as some of

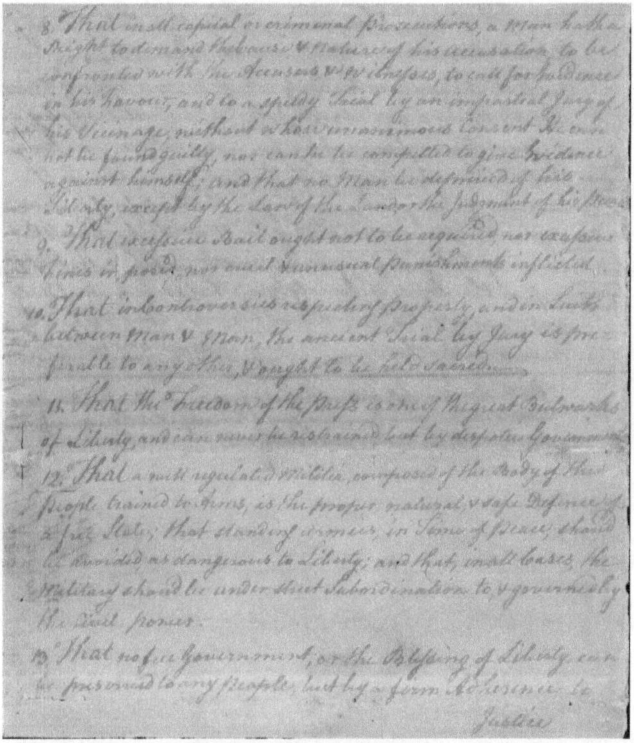

8. That in all capital or criminal Prosecutions, a Man hath a Right to demand the cause & Nature of his accusation, to be confronted with the Accusers & Witnesses, to call for Evidence in his Favour, and to a speedy Trial by an impartial Jury of his Vicinage, without whose unanimous Consent he can not be found guilty, nor can he be compelled to give Evidence against himself; and that no Man be deprived of his Liberty, except by the Law of the Land or the Judgment of his Peers.
9. That excessive Bail ought not to be required, nor excessive Fines imposed, nor cruel & unusual Punishments inflicted.
10. That in Controversies respecting Property, and in Suits between Man & Man, the ancient Trial by Jury is preferable to any other, & ought to be held sacred.
11. That the Freedom of the Press is one of the great Bulwarks of Liberty, and can never be restrained but by despotic Governments.
12. That a well regulated Militia, composed of the Body of the People, trained to Arms, is the proper, natural, & safe Defence of a free State; that standing Armies, in Time of Peace, should be avoided as dangerous to Liberty; and that, in all Cases, the Military should be under strict Subordination to, & governed by the Civil Power.
13. That no free Government, or the Blessing of Liberty can be preserved to any People, but by a firm Adherence to Justice

Figure 1.2 The Virginia Declaration of Rights (1776). Copy of the first draft 1776. (Courtesy of Virginia Memory, University of Virginia.)

[139] Dickinson-Politics 194.

[140] The Thoughts of a Tory Author Concerning the Press 7, 12 (A. Baldwin, London 1712).

[141] Robbins 77 (Lord Somers), 123 & n.83 (John Toland), 127 & n.93 (Anthony Collins), 199 & nn.48–49 (Robert Wallace); *see id.* 66 (Sir Isaac Newton).

[142] 3 Burgh 246–66.

[143] William Molyneux, The Case of Ireland's Being Bound by Acts of Parliament in England Stated 3 (Joseph Ray, Dublin 1698), mentioned in Robbins 136–37 & n.9.

those inherent rights, began to be made more and more by various moderate[144] and radical Whigs.[145]

By the time of the American Revolution, freedoms of press and speech in England proved insufficient to protect Wilkes and Junius from prosecution, but had broadened from the Stuart period. One measure of that growth was that the Whig opposition could question Tory prosecution of the war,[146] at least in parliamentary speech,[147] and another measure was that England's press multiplied its books and pamphlets.[148] By 1775, freedom of press had almost no relation to freedom from licensing, which had not existed for eighty years. Freedom of speech never had any relation to freedom from licensing, since speech had never been licensed (except preaching and theater). Still, freedoms of press and speech enjoyed only toleration but no security as rights.[149]

The Developing Freedoms of Press and Speech in Eighteenth-Century America

Those events in English history figured large in the American colonies, and were endlessly cited as the colonists' own heritage.[150] The political philosophers in

[144] [HORACE WALPOLE], A LETTER TO THE WHIGS 12 (M. Cooper, London 1747) (liberty of the press); [THOMAS HAYTER], AN ESSAY ON THE LIBERTY OF THE PRESS 7 (J. Raymond, London 1755); DAVID WILLIAMS, A LETTER TO THE BODY OF THE PROTESTANT DISSENTING MINISTERS OF ALL DENOMINATIONS 23–24 (1777), quoted in DICKINSON 202; *accord* H. T. Dickinson, *Whiggism in the Eighteenth Century*, in THE WHIG ASCENDANCY: COLLOQUIES ON HANOVERIAN ENGLAND 28, 32 (John Cannon ed., Edward Arnold, London 1981).

[145] GEORGE STEPHENS, NATIONAL RIGHTEOUSNESS, THE FOUNDATION OF PUBLIC PROSPERITY 21 (T. Cox, London 1728) (natural right of inquiry); A COLLECTION OF LETTERS PUBLISH'D IN OLD ENGLAND: OR, THE CONSTITUTIONAL JOURNAL 59 (W. Webb, London 1742) (freedom of press); [JOHN ASGILL], AN ESSAY FOR THE PRESS (A. Baldwin, London 1712), 4 KEMP 245, 245. However, freedom of press was not sufficiently accepted as a core freedom to appear in Richard Price's definition of civil and religious liberty in 1776. RICHARD PRICE, OBSERVATIONS ON THE NATURE OF CIVIL LIBERTY 21–22 (2d ed. T. Cadell, London 1776).

[146] JAMES E. BRADLEY, RELIGION, REVOLUTION, AND ENGLISH RADICALISM: NONCONFORMITY IN EIGHTEENTH-CENTURY POLITICS AND SOCIETY 7–18, 147–53 (CUP, Cambridge 1990); THOMAS 175; 3 Edmund Burke, *An Appeal from the New to the Old Whigs* (1791), in 3 WORKS OF EDMUND BURKE 1, 30 (Bohn's Standard Library, London 1886).

[147] The "Junius" letter prosecuted in 1770 was nonparliamentary criticism of the King's approach to America.

[148] Michael F. Suarez, *Towards a Bibliometric Analysis of the Surviving Record, 1701–1800*, in 5 CHB 39, 43 (England, Scotland, and Wales).

[149] *See* 8 OXFORD HISTORY 289. Cressy disagrees, CRESSY 235, 239, 243, but his numerous examples of eighteenth-century prosecution of words for sedition show restricted freedom. *Id.* 226–35, 236–58.

[150] *E.g.*, Trial of Mr. John Peter Zenger, 17 State Trials 675, 682, 697, 707, 711, 717, 723 (N.Y.S.Ct. 1735); WILLIAM BOLLAN, THE FREEDOM OF SPEECH AND WRITING UPON PUBLIC

English history also figured large in the constitutional period, though which ones were most influential in America remains hotly debated. Earlier assumptions that Locke was the dominant influence were questioned by Robbins's discussion of the "Commonwealthmen" and by others,[151] and were directly attacked[152] by the republican synthesis, led by Bailyn's and Wood's broader ideological origins and Pocock's classical and renaissance influences.[153] Neolockeans counterattacked and rejected a republican-Locke antithesis,[154] and condemned the "contemporary infatuation with 'classical republicanism' and the synthesis itself."[155] Others joined them in objecting to undue emphasis on classical republicanism over individualistic liberalism,[156] and in denying that Machiavelli's "long, somber shadow" had much to do with American political thought.[157]

Though political philosophy flourished more in England, it was in America that freedoms of press and speech were exercised more freely and were secured more effectively. The reasons why these freedoms grew more in America included the distance and de facto freedom from London government,[158] the relative

---

AFFAIRS CONSIDERED (S. Baker, London 1766); WILSON'S CONSIDERATIONS 9–13; FEDERALIST No.5, at 24. That was part of a growing "turn to history." DAVID M. RABBAN, LAW'S HISTORY: AMERICAN LEGAL THOUGHT (CUP, New York 2013).

151 ROBBINS 19–51, 52–129, 216–312; IDEOLOGICAL ORIGINS 34–35; CREATION 14, 50; ROBERT MIDDLEKAUFF, THE GLORIOUS CAUSE: THE AMERICAN REVOLUTION, 1763–1789, at 51 (rev. ed. OUP, New York 2007); JAMES HARRINGTON, THE COMMONWEALTH OF OCEANA AND A SYSTEM OF POLITICS xv (J. G. A. Pocock ed., CUP, Cambridge 1992); Jenni Parrish, *Law Books and Legal Publishing in America, 1760–1840*, 72 LAW LIBRARY J. 355, 356–57 (1979).

152 BERNARD BAILYN, THE ORIGINS OF AMERICAN POLITICS ix-x, 57 (Knopf, New York 1968); IDEOLOGICAL ORIGINS 34–35; CREATION 29; *accord* Robert E. Shalhope, *Toward a Republican Synthesis*, 29 WILLIAM & MARY Q. (3d ser.) 49, 49 & n.1, 51 (1972).

153 IDEOLOGICAL ORIGINS 23–42; CREATION 47, 49, 114–17; J.G.A. POCOCK, THE MACHIAVELLIAN MOMENT (PUP, Princeton 1975); *accord* 1 QUENTIN SKINNER, THE FOUNDATIONS OF MODERN POLITICAL THOUGHT 3–22, 49–65, 71–84, 139–89 (CUP, Cambridge 1978) (medieval and Renaissance); 2 *id.* 12–19, 241–54 (Reformation).

154 *E.g.*, THOMAS L. PANGLE, THE SPIRIT OF MODERN REPUBLICANISM: THE MORAL VISION OF THE AMERICAN FOUNDERS AND THE PHILOSOPHY OF LOCKE 28–39 (UChiP, Chicago 1988); JEROME HUYLER, LOCKE IN AMERICA 31–41, 175–273 (UPKan, Lawrence 1995); *cf.* J.G.A. Pocock, *Empire, Revolution and an End of Early Modernity*, in VARIETIES 283, 287.

155 *E.g.*, *id.* at 29; ZUCKERT 150–83, esp.164–66; CLARK 24, 25–29.

156 *E.g.*, Isaac Kramnick, *Republican Revisionism Revisited*, 87 AM. HISTORICAL REV. 629, 634–55 (1982); M. N. S. SELLERS, THE SACRED FIRE OF LIBERTY: REPUBLICANISM, LIBERALISM, AND THE LAW ix (NYUP, New York 1998); DAVID J. BEDERMAN, THE CLASSICAL FOUNDATIONS OF THE AMERICAN CONSTITUTION 1–49 (CUP, Cambridge 2008); *cf.* IDEOLOGICAL ORIGINS 351–52.

157 *E.g.*, KENNETH PENNINGTON, THE PRINCE AND THE LAW, 1200–1600: SOVEREIGNTY AND RIGHTS IN THE WESTERN LEGAL TRADITION 269 (UCP, Berkeley 1993); 1 CATO'S LETTERS 230 (no.32).

158 IDEOLOGICAL ORIGINS 204; TRANSATLANTIC 1, 2, 4.

weakness of colonial government,[159] the much larger percentage of religious dissenters,[160] the correspondingly reduced influence of the Church of England, and the minimal obstructions to "Commonwealthmen" and radical Whig thought. However, above all, the reason was the colonial crisis and the American Revolution, which impelled the articulation, defense, and ultimate securing of those rights.

Dissenting Press and Speech at the Beginning of the Eighteenth Century

While freedom of conscience gained protection in much of colonial America even before the eighteenth century,[161] freedoms of press and speech were slower to be secured. Glimmers of a new conceptual framework appeared in the founding agreement of Rhode Island in 1637, which stated that the colony's powers reached "only . . . civill things,"[162] but subsequent documents used only "liberty of conscience" language.[163]

The primary reason why freedom of press enjoyed only slight American discussion in the seventeenth century was that the press barely existed in the colonies then. It consisted only of a first printing press in Massachusetts in 1638, a second colonial press in the same shop in 1660,[164] and a few presses thereafter. A lone newspaper died after the first issue in 1690,[165] and the first continuing newspaper in the colonies only began in 1701.[166] Licensing came to Massachusetts the same year as England's Licensing Act of 1662, and came to the colonies generally

[159] Jack P. Greene, Peripheries and Center: Constitutional Development in the Extended Polities of the British Empire and the United States, 1607–1788, at 79–150 (W.W. Norton, New York 1990); Ideological Origins 203.

[160] Edwin S. Gaustad, New Historical Atlas of Religion in America 7, 8, 399 (OUP, Oxford 2001); 2 William G. McLoughlin, New England Dissent, 1630–1833, at 833–54 (HUP, Cambridge 1971); 1 *id.* 329–417, 420–76; Clark 205, 208, 209–10, 212, 268.

[161] The best collection of relevant documents and discussion is Daniel L. Dreisbach & Mark D. Hall, The Sacred Rights of Conscience: Selected Readings on Religious Liberty and Church-State Relations in the American Founding (LF, Indianapolis 2009).

[162] 1 Thomas W. Bicknell, History of the State of Rhode Island 196 (AHS, New York 1920).

[163] Plantation Agreement (27 Aug.-6 Sept.1640), in 6 Federal-State Constitutions 3205, 3206; Determinations of General Court of Election (16–19 Mar.1641), in 6 *id.* at 3207, 3208; Charter ¶¶1, 2 (8 July 1663), in 6 *id.* at 3211, 3212.

[164] Press-Mass. 22–23, 42.

[165] *Id.* 68–69; Tyranny 29.

[166] Charles E. Clark, *Early American Journalism: News and Opinion in the Popular Press*, in The Colonial Book in the Atlantic World 347, 351 (Hugh Amory & David D. Hall eds., CUP, Cambridge 2000).

in royal instructions in 1683,[167] but it was rarely enforced and its ghost vanished after a last abortive effort of enforcement in 1723.[168]

Freedom of speech received its first legal protection in the English-speaking world in Massachusetts in 1641, as the "Body of Liberties" provided that "every man" had "libertie to come to any publique court, councel, or towne meeting, and either by speech or writeing to move any lawfull, seasonable, and materiall question."[169] That preceded even the radical army proposals in England of 1647. However, with most speech taking the form of petitions[170] to distant government, the concept of freedom of speech took longer than freedom of press to become a popular demand, until there were threats against prerevolutionary expression.

In America as in England, freedoms of press and speech were practiced, but not secured. However, demands for security grew throughout the eighteenth century, as did criticism and rejection of seditious libel as a threat to those freedoms.

Treatment of Dissenting Press and Speech and the Zenger Trial

Freedom of speech was often suppressed in colonial America, as Eldridge and others have thoroughly chronicled.[171] After frequent prosecution of seditious words in the seventeenth century,[172] freedom in practice for spoken words grew in the next century,[173] though that freedom was not secured in law.

Colonial laws continued to make it a crime to "speak any seditious words or speeches, or spread abroad false news, [to] write or disperse scurrilous libels

167 *Id.* 41–42; PRELUDE 61; 2 ROYAL INSTRUCTIONS 495 (No.719).

168 *Id.* 98–102; PRINTERS 97–104.

169 The Body of Liberties of the Massachusetts Collonie in New England §12 (10 Dec.1641), in 8 COLLECTIONS OF THE MASS. HISTORICAL SOC. (3d ser.) 216, 218. It was less charitable toward blasphemy, sec.94(3), 8 *id.* at 232, which the courts regularly prosecuted along with profane swearing and women's preaching. JANE KAMENSKY, GOVERNING THE TONGUE: THE POLITICS OF SPEECH IN EARLY NEW ENGLAND 7, 74–98 (OUP, Oxford 1997). The provision was continued in the Laws and Liberties of Massachusetts (1648). THE LAWS AND LIBERTIES OF MASSACHUSETTS: REPRINTED FROM THE COPY OF THE 1648 EDITION 35 (Thomas G. Barnes ed., Legal Classics Library, Birmingham 1982).

170 EDMUND S. MORGAN, INVENTING THE PEOPLE: THE RISE OF POPULAR SOVEREIGNTY IN ENGLAND AND AMERICA 227, 229–30 (Norton, New York 1988); EMPIRE 59.

171 LARRY D. ELDRIDGE, A DISTANT HERITAGE: THE GROWTH OF FREE SPEECH IN EARLY AMERICA 5–19, 23–41, esp.14–19 (on criticism of government) (NYUP, New York 1994); LEVY 16–88.

172 Larry D. Eldridge, *Before Zenger: Truth and Seditious Speech in Colonial America, 1607–1700*, 39 AM. J. LEGAL HISTORY 337, 337 (1995); *e.g.*, GEORGE L. HASKINS, LAW AND AUTHORITY IN EARLY MASSACHUSETTS 28, 183, 196 (Macmillan, New York 1960).

173 ELDRIDGE, *supra* note 171, at 65–66, 77, 91–113, 114, 132.

against the present government," or to "instigate others to sedition."[174] Legislatures often charged critics with "writing, signing and publishing a false, scandalous, virulent and seditious libel against the last house of assembly," and jailed authors and accomplices.[175] Governors intermittently sought to prosecute newspaper critics of government for seditious libel.[176] Court prosecutions were frequently threatened, though less frequently brought, against authors for seditious libel.[177]

Judicial suppression of printing reached a decisive point in the 1735 trial of John Peter Zenger in New York,[178] for publishing seditious libel consisting of criticism of the governor and Crown ministers.[179] Zenger's defense relied primarily on the arguments that truth could not be libelous, and that the jury should decide whether words were false and libelous,[180] both contrary to English law until the jury's role was changed in 1792. Though the judge rejected those arguments, the jury ignored his instructions and acquitted Zenger,[181] after deliberating only ten minutes.[182] The practical effect of the Zenger trial was to introduce those potential ameliorations of seditious libel law to the American colonies (a truth defense and a general verdict), and to deter colonial officials from bringing many seditious libel cases out of fear that juries would again acquit the accused.

[174] *E.g.*, Act for the More Effectual Observing of the Queen's Peace (1713), in 1 COLLECTION OF ALL THE ACTS OF ASSEMBLY, OF THE PROVINCE OF NORTH-CAROLINA 8 (James Davis, Newbern 1765); *accord* Act against Intemperance, Immorality and Prophaneness, ACTS AND LAWS, PASSED BY THE GREAT AND GENERAL COURT . . . MASSACHUSETTS-BAY [1711–1712] 371 (n.p., Boston 1712); JOURNAL OF THE VOTES AND PROCEEDINGS OF THE HOUSE OF REPRESENTATIVES OF THE PROVINCE OF PENNSYLVANIA 30 (n.p., Philadelphia 1727) (requesting enforcement); Act Against Spreading False News and Defamation (1741), in LAWS OF THE GOVERNMENT OF . . . DELAWARE 217 (James Adams, Wilmington 1763).

[175] *E.g.*, 4 VOTES AND PROCEEDINGS OF THE HOUSE OF REPRESENTATIVES OF THE PROVINCE OF PENNSYLVANIA 769 (Henry Miller, Philadelphia 1774) (William Moore-William Smith, 1758); *accord* JOURNAL OF THE VOTES AND PROCEEDINGS OF THE GENERAL ASSEMBLY OF THE COLONY OF NEW-YORK [1769–1770] 49, 51 (Hugh Gaine, New York 1770) (Legion-John Lamb, 1769); PRELUDE 62–64.

[176] *E.g.*, LETTERS TO THE MINISTRY FROM GOVERNOR BERNARD, GENERAL GAGE, AND COMMODORE HOOD 6–7 (Samuel Hall, Salem 1769) (Boston Gazette, 1768); Gov. William Cosby, A Proclamation (n.p., New York 1734); *accord* Lt. Gov. Spencer Phips, A Proclamation (John Draper, Boston 1751).

[177] PRELUDE 63–64; LEVY 17.

[178] Trial of Mr. John Peter Zenger, 17 State Trials 675 (N.Y.S.Ct. 1735).

[179] "Information," 17 *id.* at 692; JAMES ALEXANDER, A BRIEF NARRATIVE OF THE CASE AND TRIAL OF JOHN PETER ZENGER (Stanley N. Katz ed., BP-HUP, Cambridge 1968).

[180] 17 *id.* at 693, 694, 704, 705, 713, 716, while not directly attacking seditious libel, LEVY 127–28.

[181] 17 *id.* at 699, 706, 722, 723.

[182] OPEN PRESS 49.

The Central Place of Dissenting Press and Speech in Prerevolutionary Debates

The colonies were jarred out of a century of "salutary neglect"[183] by the Stamp Act[184] crisis of 1765 and, after its repeal, by a series of further crises as Parliament attempted to govern the colonies. Parliament asserted authority over the colonies during 1763–1767[185] by laws including the Declaratory Act[186] of 1766, and attempted to collect taxes during 1767–1773[187] with the Townshend duties.[188] Outraged by the Boston Tea Party,[189] Parliament passed the punitive Coercive Acts,[190] and the conflict spiraled to armed battle and independence in 1775 and 1776.[191]

Those provocations unleashed a torrent of colonial dissent—press, speech, and petition—which brought increasing awareness of dissent's precarious legal status. "Patriot newspapers were one of the most important factors in turning American public opinion,"[192] and American newspapers doubled from twenty to

[183] 8 OXFORD HISTORY 171–72; Jacob M. Price, *Who Cared about the Colonies?*, in STRANGERS WITHIN THE REALM 395, 396 (Bernard Bailyn & Philip D. Morgan eds., UNCP, Chapel Hill 1991). For an outstanding discussion of the growing right to dissent, see ROBERT W.T. MARTIN, GOVERNMENT BY DISSENT: PROTEST, RESISTANCE, AND RADICAL DEMOCRATIC THOUGHT IN THE EARLY AMERICAN REPUBLIC (NYUP, New York 2013).

[184] 5 Geo 3 c12 (22 Mar.1765); 26 STATUTES 179; along with the Revenue Act, 4 Geo 3 c15 (1764); 26 STATUTES 33; and Quartering Act, 5 Geo 3 c33 (15 May 1765); 26 STATUTES 305.

[185] *E.g.*, PETER D.G. THOMAS, BRITISH POLITICS AND THE STAMP ACT CRISIS 85–114, 131–84, 185–252 (CP, Oxford 1975); EDMUND S. MORGAN, PROLOGUE TO REVOLUTION: SOURCES AND DOCUMENTS ON THE STAMP ACT CRISIS, 1764–1766 (UNCP, Chapel Hill 1959).

[186] 6 Geo 3 c12 (18 Mar.1766); 27 STATUTES 19; adopted the same day as the Stamp Act was repealed, Act Repealing the Stamp Act, 6 Geo 3 c11 (18 Mar.1766); 27 STATUTES 19.

[187] *E.g.*, PETER D.G. THOMAS, THE TOWNSHEND DUTIES CRISIS 18–75, 76–141, 161–79 (CP, Oxford 1987).

[188] Act Creating the American Board of Customs Commissioners, 7 Geo 3 c41, c46 (29 June 1767); 27 STATUTES 447, 505; repealed 10 Geo 3 c17 (1770).

[189] Following the Tea Act, 13 Geo 3 c44 (1773); *see* 7 Geo 3 c56 (1766); 27 STATUTES 600. *E.g.*, BENJAMIN W. LABAREE, THE BOSTON TEA PARTY 126–35 (OUP, Oxford 1964); BERNARD KNOLLENBERG, GROWTH OF THE AMERICAN REVOLUTION, 1766–1775, at 90–102 (Free Press, NY 1975).

[190] Boston Port Act, 14 Geo 3 c19 (31 Mar.1774); 30 STATUTES 336; Massachusetts Administration of Justice Act, 14 Geo 3 c39 (20 May 1774); 30 STATUTES 367; Massachusetts Government Act, 14 Geo 3 c45 (20 May 1774); 30 STATUTES 381; Quartering Act, 14 Geo 3 c54 (2 June 1774); 30 STATUTES 410; Quebec Act, 14 Geo 3 c83 (22 June 1774).

[191] *E.g.*, PETER D.G. THOMAS, TEA PARTY TO INDEPENDENCE 26–142, 220–319, 320–34 (CP, Oxford 1991); MIDDLEKAUFF, *supra* note 151, at 180–339; DAVID MCCULLOUGH, 1776 (Simon & Schuster, New York 2005).

[192] TYRANNY 33; PRELUDE 51–301; Robert M. Weir, *The Role of the Newspaper Press in the Southern Colonies*, in THE PRESS AND THE AMERICAN REVOLUTION 99, 99 (Bernard Bailyn & John B. Hench eds., American Antiquarian Society, Worcester 1980).

forty-three between 1762 and 1775.[193] Colonial legislatures increasingly spoke and voted in opposition to Crown measures.[194]

This growing dissent brought development of theories of colonists' rights. As conflict grew, the "ancient constitution" was increasingly seen as corrupted,[195] and the ill-defined and restricted nature of English rights demanded alternate grounds,[196] which were natural rights and charter rights (later replaced by revolutionary declarations of rights).[197] Colonial theorists most often relied on the "radical Whig understanding of politics,"[198] which was much more widely adopted in America than in England.[199] That was in part because America was in search of a theory for challenging Parliament, and in part because "radical Whigs were only dissenting Protestants, once removed"[200]—and the majority of Americans were religious dissenters.[201]

"'Rights' obviously lay at the heart of the Anglo-American controversy,"[202] as Bailyn noted and as American petitions showed.[203] Beyond that common denominator, theories of the origin of the Revolution have varied enormously from the "republican synthesis" and its "repudiation not only of parliamentary sovereignty over the colonies, but . . . as an acceptable form of government" along with

[193] CHRONOLOGICAL TABLES 6–9, 9–13 (including partial-year ones); TYRANNY 33.

[194] GREENE, *supra* note 159, at 79–150; JACK P. GREENE, THE QUEST FOR POWER: THE LOWER HOUSES OF ASSEMBLY 357–79 (UNCP, Chapel Hill 1963).

[195] CREATION 28–36, bringing a "pattern of tyranny," *id.* at 36–43; IDEOLOGICAL ORIGINS 129–40.

[196] TRANSATLANTIC 7; GREAT RIGHTS 24.

[197] *E.g.*, Samuel Adams, *The Rights of the Colonists* (Nov.1772), in 2 THE WRITINGS OF SAMUEL ADAMS 350, 351, 356 (Harry A. Cushing ed., Putnam's Sons, New York 1904–08); *accord* DICKINSON'S ESSAY 114; WILSON'S CONSIDERATIONS 2; LAMP 190; CREATION 9–10; IDEOLOGICAL ORIGINS 77–78, 191–93, 307; CLARK 2, 4, 18.

[198] GLORIOUS CAUSE 51; *accord* CREATION 13, 15–17, 49, 200; LAMP 185–86, 9–10; CLARK 271.

[199] J.G.A. POCOCK, VIRTUE, COMMERCE, AND HISTORY: ESSAYS ON POLITICAL THOUGHT AND HISTORY, CHIEFLY IN THE EIGHTEENTH CENTURY 253–73 (CUP, Cambridge 1985); LAMP 59–193; KENYON 205; CREATION 13, 14, 15–17, 49, 200.

[200] EDWIN S. GAUSTAD, NEITHER KING NOR PRELATE: RELIGION AND THE NEW NATION, 1776–1826, at 34 (Eerdmans, Grand Rapids 1993); *accord* GLORIOUS CAUSE 52.

[201] PATRICIA U. BONOMI, UNDER THE COPE OF HEAVEN: RELIGION, SOCIETY, AND POLITICS IN COLONIAL AMERICA 188 (OUP, Oxford 1986); *accord* John Adams to Abigail Adams (16 Sept.1774), THE BOOK OF ABIGAIL AND JOHN: SELECTED LETTERS OF THE ADAMS FAMILY 75, 76 (L.H. Butterfield et al. eds., HUP, Cambridge 1975); [JOSEPH PRIESTLEY], AN ADDRESS TO PROTESTANT DISSENTERS 5 (Thomas and John Fleet, Boston 1774), quoted in CLARK 45; *id.* at 13, 203; FEDERALIST Nos.10, 51, at 65, 351–52.

[202] IDEOLOGICAL ORIGINS 307.

[203] *E.g.*, Declarations of the Stamp Act Congress ¶2 (19 Oct.1765), 9 EHD 672; JOHN P. REID, CONSTITUTIONAL HISTORY OF THE AMERICAN REVOLUTION: THE AUTHORITY OF RIGHTS 4 (UWP, Madison 1986); CLARK 383–85.

monarchy,[204] to post-revisionist critics returning to the centrality of natural rights[205] or constitutional rights,[206] to others seeing the Revolution as an outgrowth from radical Whig ideology[207] or from other philosophies.[208]

Colonial theorists typically discussed the rights to life, liberty, and property,[209] or rights to representation and to taxation with consent,[210] but they sometimes moved to specific rights such as press and speech. Dulany began his influential 1765 pamphlet by noting that "the Liberty of the Press is of the most momentous consequence" in disseminating truth, and by protesting that petitions were often deemed seditious libels.[211] In the first Continental Congress, the Address to the Inhabitants of Quebec was unequivocal in exalting freedom of press as the last of five "grand rights" or "invaluable rights" without which "a people cannot be free." It was the "first declaration by an official assembly" anywhere proclaiming that freedom.[212] It listed as one benefit of the press that "oppressive officers are shamed or intimidated, into more honourable and just modes of conducting affairs,"[213] which made clear that freedom of press must include liberty to criticize government officials. Many

[204] J.G.A. Pocock, *The Varieties of Whiggism from Exclusion to Reform*, in J.G.A. Pocock, Virtue, Commerce, and History: Essays on Political Thought and History, Chiefly in the Eighteenth Century 216–18 (CUP, Cambridge 1985); *accord* J.G.A. Pocock, The Machiavellian Moment: Florentine Political Thought and the Atlantic Republican Tradition 83–422 (PUP, Princeton 1975); Ideological Origins 22; Creation 47; Empire 6–7.

[205] *E.g.*, Thomas Pangle, The Spirit of Modern Republicanism 35–36, 32–34, 247–49 (UChiP, Chicago 1988); Zuckert 164–66.

[206] Jack P. Greene, The Constitutional Origins of the American Revolution 18 (CUP, New York 2011), richly documenting developing colonial arguments, *id.* at 19–186; Jack P. Greene, *Law and the Origins of the American Revolution*, in 1 Cambridge History of Law in America 447, 447–80 (Michael Grossberg ed., CUP, Cambridge 2008); John P. Reid, Constitutional History of the American Revolution: The Authority of Law 172–73 (UWP, Madison 1993).

[207] Glorious Cause 51; Lamp 193.

[208] Clark 295, 22–23; J.C.D. Clark, Revolution and Rebellion: State and Society in England in the Seventeenth and Eighteenth Centuries 4, 93, 169 (CUP, Cambridge 1986); Alan Heimert, Religion and the American Mind, from the Great Awakening to the Revolution (HUP, Cambridge 1966); Jack P. Greene, Interpreting Early America 311–33, 41–59, 493–509 (UPV, Charlottesville 1996).

[209] *E.g.*, Dickinson's Essay 41; Wilson's Considerations 18.

[210] *E.g.*, [Daniel Dulany], Considerations on the Propriety of Imposing Taxes in the British Colonies 6, 30 (John Holt, New York 1765); Dickinson 217–18, 215–16; Ideological Origins 162–75; Brewer-Party 208–16.

[211] *Id.* 4 (he also commended "the excellent *Letter Concerning Libels*," *id.* at 33n.).

[212] 1 Bill of Rights 221.

[213] Address to the Inhabitants of Quebec (26 Oct.1774), 1 JCC 105, 108. Similarly, the Declaration of Colonial Rights adverted to freedom of speech when it affirmed the right to assemble and "consider of their grievances." Declaration of Colonial Rights and Grievances (14 Oct.1774), 1 JCC 63, 70.

essayists such as Dickinson warned that the Crown claimed the right of "stopping the press."[214] Cato was regularly reprinted on freedom of speech.[215] These examples and many others show growing colonial demands for secure freedoms of press and speech.[216] This culminated in the new states' declarations of rights.

State Declarations of Rights and Freedoms of Press and Speech

Rights remained at center stage as most new states adopted declarations of rights, or similar provisions in new constitutions. Seven of the thirteen new states (plus independent Vermont) adopted such declarations, and four others listed various rights in new constitutions; the remaining two continued under their old, more republican charters.[217]

Freedom of press was guarded by nine of the revolutionary declarations and constitutions (ten including Vermont). The first to protect freedom of press, Virginia's Declaration of Rights of 1776 (reproduced in Figure 1.2), provided

> That the freedom of the press is one of the great bulwarks of liberty, and can never be restrained but by despotic governments.[218]

This was "the first enactment, constitutional or statutory, expressly protecting freedom of the press" in history.[219] The next, Pennsylvania's Declaration of Rights, affirmed the right "of writing, and publishing their sentiments," and provided that "freedom of the press ought not to be restrained." Delaware, in September 1776, declared that "the liberty of the press ought to be inviolably preserved."[220] Six other states adopted variations of these (seven with Vermont).[221]

[214] DICKINSON'S ESSAY 63, 66; and had done so, TRADESMAN OF PHILADELPHIA [JOHN DRINKER], OBSERVATIONS ON THE LATE POPULAR MEASURES 5 (n.p., Philadelphia 1774).

[215] *E.g.*, Zenger's *New-York Weekly Journal*, 11 Nov.1734, at 1 (quoting No.15); Franklin's *New-England Courant*, PRINTERS 9 (same).

[216] Richard Buel, *Freedom of the Press in Revolutionary America*, in THE PRESS, *supra* note 192, at 59, 72–82.

[217] Act Containing an Abstract and Declaration of the Rights and Privileges of the People of This State (Conn.1776), 1 FEDERAL-STATE CONSTITUTIONS-POORE 257; *accord* CREATION 133; TRANSATLANTIC 5; WILLI P. ADAMS, THE FIRST AMERICAN CONSTITUTIONS: REPUBLICAN IDEOLOGY AND THE MAKING OF THE STATE CONSTITUTIONS IN THE REVOLUTIONARY ERA 67, 73, 75, 76, 79, 80, 82, 83, 85, 91 (UNCP, Chapel Hill 1980).

[218] Va. D.O.R. sec.12 (1776), 7 FEDERAL-STATE CONSTITUTIONS 3812, 3814.

[219] GREAT RIGHTS 71.

[220] Pa. D.O.R. art.XII (1776), 5 FEDERAL-STATE CONSTITUTIONS 3081, 3083; Del. D.O.R. sec.XXIII (1776), in IN CONVENTION, AT NEW-CASTLE, FOR THE DELAWARE STATE, BEGUN THE 27TH DAY OF AUGUST, 1776, at 4 (James Adams, Wilmington 1776).

[221] Md. D.O.R. art.XXXVIII (1776), 3 *id.* at 1686, 1690; N.C. D.O.R. art.XV (1776), 5 *id.* at 2787, 2788; Ga. Const. art.LXI (1777), 1 *id.* at 777, 784; Vt. D.O.R. art.XIV (1777), 6 *id.* at 3737,

Three things stand out most about these protections of freedom of press. Press provisions were the most prevalent of the dozens of new state protections, except for free exercise of religion (eleven states plus Vermont) and jury trial (ten plus Vermont). All nine press provisions employed broad language and gave no restriction. Conversely, not one said it was adopting freedom of press as it existed, or as it was restricted, under English law. Finally, most began by quoting or paraphrasing Blackstone's language on the indispensability of freedom of press, but then ended with a stark contradiction of his language on its common law limitations.[222]

Freedom of speech, too, was protected by Pennsylvania's revolutionary declaration (and was copied by Vermont), and this also was for "the first time in any constitutional enactment"[223] (outside legislative speech). It said that "the people have a right to freedom of speech," as well as of writing and publishing their sentiments.[224] While the newer phraseology of freedom of speech did not find its way into the other declarations of rights, the older freedom of petition, the common form of nonlegislative speech, was secured by five states.[225] Thirteen years later, freedom of speech did find its way into the federal Bill of Rights.

The Federal Bill of Rights and Freedom for Dissent

During the years of the Continental Congress, freedom of press was discussed on at least four occasions, after the Address to the Inhabitants of Quebec. Each occasion involved objections to newspaper criticisms of Congress or its members, and each resulted in lopsided congressional majorities refusing to prosecute press criticism under doctrines of seditious libel or legislative privilege.[226]

3741; S.C. Const. art.XLIII (1778), 6 *id.* at 3248, 3257; Mass. D.O.R. art.XVI (1779), 3 *id.* at 1888, 1892; N.H. B.O.R. art.XXII (1783), 4 *id.* at 2453, 2456.

[222] OPEN PRESS 97; *e.g.*, Mass. Const. art.VI §6 (1779), 3 FEDERAL-STATE CONSTITUTIONS 1888, 1910; N.H. Const. pt.II (1776), 4 *id.* at 2451, 2469.

[223] GREAT RIGHTS 73.

[224] Pa. D.O.R. art.XII (1776), 5 FEDERAL-STATE CONSTITUTIONS 3081, 3083; Vt. D.O.R. art. XIV (1777), 6 *id.* at 3739, 3741.

[225] Pa. D.O.R. art.XVI (1776); Del. D.O.R. art.IX (1776); Md. D.O.R. art.XI (1776); Mass. D.O.R. art.XIX (1780); N.H. B.O.R. art.XXXII (1783).

[226] In December 1778, the president of Congress, Henry Laurens, objected that an address Silas Deane published in the *Pennsylvania Packet* was a libel that "created anxieties" and "excited tumults" by insulting Congress and the United States; but Laurens could not even garner support for appointing a committee to consider prosecution of the published address, and consequently resigned his position. 12 JCC 1203, 1205, 1206 (9 Dec.1778).

In May 1779, the tables were turned as Laurens was blamed for a letter "derogatory to the honor of Congress" and the United States; but a unanimous vote of states declined to require him "to declare whether he wrote that letter" (the prelude to prosecution), and a majority even declined to enter the movant's written apologia into the legislative journal. 14 *id.* at 588, 591–92, 610–11 (14, 18 May 1779); Henry Laurens to John Houstoun (27 Aug.1778), 10 LETTERS OF DELEGATES 509, 511 n.4.

At the Constitutional Convention,[227] no one opposed the rights of press and speech, though there was opposition to the advisability of a bill of rights. As Washington himself noted, "there was not a member of the convention, I believe, who had the least objection to what is contended for by the advocates for a *Bill of Rights* and *Tr[i]al by Jury*."[228] In fact, a provision for freedom of press was proposed several times, discussed, and at one point supported by a majority of states.[229] Failure to approve it, which was on the ground that a bill of rights was unnecessary when there was no enumerated power that could infringe freedom of press, turned out to be a major political miscalculation by supporters of the Constitution.

Two months later, the publisher of a pseudonymous attack on Congress over national finance in the *Pennsylvania Packet* was assailed by a motion to bring him before that body; but the motion was unanimously rejected by the states and only drew the support of two legislators. 14 *id.* at 799, 800 (3 July 1779); Henry Laurens' Notes of Debates (3 July 1779), in 13 LETTERS OF DELEGATES 139. Instead, opponents warned of dire consequences "[w]hen the liberty of the press shall be restrained," and declaimed that the "liberty of the press ought not to be restrained." 13 LETTERS OF DELEGATES 139.

Finally, in December 1782, a member of Congress, who acknowledged writing a letter reprinted in the *Boston Gazette* that commented on presumptively secret discussion of loan negotiations, objected to appointment of a committee to investigate the publication, as "establish[ing] a precedent dangerous to the freedom of the press" and violating his legislative freedom "by deterring the minority from writing freely to their constituents." 23 JCC 814, 815, 816 (18 Dec.1782). Congress, though rejecting his motion condemning the committee on those grounds and instead upholding diplomatic secrecy, did not prosecute him and temporized by appointing a committee "to report such measures" as would be proper. 23 *id.* at 816–18, 818–19.

[227] DAVID O. STEWART, THE SUMMER OF 1787 (Simon & Schuster, New York 2007); MAX FARRAND, THE FRAMING OF THE CONSTITUTION (YUP, New Haven 1913).

[228] George Washington to Lafayette (28 Apr.1788), 6 WASHINGTON PAPERS-CONFEDERATION 242, 244; *accord* James Madison to Thomas Jefferson (17 Oct.1788), 11 MADISON PAPERS 295, 297–300; James White to Richard Caswell (13 Nov.1787), 24 LETTERS OF DELEGATES 554.

[229] As the Convention began, Charles Pinckney offered a draft constitution prohibiting Congress from "touching or abridging the liberty of the press." 1 ELLIOT'S DEBATES 145, 148 (29 May 1787); *see* 3 FARRAND'S RECORDS 604, 609. He later "most anxiously," 2 FARRAND'S RECORDS 290 (Luther Martin), proposed to add to the draft Constitution "that the liberty of the press should be inviolably observed," and there was enough support that an affirmative vote sent the proposal to the committee of detail. 2 *id.* at 334, 340–41 (20 Aug.1787); 1 ELLIOT'S DEBATES 249. Later, Gerry's and Mason's motion "for a committee to prepare a bill of rights" was rejected by all ten states voting. 2 FARRAND'S RECORDS 588 (12 Sept.1787). The reason given for opposition was that "[i]t is unnecessary–The power of Congress does not extend to the press," 2 *id.* at 618 (Roger Sherman), as Pinckney's cousin Charles Cotesworth Pinckney reported back to South Carolina, 3 *id.* at 256—not opposition to that right itself or its breadth, as was evident in Pinckney's later assurances. 4 ELLIOT'S DEBATES 259; *accord* 3 *id.* at 203 (Randolph). Yet again, Pinckney renewed that proposal, and it was narrowly defeated by a vote of five to six states. 2 FARRAND'S RECORDS at 611, 617–18, 620 (14 Sept.1787); 5 ELLIOT'S DEBATES 545, 1 *id.* 310; *see* PRELUDE 299. Richard Henry Lee introduced his own proposed bill of rights with a free press provision. Richard Henry Lee to Elbridge Gerry (29 Sept.1787), 24 LETTERS OF DELEGATES 451, 452; 33 JCC 540–44 (27 Sept.1787). Toward the end of the convention, proposals for a bill of rights by Pinckney, Mason and Gerry, and Randolph similarly failed. 2 FARRAND'S RECORDS 340–41, 587–88, 631, 633.

While the federalists contributed the Constitution, the anti-federalists ultimately contributed the Bill of Rights.[230] Together those documents have been called the "third phase of the revolution."[231]

The anti-federalist attack in newspaper essays built upon "their strong hold,"[232] the lack of a bill of rights, and particularly the lack of protection of freedom of press[233] and of the other "great rights" (as Madison referred to them, listing jury trial, press, and conscience).[234] In response, the federalist argument for why a bill of rights was superfluous emphasized that the federal government had no power to invade the rights at issue,[235] and that a list was both "unnecessary" and "dangerous" in implying that such federal power existed, as *The Federalist* contended.[236]

The state ratification debates,[237] particularly the later ones where federalists were less dominant, witnessed frequent anti-federalist criticism of the absence of a bill of rights, and of the lack of protection of freedom of press[238]—as Patrick Henry thundered, "liberty of the press" is rendered "insecure, if not lost."[239] They

[230] IDEOLOGICAL ORIGINS 350–51; SAUL CORNELL, THE OTHER FOUNDERS: ANTI-FEDERALISM AND THE DISSENTING TRADITION 26–42 (UNCP, Chapel Hill 1999).

[231] BERNARD BAILYN, FACES OF REVOLUTION 228 (Knopf, New York 1990).

[232] Aristides [Alexander C. Hanson], *Remarks on the Proposed Plan of a Federal Government* (1788), in PAMPHLETS-CONSTITUTION 217, 241.

[233] For press, *e.g.*, Plebeian [Melancton Smith], *Address to the People of New-York* (1788), in PAMPHLETS-CONSTITUTION 87, 113–14; George Mason, *Objections of the Hon. George Mason* (1787), *id.* at 327, 331; Federal Farmer [Richard Henry Lee], *Observation Leading to a Fair Examination of the System of Government* (1787), *id.* at 277, 315–17; [Elbridge Gerry], *Observations on the New Constitution* (1788), *id.* at 2, 9, 12–13; Luther Martin, *Letters of Luther Martin* (7 Mar.1788), in ESSAYS-CONSTITUTION 337, 365; Hugh H. Brackenridge, *Cursory Remarks by Hugh Henry Brackenridge* (Apr.1788), *id.* at 315, 365; Brutus, *Letters of Brutus* (1788), in 1 BILL OF RIGHTS 505, 509.

[234] CREATING BILL OF RIGHTS 69, 85 (8 June 1789); 2 BILL OF RIGHTS 1028; *accord* 10 MADISON PAPERS 199; 4 ELLIOT'S DEBATES 259, 3 *id.* 587; RICHARD LABUNSKI, JAMES MADISON AND THE STRUGGLE FOR THE BILL OF RIGHTS 178–212 (OUP, Oxford 2006).

[235] *E.g.*, FEDERALIST No.84, at 579 (Hamilton); John Jay, *An Address to the People of the State of New-York* (1788), in PAMPHLETS-CONSTITUTION 67, 76–77; Marcus [James Iredell], *Answers to Mr. Mason's Objections* (1788), *id.* at 333, 360–61; Citizen of America [Noah Webster], *An Examination into the Leading Principles* (1787), *id.* at 25, 48; Landholder [Oliver Ellsworth], *The Letters of a Landholder* (1787–88), in ESSAYS-CONSTITUTION 135, 163–64; Countryman [Roger Sherman], *Letters of a Countryman* (Nov.-Dec.1787), *id.* at 213, 218–19; James Wilson, *State House Yard Speech* (6 Oct.1787), 1 WILSON WORKS 171, 172.

[236] *E.g.*, FEDERALIST No.84, at 579; 2 BILL OF RIGHTS 1028 (Madison); Hugh Williamson, *Remarks on the New Plan of Government* (1788), in ESSAYS-CONSTITUTION 393, 398.

[237] *See generally* PAULINE MAIER, RATIFICATION: THE PEOPLE DEBATE THE CONSTITUTION, 1787–1788, at 97–434 (Simon & Schuster, New York 2010).

[238] *E.g.*, 1 ELLIOT'S DEBATES 503 (R.H. Lee), 2 *id.* 399 (Tredwell), 552 (Md. minority); 3 *id.* 44–45, 149, 442 (Mason), 448–49, 462, 587–88, 594 (Henry); 4 *id.* 205 (Lenoir), 314–15 (Lincoln); 2 DHRC 204, 288, 310, 441, 453, 454, 504, 597; 3 *id.* 243; 5 *id.* 587, 780, 782; 10 *id.* 1326; 20 *id.* 624; *see* 1 COMPLETE ANTIFEDERALIST 64; 12 JEFFERSON PAPERS 438, 440; 14 *id.* 649, 650.

[239] 3 ELLIOT'S DEBATES at 44.

also heard federalist replies that protections were unnecessary[240]—as James Wilson said, "there is given to the general government no power whatsoever concerning it; and no law . . . can possibly be enacted to destroy that liberty."[241]

Virginia, the largest state, ratified the Constitution subject to reservations or subsequent amendments including "[t]hat the people have a right to freedom of speech, and of writing and publishing their sentiments; that the freedom of the press is one of the greatest bulwarks of liberty, and ought not to be violated."[242] Similarly, New York proposed amendments including that "freedom of the press ought not to be violated," which Rhode Island later echoed; and North Carolina, rejecting ratification, asked for similar amendments.[243] Minority reports in three more states demanded protection of the press and, in Pennsylvania's case, of speech as well.[244]

The first Congress appeased these calls by approving the Bill of Rights in September 1789, with the support of both federalists and anti-federalists.[245] Particularly interesting among the discussion of freedoms of speech[246] and press[247] was Madison's explanation of the committee-approved language: "The right of freedom of speech is secured; the liberty of the press is expressly declared to be beyond the reach of this Government."[248] Nine states ratified the Bill of Rights by June 1790,[249] but with admission of new states eleven were required. Virginia became that eleventh state on the fifteenth of December 1791.[250]

The First Amendment now provided that Congress may not pass any law "abridging the freedom of speech, or of the press," but what did that mean? The next two chapters will discuss its background, and then Chapters 4–5 will discuss how the early justices of the Supreme Court understood those freedoms, before the crisis of the Sedition Act of 1798 caused some justices to rethink their understanding of freedoms of press and speech.

240 *E.g.*, 1 *id.* at 497–98 (Jay); 2 *id.* at 449, 468 (Wilson); 3 *id.* at 103, 246 (Nicholas), 203, 469 (Randolph); 4 *id.* at 208–09 (Spaight), 259 (C. Pinckney), 315 (C.C. Pinckney); 2 DHRC 168, 454–55 (Wilson).

241 2 *id.* at 449.

242 3 *id.* at 659 (27 June 1788).

243 1 *id.* at 328 (N.Y. 26 July 1788), 332; 4 *id.* at 244 (N.C. 1 Aug.1788); 1 *id.* at 335 (R.I. 29 May 1790); 4 DHFFC 21 (N.Y.); The Anti-Federalist Writings of the Melancton Smith Circle 344, 347 (Michael P. Zuckert & Derek A. Webb eds., LF, Indianapolis 2009) (N.Y. proposals July 1788).

244 *See* 2 DHRC 618, 623, 631 (Pa. minority 18 Dec.1787); 17 *id.* at 244 (Md. minority); Complete Bill of Rights-Sources 93 (Mass. minority 6 Feb.1788).

245 4 DHRC 9–48; 1 DHFFC 134–99.

246 2 Bill of Rights 1026, 1089–90, 1096, 1104, 1122, 1148–49, 1153.

247 2 *id.* at 1026, 1034–35, 1042, 1089–90, 1096, 1104, 1148–49, 1153, and provisions restricting state abridgment, 2 *id.* at 1027, 1033, 1112–13.

248 1 Annals 766 (15 Aug.1789).

249 2 DHC 325, 330, 335, 340, 345, 347, 352, 357, 363.

250 2 *id.* at 373, 374–76, 377; *accord* J. Gordon Hylton, *Virginia and the Ratification of the Bill of Rights, 1789–1791*, in 25 U. Richmond L. Rev. 433, 450–56, 456–68, 460–64 (1991).

2

The Crime of Seditious Libel, and England's Evisceration of Freedoms of Press and Speech

> The liberty of the press . . . consists in laying no previous restraints upon publications, and not in freedom from censure for criminal matter when published. . . .
>
> —Blackstone's *Commentaries*

Sir William Blackstone, in the last volume of his *Commentaries* in 1769,[1] undertook to summarize the common law "liberty of the press." He described it as meaning only protection against prior restraints such as licensing, and not protection against any other restraints such as seditious libel prosecutions:

> In this, and the other instances which we have lately considered, where blasphemous, immoral, treasonable, schismatical, seditious, or scandalous libels are punished by the English law, . . . the *liberty of the press*, properly understood, is by no means infringed or violated. The liberty of the press is indeed essential to the nature of a free state: but this consists in laying no *previous* restraints upon publications, and not in freedom from censure for criminal matter when published. Every freeman has an undoubted right to lay what sentiments he pleases before the public: to forbid this, is to destroy the freedom of the press: but if he publishes what is improper, mischievous, or illegal, he must take the consequence of his own temerity. . . .[2]

[1] Blackstone is cited herein as influential in America in the later eighteenth century, not as authoritative (which the *Commentaries* are not). 1 OHLE 75. A list of abbreviated titles is at the end of this book.

[2] 4 Sir William Blackstone, Commentaries on the Laws of England 151–52 (CP, Oxford 1765–69) (4 vols.) (emphasis in original). This book's focus is on seditious libel, so blasphemous libel and obscene libel are not discussed.

That passage immediately followed Blackstone's description of the crime of seditious libel (which is quoted below)[3]; that crime is what he principally meant in referring to "censure for criminal matter when published." It immediately preceded Blackstone's summary of liberty of speech, which he described in similar narrow terms with similar restriction of seditious words: "[n]either is any restraint hereby laid upon freedom of thought or enquiry," because only "the disseminating, or making public, of bad sentiments, destructive of the ends of society, is the crime which society corrects."[4] For Blackstone, "bad sentiments" could be a crime, with seditious words subject to parallel rules as for seditious libel; some prosecutions involved only spoken words. Was Blackstone's passage an accurate summary of the common law of liberties of press and speech, and did an ancient and impartial historical process result in the common law of seditious libel as it then stood?

This chapter summarizes the development of the English common law of seditious libel. Its review of the leading cases and the references to freedoms of press and speech reveals nothing resembling Blackstone's summary of the English common law of liberty of press and speech—that liberty of the press meant only protection from prior restraints such as licensing, and not protection from other restraints such as seditious libel prosecutions. It instead shows that Blackstone's summary was no summary at all—it had never been expressed in the English common law that he claimed to summarize. Instead, Blackstone's summary was only introduced into the English common law the year *after* he published it, when his formulation was adopted by Lord Chief Justice Mansfield[5] of the Court of King's Bench, in the trials of the publishers of *Letters of Junius* (and so it is referred to here as the Blackstone-Mansfield definition).[6] Blackstone and Mansfield said, in essence, that a writer or printer fully enjoyed freedom of the press if he did not have to apply for a license before publishing a book, pamphlet, or

[3] 4 *id.* at 150.

[4] 4 *id.* at 152.

[5] William Murray, Baron Mansfield 1756 and first Earl of Mansfield 1776. 1 THE MANSFIELD MANUSCRIPTS AND THE GROWTH OF ENGLISH LAW IN THE EIGHTEENTH CENTURY 8–43 (James Oldham ed., UNCP, Chapel Hill 1992); 39 ODNB 992.

[6] Case of Henry Sampson Woodfall, (1770) 20 State Trials 895, 903; Lofft 776, 781, 98 Eng. Rep. 914, 916 (K.B.) (Mansfield stated that "the liberty of the press is, that a man may print what he pleases without a licenser: as long as it remains so, the liberty of the press is not restrained."); *s.c.* 5 Burr. 2661, 98 Eng. Rep. 398; 2 Strange 1131, 93 Eng. Rep. 1082; Trial of John Almon, (1770) 20 State Trials 803, 836; 5 Burr. 2686, 98 Eng. Rep. 411 (K.B.) (Mansfield ruled that, "[i]f an author is at liberty to write, he writes at his peril, if he writes or publishes what is contrary to law"); Proceedings . . . against Rev. William Davies Shipley, Dean of St. Asaph, (1784) 21 State Trials 847, 1040 (K.B.) (Mansfield ruled that "[t]he *liberty of the press* consists in printing without any previous license, subject to the consequences of law"); *s.c.* 3 T.R. 428, 100 Eng. Rep. 657; 4 Dougl. 73, 99 Eng. Rep. 774; *see* R v. Wilkins, (1787) 22 State Trials 209, 213 (K.B.) (Justice Buller rejected a freedom of press defense because "it goes to give a general licence to printers to print whatever they may think proper; which cannot be endured in this or in any other country.").

newspaper article, though he could be indefinitely imprisoned, brutally whipped, and prohibitively fined for his disapproval of a government official or of government measures in that publication. Thus, freedom of press was complete if there was no license requirement, even if something after being published or spoken could be criminally prosecuted. Furthermore, much the same was true of the common law of seditious libel and seditious words—it had been quite intentionally formulated over the past seventy-three years to restrict printing and speech by creating six unique rules different from rules governing other criminal prosecutions (only the first predated 1696 and was then adopted by King's Bench). They were summarized as part of the common law of seditious libel by Blackstone,[7] and were represented as ancient principles by Mansfield, who was their foremost judicial exponent.

Nearly everything material to conviction for seditious libel deviated from English law for other crimes and for other defamations in a way that assisted arresting or imprisoning the political opposition and that thwarted a successful legal defense. Thus, while truth was a defense for other crimes involving falsehood and for other defamation of persons, it was not a defense to a charge of seditious libel, though that crime required falsehood; and in fact the truth of a statement was an aggravation of the crime. While criminal intent had to be proved for other crimes including criminal defamation, it did not have to be shown in a seditious libel prosecution because courts assumed it from the mere fact of publishing something. While other defamation could only be prosecuted if it was of specific identifiable persons, seditious libel could be prosecuted for criticism of the government as a whole, which courts assumed, without proof, had "a tendency" to "weaken" the subject's affection for the government. While other defamation cases and other criminal cases required jury findings of a crime and of criminal intent, seditious libel cases withheld those issues from juries and empowered judges to find a crime and criminal intent. Further, seditious libel cases tricked the jury into thinking it was only determining if the defendant was guilty of writing or printing the questioned publication and if such abbreviations as "K—g" meant the King, when in fact the courts treated that as a jury determination of guilt on all issues. While most criminal documents and contraband could only be searched for under a specific search warrant identifying the items and place, seditious libel was generally searched for under a general warrant that did not identify item or place, and that instead allowed looking for virtually anything anywhere. These deviations of seditious libel from other criminal law and from other defamation law are described in this chapter, and they came as major steps in the historical

[7] 4 Blackstone's Commentaries 150 (restricted criticism of magistrates, truth irrelevant, tendency rather than intent is sole consideration); 151 (only jury issues are making or publishing the book or writing, and whether it is criminal, not intent); 152 (criticism of government can undermine government, and "bad sentiments" are restrained).

development by English courts of the common law of seditious libel. However, not until Blackstone and Mansfield was the quantum step taken of defining liberties of press and speech as only freedom from prior restraint, and of neutralizing those liberties from interfering with criminalization of seditious libel and seditious words, as the end of this chapter describes.

These unique rules for seditious libel largely came from three luminaries in the English judiciary. The first came from an argument, misdescribed as the court's opinion, by Lord Chief Justice Edward Coke (1552–1634) (portrayed in Figure 2.1). Most came from an active quest to find cases and to reformulate the rules for seditious libel and seditious speech by Lord Chief Justice John Holt (1642–1710) (Figure 2.2). Summarized by Blackstone (Figure 2.3), they were championed by Lord Chief Justice Mansfield (1705–1793) (Figure 2.4). (For simplicity, these unique rules are sometimes referred to here as the Blackstone-Mansfield framework for prosecuting seditious libel, accompanying their definition of freedom of press and speech.) The one thing these six unique rules had in common is that they restricted criticism of government, its officials, and its measures—which was the core of the crime of seditious libel. This chapter looks backward at how seditious libel and its unique rules were contrived, along with how the common law of liberties of press and speech stood when Blackstone published. The next chapters look forward at whether the Blackstone-Mansfield definition and framework were embraced by any of the early Supreme Court justices before the Sedition Act crisis of 1798–1801, and whether they were embraced by all of those justices during 1798–1801.

Figure 2.1 Sir Edward Coke (1552–1634). Engraving by David Loggan 1666. (Courtesy of, and copyright, National Portrait Gallery, London.)

Figure 2.2 Lord Chief Justice John Holt (1642–1710). Portrait by Richard van Bleeck c.1700. (Courtesy of, and copyright, National Portrait Gallery, London.)

Introduction: Development of the English Crime of Seditious Libel

The crime of seditious libel as it existed in England and in colonial America around the time of the American Revolution was summarized by Blackstone as follows:

> Of a nature very similar to challenges are *libels, libelli famosi*, which . . . in the sense under which we are now to consider them, are malicious defamations of any person, and especially a magistrate, made public by either printing, writing, signs, or pictures, in order to provoke him to wrath, or expose him to public hatred, contempt, and ridicule. The direct tendency of these libels is the breach of the public peace, by stirring up the objects of them to revenge, and perhaps to bloodshed. . . . [8]

(A "libel" meant "literally a little book,"[9] but commonly referred to "any defamation in writing or permanent form"[10] and in seditious libel prosecutions referred to a "seditious libel."[11])

[8] 4 *id.* 150 (emphasis in original).

[9] Giles Jacob, A New Law-Dictionary [unnumbered under "Libel"] (Nutt, London 1729). Libel also meant a statement of claim (and hence a claim more generally) in ecclesiastical courts and admiralty courts. 1 OHLE 321–23.

[10] *Id.*; 3 Bacon 490; 3 Blackstone's Commentaries 126.

[11] *E.g.*, 10 Calendar-William 350–51, 364, 400 (calling same publication a "seditious libel" and "false, scandalous and traitorous libel"); 3 Calendar-Anne no.112, 138, 660 (calling same publications "scandalous libels" and "libel[s]"); 1 Hawkins 193; R v. Woodfall, (1770) 5 Burr. 2661, 2665, 98 Eng. Rep. 398, 400 (K.B.).

Broadly, the common opinion of legal historians for many years has been that the doctrine of seditious libel "largely derive[d] from . . . work of the [S]tar [C]hamber" in the seventeenth century,[12] as did criminal libel generally,[13] and it continued when the King's Bench during the Restoration adopted the former Court of Star Chamber's jurisdiction.[14] That judicial choice to follow Star Chamber precedent for seditious libel, which deviated from the existing defamation law and criminal law of the King's Bench, rather than to apply prevailing rules for defamation and crime (or even to question the legitimacy of seditious libel itself) amounted to a political choice by English judges[15] to facilitate Crown prosecution of dissidents and to minimize jury interference with successful prosecutions. After the Revolution of 1688, Holt chose to continue following that Star Chamber precedent.

Eighteenth-century English courts did borrow significantly from that Star Chamber precedent in developing seditious libel doctrine.[16] However, Hamburger suggests that "prior to the eighteenth century the law of seditious libel was a relatively insignificant means of restraining the printed press and was the basis of a relatively small number of prosecutions."[17] He instead identifies the basis of

[12] MILSOM 390; *accord id.* 388–89; FIFOOT 131, 128 n.14; BRANT 5, 11; *e.g.*, R v. Lucas, (1515) 2 Hudson 102 (Star Chamber) ("scandalous words against the lord cardinal," Wolsey); J.A. Guy, *Wolsey, the Council and the Council Courts*, 91 ENG. HISTORICAL REV. 481, 484 (1976) (1516 case involving "two sclaunderous bills aswell againste the kinges heighnes" and Council); R v. Perkins, (1625) Rushworth 8 (Star Chamber); Proceedings against Wm. Prynn, (1632–33) 3 State Trials 561, 576, 579, 580 (Star Chamber).

[13] BAKER-INTRODUCTION 119, defined in 4 BLACKSTONE'S COMMENTARIES 151; LEVY 7.

[14] FIFOOT 131; *see* THEODORE F.T. PLUCKNETT, A CONCISE HISTORY OF THE COMMON LAW 496 (5th ed. Butterworth, London 1956); *e.g.*, Trial of Dover, Brewster, and Brooks, (1663) 6 State Trials 539, 563, 547 (K.B.); Trial of Benjamin Harris, (1680) 7 State Trials 925 (K.B.); Trial of Sir Samuel Barnardiston, (1684) 9 State Trials 1333, 1351 (K.B.); Proceedings against Richard Baxter, (1685) 11 State Trials 493, 493, 497 (K.B.); *s.c.* 3 Mod. 68, 87 Eng. Rep. 43; R v. Johnson, (1685) 2 Show. K.B. 488, 89 Eng. Rep. 1058 (K.B.); Trial of the Seven Bishops, (1688) 12 State Trials 183, 426, 426–27, 427–28, 429 (K.B.); *s.c.* 3 Mod. 212, 87 Eng. Rep. 136.

The accuracy of *State Trials* has been questioned (like that of most nominate reports). *E.g.*, John H. Langbein, *The Criminal Trial Before the Lawyers*, 45 U. CHI. L. REV. 263, 265–67 (1978). However, after 1688 most proceedings in *State Trials* were "[t]aken down in short hand, and transcribed into long hand," Trial of Mr. Richard Francklin, (1731) 17 State Trials 625, 625 n. (K.B.); *e.g.*, Trial of John Almon, 20 State Trials 803, 803. Hale and Hawkins treated *State Trials* "as a source of legal authorities." M. R. T. Macnair, *Review*, 11 LAW & HIST. REV. 450, 452 (1993); 1 HALE 112n(n), 116n(z), 118n(h)-(i), 168n(m), 370n(i), 390n(e), 502n(e), 697 *passim*; 2 HAWKINS 259, 364, 391, 395, 397, 401, 406, 409, 412, 413, 418, 420, 422, 424, 425, 428, 429, 430 *passim*.

[15] *See* HAMBURGER 752–63; GREEN 68.

[16] HAMBURGER 691–97, 701, 703, 712, 730, 740.

[17] *Id.* 663. He identifies most of those pre-eighteenth century prosecutions as "against manuscripts rather than printed material," since manuscripts could not support prosecution under licensing requirements. *Id.* 665.

most prosecutions as statutes governing scandalous language about magnates (*scandalum magnatum*), cases on infamous libel (*libellis famosis*) which he sees as then limited to magistrates, and particularly licensing ordinances and laws[18] such as those of 1637 and 1662.[19] Disagreeing with legal historians of earlier generations who indiscriminately treated Star Chamber and other prosecutions for seditious words and seditious publications as prosecutions for seditious libel,[20] or for an "offence of sedition,"[21] Hamburger instead dates the beginning of extensive reliance on and development of seditious libel just after the final lapse of press licensing in 1695[22] as replacement restraints on the press were sought.[23] Thus, the defining decisions on seditious libel occurred between 1695 and 1704, and prosecutions followed after that.

Hamburger's view has been broadly accepted.[24] Its correctness is shown by four additional facts: a decision of the administration in 1695 to use seditious

[18] *Id.* 763–65, 664, 674; *accord* 2 MANSFIELD MANUSCRIPTS 775.

[19] A Decree of Starre-Chamber, Concerning Printing (11 July 1637), 4 ARBER 528; 1 KEMP 346; Licensing Act (1662), 13–14 Car 2 c33; 8 EHD 67.

[20] 2 SIR JAMES F. STEPHEN, A HISTORY OF THE CRIMINAL LAW OF ENGLAND 316, 343, 348, 300–01, 307–33 (Macmillan, London 1883); FRED S. SIEBERT, FREEDOM OF THE PRESS IN ENGLAND, 1476–1776: THE RISE AND DECLINE OF GOVERNMENT CONTROLS 117–26, 269–70, 302, 80–81 (UIP, Urbana 1952); 10 SIR WILLIAM S. HOLDSWORTH, A HISTORY OF ENGLISH LAW 674 (Methuen, London repr. 1966), 5 *id.* at 208–12, 8 *id.* at 338–42, though Holdsworth is overstated as advocating continuity between pre-1695 and post-1695 decisions, 10 *id.* at 673–74, 676, 695 and William S. Holdsworth, *Press Control and Copyright in the 16th and 17th Centuries*, 29 YALE L.J. 841, 857 (1920); *cf.* HAMBURGER 663, 759–60.

[21] Roger B. Manning, *The Origins of the Doctrine of Sedition*, 12 ALBION 99, 100 (1980). Hamburger is supported by the paucity of descriptions of a sedition offense in treatises. *E.g.*, 4 BACON 409–65 (no section); 5 SIR JOHN COMYNS, A DIGEST OF THE LAWS OF ENGLAND 688 (H. Woodfall, London 1762) (not in index).

[22] During prior lapses, the Crown brought seditious libel prosecutions under claimed prerogative power to prosecute seditious libels under proclamations, Trial of Henry Carr [Care], (1680) 7 State Trials 1111, 1114 (K.B.) (describing decision of all judges); and the judges claimed authority to punish books "scandalous to the government" under common law, *Harris*, 7 State Trials at 929–30, 931–32; *accord Dover*, 6 State Trials at 563, 564, 548, and libel, Memorandum, Cro. Jac. 37, 79 Eng. Rep. 30 (Assemblage of all Justices 1604) (false rumors of King were indictable "by the rules of the common law"); *Dover*, 6 State Trials at 548(from private libels); *Seven Bishops*, 12 State Trials at 426 (from *libellis famosis*).

[23] He reasons that most prior prosecutions were for violation of licensing requirements, and so were not "historical evidence of seditious libel doctrine." HAMBURGER 674. In 1695, the Commons stated that offenders of the former Licensing Act could "be punished at common law." *Id.* 717 n.168, citing 11 JHC 305 (17 Apr. 1695).

[24] *E.g.*, 2 MANSFIELD MANUSCRIPTS 778; B&M 778; SHANNON C. STIMSON, THE AMERICAN REVOLUTION IN THE LAW 162 n.87 (PUP, Princeton 1990); Lois G. Schwoerer, *Liberty of the Press and Public Opinion: 1660–1695*, in J.R. JONES, LIBERTY SECURED? BRITAIN BEFORE AND AFTER 1688, at 199, 208 (SUP, Stanford 1992); REPRESSIVE JURISPRUDENCE 54; RECLAIMING 188 n.70.

libel, an increase in prosecutions initiated on that basis, formal instructions to the Crown judges, and a decision of the Commons to follow essentially the same approach.[25] Thus, immediately after the Licensing Act lapsed, the ministry, in May 1695, posed the question to the Solicitor General "what may be done according to law (now that the act about licensing is expired) for preventing the abuses of the press," in order to confirm the legitimacy of a warrant "for suppressing all scandalous and seditious books and pamphlets" and newspapers.[26] The Attorney General and Solicitor General responded that seditious publications "were still punishable when detected,"[27] and a round of warrants for "seditious and treasonable books, papers and printing presses"[28] soon followed.[29] Reacting to a particularly infuriating publication in 1696, the King asked the Attorney General "how far the writer, printer and dispersers of them may be punished," and declared he was "resolved to have the prosecutions thereof carried as far as the law may be."[30] As substitute authority for the licensing statute, the Crown relied on proclamations proscribing seditious publications and issued additional ones,[31] and supplemented those with periodic instructions to prosecute particular publications.[32]

The Crown's prosecutions of print, writing, and speech after the 1695 lapse of licensing that are mentioned in the *Calendar of State Papers* were indeed primarily based on allegations of seditious libel, during the remaining seven years of William III's reign and the first five years of Anne's reign. In the seventy Crown prosecutions that are listed, the focus was on "seditious libel" (12),[33] or the equivalent

[25] The Commons adopted a rule "that to print, or publish, any books or libels, reflecting upon the proceedings of the House of Commons, or any member thereof, for, or relating to, his service therein, is a high violation of the rights and privileges of the House of Commons." 13 JHC 767 (26 Feb.1701). It enforced the rule by the legislative prosecutions, and recommendations for Crown prosecutions, cited in Chapter 1.

[26] 5 CALENDAR-WILLIAM 465 (9 May 1695).

[27] 5 *id.* at 483 (30 May 1695).

[28] 5 *id.* at 498 (18 June 1695); *accord,* 6 *id.* at 29, 30, 49 (July-Aug.1695); CRESSY 228–29.

[29] Attempts to prosecute dissenting press for treason collided with the Trial for Treason Act of 1696. 7&8 Wm 3 c3, 8 EHD 89; 7 STATUTES 6–7; HAMBURGER 722–23.

[30] Sir William Trumbull (Secretary of State) to Attorney General (26 Oct.1696), 7 CALENDAR-WILLIAM 424.

[31] Proclamation for the Better Discovery of Seditious Libellers (no.4101) (13 Sept.1692), 1 TUDOR-STUART PROCLAMATIONS 491; Proclamation, for Restraining the Spreading of False News, and . . . Seditious Papers and Libels (26 Mar.1702), 4 KEMP 107; 1 TUDOR-STUART PROCLAMATIONS 514, reissued 518 (25 Feb.1703); Proclamation for Preventing and Punishing Immorality and Profaneness (24 Feb.1698), 9 CALENDAR-WILLIAM 107 (heresy). Thus, Tutchin's prosecution was "according to the proclamation." 4 CALENDAR-ANNE no.80 (15 May 1704).

[32] 6 CALENDAR-WILLIAM 72–73; 7 *id.* 431; 9 *id.* 261–62;10 *id.* 255; 3 CALENDAR-ANNE no.138; Proclamation, for Apprehending John Tutchin (no.4368) (24 Feb.1704), 1 TUDOR-STUART PROCLAMATIONS 519.

[33] 6 *id.* 30, 49, 117; 7 *id.* 425, 431, 432; 8 *id.* 51, 262; 10 *id.* 237–38, 350–51; 3 CALENDAR-ANNE no.690; 4 *id.* no.796.

"seditious books and pamphlets" (17)[34] or "seditious news" (15),[35] or sometimes just "libels" (16),[36] along with treasonous (4) or heretical (6) publications.[37] The government's twenty similar prosecutions were also primarily based on seditious words in unpublished writings (3),[38] and seditious or scandalous spoken words (17).[39] In framing those cases, prosecutors followed the lines of seditious libel doctrine from the Star Chamber.[40] Indictments included elements drawn, instead of from licensing statutes or ordinances, from defamation and *scandalum magnatum*,[41] and allegations of treason by words[42] (though those only constituted overt acts[43]). Reliance on seditious libel and the use of prosecutions continued, as "from 1702 to 1756, there were 123 prosecutions for political libels," and "a further sixty-six in the years 1760–89,"[44] followed by an explosion of about two hundred prosecutions of seditious libel and seditious words in the 1790s.[45]

[34] 5 *id.* 498(2); 6 *id.* 72–73, 73; 7 *id.* 422, 424, 488; 8 *id.* 257, 301; 9 *id.* 422; 10 *id.* 253(2); 11 *id.* 352; 2 CALENDAR-ANNE 474, 476; 3 *id.* no.22; 4 *id.* no.1278.

[35] 6 *id.* 29, 30; 8 *id.* 171, 175; 8 *id.* 316, 426; 10 *id.* 220, 249, 255(2), 341; 2 CALENDAR-ANNE 471, 477(2), 535.

[36] 8 *id.* 249, 274; 9 *id.* 261–62; 11 *id.* 109, 425–26, 456; 1 CALENDAR-ANNE 336, 540–41; 2 *id.* 39, 60; 3 *id.* no.112, 138, 660, 2215; 4 *id.* no.366, 945.

[37] Treason: 6 *id.* 53, 73; 8 *id.* 222; 10 *id.* 364 (same at 10 *id.* 400). Heresy: 8 *id.* 300, 388; 9 *id.* 107 (same at 8 *id.* 301); 2 CALENDAR-ANNE 49; 3 *id.* no.967, 1372 (same at no.1023).

[38] 7 *id.* 422 (same in other at 7 *id.* 422); 10 *id.* 85, 256; *accord* CALENDAR OF THE MIDDLESEX COUNTY RECORDS, SESSION BOOKS 1689 TO 1709, at 327, 351 (W.J. Hardy ed., Harrison, London 1903) (John Denton, Thomas Pudsey).

[39] 6 *id.* 49; 7 *id.* 415(2), 437; 8 *id.* 53, 461; 10 *id.* 179, 300, 400; 11 *id.* 52, 149, 349; 1 CALENDAR-ANNE 66, 124, 509(2); 2 *id.* 147–48, in addition to treasonable words.

[40] As discussed in the remainder of this chapter.

[41] By calling publications "scandalous," *e.g.*, 7 CALENDAR-WILLIAM 425; 8 *id.* 53; 10 *id.* 364; 2 CALENDAR-ANNE 476; 3 *id.* no.22, 112; 4 *id.* no.366, 796, 945; and by calling newspapers "false news," 6 *id.* 29, 30; 7 *id.* 431; 8 *id.* 171, 175; 10 *id.* 249; 2 CALENDAR-ANNE 477; 4 *id.* no.945.

[42] By often calling publications and words treasonable as well as seditious, *e.g.*, 5 CALENDAR-WILLIAM 498; 6 *id.* 30, 49(2), 117; 7 *id.* 422; 8 *id.* 262; 10 *id.* 364, 400; 1 CALENDAR-ANNE 90. *See* ORR 11–29.

[43] 4 BLACKSTONE'S COMMENTARIES 79–80; 1 HAWKINS 38–39; *e.g.*, Case of Hugh Pine, (1628) Cro. Car. 117, 79 Eng. Rep. 703 (K.B.); R v. Tayler, (1703) 3 Salkeld 198, 91 Eng. Rep. 775; 2 Ld. Raym. 879, 92 Eng. Rep. 88 (Q.B.) (treasonable words); R v. Whitmore, (1749) 1 Black. W. 37, 96 Eng. Rep. 20 (K.B.) ("speaking treasonable words").

[44] Michael Lobban, *From Seditious Libel to Unlawful Assembly: Peterloo and the Changing Face of Political Crime* c1770–*1820*, OXFORD J. LEGAL STUDIES 307, 309 n.11 (1990); *accord* HARLING 108; HAMBURGER 724–25 ("at least 115" in King's Bench, with additional ones in Common Pleas).

[45] Clive Emsley, *Repression, "Terror" and the Rule of Law in England During the Decade of the French Revolution*, 100 ENG. HISTORICAL REV. 801, 824 (1985); *accord* Michael Lobban, *Treason, Sedition and the Radical Movements in the Age of the French Revolution*, 22 LIVERPOOL L. REV. 205, 206–10, 210–24, 224–30, 230–34 (2000) (seditious libel, treason, gag act prosecutions, then detentions).

The Crown also gave instructions to the judges "to have a watchful eye over the writers, printers and dispersers of false and seditious news" and to prosecute them, in 1697, and repeated those instructions two years later.[46] The King in Council instructed judges to include in their charges for grand juries, in 1700, "to proceed against the printers, vendors and disposers of popish books and of other seditious books" and "to proceed against writers and dispersers of false news."[47]

The judges complied with those instructions, just as the prosecutors had, by shaping the distinctive eighteenth-century form of seditious libel that Blackstone described. With the Stuarts fallen and licensing expired, the courts, particularly King's Bench, faced the implicit question whether seditious libel would remain a crime, and the explicit question whether it would be governed by Star Chamber precedent for seditious words and seditious libel, or instead by the common law of libel and of criminal law generally. The choice was made by the Lord Chief Justice at the time licensing lapsed in 1695, John Holt,[48] and after little attention for a half century was reaffirmed by his successors,[49] to base seditious libel on Star Chamber precedent from the early Stuarts[50] and on King's Bench precedent from the later Stuarts,[51] with the fatuous claim that the Star Chamber was only abolished because all offenses punishable there were also punishable in King's Bench.[52] They did so even though those seditious libel precedents diverged starkly from rules governing other libel actions and other criminal actions. Those divergences were not logically unified, except for their Star Chamber derivation and their uniform beneficence to prosecutors and their corresponding disastrous effect on the accused.

The rules governing criminal prosecution of seditious libel, particularly their transparent bias and facilitation of prosecutions, brought swelling criticism of their deviation from general libel law and other criminal law, and for their restraint on freedoms of press and speech. The six unique rules that drew the most

46 8 CALENDAR-WILLIAM 171 (27 May 1697); *accord* 10 *id.* 237–38 (13 July 1699).

47 10 *id.* 388 (22 Feb.1700).

48 J.R., THE LIFE OF THE RIGHT HONOURABLE SIR JOHN HOLT ... WITH A TABLE OF REFERENCES TO ALL HIS LORDSHIP'S ARGUMENTS (J. Worrall, London 1764); *see* 27 ODNB 830.

49 Proceedings ... against Rev. William Davies Shipley, Dean of St. Asaph, (1784) 21 State Trials 847, 1036 (K.B.) (following *Bear* and *Tutchin*); *accord* 2 MANSFIELD MANUSCRIPTS 777, 789.

50 Prynn's Case, (1690) 5 Mod. 459, 87 Eng. Rep. 764, abridged in Holt K.B. 362, 90 Eng. Rep. 1100 (K.B.); *e.g.*, R v. Bear, (1699) 2 Salkeld 417, 419, 91 Eng. Rep. 363, 365 (K.B.); HAMBURGER 730& n.212.

51 In fact, Holt prosecuted some of those seditious libel trials. Trial of Francis Smith, (1680) 7 State Trials 931, 931 (K.B.); Trial of Jane Curtis, (1680) 7 *id.* at 959, 959 (K.B.); *accord* 27 ODNB 830, 830.

52 *Prynn's Case*, 5 Mod. at 464, 87 Eng. Rep. at 767, adopting the argument of Sir William Williams for the Crown.

criticism, and that appeared again and again in essays advocating broader freedom of press and speech, were (1) rejection of a defense of truth, (2) elimination of a requirement to prove criminal intent, (3) criminalization of criticism of government officials, (4) criminalization of criticism of government generally, (5) withholding from jury determination the issues of crime and criminal intent, and (6) use of general warrants, in addition to (7) adopting a narrow definition of liberties of press and speech and claiming it was part of the common law.[53]

That criticism provoked defenses, and the most influential was Lord Mansfield's. Mansfield applied and championed these six unique rules as a framework for seditious libel, and also recognized the threat that liberties of press and speech posed. His insertion into the English common law of what was essentially Blackstone's purported summary of that common law of liberties of press and speech is discussed at the end of this chapter.

Rejection of a Defense of Truth

Defamation liability[54] developed in the sixteenth century[55] through the action on the case for words (slander),[56] which remained the dominant basis of liability until well into the eighteenth century.[57] The era was a time of widespread abusive language,[58] and courts developed limitations on actionable invective.

[53] This section undertakes to discuss only cases relevant to development of criminal libel, not all decisions on libel or licensing.

[54] There is an extensive literature displaying variant views on its development. MILSOM 379–92; B&M 686–716; D.J. IBBETSON, A HISTORICAL INTRODUCTION TO THE LAW OF OBLIGATIONS 112–25 (OUP, Oxford 1999); PAUL MITCHELL, THE MAKING OF THE MODERN LAW OF DEFAMATION (Hart Publishing, Oxford 2005).

[55] Paralleling its development by canon law in ecclesiastical courts, HELMHOLZ 58–61; HELMHOLZ-CASES xxvi–xli; 2 BAKER 236, 238–40; 1 OHLE 564–98; 6 *id.* 788–91; B&M 686–91; MILSOM 380–84; FIFOOT 126–28; David Hewitt, *Some Cases from the Defamation Jurisdiction of the Archdeaconry of Richmond*, 19 J. LEGAL HISTORY 251, 253–66 (1998). Defamation "largely died out by 1400" in local courts. IBBETSON 113; *see* Sandy Bardsley, *Sin, Speech and Scolding in Medieval England*, in FAMA: THE POLITICS OF TALK AND REPUTATION IN MEDIEVAL EUROPE 145, 152–61 (Thelma Fenster & Daniel L. Small eds., CorUP, Ithaca 2003).

[56] 2 BAKER 237–44; *id.* 239–40, quoting and translating [RICHARD PYNSON], NATURA BREVIU[M] NEWLY AND MOOST TREWLY CORRECTED clxxxv–clxxxvi (n.p. [1528]); 6 OHLE 783–88; HELMHOLZ 56; HELMHOLZ-CASES lxxxvii–cvi; FIFOOT 129–37.

[57] CRESSY 235, 240; *e.g.*, R v. Edgar, (1724) Sess. Cas. 133, 93 Eng. Rep. 135; Sess. Cas. 128, 93 Eng. Rep. 129 (K.B.).

[58] Worsley v. Lyddal, (1669) 3 Sid. 433, 82 Eng. Rep. 1201; 2 Keble 577, 581, 84 Eng. Rep. 363, 366 (K.B.); LAURA GOWING, DOMESTIC DANGERS: WOMEN, WORDS, AND SEX IN EARLY MODERN LONDON 121 (CP, Oxford 1996); CRESSY 17–38; *but see* Robert B. Shoemaker, *The Decline of Public Insult in London 1660–1800*, 169 PAST & PRESENT 97, 99–103 (2000).

Truth was a defense across a wide spectrum of law. The very "gist of the action on the case for slander was the speaking of false words," Baker says of common law courts,[59] and truth was from the outset a defense to slander.[60] The same applied to civil actions for libel,[61] which "may be justified in an action upon the case" in the seventeenth century,[62] once distinction began to be made between libel and slander in the latter part of that century,[63] on the theory that written words were more readily found actionable[64] and malicious or damaging.[65] In the early eighteenth century, some commentators and judges said that truth could not be pleaded in actions on the case for libel, any more than in criminal libel.[66]

[59] 2 BAKER 245, 247; 6 OHLE 794; HELMHOLZ-CASES cvii.

[60] Reymond v. Lord Fitzwauter, (1521) Spelman 1, 93 Selden Society 2 (K.B.) ("if he was a villein in fact, then he has no cause of action"); Legat v. Bull, (1533) Spelman 6, 93 Selden Society 6 (K.B.) (one judge); SHEPPARD 6, 7, 12; 3 BACON 495; 4 *id.* 516; 3 BLACKSTONE'S COMMENTARIES 125.

[61] 6 OHLE 796 (after 1533 "truth seems to have been generally accepted as a distinct defence"); IBBETSON 115; Lloide v. Breverton, (1604) 2 Hudson 101 (Star Chamber) ("defendant would have undertaken to have proved the contents of the letter to have been true"); *see* Edwardes v. Woo[l]ton, (1607) 12 Co. Rep. 35, 77 Eng. Rep. 1316; B&M 708 (Star Chamber) ("honesty . . . of the said complainant"); [Col.] King v. Lake, (1667) Hardres 470, 145 Eng. Rep. 552 (Exch.) ("a false libel," per Hale, C.B.).

[62] Lake v. Hatton, (1619) Hobart 252, 253, 80 Eng. Rep. 398, 399; Hobart 253, 80 Eng. Rep. 400 (Star Chamber) (though not in a criminal prosecution).

[63] Austin v. Culpeper, (1683) 2 Shower K.B. 313, 89 Eng. Rep. 960; Skinner 122, 90 Eng. Rep. 57 (K.B.); Yoxon v. Bennet, (1702) 7 Mod. 91, 87 Eng. Rep. 1115 (K.B.); *accord* SHEPPARD 1, 3; MILSOM 388; FIFOOT 132; PAUL MITCHELL, THE MAKING OF THE MODERN LAW OF DEFAMATION 4 (Hart Publishing, Oxford 2005). Mitchell argues persuasively that *Austin* and the earlier *King v. Lake* were actions on the case for words, and used the term "libel" only to indicate the existence of writing and to use it to escape the *mitior sensus* rule, rather than to designate an independent cause of action.

[64] [Col.] King v. Lake, (1667) Hardres 470, 145 Eng. Rep. 552, 553; Hardres 364, 388, 145 Eng. Rep. 499, 511 (Exch.); *accord* R v. Summer [Somers] & Hillard, (1665) 1 Sid. 270, 271, 82 Eng. Rep. 1099, 1100 (K.B.); R v. Langley, (1703) 2 Ld. Raym. 1029, 92 Eng. Rep. 184; 6 Mod. 124, 87 Eng. Rep. 882; 2 Salkeld 697, 91 Eng. Rep. 590; 3 Salkeld 190, 91 Eng. Rep. 769; Holt K.B. 654, 90 Eng. Rep. 1261 (Q.B.); Harman v. Delany, (1731) Fitz-G. 253, 254, 94 Eng. Rep. 743, 744; 1 Barn. K.B. 289, 438, 94 Eng. Rep. 197, 294 (K.B.). Holt K.B. reports are not always accurate, and here are copies and abridgments of other reports by William Nelson.

[65] R v. Roberts, (1734) Cunningham 94, 94 Eng. Rep. 1084; 1 Barn. K.B. 90, 94 Eng. Rep. 62 (K.B.).

[66] 3 BACON 495; 4 *id.* 516 ("no scandal in writing is any more justifiable in a civil action . . . than in an indictment or information"). King's Bench still could decline "granting an information for an offence" if the "libel happens to be true." 3 BACON 492. Words were still not actionable if adequately "explained by other words." 1 COMYNS 207. There was similar confusion in ecclesiastical courts, which for defamation actions similarly required "that the imputation of a crime had been a false one," and "truth could in some circumstances serve legally to excuse defamatory utterances," though "truth in itself was not a sufficient justification." 6 OHLE 582; *see* HELMHOLZ 64 & n.32, modifying HELMHOLZ-CASES xxx.

Perhaps that resulted from confusion as King's Bench integrated its libel jurisdiction with its inherited Star Chamber jurisdiction including criminal libel, or perhaps it resulted from bringing criminal libel rules into the emerging action on the case for libel. That exclusion of truth from actions on the case was never consistently followed and had been rejected by the time of Lord Mansfield.[67] Criminal law outside libel also allowed truth-based defenses, such as (taking examples from Holt decisions when he was not punishing seditious libel) the defense to fraud and deceit that amounts due were actually paid,[68] the defense to forgery that the bond was valid and not a forgery,[69] and the defense to prosecution of a cheat and imposter that "he did not counterfeit" facts[70] or that his claims "are true."[71]

By contrast, truth was not a defense in the Star Chamber in criminal prosecutions for seditious words or seditious writings.[72] There, the *Case de Libellis Famosis* early in the seventeenth century held, at least as it was tendentiously described by Sir Edward Coke, that "[i]t is not material whether the libel be true."[73] (Coke acknowledged the deviation from civil cases, saying in Star Chamber in a civil libel case about alleged poisoning that "if it had been true, . . . Hatton might have justified the writing."[74]) Truth was similarly excluded as a defense by the Star Chamber, where most such actions were heard,[75] in criminal prosecutions for

[67] *In re* Anonymous, (1706) 11 Mod. 99, 88 Eng. Rep. 921, 921–22 (K.B.) (per Holt, "A man may justify in an action upon the case for words, or for a libel"); Cropp v. Tilney (Tylney), (1706) 3 Salkeld 225, 91 Eng. Rep. 791; abridged in Holt K.B. 422, 90 Eng. Rep.1132 (K.B.) (incorrectly dated in reports); Hargrave v. Le Breton, (1769) 4 Burr. 2422, 2425, 98 Eng. Rep. 269, 271 (K.B.) (per Mansfield: suits against employers for "giving the true character of a servant" nonactionable); Ward v. Mortimer, (1776) 2 Mansfield Manuscripts 844 (K.B.); Weatherston v. Hawkins, (1786) 1 T.R. 110, 111–12, 99 Eng. Rep. 1001, 1002 (K.B.) (in such suits plaintiffs must "prove the falsehood"); Giles Jacob, A New Law-Dictionary [unnumbered under "Libel"] (Nutt, London 1729) ("in actions on the case, one may justify that the matter is true," but not in criminal prosecutions); 3 Blackstone's Commentaries 126; 4 *id.* 150.

[68] Trial of Charles Duncombe, (1699) 13 State Trials 1061, 1104 (K.B.); *s.c.* 12 Mod. 224, 88 Eng. Rep. 1278, though the judges disagreed.

[69] Trial of Mary Butler, (1699) 13 State Trials 1249, 1262 (K.B.), other than where forgery was admitted.

[70] Trial of Richard Hathaway, (1702) 14 State Trials 639, 689–90 (K.B.).

[71] Trial of William Fuller, (1702) 14 State Trials 517, 534 (K.B.).

[72] 2 Hudson 102; *accord* Milsom 390, 389; Green 41.

[73] Case de Libellis Famosis, (1605) 5 Coke's Rep. 125a, 77 Eng. Rep. 250, 250 (Star Chamber), which is Coke's report stating his argument as attorney general but describing it as the judgment of the court in the case of Attorney General v. Pickering, (1605) Hawarde 222, 225 (Star Chamber). *Accord* Sheppard 116; Milsom 389 (whether written or spoken).

[74] Lake v. Hatton, (1619) Hobart 252, 253, 80 Eng. Rep. 398, 399 (Star Chamber) (dissent).

[75] John C. Lassiter, *Defamation of Peers: The Rise and Decline of the Action for* Scandalum Magnatum, *1497–1773*, 22 Am. J. Legal Hist. 216, 217 (1978).

scandalum magnatum,[76] even though the statutes defined the offense as "false news" about magnates[77] and seemed to allow truth as a defense.[78] That same rule came to apply to all libel actions in Star Chamber, whether brought by the Crown or by private litigants[79]: while "the defendant may justify . . . as true" any spoken words, "if he put the scandal in writing, it is then past any justification."[80] During the Restoration, King's Bench followed the Star Chamber rule that "whether true or faux" is irrelevant (though the chief justice dissented).[81] The Restoration ended with a split of judges in the *Seven Bishops* case: only Justice Powell's opinion required that to be seditious libel "it must be false," while Justice Allybone's position was that "there may be every tittle of a libel true, and yet it may be a libel still."[82]

Holt followed that Star Chamber rule for the crimes of libel and seditious libel, that truth was irrelevant,[83] even while recognizing that in private actions for libel the defendant "may justify" the printed or spoken words, when he added that the rule was "otherwise in an indictment" where no justification of truth was

[76] 3 Edw 1 c34 (1275); 2 Rich 2, stat 1, c5 (1378); 12 Rich 2 c11 (1388); 1 & 2 Mary c3 (1554); 1 Elizabeth 1 c6 (1559); SHEPPARD 16; 3 BLACKSTONE'S COMMENTARIES 123; *e.g.*, Duke Schomberg v. Murrey, (1701) 12 Mod. 420, 88 Eng. Rep. 1423 (K.B.); Holt K.B. 640, 90 Eng. Rep. 1254 (K.B.); SELECT CASES BEFORE THE KING'S COUNCIL IN THE STAR CHAMBER . . . 1477–1509, at 36–37 n. (I.S. Leadam ed., Selden Society v.16, Bernard Quaritch, London 1903); *accord* 2 BAKER 244–45; 6 OHLE 781; FIFOOT 128.

[77] EDWARD COKE, THE SECOND PART OF THE INSTITUTES OF THE LAWS OF ENGLAND 227 (Brooke, London 1797); 3 Edw 1 c34 (1275) (Coke's translation, *id.* 225: "to tell or publish any false news or tales, whereby discord, or occasion of discord or slander may grow between the king and his people, or the great men of the realm."); SHEPPARD 17; 1 COMYNS 187; 4 BLACKSTONE'S COMMENTARIES 149.

[78] SHEPPARD 17 (undifferentiated); 2 HUDSON 104 (if spoken, not if written); *accord* [CAPEL LOFFT], AN ESSAY ON THE LAW OF LIBELS 31 (C. Dilly, London 1785); HAMBURGER 668–69.

[79] The Star Chamber heard nonseditious libel cases as well. Frize v. Bennet, (1625) Rushworth 6 (Star Chamber); Moore v. Mercer, (1632) 3 Rushworth 35 (Star Chamber); R v. Walker, (1633) 3 Rushworth 59 (Star Chamber); RICHARD CROMPTON, STAR-CHAMBER CASES, SHEWING WHAT CAUSES PROPERLY BELONG TO THE COGNIZANCE OF THAT COURT 10 (John Grove, London 1630).

[80] 2 HUDSON 104; *accord* Wants Case, (1601) Moore K.B. 627, 72 Eng. Rep. 802 (Star Chamber) ("un libeller est punishable, coment que le matter del libel soit vray"); Caston v. Hitcham, (1632) Rushworth 35, 36 (Star Chamber); *see* Smith v. Tuston, (1632) 3 Rushworth 47 (Star Chamber).

[81] R v. Banks, (1666) 2 Keble 22, 84 Eng. Rep. 14 (K.B.); *s.c.* 2 Keble 4, 84 Eng. Rep. 3. One later treatise said the most an accused could do was to "explain the words by shewing the occasion." 4 BACON 408.

[82] (1688) 12 State Trials 183, 426–27, 429 (K.B.).

[83] THEODORE F. T. PLUCKNETT, A CONCISE HISTORY OF THE COMMON LAW 496 (5th ed. Butterworth, London 1956); THOMAS A. GREEN, VERDICT ACCORDING TO CONSCIENCE: PERSPECTIVES ON THE ENGLISH CRIMINAL TRIAL JURY, 1200–1800, at 253 (UChiP, Chicago 1985).

allowed.[84] Thus in the years after 1688, the Crown's charges against publications or words rarely alleged falsity,[85] except in charges against seditious news that generally recited that it was "false news,"[86] probably seeking to build upon *scandalum magnatum*. In Crown prosecutions for seditious libel and other criminal libel during the eighteenth century, truth was no defense[87] and was "immaterial . . . since the provocation, and not the falsity, is the thing to be punished criminally."[88] Mansfield, like other judges, acknowledged (and defended) the inconsistency: "In the case of a civil action, it is different."[89]

There is no logical reason why truth should not be a defense to seditious libel, or why its admissibility in civil actions for libel should not apply to criminal actions involving libel of the King or magistrates. The obvious real reason is that government wanted power to punish criticism, even if true. The illogic underlying that rule was shown by decisions and treatises carrying the point further: it was not just neutral (no justification) that the seditious libel was true, but it was an aggravating factor that the libel was true.[90] True criticism was a worse crime than false criticism!

Those counterintuitive standards began to be challenged by the late seventeenth century, most notably in the *Harris* case and the *Seven Bishops* case (where the attempt to raise truth as a defense was rebuffed[91] but the even division of the judges allowed the jury to decide all issues and to reach a general verdict of acquittal[92]). Challenges, rejected by Holt, continued to be rejected by his

[84] *In re* Anonymous, (1706) 11 Mod. 99, 88 Eng. Rep. 921, 921–22 (K.B.), evidently same case as Cropp v. Tilney (Tylney), (1706) 3 Salkeld 225, 91 Eng. Rep. 791; Holt K.B. 422, 90 Eng. Rep.1132 (K.B.); *accord* 1 HAWKINS 194; GREEN 41.

[85] 10 CALENDAR-WILLIAM 249, 255, 256, 364, 400; R v. Orme and Nutt, (1699) 1 Ld. Raym. 486, 91 Eng. Rep. 1224 (K.B.).

[86] 6 CALENDAR-WILLIAM 29, 30; 7 *id.* 431; 8 *id.* 171, 175; 10 *id.* 249; 4 CALENDAR-ANNE no.945; *e.g.*, Trial of Mr. Richard Francklin, (1731) 17 State Trials 625, 628, 655 (K.B.).

[87] R v. Dormer, (1726) 1 Barn. K.B. 13, 94 Eng. Rep. 9 (K.B.); R v. Lofeild, (1731) 2 Barn. K.B. 128, 152, 193, 94 Eng. Rep. 399, 416, 442 (K.B.) (rejecting defense); R v. Griffin and Banyere, (1733) 2 Barn. K.B. 558, 94 Eng. Rep. 558; W. Kel. 292, 25 Eng. Rep. 621 (K.B.);R v. Roberts, (1734) Cunningham 94, 94 Eng. Rep. 1084 (K.B.) ("you may justify for words spoken, but not for words put into writing," because words in writing are more "deliberate" and are "supposed to spread the scandal").

[88] 4 BLACKSTONE'S COMMENTARIES 150; 3 *id.* 125–26; *accord* 3 BACON 491; *St. Asaph*, 21 State Trials at 1034.

[89] Earl of Sandwich v. Miller, (1773) 2 Mansfield Manuscripts 806 (K.B.); *s.c.* Lofft 210, 98 Eng. Rep. 614, citing THE EVIDENCE, (AS TAKEN DOWN IN COURT) IN THE TRIAL WHEREIN THE RT. HON. JOHN, EARL OF SANDWICH, WAS PLAINTIFF, AND J. MILLER, DEFENDANT 33 (G. Kearsley, London 1773); Onslow v. Horne, (1770) 2 Mansfield Manuscripts 839, 840 n.8; 2 Black. W. 750, 96 Eng. Rep. 439 (K.B.); 3 Blackstone's Commentaries 125–26.

[90] 2 HUDSON 102; 3 BACON 495.

[91] Trial of the Seven Bishops, (1688) 12 State Trials 183, 427, 429 (K.B.); HAMBURGER 709.

[92] 12 *id.* at 425–29, 430–31.

successors,[93] including Mansfield, who found it "totally immaterial" whether the "libel" was "true or false,"[94] and ultimately by all the judges.[95]

Elimination of the Requirement to Prove Criminal Intent

In the law of defamation generally, malicious intent had to be shown throughout the sixteenth[96] and seventeenth centuries.[97] Private actions continued to treat malice as "the 'foundation' of the action for defamation" and as "an essential aspect of the plaintiff's claim"[98] through the next century. For slander, similarly, "malice is the gist of this action."[99] Criminal libel consisted of "malicious defamations,"[100] and seditious libel alleged malice. Other criminal law, too, made criminal intent a requirement,[101] as Holt recognized.[102]

The Star Chamber, however, began to imply criminal intent when it found a libel seditious. A 1610 case stated its older rule for civil libel actions, that "every one who

[93] Trial of Mr. Richard Francklin, (1731) 17 State Trials 625, 659 (K.B.), where the defense was well argued, 17 *id.* 659–60.

[94] Trial of John Almon, (1770) 20 State Trials 803, 836 (K.B.); *s.c.* 5 Burr. 2686, 98 Eng. Rep. 411; *accord* Case of Henry Sampson Woodfall, (1770) 20 State Trials 895, 902 (K.B.); *s.c.* Lofft 776, 98 Eng. Rep. 914; 5 Burr. 2661, 98 Eng. Rep. 398; 2 Strange 1131, 93 Eng. Rep. 1082; Earl of Sandwich v. Miller, (1773) 2 MANSFIELD MANUSCRIPTS 806 (K.B.); R v. Horne, (1777) 2 Cowp. 672, 679, 98 Eng. Rep. 1300, 1304 (K.B.); R v. Dean of St. Asaph, (1784) 3 T.R. 428, 429, 100 Eng. Rep. 657, 658 (K.B.) ("published without a lawful excuse").

[95] Opinion of the Judges, (1792) 22 State Trials 297, 298–99 (H.L.).

[96] Brook v. Montague, (1605) Cro. Jac. 90, 91, 79 Eng. Rep. 77, 78 (K.B.) (describing decision of Wray, C.J., who died 1592, as good law); *accord* IBBETSON 115 & nn.114–16.

[97] Peacock v. Reynal, (1612) 2 Brownlow & Goldesborough 151, 123 Eng. Rep. 868 (Star Chamber) ("with what mind it was made is to be respected," and "the defendant intended his profit, and his own benefit," whereas the same words to apprise a father of a wayward child would lack defamatory intent); R v. Eades, (1686) 2 Show. K.B. 468, 89 Eng. Rep. 1046 (K.B.) (though that exception was later waived in the case); SHEPPARD 7 (slander); *accord* 6 OHLE 785; HAMBURGER 730.

[98] Paul Mitchell, *Duties, Interests, and Motives: Privileged Occasions in Defamation*, 18 OXFORD J. LEGAL STUDIES 381, 381–82 (1998); *accord* 3 BACON 490 (libel); 1 COMYNS 212.

[99] Smith v. Richardson, (1737) Willes 20, 24, 125 Eng. Rep. 1034, 1036 (Exch.); *e.g.*, Cr[a]wford v. Middleton, (1662) 1 Lev. 82, 83 Eng. Rep. 308; 1 Keble 344, 353, 377, 83 Eng. Rep. 984, 990, 1004 (K.B.) ("non-suit, for it was not maliciously").

[100] 4 BLACKSTONE'S COMMENTARIES 150.

[101] 4 *id.* at 27; *accord* 1 HALE 532, 683, 425, 439–40, 443–44, 475–76, 508–09, 519–22, 548–51 (all listed felonies); 4 BLACKSTONE'S COMMENTARIES 4–5 (criminal law); BAKER-INTRODUCTION 523 (felonies).

[102] Among Holt decisions, *e.g.*, Trial of Sarah Baynton et al., (1702) 14 State Trials 597, 629 (K.B.); *see* Trial of Charles Duncombe, (1699) 13 State Trials 1061, 1106 (K.B.).

shall be convicted ought to be a contriver, procurer, or publisher of it, knowing it to be a libel."[103] However, cases during the Laudian days dispensed with any requirement of knowledge or intent, such as when Prynne was told "you can never make any defence at all out of that" because his words were "plain" and "wicked, infamous, scandalous, and seditious libel."[104] Cases in the Restoration, such as of the printers and booksellers in the 1684 *Barnardiston* case, similarly held that if anyone "write libels, or publish any expressions which in themselves carry sedition and faction, and ill-will towards the government," "proof of the thing itself proves the evil mind" and is "proof enough of the words maliciously, seditiously, and factiously."[105] In the last seditious libel decision before the Revolution of 1688, *Seven Bishops*, a judicial fracture appeared as two of four judges required a seditious libel to have "an ill intention of sedition," and to be shown to be malicious.[106] However, the other judges were followed by Holt.

The first seditious libel decision by King's Bench after the Licensing Act lapsed in 1695 was *R v. Paine*.[107] There, Holt confronted a defendant who physically wrote but did not compose a libel (it was "dictated to him by another"), which was deemed seditious because it was "against the late Queen"; but the libel was "by mistake delivered" and not intentionally published (his servant picked up the wrong sheet of paper).[108] Counsel for the defense argued that something "delivered by mistake" lacked "proof of a malicious and seditious publication of this paper."[109] Holt disagreed entirely, ruling that the person "who writes it" as dictated "is maker of a libel,"[110] and even though "delivering it by mistake is no publication," the "making a libel is an offence, though never published" and the reading by either the recipient or the scribe "is a publication."[111] In doing so, Holt applied the rule of the Star Chamber and the later Stuart cases that inferred criminal intent,[112] and also applied the rule of the Star Chamber that did not require

[103] Lamb's Case, (1610) 9 Co. Rep. 59b, 77 Eng. Rep. 822; 5 Co. Rep. 23b, 77 Eng. Rep. 85 (Star Chamber); *accord* Wants Case, (1601) Moore K.B. 627, 72 Eng. Rep. 802 (Star Chamber); *see* Brant 6–7.

[104] Proceedings against Wm. Prynn, (1632–33) 3 State Trials 561, 580 (Star Chamber); 3 *id.* at 576, 579–80; *see* Proceedings against Mr. Wraynham, (1618) 2 State Trials 1059, 1072–73 (Star Chamber); Milsom 391.

[105] Trial of Sir Samuel Barnardiston, (1684) 9 State Trials 1333, 1352 (K.B.); *accord* Trial of Dover, Brewster and Brooks, (1663) 6 State Trials 539, 547, 559 (K.B.).

[106] (1688) 12 State Trials 183, 426, 427 (K.B.) (Holloway and Powell, JJ.).

[107] R v. Paine, (1696) 5 Mod. 163, 87 Eng. Rep. 584; Comberbach 358, 90 Eng. Rep. 527; abridged Holt K.B. 294, 90 Eng. Rep. 1062; Carthew 405, 90 Eng. Rep. 834; 1 Ld. Raym. 729, 91 Eng. Rep. 1387 (K.B.); discussed in Hamburger 729.

[108] 5 Mod. at 163, 87 Eng. Rep. at 584.

[109] 5 Mod. at 165, 87 Eng. Rep. at 585.

[110] Comberbach at 359, 90 Eng. Rep. at 527.

[111] 5 Mod. at 167, 87 Eng. Rep. at 585–86.

[112] Even if the printer or seller was ignorant of a publication's content. *E.g., Dover,* 6 State Trials at 564.

publication for a criminal action,[113] even though that was contrary to more recent precedents of King's Bench requiring publication.[114] Holt made clear where he stood on seditious libels, concluding with comparison of "murdering a man's reputation" to murdering a life,[115] although the court adjourned without clearly entering a final decision against such "murders." The jury found Paine guilty of writing the libel (though not publishing it). That was challenged primarily on the ground that the jury "found nothing as to the intent," and that a criminal intent was required in any case such as perjury, where the verdict is void "if the jury find only the false swearing, and say nothing as to the corruption and malice."[116] The court, apparently standing on implied criminal intent, upheld the verdict on the counterintuitive basis that Paine writing what was dictated committed criminal libel, while "[h]e who dictated cannot be indicted for making this libel, because he did not write it."[117] Holt made the same point more explicitly in a case involving treasonable words in 1703, *R v. Tayler.* Responding to the objection that no intent to injure the Queen or Government had been alleged, he held that "there needs no averment that they were spoken with an intent to injure the Government, for the words import a crime of themselves."[118]

Subsequent cases reaffirmed that it is not material "whether he who disperses a libel knew any thing of the contents or effect of it,"[119] finding the absence of intent no defense.[120] They inferred criminal intent from seditious libels,[121] even finding that "the circumstances of malice are [e]ntirely immaterial."[122] As Mansfield directed a jury, the "inference of law" of intent that was "drawn upon the printing and publishing a libel" was supported by "the lowest to the highest degree of guilt,

[113] Barrow v. Lewellin, (1603–25) Hobart 62, 80 Eng. Rep. 211 (Star Chamber).

[114] *Barnardiston,* 9 State Trials at 1356.

[115] *Paine,* 5 Mod. at 167, 87 Eng. Rep. at 587.

[116] Carthew 405, 406, 90 Eng. Rep. 834, 835.

[117] *Id.*

[118] R v. Tayler, (1703) 3 Salkeld 199, 91 Eng. Rep. 775; 2 Ld. Raym. 879, 92 Eng. Rep. 88 (Q.B.).

[119] 1 HAWKINS 195; *accord* R v. Clerk, (1728) 1 Barn. K.B. 304, 94 Eng. Rep. 207 (K.B.); R v. Knell, (1728) 1 Barn. K.B. 305, 306, 94 Eng. Rep. 207, 208 (K.B.); *In re* Anonymous [R v. Mayer & Dowling], (1731) 2 Barn. K.B. 43, 94 Eng. Rep. 345 (K.B.); HAMBURGER 749.

[120] R v. Nutt, (1728) 1 Barn. K.B. 306, 94 Eng. Rep. 208; Fitz-G. 47, 94 Eng. Rep. 697 (K.B.) (same for bedridden bookseller selling or illiterate servant carrying libel, though jury refused to render general verdict and Attorney General created mistrial); *Francklin,* 17 State Trials at 674–75; *Almon,* 20 State Trials at 838; R v. Miller, (1776) 2 MANSFIELD MANUSCRIPTS 847, 848 n.1 (K.B.); *accord* 3 BACON 497; HAMBURGER 752.

[121] *E.g., Francklin,* 17 State Trials at 675, 659; *Almon,* 20 State Trials at 836; *Woodfall,* 5 Burr. at 2666–67, 98 Eng. Rep. at 401; *Woodfall,* 20 State Trials at 913; *Miller,* 20 State Trials at 894; R v. Horne, (1777) 2 Cowp. 672, 681, 98 Eng. Rep. 1300, 1305 (K.B.); *St. Asaph,* 3 T.R. at 429, 100 Eng. Rep. at 659. Willes, J. dissented on this point. *St. Asaph,* 21 State Trials at 1040–41; 4 Dougl. 171, 99 Eng. Rep. 824 (1784).

[122] R v. Clerk, (1728) 1 Barn. K.B. 304, 94 Eng. Rep. 207 (K.B.).

even to a very venial degree of guilt."[123] Decisions similarly inferred intent from the fact of publication of alleged criminal libels.[124] When the House of Lords addressed the issue, it determined that the "criminal intention charged" for a seditious libel "requir[ed] no proof" by the prosecutor and "admitt[ed] no proof" by the accused, and that the same was true of the "criminality or innocence" of the publication.[125]

Criminalization of Criticism of Government Officials

Spreading false news about the King or a limited class of "magnates" and officials—*scandalum magnatum*—had been criminalized since 1275 (with amendments in 1378 and 1388). However, the statute did not prohibit making true statements, or false statements about lesser magistrates or other prominent people.

The Star Chamber found the statutory framework inadequate. Its decision in *Pickering's Case* (*Case de Libellis Famosis*) in the early seventeenth century,[126] as reported by Coke, slightly extended *scandalum magnatum* to libeling the deceased Archbishop of Canterbury. In his printed report, Coke tagged the case with the name of the capital offense in late Roman law,[127] and further expanded the *scandalum magnatum* concept into the claim that a libel "against a magistrate, or other public person," is a "greater offence" than against a private person. That report gave the rationale that such a libel "concerns not only the breach of the peace, but also the scandal of Government; for what greater scandal of Government can there be than to have corrupt or wicked magistrates to be appointed and constituted by the King to govern his subjects under him?"[128] Coke's report misleadingly claimed to restate the common law, when in fact it fabricated a new crime of seditious libel.[129] The Star Chamber regularly found censure of magistrates and

[123] *Miller*, 20 State Trials at 894; *accord* R v. Cook, (1758) 2 MANSFIELD MANUSCRIPTS 810, 811 (K.B.); R v. Wilkie, (1776) 2 *id.* at 849 (K.B.).

[124] *E.g.*, 4 BLACKSTONE'S COMMENTARIES 151 (whether the book or writing "be criminal"); R v. Topham, (1791) 4 T.R. 126, 127–28, 100 Eng. Rep. 931, 932 (K.B.).

[125] Opinion of the Judges, (1792) 22 State Trials 297, 300, 297–98 (H.L.).

[126] Also called Attorney General v. Pickering, (1605) Hawarde 222, 2 Hudson 103 (Star Chamber); background in COLCLOUGH 217–19; BRANT 4–10.

[127] The civil law offense *de famosis libellis*, CODEX JUSTINIANUS §9.36, at 856 (Paulus Krueger ed., Weidmann, Berlin 1877).

[128] Case de Libellis Famosis, (1605) 5 Coke's Rep. 125a, 77 Eng. Rep. 250, 251 (Star Chamber); *accord* SHEPPARD 115, 117; 1 HAWKINS 194; 1 COMYNS 195.

[129] BRANT 5, 7–10; though 1 BAKER lxxii–lxiii cited Star Chamber proceedings against seditious books from the 1560s.

bishops to be criminal libel,[130] and in the 1620s through the 1630s stretched the jurisdiction further to public criticism of "the King and State"[131] or of "all magistrates, and particularly against the king"[132] as seditious libels. King's Bench under Charles I gladly followed that.[133]

King's Bench in the Restoration and after continued to treat criticism of magistrates as *libellis famosis*[134] or seditious libel.[135] Even after *Seven Bishops*, it followed the Crown's view of "publick magistrates" that "every charge of abuse in the execution of that office is libellous" (even if true), "as reflecting upon their persons in particular" and as "also a reflection upon the Government."[136] Consequently, throughout the eighteenth century, prosecutions were brought against critics of governmental officials as criminal libels[137] or seditious libels,[138] under that century's fortified doctrine of seditious libel.

The rationale for why libel of magistrates was deemed more serious than libel of private persons, "that it tends to scandalize the Government,"[139] generated

[130] *Proceedings against Mr. Wraynham*, (1618) 2 State Trials at 1059; *s.c.* Wrennum's Case, Popham 135, 79 Eng. Rep. 1237 (Star Chamber) (slander); Whitacle v. Moody, (1627) Rushworth 7 (Star Chamber); Thelwel v. Holman, (1627) *id.* 12 (Star Chamber); Bishop of Worcester v. Boyer, (1629) *id.* 21 (Star Chamber); R v. Norton, (1630) *id.* 29, 30 (Star Chamber); R v. Jones, (1630) *id.* 31 (Star Chamber); R v. Morgan, (1630) *id.* 33 (Star Chamber); R v. Reignolds, (1633) *id.* 58 (Star Chamber); R v. Bowyer, (1633) *id.* 61 (Star Chamber). *Wraynham, Bishop of Worcester, Reignolds,* and *Bowyer* were under the Act of 1381, and the others involved extension to other judicial officials.

[131] R v. Perkins, (1627) Rushworth 8 (Star Chamber).

[132] *Prynn*, 3 State Trials at 575; *see* R v. Cawley, (1602) Hawarde 146 (Star Chamber) ("infamous libel" that officials embezzled).

[133] Case of Eliot, Hollis and Valentine, (1629) 3 State Trials 293, 308 (K.B.); *s.c.* Cro. Car. 181, 605, 79 Eng. Rep. 759, 1121; Jeffes' Case, (1629) Cro. Car. 175, 79 Eng. Rep. 753 (K.B.).

[134] *E.g.*, R v. Banks, (1666) 2 Keble 22, 84 Eng. Rep. 14 (K.B.); R v. Dangerfield, (1685) 3 Mod. 68, 87 Eng. Rep. 43 (K.B.); R v. Dutton, (1698) 12 Mod. 250, 88 Eng. Rep. 1298 (K.B.); R v. Orme and Nutt, 1 Ld. Raym. 486, 91 Eng. Rep. 1224; *s.c.* Alme & Nott, (1699) 3 Salkeld 224, 91 Eng. Rep. 790 (K.B.).

[135] *E.g., Seven Bishops*, 12 State Trials at 426, 427, 429; R v. Bell, (1700) 12 Mod. 348, 88 Eng. Rep. 1372 (K.B.).

[136] R v. Griffin, (1733) W. Kel. 292, 294, 25 Eng. Rep. 621, 622 (K.B.).

[137] R v. Bedford, (1702–15) Gilb. Cas. 297, 93 Eng. Rep. 334 (Q.B.) (seditious libel); R v. Smith, (1725) Sess. Cas. 134, 93 Eng. Rep. 135 (K.B.); R v. How, (1725) Sess. Cas. 134, 93 Eng. Rep. 136; 2 Strange 699, 93 Eng. Rep. 793 (K.B.) (though judgment for defendant because indictment inadequately specific); R v. Dormer, (1726) 1 Barn. K.B. 13, 94 Eng. Rep. 9 (K.B.); *In re* Anonymous, (1731) 2 Barn. K.B. 43, 94 Eng. Rep. 345 (K.B.); R v. Pownell, (1731) W. Kel. 68, 25 Eng. Rep. 488 (K.B.); R v. Griffin and Banyere, (1733) 2 Barn. K.B. 558, 94 Eng. Rep. 558 (K.B.); Bolingbroke v. Woodfall, (1777) 2 MANSFIELD MANUSCRIPTS 847 (K.B.); R v. Bew, (1781) 2 *id.* 853 (K.B.); R v. Jolliffe, (1791) 4 T.R. 285, 100 Eng. Rep. 1022; 2 T.R. 90, 100 Eng. Rep. 50 (K.B.).

[138] *E.g., Francklin*, 17 State Trials at 659; Trial of William Owen, (1752) 18 State Trials 1203 (K.B.); *s.c.* Sayer 30, 96 Eng. Rep. 792; *Almon*, 20 State Trials at 803; *Miller*, 20 State Trials at 869; *In re* Information, (1772–74) Lofft 462, 98 Eng. Rep. 748 (K.B.); *In re* Information, (1772–74) Lofft 544, 98 Eng. Rep. 791 (K.B.).

[139] 1 HAWKINS 194; *accord* 3 BACON 491; COLCLOUGH 217.

constant pressure to treat libel of the government generally as a still more serious offense. Laws such as those of the Cavalier Parliament often trumpeted the threat of spoken or published words to government. The Licensing Act of 1662 castigated "heretical, schismatical, blasphemous, seditious and treasonable books, pamphlets and papers" during the late war, and prohibited printing such publications that "tend or be to the scandal of religion, or the Church, or the government or governors of the Church, State or commonwealth" (to be enforced by denial of licensing). The Act for the Preservation of the King of 1661 criminalized criticism of King or government,[140] and the Act against Tumultuous Petitioning that year criminalized many petitions disparaging laws or government.[141] Royal decrees on dissent, political and religious, more and more proscribed expression critical of government as well as governors.[142] Supporting those royal decrees, the Crown judges gave an opinion to Charles II that publications "scandalous to the government" may be seized and their authors and printers punished under common law.[143] After the Revolution of 1688, monarchs were particularly sensitive to criticism as the ex-King and the ex-Prince sat across the channel, and the royal reaction was predictable as criticism of the government multiplied with the expansion of newspapers and periodicals after the lapse of licensing in 1695.

Suppression of criticism of government was a punishment in search of a crime, reaching its apogee in Justice Allybone's opinion in *Seven Bishops* that "no private man can take upon him to write concerning the government at all," because "it is the business of subjects to mind only their own properties and interests," or else that person is "a libeller"—and "every libel against the government carries in it sedition."[144] The Lord Chief Justice agreed, frantically stretching libel, that "any thing that shall disturb the government . . . is certainly within the case of 'Libellis Famosis.'"[145] Judges had long festooned seditious libel cases with declarations about the wickedness of criticizing the government,[146] though in dicta.[147] The Crown's charges in seditious libel cases had long alleged libel of the Government as well as of the King or particular officials, before[148] and after the

140 13 Car 2, stat 1, c1 (1661); 8 EHD 63–64 §§I–II.

141 13 Car 2, stat 1, c5 (1661); 8 EHD 66 §I (petitions disparaging laws or raising grievances against government if signed by more than twenty persons or delivered by more than ten).

142 *E.g.*, 13–14 Car 2 c33 (1662); 8 EHD 67 §I.

143 *Harris*, 7 State Trials at 929; *see* BRANT 12, 13.

144 *Seven Bishops*, 12 State Trials at 428, 429.

145 12 *id.* at 426.

146 *E.g.*, *Dover*, 6 State Trials at 540 n., 548, 558, 564; *Barnardiston*, 9 State Trials at 1351, 1353, 1365, 1367, 1369.

147 HAMBURGER 701, 714; *accord* R v. Prin [Pym], (1664) 1 Keble 773, 83 Eng. Rep. 1235; 1 Sid. 219, 82 Eng. Rep. 1068 (K.B.).

148 *Prynn*, 3 State Trials at 574; *Seven Bishops*, 3 Mod. at 213, 214, 87 Eng. Rep. at 137.

Revolution,[149] doubtless recognizing that censure of "the Government" had the same effect as censure of the King or the Secretary of State. Such charges became much more common after 1695.[150]

Criminalization of Criticism of Government Generally

The law of defamation generally required that a writing "must descend to particulars and individuals to make it a libel."[151] It was actionable only if "the person who is scandalised is certain."[152] Consequently, cases for libel of a large group could not be maintained.[153] Generally in criminal law, a specific victim was required—a person murdered, a person robbed. That allowed critics of government generally, rather than of a specific official or measure, to escape suppression, unless they performed actions amounting to treason.

The Star Chamber led the way away from that principle when it found publications to be seditious libels, by interlacing discussion of their negative reflection on the King with their negative reflection on government generally,[154] ignoring that criticism of government generally does not "descend to particulars and individuals." Holt extended that Star Chamber approach, departing from the usual defamation approach.

Holt appears to have embarked on a search for the right case to expand seditious libel doctrine to prohibit criticism of government. In 1699 he wrote that "transcribing and collecting" material critical of government "was highly criminal, without publishing it, and . . . was of dangerous consequence to the

149 R v. Bear, (1699) Holt K.B. 422, 422, 423–24, 90 Eng. Rep. 1132, 1132, 1133 (abridgment); 1 Ld. Raym. 414, 91 Eng. Rep. 1175; 1 Salkeld 324, 91 Eng. Rep. 287; 2 Salkeld 417, 646, 91 Eng. Rep. 363, 547; 3 Salkeld 226, 91 Eng. Rep. 791; Carthew 407, 90 Eng. Rep. 836; (*Beere*) 12 Mod. 218, 88 Eng. Rep. 1274 (K.B.); R v. Tayler, (1703) 3 Salkeld 199, 91 Eng. Rep. 775; 2 Ld. Raym. 879, 92 Eng. Rep. 88 (Q.B.); R v. Langley, (1703) 6 Mod. 124, 87 Eng. Rep. 882 (Q.B.).

150 1 HAWKINS 194; 6 CALENDAR-WILLIAM 30, 117; 7 *id.* at 425, 431, 488; 8 *id.* at 51, 53; 10 *id.* at 364; 4 CALENDAR-ANNE no.945. Some alleged libel of Parliament. 7 CALENDAR-WILLIAM 431, 488.

151 R v. Alme & Nott, (1699) 3 Salkeld 224, 91 Eng. Rep. 790; *s.c.* Alme & Nott, 3 Salkeld 224, 91 Eng. Rep. 790 (K.B.); *accord* 1 HAWKINS 195; 6 OHLE 795.

152 Jeames v. Rutlech, (1599) 4 Co. Rep. 17a, 17b, 76 Eng. Rep. 900; B&M 702, 703 (K.B.); *accord* 3 BACON 493; 1 COMYNS 207.

153 R v. Osborne, (1732) W. Kel. 230, 25 Eng. Rep. 584; 2 Barn. K.B. 166, 94 Eng. Rep. 425 (K.B.); *see In re* Anonymous, (1731) 2 Barn. K.B. 138, 94 Eng. Rep. 406 (K.B.) (though different result stated in Kelynge report).

154 R v. Perkins, (1627) Rushworth 8 (Star Chamber); and in cases alleging miscarriage of justice, treated as defamation of judges, R v. Mady, (1628) *id.* 15 (Star Chamber); Smith v. Crokey, (1632) *id.* 37 (Star Chamber); *see* Whitacle v. Moody, (1627) *id.* 7 (Star Chamber).

Government."[155] However, he did not dispose of the case on that basis because it was enmeshed in challenges to the wording of the indictment. In 1703 he characterized spoken words calling a mayor "a rogue and a rascal" as "a disparagement of the Government, who put an ill man into office." However, he did not base the decision on that ground where the words were not written but spoken, acknowledging that "this is an extraordinary thing to indict a man for these [spoken] words."[156] On further argument, Holt remained "not satisfied that these words will maintain an indictment," but ominously added that if Langley "had abused him in writing, that would have been indictable."[157] A year later, a case involved exactly that.

John Tutchin, publisher of the *Observator*, regularly printed such criticisms as "that the Government is maladministred by corrupt persons."[158] Prosecuted for seditious libel in *R v. Tutchin* in 1704,[159] his primary defense was that "there can be no libel, where no person certain is reflected upon, or scandalized."[160] Holt rejected the defense and ruled that "a libel, reflecting on the Government," could be prosecuted as appropriately as criticism of particular officials could. Holt's justification for extending the bounds of seditious libel was overtly partisan[161]:

> If men should not be called to account for possessing the people with an ill opinion of the Government, no Government can subsist; for it is very necessary for every Government, that the people should have a good opinion of it. And nothing can be worse to any Government, than to endeavour to procure animosities as to the management of it. This has been always look'd upon as a crime, and no Government can be safe unless it be punished.[162]

[155] R v. Bear, (1699) Carthew 407, 409, 90 Eng. Rep. 836, 837 (K.B.).

[156] R v. Langley, (1703) 2 Ld. Raym. 1029, 1029–30, 92 Eng. Rep. 184, 184; 6 Mod. 124, 87 Eng. Rep. 882 (Q.B.). Raymond's report is far superior to Modern's.

[157] 2 Ld. Raym. at 1031, 92 Eng. Rep. at 185.

[158] Trial of John Tutchin, (1704) 14 State Trials 1095, 1125 (K.B.); *s.c.* 6 Mod. 164, 268, 90 Eng. Rep. 922, 1014; 2 Ld. Raym. 1061, 92 Eng. Rep. 204; 1 Salkeld 51, 91 Eng. Rep. 50; Holt K.B. 56, 424, 90 Eng. Rep. 929, 1133; *see* 55 ODNB 708. *State Trials* provides the most thorough report, based on a courtroom stenographer.

[159] Holt K.B. at 424, 90 Eng. Rep. at 1133; Holt K.B. 56, 90 Eng. Rep. 929; 6 Mod. 268, 90 Eng. Rep. 1014; 14 State Trials at 1125–28.

[160] 14 State Trials at 1119.

[161] As was Holt's reversal on a technicality as Tory power waned and Whig power grew. Holt K.B. at 425, 90 Eng. Rep. at 1134; Holt K.B. 56, 57, 90 Eng. Rep. 929; 6 Mod. 268, 90 Eng. Rep. 1014; 2 Ld. Raym. 1061, 92 Eng. Rep. 204 (1704); *accord* Lee S. Horsley, *The Trial of John Tutchin, Author of the "Observator,"* 3 Yearbook of English Studies 124, 136–37 (1973); Kenyon 109. The Raymond report is more precise than Modern, which is abridged in Holt.

[162] Holt K.B. at 424, 90 Eng. Rep. at 1133–34; *accord* 14 State Trials at 1128; Hamburger 735.

Consequently, he instructed the jury to "consider, whether these words I have read to you, do not tend to beget an ill opinion of the administration of the government?"[163] Though dicta existed to that effect, Holt is described as "the first to rely upon this doctrine in a decision,"[164] at least other than *R v. Pym* in 1664.[165] This dramatic extension of seditious libel doctrine occurred only five years after Holt followed the longstanding rule, holding that a libel "must descend to particulars and individuals to make it a libel"![166]

Libel of government quickly became the central claim in seditious libel prosecutions,[167] such as the prosecution of printer Richard Francklin for publishing a diplomatic letter that was charged with tending to "vilify the administration of his present majesty's government."[168]

The amorphous nature of expanding seditious libel to criticism of government generally was reflected in legal treatises. A 1662 treatise asserted that "there is a slander of the state" without categorizing it,[169] and one in 1716 listed "contempts against the King's person or government" (including "any thing which may lessen him in the esteem of his subjects, and weaken his Government") without calling it sedition.[170] Neither listed seditious libel or seditious words as a "plea of the Crown."[171] However, Holt's necessity of state reasoning took hold. Even near the

[163] 14 State Trials at 1128.

[164] HAMBURGER 735, 736. Two years earlier, Holt told an accused the law forbad him "to make libels, nor traduce ministers of state." TRYAL OF WILLIAM FULLER 12 (Isaac Cleave, London 1702); *accord* Trial of William Fuller, (1702) 14 State Trials 517, 536 (K.B.).

[165] R v. Pym, (1664) 1 Sid. 219, 82 Eng. Rep. 1068 (K.B.) ("containe matter de grand scandal al government car fist le late government melior que cel"—contains matter of great scandal to government of the city by representing the late government was better than the present).

[166] R v. Alme & Nott, (1699) 3 Salkeld 224, 91 Eng. Rep. 790 (K.B.). That rule was still being stated in 1716. 1 HAWKINS 195.

[167] *E.g.*, R v. Earbury, (1732) 2 Barn. K.B. 293, 94 Eng. Rep. 509; 2 Barn. K.B. 346, 374, 94 Eng. Rep. 544, 562; Fortescue 37, 92 Eng. Rep. 751 (K.B.); *s.c.* 19 State Trials 1016; R v. Rayner, (1732) 2 Barn. K.B. 232, 293, 94 Eng. Rep. 469, 509 (K.B.); *Owen*, 18 State Trials at 1204; *Almon*, Wilm. at 243–44, 97 Eng. Rep. at 95; *Almon*, 20 State Trials at 803; *Woodfall*, 20 State Trials at 902; R v. Bostock, (1790) 22 State Trials 308 (K.B.). The same is true of the *Miller, Williams, Horne, St. Asaph/Shipley, Gordon,* and *Stockdale* cases.

[168] Trial of Mr. Richard Francklin, (1731) 17 State Trials 625, 628 (K.B.); *see* 20 ODNB 752.

[169] SHEPPARD 2, other than differentiating it from *scandalum magnatum* or *libellis famosis, id.* 16, 115.

[170] 1 HAWKINS 60; *accord* 4 BLACKSTONE'S COMMENTARIES 123 (relying on Hawkins); STATE LAW: OR, THE DOCTRINE OF LIBELS, DISCUSSED AND EXAMINED 67 (2d ed. Nutt, London [1714]) (seditious libel).

[171] Hale's discussion of crimes was limited to felonies. 1 HALE i–iv, 2 *id.* i–iv (though there were occasional references to sedition, 1 *id.* 77–78, 115, 311–12, 319, 324, 333–34, 681; 2 *id.* 28, 115); *accord* MATTHEW HALE, PLEAS OF THE CROWN i–v (Richard Atkyns, London 1682). Blackstone reflected continuing confusion in 1769 by describing "speaking or writing" against "the king's

end of the eighteenth century, the chief justice, allowing criminal prosecution of criticism of a court decision, declared that nothing was "of greater importance to the welfare of the public than to put a stop to the animadversions and censures which are so frequently made on courts of justice." He was joined by another justice bewailing that "there is no case which calls more loudly for the interference of this court" by allowing prosecution.[172]

Elimination of Jury Finding of a Crime and Criminal Intent

A recurring problem for the Crown was that juries often acquitted defendants charged with seditious libel.

Trial by jury was often described as "the palladium of English liberty" and figured large in "the 'ancient constitution' ideology,"[173] though juries frequently were packed by prosecutors[174] and frequently deferred to judges' instructions that were "pointed and leading, if not coercive."[175] Common law enshrined the jury's right to determine factual matters[176] and to apply law given by the judge to those facts. In criminal law generally, the jury determined if the accused "be guilty or not guilty,"[177] which included whether the facts constituted a criminal offense and whether the accused acted with criminal intent. Holt himself described the normal provinces of jury and judge in criminal cases, saying that criminal intent "is matter of evidence for a jury to find the fact, and not for judges to intend it" or

---

person and government" as a different crime from seditious libel toward magistrates. 4 Blackstone's Commentaries 123, 150 (though the first reference treated sedition as a type of contempt, and the second as criminal defamatory libel).

[172] R v. Watson, (1788) 2 T.R. 199, 205, 207, 100 Eng. Rep. 108, 113 (K.B.).

[173] Baker-Introduction 508; Michael R.T. Macnair, The Law of Proof in Early Modern Equity 286 (Duncker & Humblot, Berlin 1999); *see id.* 288; *accord* Bill of Rights (1689), 8 EHD 122, 124.

[174] Harling 116–17; 2 Mansfield Manuscripts 783, 835; *e.g.*, [George Lyttleton], Considerations upon the Present State of Our Affairs 36 (T. Cooper, London 1749).

[175] Thomas A. Green, Verdict According to Conscience 271 (UChiP, Chicago 1985); *accord* 2 Mansfield Manuscripts 835 n.1; *e.g.*, Trial of Benjamin Harris, (1680) 7 State Trials 925, 929–30 (K.B.).

[176] 2 Hale 277.

[177] 2 *id.* 294; for examples in Holt's cases, Trial of Charles Duncombe, (1699) 13 State Trials 1061, 1106, 1103 (K.B.) (fraud and deceit); Trial of Mary Butler, (1699) 13 State Trials 1249, 1262 (K.B.) (forgery); Trial of Haagen Swendsen, (1702) 14 State Trials 597, 596 (K.B.) (criminal seduction). In nonfelonies where offences did not involve forfeiture, "the jury need not find the special matter" but could render a general verdict. 2 Hale 303; *accord* 2 Mansfield Manuscripts 928, 1069–70.

to "condemn him as guilty of it."[178] In the law of defamation generally, the province of the jury presumptively was to determine if the defendant was guilty or liable (as in *Seven Bishops* and *Owen*[179]), and that would incorporate the factual determinations whether the words or writing were defamatory, and whether the defendant acted with malicious intent.[180] However, the courts narrowed the scope of jury determinations uniquely in cases of libel.

The Star Chamber had determined seditious libel and other criminal cases without grand jury indictments,[181] though that had been challenged,[182] and without trial juries.[183] King's Bench, which followed the Star Chamber's elimination of a defense of truth and of an affirmative showing of malice or criminal intent in seditious libel and other criminal libel prosecutions, also followed the Star Chamber in restricting juries. King's Bench often avoided grand juries by adopting[184] the Star Chamber practice of using informations for seditious libel[185] (and other cases), particularly after 1690.[186] During the later Stuart reigns, King's Bench restricted juries to finding the accused guilty or innocent of publication: "the question before you is, whether the defendant be guilty of writing these malicious, seditious letters."[187] The judges then determined whether the writings were "seditious, and malicious" publications.[188]

The risk of a jury acquitting the accused of seditious libel was highlighted by *Seven Bishops*,[189] by *Paine* eight years after,[190] and by later cases.[191] Leaving to the

[178] R v. Plummer, (1701) 12 Mod. 627, 627–28, 88 Eng. Rep. 1565, 1565; Kelyng 109, 84 Eng. Rep. 1103 (K.B.).

[179] *Seven Bishops*, 12 State Trials at 430; *Owen*, 18 State Trials at 1228.

[180] R. H. Helmholz, *Civil Trials and the Limits of Responsible Speech*, in R. H. Helmholz & Thomas A. Green, Juries, Libel and Justice 1, 22 (Clark Memorial Library, Los Angeles 1984).

[181] Baker-Introduction 506–07; *e.g.*, *Prynn*, 3 State Trials at 561.

[182] Prynn's Case, (1690) 5 Mod. 459, 463–64, 87 Eng. Rep. 764, 766; Holt K.B. 362, 90 Eng. Rep. 1100 (K.B.); 2 Mansfield Manuscripts 775. Modern's report is more detailed and accurate than Holt's.

[183] 6 OHLE 351, 197; Baker-Introduction 119.

[184] *E.g.*, *Barnardiston*, 9 State Trials at 1333; *Baxter*, 11 State Trials at 497; *Seven Bishops*, 12 State Trials at 430.

[185] Baker-Introduction 507; *e.g.*, *Harris*, 7 State Trials at 925; *Barnardiston*, 9 State Trials at 1333; *Tutchin*, Holt K.B. at 56, 90 Eng. Rep. at 929; Holt K.B. at 424, 90 Eng. Rep. at 1133; *Francklin*, 17 State Trials at 625.

[186] Baker-Introduction 507; 2 Mansfield Manuscripts 775.

[187] *Barnardiston*, 9 State Trials at 1355; *accord* 9 *id.* at 1352; *Dover*, 6 State Trials at 563; *Seven Bishops*, 12 State Trials at 425; *see* 2 Hudson 103. Where reference was indirect, another issue was whether words referred to particular officials. *Baxter*, 11 State Trials at 501.

[188] *Barnardiston*, 9 State Trials at 1352; *accord* 9 *id.* at 1355; *Seven Bishops*, 12 State Trials at 425.

[189] *Seven Bishops*, 12 State Trials at 430–31.

[190] *Paine*, 5 Mod. at 165, 87 Eng. Rep. at 585 (verdict of physical writing but not "composing and making the libel").

[191] R v. Bear, (1699) 2 Salkeld 417, 417, 419, 91 Eng. Rep. 363, 363, 365 (K.B.) (verdict of physical writing but not composing); Hamburger 729 (other case).

jury whether the publication was a seditious libel, as *Seven Bishops* effectively did because of the even division of the bench,[192] had been lethal to prosecution.

Holt and his colleagues reaffirmed the Star Chamber and subsequent King's Bench rule that the determination whether content was libelous should be by judge rather than jury,[193] and took a further step to keep it that way, in *R v. Bear* in 1699.[194] Bear was found guilty of copying "false and scandalous libels" about "the King and Government," though not of writing or publishing them.[195] Holt ruled that "the Court must be judge of the words themselves," and he required the indictment or information to give "a transcript" of the accused's words,[196] obviously to make that possible without jury fact-finding. That new requirement again broke with precedent[197]; while the practice of seventeenth-century informations generally was to recite the libelous words,[198] prior decisions held that only the substance of the libelous words need be pleaded.[199]

Holt and the other judges likewise reaffirmed the rule (discussed above) that malice or criminal intent need not be affirmatively proved, but instead was inferred by the judges from writings. In *Bear*, he held that the person "putting the infamous matter into writing" is "highly criminal" and "cannot be construed to be innocent" of the crime, and the same was true of each person who rewrote or printed it.[200] This, too, broke with precedent[201] that it was necessary for the accused to have known of publication or to have intended to publish.[202]

[192] *Seven Bishops*, 12 State Trials at 425–29; *accord* Green 41–42.

[193] 2 Mansfield Manuscripts 781.

[194] R v. Bear, (1699) (spelled as *Beare*) 1 Ld. Raym. 414, 91 Eng. Rep. 1175; 1 Salkeld 324, 91 Eng. Rep. 287; 2 Salkeld 417, 646, 91 Eng. Rep. 363, 547; 3 Salkeld 226, 91 Eng. Rep. 791; Carthew 407, 90 Eng. Rep. 836; Holt K.B. 422, 90 Eng. Rep. 1132; (under spelling *Beere*) 12 Mod. 218, 88 Eng. Rep. 1274 (K.B.); *accord* Hamburger 728–34. The report by Lord Raymond gives by far the most detail; Holt appears to abridge Carthew and is limited; Salkeld is still more abbreviated.

[195] 1 Ld. Raym. at 414–15, 91 Eng. Rep. at 1175; Holt K.B. at 422, 90 Eng. Rep. at 1132. Bear's first of eight ballads about King William was unflatteringly entitled the "Belgick Boar."

[196] 2 Salkeld at 417, 91 Eng. Rep. at 364. The indictment must state "the specific words mentioned in the libel"; giving the libelous words "in effect" would be insufficient, 1 Ld. Raym. at 415, 91 Eng. Rep. at 1175, 1176; *accord* Holt K.B. at 423, 90 Eng. Rep. at 1133; 3 Salkeld at 226, 91 Eng. Rep. at 791–92; *accord* Hamburger 729.

[197] Hamburger 731.

[198] 2 Baker 238, 243 (*but see* 2 *id.* at 238); 6 OHLE 784–85.

[199] Sheppard 19, 114.

[200] 2 Salkeld 417–18, 91 Eng. Rep. at 364; *accord* Holt K.B. at 423, 90 Eng. Rep. at 1133 ("highly criminal, without publishing it"); *accord* Hamburger 732, 733. The mere putting a libel into writing, without composing it, makes one "a libeller" and "is criminal." 1 Ld. Raym. at 416, 91 Eng. Rep. at 1176. Holt's list of elements of the crime did not include either publication or intent. 1 Ld. Raym. at 417, 91 Eng. Rep. at 1177; 2 Salkeld at 419, 91 Eng. Rep. at 365; *Tutchin*, Holt K.B. at 424, 90 Eng. Rep. at 1133.

[201] Hamburger 730.

[202] *See In re* Anon., (1562) B&M 707 (K.B.) (not defamation if written statement "neither published nor made known to others"); Edwardes v. Woo[l]ton, (1607) 12 Co. Rep. 35, B&M 708 (Star Chamber); *Dover*, 6 State Trials at 563; *accord* 6 OHLE 798; Ibbetson 116–17.

Anticipating those criticisms, Holt ended by brandishing the claim that "this notion of libelling is as old as the law," and again filled in what relevant precedent did not provide with necessity of state:

> And if the law were otherwise it might be very dangerous, for then men might take copies of [libels] with impunity; and for the same reason the printing of them would be no offence; and then farewel[l] to all government.... Libelling against a private man is a moral offence; but when it is against a government, it tends to the destruction of it.[203]

Both rulings greatly assisted prosecution of dissent, not only by adopting Star Chamber rules but by adding further jury impediments. Juries could not properly acquit dissidents by finding their writings nonlibelous, by finding that the accused lacked criminal intent, or by finding publication unintentional or unknown to the accused. Courts in seditious libel cases bypassed any jury determination of a criminal writing or criminal intent.

The ruling that the indictment or information must give a transcript of the libelous words was followed in *R v. Drake*[204] in 1706. There, Holt stated that, unlike an information saying the defendant wrote words "to the effect following," which would "leave the construction of it to the jurors," specifying the words leaves interpretation "to conclude the court."[205] If Modern's report is accurate,[206] Holt encouraged prosecutors to quote libels in Latin (which was more readily understood by judges than jurors), rather than in English,[207] by creating the different standards that any variance (even one letter) "in these English words . . . spoils the whole information" and requires judgment for the accused, while "[i]f it had been in Latin it had been good."[208]

Mansfield later interpreted *Bear* in the same way: the reason for requiring "that the writing complained of must be set out" is that "the court may judge of the very words themselves; whereas, if it was to be *according to the effect*, that judgment

[203] 1 Ld. Raym. at 417–18, 91 Eng. Rep. at 1177; *accord* Holt K.B. at 424, 90 Eng. Rep. at 1133.

[204] R v. Drake, (1706) 3 Salkeld 224, 91 Eng. Rep. 790; 2 Salkeld 660, 91 Eng. Rep. 563; 11 Mod. 95, 88 Eng. Rep. 919; Holt K.B. 347, 349, 350, 425, 90 Eng. Rep. 1092, 1093, 1093, 1134 (Q.B.); *accord* HAMBURGER 736–37.

[205] HAMBURGER 736–37, quoting R v. Drake, Hardwicke Papers at 13–14 (British Library Add. M.S. 35980), though the point is not mentioned in other reports. Holt upheld judgment for the defendant because the information misquoted the libel, though by only one letter. 3 Salkeld at 225, 91 Eng. Rep. at 791.

[206] Holt's and Salkeld's reports do not contain the statement that the quotation in Latin would have been good. Salkeld's report is more precise than Holt's, which appears to copy him.

[207] As they commonly were recited, 6 OHLE 784–85, 786; *e.g.*, R v. Harrison, (1677–78) 3 Keble 841, 84 Eng. Rep. 1044 (K.B.).

[208] 11 Mod. at 96–97, 88 Eng. Rep. at 920. Latin indictments ended in 1731. 4 Geo 2 c26.

must be left to the jury."[209] Thus, "the question remains entirely for the Court" whether the writing was criminal, and the issue for the jury is limited to "the fact of publication" and whether any innuendos meant the person defamed.[210] Mansfield bootstrapped that requirement for setting out the libelous words to create a mandate that the judge rather than the jury must determine whether a publication is libelous: "It is almost peculiar to the form of the prosecution for a libel, that the question of law remains entirely for the Court *upon record*," and that availability of the publication "open upon the record" creates a "duty of the judge to advise the jury to separate . . . the question of law."[211] He thereby acknowledged the "peculiar" deviation from what a jury determined in other areas of criminal law.

The effect of Holt's rulings was to narrow to triviality what the jury was to determine. Holt began to state that the issue to be determined by the jury was whether the accused "is guilty of writing, composing, or publishing these libels."[212] Lord Chief Justice Raymond stated the jury issues similarly in *R v. Francklin*, as simply whether the accused published the item and whether its expressions refer to the libeled persons, leaving to the judge "[w]hether these defamatory expressions amount to a libel."[213] Lord Chief Justice Lee did the same in *R v. Owen*, adding that "the fact of publication was fully proved" so "the jury ought to find the defendant guilty,"[214] at the urging of then-Solicitor General Murray over the opposition of then-defense counsel Pratt.[215]

The battle was joined in the cases of John Wilkes and "Junius," both well publicized and closely watched in America,[216] as Murray became Lord Chief Justice

[209] *St. Asaph*, 21 State Trials at 1036; *accord Woodfall*, 5 Burr. at 2666, 98 Eng. Rep. at 400; Hamburger 737 n.232.

[210] *St. Asaph*, 3 T.R. at 428, 100 Eng. Rep. at 658–59, 660; *accord Woodfall*, 20 State Trials at 902.

[211] *St. Asaph*, 21 State Trials at 1035; *accord Woodfall*, 5 Burr. at 2666, 98 Eng. Rep. at 400 ("upon the face of the record").

[212] *Tutchin*, Holt K.B. at 424, 90 Eng. Rep. at 1133; *accord* The Tryal of William Fuller 13 (Isaac Cleave, London 1702). And if relevant, whether words were irony. R v. Dr. Browne, (1706) Holt K.B. 425, 90 Eng. Rep. 1134 (Q.B.).

[213] *Francklin*, 17 State Trials at 671–72.Not surprisingly he was found guilty, *id.* 676, and the verdict was upheld over posttrial motions. R v. Franklin, (1731) W. Kel. 76, 25 Eng. Rep. 499; Sess. Cas. 220, 93 Eng. Rep. 222; 2 Barn. K.B. 117, 94 Eng. Rep. 393; Fitz-G. 5, 94 Eng. Rep. 628 (K.B.); W. Kel. 86, 25 Eng. Rep. 504 (1732). *Accord* R v. Clerk, (1728) 1 Barn. K.B. 304, 94 Eng. Rep. 207 (K.B.). For background, *see* Harris-Newspapers 146–53.

[214] Trial of William Owen, (1752) 18 State Trials 1203, 1228 (K.B.).

[215] 18 *id.* at 1222–23, 1228, 1226; 29 Parliamentary History 1408 (31 May 1792); *see* C.H.S. Fifoot, Lord Mansfield 44–45 (OUP, Oxford 1936). The jury acquitted Owen of seditious libel for selling a publication that reflected negatively on the Commons. *Id.* 1228–29.

[216] Pauline Maier, *John Wilkes and American Disillusionment with Britain*, 20 William & Mary Q. 373, 374 (1963); *e.g.*, An Authentick Account of the Proceedings against John Wilkes (n.p., [Boston] 1763); An Interesting Appendix to Sir William Blackstone's Commentaries . . . The Case of the Late Election of the County of Middlesex 59, 61–63, 103–04 (Robert Bell, Philadelphia 1772); The Palladium of Conscience . . . Containing, . . . Blackstone's Case of the Middlesex Election (Robert Bell, Philadelphia 1774).

Mansfield and Pratt became Lord Chief Justice Pratt and, in 1766, Lord Chancellor Camden.[217] As Wilkes was prosecuted for seditious libel for criticizing the King's speech in his newspaper *North Briton No. 45* in 1763, Pratt released him based on Wilkes's parliamentary privilege.[218] Pratt later ruled that the general warrant by which Wilkes and his papers were seized was illegal, after which the jury awarded Wilkes damages.[219] Though the House of Commons disagreed that seditious libel was protected by parliamentary privilege, concern about the doctrine was sufficiently stirring that seventeen of the House of Lords dissented and challenged "the severity of the law touching libels" and its propensity "to be abused by outrageous and vindictive prosecutions."[220] A year after Camden's decisions, Mansfield presided over Wilkes's trial and conviction for seditious libel, which was upheld.[221]

Mansfield limited the jury issues in the *Wilkes* trial, and in other seditious libel actions, in the same way as Holt, Raymond, and Lee.[222] By the end of his career he said he had "uniformly" in seditious libel cases limited juries to determining whether the accused published the libel and whether "the meanings of the innuendos were as stated," and had instructed juries that if they found those points proved, "they ought to find the defendant guilty."[223] (Mansfield also said juries routinely followed his directions "except in political causes."[224]) Camden, by contrast, believed juries should render general verdicts on all issues, as he had instructed his *Wilkes* jury to do,[225] including determining whether writings were libelous and whether statements were with criminal intent.[226]

[217] Charles Pratt, first Baron Camden 1765, first Earl of Camden 1786. 45 ODNB 211.

[218] R v. Wilkes, (1763) 2 Wils. K.B. 151, 159–60, 95 Eng. Rep. 737, 742 (C.P.); 19 State Trials 982, 990–93; *accord* RUDÉ 26–27; THOMAS 30–31.

[219] Wilkes v. Wood, (1763) Lofft 1, 19, 98 Eng. Rep. 489, 499 (C.P.); 19 State Trials 1153, 1166–67; *accord* RUDÉ 28–30; THOMAS 32–35, 46.

[220] 19 State Trials 994–99; 30 JHL 426 (29 Nov.1763), reprinted in SELECT STATUTES-CASES 302, 305, 308; *accord* THOMAS 45.

[221] The seditious libel prosecutions in 1764, along with subsequent proceedings, are described in Wilkes v. R, (1769) Wilm. 322, 323, 339–40, 97 Eng. Rep. 123, 124, 130; 4 Brown P.C. 360, 2 Eng. Rep. 244 (H.L.). Mansfield reversed Wilkes's outlawry, and the judges sentenced Wilkes to fines totaling £1000 and imprisonment of twenty-two months. R v. Wilkes, (1768–70) 4 Burr. 2527, 2565–66, 2574, 98 Eng. Rep. 327, 349, 353–54 (K.B.).

[222] *Woodfall*, 5 Burr. at 2666, 98 Eng. Rep. at 400; R v. Horne, (1777) 2 Cowp. 672, 679, 98 Eng. Rep. 1300, 1304 (K.B.); *accord* 2 MANSFIELD MANUSCRIPTS 777; R v. Nutt, (1755) 2 *id.* 784 (K.B.) (as prosecutor).

[223] *St. Asaph*, 21 State Trials at 1038, though Mansfield arrested judgment for deficiency in indictment, 21 *id.* at 1044. The trial judge, Buller, similarly limited the jury issues. 21 *id.* at 946.

[224] 7 PRIVATE PAPERS OF JAMES BOSWELL 177 (Frederick A. Pottle & Marion S. Pottle eds., YUP, New Haven 1950); *accord* 2 MANSFIELD MANUSCRIPTS 835 n.1.

[225] Wilkes v. Wood, (1763) Lofft 1, 17, 98 Eng. Rep. 489, 498 (C.P.).

[226] *Owen*, 18 State Trials at 1227 (Pratt's argument); *see* R v. Shipley, (1784) 4 Dougl. 73, 171, 175, 99 Eng. Rep. 774, 826 (K.B.) (Willes, J., dissenting).

Mansfield and Camden disagreed over broader issues of constitutionalism as well. Mansfield claimed and practiced judicial power to imply "exceptions" that soon "form a system of law,"[227] to the point of using prior common law rules to avoid specific limitations of statutes, which Camden led in reversing.[228] Camden stressed a duty of judges to apply the law as they found it and to leave lawmaking to the legislature.[229] Their divergences spilled over to such other issues as the American war, with Mansfield supporting prosecution[230] and Camden advocating conciliation as hostilities spread (citing Locke on resistance to absolutism).[231]

The trials of the printers and sellers of the "Junius" essays in 1770,[232] which had censured corruption in Britain's administration[233] and Mansfield's decisions,[234] repeated the controversy. Counsel for the defense echoed Pratt's arguments in *Owen*, and Mansfield again limited the jury to determining "whether he did publish" the pamphlet and "whether the construction . . . where there are dashes . . . is to be made to the king, to the administration of his government, to his ministers."[235] Mansfield said the jury "were not to concern themselves" with malice or seditiousness; "the Court would consider of that" and "were the only proper judges of that" as "inferences of law" from the fact of publication.[236] Juries convicted one newspaper printer, Almon,[237] but ignored Mansfield's instructions and

[227] 1 Mansfield Manuscripts 199; *accord* 1 *id.* at 197.

[228] Millar v. Taylor, (1769) 4 Burr. 2303, 98 Eng. Rep. 201 (K.B.), *rev'd*, 4 Burr. 2416–17, 98 Eng. Rep. 262 (1769); Donaldson v. Beckett, (1774) 2 Brown P.C. 129, 1 Eng. Rep. 837 (H.L.) (Copyright Act); *accord* 1 Mansfield Manuscripts 199–200; *cf.* Perrin v. Blake, (1770) 1 Black. W. 672, 96 Eng. Rep. 392; 4 Burr. 2579, 98 Eng. Rep. 355 (K.B.) (modifying rule in *Shelley's Case*), *rev'd* (1772) 1 Black. W. 67, 96 Eng. Rep. 393 (Exch.); William R. Leslie, *Similarities in Lord Mansfield's and Joseph Story's View of Fundamental Law*, 1 Am. J. Legal History 278, 279–84 (1957).

[229] Entick v. Carrington, (1765) 2 Wils. K.B. 275, 291, 292, 95 Eng. Rep. 807, 817, 818 (C.P.).

[230] 1 Mansfield Manuscripts 30; 39 ODNB 997.

[231] 6 Proceedings and Debates of the British Parliaments Respecting North America, 1754–83, at 53–54, 252–53 (R.C. Simmons & P.D.G. Thomas eds., Kraus, Millwood 1982–87); 45 ODNB 213–14.

[232] Trial of John Almon, (1770) 20 State Trials 803; 5 Burr. 2686, 98 Eng. Rep. 411 (K.B.); Case of Henry Sampson Woodfall, (1770) 20 State Trials 895; Lofft 776, 98 Eng. Rep. 914; 5 Burr. 2661, 98 Eng. Rep. 398; 2 Strange 1131, 93 Eng. Rep. 1082 (K.B.); Trial of John Miller, (1770) 20 State Trials 869 (K.B.); R v. Baldwin, (1770) 2 Mansfield Manuscripts 842 (K.B.).

[233] Junius 25, 320; *see* Brewer-Party 154–55; Thomas 126. The identity of Junius is summarized in T.H. Bowyer, *Junius, Philip Francis and Parliamentary Reform*, 27 Albion 397, 397 n.1 (1995).

[234] Junius 15–18, 302 (no.61) (17 Oct.1771), 320 (no.68) (21 Jan.1772).

[235] 20 State Trials at 836; *accord Woodfall*, 20 *id.* at 902; *Miller*, 20 *id.* at 893.

[236] *Woodfall*, 20 State Trials at 901–02, 918; *accord Miller*, 20 State Trials at 893–94.

[237] *Almon*, 20 State Trials at 839; *see* 2 Mansfield Manuscripts 833. Almon is chronicled, poorly, in Deborah D. Rogers, Bookseller as Rogue: John Almon 19–42, 43–56 (Peter Lang, New York 1986).

found another printer, Woodfall, "guilty of printing and publishing only,"[238] and acquitted two other newspaper printers, Miller[239] and Baldwin.[240]

The Junius trials ignited debates in the House of Lords over seditious libel in 1770–71, which again pitted Mansfield and allies against Camden and supporters,[241] following debates in the Commons.[242]

Camden had the better of the argument on the issues for the jury in a libel case. Mansfield's severe limitation of the jury's issue for decision left almost nothing for the jury to decide except the "virtually undeniable" fact of whether the accused wrote or published[243] what already had been determined to be a seditious libel with what already had been implied as criminal intent, thereby causing "the jury's role in seditious libel cases . . . to be uniquely and awkwardly restricted" in comparison to other criminal cases, as he conceded.[244] Mansfield nominally said that the legal inference of criminal intent was rebuttable: "the proof of justification, or excuse, lies on the defendant"[245]; but he prohibited the logical justifications or excuses that the publication was true and was without criminal intent.[246] In doing that, Mansfield effectively tricked the jury into giving a special verdict on two minor issues that was then treated as a general verdict on all issues.[247] When Mansfield instructed the jury, if it found publication was by the accused and innuendos referred to the government or ministers, "to find the defendant *guilty*," he did not tell them the court had already made a determination of law that the jury was effectively incorporating and applying ("in that shape they take the opinion of the Court upon the law" since "the judge is not called upon necessarily to tell them his own opinion"[248]), or what his determination of law was in terms of the accused's publication being a criminal libel with criminal intent. Camden, claiming that violated the fundamental right to jury trial, said "the Court ought not . . . to take away of the office of a jury," but ought to leave the jury's role the same as in other criminal cases, applying the law given in the judge's instructions to the facts

[238] *Woodfall*, 5 Burr. at 2667, 98 Eng. Rep. at 401; *see* 2 MANSFIELD MANUSCRIPTS 837. This led to his being granted a new trial, 20 State Trials at 921, which was never held, ostensibly because the evidentiary copy of his newspaper was misplaced, and really because the Miller-Baldwin acquittals made a guilty verdict unlikely.

[239] *Miller*, 20 State Trials at 896; *see* 2 MANSFIELD MANUSCRIPTS 841.

[240] R v. Baldwin, (1770) 2 MANSFIELD MANUSCRIPTS 842 (K.B.).

[241] 16 PARLIAMENTARY HISTORY 1312 (10 Dec.1770), where Camden directed written questions to Mansfield addressing all these issues, 16 *id.* at 1321 (11 Dec.1770); *Woodfall*, 20 State Trials at 921–22.

[242] 16 PARLIAMENTARY HISTORY 1175, 1211 (27 Nov.1770).

[243] GREEN 65.

[244] 1 MANSFIELD MANUSCRIPTS 201; *St. Asaph*, 21 State Trials at 1035.

[245] *Woodfall*, 20 State Trials at 919.

[246] 20 *id.* at 902, 913, 918, 919.

[247] As Erskine argued about Buller's instructions, which Mansfield upheld. *Shipley*, 4 Dougl. at 134, 99 Eng. Rep. at 805 (1784); *St. Asaph*, 21 State Trials at 984–88; *accord* PHILELEUTHERUS ANGLICANUS [HENRY S. WOODFALL], A SUMMARY OF THE LAW OF LIBEL 13 (S. Bladon, London 1771).

[248] *St. Asaph*, 21 State Trials at 1035.

of the case,[249] including on issues of libelous content and criminal intent.[250] Despite swirling controversy, judges generally followed Mansfield's limitation of juries to the issues of publication and innuendo,[251] until 1792.

The central pillar in Camden's argument was adopted, and in Mansfield's and the other royal judges' was rejected,[252] by Parliament in Fox's Libel Act of 1792. The Act provided that juries in criminal libel actions may give general verdicts and may not be required "to find the defendant or defendants guilty, merely on the proof of the publication by such defendant . . . and of the sense ascribed to the same in such indictment or information."[253] The reform attempted to reset the balance between judge and jury in seditious libel cases, and to restore the jury's roles as a "safeguard against tyranny" and a potential force of mitigation.[254] However, the Libel Act did not decriminalize seditious libel, and did not succeed in protecting freedom of press. Instead, prosecutions escalated with the French Revolution and the wars it detonated in the 1790s[255] to nearly two hundred cases,[256] and conviction rates increased as well because juries often functioned as rubber stamps.

Use of General Warrants

Each Star Chamber licensing ordinance and decree expressly authorized general searches of any premises where unlicensed or seditious publications were suspected to be, and general arrests of any persons in possession.[257] Prosecutors certainly preferred fishing expeditions to limited searches of named places and persons.

[249] *Wilkes*, 19 State Trials at 992; GREEN 64–65.

[250] 29 PARLIAMENTARY HISTORY 1405–06 (31 May 1792).

[251] R v. Shipley, (1784) 4 Dougl. 73, 82, 99 Eng. Rep. 774, 779 (K.B.) (Buller, J.); R v. Gordon, (1787) 22 State Trials 175, 207 (K.B.); R v. Watson, (1788) 2 T.R. 199, 206, 100 Eng. Rep. 108, 113 (K.B.); R v. Stockdale, (1789) 22 State Trials 237, 292 (K.B.); R v. Withers, (1789) 3 T.R. 428, 429–30, 100 Eng. Rep. 657, 657–58 (K.B.); R v. Topham, (1791) 4 T.R. 126, 127, 100 Eng. Rep. 931, 931 (K.B.); Opinion of the Judges, (1792) 22 State Trials 297, 303–04 (H.L.); *contra St. Asaph*, 21 State Trials at 1040–41; 4 Dougl. 171, 99 Eng. Rep. 824 (1784) (Willes, J., dissenting).

[252] 8 OXFORD HISTORY 302; Opinion of the Judges, (1792) 22 State Trials 297 (H.L.).

[253] 32 Geo 3 c60; 11 EHD 363; 37 STATUTES 627; *accord* GREEN 67–72.

[254] GREEN 69–71.

[255] *E.g.*, 22 State Trials at 317, 753, 785, 953, 1033, 1189, 1237; and seditious words, 22 *id.* at 471, 823, 875, 909, 1019; *accord* JOHN BARRELL, IMAGINING THE KING'S DEATH: FIGURATIVE TREASON, FANTASIES OF REGICIDE 1793–1796, at 108–12, 630–31, 633–37 (OUP, Oxford 2000).

[256] BOYD HILTON, A MAD, BAD, AND DANGEROUS PEOPLE? ENGLAND 1783–1846, at 72–73 (CP, Oxford 2006); HARLING 108–09; *see* Clive Emsley, *An Aspect of Pitt's "Terror": Prosecutions for Sedition during the 1790s*, 6 SOCIAL HISTORY 155 (1981).

[257] Star-Chamber Ordinance (23 June 1586), SELECT STATUTES 169, 169; A Decree of Starre-Chamber, Concerning Printing (11 July 1637), 4 ARBER 528. *See generally* WILLIAM J. CUDDIHY, THE FOURTH AMENDMENT: ORIGINS AND ORIGINAL MEANING, 1602–1791, at 446–58 (OUP, Oxford 2009).

Subsequent courts chose to continue use of general warrants in seditious libel cases, relying primarily on the Licensing Act of 1662, which was modeled on the Star Chamber Decree of 1637. For a brief time after the statutory authorization lapsed in 1695, the King's attorney concluded that "a general warrant could not now be granted to search houses for printing presses, but it must be done upon particular informations upon oath."[258] However, after repeated failures to reenact a licensing law, the government reversed itself and reverted to the practice of general warrants without a supporting statute, and the courts upheld that.[259]

The most relentless objection to general warrants was made by Wilkes, after suffering search and arrest under such a warrant. Steering the case to Pratt, he was not disappointed with the decision that general warrants were "illegal, and contrary to the fundamental principles of the constitution," as well as "totally subversive of the liberty of the subject."[260] Pratt reaffirmed this in another libel case, *Entick v. Carrington*, stating that no law authorized general warrants and that judicial practice "cannot make law" or provide authority.[261] The popular cat being already out of the bag, Mansfield also rejected such warrants, on the basis of insufficiently long practice rather than insufficient statutory authorization.[262]

Other invasions of rights were debated besides general warrants, such as the use of informations in lieu of grand jury indictments to prosecute seditious libels and other crimes,[263] and the practice of prosecution followed by a *nolle prosequi* to intimidate authors and printers.[264] All figured in criticisms of seditious libel.

However pathbreaking Holt's other contributions and Mansfield's commercial law decisions, their various decisions about seditious libel and other criminal libel were unified only by promoting successful prosecution of dissent, as they ruled that the truth of speech or writing was irrelevant and even exacerbated a seditious libel, and that criminal intent was inferred from the mere fact of publishing or copying a libel; that it was criminal speech to criticize individual officials, or even to criticize the government as a whole; that Crown-appointed judges determined libelousness

258 5 CALENDAR-WILLIAM 483 (30 May 1695).

259 R v. Derby, (1711) Fortescue 140, 144, 92 Eng. Rep. 794, 796 (Q.B.); 4 BLACKSTONE'S COMMENTARIES 288 n.

260 Wilkes v. Wood, (1763) Lofft 1, 19, 18, 98 Eng. Rep. 489, 499, 498 (C.P.).

261 Entick v. Carrington, (1765) 2 Wils. K.B. 275, 292, 95 Eng. Rep. 807, 818; 22 State Trials 237 (C.P.).

262 Money v. Leach, (1765) 3 Burr. 1742, 1766–67, 97 Eng. Rep. 1075, 1088; 3 Burr. 1692, 97 Eng. Rep. 1050; 1 Black. W. 555, 96 Eng. Rep. 320 (K.B.).

263 2 MANSFIELD MANUSCRIPTS 775; Case of Mr. Earbery, (1737) 19 State Trials 1016 (K.B.).

264 James Oldham, *The Work of Ryder and Murray as Law Officers of the Crown*, in LEGAL RECORD AND HISTORICAL REALITY 157, 173 (Thomas G. Watkin ed., HP, London 1989); HARLING 110–11, 112–20, though prosecutors encountered obstacles, *id.* 120–33; *e.g.*, R v. Almon, (1765) Wilm. 243, 243 n.(a), 97 Eng. Rep. 94 (K.B.). Or the exclusion of testimony by parties. James Oldham, *Truth-Telling in the Eighteenth-Century English Courtrooma*, 12 LAW & HISTORY REV. 95, 107–12 (1994).

and criminal intent while the jury only determined the generally undisputed detail of publication; and that authors, printers, and booksellers could be searched, arrested, imprisoned, and brought to trial under general warrants merely identifying a publication as a seditious libel. One more step remained that Mansfield would take, as relentless claims were made that this framework of six unique rules violated freedoms of press and speech, and it was a step that dwarfed the prior ones.

Figure 2.3 Sir William Blackstone (1723–1780). Portrait by unknown artist c.1755. (Courtesy of, and copyright, National Portrait Gallery, London.)

Figure 2.4 Lord Chief Justice Mansfield (1705–1793). Portrait by John Singleton Copley c.1783. (Courtesy of, and copyright, National Portrait Gallery, London.)

Narrow Definition of Freedoms of Press and Speech and the Claim that it was Part of the English Common Law

Defense counsel in the seditious libel cases began to mention, and then to argue, that prosecution for seditious libel violated freedom of the press. In *Francklin* in 1731, counsel cautioned that prohibiting true as well as false news of public affairs as seditious libel, on the ground it reflected negatively on the King or his ministers, threatened "suppression of the liberty of the press" and would bring "dangerous and fatal consequence" and would result in life "in darkness and ignorance."[265] Lord Chief Justice Raymond responded by ending his jury charge with the admonition that a newspaper publisher is not "to take the liberty to print what he pleases; for the liberty of the press is only a legal liberty, such as the law allows; and not a licentious liberty."[266] Of course, "liberty . . . such as the law allows" was tautologous and manipulable. In *Owen* in 1752, Pratt's co-counsel warned the jury that if a court decision was "not to be called in question" and if a parliamentary vote could not be complained of as wrong, then the legal right to "complain or petition for redress" would be meaningless.[267] However, in none of the seditious libel cases, before Mansfield's opinions in the Junius cases, was there any judicial opinion that liberty of press or speech meant only freedom from prior restraint and not from seditious libel punishment, or anything remotely like Blackstone's claimed summary of the common law of those freedoms. There were cases prosecuting seditious libel and seditious words, and there were widespread affirmations of liberty of press and liberty of speech, but there were no cases—there was no English common law—that established how these concepts interacted or that said that seditious libel or seditious words were unprotected by liberty of press or liberty of speech. The English common law only addressed that subject the year after Blackstone's fourth volume summarized nonexistent English common law, when Mansfield addressed the subject in 1770.

In the Junius trials that year, Almon's counsel argued "that the freedom of political discussion is of the utmost consequence to all our liberties," and included "censur[ing] the acts of government," though he timidly conceded that "liberty of the press," though "the most sacred of all" other liberties, if abused was criminal.[268] Representing Woodfall, the same defense counsel cautioned that "the liberty of the press" was "in some degree of danger"[269] because "the people needed that kind of information," and the printer's intent was the "laudable motive

[265] *Francklin,* 17 State Trials at 655, 660; *accord* 17 *id.* at 659.

[266] 17 *id.* at 675.

[267] *Owen,* 18 *id.* at 1223–24.

[268] *Almon,* 20 *id.* at 832, 834.

[269] *Woodfall,* Lofft at 778, 98 Eng. Rep. at 914.

of informing his fellow-subjects." Further, "the public acts of government often demanded public scrutiny," all of which would be thwarted if "ministerial scribblers" could with impunity abuse those not in office, while for the opposition it was "dangerous to answer them" so that "the hands of every publisher would be tied."[270] These arguments did not ask the jury to acquit on grounds that seditious libel prosecution conflicted with that liberty of the press, but did ask the jury to acquit, within the existing legal framework, because the publication was not a seditious libel and the printer's intent was nonmalicious.[271]

Mansfield responded to these arguments by adopting Blackstone's restrictive description of liberty of press. In the *Woodfall* case, he ruled that "the liberty of the press is, that a man may print what he pleases without a licenser: as long as it remains so, the liberty of the press is not restrained"[272]; and so he allowed criminal prosecution for seditious libel of a publisher of Junius's letters. In the *Almon* case, he ruled that "[i]f an author is at liberty to write, he writes at his peril, if he writes or publishes that which is contrary to law"[273]; and so he allowed a similar prosecution of a seller of the same letters. Prosecutors and other judges joined Mansfield in fighting back, such as the government claim in the *Williams* case in 1774 that "liberty of the press" must be restrained from such "excess" as seditious libel, and Justice Aston's agreement that the liberty is "frequently abused" by such attacks (he was silent on whether liberty was abused by seditious libel prosecutions).[274] Over the next two decades most royal judges held the line[275]—for example, Justice Ashhurst, after referring to liberty of the press, said one function of the law is "to restrain them of that liberty which they so grossly abuse."[276]

Junius immediately disputed Mansfield's new doctrine of freedom of press. He boldly published a public letter to Mansfield soon after the 1770 trials of Almon,

270 *Woodfall*, 20 State Trials at 899.

271 *Id.; accord* R v. Woodfall, (1774) Lofft 776, 781, 98 Eng. Rep. 914, 914 (K.B.).

272 Case of Henry Sampson Woodfall, (1770) 20 State Trials 895, 903; 5 Burr. 2661, 98 Eng. Rep. 398; 2 Strange 1131, 93 Eng. Rep. 1082 (K.B.); *accord* Proceedings . . . against Rev. William Davies Shipley, Dean of St. Asaph, (1784) 21 State Trials 847, 1040; 3 T.R. 428, 100 Eng. Rep. 657; 4 Dougl. 73, 99 Eng. Rep. 774 (K.B.) (in first source, Mansfield ruled that "[t]he *liberty of the press* consists in printing without any previous license, subject to the consequences of law").

273 Trial of John Almon, (1770) 20 State Trials 803, 836; 5 Burr. 2686, 98 Eng. Rep. 411 (K.B.); *accord* Trial of John Miller, (1770) 20 State Trials 869, 894 (K.B.); R v. Woodfall, (1774) Lofft 776, 781, 98 Eng. Rep. 914, 916 (K.B.).

274 R v. Williams, (1774) Lofft 759, 763, 98 Eng. Rep. 905, 907 (K.B.) (Aston, J.); *accord* Proceedings . . . against John Stockdale, (1789) 22 State Trials 237, 291 (K.B.) (prosecution argument).

275 Charges to the Grand Jury 1689–1803, at 402, 452, 473–74, 492–93 (Georges Lamoine ed., RHS, London 1992).

276 Trials of George Gordon, (1787) 22 State Trials 176, 233–34 (K.B.); *accord* R v. Wilkins, (1787) 22 *id.* 209, 213 (K.B.) (Justice Buller rejected a freedom of press defense because "it goes to give a general licence to printers to print whatever they may think proper; which cannot be endured in this or in any other country.").

Woodfall, Miller, and Baldwin, which warmed up by reminding the public that the "language has no term of reproach . . . which has not already been happily applied to you," that Mansfield had been a Jacobite, and that his apparent plan was "to enlarge the power of the crown, at the expense of the liberty of the subject."[277] Junius then responded to the trials by stating that Mansfield's doctrine "in cases of libel" showed "a settled plan to contract the legal power of juries," which "in effect, attack[ed] the liberty of the press," particularly by limiting the jury issues, ignoring criminal intent that other crimes required, and disallowing a general verdict.[278] The unmistakable claim was that Mansfield's doctrine of seditious libel violated freedom of press, though Junius chose to argue on judge-made features different from other criminal law rather than on irreconcilability with liberty of press and speech. In Junius's estimation, England did not enjoy liberty of press; instead, there was "distress and danger with which the press is threatened" because of Mansfield and his doctrine.[279]

Mansfield, in his last seditious libel decision in *St. Asaph* in 1784, clearly saw the threat posed by advocates of freedom of press to his newly minted common law of liberties of press and speech and to the recently created common law of seditious libel. In that case, the most forceful attack by any defendant's counsel was directed at the incongruence of seditious libel with other criminal law, and among the many grounds argued was "the danger which has often attended the liberty of the press in former times, from the arbitrary proceedings of abject, unprincipled, and dependent judges," from licensors and the Star Chamber, and from government perception of "the seeds of its destruction in a free press."[280] Mansfield again followed Blackstone by proclaiming that "[t]he *liberty of the press* consists in printing without any previous license, subject to the consequences of law" (prosecutions), which were necessary "to protect individuals, or to guard the state."[281]

Mansfield did not stop with rewriting the English common law of liberties of press and speech, however; he also rewrote the history of seditious libel in *St. Asaph*, claiming that his rulings followed "the *uniform* judicial practice since the [1688] Revolution."[282] He took "up an eighteenth-century formulation of seditious libel and

[277] Junius 206, 207, 208 (Letter 46) (14 Nov. 1770).

[278] *Id.* 211, 211–12.

[279] *Id.* 207.

[280] *St. Asaph*, 21 State Trials at 900, 924, 1023. The jury found the Dean "guilty of publishing only," like *Woodfall*. 21 *id.* at 950. Erskine, defendant's counsel, was even more eloquent in Thomas Paine's case after the period relevant to the First Amendment. R v. Paine, (1792) 22 State Trials 357, 414–15 (K.B.).

[281] *St. Asaph*, 21 State Trials at 1040; 4 Dougl. 73, 170, 99 Eng. Rep. 774, 824 (emphasis in original).

[282] Proceedings . . . against Rev. William Davies Shipley, Dean of St. Asaph, (1784) 21 State Trials 847, 1035, 1040 (K.B.); *s.c.* 3 T.R. 428, 100 Eng. Rep. 657; 4 Dougl. 73, 99 Eng. Rep. 774, responding to defense argument to Justice Buller that doctrines of seditious libel were "new doctrines" not supported by "ancient precedents," 21 State Trials at 923; *accord* Hamburger 756.

treated it as age-old," as Oldham notes.[283] He misstated that "every lawyer for near 100 years, has so far acquiesced,"[284] and misstated that "[n]o counsel ever complained" of such narrow jury issues,[285] ignoring the defense protests in the *Francklin, Owen,* Junius, and other cases. Mansfield chose the starting point, for his history of seditious libel, to be the Holt decisions, entirely ignoring the contrary authority of *Seven Bishops* just eight years before *Paine,*[286] and claiming nothing was inconsistent in *Owen* three decades before he wrote.[287] He was correct only in identifying the "true creator" of the newly minted doctrine of seditious libel as "Chief Justice Holt at the turn of the eighteenth century."[288] The persistence of Mansfield's tale results not only from his towering stature but from his tale's acceptance by such English legal historians as Stephen and Holdsworth.[289]

The Blackstone-Mansfield definition and framework were not merely reactive at the end of Mansfield's career, but underlay all his seditious libel opinions. Early in his legal career in 1747, it was apparently Mansfield who wrote about liberty of the press that the patience of government was "provoked to *stretch power*" because "vermin" or "the sons of sedition *overstrain liberty*."[290] Shortly before taking the bench, he argued that in seditious libel cases, "uncommon pains [were] taken to misapply the principles of the liberty of the press," a liberty he defined meaninglessly (following *Francklin*) as "printing *everything that don't offend the laws*."[291] His conclusion in that case, as in every seditious libel case coming before him on the bench,[292] was that "[i]f defendant is concerned in the publication, none of this

[283] 2 Mansfield Manuscripts 775; *e.g., St. Asaph,* 21 State Trials at 1036; R v. Almon, (1770) 2 Mansfield Manuscripts 833, 836 (K.B.) ("an established rule from the beginning of time"). Mansfield also altered a ballad in *St. Asaph,* 21 State Trials at 1037–38; *see* Trial of Mr. Richard Francklin, (1731) 17 State Trials 625, 672 n. (K.B.).

[284] *Contra* the eloquent defense counsels' challenges in *Owen, Wilkes, Almon, Woodfall, Miller,* and especially *St. Asaph.*

[285] *Contra Owen,* 18 State Trials at 1225–27; R v. Cook, (1758) 2 Mansfield Manuscripts 810 (K.B.); *Woodfall,* 20 State Trials at 899, 904–05; R v. Wilkie, (1776) 2 State Trials 849 (K.B.); *St. Asaph,* 21 State Trials at 923, 1031, 1032, 1041.

[286] 2 Mansfield Manuscripts 807; *accord* 2 *id.* 777, 782, 836 n.1.

[287] Trial of William Owen, (1752) 18 State Trials 1203 (K.B.); *s.c.* Sayer 30, 96 Eng. Rep. 792. Mansfield claimed the report in *State Trials* was false, which its later editor disputed. *Id.* 1203 n.

[288] James Oldham, English Common Law in the Age of Mansfield 209 (UNCP, Chapel Hill 2004); *see St. Asaph,* 21 State Trials at 1036.

[289] 2 Sir James F. Stephen, A History of the Criminal Law of England 316, 343, 347, 350, 355, 358 (Macmillan, London 1883); 10 Sir William S. Holdsworth, A History of English Law 680 (Methuen, London repr. 1966) ("[t]he view of the law held by Lord Mansfield and the other judges was the historically correct view of the law"); *accord id.* 687–88, 692, 674, 677, 683, 684, 687.

[290] Aretine [William Murray], The Thistle . . . The Rose: Being a Detection of the Pernicious Tendency of Two Libels 31, 30 (3d ed. n.p., London 1747).

[291] R v. Nutt, (1755) 2 Mansfield Manuscripts 784 (K.B.) (quoting Ryder shorthand manuscript).

[292] *See* 2 Mansfield Manuscripts 808.

jury *can have a doubt* of his guilt."[293] Midway through his judicial years was when he adopted Blackstone's definition in the Junius cases. Mansfield, the trailblazer for modern commercial law, led the rear guard against liberalizing seditious libel.[294] He effectively argued that any published "reflection" on government was the crime of seditious libel. That left no protection for freedom of press and speech about things that mattered the most to many people, as was evident in his contentless definition of freedom of press as mere freedom from licensing. That was freedom from a historical phantom that had not existed for nearly a century.

What had existed was arrest and further prosecution for criticism of government or its officials. Seditious libel and seditious words figure in the following discussion for three reasons. First, the Blackstone definition that is said to be the revolutionists' and the framers' definition, that liberty of press "consists in laying no *previous* restraints upon publications, and not in freedom from censure for criminal matter when published," was stated negatively as not freedom for seditious libel (which is what "criminal matter when published" meant[295]). Second, the right to speak and write freely about government and its officials is one of the most important components of speech and press to many people historically as well as today, though that is not the only measure of the breadth or narrowness of views of freedoms of press or speech, as Rabban points out.[296] A definition of freedom of press or speech that allows criticism of government and its officials is far broader than a definition that treats such criticism as a crime. Finally, the threats and prosecutions confronted by the revolutionary generation were mostly about seditious libel or about Parliamentary authority. There was no freedom of press or speech to the extent nonviolent publications and speeches were criminalized as seditious libel and seditious words.

If an English common law of liberties of press and speech was indeed created by Blackstone in 1769 and first appeared in judicial opinions by Mansfield in 1770, it would be reasonable to expect that the Blackstone-Mansfield definition and framework were not universally accepted in England or America in the 1770s and 1780s, and that other views of liberties of press and speech would be discussed as well. In fact, none of the early Supreme Court justices embraced the Blackstone-Mansfield definition or framework before the Sedition Act crisis of 1798–1801, as Chapters 4–5 will discuss; and other views were widespread.[297]

293 2 *id.* at 785 (emphasis in original).

294 2 *id.* at 808.

295 A "definition of freedom of the press as a freedom from prior restraints, or, what amounts to the same thing, a freedom circumscribed by the penalties for criminal libel." LEVY 170.

296 David M. Rabban, *The Ahistorical Historian: Leonard Levy on Freedom of Expression in Early American History*, 37 STAN. L. REV. 795, 802–03 (1985).

297 Wendell Bird, *Liberties of Press and Speech: "Evidence Does Not Exist To Contradict the . . . Blackstonian Sense" in Late Eighteenth Century England?*, 36 OXFORD J. OF LEGAL STUDIES — (forthcoming 2016); Wendell Bird, Freedoms of Press and Speech in the First Decade of the U.S. Supreme Court 100–43 (2012) (unpublished D.Phil. thesis in legal history, University of Oxford).

3

The Collision of Seditious Libel and Freedoms of Press and Speech in America's Constitutional Period

> Were it not for such writings as have been called libels, there would have been no revolution either in England or America, nor the least vestige or jot of civil liberty remaining among us.
>
> —Philadelphia newspaper (a week after Madison introduced the Bill of Rights, 1789)[1]

What William Blackstone claimed was a summary of the English common law liberty of press and speech appeared in the fourth volume of his *Commentaries* in 1769. He said that "liberty of the press . . . consists in laying no *previous* restraints upon publications, and not in freedom from censure for criminal matter when published,"[2] so that if someone "publishes what is improper, mischievous, or illegal, he must take the consequence of his own temerity."[3] Thus, when "seditious, or scandalous libels are punished . . . the *liberty of the press*, properly understood, is

[1] *Philadelphia, June 15*, INDEPENDENT GAZETTEER (Philadelphia), 15 June 1789, at 2. A list of abbreviated titles is at the end of this book.

[2] "Criminal matter when published" referred primarily to seditious libel, which is at core the crime of criticism of government or its officers. Trial of John Tutchin, (1704) 14 State Trials 1095, 1128; Holt K.B. 56, 424, 90 Eng. Rep. 929, 1133; 6 Mod. 164, 268, 90 Eng. Rep. 922, 1014; 2 Ld. Raym. 1061, 92 Eng. Rep. 204; 1 Salkeld 51, 91 Eng. Rep. 50 (K.B.); 3 GENTLEMAN OF THE MIDDLE TEMPLE [MATTHEW BACON], A NEW ABRIDGMENT OF THE LAW 491 (E. & R. Nutt, London 1740); 1 WILLIAM HAWKINS, A TREATISE OF THE PLEAS OF THE CROWN 194 (3d ed. E. & R. Nutt, London 1739).

[3] 4 SIR WILLIAM BLACKSTONE, COMMENTARIES ON THE LAWS OF ENGLAND 151–52 (CP, Oxford 1765–69) (4 vols.) (emphasis in original).

by no means infringed or violated."[4] He then gave a similar summary of liberty of speech, because while "liberty of private sentiments is still left; the disseminating, or making public, of bad sentiments, destructive of the ends of society, is the crime which society corrects."[5] As we saw in the preceding chapter, Blackstone's summary of the English common law of liberties of press and speech did not actually describe any existing common law decisions in Britain, and was only inserted into the English common law the *next* year by Lord Mansfield, Chief Justice of King's Bench. While Mansfield presided over a prosecution for the crime of seditious libel for publishing Junius's criticism of the British government, he declared that "the liberty of the press is, that a man may print what he pleases without a licenser: as long as it remains so, the liberty of the press is not restrained."[6] Mansfield held to that formulation for the rest of his tenure, as well as to his framework of rules for prosecuting seditious libel,[7] and was followed by most Crown judges. That approach continues to be referred to here as the Blackstone-Mansfield definition and framework.

Blackstone was certainly influential in America,[8] as in Britain,[9] for the rest of the eighteenth century and into the next century. However, he was far from unquestioned, as his British critics were read in America,[10] and his American critics abounded including Thomas Jefferson and James Madison, and to some degree

[4] 4 *id.* 151 (emphasis in original).

[5] 4 *id.* 152.

[6] Case of Henry Sampson Woodfall, (1770) 20 State Trials 895, 903; Lofft 776, 98 Eng. Rep. 914; 5 Burr 2661, 98 Eng. Rep. 398; 2 Strange 1131, 93 Eng. Rep. 1082 (K.B.); *accord* Trial of John Almon, (1770) 20 State Trials 803, 836; 5 Burr. 2686, 98 Eng. Rep. 411 (K.B.); *Postscript*, London Evening Post, 12–14 June 1770, at 4; *For the Middlesex Journal*, Middlesex Journal or Chronicle of Liberty (London), 14–16 June 1770, at 1.

[7] Proceedings . . . against Rev. William Davies Shipley, Dean of St. Asaph, (1784) 21 State Trials 847, 1040; 3 T.R. 428, 100 Eng. Rep. 657; 4 Dougl. 73, 99 Eng. Rep. 774 (K.B.); *accord* Norman S. Poser, Lord Mansfield: Justice in the Age of Reason 244–59 (McGill, Montreal 2013).

[8] Dennis R. Nolan, *Sir William Blackstone and the New American Republic: A Study of Intellectual Impact*, 51 N.Y.U.L. Rev. 731 (1976); Ideological Origins 30–31; *see* Wilfrid Prest, Blackstone and His Commentaries (Hart Publishing, Oxford 2009).

[9] Tariq A. Baloch, *Law Booksellers and Printers as Agents of Unchange*, 66 Cambridge L.J. 389, 405 n.85, 404–08 (2007); S.F.C. Milsom, Studies in the History of the Common Law 198 (HP, London 1985).

[10] *E.g.*, An Interesting Appendix to Sir William Blackstone's Commentaries . . . Containing Priestley's Remarks . . . Furneaux's Letters 5, 51, 120 (Robert Bell, Philadelphia 1772); The Palladium of Conscience . . . Containing, Furneaux's Letters to Blackstone. Priestley's Remarks on Blackstone (Robert Bell, Philadelphia 1773); 3 Burgh 275, 285, 303; [Jeremy Bentham], A Fragment on Government; Being An Examination of . . . Sir William Blackstone's Commentaries iii *passim* (T. Payne, London 1776); An Interesting Address to the Independent Part of the People 16–17 *passim* (G. Kearsly, London 1777) (disputing Blackstone on informations).

John Adams.[11] They and other American revolutionists differed with Blackstone sharply on parts of English law based on monarchical and antirepublican premises.[12] Criminal law in Book IV of his *Commentaries*,[13] including the crime of seditious libel and countervailing liberty of press,[14] was one of the parts based on those rejected premises. American revolutionists could not fail to notice the Crown's use of the crimes of seditious libel and seditious speech to threaten opposition expression, and many criticized this. America's ubiquitous religious dissenters similarly rejected Blackstone's parallel definition of religious liberty as meaning mere toleration of qualifying sects,[15] and their disagreement was intensified by Blackstone's inept apologia that conceded that "*non-conformity* is still a crime" on the part of those dissenters not qualifying for toleration, and that "*reviling the ordinances of the [Anglican] church* is a crime" on the part of any dissenter.[16]

Opposing definitions of freedoms of press and speech were expressed by William Bollan, Junius, Junius Wilkes, Eleazer Oswald, and many others on both sides of the Atlantic, in the years before 1789, and I have discussed those elsewhere.[17]

[11] *E.g.*, Thomas Jefferson, Communication from House of Delegates to Senate Concerning Money Bills (9 Jan.1778), 2 JEFFERSON PAPERS 54, 57; 2 *id.* 43; Thomas Jefferson to John Tyler (17 June 1812), 5 JEFFERSON PAPERS-RETIREMENT 134, 136; [John Adams], *Novanglus No.X* (3 Apr.1775), in THE REVOLUTIONARY WRITINGS OF JOHN ADAMS 262, 267–68 (C. Bradley Thompson ed., LF, Indianapolis 2000).

[12] *E.g.*, Chisholm v. Georgia, 2 U.S. (2 Dall.) 419, 458, 460,462 (1793); 1 WILSON WORKS 4, 25, 190, 196, 443, 467–68, 471–74, 549; 2 *id.* 1049; WILSON'S CONSIDERATIONS 2–3, 27–28; DICKINSON'S ESSAY 38–39, 97 n.; *accord* Albert W. Alschuler, *Rediscovering Blackstone*, 145 U. PA. L. REV. 1, 9–16 (1996); PRINTERS 61–62; IDEOLOGICAL ORIGINS 171; CREATION 7, 375, 530, 599.

[13] *E.g.*, 4 BLACKSTONE'S COMMENTARIES 2, 74–75, 82, 94, 102, 119, 127. Many recognized, as Blackstone did not, the inconsistency of his parliamentary supremacy with other Whig principles, including the Revolution of 1688, the right of revolution, contractarian theory, and natural rights. Michael Lobban, *Blackstone and the Science of Law*, 30 HISTORICAL J. 311, 326–27, 328–29 (1987); H.T. Dickinson, *The Eighteenth-Century Debate on the Sovereignty of Parliament*, 26 TRANSACTIONS OF THE ROYAL HISTORICAL SOC. (5th ser) 189 (1976).

[14] 4 *id.* 150–51, 123. Thus, Chipman, showing queasiness about English criminal law, complained that Blackstone defended all English laws "not the least those, which are the most faulty." Nathaniel Chipman, *Sketches of the Principles of Government* (1793), in THE LEGAL MIND IN AMERICA 19, 29 (Perry Miller ed., CorUP, Ithaca 1969).

[15] 4 BLACKSTONE'S COMMENTARIES 53, 425.

[16] William Blackstone, *A Reply to Dr. Priestley's Remarks* (1769), in THE PALLADIUM OF CONSCIENCE 37, 40, 41 (Robert Bell, Philadelphia 1773); *accord* 4 BLACKSTONE'S COMMENTARIES 50–58.

[17] Wendell Bird, *Liberties of Press and Speech: "Evidence Does Not Exist To Contradict the . . . Blackstonian Sense" in Late Eighteenth Century England?*, 36 OXFORD J. OF LEGAL STUDIES — (forthcoming 2016). That is also the subject of a forthcoming book.

We will first look briefly at the adoption of the revolutionary state protections for freedoms of press and speech, and of the First Amendment, and at their historical context. The second section will address whether the narrow Blackstone-Mansfield definition of those freedoms and those jurists' framework for seditious libel limited the protections of the First Amendment, by means of English common law applying to the new federal courts and giving them both a Blackstone-Mansfield definition of freedoms of press and speech and a jurisdiction of crimes under the common law. The final section will discuss underlying reasons for why the early justices of the United States Supreme Court came to disagree on freedoms of press and speech, the crimes of seditious libel and seditious speech, a federal common law, and other important issues, as the Sedition Act of 1798 was enacted and enforced.

Figure 3.1 Federal Hall, New York (1789), where President George Washington was sworn in, where Congress approved the Bill of Rights. Engraving by Peter Lacour 1789. (Courtesy of Art Resource, New York.)

The State and Federal Protections of Freedoms of Press and Speech

Before the American Revolution, Britain's Privy Council warned royal governors that "seditious and libellous publications have been put forth . . ., having a tendency and apparently manifesting a design to incite the people to acts of violence, and opposition to the laws, and to the authority of Parliament."[18] The royal governors complied by condemning sedition and threatening speakers and publications.[19] The leaders of the patriot party were repeatedly treated as seditious,[20] and those incidents were widely reported in American newspapers.[21] The King and his council continued to demand suppression of sedition.[22]

The "printing presses were notoriously the great instruments of the American Revolution," as Samuel Bryan recalled,[23] from the Stamp Act controversy to 1770[24] and thereafter to the Revolution.[25] The popular party identified with freedoms of press and speech, impelled by those royal threats, and cemented that identification with suspicions of British conspiracy against American liberties.[26] Threats against the popular party's press and speech fostered the belief that those freedoms were endangered and needed solid legal protection.

[18] 5 Privy Council-Colonial 246, 262 §155 (1770); *accord* Lord Dartmouth to Gen. Thomas Gage (3 June 1776), in 2 Correspondence of General Thomas Gage 163, 165 (Clarence E. Carter ed., YUP, New Haven 1931).

[19] *E.g.*, Gov. Horatio Sharpe to Lower House (20 June 1768), 61 Maryland Archives 399; Gov. Francis Bernard to House of Representatives (1 Mar.1768), in Speeches of the Governors of Massachusetts, 1765–1775, at 118 (Alden Bradford ed., Russell & Gardner, Boston 1818); *see* Lt. Gov. Cadwallader Colden to Admiral Graves (20 Feb.1775), 10 Collections of the New-York Historical Society 387 (NYHS, New York 1878); Copy of Letters Sent to Great Britain 10 (Edes & Gill, Boston 1773); Gov. Francis Bernard to Earl of Hillsborough (25 Jan.1769), 13 Journal of the Commissioners for Trade and Plantations 125 (HMSO, London 1937); Quincy 236–37, 242–43, 262–64, 305.

[20] 3 Adams Works 457; 3 Elliot's Debates 45; *see* Press-Mass. 123–24.

[21] *E.g., Extract of a Letter*, New-York Gazette, 13 Feb.1769, at 3; *Annapolis*, Boston Chronicle, 23–27 Feb.1769, at 67; *New-York, February 11*, New-York Gazette, 11 Feb.1765, at 2.

[22] *King's Proclamation for Suppressing Rebellion and Sedition* (23 Aug.1775), 9 EHD 850; *accord* 5 Privy Council-Colonial 417 §322 (23 Aug.1775); Samuel Ward to Henry Ward (2 Nov.1775), 2 Letters of Delegates 290, 291.

[23] Samuel Bryan to Aedanus Burke (post-5 Dec.1789), 17 DHFFC 1732, 1738; *see* Prelude 51–301.

[24] Alexander McDougall, *To the Freeholders*, Boston Evening-Post, 26 Feb.1770, at 4; Alexander McDougall, *To the Freeholders*, Boston Gazette, 26 Feb.1770, at 2, 3.

[25] 2 David Ramsay, History of the American Revolution 319 (R. Aitken, Philadelphia 1789); *see* Prelude 297.

[26] Ideologica Origins 144–59; Creation 40–42; 2 DHRC 643; Clark 277–78.

Nine of the new states, in adopting declarations of rights or constitutions, protected freedom of press. That is notable, because only eleven of the thirteen states adopted new fundamental laws, and more secured freedom of press than any other liberty except freedom of conscience and the right of jury trial. Moreover, every one of the nine used unrestricted wording for the freedom of press provision, such as the first (Virginia's): "freedom of the press is one of the great bulwarks of liberty, and can never be restrained but by despotick governments."[27] The first half of it quoted Cato, and the second half paraphrased Cato.

The new states also provided that English common law was received (or adopted).[28] However, all of them subordinated that to the rights established under their new declarations of rights or constitutions, which were fundamental laws.[29] Most of the new states also, during the Revolutionary War, enacted laws against seditious words or seditious libels.[30] They did so as part of broader laws against loyalists, which provided for suppression of loyalist speech[31] and confiscation and forfeiture of loyalist property, disenfranchisement, and other penalties and restrictions for loyalists.[32] The laws against sedition were not enforced against revolutionist speech or press.

After the Revolution, Virginia took a major step in defining the spheres of government regulation and of private liberty of opinion. It enacted its Statute of Religious Liberty in 1785, written by Jefferson and sponsored by Madison.[33] That statute provided that

> to suffer the civil magistrate to intrude his powers into the field of opinion, and to restrain the profession or propagation of principles on

[27] Va. Decl. of Rights sec.12 (1776), 7 FEDERAL-STATE CONSTITUTIONS 3812, 3814. The other provisions are cited in Chapter 1.

[28] Ford W. Hall, *The Common Law: An Account of Its Reception in the United States*, 4 VANDERBILT L. REV. 791, 799–800, 806–07 (1951); TRANSATLANTIC 187.

[29] N.J. Const. art. XXII (1776), 5 FEDERAL-STATE CONSTITUTIONS 2594, 2598; Del. Const. art. XXV (1776), 1 *id.* 562, 566–67; Md. D.O.R. art. III (1776), 3 *id.* 1686, 1686; N.Y. Const. art. XXXV (1777), 5 *id.* 2623, 2635–36; Mass. Const. art. VI, §6 (1779), 3 *id.* 1888, 1910; *see* N.H. Const. pt. II (1776), 4 *id.* 2451, 2469; 9 HENING'S STATUTES-VA. 127 (1776).

[30] CLAUDE HALSTEAD VAN TYNE, LOYALISTS IN THE AMERICAN REVOLUTION 327–29 (MacMillan Co, New York 1902); *e.g.*, Act for Restraining and Punishing Persons, Who Are Inimical to the Liberties of This, and the Rest of the United Colonies (Conn. 1775) (broadside); Act To Prevent Sedition and Punish Insurgents (4 Apr.1776), JOURNALS OF GENERAL ASSEMBLY-S.C. 29; Act for the Punishment of Certain Offences (Oct.1776), 9 HENING'S STATUTES-VA. 170; An Ordinance Declaring Certain Practices Misdemeanors (1776), 23 COLONIAL RECORDS-N.C. 998.

[31] PRELUDE 216–17, 297; LEVY 173; PRESS-MASS. 131.

[32] PRELUDE 74–79, 297–98, 107–08, 174–76, 185, 189–90, 210–11, 215, 221, 239–40; DAVIDSON 251, 252, 254, 256–57, 259, 260–61; VAN TYNE, *supra* note 30, at 327–41. John Adams saw a benefit of independence, and its test oaths, as that "[t]he presses will produce no more seditious or traitorous speculations" and "[s]landers upon public men and measures will be lessened." John Adams to John Winthrop (23 June 1776), 4 ADAMS PAPERS 331, 332.

[33] 2 JEFFERSON PAPERS 545, 305 n.; 8 MADISON PAPERS 399, 401 n.1.

> supposition of their ill tendency, is a dangerous fallacy . . .; that it is time enough for the rightful purposes of civil government, for its officers to interfere when principles break out into overt acts against peace and good order. . . .[34]

Though the statute protected religion, abandoning mere toleration for full religious freedom, its principle equally invalidated government prosecution of unorthodox religious principles and government prosecution of seditious libel or seditious words. Further, its overt acts test established a very high bar for governmental interference.

As the Constitution was drafted in 1787 and its ratification was debated, many issues divided anti-federalists and federalists, but there were two points of near unanimity on freedom of press. First, both sides agreed that the new federal government had no legitimate power to restrict the press (though no one questioned state laws protecting reputation against defamation). Thus, federalist speeches and essays followed James Wilson's argument against the need for a bill of rights provision, that "the proposed system possesses no influence whatever upon the press," so no "controul can proceed from the foederal government to shackle or destroy that sacred palladium of national freedom."[35] Anti-federalist essays generally objected to the absence of a bill of rights, and many joined Melancton Smith in expressing alarm about the lack of a bill of rights provision, "that by the indefinite powers granted to the general government, the liberty of the press may be restricted by duties, &c. and therefore the constitution ought to have stipulated for its freedom."[36] In state ratification conventions, the same point of agreement continued, even as federalists maintained their same argument[37] and anti-federalists

[34] Act for Establishing Religious Freedom (1785), 12 HENING'S STATUTES-VA. 84, 85; SOURCES AND DOCUMENTS ILLUSTRATING THE AMERICAN REVOLUTION 1764–1788, at 206, 207 (Samuel E. Morison ed., 2d ed. CP, Oxford 1929).

[35] James Wilson, *State House Yard Speech* (6 Oct.1787), 13 DHRC 339; 1 WILSON WORKS 171; *accord* FEDERALIST No. 84, at 575, 579 (Alexander Hamilton); *accord* 2 DHRC 168, 190, 192, 454–55 (Pa.); 5 *id.* at 736–37, 489–90 (Mass.); 3 *id.* at 243, 247 (Ga.), 524, 525 (Conn.); Citizen of America [Noah Webster], *An Examination into the Leading Principles of the Federal Constitution*, in PAMPHLETS-CONSTITUTION 25, 48; John Jay, *An Address to the People of the State of New-York* (1788), in *id.* at 67, 76; Marcus [James Iredell], *Answers to Mr. Mason's Objections to the New Constitution* (1788), in *id.* at 333, 361; 16 DHRC 162, 382; Landholder [Oliver Ellsworth], *Landholder VI* (10 Dec.1782), in 3 DHRC 487, 490; Citizen of New-Haven, *Observations on the New Federal Constitution*, CONNECTICUT COURANT (Hartford), 7 Jan.1788, at 2; Anti-Cincinnatus, *Mr. Printer*, HAMPSHIRE GAZETTE (Northampton), 19 Dec.1787, at 2.

[36] Plebeian [Melancton Smith], *An Address to the People of the State of New-York*, PAMPHLETS-CONSTITUTION 87, 114 (1788); *accord* Centinel [Samuel Bryan], *Centinel No. II*, NEW-YORK JOURNAL, 1 Nov.1787, at supp.1, 2; 1 DEBATE 77, 80 (first published 24 Oct.1787).

[37] *E.g.*, 2 DHRC 168, 454–55 (Wilson); 1 ELLIOT'S DEBATES 497–98 (Jay); 4 *id.* 315 (C.C. Pinckney); 3 *id.* 203, 469 (Randolph); 2 *id.* 449 (Wilson); 4 *id.* 208 (Spaight), 259 (C. Pinckney); 4 *id.* 315 (18 Jan. 1788); 3 FARRAND'S RECORDS 255, 256.

continued theirs,[38] until some states ratified on the understanding that a bill of rights would be adopted after the Constitution was ratified, under a compromise generally agreed to by federalists.

Second, both sides agreed that a freedom of press provision in the bill of rights would prevent the federal government from having or exercising any power to restrict the press (again, not questioning state defamation law). Many anti-federalist essays said that preventing the federal government from restricting liberty of press by seditious libel prosecutions was an important reason for a bill of rights provision securing the press.[39] Many anti-federalists joined John Smilie of Pennsylvania in understanding that a freedom of press provision would deprive Congress of "a power, or right, *to declare* what is a *libel*," or "to pass an act for the punishment of libels and restrain the liberty of the press."[40] Federalists agreed that a freedom of press provision would preclude such a power. When a North Carolina delegate argued that the lack of press protection meant "[t]hey might make it treason to write against the most arbitrary proceedings,"[41] federalist Richard Spaight (a Constitutional Convention participant) responded that the Constitution "can do nothing to injure" the press and that "the constitution of every state" secures it,[42] acknowledging that a state freedom of press provision had the effect of barring such restraint of the press. James Iredell added that the first delegate was mistaken because Congress "have no power to define any other crime whatever," asking, "Where is the power given to them to do this?"[43]

[38] 2 DHRC 441 (Smilie); 2 *id.* 204, 288, 310, 504, 597; 3 *id.* 243; 5 *id.* 587; 20 *id.* 624; 4 ELLIOT'S DEBATES 259 (C. Pinckney); *e.g.*, 1 *id.* 496 (Mason), 503 (R.H. Lee); 2 *id.* 399 (Tredwell); 3 *id.* 44–45, 149 (Henry); 4 *id.* 205 (Lenoir), 314 (Lincoln); *see* 1 COMPLETE ANTI-FEDERALIST 64; 12 JEFFERSON PAPERS 438, 440; 14 *id.* 649, 650.

[39] Cincinnatus [Arthur Lee], *Cincinnatus I*, in 1 DEBATE 92, 95–96; Cincinnatus [Arthur Lee], *Number I*, NEW-YORK JOURNAL, 1 Nov.1787, at 2; *accord* Cincinnatus [Arthur Lee], *Number II*, NEW-YORK JOURNAL, 8 Nov.1787, at 2; Democratic Federalist, *Messieurs Printers*, PENNSYLVANIA PACKET (Philadelphia), 23 Oct.1787, at 2; 1 DEBATE 70; Confederationalist, *To the Editor*, PENNSYLVANIA HERALD (Philadelphia), 27 Oct.1787; AN OFFICER OF THE LATE CONTINENTAL ARMY [WILLIAM FINDLEY], ADDRESS FROM AN OFFICER IN THE LATE CONTINENTAL ARMY 2 (n.p., Philadelphia 1787); 1 DEBATE 97, 98–99; One of the Common People, *Messieurs Edes*, BOSTON GAZETTE, 3 Dec.1787, at 2; *From the New-York Journal*, HAMPSHIRE GAZETTE (Northampton), 5 Dec.1787, at 2; Philadelphiensis [Benjamin Workman], *Philadelphiensis No. IX*, FREEMAN'S JOURNAL (Philadelphia), 6 Feb.1788, at 2.

[40] 2 DHRC 453 (1 Dec.1787), 441 (30 Nov.1787); a concern Whitehill joined in, 2 *id.* 454, *see* 2 *id.* 597; *accord* Foreign Spectator, *Remarks on the Amendments to the Federal Constitution, Proposed by the Conventions... Number XXVIII*, FEDERAL GAZETTE (Philadelphia), 16 Feb.1789, at 2, 3 & n.; Foreign Spectator, *Remarks on the Amendments to the Federal Constitution, Proposed by the Conventions... Number XXVIII*, NEW-YORK DAILY GAZETTE, 6 July 1789, at 654; 10 DHRC 1326 (16 June 1788); 3 ELLIOT'S DEBATES 442.

[41] 4 ELLIOT'S DEBATES 205 (Lenoir); *see* GREAT RIGHTS 154–56.

[42] 4 *id.* 209.

[43] 4 *id.* 219.

The post-ratification amendments to the Constitution that were proposed by several states, as they ratified, sought greater protection for freedom of press, while none sought to ensure an unmodified common law or continuation of seditious libel. Virginia called in its form of ratification for a provision that "liberty . . . of the press, cannot be cancelled, abridged, restrained, or modified, by any authority of the United States,"[44] and proposed the amendment that "the people have a right to freedom of speech, and of writing and publishing their sentiments; that the freedom of the press is one of the greatest bulwarks of liberty, and ought not to be violated."[45] New York's form of ratification posited that "freedom of the press ought not to be violated." Rhode Island later reiterated that proposition, and North Carolina called for an amendment to that effect.[46]

James Madison, in proposing the First Amendment[47] in June 1789, said that the freedom of press and freedom of conscience provisions were necessary because "government should be disarmed of powers which trench upon those particular rights," but he did not merely formalize British common law, because those rights "are unguarded in the British constitution."[48] When the house committee (which he chaired) approved language similar to the current First Amendment, Madison described it as going beyond a restatement of common law. "The right of freedom of speech is secured; the liberty of the press is expressly declared to be beyond the reach of this Government. . . ."[49]

Three weeks before that committee approval, the House committee rejected replacement language in the First Amendment that limited freedoms of press and speech to decent expressions,[50] and three weeks after, the Senate rejected substitute wording that limited freedoms of press and speech to what was "secured by the common law."[51]

Congress approved the Bill of Rights by the required two-thirds majority in September 1789 (the location is depicted in Figure 3.1), and most of the states

[44] 1 *id.* 327; 3 *id.* 656 (26 June 1788); 4 DHFFC 15–17. Virginia was critical as the largest state. Great Rights 134.

[45] 4 DHFFC 15, 16–17; 3 Elliot's Debates 659 (27 June 1788).

[46] 4 DHFFC 19, 21 (N.Y. 26 July 1788); 1 Elliot's Debates 328 (N.Y. 26 July 1788), 332; 4 *id.* 244 (N.C. 1 Aug.1788); 1 *id.* 335 (R.I. 29 May 1790); The Anti-Federalist Writings of the Melancton Smith Circle 344, 347 (Michael P. Zuckert & Derek A. Webb eds., LF, Indianapolis 2009) (N.Y. proposals July 1788).

[47] It then was the fourth of nineteen amendments, and when ratified was the third of twelve amendments, the first two of which failed to be ratified.

[48] Creating Bill of Rights 85, 80 (8 June 1789), reprinting 1 Congressional Register 437–38 (8 June 1789); 11 DHFFC 825–26, 822.

[49] 1 Annals 766 (15 Aug.1789).

[50] Creating Bill of Rights 266, 267 (21–28 July 1789); Complete Bill of Rights-Sources 83.

[51] 1 DHFFC 152 (3 Sept.1789); 4 *id.* 36 n.9.

ratified it over the next half year. The required three-quarters was reached in December 1791.

The Sedition Act of 1798 forced thought and development of theory on the breadth of the First Amendment and its effect on seditious libel. In the fierce debate around the Act, James Madison, the "father of the Bill of Rights," best formulated the argument that the First Amendment prohibited criminalization of discussion of public officials and measures, and that it and the American Revolution overrode the Blackstone-Mansfield definition.[52] He explicitly rejected Blackstone's definition as inconsistent with American bills of rights:

> this idea of the freedom of the press can never be admitted to be the American idea of it; since a law inflicting penalties on printed publications would have a similar effect with a law authorizing a previous restraint on them. It would seem a mockery to say that no laws should be passed preventing publications from being made, but that laws might be passed for punishing them in case they should be made.[53]

Alexander Hamilton, by contrast, contended that freedom of press in the First Amendment meant the same thing in English common law as summarized by Blackstone, and he believed that English common law applied to the federal courts and conferred jurisdiction of common law crimes including seditious libel and seditious words. As a consequence, the Constitution allowed "laws for restraining and punishing incendiary and seditious practices," including "writings &c which at common law are libels if levelled against any officer whatsoever of the U[nited] States."[54]

Those two views have continued to be advocated through the years, and the discussion has focused on whether the broad or narrow approach to freedoms of press and speech was embodied in state declarations of rights as they were adopted during 1776–1780, and in the First Amendment as it was ratified during 1789–1791. Throughout the nineteenth century, the Blackstone-Mansfield definition of freedoms of press and speech and those jurists' framework for seditious libel remained influential,

[52] James Madison, *Report on the Virginia Resolutions* (Dec.1799-Jan.1800), 4 ELLIOT'S DEBATES 546, 561, 569; reprinting REPORT OF THE COMMITTEE TO WHOM WAS COMMITTED THE PROCEEDINGS OF SUNDRY OF THE OTHER STATES, IN ANSWER TO THE RESOLUTIONS (General Assembly, Richmond [7 Jan.1800].

[53] 4 *id.* 569; *accord* ST. GEORGE TUCKER, *Of the Right of Conscience; and of the Freedom of Speech and of the Press*, in VIEW OF THE CONSTITUTION OF THE UNITED STATES 371, 379–94 (Clyde N.Wilson ed., LF, Indianapolis 1999) (original edition was 1803).

[54] Alexander Hamilton to Jonathan Dayton (Oct.-Nov.1799), 23 HAMILTON PAPERS 599, 604; *accord* Alexander Hamilton, An Address to the Electors (21 Mar.1801), 25 *id.* 349, 364. He later argued for the common law of seditious libel with *Zenger* amelioration. People v. Croswell, 3 Johns. Cas. 337 (N.Y. 1804); 1 THE LAW PRACTICE OF ALEXANDER HAMILTON 808, 809 (Julius Goebel et al. eds., ColUP, New York 1964–81).

though an expansive definition of those freedoms was championed by some legal treatises and their objections to Blackstone and Mansfield were noted by Cooley.[55] Through the first half of the twentieth century, divergence between those approaches continued, as the First Amendment was understood to embody the Blackstone-Mansfield definition of freedoms of speech and press by various professors[56] and justices,[57] and, contrariwise, to embody the Madison approach by other professors[58] and

[55] JOSEPH STORY, A FAMILIAR EXPOSITION OF THE CONSTITUTION OF THE UNITED STATES 317–18 (Harper, New York 1859); THOMAS M. COOLEY, A TREATISE ON THE CONSTITUTIONAL LIMITATIONS 421 (LB, Boston 1868) ("commentators seem to be agreed in the opinion that the term itself means only that liberty of publication without the previous permission of the government"; Blackstone "has been followed by American commentators of standard authority"; but see discussion of seditious libel, *id.* at 426–30); 7 NATHAN DANE, A GENERAL ABRIDGMENT AND DIGEST OF AMERICAN LAW 52–53 (Cummings Hilliard, Boston 1824) (9 vols.) (Mansfield definition); WILLIAM RAWLE, A VIEW OF THE CONSTITUTION OF THE UNITED STATES OF AMERICA 120 (H.C. Carey & L. Lea, Philadelphia 1825) (Blackstonian view). Advocates of an expansive definition included ST. GEORGE TUCKER, BLACKSTONE'S COMMENTARIES: WITH NOTES OF REFERENCE Pt. II (Appendix), 11–30 (William Young Birch & Abraham Small, Philadelphia 1803) (appendix was separately paginated); HORTENSIUS [GEORGE HAY], AN ESSAY ON THE LIBERTY OF THE PRESS (Aurora, Philadelphia 1799); TUNIS WORTMAN, A TREATISE CONCERNING POLITICAL ENQUIRY AND THE LIBERTY OF THE PRESS (George Forman, New York 1800); THOMAS COOPER, POLITICAL ESSAYS 59, 62–88 (2d ed. Robert Campbell, Philadelphia 1800); JOHN THOMSON, AN ENQUIRY CONCERNING THE LIBERTY AND LICENTIOUSNESS OF THE PRESS (Johnson & Stryker, New York 1801).

[56] E.g., Edward S. Corwin, *Freedom of Speech and Press under the First Amendment: A Résumé*, 30 YALE L.J. 48, 49 (1920); Thomas F. Carroll, *Freedom of Speech and of the Press in the Federalist Period: The Sedition Act*, 18 MICH. L. REV. 615, 636–37, 648 (1920); WESTEL W. WILLOUGHBY, THE CONSTITUTIONAL LAW OF THE UNITED STATES 1196 (2d ed. Baker, New York 1929).

[57] Robertson v. Baldwin, 165 U.S. 275, 281 (1897) (Brown, J.) ("'Bill of Rights,' were not intended to lay down any novel principles of government, but simply to embody certain guaranties and immunities which we had inherited from our English ancestors, and which had, from time immemorial, been subject to certain well-recognized exceptions. . . . Thus, the freedom of speech and of the press (article 1) does not permit the publication of libels, blasphemous or indecent articles. . . ."); Patterson v. Colorado, 205 U.S. 454, 462 (1907) (Holmes, J., before *Abrams*) ("the main purpose of such constitutional provisions is 'to prevent all such *previous restraints* upon publications as had been practised by other governments,' and they do not prevent the subsequent punishment of such as may be deemed contrary to the public welfare."); *see* Alexander v. United States, 509 U.S. 544, 569 (1993) (Kennedy, Blackmun & Stevens, JJ., dissenting) ("our earliest cases tended to repeat the suggestion by Blackstone that prior restraints were the sole concern of First Amendment protections").

[58] Henry Schofield, *Freedom of the Press in the United States*, 9 PAPERS AND PROCEEDINGS, NINTH ANNUAL MEETING, AMERICAN SOCIOLOGICAL SOC. 67 (1914); Henry Schofield, *Freedom of the Press in the United States*, in 2 HENRY SCHOFIELD, ESSAYS ON CONSTITUTIONAL LAW AND EQUITY 510, 511, 535 (Chipman, Boston 1921) (2 vols.); ZECHARIAH CHAFEE, FREEDOM OF SPEECH 10, 23 (Harcourt Brace, New York 1920); THEODORE SCHROEDER, FREE SPEECH BIBLIOGRAPHY (H.W. Wilson Co., New York 1922); *accord* ZECHARIAH CHAFEE, FREE SPEECH IN THE UNITED STATES 18, 21 (HUP, Cambridge 1941).

justices.[59] The same was true of the second half of the twentieth century, and since, as the narrow view (to quote Blumberg's recent version) that "American courts without exception followed Blackstone" and "gave the provisions for 'free speech' and 'free press' no more scope than the cramped meaning that the English law had fashioned" has continued to prevail among scholars[60] (and has been described as the "new orthodoxy" or as highly influential not only by supporters[61] but by many who could not

[59] Abrams v. United States, 250 U.S. 616, 630–31 (1919) (Holmes, J., dissenting with Brandeis, J.), though Holmes had migrated from an inconsistent prior opinion in *Patterson*; Thornhill v. Alabama, 310 U.S. 88, 101–02 (1940); Chaplinsky v. New Hampshire, 315 U.S. 568, 572 n.3 (1942).

[60] REPRESSIVE JURISPRUDENCE 5–9, 52–71. E.g., 2 PAUL A. FREUND ET AL., CONSTITUTIONAL LAW: CASES AND OTHER PROBLEMS 1545 (2d ed. Little Brown, Boston 1961); LEONARD W. LEVY, LEGACY OF SUPPRESSION: FREEDOM OF SPEECH AND PRESS IN EARLY AMERICAN HISTORY vii, ix, x, 176–248 (HUP, Cambridge 1960); CREATION 63; Jerome L. Merin, *Libel and the Supreme Court*, 11 WM. & MARY L. REV. 371, 375, 376, 377–78, 379 (1969); Walter Berns, *Freedom of the Press and the Alien and Sedition Acts: A Reappraisal*, 1970 SUP. CT. REV. 109; WALTER BERNS, THE FIRST AMENDMENT AND THE FUTURE OF AMERICAN Democracy 84 (Basic Books, New York 1976); LEONARD W. LEVY, EMERGENCE OF A FREE PRESS xi–xii, 170–72 (OUP, New York 1985); Philip D. Kurland, *The Original Understanding of the Freedom of the Press Provision of the First Amendment*, 55 MISS. L.J. 225, 234, 236, 237, 246 (1985); HAMBURGER 745–46 n.261; JOHN P. REID, 1 CONSTITUTIONAL HISTORY OF THE AMERICAN REVOLUTION: THE AUTHORITY OF RIGHTS 4 (UWP, Madison 1986); Michael T. Gibson, *The Supreme Court and Freedom of Expression from 1791 to 1917*, 55 FORDHAM L. REV. 263, 327, 331 (1986); Stanley C. Brubaker, *Original Intent and Freedom of Speech and Press*, in THE BILL OF RIGHTS: ORIGINAL MEANING AND CURRENT UNDERSTANDING 82, 83 (Eugene W. Hickok ed., UPV, Charlottesville 1991); FEDERALISM 700 & n.25; DAVID P. CURRIE, THE CONSTITUTION IN CONGRESS: THE FIRST CONGRESS, 1789–1801, at 261 & n.198 (UChiP, Chicago 1994); WALT BROWN, JOHN ADAMS AND THE AMERICAN PRESS 32–34 (McFarland, Jefferson 1995); William R. Casto, *Oliver Ellsworth*, 1996 J. SUP. CT. HISTORY 73; Norman L. Rosenberg, *Seditious Libel*, OCSC 765, 766; James P. Martin, *When Repression Is Democratic and Constitutional: The Federalist Theory of Representation and the Sedition Act of 1798*, 66 U. CHI. L. REV. 117, 125–26 nn.14–15 (1999); Michael I. Meyerson, *The Neglected History of the Prior Restraint Doctrine*, 34 IND. L. REV. 295, 311–13, 320 & n.178, 321–22 (2001); Richard D. Brown, *The Shifting Freedoms of the Press in the Eighteenth Century*, in THE COLONIAL BOOK IN THE ATLANTIC WORLD 366, 375 (Hugh Amory & David D. Hall eds. CUP, Cambridge 2000) (1st of 5 vols. of *A History of the Book in America* as reissued by UNCP 2007); WILLIAM COHEN, THE FIRST AMENDMENT: CONSTITUTIONAL PROTECTION OF EXPRESSION AND CONSCIENCE 5 (Foundation Press, New York 2003); ERIC BARENDT, FREEDOM OF SPEECH 163–64 & n.47 (OUP, New York 2005); RICHARD LABUNSKI, JAMES MADISON AND THE STRUGGLE FOR THE BILL OF RIGHTS 258 & n.16 (OUP, New York 2006); RUSSELL L. WEAVER & DONALD E. LIVELY, UNDERSTANDING THE FIRST AMENDMENT 6, 4 (2d ed., Lexis-Nexis, Newark 2006); EMPIRE 258; *see* Merrill Jensen, *Review*, 75 HARV. L. REV. 456, 458 (1961); Philip A. Hamburger, *Natural Rights, Natural Law, and American Constitutions*, 102 YALE L.J. 907, 911–12 (1993). Older supporters are cited in David M. Rabban, *The Ahistorical Historian: Leonard Levy on Freedom of Expression in Early American History*, 37 STAN. L. REV. 795, 797 n.7 (1985).

[61] Richard D. Brown, *supra* note 60, at 375. *Accord* 2 FREUND, *supra* note 60, at 1545; BERNS, *supra* note 60, at 84; Norman L. Rosenberg, *Another World: Freedom of Press in the Eighteenth Century*, 16 REVIEWS IN AM. HIST. 554, 554 (1988); CURRIE, *supra* note 60, at 261 & n.198; WEAVER & LIVELY, *supra* note 60, at 6, 4.

bring themselves to embrace that thesis[62]), as well as being the position of various justices,[63] while the Madisonian position has been embraced by many other scholars[64] and justices.[65]

One group whose views have not been studied, but whose views are highly relevant to whether the First Amendment incorporated or presupposed the narrow Blackstone-Mansfield definition of freedoms of press and speech, or an expansive definition of those freedoms, is the early justices of the Supreme Court of the United States, the highest ranking jurists of the new country. From the Revolution

[62] Rabban, *supra* note 60, at 797. *Accord* Gerald A. Berlin, *Legacy of Suppression*, 72 YALE L.J. 631, 636 (1963) (book review); Alexander Meiklejohn, *The First Amendment Is an Absolute*, 1961 SUP. CT. REV. 245, 264; Dwight L. Teeter, A Legacy of Expression: Philadelphia Newspapers and Congress During the War for Independence, 1775–1783, at i (1966) (unpublished Ph.D. dissertation, University of Wisconsin); David A. Anderson, *The Origins of the Press Clause*, 30 UCLA L. REV. 455, 461 n.38, 534 (1983); William T. Mayton, *Seditious Libel and the Lost Guarantee of a Freedom of Expression*, 84 COLUM. L. REV. 91, 92 (1984); Ellen K. Solender, *Book Review: Emergence of a Free Press*, 62 NOTRE DAME L. REV. 145, 146 (1986); Rabban, *supra* note 60, at 802, 797; Loren P. Beth, *Emergence of a Free Press*, 91 AM. HISTORICAL REV. 1266 (1986) (book review); William W. van Alstyne, *Congressional Power and Free Speech: Levy's* Legacy *Revisited*, 99 HARV. L. REV. 1089, 1089 (1986); Howard O. Hunter, *Problems in Search of Principles: The First Amendment in the Supreme Court from 1791–1930*, 35 EMORY L.J. 59, 62 (1986); Robert Palmer, *Liberties*, in WILLIAM E. NELSON & ROBERT C. PALMER, CONSTITUTION AND RIGHTS IN THE EARLY AMERICAN REPUBLIC 55, 57 (College of William & Mary, Williamsburg 1987); Robert C. Post, *Defaming Public Officials: On Doctrine and Legal History*, 12 AM. BAR FOUNDATION RESEARCH J. 539, 541–42 (1987) (though disagreeing, as do all others in this footnote); LARRY D. ELDRIDGE, A DISTANT HERITAGE: THE GROWTH OF FREE SPEECH IN EARLY AMERICA 1 (NYUP, New York 1994); KATHLEEN M. SULLIVAN & GERALD GUNTHER, FIRST AMENDMENT LAW 3 (3d ed. Foundation Press, New York 2007); JOHN E. NOWAK & RONALD D. ROTUNDA, CONSTITUTIONAL LAW 1268 (8th ed. West, Minneapolis 2010); Randall P. Bezanson, *Whither Freedom of the Press?*, 97 IOWA L. REV. 1259, 1264 (2012) ("the most prominent twentieth-century historian of the free-press guarantee").

[63] The Supreme Court majority cited Leonard Levy's book in New York Times Co. v. Sullivan, 376 U.S. 254, 273 (1964); as did the plurality in Curtis Publishing Co. v. Butts, 388 U.S. 130, 149 n.13 (1967) (plurality opinion of Harlan, J., with Clark, Stewart & Fortas, JJ.); and more recently the four dissenters in Citizens United v. FEC, 558 U.S. 310, 393, 432 & n.58 (2010) (Stevens, J., concurring and dissenting with Ginsburg, Breyer & Sotomayor, JJ.) (on seeing indeterminacy of meaning of the speech and press provisions). Chief Justice Warren Burger cited Levy's book favorably in a concurrence in First National Bank v. Bellotti, 435 U.S. 765, 799 (1978) (on the eighteenth-century equivalent use of speech and press). Justice Byron White extensively cited and followed Levy's thesis in a dissent in Gertz v. Robert Welch, Inc., 418 U.S. 323, 381–82 (1974) ("Contrary to some popular notions, freedom of the press was sharply curtailed in colonial America. [Footnote omitted.] Seditious libel was punished as a contempt by the colonial legislatures and as a criminal offense in the colonial courts. [Citing Levy.].... Moreover, consistent with the Blackstone formula, these common-law actions did not abridge freedom of the press. See generally L. Levy, Legacy of Suppression....").

[64] The leading ones were Smith, Rabban, and Anderson. JEFFERY A. SMITH, PRINTERS AND PRESS FREEDOM: THE IDEOLOGY OF EARLY AMERICAN JOURNALISM >4–12, 13, 170 (OUP, Oxford 1988); David M. Rabban, *The Ahistorical Historian: Leonard Levy on Freedom of Expression in Early American History*, 37 STAN. L. REV. 795, 795, 795–96, 801, 821–41, 841–49, 802–20 (1985); David

to 1798, those who became the twelve earliest justices of the Supreme Court did not show any support for the narrow Blackstone-Mansfield definition or framework, and spoke consistently with a broad definition, as we will see in the next two chapters. However, in 1798 they split almost evenly between adopting that Blackstone-Mansfield view and retaining a more expansive view of freedoms of press and speech, as we will discuss in Chapters 6–8. Their responses were similar on the concept of a federal common law of crimes, as before 1798 none adopted that concept except Justice Iredell in 1796 (though all found the law of nations applicable), while during the crisis years of 1798–1801 about half adopted a federal common law of crimes and justified criminalization of seditious libel and seditious words.

Figure 3.2 Alexander Hamilton. Portrait by John Trumbull c.1792. (Courtesy of National Gallery of Art.)

A. Anderson, *The Origins of the Press Clause*, 30 UCLA L. Rev. 455, 462–85, 494–509, 522 (1983); David A. Anderson, *Levy vs. Levy*, 84 Mich. L. Rev. 777 (1986). *E.g.*, Freedom's Fetters 427–31; Berlin, *supra* note 62, at 637; Harry Kalven, *The New York Times Case: A Note on "The Central Meaning of the First Amendment,"* 1964 S. Ct. Rev. 191, 205–06, 221 & n.124; Brant 17; Vincent Blasi, *The Checking Value in First Amendment Theory*, 2 Am. B. Found. Res. J. 521 (1977) (though is limited to Levy's historical evidence); Thomas A. Green, *The Jury, Seditious Libel, and the Criminal Law*, in R.H. Helmholz & Thomas A. Green, Juries, Libel and Justice 37, 40 (Clark Memorial Library, Los Angeles 1984);` Mayton, *Seditious Libel, supra* note 62, at 91, 93, 95, 96–99, 114; William T. Mayton, *From a Legacy of Suppression*, 39 Stan. L. Rev. 139, 147–48 (1986); Lucas A. Powe, Jr., The Fourth Estate and the Constitution 27, 47 (UCalP, Berkeley 1991); Akhil R. Amar, *The Bill of Rights and the Fourteenth Amendment*, 101 Yale L.J. 1193, 1266–67 (1992); Harling 112; Geoffrey R. Stone, Perilous Times 42 (Norton, New York 2004); George Anastaplo, The Constitutionalist 103–04, 509 n.34, 513 n.43 (rev. ed., Lexington Books, Lanham 2005).

[65] Times Film Corp. v. City of Chicago, 365 U.S. 43, 54 (1961) (Warren, C.J., dissenting, with Black, Douglas & Brennan, JJ.); Communist Party v. Subversive Activities Control Bd., 367 U.S. 1, 159 n. 46 (1961) (Black, J., dissenting); New York Times Co. v. Sullivan, 376 U.S. 254, 273–74 (1964); First National Bank v. Bellotti, 435 U.S. 765, 776 (1978); and various cases thereafter.

Figure 3.3 James Madison. Portrait by Gilbert Stuart c.1821. (Courtesy of National Gallery of Art.)

The Question of a Federal Common Law of Crimes: Whether the Narrow Definition of Freedoms of Press and Speech, and The Wide-Ranging Crime of Seditious Libel, Were Incorporated into Federal Law

Criminal law before and during the eighteenth century, both in England and America, was largely "a common law field," as Langbein notes,[66] though it was steadily being modified by statute.[67] Crimes under English common law included "writing a libel and publishing it," which was "a matter indictable at common law."[68] However, not all of English common law carried over to the new *states*, as most provided and the rest assumed that common law repugnant with their constitution or laws was not received. Whether any common law carried over to the new *federal* government, to create additional federal crimes and additional federal court jurisdiction, soon generated a storm.

The Hamiltonian view soon became that America had a federal common law of crimes as well as state common law, since the Constitution expressly authorized very few crimes such as treason. The Madisonian view soon became that there was

[66] John H. Langbein, *Shaping the Eighteenth-Century Criminal Trial: A View from the Ryder Sources*, 50 U. Chi. L. Rev. 1, 40 (1983); *accord* 1 Leon Radzinowicz, A History of English Criminal Law and Its Administration from 1750, at ix (Stevens, London 1948–86); J.M. Beattie, Crime and the Courts in England, 1660–1800, at 5, 113, 140, 182 (CP, Oxford 1986).

[67] 1 Radzinowicz, *supra* note 66, at 611–726; Peter Linebaugh, The London Hanged 74–82 (CUP, Cambridge 1992).

[68] *In re* A Prohibition, (1687–88) Comberbach 71, 90 Eng. Rep. 350 (K.B.); *accord* Opinion of the Judges, (1792) 22 State Trials 297, 300 (H.L.).

no federal common law of crimes, because the Constitution did not enumerate such a federal power and the Bill of Rights rejected much of English common law. (Hamilton and Madison are portrayed in Figures 3.2 and 3.3.) Between these viewpoints, there was no controversy that states adopted the bulk of English common law not repugnant to state constitutions and laws, or that Americans extolled the ideal of the common law as a repository of English rights[69] and particularly jury trial rights,[70] canonized by prerevolutionary "identification of English rights with natural rights."[71] However, even then the common law was seen as "not sufficient, to secure [people] from oppression," as Dulaney said in his influential 1728 pamphlet.[72] The controversy between these viewpoints has been thoroughly discussed by Jay and Palmer,[73] and so is summarized and supplemented principally with sources they do not cite. That controversy determined whether the federal government inherited a federally enforceable common law, two years before ratification of First Amendment protections for press and speech. (We will not revisit the point of Chapter 2, that the English common law did not include the Blackstone-Mansfield definition of freedoms of press and speech until the middle of the colonial storm in 1770, and that its insertion then was of suspect origin to America's revolutionaries.)

Discussion of the Common Law of Seditious Libel During the Ratification Period

Nine days after the first Congress rejected the amendment limiting freedoms of speech and press to "as ample a manner as hath at any time been secured by the common law," and thirteen days before it adopted what became the First Amendment, a Philadelphia essayist described the status of seditious libel and the impact of state and federal freedoms of speech and press:

> It is really often curious to see some of our *Lawyers* attempting to restrain the press, by quoting as LAW for this country, the opinions of arbitrary and corrupt *English* judges; some of whom have done their utmost to change and new model the *British* constitution, . . . without the liberty of speech, or of press. . . . It is high time to make use of our own common

[69] *E.g.*, 2 DHSC 179, 402, 415–16 (Wilson); 4 DHFFC 19, 21 (N.Y. ratification); 1 ELLIOT'S DEBATES 328, 494; 3 *id.* 508 (Mason), 446 (Henry).

[70] *E.g., Declaration of Colonial Rights and Grievances* (10 Oct.1774), in 9 EHD 805, 807.

[71] LAMP 189; *see* DAVID MCCULLOUGH, 1776, at 54 (Simon & Schuster, New York 2005).

[72] DANIEL DULANEY, THE RIGHT OF THE INHABITANTS OF MARYLAND TO THE BENEFIT OF THE ENGLISH LAWS 18 (W. Parks, Annapolis 1728).

[73] Stewart Jay, *Origins of Federal Common Law, Part I*, 133 U. PA. L. REV. 1003 (1985); Stewart Jay, *Origins of Federal Common Law, Part II*, 133 U. PA. L. REV. 1231 (1985); Robert C. Palmer, *The Federal Common Law of Crime*, 4 LAW & HISTORY REV. 267 (1986); *see* 1 HISTORY OF SUPREME COURT 623–33.

> sense, and be guided by the spirit of our own constitutions, if we mean to preserve that invaluable liberty for which we so ardently struggled. And should we apply this doctrine of the tyrant Lord Mansfield, even to private life, in what a disagreeable predicament will it place our printers. . . .
>
> . . . . Surely such slavish, such childish doctrines, will not prevail in America; rather let the sophistry and maxims of court casuists be disregarded, and the language of our new government alone become the guide of freemen—"*No state shall infringe the freedom of speech, or of the press.*"[74]

It was the pending Bill of Rights of which the essay spoke, because the quotation in the last sentence was part of Madison's proposed wording for freedom of speech and press, not any state constitution.[75] The essayist viewed "the opinions of arbitrary and corrupt *English* judges," including their rule excluding a defense of truth, not to be "law for this country," and instead to "restrain the press" in conflict with the law of this country, which secured freedoms of speech and press both in "our own constitutions" (state) and in "our new government" Bill of Rights (federal). He rejected "this doctrine of the tyrant Lord Mansfield" that left a British constitution "without the liberty of speech, or of press."

He was not alone. The day after the Bill of Rights was approved, "Libero," finding imprisonment of printers for libels "contrary to the spirit of the constitution," proclaimed that "our laws have not drawn a line between the liberty and licentiousness of the press."[76] Days after the first state ratification, another writer queried, "Shall we, who have renounced the tyranny of *England*, acknowledge the most *tyrannic* part of its laws?," referring to "the *Star-Chamber* practice" of seditious libel.[77] The point was not that English common law was not adopted by the American states, but that the parts repugnant to their rights and powers were not received but rejected. As an article said a year earlier, though freedom of press was claimed as the "bulwark of *English* liberty," it "is but a name" there and "is not *secured*" under English common law, whereas the situation of Pennsylvanians differed because in addition to "the advantages assigned by the *common law* of England, our rights and privileges are ascertained and fixed . . . by the *constitution* of the state."[78] Consequently, while for common law generally Blackstone was influential, for the purpose of defining our rights "[w]e have no business nor

[74] *Mr. Oswald*, Independent Gazetteer (Philadelphia), 12 Sept.1789, at 3.

[75] Proposal (8 June 1789), 4 DHFFC 9, 10, 11; Articles of Amendment (24 Aug.1789), 4 *id.* 35, 39, until amended 9 September, 4 *id.* 45. The essayist was not aware of the current language yet, because the first Congress was distant in New York.

[76] Libero, *Mr. Oswald*, Independent Gazetteer (Philadelphia), 26 Sept.1789, at 2.

[77] *Philadelphia, Friday, November 20*, Independent Gazetteer (Philadelphia), 20 Nov.1789, at 3; *accord There Is Something*, Middlesex Gazette (Middletown), 12 Dec.1789, at 1.

[78] *Philadelphia, August 13*, Independent Gazetteer (Philadelphia), 13 Aug.1788, at 3.

necessity, like the people of England, to refer to *Blackstone*, or any other writer and commentator on the laws of England."[79] The common law did not define the boundary of freedom of press or of rights generally, nor did the restrictions that "mutilated" it; English rights had "precarious" security, were "undefined," and depended on "a mass of mutilated laws, *in volumes of contradictory reports*."[80]

Effect of the First Amendment, and the Bill of Rights Generally, in Modifying Common Law

The Hamilton view faced a severe difficulty, in claiming a federal common law of crimes including seditious libel. That would require state declarations of rights and the new Bill of Rights to incorporate the English common law meaning of freedom of press, as mere freedom from prior restraint, in order for seditious libel not to be repugnant. Yet the effect of every other clause of the First Amendment, and of most other amendments,[81] was seriously to modify common law and statutory law to broaden rights and eliminate restrictions.

Thus, in the First Amendment, the Free Exercise Clause recognized a right in place of English toleration of some faiths[82] and criminalization of other faiths.[83] The Establishment Clause rejected the English common law establishing religion.[84] The Assembly Clause secured a right that overrode English restrictions on assemblies exceeding twelve individuals and criminalization after warning.[85] The Petition Clause greatly expanded the ineffectual English right and terminated English restrictions criminalizing petitions with more than twenty signatories or ten deliverers, and criminally prosecuting "indecent" petitions as seditious libel.[86] If the Petition Clause overrode the common law crime of indecent petitions being

[79] *Id.*

[80] One of the Common People, *Messieurs Edes*, BOSTON GAZETTE, 3 Dec.1787, at 2.

[81] As was conceded in LEONARD W. LEVY, ORIGINS OF THE BILL OF RIGHTS 4 (YUP, New Haven 1999).

[82] 4 BLACKSTONE'S COMMENTARIES 53–54, 54–55; Toleration Act (1689), 1 W&M c18.

[83] 4 *id.* 50–59; William Blackstone, *A Reply to Dr. Priestley's Remarks* (1769), in THE PALLADIUM OF CONSCIENCE 37, 40, 41 (Robert Bell, Philadelphia 1773).

[84] 4 *id.* 49–53, 57–58; 2 ROYAL INSTRUCTIONS 482; Mark McGarvie & Elizabeth Mensch, *Law and Religion in Colonial America*, in 1 CAMBRIDGE HISTORY OF LAW IN AMERICA 324, 326–62 (Michael Grossberg ed., CUP, Cambridge 2008). Madison criticized the common law for importing "the *ecclesiastical hierarchy itself*." James Madison to George Washington (18 Oct.1787), 10 MADISON PAPERS 196, 197.

[85] 4 *id.* 142–43. English law prescribed hanging for assemblies of twelve or more persons who failed to disperse when ordered, or fine and imprisonment if three to eleven persons. 4 *id.* 146.

[86] 4 *id.* 147; 1 *id.* 143; Act against Tumultuous Petitioning (1661), 13 Car 2, stat 1, c5. English law imposed up to £100 fine and three months' imprisonment when petitions to King or Parliament exceeded those limits, and called for "alteration of matters established by law in church or state" without prior approval. 4 BLACKSTONE'S COMMENTARIES 147.

seditious libel, is it not likely that the Press and Speech Clauses similarly overrode the common law of printed and spoken words being seditious libel? If the Free Exercise, Establishment, Assembly, and Petition Clauses rejected English common law, is it not probable that the Speech and Press Clauses did so as well? Much of the rest of the Bill of Rights overturned major parts of English common law of crime, which Wilson and other contemporaries called "defective to a degree both gross and cruel,"[87] with the "ensanguined hue" of 160 capital offenses,[88] the denial of counsel and confronting witnesses,[89] and inquisitorial extraction of confessions and limitation of jury trial rights[90] (or what Milsom similarly called "[t]he miserable history of crime in England" with its "savage laws"[91] and unjust judges).[92]

Madison said as much in his speech introducing the Bill of Rights: "freedom of the press and rights of conscience . . . are unguarded in the British constitution"; and according to his notes, Britain offered "no freedom of press—conscience," so that the Bill of Rights was needed as a "check on . . . common law."[93] Governor Edmund Randolph, the other federalist leader in the most critical state's ratification convention, declared that constitutionalizing the common law "would in many respects be destructive to republican principles," such as enforcing "the writ of burning heretics" and other examples in "many parts of the common law."[94] The argument that the First Amendment, with unrestricted language and without saying so, incorporated the parts of English common law most restrictive of press and speech (the Blackstone-Mansfield definition of freedom of press, and the Blackstone-Mansfield framework of six unique rules for seditious libel) conflicts with its raison d'être, just as much as incorporating common law on conscience and establishment, or on assembly and petition.

[87] 2 WILSON WORKS 1104.

[88] 2 DHSC 167, 189, and the "savage butchery" that "disgraces humanity" of treason penalties, 2 *id.* 145; *accord* 2 *id.* 186, 223 (Iredell). The total of 160 comes from 4 BLACKSTONE'S COMMENTARIES 18, and includes innumerable petty offenses, such as 4 *id.* 238, 56, 93, 97, 99, 124, 131–32, 143.

[89] 2 *id.* 188; *accord* 2 *id.* 314 (Iredell); John H. Langbein, *The Origins of Public Prosecution at Common Law*, 17 AM. J. LEGAL HISTORY 313, 316 (1973).

[90] J.H. Baker, *Criminal Courts and Procedure at Common Law 1550–1800*, in CRIME IN ENGLAND, 1550–1800, at 15, 21–22, 24–25 (J.S. Cockburn ed., PUP, Princeton 1977); JOHN H. LANGBEIN, PROSECUTING CRIME IN THE RENAISSANCE: ENGLAND, GERMANY, FRANCE 16–20, 77–97 (HUP, Cambridge 1974); *id.* 9–15 (excessive bail).

[91] MILSOM 403.

[92] Similarly, the Constitution overturned parts of common law such as defining treason, J.G. BELLAMY, THE LAW OF TREASON IN ENGLAND IN THE LATER MIDDLE AGES 212–15 (CUP, Cambridge 1970); 4 BLACKSTONE'S COMMENTARIES 74–93; and the Revolution jettisoned parts of common law such as conflict of laws rules. William E. Nelson, *The American Revolution and the Emergence of Modern Doctrines of Federalism and Conflict of Laws*, in LAW IN COLONIAL MASSACHUSETTS, 1630–1800, at 419, 441–51 (Colonial Soc. of Mass., Boston 1984).

[93] 11 DHFFC 818, 821–22 (8 June 1789); 16 *id.* 724, 725 (8 June 1789).

[94] 10 DHRC 1353 (17 June 1788); 3 ELLIOT'S DEBATES 469–70; *see* 4 *id.* 63 (MacLaine-N.C.).

Actions of the First Congress Relevant to Federal Adoption of Common Law Crimes and Seditious Libel

The first Congress, in adopting the first Judiciary Act, used language about lower federal court jurisdiction that advocates of a federal common law of crime would cite: they would have "cognizance of all crimes and offences that shall be cognizable under the authority of the United States."[95] Facially, this was silent on common law crimes. If it had given federal courts jurisdiction over common law crimes, the Crimes Act was not needed, because English common law addressed all the crimes it prescribed.

Instead, that first Congress, a half year later, saw the Crimes Act as necessary, and more significantly, did not reference common law crimes, or prescribe a large collection mirroring the common law.[96] Oliver Ellsworth and William Paterson, drafting committee members,[97] said the bill would "define the crimes and offences that will be cognisable under the authority of the United States,"[98] thereby ruling out incorporation of common law crimes as federal crimes, though a decade later they reversed that position. The bill defined federal crimes, and consistent with the assurance that the new federal government was one of enumerated powers, created only federal crimes arising from constitutional provisions.[99] Those crimes were treason, acts on federal military bases and property, acts on high seas and nonstate waters, counterfeiting federal securities, forging federal court records, stealing federal property, other offenses toward federal courts, and offenses toward foreign envoys,[100] along with revenue crimes. It was a draft of this act that made it a crime to "defame, libel, or slander any Ambassador"—a provision that was jettisoned.[101]

In that first Congress, Abraham Baldwin noted that "we have not adopted the common law,"[102] and others acted consistently with that thought. The first Congress showed no objection to federal court enforcement of the law of nations,[103] or definition of non-self-defining terms with common law principles that were not inconsistent with the Bill of Rights,[104] but that was different from incorporating

[95] Judiciary Act §9, 1 Stat.73 (24 Sept.1789); 5 DHFFC 1150, 1153.

[96] PALMER 271–72, 280–84; PREYER 225–26

[97] 6 DHFFC 1741.

[98] Oliver Ellsworth to Charles Chauncey (15 June 1789), Chauncey Family Manuscripts (YUL, Box 2, Folder 17).

[99] An Act for the Punishment of Certain Crimes, 1 Stat. 112 (30 Apr.1790); 6 DHFFC 1733.

[100] *Id.* §§1–2, 3–7, 8–13, 14, 15, 16–17, 18–23, 24–27.

[101] 6 DHFFC 1730 & n.81.

[102] 1 ANNALS 1108 (20 Jan.1790); PALMER 279.

[103] 1 *id.* 828 (29 Aug.1789).

[104] James Wilson's Charge (23 May 1791), 2 DHSC 166, 176; 3 ELLIOT'S DEBATES 531 (Madison).

common law and enforcing common law crimes. The fact that Congress a decade later saw the Sedition Act as necessary also implied that common law did not already create a federal crime of seditious libel.[105]

Statements of the Early Supreme Court Justices for and Against Federal Adoption of Common Law Crimes and Seditious Libel

The first Supreme Court justices individually addressed the issue of whether there are federal crimes under common law. Levy assured us that "[a]ll the early Supreme Court judges . . . assumed the existence of a federal common law of crimes,"[106] Stewart Jay called them "virtually unanimous," and Horwitz and others concurred.[107] With equal confidence, Preyer stated that the evidence "is hardly conclusive for the proposition that there was a widely shared view among the early federal judges supportive of a federal common law of crimes," finding "only Wilson, Jay, Iredell and Ellsworth" to share that view.[108] Her characterization of Wilson's and Jay's views, and Iredell's before 1796, was overblown, as their grand jury charges and opinions show, though as 1798 arrived Ellsworth and other sitting justices shifted as they entered the fray over the Sedition Act. Palmer was most accurate in finding little acceptance of *federal* common law by any justices until 1797.[109]

The early Supreme Court justices, when they traveled on circuit, charged grand juries, and tried cases, generally treated the body of federal crimes as those proscribed in express federal laws and those supported by express constitutional provisions. Before the Crimes Act was passed in April 1790, Jay, after discussing the law of nations and federal revenue laws, ended his charge by addressing official corruption and encouraging indictment of "all offences of every kind committed against the United States,"[110] which Palmer persuasively found to refer to statutes and the law of nations.[111] Jay with Cushing then presided over an indictment and trial for

[105] 2 History of Supreme Court 638; Anderson 505.

[106] Levy-Liberty 29; *accord id.* 275.

[107] Jay 1016; Morton J. Horwitz, Transformation of American Law, 1780–1860, at 9 (HUP, Cambridge 1977); *accord* 1 Warren 433; Misunderstanding 96; Stephen B. Presser, *A Tale of Two Judges: Richard Peters, Samuel Chase, and the Broken Promise of Federalist Jurisprudence*, 73 Nw. L. Rev. 26, 70 (1978); Ellsworth 115; Reclaiming 44 (except Chase); Repressive Jurisprudence 5 n.6.

[108] Kathryn Preyer, *Jurisdiction To Punish: Federal Authority, Federalism and the Common Law of Crimes in the Early Republic*, 4 Law & History Rev. 223, 231 (1986); *accord* Levy 279. Warren and Presser add Justices Patterson, Washington, and Cushing. 1 Warren 433–34; Stephen B. Presser, *The Supra-Constitution, the Courts, and the Federal Common Law of Crimes: Some Comments on Palmer and Preyer*, 4 Law & History Rev. 325, 326 (1986).

[109] Palmer 272, 285–306; *accord* 1 History of Supreme Court 229–30, 496, 623–33.

[110] John Jay's Charge (12 Apr. 1790), 2 DHSC 25, 30; Notes, 1 *id.* 8 (13–14 Apr. 1790).

[111] Palmer 289–90 n.145; *contra* Jay 1040.

mutiny and murder on the high seas, which was consistent with his reference to the law of nations, admiralty, and maritime jurisdiction.[112] Wilson listed only treason under the Constitution and acts criminalized by revenue laws,[113] and Cushing, urging completion of the criminal statute, feared "what predicament our courts will be [in] as to carrying into execution punishments for pyracies & felonies on the h[igh] seas & some other matters."[114] Earlier during ratification debates, Iredell had stated that Congress "have no power to define any other crime whatever."[115]

After the Crimes Act was passed, Wilson "enumerated . . . the crimes and offences known to the constitution and the laws of the United States" by listing every offence in that act and in revenue acts, and identified the role of the common law as "for the definition or description of the crimes and offences, which, in the laws of the United States, have been *named,* but have not been *described* or *defined.*"[116] That statement is inconsistent with belief that the common law created additional federal crimes, but consistent with Wilson's statement at the Constitutional Convention that strictness or precision is "necessary in enacting" federal criminal laws.[117] Jay, consistent with his earlier misunderstood charge, now identified crimes under the penal law and excise laws, and under the law of nations and treaties,[118] but did not list crimes under common law. Iredell, agreeing that crimes should be specified "by fixed and general laws," read the Crimes Act in its entirety to the grand jury,[119] and later stressed the "express authority given in the Constitution to define and punish" the various crimes including "offences against the law of nations."[120] Even in 1795, he described federal "authority in regard to the criminal law" by listing the specific constitutional provisions for punishing crimes.[121] That same year, Paterson stated that "the penal code of the U. States is

[112] *Cf.* Palmer 286–90.

[113] James Wilson's Charge (12 Apr.1790), 2 DHSC 33, 42–44.

[114] William Cushing to John Lowell (4 Apr.1790), 2 DHSC 21, 22.

[115] 4 Elliot's Debates 219 (30 July 1788); *accord* Marcus [James Iredell], *Answers to Mr. Mason's Objections* (1788), in 16 DHRC 379, 381.

[116] James Wilson's Charge (23 May 1791), 2 DHSC 166, 181, 176; James Wilson's Charge (21 Feb.1791), 2 *id.* 142, 144–52, 147; *accord* 2 Wilson Works 1104 (listing all federal crimes); *contra* Jay 1041.

[117] 3 Farrand's Records 315 (17 Aug.1787); *accord* 1 Wilson Works 226.

[118] John Jay's Charge (5 Apr.1792), 2 DHSC 253, 255–56; John Jay's Charge (25 June 1792), 2 *id.* 282, 283–85; John Jay's Charge (22 May 1793) (under Neutrality Proclamation), 2 *id.* 380, 381; *see* Jay 1045. He stated that Congress could criminalize "oppos[ing] the operation of this Constitution and of the Government," apparently when by armed force, but did not claim judicial capability of prosecuting it without statute. 2 *id.* 390.

[119] James Iredell's Charge (17 Oct.1791), 2 DHSC 216, 219, 220; *see* James Iredell's Charge (26 Apr.1792), 2 *id.* 263, 264, 265; James Iredell's Charge (12 Oct.1792), 2 *id.* 308, 314–15.

[120] James Iredell's Charge (2 Apr.1793), 2 DHSC 348, 355; *accord* 2 *id.* 268; 3 *id.* 19, 79–80; Jay 1041; *see* United States v. Mundel, 10 Va. (6 Call) 245, 257 (C.C.D. Va. 1795).

[121] James Iredell's Charge (6 Apr.1795), 3 DHSC 14, 19.

plain and concise, and reduced, in its most important points, to written exactitude and precision," before describing several provisions of the criminal code.[122] The other justices continued defining crimes in that manner until partisan escalation in 1797,[123] and added violations of the Neutrality Proclamation of 1793[124] and Neutrality Act of 1794,[125] and treason during the Whiskey Rebellion.[126]

Though Iredell spoke of the law of nations[127] when he stated that "the common law therefore as to such offences [of neutrality] is still in force,"[128] he became the first to break out of the box of constitutional and statutory crimes (including the law of nations) in 1796, when he stated that a violation of the law of nations "is an offence at common law, in the same manner . . . as any other offence committed against the common law," when no federal statute addressed the act.[129] Not until 1798 did Iredell apply that to seditious libel, nor did any other justices begin to join him, except Blair, who off the bench in 1797 acted as if common law crimes existed.[130] Thus, before the political polarization leading to the Sedition Act of 1798, no grand jury charge or opinion from a Supreme Court justice expressly took the position that all common law crimes were indictable as federal crimes (though Iredell implied that in 1796 and Chase rejected that in early 1798), or the position that seditious libel was indictable. Yet if proponents of a federal common law of crime are correct, all the justices should have done so, even before the Crimes Act created the first federal crimes. Instead, John Marshall, in the midst of partisan strife and differing with his party in 1800, denied that even "one man can be found who maintains" that the common law of England was "adopted as the common law of America by the constitution."[131]

[122] William Paterson's Charge (4 May 1795), 3 *id.* 40, 41; *accord* William Paterson's Charge (2 Apr.1795), 3 *id.* 10, 11.

[123] James Iredell's Charge (6 Apr.1795), 3 *id.* 14, 19–22; James Iredell's Charge (25 Apr.1795), 3 *id.* 28, 30; John Blair's Charge (27 Apr.1795), 3 *id.* 31, 37; [Oliver Ellsworth], ESSAYS-CONSTITUTION 155, 159, 164.

[124] James Wilson's Charge (22 July 1793), 2 DHSC 414, 420–21; James Iredell's Charge (12 May 1794), 2 *id.* 454, 455–57, 459–61.

[125] William Cushing's Charge (7 Nov.1794), 2 *id.* 491, 495, as well as statutory crimes, 493–94; William Paterson's Charge (8 June 1795), 3 *id.* 57, 58.

[126] John Blair's Charge (27 Apr.1795), 3 DHSC 31, 32; William Paterson's Charge (4 May 1795), 3 *id.* 40, 41–42; James Iredell's Charge (23 Nov.1795), 3 *id.* 74, 77–78.

[127] PALMER 299, 301; *contra* JAY 1041.

[128] James Iredell's Charge (12 May 1794), 2 DHSC 454, 469, 467; *see* James Iredell's Charge (23 Nov.1795), 3 *id.* 74, 75; PALMER 299. Paterson agreed in a draft charge, PATERSON PAPERS-NYPL, which Stewart Jay called an "original," JAY 1052 n.243, but which is a nineteenth-century handwritten copy of the original at Rutgers.

[129] James Iredell's Charge (12 Apr.1796), 3 *id.* 106, 111.

[130] Oliver Ellsworth's Charge (7 May 1799), 3 *id.* 357, 358; PATERSON'S DRAFT OPINIONS 45–46; Presentment of the Grand Jury (22 May 1797), 3 DHSC 181. 1798 is where Levy's summary begins of the justices' charges. *See* LEVY 277–78.

[131] John Marshall to St. George Tucker (27 Nov.1800), 6 MARSHALL PAPERS 23; cited in PREYER 237 n.47; JAY 1326–28.

Decisions of the Early Supreme Court Justices about Federal Common Law Crimes and Seditious Libel

The early justices' decisions in circuit courts were consistent with their grand jury charges, though their decisions in *Henfield's Case,*[132] *Ravara,*[133] *Smith,*[134] and other cases have been cited to show acceptance of federal common law of crimes. Much of the confusion arises from inverting the common statement that the law of nations was "adopted in" the common law,[135] into an assertion that prosecution under the law of nations was identical to prosecution under all the common law. Instead, the early justices generally used law of nations references and authorities in decisions, not to import the entire common law,[136] but to implement constitutional provisions empowering Congress "[t]o define and punish . . . offences against the law of nations" (and under corresponding Crimes Act sections), or empowering the courts to adjudicate "cases affecting ambassadors, other public ministers and consuls" (and corresponding Crimes Act sections) and "admiralty and maritime jurisdiction."[137]

Thus, *Henfield's Case,* in which Wilson and Iredell allowed federal prosecution for treaty violations, was under the law of nations and treaties,[138] not under general common law.[139] *United States v. Ravara,* in which the same justices sanctioned federal court indictment of a foreign consul, likewise was under constitutional and statutory jurisdiction involving consuls,[140] not under general common law.[141] *Wiscart v. Dauchy,* in which Ellsworth ruled an enabling statute is required for appellate jurisdiction,[142] did not recognize federal common law, and in fact would seem to preclude it because there was no enabling statute. *United States v. Smith,* in which unnamed justices permitted federal prosecution for counterfeiting bills of the congressionally authorized Bank of the United States, stated that it arose under federal law and, without federal statutory punishments, that it used punishments under state law, while noting that the offense could also be prosecuted under *state*

[132] Charles G. Haines, The Role of the Supreme Court 126–27 (UCalP, Berkeley 1944); Editor's note in Henfield's Case, 11 F.Cas.1099, 1099 n.1 (C.C.D. Pa.1793); 1 Wilson Works xxiv; Levy 126; *see* Jay 1253.

[133] *Id.* 126; Levy 126.

[134] Editor's headnote in United States v. Smith, 27 F.Cas.1147, 1147 (C.C.D. Mass. [1797]) (No.16,323); Levy 126.

[135] *See* 4 Blackstone's Commentaries 67.

[136] Palmer 275 n.61.

[137] U.S.Const. art.I, §8, cl.10; art.III, §2; *accord* Federalist No.42, at 279.

[138] 11 F.Cas. at 1120; *see* Palmer 290–99. They were joined by a district judge, Peters.

[139] 1 History of Supreme Court 624; Preyer 230; *cf.* Jay 1054.

[140] United States v. Ravara, 27 F.Cas.713, 714 (C.C.D. Pa. 1793) (Nos.16,122, 16,122a); *see* Palmer 301–05; Jay 1063–64.

[141] *Se* 1 History of Supreme Court 627; Preyer 230.

[142] Wiscart v. Dauchy, 3 U.S. (3 Dall.) 321, 327 (1796); *see* Palmer 306–09.

common law in state courts.[143] That obviously did not affirm a general federal common law of crimes,[144] but instead adapted the Judiciary Act authorization for federal diversity cases to use state law including state common law.[145] In *United States v. Worrall,* Chase split the panel by holding that "the United States, as a federal government, have no common law."[146] However, he did not hold that position for long because he immediately joined in sentencing Worrall,[147] and then "reversed himself" a year later[148] after helping establish the necessity of the Sedition Act (as discussed in Chapter 6, though some argue his opposition continued[149]).

As the crisis of 1798 arrived, several justices did begin to support federal common law crimes including seditious libel in cases,[150] as well as in grand jury charges.[151] However, *United States v. McGill* is not one of them, though it is called "the clearest case" of endorsing the concept.[152] Its sentence beginning that "federal courts have a common law jurisdiction in criminal cases" is less quoted for its ending: coming under "admiralty and maritime jurisdiction" rather than common law, and without an enabling act, "the indictment cannot be sustained."[153] The status of federal common law of crimes was finally resolved in 1812, when the Marshall Court[154] ruled that there is none, in a case involving libels against the President and Congress.[155]

[143] United States v. Smith, 27 F.Cas.1147, 1147–48 (C.C.D. Mass. [1797]) (No.16,323); *see* PALMER 212–14; JAY 1064 n.306. Its reported date was corrected by Goebel. 1 HISTORY OF SUPREME COURT 630 n.82; PALMER 212 n.282.

[144] 1 HISTORY OF SUPREME COURT 630; PREYER 230.

[145] Judiciary Act §34, 1 Stat. 92.

[146] United States v. Worrall, 28 F.Cas.774, 779 (C.C.D. Pa. 1798) (No.16,766). Judge Peters disagreed, *id.* 779–80. *See* 1 HISTORY OF SUPREME COURT 631–33; JAY 1067–73.

[147] Editor's note, *id.* 780 n.; Wharton's State Trials 199 n.

[148] Stephen B. Presser & Becky B. Hurley, *Saving God's Republic: The Jurisprudence of Samuel Chase,* 1984 U. ILL. L. REV. 771, 796 n.164, 798–99; 3 DHSC 322 n.29; LEVY 278 & n.146; *contra* JAY 1070 n.332.

[149] PREYER 235–36; *id.* 240, citing Richard Peters to Timothy Pickering (8 Dec.1806), 27 PICKERING PAPERS 334; Richard Peters to Timothy Pickering (5 Dec.1807), 28 *id.* 99.

[150] United States v. Greenleaf, discussed in 1 HISTORY OF SUPREME COURT 629; PREYER 230; PALMER 305–06; *contra* LEVY 276; *accord In re* Anonymous, 1 F.Cas.1032 (C.C.D. Pa. 1804) (Washington, J.); *see* Williams's Case, 29 F.Cas.1330, 1331 (C.C.D. Conn. 1799) (No.17,708) (Ellsworth, C.J.); PALMER 319 n.330; *contra* LEVY 277 & n.142; JAY 1086 n.406.

[151] Oliver Ellsworth's Charge (C.C.D. S.C. 7 May 1799), 3 DHSC 357, 357–58; 45 (n.d.); PATERSON THIRD OPINION 530 (n.d.).

[152] JAY 1017 n.52.

[153] United States v. McGill, 26 F.Cas.1088, 1090 (C.C.D. Pa. 1806) (No.15,676); *see* PALMER 276 n.62.

[154] A biographer suggests Marshall disagreed, ROBERT K. FAULKNER, THE JURISPRUDENCE OF JOHN MARSHALL 88 (PUP, Princeton 1968); JAY 1332–33; but that is incorrect, John Marshall to St. George Tucker (27 Nov.1800), 6 MARSHALL PAPERS 23, 24; *accord* PREYER 246–47; R. KENT NEWMYER, SUPREME COURT JUSTICE JOSEPH STORY 101 (UNCP, Chapel Hill 1985).

[155] United States v. Hudson & Goodwin, 11 U.S. (7 Cranch) 32, 34 (1812) (Johnson, J.); *accord* United States v. Coolidge, 14 U.S. (1 Wheat.) 415 (1816); Wheaton v. Peters, 33 U.S. (8 Pet.) 591,

Even so, the First Amendment status of seditious libel had to wait a century and a half for its denouement, until 1964, in *New York Times Co. v. Sullivan* and *Garrison v. Louisiana*.[156] Even then, seditious libel was not held unconstitutional under the First Amendment, but was only held contrary to long-standing public opinion, "the court of history."[157] The continuing travails of criminal libel in nineteenth-century America, after the period covered here, are interestingly chronicled by Blumberg.[158]

How could the early justices divide over federal common law crimes, the definition of freedoms of press and speech, and the Sedition Act? That was closely related to their division over the right to dissent.

Differing Understandings of Limits to the Right of Dissent, or of the Scope of Freedoms of Press and Speech

Hand-in-hand with debate before the American Revolution about the scope of liberties of press and speech was debate about the scope of legitimate dissent, and ultimately about the characteristics of republicanism. As the Constitution was framed in 1787, permanent political parties did not exist in the states, and federalists widely expected that the new government's administration would be as generally supported as George Washington would soon be for president. Would it be legitimate or not to oppose the administration, and for an ongoing opposition to be formed? Also, English Whigs had long proclaimed a right of revolution against usurpation, when unjust laws could be deemed void and disobeyed. Was there ever a time short of a new revolution when citizens could treat laws as void, and disobey them? The new general government would start with few statutes, and much of the

658 (1834); *see* PREYER 242–49, 253–61. For the history of civil federal common law, *see* Note, *Federal Common Law and Article III: A Jurisdictional Approach to Erie*, 74 YALE L.J. 325 (1964).

[156] New York Times Co. v. Sullivan, 376 U.S. 254, 272–73, 273–77 (1964) (civil libel restricted and Sedition Act questioned); *see* Garrison v. Louisiana, 379 U.S. 64, 74–78 (1964) (criminal libel restricted but not invalidated); Robert C. Post, *The Social Foundations of Defamation Law: Reputation and the Constitution*, 74 CAL. L. REV. 691, 721–39 (1986). For an insightful overview of doctrinal factors and social currents, *see* Robert C. Post, *Defaming Public Officials: On Doctrine and Legal History*, 12 AM. BAR FOUNDATION RESEARCH J. 539, 542–46, 550–57 (1987).

[157] New York Times Co. v. Sullivan, 376 U.S. at 276.

[158] PHILLIP L. BLUMBERG, REPRESSIVE JURISPRUDENCE IN THE EARLY AMERICAN REPUBLIC: THE FIRST AMENDMENT AND THE LEGACY OF ENGLISH LAW 8–12, 148–373 (CUP, Cambridge 2010); *accord* Alfred H. Kelly, *Constitutional Liberty and the Law of Libel: A Historian's View*, 74 AM. HISTORICAL REV. 429, 432–52 (1968); Michael T. Gibson, *The Supreme Court and Freedom of Expression from 1791 to 1917*, 55 FORDHAM L. REV. 263, 266–67 n.15 (1986); Norman L. Rosenberg, *The Law of Political Libel and Freedom of the Press in Nineteenth Century America: An Interpretation*, 17 AM. J. LEGAL HISTORY 336, 337–52 (1973).

English legal heritage was common law. Would the new government carry over English common law, with federal courts exercising common law jurisdiction in addition to constitutionally conferred jurisdiction, and as part of that would it carry over English common law restrictions on liberty of press and liberty of speech?

The early justices of the Supreme Court held divergent views about these issues, which defined the limits of legitimate dissent, and that divergence was a major reason for their later division over the Sedition Act. Their positions derived principally from the English legal history of the right to dissent, and fell into at least seven principal points of disagreement: (1) the legitimacy of factions and parties, (2) the legitimacy of opposition to the existing administration, (3) a right to evaluate laws as illegal and void, (4) a right to disobey unconstitutional laws, (5) the nonextension of treason to an opposition, (6) the nonexistence of a federal common law of crimes, and, most importantly, (7) the effect of state and federal provisions for freedoms of press and speech on the Blackstone-Mansfield definition and on seditious libel law. Though different, these views parallel the "two strains of English and American jurisprudence" described by Presser, and the two strains of Federalism described by Dauer.[159]

The ongoing American debate was not the first time those issues had been faced, though it was the first time they had been confronted all at once and with the complicating factor of new declarations of rights. Parallel divergences had distinguished Grotius from Sidney, Locke, and other republicans,[160] the moderate Whigs from radical Whigs in and after 1688,[161] the New Whigs from Old Whigs of Hanoverian times,[162] and classical republicans and Federalists from liberals and Republicans.[163] Such Grotian-moderate Whig[164] and Lockean-radical Whig differences about the permitted scope of dissent and the nature of republicanism continued to influence the constitutional generation's beliefs and the early justices' beliefs. For example, Iredell and Chase viewed Grotius as "of very high authority,"[165] while Wilson was highly critical of Grotius[166] but laudatory toward

[159] MISUNDERSTANDING 9, 47–54; SAVING 777–78, 784–85, 788–90; MANNING J. DAUER, THE ADAMS FEDERALISTS 218–37, 266–67 (JHUP, Baltimore 1953).

[160] *E.g.*, 2 JOHN LOCKE, TWO TREATISES OF GOVERNMENT ¶¶202, 206, 207, 222, 223–30, 228, 232, 237–39, 242 (Black Swan, London 1698); *accord* ASHCRAFT 297, 307, 305, 315, 319.

[161] ROBBINS 82–83, 84; DICKINSON 126–28.

[162] 3 BURKE 44, 115; KENYON 170.

[163] JOYCE O. APPLEBY, CAPITALISM AND A NEW SOCIAL ORDER: THE REPUBLICAN VISION OF THE 1790S, at 22 (NYUP, New York 1984).

[164] RICHARD TUCK, NATURAL RIGHTS THEORIES: THEIR ORIGIN AND DEVELOPMENT 58 (CUP, Cambridge 1979); KENYON 31; MICHAEL P. ZUCKERT, NATURAL RIGHTS AND THE NEW REPUBLICANISM 119 (PUP, Princeton 1994).

[165] Talbot v. Janson, 3 U.S. (3 Dall.) 133, 160 (1795); Ware v. Hylton, 3 U.S. (3 Dall.) 199, 230, 258–59 (1796).

[166] 1 WILSON WORKS 480–82, 528–29; WILSON 37, 43–45.

Locke.[167] Those differences included belief in noncontractarian[168] or singular contract theories[169] versus full contractarianism;[170] in natural law without natural equality[171] or original sovereignty in the people[172] versus natural law with both; in surrender of rights to civil government[173] versus retention of inalienable rights;[174] in narrow natural rights[175] versus extensive natural rights;[176] in a very limited right of revolution[177] versus an ongoing right to resist tyranny;[178] and in acceptance of mere freedom from prior restraint versus insistence also on freedom from subsequent punishment for press and speech. The influences on the American debate were both classical republican and Lockean liberal ones, though the former more guided the High Federalists and the latter more guided the Republican Party and some moderate Federalists.

The divergence on each of those issues had echoed through much of English legal history, and it continued to appear in statements by the early justices of the Supreme Court.

Illegitimacy of Parties and Factions?

Classical and English history and philosophy condemned parties and factions. Alexander Pope pronounced a "curse on the word *party*,"[179] and David Hume

[167] 1 *id.* at 213, 433, 473, 484, 604–05, 610.

[168] Dickinson 65, 132–40; *accord* English Society 56, 55, 57; Zuckert 105.

[169] Zuckert 105, 106–13, 120; Kenyon 7–8; Dickinson 61; Tuck 77, 68; Harro Höpfl and Martyn P. Thompson, *The History of Contract as Motif in Political Thought*, 84 Am. Historical Rev. 919, 937–41 (1979) (taxonomy of contractarianisms).

[170] Richard Ashcraft, Revolutionary Politics & Locke's Two Treatises of Government 193–96, 560, 563 (PUP, Princeton 1986); Kenyon 57–58; 2 Locke ¶¶149, 212–17, 219, 220, 221, 224–28, 243.

[171] Zuckert 104; Ashcraft 210.

[172] Zuckert 111; John N. Figgis, Studies of Political Thought from Gerson to Grotius 185 (2d ed., CUP, Cambridge 1916 repr. 1956); Tuck 78; Hugo Grotius, The Law of War and Peace Bk I, c3.8.1 (new ed. Johan Bleu, Amsterdam 1646); *see id.* Bk I, c3.8.14.

[173] Tuck 79–80, 66, 71, 77–78; Zuckert 111; Knud Haakonssen, *Hugo Grotius and the History of Political Thought*, in 2 Grotius 343 (John Dunn & Ian Harris eds., Edward Elgar, Cheltenham 1997); Grotius Bk I, c1.3.8, c3.8.3, c4.2, 6.

[174] Ashcraft 397–98; Dickinson 58; 2 Locke ¶¶23, 24, 209, 220, 222 *passim.*

[175] Zuckert 141; Tuck 67, 74–75; David Kennedy, *Primitive Legal Scholarship*, 27 Harv. International L.J. 1, 87–88 (1986); Haakonssen, *supra* note 173, at 342; Grotius Bk I, c3.8.1, c3.8.4, c4.7.7 (speech); *see id.* c3.16.1.

[176] Ashcraft 577; Robbins 76; Dickinson 65, 66, 67; Dickinson-Politics 192, 193; 2 Locke ¶¶149, 119, 243.

[177] Tuck 78–79, 63, 65; Zuckert 115, 123; Haakonssen, *supra* note 173, at 344; Jonathan Scott, Commonwealth Principles: Republican Writing of the English Revolution 110–11 (CUP, Cambridge 2004); Grotius Bk I, c4.2.1, 4.6.1, 4.9–11 (abdicating, alienating kingdom, openly enemy of people), 4.13, 4.15.1, 4.19.1, 3.8.1, 3.16.1; *cf.* Dickinson 131 (Blackstone).

cautioned that "[f]actions subvert government, render laws impotent, and beget the fiercest animosities."[180] Yet eighteenth-century parties dominated Britain (both Tory-Whig[181] and Court-Country[182])—though each party generally denied its existence while giving dire warnings about opposing factions and parties.[183]

American colonists generally attributed factions to the corruption of the English court and legislature,[184] and similarly condemned them.[185] Madison's famous discussion of "the spirit of party and faction" in *The Federalist* treated it as baneful, though inevitable, like crime "sown in the nature of man."[186] Similar views prevailed in the 1790s.[187] Because Americans in the 1790s expected "civic harmony and consensus," they "unconsciously interpreted political events along *sectional* and *partisan* lines," as Sharp described, and "with great conviction and great sincerity . . . could believe that [their] policies *alone* reflected and served the national public good."[188] Thus, once the federalist–anti-federalist debates ended, there were no defined parties. As the political elites failed to achieve consensus, divisions deepened and "interests" or "proto-parties" emerged during 1792–1798, and even in the "crisis of the union" during 1798–1801, the word "party" was

---

[178] ZUCKERT 216–88; DICKINSON 61–62, 65, 66, 67, 70, 77; ASHCRAFT 190, 315; ROBBINS 3, 40 (Sidney), 70 (radical Whigs, Tyrrell), 76 (Somers), 183 (Hutcheson); KENYON 52, 46, 57, 156; ENGLISH SOCIETY 219, 239; DICKINSON-POLITICS 171 (radical Whigs and Locke); 2 LOCKE ¶¶134, 231, 233 *passim*; [MATTHEW TINDAL], *Of Obedience to the Supreme Powers*, in FOUR DISCOURSES 1 (n.p., London 1709).

[179] Alexander Pope to Charles Jervas (27 Aug.1714), 2 THE CORRESPONDENCE OF ALEXANDER POPE 244, 245 (George Sherburn ed., CP, Oxford 1956).

[180] DAVID HUME, *Of Parties in General* (1742), in ESSAYS MORAL, POLITICAL AND LITERARY 54, 55 (OUP, Oxford 1963).

[181] DICKINSON 8, 13–90; CLAYTON ROBERTS, THE GROWTH OF RESPONSIBLE GOVERNMENT IN STUART ENGLAND 197–99 (CUP, Cambridge 1966 repr. 2008).

[182] DICKINSON 121–23, 123–92, revised by DICKINSON-POLITICS 198–99 (from c.1714–1760s).

[183] [JOHN DOUGLAS], SEASONABLE HINTS FROM AN HONEST MAN ON THE PRESENT IMPORTANT CRISIS 18–34 (A. Millar, London 1761); ROBBINS 47 (Marchamont Needham), 50 (Andrew Marvell), 287 (Edward Montagu), 303 (John Brown); *accord* DICKINSON 153–54; BREWER-PARTY 39–54, 55–76; ALISON G. OLSON, ANGLO-AMERICAN POLITICS, 1660–1775, at 159–82 (OUP, Oxford 1973).

[184] 1 WILSON WORKS 733; DICKINSON 102, 110, 112, 169–75; DICKINSON-POLITICS 175.

[185] BERNARD BAILYN, THE ORIGINS OF AMERICAN POLITICS 64–65 (Knopf, New York 1968); FEDERALISM 533; 1 WILSON WORKS 427, 733; 1 AMES WORKS 260.

[186] FEDERALIST No.10, at 59, 58, 61 (Madison); *accord* MORTON WHITE, PHILOSOPHY, THE FEDERALIST, AND THE CONSTITUTION 56–61, 72–74 (OUP, Oxford 1987).

[187] *E.g.*, EMPIRE 207; CRISIS 10–11; RICHARD HOFSTADTER, THE IDEA OF A PARTY SYSTEM: THE RISE OF LEGITIMATE OPPOSITION IN THE UNITED STATES, 1780–1840, at 80–121 (UCP, Berkeley 1969).

[188] JAMES R. SHARP, AMERICAN POLITICS IN THE EARLY REPUBLIC 276 (YUP, New Haven 1993); *see* CREATION 57.

generally applied to political adversaries and not to political allies, who instead were seen as "virtuous" servants of the "common good."[189]

Newspapers became visible representatives of less visible but incipient political parties.[190] An opposition press was of disputed legitimacy, just as an opposition political party was, particularly given the colonial background of nominal newspaper neutrality[191] and the 1790s change to sharp partisanship in many papers.[192] Some newspapers, like many politicians, defined only support of the administration as nonpartisan.[193] Others, however, had long "challenged religious and political authority," and continued to carry on robust journalism with the newly adopted partisan edge, as Smith noted.[194] In that atmosphere, it was not surprising that opposition newspapers, along with opposition politicians, were the primary targets of the Sedition Act.

A few of the early Supreme Court justices reacted mildly to faction and party. Jay initially shared the common fear that factions opposing the ineffectual confederation might produce tyranny,[195] though he also noted the coexistence of two parties in Pennsylvania.[196] During the ratification debates, he lamented that America had "unhappily become divided into parties," federalist and antifederalist.[197] By the time debate raged over his treaty in 1795, Jay viewed parties as unfortunate but legitimate: "Differences in opinion, and other causes equally pure and natural, will unavoidably cause parties; . . . and are probably no less conducive to good government, than moderate fermentation is necessary to make good wine."[198] Wilson, while attributing English parties to corrupt bestowal of offices and hoping to avoid American parties as he wrote in 1790–1791,[199] acknowledged that even "friends of freedom . . . unanimous in their sentiments" could disagree

[189] *Id.* at 15–50, 51–184, 187–275, 232; *accord* Joanne B. Freeman, *The Election of 1800*, 108 YALE L.J. 1959, 1960 (1999).

[190] Note: Jefferson, Freneau, and the Founding of the National Gazette, 20 JEFFERSON PAPERS 718–53; Alexander Hamilton to Rufus King (11 Nov.1793), 15 HAMILTON PAPERS 395–96; TYRANNY 51–59, 60–78.

[191] OPEN PRESS 55–58; TYRANNY 27–28.

[192] TYRANNY 22–23; 20 JEFFERSON PAPERS 749n.; MARCUS DANIEL, SCANDAL AND CIVILITY: JOURNALISM AND THE BIRTH OF AMERICAN DEMOCRACY 8 (OUP, Oxford 2009), sometimes as printers reconceived themselves as "editor-authors," *id.* at 7.

[193] TYRANNY 55–56.

[194] PRINTERS 162, 7; *accord* EMPIRE 251–56.

[195] John Jay to Thomas Jefferson (27 Oct.1786), 3 JAY CORRESPONDENCE at 212, 213; *accord id.* at 174, 188.

[196] John Jay to John Adams (14 Oct.1785), 3 *id.* at 172, 174; John Jay to Francis Hopkinson (29 Mar.1786), 3 *id.* at 187, 188.

[197] John Jay, An Address to the People of the State of New York (1788), 3 *id.* at 294; *accord id.* at 311.

[198] John Jay to Gen. Henry Lee (11 July 1795), 4 *id.* at 178, 178–79; *accord id.* 261, 262.

[199] 1 James Wilson, *Lectures on Law* (1790–1791), WILSON WORKS 427, 733, 705.

on measures and timing.[200] Blair affirmed that citizens have a right to think of government as they please, even in sharp disagreements.[201]

Most successor justices, by contrast, anathematized faction and party. Paterson combined that with aversion to the French Revolution as he excoriated a "party-spirit" as "the madness of many for the gain of a few," which delighted in blood, as in France.[202] Ominously, his next paragraph painted American newspapers with the same brush, finding "no station so elevated, no character so pure, . . . as to escape the malignant breath of faction."[203] Earlier, Chase had been quick to attribute intrigues, including his exclusion from Congress, to "party and faction."[204] During the federalist–anti-federalist debates, Ellsworth worried that "a thousand existing factions, and acts of public injustice, thro' the temporary influence of parties," might lead to anarchy, which in turn would bring a usurper and tyranny.[205] As parties began to appear, Iredell equated the Federalist Party with the government, and described the Republicans as "the little barkings of ill-humor which are now perpetually assailing our ears."[206] Paterson still inveighed about the menace of those who are "a fool to party, or a madman in politics."[207] He protested in 1797 that "it is high time that we should be done with parties."[208] Ellsworth deplored "a spirit of party" whose "object still is to sep[a]rate the people from the government."[209] After Sedition Act prosecutions began, Iredell complained that "ever since the first formation of the present government, every act which any extraordinary difficulty has occasioned, has been uniformly opposed," and every "effort[] made to vilify and undermine the government," by the minority that trumpeted "republicanism, the perpetual theme of their declamation."[210] Cushing denounced "the clamors of faction, the unaccountable rage of pretended patriots to subvert the government" to foreign interests, including newspapers that proclaimed the "same evil spirit" of democratic societies "set up to pull down

200 1 *id.* at 710, 695, 701.

201 John Blair's Charge (C.C.D. Del. 27 Oct.1794), 2 DHSC 485, 489; *accord* 3 DHSC 35–36.

202 William Paterson, July 4 Oration (c.1792), PATERSON PAPERS-LC 2; *accord* William Paterson, Jury Charge (n.d.), PATERSON LEGAL PAPERS-LC 3; PATERSON ESSAYS 7 (c.1789).

203 *Id.*

204 Censor [Samuel Chase], *Censor IV*, MARYLAND GAZETTE (Annapolis), 21 June 1781, in 3 CARROLL PAPERS 1449, 1450, 1454.

205 Landholder [Oliver Ellsworth], *Landholder IX*, in ESSAYS-CONSTITUTION 178, 179–80.

206 James Iredell to James Wilson (24 Nov.1794), 2 IREDELL CORRESPONDENCE 429; *accord* 1 IREDELL PAPERS 383.

207 PATERSON ESSAYS 56 (at time Jay Treaty was public and debated, *id.* 56–57); *accord* 3 DHSC 57; 2 IREDELL CORRESPONDENCE 495, 496.

208 William Paterson to James Iredell (7 Mar.1797), 2 IREDELL CORRESPONDENCE 495.

209 Oliver Ellsworth's Charge (C.C.D. N.Y. 1 Apr.1797), 3 DHSC 158, 158–59; *accord* 3 *id.* at 119.

210 James Iredell's Charge (C.C.D. Pa. 11 Apr.1799), 3 DHSC 332, 350.

free republics" that spoke in "unbounded licentiousness . . . by the grossest misrepresentation of public men; and almost every measure."[211]

Illegitimacy of Opposition to the Present Administration?

Even after English dissent ceased to be ipso facto treason, opposition to the King's ministers remained at risk of being treated as sedition. Because of the King's role as head of state, disagreement with the administration was readily characterized by the ministry as challenge to the King, but was defended by those opposing the ministry as challenge to wrongdoing by his "evil counsellors" and "wicked ministers."[212] Some seventeenth-century laws overtly demanded support of the administration, particularly after the Stuart monarchy was restored. The Act for Preservation of the King prohibited words endeavoring "a change of government either in church or state,"[213] and the Act of Uniformity of 1662 required oaths by Anglican clergy forswearing "any alteration of government either in Church or State."[214] The eighteenth century still saw widespread condemnation of "opposition to the king's ministers" as faction, sedition, or even treason.[215]

Colonial America, still "dominantly British and traditional" as the Revolution approached,[216] embodied most of English society's deference and hierarchical assumptions,[217] including to the King and his ministers. Postrevolutionary America continued to reflect widespread belief that opposition to the administration, or at least to its leader, was illegitimate.[218] The "cultural context" of that continuing belief, and ultimately of the Sedition Act, was concern that America's new government was so fragile that it would survive or collapse with the public's confidence in the character of its officials, as Freeman has described, so that the government was attacked when its officials were publicly criticized.[219]

211 William Cushing's Charge (C.C.D. Va. 23 Nov.1798), 3 DHSC 305, 306.

212 1 BLACKSTONE'S COMMENTARIES 237; *accord* DICKINSON-POLITICS 206.

213 Act for the Preservation of the King §§ II, III (1661), 13 Car 2, stat 1, c1.

214 8 EHD 377, 379–80; *accord* 8 *id.* at 382, 383.

215 DICKINSON 175, 178–81. Even defenders of parties distinguished factions. 1 EDMUND BURKE, *Thoughts on the Cause of the Present Discontents*, WORKS OF EDMUND BURKE 306, 375 (Bohn's Standard Library, London 1886).

216 GORDON S. WOOD, THE RADICALISM OF THE AMERICAN REVOLUTION 12–13 (Knopf, New York 1992); *id.* 15–16, 20–23, 24–42.

217 DICKINSON 43; ENGLISH SOCIETY 25, 7; MISUNDERSTANDING 8; IDEOLOGICAL ORIGINS 301.

218 John Adams to John Quincy Adams (12 Dec.1795), 1 DHSC 811; John Adams to Abigail Adams (17 Dec.1795), 1 *id.* at 813.

219 Joanne B. Freeman, *Explaining the Unexplainable: The Cultural Context of the Sedition Act*, in THE DEMOCRATIC EXPERIMENT 20, 27–31, 41 (Meg Jacobs et al. eds., PUP, Princeton 2003); *see* JOANNE B. FREEMAN, AFFAIRS OF HONOR: NATIONAL POLITICS IN THE NEW REPUBLIC xvii–xviii (YUP, New Haven 2001).

The initial Supreme Court justices who were inclined to believe in inalienable rights that were never surrendered to government,[220] even while encouraging obedience to laws, did not press the point so far as to treat opposition to the administration as seditious. Wilson, going to the heart of the issue, disparaged identification of the government with the state and the claim of officials to be "the sovereigns of the state."[221] His lecture on government began by denying that a "change of government" was hazardous, and by instead asserting that "prostituted characters" should be turned out of office.[222] Jay allowed for differing opinions, including on political questions,[223] and distinguished criticism of government from sedition.[224]

The early justices who were prone to view most or all rights in a state of nature as surrendered when government was formed[225] instead spoke of obedience as the price of government granting civil rights. When Chase offered himself to President Washington as one of the initial justices, he pledged that "I will support the present Government."[226] He later "conclude[d] that *liberty* and *rights* (and also *property*) must arise out of civil society" and obedience to its laws, and so "must be for ever subject to the modifications of particular government."[227] Cushing, before joining the Supreme Court, charged a grand jury that "all good citizens . . . persevere peaceably in doing their duty, in supporting the magistrate in the execution of his office."[228] Later, he continued to urge "the necessity of giving our confidence and support to our own Government."[229] Iredell charged grand juries that the "security of each individual consists in a due obedience" to law, which "is the depositary of the common happiness and security of all the citizens."[230] In a subsequent charge, he extended the duty of obedience beyond the laws to "the government of the United States."[231] Paterson, before appointment to the bench, praised the industrious citizen who "has not leisure . . . to

[220] Chisholm v. Georgia, 2 U.S. (2 Dall.) 419, 457, 470–71 (1793) (Wilson, Jay); 2 Wilson Works 1054, 1055, 1057; 1 Jay Correspondence 162; 2 DHSC 27, 363 (Jay); 2 Bill of Rights 896 (Jay).

[221] Chisholm v. Georgia, 2 U.S. (2 Dall.) 419, 455 (1793).

[222] 1 James Wilson, *Lectures on Law* (1790–91), in Wilson Works 427, 689, 701.

[223] 2 DHRC 26, 27, 364.

[224] 2 DHRC 363.

[225] Chase Trial App.61; Calder v. Bull, 3 U.S. (3 Dall.) 386, 400 (1798) (Iredell) ("private rights must yield to public exigencies"); William Cushing's Charge (C.C.D. R.I. 7 Nov.1794), 2 DHSC 491, 492.

[226] Samuel Chase to George Washington (3 Sept.1789), 3 Washington Papers-Presidential 597.

[227] Samuel Chase's Charge (C.C.D. c.1803), Chase Charge Book 38, 42–43; *accord* Ware v. Hylton, 3 U.S. (3 Dall.) 199, 223 (1796); Chase Trial App.61.

[228] *Substance of the Charge Delivered at Salem*, American Herald (Boston), 27 Nov.1786, at 4.

[229] Newport Mercury, 19 June 1798, reprinted in 3 DHSC 278.

[230] James Iredell's Charge (C.C.D. N.J. 2 Apr.1793), 2 DHSC 348, 348–50.

[231] James Iredell's Charge (C.C.D. Pa. 11 Apr.1797), 3 DHSC 163, 164.

revile the government, to disseminate dangerous principles," and inveighed against the "mob of politicians" who "are occupied . . . in criticising and canvassing the acts of government."[232] Once on the bench, he charged grand juries that to support "the constitution, government, and constituted authorities of the United States" is "our primary duty—to attempt their destruction is an offence of deep malignity."[233] Ellsworth charged that the federal government was "entitled to affection, as well as support," and that an unnamed element instead "poisons the sources of public confidence."[234] Before the election of 1800, Chase charged juries that citizens must "support . . . the present administration"[235]—but after Jefferson won, he blatantly rewrote his charge to drop that phrase.[236]

That second group of justices increasingly gave as their rationale government's right of self-preservation or reasons of state. Discussing the Sedition Act, Paterson warned that "written or printed detraction" would "destroy confidence" and "alienate the affections of the people from their government," and without stopping that poison "[n]o government, indeed, can long subsist."[237] Cushing asked rhetorically whether government "has no power to protect itself by laws to prevent crimes which tend directly to its overthrow and destruction?"[238] Much earlier, Ellsworth declared that it was "justifiable and frequent, in the adjustment of national differences, to concede for the safety of the state, the rights of individuals."[239] By contrast, Wilson denounced "reasons of state" as "terrible instruments of arbitrary power."[240]

No Right to Evaluate Laws as Illegal and Void?

Parliament periodically used the formulation that Crown actions being curtailed were illegal or unconstitutional.[241] Coke was widely understood in colonial America[242] as teaching that parliamentary action, too, could be illegal and void,[243]

[232] William Paterson, July 4 Oration (c.1792), Paterson Papers-LC 3–4.

[233] William Paterson's Charge (C.C.D. Vt. 3 Oct.1798), 3 DHSC 292, 294.

[234] Oliver Ellsworth's Charge (C.C.D. N.Y. 1 Apr.1797), 3 DHSC 158, 158–59; *accord* 3 *id.* at 119, 120.

[235] Samuel Chase's Charge (C.C.D. Pa. 12 Apr.1800), 3 DHSC 408, 416.

[236] Samuel Chase's Charge (C.C.D. Md. Nov.1802), Chase Charge Book 33, 33.

[237] William Paterson's Charge (C.C.D. Vt. 3 Oct.1798), 3 DHSC 292, 293.

[238] William Cushing's Charge (C.C.D. Va. 23 Nov.1798), 3 DHSC 305, 315.

[239] Hamilton v. Eaton, 11 F.Cas. 336, 340 (C.C.D. N.C. 1792).

[240] 1 Wilson Works 706.

[241] *E.g.*, Bill of Rights (16 Dec.1689), 1 W&M (sess 2) c2 §XII; 9 Statutes 67; Speech (5 Feb.1621), 3 The Selected Writings of Sir Edward Coke 1195 (Steve Sheppard ed., LF, Indianapolis 2003).

[242] *E.g.*, 1 James Wilson, *Lectures on Law* (1790–91), in Wilson Works 427, 738–39.

[243] Dr. Bonham's Case, 8 Co. Rep. 107a, 118a, 77 Eng. Rep. 638, 652 (C.P. 1610); Raoul Berger, *Doctor Bonham's Case: Statutory Construction or Constitutional Theory?*, 117 U. Pa. L. Rev. 521, 526, 545 (1969).

though that may have been a gross misinterpretation.[244] Many reasoned that the "command of any magistrate, where he has no authority, [are] as void."[245]

American challenge to the Stamp Act and other pre-Revolution laws was commonly based on Parliament's enactments being illegal and void, because they violated ancient, charter, or natural rights. They presupposed the right of an individual writer or the Continental Congress to assess Parliament's actions as illegal and void.

All the early justices believed that a law contrary to a state constitution or the federal Constitution was void,[246] and all believed that they as state or federal judges could declare such a law unconstitutional.[247] However, they differed about how ordinary citizens should and could react to a questionable law.

Those justices more influenced by radical Whig principles generally left to each citizen a right to determine whether governmental action was illegal and void.[248] Hence, Wilson disagreed sharply with Blackstone's claim that the "power and jurisdiction of Parliament" was "transcendent and absolute," and thus incapable of being illegal or void,[249] and taught instead that "an act of parliament against law and reason is, therefore, void" and that an American "act, manifestly repugnant to some part of the constitution," similarly "is void."[250] Rutledge, while out of federal office, led a citizen rally condemning the Jay Treaty as a violation of rights. Blair, both at the inception and after the suppression of the Whiskey Rebellion, acknowledged the right to resist an unconstitutional law nonviolently, and implicitly, the right of individuals to evaluate the constitutionality of laws, while cautioning against violent resistance.[251] Jay later said people were only bound to support war as "*constitutional* laws do or shall prescribe" support.[252]

[244] *E.g.*, Charles M. Gray, *Bonham's Case Reviewed*, 116 PROC. AM. PHILOSOPHICAL SOC. 35, 46–51 (1972); J.P. SOMMERVILLE, POLITICS AND IDEOLOGY IN ENGLAND, 1603–1640, at 97–98 (Longman, London 1986).

[245] *E.g.*, 2 LOCKE ¶206; *accord* ANIMADVERSIONS UPON MIJN HEER FAGELS LETTER 6 (George Larkin, London 1688); 2 GILBERT BURNET, BISHOP BURNET'S HISTORY OF HIS OWN TIME 807 (Company of Booksellers, London 1725–34).

[246] *E.g.*, Chisholm v. Georgia, 2 U.S. (2 Dall.) 419, 433 (1793) (Iredell); Calder v. Bull, 3 U.S. (3 Dall.) 386, 388, 399 (1798) (Chase, Iredell); Samuel Chase's Charge (C.C.D. Pa. 12 Apr.1800), 3 DHSC 408, 412.

[247] *E.g.*, Samuel Chase's Charge (C.C.D. Pa. 12 Apr.1800), 3 DHSC 408, 412. The other early justices' treatment of unconstitutional laws as void, and support of judicial review, is described in the epilogue to Chapter 8.

[248] Which was a widely held view. Douglas Bradburn, *A Clamor in the Public Mind*, 65 WM. & MARY Q. 565, 590–91 (2008).

[249] 1 BLACKSTONE'S COMMENTARIES 156; *contra* 1 WILSON WORKS 552–53, 579–81, 738–40.

[250] 1 James Wilson, *Lectures on Law* (1790–91), in WILSON WORKS 427, 738–39, 742; 1 *id.*, 38.

[251] John Blair's Charge (C.C.D. Ga. 27 Apr.1795), 3 DHSC 31, 33; *accord* 2 DHSC 487.

[252] John Jay to Peter Van Schaack (28 July 1812), JAY PAPERS doc.9440.

By contrast, those justices inclined to moderate Whig principles limited the determination whether action was illegal and void to federal judges,[253] even though in revolutionary days most had been quite comfortable with the opposite.[254] Chase said it was "a vain, conceited individual who can think himself as capable to judge" whether laws violate the Constitution—only judges should do so.[255] Paterson agreed.[256] Iredell charged grand juries that "[t]he part for every man who loves his country, but who disapproves of any public authoritative decision, is to submit to it with diffidence and respect, considering... his own opinion may be really wrong."[257] Chase, even after being impeached and after stripping his charge of controversy, admonished each grand juror "to submit to the laws, although he should conscientiously believe them to be *unconstitutional, unjust*, or even *oppressive*."[258] Little room was left for dissent.

No Right to Disobey Unconstitutional Laws?

The demand for unequivocal obedience to the law had an ancient lineage, descending from Tudor statutes treating dissent as treason and from Stuart precepts of divine right. The "duty of passive obedience, or non-resistance to all their commands,"[259] was also taught by the Tory Party generally[260] and, as zealously, by the established church[261] (which some said was the same group in prayer).

However, the right of legitimate resistance also had a long pedigree[262] that included the Revolution of 1688 in all Whigs' views,[263] other times of tyranny in radical Whig theory,[264] and the Revolution of 1776 in American patriots' eyes.[265] That right was supported by England's dissenting pulpits and by their

[253] Samuel Chase's Charge (C.C.D. Md. 8 Oct.1802), CHASE CHARGE BOOK 25, 28, 29.

[254] Censor [Samuel Chase], *Censor IV*, MARYLAND GAZETTE (Annapolis), 21 June 1781, in 3 CARROLL PAPERS 1449, 1452.

[255] Samuel Chase's Charge (C.C.D. Pa. 12 Apr.1800), 3 DHSC 408, 412.

[256] PATERSON DRAFT OPINIONS 47; *accord* 3 DHSC 455.

[257] James Iredell's Charge (C.C.D. Md. 8 May 1797), 3 DHSC 173, 176.

[258] Samuel Chase's Charge (C.C.D. Md. 1 May 1805), CHASE CHARGE BOOK 47, 52.

[259] SAMUEL PARKER, RELIGION AND LOYALTY (John Baker, London 1684) (quoting subtitle); *accord id.* at 581, 583.

[260] DICKINSON 19–20, 43; ENGLISH SOCIETY 123, 124–35; *id.* at 236, 248, 259.

[261] *Id.* at 15, 28–29; ENGLISH SOCIETY 158–59, 181, 221–22, 227, 199–276; GLENN BURGESS, ABSOLUTE MONARCHY AND THE STUART CONSTITUTION 216–17 (YUP, New Haven 1996); *e.g.*, SIR ROBERT FILMER, PATRIARCHA (Walter Davis, London 1680); EDMUND BOHUN, A DEFENCE OF SIR ROBERT FILMER 5, 9 (W. Kettilby, London 1684).

[262] SCOTT, *supra* note 177, at 109–30; CLARK 257–89; BELLAMY, *supra* note 92, at 9–11.

[263] KENYON 5; DICKINSON 58, 65, 77.

[264] CREATION 23–24; ENGLISH SOCIETY 219, 239.

[265] DICKINSON'S ESSAY 40.

Reformation heritage,[266] as well as, at times, by judges.[267] Colonial "presses and . . . pulpits" taught the "obligation to disobey" tyrannical government,[268] citing such historical beacons as Coke's apparent principle that in case of conflict "the law is to be obeyed and not the [King's] proclamation,"[269] and Locke's affirmations that a ruler who violates the law "has no right to obedience"[270] and that subjects have an "inalienable right of armed resistance"[271] toward governmental violation of law. Whig leaders condemned "the most mischievous of all doctrines, that of passive obedience and nonresistance,"[272] and proclaimed that "*English* history affords frequent examples of resistance by force."[273] The two approaches were not reconciled in 1642, 1688–1689, or 1776.

Most initial Supreme Court justices approvingly acknowledged that revolutionary heritage. Jay, even in Sedition Act years, recalled favorably that the colonists resisted the Stamp Act and ultimately "recurred to arms."[274] Wilson, who during the Revolution affirmed the "right to resist every attempt upon their liberties" and believed "[w]e have taken up arms in the best of causes" to defend "constitutional rights,"[275] continued on the bench to maintain "the right of rescuing themselves from . . . oppression" by changing the form of government or by revolution.[276] Rutledge, during the colonial crisis, took the position that "the House

[266] JAMES E. BRADLEY, RELIGION, REVOLUTION, AND ENGLISH RADICALISM 154–56 (CUP, Cambridge 1990); 2 QUENTIN SKINNER, THE FOUNDATIONS OF MODERN POLITICAL THOUGHT 189–358 (CUP, Cambridge 1978).

[267] *E.g.*, Case of the Reforming Constables, Holt K.B. 485, 90 Eng. Rep. 1167 (K.B. 1708) (resistance to unlawful arrest).

[268] IDEOLOGICAL ORIGINS 304; *accord* BRADLEY, *supra* note 266, at 154–58 (Nonconformists); CLARK 274–75, 279 (nonAnglicans); *e.g.*, JONATHAN MAYHEW, A DISCOURSE CONCERNING UNLIMITED SUBMISSION AND NON-RESISTANCE 40, 52 (D. Fowle, Boston 1750), reprinted J[ONATHAN] M[AYHEW], A MYSTERIOUS DOCTRINE UNRIDDLED, OR UNLIMITED SUBMISSION AND NON-RESISTANCE (D. Carpenter, Newry 1775).

[269] Speech (5 Feb.1621), 3 COKE'S WRITINGS, *supra* note 241, at 1195.

[270] 2 LOCKE 151; *id.* ¶¶202, 206, 207, 222, 223–30, 228, 232, 237–39, 242; *accord* ASHCRAFT 297, 305, 307, 305, 315, 319.

[271] ALAN CROMARTIE, THE CONSTITUTIONALIST REVOLUTION: AN ESSAY ON THE HISTORY OF ENGLAND, 1450–1642, at 278 (CUP, Cambridge 2006); *accord* 2 Locke ¶¶209, 222, 228, 230; ASHCRAFT 319.

[272] *E.g.*, 3 JOHN ADAMS, *Dissertation on the Canon and the Feudal Law* (1765), in ADAMS WORKS 447, 454; THE INDEPENDENT REFLECTOR 27–28, 326 (Milton M. Klein ed., HUP, Cambridge 1963).

[273] FARMER [JOHN DICKINSON], LETTERS FROM A FARMER 17 (Edes & Gill, Boston 1768).

[274] John Jay to Rev. Samuel Miller (28 Feb.1800), 4 JAY CORRESPONDENCE 261; *accord* 4 *id.* at 288, 289.

[275] 1 James Wilson, *An Address to the Inhabitants of the Colonies* (1776), in WILSON WORKS 46, 52, 53.

[276] 1 James Wilson, *Lectures on Law* (1790–91), in WILSON WORKS 427, 714; *accord* 1 *id.* at 427, 2 *id.* at 1041, 1082–83.

should not submit" to royal instructions that he deemed to violate his colony's rights.[277] Blair allowed for nonforcible "resistance . . . to an unconstitutional act of Congress," as "entitled to the protection of the law," and for opposition "to any self constituted authority" as "resistance of tyranny."[278]

Most successor justices left far less freedom for legitimate dissent. Paterson, the year before appointment to the bench, prophesied that "Order is Heaven's first law" and that "habitual and cheerful submission to the laws of our country, and the powers legally established is a social duty of primary importance," ironically in a speech extolling the Revolution.[279] He had long taught that to contravene the "declared will of the people by their representatives or a majority" is "subversive of government" and is done by "tyrants in heart and traitors in practice,"[280] and while on the Supreme Court he continued to write variations with even darker overtones for dissent.[281] Iredell charged grand juries that it was "necessary that an obedience to the laws of our country be enforced."[282] Chase again changed a pre-Jefferson charge—"it is the indispensable duty of every citizen to submit to the *laws*, although ever so repugnant to his *private* opinion; until they are repealed, or declared *void*" by the judiciary[283]—to a post-election version striking that language and, for the first time, adding that unconstitutional laws need not be obeyed.[284]

Extension of Treason to Opposition to the Administration?

The English law of treason[285] had expanded like a canopied tree to encompass not only levying war but planning or imagining the king's death (including "words

[277] 38 JOURNALS OF ASSEMBLY-S.C. 432, 433; LEE'S ANSWER 35.

[278] John Blair's Charge (C.C.D. Ga. 27 Apr.1795), 3 DHSC 31, 33; *accord* 2 *id.* 487, 486.

[279] William Paterson, July 4 Oration (c.1792), PATERSON PAPERS-LC 4, 1.

[280] William Paterson, Jury Charge (n.d.), PATERSON LEGAL PAPERS-LC 2; *accord* William Paterson, Notes Apparently of the Debate in the Senate (8 Sept.1789), PATERSON PAPERS-NYPL 367, 379.

[281] William Paterson's Charge (C.C.D. Pa. 4 May 1795), 3 DHSC 40, 42; *accord* 3 *id.* at 12, 294, 463, 465. A fellow senator in the first Congress described Paterson as "a Summum Jus Man." Diary of William Maclay (12 June 1789 entry), 9 DHFFC 290 & n.15 (meaning he "believe[d] in the supreme rigor of the law and applie[d] it without concern for justice").

[282] James Iredell's Charge (C.C.D. Conn. 25 Apr.1795), 3 DHSC 28, 29; *accord* 3 *id.* at 14.

[283] Samuel Chase's Charge (C.C.D. Pa. 12 Apr.1800), 3 DHSC 408, 413. This contradicted not only Chase's 1776 position, but his 1787 position on the "right in the people to resist their rulers" when tyrannical. Samuel Chase to His Constituents (Broadside 9 Feb.1787), REPRESENTATIVE GOVERNMENT AND THE REVOLUTION: THE MARYLAND CONSTITUTIONAL CRISIS OF 1787, at 55, 60 (Melvin Yazawa ed., JHUP, Baltimore 1975).

[284] Samuel Chase's Charge (C.C.D. Md. Nov.1802), CHASE CHARGE BOOK 33, 34–35. Division on the issue was related to views of natural rights. Bradburn, *supra* note 248, at 591.

[285] ORR 11–13; BELLAMY, *supra* note 92, at 59–101. It grew out of 25 Edw 3 stat 5 c2.

[that] be set down in writing"), five other major branches as Blackstone summarized them,[286] innumerable additional limbs such as treason by words alone under Henry VIII and some successors,[287] and constructive treason.[288]

The Constitutional Convention repudiated those far-reaching definitions and limited treason to levying war or adhering to enemies.[289] As Wilson explained, "a very great part of [other governments'] tyranny over the people has arisen from the extension of the definition of treason."[290]

Thus, Wilson instructed the first grand jury that, because "[t]reasons, capricious, arbitrary and constructive, have often been the most tremendous engines of despotic or of legislative tyranny," treason only meant what the Constitution defined it as, lest as in Tudor England "so many 'pains of treason were ordained by statute, that no man knew how to behave himself, to do, speak or say, for doubt.'"[291] He defined levying war equally narrowly.[292]

In contrast, Paterson painted treason and sedition with a broad brush, apparently to enhance the culpability of sedition after passage of the Sedition Act by treating it as a variety of treason, in charges that he wrote but may not have delivered. Crimes "of a treasonable and seditious nature" required "particular attention" and shared common evils. "Treasonable and seditious offences have a tendency to deprive government of the confidence and affection [of the] people.... Hence seditious language, seditious writings, and seditious actions. Hence riots, and tumults, and insurrections."[293] Under his broad view of treason, whoever "is lawless ... is a tyrant and of course a traitor to the government."[294] Cushing similarly defined treason to include almost any armed resistance to any government action.[295] The zeal of other justices in stamping out sedition also seemed to emanate from seeing it as a sibling, if not a parent, to treason. In Iredell's case, the association went back far, as during the Revolution he had prosecuted criminal charges for sedition and treason by words.[296]

[286] 4 Blackstone's Commentaries 81, 76, 80, 74–93; *see* 1 Charles de Secondat, Baron Montesquieu, Spirit of the Laws 233 (bk.12, ch.7) (1748, repr. G. & A. Ewing, Dublin 1751).

[287] Orr 16–23; *e.g.*, Act for the Preservation of the King (1661), 13 Car 2, stat 1, c1; 8 EHD 63.

[288] 4 Blackstone's Commentaries 81; Orr 27, 28.

[289] U.S.Const. art.III, §3; 1 James Wilson, *Lectures on Law* (1790–91), Wilson Works 427; 2 *id.* 1151–52.

[290] 3 Farrand's Records 163; *accord* 2 *id.* at 348 (Franklin).

[291] James Wilson's Charge (C.C.D. Pa. 12 Apr.1790), 2 DHSC 33, 42; *accord* James Wilson's Charge (C.C.D. Va. 23 May 1791), 2 *id.* at 166, 172, precluding constructive treasons, 173.

[292] 1 James Wilson, *Lectures on Law* (1790–91), in Wilson Works 427; 2 *id.* 1153, 1154.

[293] William Paterson's Charge (No.5 c.1798), 3 DHSC 464, 465; *accord* William Paterson's Charge (No.4 c.1798), 3 *id.* at 462, 463.

[294] William Paterson, Jury Charge (n.d.), Paterson Legal Papers-LC.

[295] William Cushing's Grand Jury Charge 6, Nathan Peaslee Sargent Papers (Phillips Library of Peabody Essex Museum, Salem, Papers 1757–1809, Box 2),

[296] 1 Iredell Papers 464; 2 *id.* 124, 190; *accord* Jacobin 97.

The Fries Rebellion in 1799 placed the issue squarely. John Fries and a large armed group rescued tax protesters from confinement, and when warned by the Adams administration, they and others ceased all opposition to the unpopular tax. Fries and a number of followers were charged with treason, and Fries and two leaders were convicted and sentenced to death, in trials presided over at different times by Justices Iredell, Washington, and Chase, that are discussed in Chapter 7. For a time, opposition to the administration, accompanied by any force whatever, was treated as treason, even as words critical of the administration were treated as sedition.

Existence of a Federal Common Law of Crimes?

A recurrent contention between King and Parliament had been the former's claims of prerogative powers to create or punish offenses without legislative action or authorization.[297] Star Chamber opponents, Hume, and others applied that concern to prosecution of the press, warning of "giving very large discretionary powers to the court to punish whatever displeases them."[298]

The issue of crimes not authorized by legislation reappeared as the first federal courts grappled with whether their jurisdiction included English common law crimes under an unlegislated federal common law. The pre-1798 conclusion of the early Supreme Court justices that "the penal code of the U. States is plain and concise, and reduced . . . to written exactitude and precision,"[299] along with the law of nations for international controversies, was in 1798 altered by most sitting justices. Thus, in 1798–1800, most sitting justices (Paterson, Chase after changing position, Ellsworth, Washington, apparently Cushing, and alone in 1796, Iredell) came for the first time to the conclusion that federal law included a federal common law, which in turn incorporated a Blackstonian definition of liberty of press and speech. By contrast, the remaining justices (Jay, Rutledge, Wilson, Johnson, and Moore) had never claimed that federal law included a federal common law (only Blair assumed that in 1797), though they did understand federal law to incorporate the law of nations for international controversies. Their individual positions were discussed earlier in this chapter.

[297] Proclamations, 12 Co. Rep. 74, 77 Eng. Rep. 1352, 1353 (P.C. 1610); Bill of Rights (1689), 1 W&M (sess 2) c2; 8 EHD 122; *accord* Brooks 116–17.

[298] David Hume, *Of the Liberty of the Press* (1742), in Essays Moral, Political and Literary 8 (OUP, Oxford 1963).

[299] William Paterson's Charge (C.C.D. Pa. 4 May 1795), 3 DHSC 40, 41; *accord* James Iredell's Charge (C.C.D.N.Y. 6 Apr.1795), 3 *id.* at 14, 22.

The Effect of American Constitutions on the Blackstone-Mansfield Definition and on Criminalizing Seditious Libel?

The ultimate point of disagreement between early Supreme Court justices was whether the narrow Blackstone-Mansfield definition accurately summarized the English common law of freedoms of press and speech, and whether new state constitutions and then the new federal Constitution adopted that narrow approach or rejected it to provide broader protection for printed and spoken words and a broader right to disagree with government and officials. The Blackstone-Mansfield definition, its absence from English common law before 1770, it being picked out of an assortment of narrow and broad definitions in popular essays before then,[300] and the competing approaches to freedoms of speech and press in political discussion during 1765–1791, were discussed in Chapter 2. The early justices' acceptance of a broad definition of those freedoms, and their nonacceptance of the narrow Blackstone-Mansfield definition or framework before 1798, are addressed in Chapters 4–5. Those justices' division over that doctrine and over seditious libel in response to the Sedition Act of 1798, with most sitting justices shifting to accept the Blackstone-Mansfield definition and seditious libel prosecutions, and most remaining justices diverging from them, is the subject of Chapters 6 and 8. Divergence of the justices in 1798 is less surprising when it is viewed in light of their divergence on the seven issues touched on here.

The argument that the First Amendment, or the state constitutions, incorporated the Blackstone-Mansfield definition, that freedoms of press and speech meant only what English common law ascribed to them, a freedom from licensing that ended nearly a century earlier and not also a freedom from seditious libel prosecution that persisted, faces many difficulties. English common law did not include the Blackstone-Mansfield definition of liberty of press until 1770, as Chapter 2 discussed. Even then it was not undisputed. Instead, many American essayists

[300] Bird, *supra* note 17. For a generation before and after licensing of the press ended in 1695, writers on both sides of the issue referred to a liberty of the press from licensing requirements. However, proponents of broad liberty of the press also sought liberty of the press from other infringements or restrictions, such as arrests of printers and authors without trial as that became a government weapon of choice, and prosecutions of other printers and writers for seditious libel as that regularly occurred. Instead, those proponents increasingly advocated broad definitions of liberty of the press, such as freedom of inquiry and discussion and freedom from prosecution, particularly in the 1760s through 1780s, in both Britain and the American colonies. Opponents of broad liberty of the press, such as Thomas Hutchinson (the royalist Massachusetts chief justice and then royal governor), like Blackstone sometimes responded with the narrowest definition of liberty of press, as Hutchinson did in charging grand juries in 1767–68. Hutchinson's words were not published in law reports for a century and were not known by other judges, and his growing unpopularity with the patriot party (which soon afterward sought his impeachment) ensured their rejection in revolutionary Massachusetts.

addressing the issue saw freedoms of press and speech as inconsistent with seditious libel, and all revolutionary state constitutions addressing freedom of press conferred unqualified protection without any express seditious libel exception. As the federal Constitution was ratified, anti-federalists saw a bill of rights as adequate protection against seditious libel prosecutions, and federalists assured them that the new government possessed no power that could restrain the press. The resulting federal amendment, like the state provisions, was unqualifiedly broad. Though one scholar cavils that Virginia's "pattern for all American free press clauses . . . gave no hint of what it meant by freedom of the press or by the word 'restrained,'"[301] he defends an unstated drastic limitation while demeaning those express unqualified words that Madison and other framers thought were perspicuous, at a time when many addressing the issue called seditious libel prosecutions a restraint.

The postulated incorporation of the Blackstone-Mansfield definition and framework into the press provision faced a further difficulty when incorporated into the parallel speech provision, since the historical restraint by licensing had only applied to the press and not speech (except preaching and theater). The concept that the clauses incorporated the Blackstone-Mansfield definition left the enigma that in the First Amendment "freedom of speech" did not mean merely speech free from licensing, but "freedom . . . of the press" did mean merely press free from licensing. English common law was not incorporated by any other First Amendment provision, whether on establishment, free religious exercise, petition, or assembly, and in fact was rejected by the other provisions. It also was rejected by many other Bill of Rights provisions. As Madison said on introducing the First Amendment, "freedom of the press, and the rights of conscience . . . are not guarded by the British Constitution," and instead "should be . . . secured."[302]

If two opposite views appeared in public commentary and legislative debates on freedoms of press and speech, which view did the early justices of the Supreme Court hold toward those freedoms and, later, toward the Sedition Act of 1798? Those early justices included three major and three minor participants at the Constitutional Convention, three leaders in ratification conventions, and two major participants in the first Congress that adopted the First Amendment. The next chapter discusses the initial six justices, and the following chapter discusses their six successor justices.

[301] LEVY 184.

[302] *Sketch of Proceedings of Congress*, GAZETTE OF THE UNITED STATES (New York), 10 June 1789, at 66, 67.

4

The Initial Supreme Court Justices and Their Views on Freedoms of Press and Speech

> Judge Black[stone] says, (4 vol. p.151) the liberty of the press consists—"in laying no previous restraint upon publications," and not in freedom from censure for criminal matter when published. Wherein he refers to a public licenser or inspector of the press. *That is*, no doubt, the liberty of the press as allowed by the law of England.
>
> But the words of our article, understood according to plain English and common sense–make no such distinction, and must exclude *subsequent* restraints—as much as *previous restraints*. . . .
>
> —Supreme Court Justice William Cushing in 1789[1]

What did the early Supreme Court justices (those before Chief Justice John Marshall) understand the First Amendment to mean? Their views of freedoms of press and speech are generally not mentioned and not studied,[2] and the early justices are treated as having nothing to say about freedoms of press and speech before the battle that began in 1798.[3] Alternatively, their views are pigeonholed as uniform Federalist

[1] William Cushing to John Adams 4 (18 Feb.1789), Microfilms of the Adams Papers (MHS, Boston, reel 372). A list of abbreviated titles is at the end of this book.

[2] *E.g.*, Bernard Schwartz, A History of the Supreme Court 1–31 (OUP, New York 1993); 1 David P. Currie, The Constitution in the Supreme Court: The First Hundred Years, 1789–1888, at 1–58 (UChiP, Chicago 1985); Charles G. Haines, The Role of the Supreme Court in American Government and Politics, 1789–1835, at 7–159 (UCalP, Berkeley 1944); Charles Warren, *The First Decade of the Supreme Court of the United States*, 7 U. Chi. L. Rev. 631 (1940); John D. Cushing, A Revolutionary Conservative: The Public Life of William Cushing, 1732–1810, at 328 (1959) (unpublished Ph.D. dissertation, Clark University) ("there is nothing to indicate what, if anything, Cushing contributed . . . as a circuit judge," and "little of significance" in Supreme Court sessions); *cf.* William G. Brown, The Life of Oliver Ellsworth 200 (Macmillan, New York 1905).

[3] Examples are given at the beginning of Chapter 6.

beliefs, embracing the Blackstone-Mansfield definition and sharply limiting those freedoms by seditious libel law before 1798, and then supporting the Sedition Act with alacrity during the crisis of 1798–1801.[4] That does not accurately describe the understanding of any of the first twelve justices before 1798, or the views of roughly half of those justices about the Sedition Act. Instead, nearly all of the early justices expressed commitment to broad freedoms of press and speech before 1798, and not one of them endorsed the Blackstone-Mansfield definition of freedom of press and seditious libel before 1798. Further, roughly half did not support the Sedition Act.

That is surprising if one assumes that the narrow Blackstone-Mansfield definition of liberties of press and speech accurately summarized a long-standing common law, and that the criminality of seditious libel was universally assumed. It is unsurprising, however, if Blackstone's summary had no basis in the prior English common law, if Mansfield altered the common law to conform to Blackstone's summary after it was written, if Mansfield rewrote the history of seditious libel to make it ancient rather than relatively new, as Chapter 2 discussed, and if state and federal provisions for freedoms of press and speech used broad language without express Blackstonian limitations.

The six initial justices, all appointed by President George Washington,[5] were Chief Justice John Jay (who served 1789–1795), John Rutledge (1789–1791 and 1795), William Cushing (1789–1810), James Wilson (1789–1798), John Blair (1789–1795), and soon after, James Iredell (1790–1799).[6] (The original sixth justice, Robert Harrison, died before taking office, causing delay before Iredell was nominated.[7] Thus, Iredell could alternately be categorized as a successor justice.) Those six initial justices, who constituted the initial Court, are discussed individually in this chapter, and the six successor justices are discussed in the next chapter.

This chapter challenges assumptions about the initial justices' views of freedoms of press and speech, and fills the gap about their views in existing biographies, histories, and legal studies, by locating and summarizing each initial justice's views of freedoms of press and speech before 1798, including many passages never before quoted except as some were printed in documentary compilations or in two justices' incomplete collected works. This chapter shows that all the initial justices expressed commitment to, not opposition or indifference to, those rights before the conflict that began in 1798, while none adopted the Blackstone-Mansfield definition of freedoms of press and speech or those jurists'

[4] Examples are given at the beginning of Chapter 8.

[5] Nominations, 4 WASHINGTON PAPERS-PRESIDENTIAL 75 (24 Sept.1789); 2 DHFFC 44; confirmed two days later, DHFFC 44–45. Iredell was only nominated after Robert Harrison's declination, 5 WASHINGTON PAPERS-PRESIDENTIAL 121–22, 2 DHFFC 59; and was confirmed shortly after, 2 *id.* 61.

[6] The conventional order in which they are listed is the dates of their commissions as justices. *The First Judges of the Federal Courts*, 1 AM. J. LEGAL HISTORY 76, 77 (1957); 19 ANB 133, 134.

[7] 1 DHSC 34, 36, 37, 42; 4 DHFFC 99, 102.

framework for seditious libel before 1798, and only two of the six initial justices adopted those doctrines during 1798–1801. Later, Chapter 8 will discuss the split of the initial justices over the Sedition Act during 1798–1801, as it appears that roughly half of the initial justices and a minority of the Federalist Party generally did not support that Act or its constitutionality.

The new American government that started in 1789 and took form in the early 1790s[8] was a grand experiment, as the framers of the Constitution had recognized at the Convention of 1787.[9] The new president, George Washington, took his oath of office in April 1789,[10] but there were no Supreme Court justices to administer it. The new Congress had broader powers than the Confederation Congress, and disagreement about their breadth would break out within a year. The new Supreme Court was not nominated and confirmed until late September 1789,[11] just when the Bill of Rights was approved by Congress after consideration during the summer.[12] Soon, the Hamiltonian financial plans,[13] following a British model for a financial and military state,[14] divided Congress over the scope of

[8] *See generally* GORDON S. WOOD, EMPIRE OF LIBERTY: A HISTORY OF THE EARLY REPUBLIC, 1789–1815, at 5–173 (OUP, New York 2009); STANLEY ELKINS & ERIC MCKITRICK, THE AGE OF FEDERALISM 31–302 (OUP, New York 1993); JAMES R. SHARP, AMERICAN POLITICS IN THE EARLY REPUBLIC 17–137 (YUP, New Haven 1993).

[9] ALISON L. LACROIX, THE IDEOLOGICAL ORIGINS OF AMERICAN FEDERALISM 132–35 (HUP, Cambridge 2010); JOSEPH J. ELLIS, AMERICAN CREATION 7–17, 87–126 (Knopf, New York 2007); EMPIRE 5–52; GORDON S. WOOD, REVOLUTIONARY CHARACTERS 29–172 (Penguin, New York 2006); JOSEPH J. ELLIS, FOUNDING BROTHERS: THE REVOLUTIONARY GENERATION 8–18 (Knopf, New York 2001); GORDON S. WOOD, THE RADICALISM OF THE AMERICAN REVOLUTION 229–43, 261–65, 293–99 (Knopf, New York 1992).

[10] On Washington's presidency, *see* JOHN E. FERLING, THE ASCENT OF GEORGE WASHINGTON (Bloomsbury Press, New York 2009); JOSEPH J. ELLIS, HIS EXCELLENCY: GEORGE WASHINGTON 188–240 (Knopf, New York 2004).

[11] WILLIAM R. CASTO, THE SUPREME COURT IN THE EARLY REPUBLIC: THE CHIEF JUSTICESHIPS OF JOHN JAY AND OLIVER ELLSWORTH 54–68 (USCP, Columbia 1995); BERNARD SCHWARTZ, A HISTORY OF THE SUPREME COURT 16–17 (OUP, New York 1993).

[12] RICHARD LABUNSKI, JAMES MADISON AND THE STRUGGLE FOR THE BILL OF RIGHTS 178–240 (OUP, New York 2006); JACK N. RAKOVE, JAMES MADISON AND THE CREATION OF THE AMERICAN REPUBLIC 90–93, 96–100 (Pearson Longman, New York 2007); *see* ERIC T. KASPER, TO SECURE THE LIBERTY OF THE PEOPLE 63–79 (Northern Ill. Univ. Press, DeKalb 2010).

[13] Ron CHERNOW, ALEXANDER HAMILTON 295–306, 326–31 (Penguin, New York 2004); EDWIN J. PERKINS, AMERICAN PUBLIC FINANCE AND FINANCIAL SERVICES, 1700–1815, at 213–44 (Ohio State Univ. Press, Columbus 1994); *see* FOUNDING CHOICES: AMERICAN ECONOMIC POLICY IN THE 1790S, at 59–88 (Douglas A. Irwin & Richard Sylla eds., UChiP, Chicago 2011); EMPIRE 93–103.

[14] JOHN BREWER, THE SINEWS OF POWER: WAR, MONEY AND THE ENGLISH STATE, 1688–1783, at 25–134 (HUP, Cambridge 1990); MAX M. EDLING, A REVOLUTION IN FAVOR OF GOVERNMENT: ORIGINS OF THE U.S. CONSTITUTION AND THE MAKING OF THE AMERICAN STATE 97–98, 171 (OUP, New York 2003); *see* EMPIRE 32, 93, 103–04, 107, 149; Donald F. Swanson & Andrew P. Trout, *Alexander Hamilton, "the Celebrated Mr. Neckar," and Public Credit*, 47 WM. & MARY Q. (3d Ser.) 422, 424–29 (1990) (French influence).

federal powers under the Constitution.[15] Soon, precursors to political parties appeared,[16] and partisan newspapers spread.[17] The aftermath of the French Revolution further divided the nation, and Francophile and Anglophile sympathies and foreign policy alternatives quickly became features of the incipient Republican and Federalist interests.[18] After war between France and Britain began in early 1793, the Neutrality Proclamation (drafted by Jay and revised by the attorney general) quelled the risk of America being drawn in, and the Jay Treaty stabilized relations with Britain as it was signed in 1795.[19] That came at a cost, however, as the Jay Treaty produced further partisan and sectional divisions, which heaped abuse on the chief justice who negotiated it,[20] some of which came in an ill-fated speech by the successor chief justice, John Rutledge. The legitimacy of such criticism of the administration was still disputed, as was the legitimacy of an opposition party,[21] and those unresolved issues were at the heart of the crisis of 1798–1801.

The views of each early justice about freedoms of speech and press before the turmoil of 1798 are the subject of this chapter and the next. Their views about those freedoms during the crisis years of 1798–1801 and their opinions about the constitutionality of the Sedition Act then will be discussed in Chapters 6 and 8.

[15] Gordon S. Wood, *Launching the "Extended Republic,"* in LAUNCHING THE "EXTENDED REPUBLIC": THE FEDERALIST ERA 1, 14 (Ronald Hoffman & Peter J. Albert eds., UPV, Charlottesville 1996); Herbert E. Sloan, *Hamilton's Second Thoughts: Federalist Finance Revisited* 61, in FEDERALISTS RECONSIDERED 61, 61–76 (Doron Ben-Atar, Barbara B. Oberg eds., UPV, Charlottesville 1998); *see* AMERICAN POLITICS 34, 48.

[16] JOYCE O. APPLEBY, INHERITING THE REVOLUTION 20 (BP-HUP, Cambridge 2000); AMERICAN POLITICS 8–10, 15–50, 53, 60, 66; *see* EMPIRE 140–41, 143–44, 145–47, 152–57, 158–59, 161–64, 172–73.

[17] JEFFREY L. PASLEY, "THE TYRANNY OF PRINTERS": NEWSPAPER POLITICS IN THE EARLY AMERICAN REPUBLIC 48–104 (UPV, Charlottesville 2001); RICHARD D. BROWN, KNOWLEDGE IS POWER: THE DIFFUSION OF INFORMATION IN EARLY AMERICA, 1700–1865, at 279–82 (OUP, New York 1989); *see* EMPIRE 150–52, 251–56.

[18] Matthew Schoenbachler, *Republicanism in the Age of Democratic Revolution: The Democratic-Republican Societies of the 1790s*, 18 J. EARLY REPUBLIC 237, 243–44 (1998); JOYCE O. APPLEBY, CAPITALISM AND A NEW SOCIAL ORDER: THE REPUBLICAN VISION OF THE 1790S, at 54–58 (NYUP, New York 1984); *see* AMERICAN POLITICS 10, 69; EMPIRE 162–64, 174–208.

[19] TODD ESTES, THE JAY TREATY DEBATE 106, 75–76 (UMP, Amherst 2006); JERALD A. COMBS, THE JAY TREATY: POLITICAL BATTLEGROUND OF THE FOUNDING FATHERS, at 107–15, 137–70 (UCP, Berkeley 1970); *see* AMERICAN POLITICS 75, 117–23.

[20] *Id.* at 104–26, 35–70; WALTER STAHR, JOHN JAY: FOUNDING FATHER 335–37 (HP, New York 2005); *see* AMERICAN POLITICS 119–36.

[21] BRUCE ACKERMAN, THE FAILURE OF THE FOUNDING FATHERS 18–27 (BP-HUP, Cambridge 2005); RICHARD BUEL, SECURING THE REVOLUTION: IDEOLOGY IN AMERICAN POLITICS, 1789–1815, at 1–90 (CorUP, Ithaca 1972); RICHARD HOFSTADTER, THE IDEA OF A PARTY SYSTEM: THE RISE OF LEGITIMATE OPPOSITION IN THE UNITED STATES, 1780–1840, at 80–121 (UCP, Berkeley 1969).

Chief Justice John Jay

Figure 4.1 Chief Justice John Jay (on Supreme Court 1789–1795). Portrait by Gilbert Stuart 1794. (Courtesy of National Gallery of Art.)

John Jay (Figure 4.1) was the first chief justice of the Supreme Court, though he is better known as the most influential negotiator of the Treaty of Paris of 1783, ending the Revolutionary War, as the coauthor of *The Federalist*, and as the negotiator of the Jay Treaty of 1795, averting war with Great Britain.[22]

Jay supported the colonists' cause as a member of the New York Committee of Correspondence and as a delegate to the Continental Congress during 1774–1776.[23] He left Congress to attend New York's convention,[24] and had he not done so would have signed the Declaration of Independence,[25] which he shepherded New York's legislators to approve.[26] He chaired his state's Committee for

[22] *See generally* Herbert A. Johnson, John Jay, 1745–1829 (Office of State History, Albany 1970); Herbert A. Johnson, John Jay: Colonial Lawyer (1965) (unpublished Ph.D. dissertation, Columbia University); Richard B. Morris, John Jay, the Nation, and the Court (BUP, Boston 1967); OCSC 446; 1 Justices 3; *accord* Walter Stahr, John Jay: Founding Father 335–37 (HP, New York 2005); Fischer 6–10. Jay signed the treaty in England in 1794, but it was only ratified by the Senate and signed by the President in 1795, so the 1795 date is used.

[23] 1 JCC 14 (5 Sept.1774).

[24] 1 Constitutional History-N.Y. 471.

[25] On the day it was received, Jay as committee chair prepared a resolution approving the Declaration. 1 Jay Correspondence 72, 73. He placed its full text in the New York Constitution of 1777. 5 Federal-State Constitutions 2623, 2625–28; *see* 1 Jay Correspondence 72 n.1.

[26] Resolutions of New York Convention Approving Declaration of Independence (9 July 1776), 1 Jay Correspondence 72 & n.1; *accord* Richard B. Morris, John Jay, the Nation, and the Court 8 (BUP, Boston 1967).

Detecting and Defeating Conspiracies[27] during the first part of the Revolutionary War, and his telling the story of an assistant provided the basis for James Fenimore Cooper's first successful novel, *The Spy*.[28] Jay served as the first chief justice of the new State of New York during 1777–1779.[29] After returning to Congress in 1778,[30] he became its president from December 1778 to September 1779,[31] when he resigned to serve as the colonies' minister to Spain.[32] He was one of three ministers assigned to discuss peace with England during 1781–1783,[33] and was principally responsible for successfully negotiating the Treaty of Paris.[34] Upon returning, he served as Congress' secretary of foreign affairs, effectively the secretary of state, from 1784–1789.[35] During the national debate on the proposed Constitution, he joined with Hamilton and Madison as authors of *The Federalist*.[36]

Jay became President George Washington's first appointment to the Supreme Court, as chief justice, in September 1789.[37] He continued to hold office through

[27] *Minutes of the Committee and of the First Commission for Detecting and Defeating Conspiracies*, 57 Collections of the New York Historical Society 21, 51 (NYHS, New York 1924); Jay-Revolutionary 337, 347.

[28] 1 Correspondence of James Fenimore-Cooper 42 (James Fenimore Cooper III ed., YUP, New Haven 1922); *compare* 1 H.L. Barnum, The Spy Unmasked xii–xiii (J. & J. Harper, New York 1829) *with* J. Fenimore Cooper to Benson Lossing (2 Aug.1850), 6 Letters and Journals of James Fenimore Cooper 212 (James F. Beard ed., HUP, Cambridge 1960–68) (never heard the name Enoch Crosby).

[29] *Minutes of the Council of Appointment Apr.4, 1778 – May 3, 1779*, in 58 Collections of the New York Historical Society 20, 46–67, 51–53 (NYHS, New York 1924); 1 Journals of Provincial Congress-N.Y. 910 (3 May 1777); Historical Memoirs . . . of William Smith 128, 137 (William H.W. Sabine ed., Colburn & Tegg, New York 1958). Jay resigned in 1779. John Jay to George Clinton (18 Aug.1779), 13 Letters of Delegates 386; John Jay to George Clinton (16 Sept.1779), 13 *id.* 499.

[30] 12 JCC 1196 (7 Dec.1778).

[31] 12 *id.* 1206 (10 Dec.1778), 15 *id.* 1114 (28 Sept.1779).

[32] 15 *id.* 1113 (27 Sept.1779); Congress Proceedings as to Election and Commissioning of Plenipotentiaries (26 Sept.1779), 3 The Revolutionary Diplomatic Correspondence of the United States 335–37 (Francis Wharton ed., GPO, Washington 1889); Silas Deane to Simeon Deane (28 Sept.1779), 4 The Deane Papers 107, 108 (Charles Isham ed., NYHS, New York 1887–90). He was unsuccessful other than obtaining a $150,000 loan. John Jay to Benjamin Franklin (21 Feb.1781), 2 Jay Correspondence 1.

[33] Commission To Treat of Peace (15 June 1781), 4 Diplomatic Correspondence, *supra* note 32, at 503; Thomas Rodney to Caesar Rodney (14 June 1781), Letters to and from Caesar Rodney 412, 414 (George H. Ryden ed., UPP, Philadelphia 1933) (initially five commissioners).

[34] 2 Treaties 151. While Franklin and Adams were also negotiators, Adams acknowledged "the principal merit of the negotiation for peace was Mr. Jay's." John Adams to John Jay (24 Nov.1800), 9 Adams Works 90, 91.

[35] 26 JCC 355 (7 May 1783); 1 ASP 89, 94, 96, 107; John Jay to American Commissioners (14 Jan.1785) (accepted 21 Dec.1784).

[36] Federalist Nos. 2–5, at 8–27; No. 64, at 432–38.

[37] Nomination (24 Sept.1789), 1 DHSC 9, 2 DHFFC 44; Confirmation (26 Sept.1789), 1 DHSC 9, 2 DHFFC 45. Jay was given his choice of that position or the secretary of state position. Samuel Otis to Caleb Strong (20 Sept.1789), 17 DHFFC 1589.

his absence from May 1794 through May 1795[38] as he served as minister to Great Britain[39] and negotiated the eponymous treaty ratified in 1795.[40] Returning to the United States in May 1795, he resigned from the Court[41] to accept the governorship of New York to which he had been elected.[42] Jay's reason was not that he deemed his new office higher, but that he had long sought release from rigorous circuit riding duties that the early Court suffered.[43] At the end of his second term as governor in 1801, he retired from public life.[44] Jay never saw or led the Supreme Court as an influential institution, and stated as he declined renomination that it was "a system so defective [that] it would not obtain the energy, weight, and dignity which are essential to its affording due support to the national government, nor acquire the public confidence and respect."[45] In that he was mistaken.

The reason Washington selected Jay as the first chief justice was Jay's stature as one of the new nation's leading statesmen.[46] Thomas Jefferson, before the development of political parties, estimated Jay as "a man who has pas[sed] his life in serving the public, who has served them in every the highest stations with universal approbation, and with a purity of conduct which has silenced even party opprobrium, who tho' poor has never permitted himself to make a shilling in the public employ."[47] Alexander Hamilton characterized Jay as one of "three persons prominent in the public eye, as the successor of the actual President of the United States" (who at the time was Washington).[48] John Adams later agreed that, among the "old supporters of the Constitution and of Washington's administration," Jay was "one of more importance than any of the rest, indeed of almost as much weight as

[38] John Jay to Edmund Randolph (9 June 1794), 1 ASP 475 (arrived in Britain the preceding day); John Jay to Edmund Randolph (28 May 1795), 1 *id.* 519 (landed in New York that day).

[39] Message Nominating John Jay as Envoy (16 Apr.1794), 1 ASP 447; Commission (19 Apr.1794), 1 *id.* 470.

[40] 2 Treaties 245; John Jay to Edmund Randolph (19 Nov.1794), 1 ASP 503; George Washington to Senate (with Treaty) (8 June 1795), 1 *id.* 470; *accord* Samuel Flagg Bemis, Jay's Treaty 252–71 (Macmillan, New York 1923).

[41] John Jay to President Washington (29 June 1795), 4 Jay Correspondence 177.

[42] Opening Speech (6 Jan.1796), 2 Messages from Governors-N.Y. 358.

[43] Egbert Benson to Rufus King (18 Dec.1793), 1 DHSC 742; William L. Smith to Edward Rutledge (13 Feb.1792), 1 *id.* 732.

[44] Opening Speech (4 Nov.1800), 2 Messages from Governors-N.Y. 463.

[45] John Jay to John Adam (2 Jan.1801), 4 Jay Correspondence 284, 285.

[46] Washington had "great confidence in the abilities, and purity of Mr. Jay[']s views, as well as in his experience." George Washington to Alexander Hamilton (26 June 1796), 35 Washington Writings 101, 103.

[47] Thomas Jefferson to James Currie (28 Jan.1786), 9 Jefferson Papers 239.

[48] Camillus [Alexander Hamilton], Defence of Mr. Jay's Treaty, in 4 Works of Alexander Hamilton 371, 375 (Henry Cabot Lodge ed., Putnam's Sons, New York 1885). This was before Hamilton's public break with Adams. *See* 6 *id.* 391. Gouverneur Morris agreed that Jay was the "proper person to succeed the President." Diary (22 Aug.1795), in 2 Diary and Letters of Gouverneur Morris 113 (Anne C. Morris ed., Kegan Paul, London 1889).

all the rest."[49] Benjamin Franklin respected Jay so much that he made Jay one of four executors of Franklin's very large estate.[50] Adams showed his respect by nominating Jay to resume the chief justiceship in 1801;[51] Jay declined.[52]

Jay, as all the framers, had flaws. His dismal view of human nature[53] would find Hobbes too generous in calling it "poore, nasty, [and] brutish."[54] Jay, though republican, was not democratic,[55] and he fully accepted classical theory that unmixed democracy was dangerous[56] as well as prevailing views about an aristocracy of talent.[57] His view of representative government was that "they who own the country are the most fit persons to participate in the government."[58] He was neither highly experienced nor highly inclined as a lawyer; as Edmund Randolph said of Jay as chief justice, he had "imposing elocution" and was "clear too in the expression of his ideas," but "they do not abound on legal subjects" and his opinions had "no legal principle."[59] Jay's ideas did abound on liberty, however.[60]

He discussed freedoms of press and speech, though his views and positions have never been described.

Jay and Freedom of Press

Jay, as other justices, relied on newspapers for information.[61] He disapproved of destruction of the loyalist press of James Rivington, soon after hostilities

[49] John Adams to James Lloyd (6 Feb.1815), 10 ADAMS WORKS 114, 115; *see* John Adams to John Jay (2 Sept.1782), 13 ADAMS PAPERS 414.

[50] 3 SELECTED WRITINGS OF BENJAMIN FRANKLIN 423, 431 (Florence Hamilton ed., William Pickering, London 1996); *accord* John Vardill to William Eden (11 Apr.1778), 4 FACSIMILES OF MANUSCRIPTS IN EUROPEAN ARCHIVES 71 at 4 (Benjamin F. Stevens ed., Malby, London 1889–98).

[51] Nomination (18 Dec.1800), 1 DHSC 144; John Adams to Thomas B. Adams (23 Dec.1800), 1 *id.* 906; Confirmation (19 Dec.1800), *id.*

[52] John Jay to John Adams (2 Jan.1801), 4 JAY CORRESPONDENCE 284–85; John Jay to John Marshall (2 Jan.1801), 6 MARSHALL PAPERS 49. Adams similarly said, during the federalist–antifederalist debates, that Jay among federalists was "of more importance than any of the rest, indeed of almost as much weight as all the rest." 10 ADAMS WORKS 115.

[53] *E.g.*, John Jay to William Vaughan (26 May 1796), 4 JAY CORRESPONDENCE 215, 216; John Jay to John Hartley (8 Jan.1795), 4 *id.* 152.

[54] THOMAS HOBBES, LEVIATHAN 84 (I, c13, ¶9) (Andrew Crooke, London 1651).

[55] *E.g.*, John Jay to Thomas Jefferson (27 Oct.1786), 10 JEFFERSON PAPERS 488, 489; John Jay to Richard Peters (24 July 1809), 4 JAY CORRESPONDENCE 315, 318.

[56] CREATION 198, 363, 412–13, 484; IDEOLOGICAL ORIGINS 70; though he was a moderate Federalist on democracy. FISCHER 7–8.

[57] CREATION 209, 237.

[58] John Jay to William Wilberforce (25 Oct.1810), 4 JAY CORRESPONDENCE 335, 336; *see* 1 WILLIAM JAY, THE LIFE OF JOHN JAY 70 (Harper, New York 1833).

[59] Edmund Randolph to James Madison (12 Aug.1792), 14 MADISON PAPERS 348, 349.

[60] *E.g.*, John Jay to Thomas Jefferson (27 Oct.1786), 3 JAY CORRESPONDENCE 212, 213; Address of the Convention of the Representatives of the State of New York (23 Dec.1776), 1 *id.* 102, 103, 118.

[61] *E.g.*, John Jay to Benjamin Franklin (18 Apr.1781), 34 FRANKLIN PAPERS 554; John Jay to Alexander Hamilton (28 Sept.1783), 3 HAMILTON PAPERS 459.

began.[62] He submitted his *Federalist* essays to newspapers for publication, and other essays as well over the years. He sent statements to newspapers when the French minister, Edmond Genet, appealed over the president's head to the American people for support.[63] He saw value in the press. Nonetheless, he was, at times, also on the receiving end of the press's reproach.

Jay's first baptism by fire in the newspapers came in the form of withering criticism for the Treaty of Paris, in 1783, particularly for its protection of British claims for prerevolutionary debts and its abandonment of American claims for confiscated slaves.[64] Though the criticism was of his actions as an American envoy, he did not urge prosecution of the critics or the editors.

Jay's next baptism by fire in the press came from sustained attacks by an ingrate ward, Lewis Littlepage, in 1785, after Jay enforced debts long owed by Littlepage.[65] The attacks forced Jay to develop a view of freedom of press, which he maintained lifelong. When threatened by Littlepage, Jay responded that Littlepage should "publish when and what you please," and when newspaper attacks by Littlepage began with selective snippets from their correspondence, Jay replied simply by publishing the full text of the correspondence.[66] Though the dispute was widely publicized and enjoyed,[67] Jay never took or threatened legal action against either Littlepage or the press. Late that year, Jay had to warn Jefferson, then minister to France, that the issue may come up with the French government,[68] because Littlepage was soon to be in Paris.[69]

Jefferson replied by commiserating that a public servant could be so attacked by any individual despite "faithful services," while adding that "it is a part of the price we pay for our liberty, which cannot be guarded but by the freedom of the press, nor that be limited without danger of losing it."[70]

[62] John Jay to Nathaniel Woodhull (26 Nov.1775), 2 Letters of Delegates 394 & n.2; *see* Alexander Hamilton to John Jay (26 Nov.1775), 1 Hamilton Papers 176; *accord* Prelude 239–40.

[63] John Jay and Rufus King to *Daily Advertiser* (14 Aug.1793), 15 Hamilton Papers 233; John Jay and Rufus King to Alexander Hamilton and Henry Knox (26 Nov.1793), 15 *id.* 411.

[64] James Madison, Memorandum on a Discussion of the President's Retirement (5 May 1792), 14 Madison Papers 299, 303.

[65] John Jay to Thomas Jefferson (9 Dec.1785), 9 Jefferson Papers 86; Thomas Jefferson to Governor Patrick Henry (24 Jan.1786), 9 *id.* 212, 213; *see* Jay-Peace 218.

[66] Letters, Being the Whole of the Correspondence Between the Hon. John Jay, Esquire, and Mr. Lewis Littlepage. A Young Man Whom Mr. Jay, When in Spain Patronized and Took into His Family (Francis Childs, New York 1786); *accord* William Livingston to Susannah Livingston (12 Dec.1785), 5 Livingston Papers 14.

[67] *E.g.*, Charles Pettit to James Hutchinson (11 Dec.1785), 22 Letters of Delegates 58, 60; Lambert Cadwalader to Robert Magaw (14 Dec.1785), 22 *id.* 61; James Monroe to James Madison (26 Dec.1785), 1 Monroe Writings 109, 112; James Monroe to James Madison (10 Mar.1786), 1 *id.* 123.

[68] John Jay to Thomas Jefferson (9 Dec.1785), 9 Jefferson Papers 86–87.

[69] Thomas Jefferson to John Jay (25 Jan.1786), 9 *id.* 215.

[70] *Id.*

Jay responded in agreement with Jefferson (in a letter not in his published correspondence):

> The Liberty of the Press is certainly too important to the public, to be restrained for the sake of personal considerations; especially as it is in every man's power to frustrate calumny, by not deserving censure; for altho slander may prevail for a while, yet truth and consistent rectitude will ultimately enjoy their rights. While I possess the esteem of those who merit esteem, the effusions of unmerited malevolence will give me no greater concern, than what naturally results from the various other evils to which we are liable. We cannot indeed be insensible to them, but we may bear them with fortitude . . . .[71]

Jay was an American official, and such public criticism of public officials historically had been treated as seditious libel, as Chapter 2 discussed. Yet Jay treated liberty of the press as extending to newspaper coverage of Littlepage's criticisms, and seditious libel as not reaching them. He recognized that restraint of the press included not just prior restraints but subsequent ones, since talking legal action against completed articles would cause the press and its liberty to be "restrained." Jay did not rely on the Blackstone-Mansfield definition of freedoms of press and speech as merely freedom from prior restraint, or those jurists' rationale, but instead adopted a more republican rationale of "Liberty of the Press" and its "importan[ce] to the public." Jay's remedy, rather than any restraint on the press, was simply to bear calumny "with fortitude" and to wait for truth to prevail; he did not take private legal action or seek government prosecution.

Jay and Freedom of Speech

Jay more often extolled liberty than he discussed specific rights.[72] However, his occasional discussions of freedom of speech were consistent over his lifetime. During the turmoil of the American Revolution, Jay pointed to the foundation of liberty, and then connected it to freedom of expression (a full decade before the First Amendment was written):

> Under governments which have just and equal liberty for their foundation, every subject has a right to give his sentiments on all matters of public concern; provided it be done with modesty and decency . . . .[73]

[71] John Jay to Thomas Jefferson (5 May 1786), 9 *id.* 450.

[72] *E.g.*, John Jay, To the King['] s Most Excellent Majesty (3–19 June 1775), JAY-REVOLUTIONARY 152–53; John Jay, Address of the Convention of the Representatives of the State of New York (Dec.1776–Feb.1777), 1 JAY CORRESPONDENCE 102, 102, 103, 105, 118, 120.

[73] John Jay, A Hint to the Legislature of the State of New York (15 Jan. –2 Apr.1778), JAY-REVOLUTIONARY 461.

He and other leaders were very aware that speech and press—"petitions and affectionate remonstrances"—had been pivotal in seeking redress of grievances, and then in joining colonists against the Crown.[74] He noted that the new state constitutions provided security to "the rights of . . . private judgment."[75] (Much later, Jay gave his definition of decency, as being not "harsh and violent," and did not equate lack of decency with seditious libel.[76])

Ten years later in 1788, Jay developed the point in a published essay supporting ratification of the federal Constitution.

> They [the framers] were likewise sensible that, on a subject so comprehensive and involving such a variety of points and questions, the most able, the most candid, and the most honest men will differ in opinion. The same proposition seldom strikes many minds in exactly the same point of light. Different habits of thinking, different degrees and modes of education, different prejudices and opinions, early formed and long entertained, conspire, with a multitude of other circumstances, to produce among men a diversity and contrariety of opinions on questions of difficulty. Liberality, therefore, as well as prudence, induced them to treat each other's opinions with tenderness . . . .[77]

Jay later applied the principle equally to elections—"propriety forbids that differences in opinion respecting candidates should suspend or interrupt that mutual good-humour and benevolence which harmonizes society."[78] In saying this, he was not speaking theoretically; he had just won the governorship of New York in 1792, yet had been denied the office by vote manipulation.[79]

He expressed the same view in a draft grand jury charge, written before[80] the Neutrality Proclamation of April 1793.[81] (This, like most other grand jury charges of the 1790s, was only published as the outstanding *Documentary History of the Supreme Court* took form over the last twenty-five years.) The charge

[74] Jay's Charge to the Grand Jury of Ulster County ([9 Sept.] 1777), 1 Jay Correspondence 158, 160.

[75] 1 *id.* 162.

[76] John Jay to Peter Van Schaack (28 July 1812), 4 *id.* 360, 361.

[77] John Jay, An Address to the People of the State of New York (spring 1788), 3 *id.* 294, 309.

[78] John Jay, Jay's Reply to the New York Committee (July 1792), 3 *id.* 442, 444.

[79] Robert Troup to John Jay (13 June 1792), 3 Jay Correspondence 433; Robert Troup to John Jay (20 May 1792), 3 *id.* 424.

[80] Had it been written after the Proclamation, the charge surely would have mentioned it and discussed obligations under it, as the final charge did. Around the same time, Jay was asked by Hamilton to draft a neutrality proclamation, and did.

[81] 1 ASP 140 (22 Apr.1793). The next year, Congress passed the Neutrality Act of 1794. 1 Stat. 381.

wandered far from the path of modern jury charges, because in the early years of the republic the charges, as court sessions opened, typically sought to educate the public about the principles of the new government[82] (just as judges' charges then wandered freely in England[83]). Such charges were commonly printed in newspapers.[84] Jay wended his way to freedom of speech of citizens in peacetime:

> until[] war is constitutionally declared—the nation and all its members must observe and preserve peace, and do the duties incident to a state of peace—Such at present is our situation, and in that light gentlemen you will regard it. As free citizens we have a right to think and speak[] our sentiments on these subject[s], in terms becoming free men—that is in terms explicit and decorous—As judges and grand jurors the merits of those political questions are without our province.[85]

The draft unwaveringly affirmed freedom of speech, and did not limit it to "decent" or nonseditious speech as the 1778 charge had.[86] It left speech, even about "political questions," simply "without [the] province" of the legal system—not subject to consideration by judges and grand jurors. Shortly before in that charge, Jay instructed the grand jury to present any "seditious practices,"[87] so he clearly did not invite presentments of speech critical of the administration on political questions as seditious. This was Jay's view uninfluenced by crisis or loyalty to the administration.

Instead, Jay's reference to sedition defined it as involving much more than mere denunciatory words. "If you find any foreigners in this district committing seditious practices ende[a]voring to seduce our citizens into acts of hostility, or attempting to withdraw them from their allegiance to the United States—present them—such men are guilty of high misdemeanors."[88] That reference to seditious practices is the first known reference to sedition in any grand jury charge of a Supreme Court justice.

[82] George Clinton to Pierre Van Cortlandt, Jr. (2 Mar.1805), 3 CORRESPONDENCE OF THE VAN CORTLANDT FAMILY 185 (Jacob Judd ed., Sleepy Hollow Restorations, Tarrytown 1976–81); Ralph Lerner, *The Supreme Court as Republican Schoolmaster*, 1967 SUP. CT. REV. 127.

[83] DICKINSON 161; *e.g.*, CHARGES TO THE GRAND JURY 1689–1803, at 399–410, 549–51 (Georges Lamoine ed., RHS, London 1992).

[84] *E.g.*, for 1793, 2 DHSC 368, 373, 377, 392, 412, 414n.

[85] John Jay's Charge (Draft) (C.C.D. Va. 22 Apr.1793), 2 DHSC 359, 364.

[86] Similarly, he wrote to a friend in 1785 that he wished "that the time may soon come when all our inhabitants of every colour and denomination shall be free and equal partakers of our political liberty." John Jay to Benjamin Rush (24 Mar.1785), 3 JAY CORRESPONDENCE 139, 140.

[87] 2 DHSC 363.

[88] *Id.*

That grand jury charge for 1793 was rewritten after the Neutrality Proclamation was issued.[89] In revising most of it, Jay replaced the passage on freedom of speech with the obligations of citizens under the Proclamation.

> It is natural in all contests, even for the best men to take sides, and wish success to one party in preference to the other. Our wishes and partialities becoming inflamed by opposition, often cause indiscretions and lead us to say and to do things that had better have been omitted. It is not certain that the irritability of the belligerent powers, combined with some indiscretions on our part, will not involve us in war with some of them. . . . It is very desir[]able that such an event do not find us divided into parties, and particularly into parties in favor of this or that foreign nation.[90]

While Jay encouraged "union and harmony among ourselves," his words were only hortatory, and he recognized that it was possible "such parties should arise among the people." He did not warn that parties would verge on seditious libel, but merely reasoned with his audience about the ill effects of parties, as Madison recently had done in *The Federalist*.[91] Continuing, Jay instead cited the Bill of Rights (his only reference to it in his grand jury charges or Supreme Court opinions), and the importance of government recognition that citizens "are entitled to be protected" in their rights:

> Happy it would be for mankind, and greatly would it promote the cause of liberty and the equal rights of men, if the free and popular governments which from time to time may take place, should be so constructed, so bal[]anced, so organized and administered, as to be evidently and em[i]nently productive of a higher and more durable degree of happiness than any of the other forms [of government.]—It is not sufficient to tell men by a Bill of Rights, that they [word inked out] are free, that they have equal rights, and that they are entitled to be protected in them—men will not believe they are really free, while they experience oppression—they will not think their title to equal rights, realized, until[] they enjoy them; nor will they esteem that a good government, whatever may be its name, which does not uniformly impartially and effectually protect them.[92]

[89] It may also have been revised because of comments from Alexander Hamilton, since Jay and he discussed drafts of a neutrality proclamation. Alexander Hamilton to John Jay (9 Apr.1793), 3 Jay Correspondence 472; Alexander Hamilton to John Jay (9 Apr.1793), 3 *id.* 473; John Jay to Alexander Hamilton (11 Apr.1793), 3 *id.* 473; Draft of Proclamation of Neutrality, by John Jay (1793), 3 *id.* 474.

[90] John Jay's Charge (C.C.D. Va. 22 May 1793), 2 DHSC 380, 389.

[91] Federalist No.10, at 56, 57.

[92] 2 DHSC 390. Jay went on to say that "[t]he more free the people are, the more strong and efficient ought their governm[en]t to be," in order to protect a large number of rights. *Id.*

Though it was a dangerous time when war with Britain or France easily could be provoked, Jay here, after describing the legal requirements of the Neutrality Proclamation, reaffirmed the First Amendment protections for expression. Moreover, he appeared to allow people to evaluate the federal government as not "a good government," which bordered on seditious libel, and to require the government to "impartially and effectually protect" their rights under the Bill of Rights.

Jay's revision also changed his draft's mention of sedition, warning that "[t]o oppose the operation of this Constitution and of the government established by it, would be to violate the sovereignty of the people, and would justly merit reprehension & punishment."[93] His reference was not to opposing the operation of government by speech, but by unneutral acts risking war, because the reference to sedition was made between the two quoted passages on rights. Another indicator that he meant not speech, but unneutral acts, was that he began the charge by summarizing the law of nations (including the Neutrality Proclamation) and federal criminal laws and ended it with an exhortation that "the laws be observed and irresist[i]bly executed."[94] Still another indicator is his draft of the proclamation itself.

It was Jay who drafted the Neutrality Proclamation of 1793, at Washington's request through Hamilton, at a precarious time when unneutral acts could cause war, and when speeches and newspapers were reaching new levels of attack on government policy. Jay's draft sternly mandated neutral conduct and enjoined unneutral actions by American citizens,[95] but it couched two provisions as merely a "recommend[ation]" and a "wish"—those on speech and press:

> I do also recommend it to my fellow-citizens in general to omit such public discussions as may tend not only to cause divisions and parties among ourselves, and thereby impair that union on which our strength depends, but also give unnecessary cause of offence and irritation to foreign powers. And I cannot forbear expressing a wish that our printers may study to be impartial in the representation of facts, and observe much prudence relative to such strictures and animadversions as may render the disposition of foreign governments and rulers unfriendly to the people of the United States.[96]

The transition in language from command (he believed the proclamation to have the force of law[97]) to precation was striking and intentional. Jay's reason was not

[93] *Id.*

[94] 2 *id.* 380–88, 391.

[95] Draft of Proclamation of Neutrality, by John Jay (Apr.1793), 3 Jay Correspondence 474, 476.

[96] 3 *id.* 476–77. Hamilton's copy differed in sequence, but was the same in substance. A Proclamation, 14 Hamilton Papers 308–10.

[97] John Jay's Charge (C.C.D. Va. 22 May 1793), 2 DHSC 380, 382–83.

practical concern that strong requirements would not be upheld, because President Washington was still extremely popular, Congress was dominated by his supporters, and the Supreme Court was solidly supportive as well. Jay instead softened the speech and press provisions because of his principles, principles he identified in his grand jury charge that he had just drafted, including that "we have a right to think and speak[] our sentiments on these subject[s]."[98]

Rights and Declarations of Rights in the Continental Congress, the New York Constitution, and the Bill of Rights

Jay showed the same ebullience for freedom and concern for rights in the prelude to the Revolutionary War. At the first Continental Congress in 1774, he took a leading role as draftsman of numerous addresses and messages, such as his[99] "Address to the People of Great Britain."[100] The address repeatedly proclaimed "the rights of men and the blessings of liberty" under the British constitution of government, and listed a half dozen rights that were widely recognized.[101] The address did not undertake to list liberties with weaker grounding in British law, such as speech or press, but was sufficiently in the vanguard of thought at that time that Jefferson praised it as "a production of the finest pen in America."[102]

At the second Continental Congress the next year, Jay's[103] "Letter from Congress to the 'Oppressed Inhabitants of Canada'"[104] shifted the argument from the ancient rights of the English[105] to natural rights ("rights bestowed by the Almighty"), and strengthened the plea for liberty to a "determin[ation] to live free, or not at all."[106] He urged Canada to rise in "defence of our common liberty" and "the rights of mankind."[107]

At the Provincial Congress of New York, after Jay led the campaign to approve the Declaration of Independence in July 1776,[108] he was the principal

[98] John Jay's Charge (Draft) (C.C.D. Va. 22 Apr.1793), 2 DHSC 359, 364.

[99] 1 JCC 81 n.2; Thomas Jefferson to William Wirt (4 Aug.1805), 1 Letters of Members 79 n.3; John Jay to Richard Henry Lee (12 Feb.1823), 4 Jay Correspondence 468, 469–70; 1 *id.* 17 n.1.

[100] John Jay, Address to the People of Great Britain (5 Sept.1774), 1 Jay Correspondence 17.

[101] 1 *id.* 18,19, 28.

[102] Thomas Jefferson to William Wirt (4 Aug.1805), 1 Letters of Members 158 n.2; *accord* Thomas Jefferson's Notes on Patrick Henry (ante 12 Apr.1812), 4 Jefferson Papers-Retirement 598, 601.

[103] 2 JCC 68 n.2.

[104] 1 Jay Correspondence 32.

[105] In September 1774, Adams quoted Jay as arguing it "is necessary to recur to the laws of nature" along with the British Constitution. Diary (8 Sept.1774), 2 Adams Works 370.

[106] 1 Jay Correspondence 34, 35.

[107] *Id.* 36.

[108] Resolutions of New York Convention Approving Declaration of Independence (9 July 1776), 1 Jay Correspondence 72 & n.1.

author[109] of the state constitution that was adopted the following April.[110] The preamble gave as the purpose "to secure the rights and liberties of the good people of this state."[111] However, the instrument did not provide a comprehensive list of those rights, instead following the approach of all of the colonial charters and of three other state constitutions during the Revolution,[112] by listing four rights in the body of the constitution.[113] Those did not include freedom of press, which nine of the revolutionary constitutions ultimately listed,[114] or freedom of speech, which had recently been accorded protection for the first time[115] in the Pennsylvania and Vermont bills of rights,[116] though not yet by other states.

Jay's lack of a declaration of rights did not signify antipathy to declarations of rights, which Virginia had only recently broken ground in adopting. The most

[109] He was on the committee of fourteen to draft it. *New-York Convention and Committee of Safety*, 3 AMERICAN ARCHIVES 201, 202. He was one of the three legislators who dominated discussion of the state constitution, in the convention journal. Correspondence immediately after the constitution was adopted called various provisions "your ideas." Robert Livingston and Gouverneur Morris to John Jay (26 Apr.1777); Reply (29 Apr.1777). He is generally described as the chair of the committee and the "chief author." 1 CONSTITUTIONAL HISTORY-N.Y. 471; 5 FEDERAL-STATE CONSTITUTIONS 2624 n.; *accord* PATRICK T. CONLEY AND JOHN P. KAMINSKI, THE CONSTITUTION AND THE STATES 235 (Madison House, Madison 1988); BERNARD SCHWARTZ, GREAT RIGHTS OF MANKIND: A HISTORY OF THE AMERICAN BILL OF RIGHTS 80 (OUP, New York 1977); 1 BILL OF RIGHTS 301; RICHARD B. MORRIS, JOHN JAY, THE NATION, AND THE COURT 10 (BUP, Boston 1967); FRANK MONAGHAN, JOHN JAY 94 (Bobbs-Merrill, New York 1935); GEORGE PELLEW, JOHN JAY 58 (Houghton Mifflin, Boston 1890) (chair); E. Wilder Spaulding, *The State Government Under the First Constitution*, in 4 HISTORY OF THE STATE OF NEW YORK 156 (Alexander C. Flick ed., ColUP, New York 1933); 1 WILLIAM JAY, LIFE OF JOHN JAY: SELECTIONS FROM HIS CORRESPONDENCE AND MISCELLANEOUS PAPERS 69 (J. & J. Harper, New York 1833). His son stated that the committee's draft was "in Mr. Jay's handwriting," 1 LIFE OF JOHN JAY 69, but that draft is not extant. 1 CONSTITUTIONAL HISTORY-N.Y. 496–97. Jay's proposal of a number of amendments as the draft was debated may indicate that the draft was not entirely or even primarily his. 1 CONSTITUTIONAL HISTORY-N.Y. 425, 432, 535, 544–45, 554; 1 SELECTED PAPERS OF JOHN JAY 400–01n. (Elizabeth M. Nuxoll ed., UVP, Charlottesville 2010). However, his son as plausibly states that Jay intentionally left controversial points for amendments in order not to kill the draft. 1 LIFE OF JOHN JAY 69.

[110] 5 FEDERAL-STATE CONSTITUTIONS 2623.

[111] 5 *id.* 2623, 2636–37, 2628.

[112] 5 *id.* 2594 (N.J.); 2 *id.* 777 (Ga.); 6 *id.* 3241 (S.C.).

[113] Those were liberty of conscience, the right to counsel, trial by jury, and protection from attainders. 5 *id.* 2636–37, 2635, 2637.

[114] 7 *id.* 3814 (VA. DECL. OF RIGHTS §12), 5 *id.* 3083 (PA. DECL. OF RIGHTS art.XII), 1 *id.* 562 (DEL. DECL. OF RIGHTS §23), 3 *id.* 1690 (MD. DECL. OF RIGHTS art.XXXVIII), 5 *id.* 2788 (N.C. DECL. OF RIGHTS art.XV), 2 *id.* 785 (GA. CONST. art.LXI), 6 *id.* 3257 (S.C. CONST. art.XLIII), 3 *id.* 1892 (MASS. DECL. OF RIGHTS art.XVI), 4 *id.* 2456 (N.H. BILL OF RIGHTS art.XXII), plus Vermont's, 6 *id.* 3741 (VT. DECL. OF RIGHTS art.XIV).

[115] Other than for legislators in legislative proceedings.

[116] 5 *id.* 3083 (PA. DECL. OF RIGHTS art.XII), 6 *id.* 3741 (VT. DECL. OF RIGHTS art.XIV).

obvious explanation is that Jay simply followed the approach of his state's and others' colonial charters[117] and of the revolutionary constitutions of nearby New England states.[118] Similarly, the absence of declarations of rights in the New Jersey, Georgia, and South Carolina constitutions,[119] and in the Declarations and Resolves of the Continental Congress,[120] did not reflect lack of commitment to rights. New York itself did not add provisions for freedom of speech and press, even when the Republicans gained control of the legislature in the elections of 1800, or thereafter until the constitutional revision of 1821.[121] Another reason is that Jay believed that unlisted rights were granted and already protected by natural law, and so were "inviolate" without need for enumeration, as he said in his first grand jury charge for the state supreme court after the adoption of the state constitution:

> the highest respect has been paid to those great and equal rights of human nature, which should forever remain inviolate in every society . . . . Your lives, your liberties, your property, will be at the disposal only of your Creator and yourselves. . . .
>
> Adequate security is also given to the rights of conscience and private judgment. They are by nature subject to no control but that of the Deity, and in that free situation they are now left.[122]

While "the rights of conscience" were protected by a paragraph of the New York constitution, the rights of "private judgment" were seen by Jay as equally inviolate even without an explicit paragraph, because they were conferred by natural law and immune from any "control."[123]

[117] 1 FEDERAL-STATE CONSTITUTIONS 519, 523, 529 (Connecticut), 557, 558, 560 (Delaware, except conscience and criminal witnesses-counsel); 2 *id.* 765 (Georgia); 3 *id.* 1870 (Massachusetts); 4 *id.* 2445 (New Hampshire); 5 *id.* 2535, 2537 (New Jersey, except conscience), 2743, 2752–53 (Carolinas, except conscience); 6 *id.* 3211, 3213 (Rhode Island, except conscience); 7 *id.* 3802 (Virginia); *contra* 5 *id.* 3047 (Pennsylvania).

[118] Massachusetts did not adopt a declaration of rights until 1780; Connecticut's new act did not list many rights; and Rhode Island never adopted a declaration of rights or constitution during the Revolution or Confederation. 3 *id.* 1888 (Mass.); 1 FEDERAL-STATE CONSTITUTIONS-POORE 257 (Conn.).

[119] 5 FEDERAL-STATE CONSTITUTIONS 2594 (N.J.), 2 *id.* 777 (Ga.), 6 *id.* 3241 (S.C.).

[120] 1 JCC 67–71.

[121] 1 CONSTITUTIONAL HISTORY-N.Y. 215 (reprinting it).

[122] Jay's Charge to the Grand Jury of Ulster County ([9 Sept.] 1777), 1 JAY CORRESPONDENCE 158, 162. His reasoning was evidently, as in 1788 ratification debates, that the state only had enumerated powers and no such power to interfere with rights.

[123] He believed strongly in natural law and natural rights. *E.g.*, John Jay, Letter from Congress to the "Oppressed Inhabitants of Canada" (spring 1775), 1 JAY CORRESPONDENCE 32, 34; John Jay to John Murray (15 Apr. 1818), 4 *id.* 403.

Jay's approach to rights did not reflect allegiance to property rights to the neglect of personal rights. He did not add a clause protecting property rights, either. In fact, he periodically lamented the "private rage for property [that] suppresses public considerations."[124] On at least two occasions, at the beginning and end of the Revolution, Jay addressed the relative importance he ascribed to personal liberty and to property. He wrote that "we do not fight for a few acres of land, but for freedom—for the freedom and happiness of millions yet unborn." Thus,

> Provided we preserve our liberty and independence I shall be content, under their auspices, in a fruitful country and by patient industry, a competence may always be acquired; and I shall always think myself a gainer when I find my civil rights secured at the expense of my property.[125]

At New York's ratification convention in 1788, "Mr. Hamilton, Mr. Jay and Chancellor Livingston had conducted the federalists,"[126] and it was Jay who made the successful motion to ratify the Constitution.[127] He had already encouraged ratification by publishing an essay.[128] The divided convention was only able to approve ratification with language that it acted "in full confidence" that amendments would be adopted, and with a proposed bill of rights attached.[129] That proposed bill of rights included the provision "[t]hat the freedom of the press ought not to be violated or restrained."[130]

Jay agreed with Madison's initial position[131] that a bill of rights was not necessary, because the Constitution did not enumerate any power for the federal government to abridge freedom of press, trial by jury, or other rights.[132] Thus, he disagreed

[124] John Jay to George Washington (27 June 1786), 4 WASHINGTON PAPERS-CONFEDERATION 130, 131; *accord* John Jay to Thomas Jefferson (27 Oct.1786), 10 JEFFERSON PAPERS 488, 489.

[125] [John Jay], Address of the Convention of the Representatives of the State of New York (23 Dec. 1776), 1 JAY CORRESPONDENCE 102, 113; John Jay to Elbridge Gerry (9 Jan.1782), JAY-PEACE 123. He revised the nonbelletristic final clause to say "I shall never cease to prefer a little with freedom, to op[]ulence without it." *Id.*

[126] James Madison to Thomas Jefferson (17 Oct.1788), 25 LETTERS OF DELEGATES 426, 427; *accord* Edward Carrington to William Short (26 July 1788), 25 *id.* 249, 250.

[127] 2 ELLIOT'S DEBATES 410 (11 July 1788); *see* 18 DHRC 295.

[128] JOHN JAY, An Address to the People of the State of New York (1788), 3 JAY CORRESPONDENCE 294; *see* 17 DHRC 103, 103–05.

[129] 18 DHRC 297 (23 July 1788); 2 ELLIOT'S DEBATES 412.

[130] 18 DHRC 300.

[131] James Madison to Edmund Randolph (10 Apr.1788), 11 MADISON PAPERS 18, 19; George Turberville to James Madison (16 Apr.1788), 11 *id.* 23 (responding to "those powerful reasons that may be urged agt. the adoption of a Bill of Rights"); James Madison to Thomas Jefferson (10 Aug.1788), 11 *id.* 226, 226; *accord* FEDERALIST No.84, at 579 (Hamilton).

[132] John Jay, An Address to the People of the State of New York (1788), 3 JAY CORRESPONDENCE 294, 305.

"that the liberty of the press is left insecure," finding it "absurd to construe the silence . . . relative to a great number of our rights, into a total extinction of them"; and consequently he disagreed that the Constitution should be "accompanied by a bill of rights," noting that the government may "exercise no rights but such as the people commit to them."[133] However, his disagreement was not adamant, because he supported ratification with those additions.[134] His significance at New York's ratification convention was acknowledged by George Washington, who wrote to "congratulate you on the success of your labours" in bringing about ratification.[135]

In fact, Jay's view of the superfluity of a bill of rights was not opposition to its substance. He wrote[136] the circular letter that the governor of New York sent to the other states, with the state's proposed bill of rights, in August 1788. It reaffirmed that "nothing but the fullest confidence of obtaining a revision" of the Constitution could permit states to ratify "without stipulating for previous amendments," and that "amendments have been proposed" that made it important to call a constitutional convention.[137] In truth, Jay's personal view had changed by that time, because in a private letter he supported a second convention to propose amendments, though he preferred to wait three or four years so the new Constitution could first gain popular support.[138]

Jay and the other initial justices did not participate in Congress' approval of the Bill of Rights, because they served in other branches of government and not in Congress in 1789. They could not participate in the states' ratifications of the Bill of Rights, because during the week when Congress approved the Bill of Rights to be sent to the states, Jay and others were appointed to the Supreme Court, in late September 1789.[139]

Freedoms of Press and Speech in Practice in the 1790s

Jay, like the other early justices, remained well aware of the importance of the press to the Revolution. He had seen the press as also important to the Constitution, as

[133] *Id.* 305, 306.

[134] 18 DHRC 300 (26 July 1788) (30–27 margin); 2 ELLIOT'S DEBATES 413; 2 BILL OF RIGHTS 897.

[135] George Washington to John Jay (3 Aug.1788), 6 WASHINGTON PAPERS-CONFEDERATION 419.

[136] 3 JAY CORRESPONDENCE 353; *accord* 1 WASHINGTON PAPERS-REVOLUTIONARY 81n.; 18 DHRC 296; RICHARD B. MORRIS, JOHN JAY, THE NATION, AND THE COURT 37 (BUP, Boston 1967).

[137] Circular Letter from the Convention of the State of New York, to the Executives of the Different States (Aug.1788), in 3 JAY CORRESPONDENCE 353; *accord* 2 ELLIOT'S DEBATES 413–14.

[138] John Jay to George Washington (21 Sept.1788), 6 WASHINGTON PAPERS-CONFEDERATION 527, 528.

[139] Except James Iredell, who was still working toward North Carolina's ratification of the Constitution itself, which occurred 21 Nov.1789, 22 STATE RECORDS-N.C. 48–49, before he was appointed to the Supreme Court on 8 Feb.1790. 2 DHFFC 60, 61.

he with Hamilton conceived the idea of encouraging ratification by publishing essays and hoping for dissemination by newspapers across the nation (which later were collected as *The Federalist*); they then enlisted Madison in the project.[140] Though Jay's essays were fewer in number than originally planned,[141] because of illness,[142] his participation was important because he was (in Madison's words) "more known by character throughout the United States" than his coauthors.[143] The essays lived up to their purpose, proving significant in securing ratification. Jay's only reference in those essays to the press was negative—"it is fresh in our memories how soon the press began to teem with pamphlets and weekly papers against those very measures" recommended by the Continental Congress[144]—but at the same time his only reference to the press was favorable in another published essay.[145]

Jay's view of freedoms of press and speech, which had been molded in the Treaty of 1783 debate, the Littlepage fracas, and the Neutrality Proclamation dispute, continued in the later 1790s when Jay had the political power to spur prosecution of a libelous and vitriolic press, and very consciously did not exercise it in any way.

The negotiator along with his Jay Treaty of 1795 were the subject of unparalleled excoriation in the press and in speeches, some even given as Jay was burned in effigy.[146] One of the milder was Thomas Paine calling him a "sycophant of every thing in power" and a "disguised traitor."[147] Even friends like Gouverneur Morris believed the attack was so clamorous that the treaty would "hang about Mr. Jay's neck like a millstone in his political voyages."[148] Jay did not attempt to silence the press in any way, though his political influence could have spurred

[140] James Madison to Thomas Jefferson (10 Aug.1788), 2 MADISON PAPERS 225, 227.

[141] FEDERALIST Nos.2–5, at 8–27; No. 64, at 432–38.

[142] James Madison to Thomas Jefferson (10 Aug.1788), 2 MADISON PAPERS 225, 227.

[143] James Madison to Thomas Jefferson (27 May 1789), 12 JEFFERSON PAPERS 185, 185 & 186 n.4 (Madison's correction of quotation).

[144] FEDERALIST No.2, at 11.

[145] If a new constitutional convention were held, we would "again see the press teeming with publications for and against it." Address to the People and State of New York, 3 JAY CORRESPONDENCE 294, 314.

[146] JAMES CALLENDER, SKETCHES OF THE HISTORY OF AMERICA 145 (Snowden & McCorkle, Philadelphia 1798); 1 WILLIAM COBBETT, PORCUPINE'S WORKS 333 (Cobbett & Morgan, London 1801); MEMOIRS OF HIS OWN TIME, BY ALEXANDER GRAYDON 376–77 (John S. Littell ed., rev. ed. Lindsay & Blakiston, Philadelphia 1846); *accord* TODD ESTES, THE JAY TREATY DEBATE 106, 75–76 (UMP, Amherst 2006); OPPOSITION 177–235.

[147] THOMAS PAINE, LETTER FROM THOMAS PAINE TO GEORGE WASHINGTON (2d ed. H.D. Symonds, London 1797).

[148] Diary (14 June 1795), in 2 DIARY AND LETTERS OF GOUVERNEUR MORRIS 91 (Anne C. Morris ed., Kegan Paul, Trench, London 1889).

federal prosecutions or congressional action. Instead, he wrote privately at the peak of the storm:

> The treaty is as it is; and the time will certainly come when it will very universally receive exactly that degree of commendation or censure which, to candid and enlightened minds, it shall appear to deserve. In the meantime I must do as many others have done before me—that is, regretting the depravity of some, and the ignorance of a much greater number, bear with composure and fortitude the effects of each. It is as vain to lament that our country is not entirely free from these evils, as it would be to lament that our fields produce weeds as well as corn.
>
> Differences in opinion, and other causes equally pure and natural, will unavoidably cause parties; but such parties . . . are probably no less conducive to good government, than moderate fermentation is necessary to make good wine.
>
> My good friend, we must take men and things as they are, and enjoy all the good we meet with. I enjoy the good-will to which I am indebted for your letter . . . .[149]

He continued his 1783 and 1785 approach to press attack, trusting the judgment of the future, accepting differences in opinion, and treating such criticism as permissible.

A half decade later and after the Sedition Act was passed, Jay was still the victim of demonstrable falsehoods in the press about his diplomatic mission. He quoted an example from "Greenleaf's paper,"[150] which misstated the expenses of his diplomatic mission as $52,721 instead of $18,000, and was "calculated . . . to impress an opinion . . . that I derived extravagant emoluments from it," even though he received no compensation except his continuing Supreme Court salary. Jay had taken no action in the two and a half years since that and similar publications, though the Sedition Act had been passed, believing that calumny "is without remedy, and consequently is to be borne patiently."[151] That virtually echoed his conclusion during the Littlepage assault. Again, Jay showed no thought of using seditious libel laws, though he was a high government official and the attacks were on his governmental mission.

Jay, as governor of New York when the Sedition Act was passed, again had the opportunity to cause prosecution of Greenleaf's newspaper and other critics, either by federal prosecutors under the Sedition Act, or by state prosecutors under the common law of seditious libel. Yet there is not one example of Jay seeking prosecutions during his five years as governor, even with Federalist control of both the federal government and the state government. Jay impeded not his critics, but the Sedition Act itself, as described in Chapter 8.

[149] John Jay to General Henry Lee (11 July 1795), 4 Jay Correspondence 178, 178–79.

[150] Unrelated to Jay's concern, Greenleaf's widow and the very Republican *Argus* suffered Sedition Act prosecution in 1799–1800 (discussed in Chapter 6).

[151] John Jay to Henry Van Schaack (23 Sept.1800), 4 *id.* 275, 276.

Justice John Rutledge

Figure 4.2 Justice John Rutledge (on Supreme Court 1789–1791, also briefly chief justice 1795). Portrait attributed to John Trumbull c.1791. (Courtesy of National Portrait Gallery, Smithsonian Institution/Art Resource.)

John Rutledge (Figure 4.2), one of the two initial justices who received their legal training in the Inns of Court,[152] was a leading member of the Constitutional Convention. Upon Jay's resignation, Rutledge briefly served as the second chief justice by recess appointment, but became the first federal appointee denied confirmation, ironically because of his exercise of freedom of speech about his predecessor's treaty.[153]

Within months of returning from law studies in England in 1761 and admission to the bar,[154] Rutledge entered South Carolina's colonial legislature,[155] the Commons House of Assembly. There, he helped generate some of the colonial storms, which are described below. His support of the colonists' cause began with the Stamp Act Congress of 1765,[156] and his role became major in the Continental Congresses of 1774–1775.[157] He led the writing of South Carolina's constitution of early

[152] E. Alfred Jones, American Members of the Inns of Court 189 (Saint Catherine Press, London 1924); C. E. A. Bedwell, *American Middle Templars*, 25 Am. Historical Rev. 680 (1920). John Blair was the other.

[153] *See generally* James A. Haw, John and Edward Rutledge of South Carolina (UGP, Athens 1997) (the best biography); OCSC 750; 1 Justices 33.

[154] Rutledge was practicing law by November 1763. Judgment, Davison v. Flyn & Mollett (proposed Nov.1763, entered 21 Sept.1766), John Rutledge [Sr.] Papers, 1762–1776 (DU, Durham, Ms. Section A).

[155] The governor's council claimed to be the upper house of the legislature, similar to the House of Lords, which colonial advocates disputed.

[156] Stamp Act Congress Journal 195, 197, 198, 203; *accord* Edmund S. Morgan, The Stamp Act Crisis (3d ed. UNCP, Chapel Hill 1995).

[157] 1 JCC 26–28, 75–81, 53, 113, 121; 2 *id.* 105, 79, 307.

1776,[158] months before the Declaration of Independence, and soon after was elected the first governor (called president) of the new state and the commander in chief of its military.[159] This required Rutledge's return to South Carolina and his replacement as a delegate to the Continental Congress,[160] where otherwise he would have signed the Declaration of Independence[161] as his brother Edward Rutledge did.[162] When South Carolina's legislature adopted a new constitution in 1778, Rutledge vetoed it as improperly adopted and resigned the presidency,[163] but within a year was reelected governor for the period 1779–1782.[164] Just after the Revolutionary War, he became a judge of the state's chancery court,[165] its highest court, and served concurrently in the state house of representatives from 1784–1790.[166]

Rutledge played a major role in the federal Constitutional Convention of 1787,[167] chairing the committee of detail that drafted the Constitution,[168] apparently supporting his fellow South Carolinians in voting to insert in it a provision "that the liberty of the press should be inviolably preserved,"[169] proposing the supremacy clause,[170] and signing the final document.[171] He then supported the Constitution in his state's ratification convention.[172]

Rutledge was the second, by commission date, of the original appointees to the United States Supreme Court in 1789.[173] After holding that office a year and a half,

[158] *See* JOURNALS OF PROVINCIAL CONGRESS-S.C. 185, 252.

[159] *Id.* 265, 267 (26 Mar.1776).

[160] JOURNAL OF THE GENERAL ASSEMBLY OF SOUTH CAROLINA, March 26, 1776-April 11, 1776, at 54 & n. (Alexander S. Salley ed., HCSC, Columbia 1906).

[161] Rutledge supported independence, though a 1776 speech is sometimes misinterpreted to hope for reconciliation. *E.g.*, Speech of John Rutledge (19 Sept.1776), 2 AMERICAN ARCHIVES 392–93 (where Rutledge stated that independence was "not only justifiable but unavoidable"); JOURNAL OF THE GENERAL ASSEMBLY OF SOUTH CAROLINA, SEPTEMBER 17, 1776-OCTOBER 20, 1776, at 9 (Alexander S. Salley ed., HCSC, Columbia 1909) (same); John Rutledge to Henry Laurens (15 June 1778), John Rutledge Papers (LC, Washington).

[162] 5 JCC 515.

[163] John L. Gervais to Henry Laurens (16 Mar.1778), 13 LAURENS PAPERS 2, 3; *accord* CREATION 278.

[164] JOURNALS OF GENERAL ASSEMBLY-S.C. 179, 233.

[165] JOURNALS OF HOUSE-S.C. 611 (1783–1784) (selected 24 Mar.1784); *id.* 310 & n.6 (1789–1790) (resigned 17 Dec.1789). He became its senior judge. 1 S.C.Eq. (1 Des.) 183, 107.

[166] *Id.* 635 (1783–1784); *id.* 601 (1785–1786); *id.* 633 (1787–1788); *id.* 379 (1789–1790).

[167] James Madison to Thomas Jefferson, 24 LETTERS OF DELEGATES 303; 3 FARRAND'S RECORDS 559.

[168] 2 FARRAND'S RECORDS 97, 106 (24 June 1787).

[169] 2 *id.* 617–18 (14 Sept.1787); 5 ELLIOT'S DEBATES 545, 1 *id.* 310; *see* PRELUDE 299. Rutledge was present and participating that day. 2 FARRAND'S RECORDS 614.

[170] 2 *id.* 176, 177, 389.

[171] 33 JCC 500.

[172] 4 ELLIOT'S DEBATES 339.

[173] Nomination (24 Sept.1789), 1 DHSC 9, 2 DHFFC 44; Confirmation (26 Sept.1789), 1 DHSC 9, 2 DHFFC 45.

he resigned because of the rigors of circuit riding,[174] to become chief justice of South Carolina, where he served 1791–1795.[175] When he was named by President Washington as the successor to Jay as chief justice in 1795,[176] he filled that position for the half year until the Senate vote on his confirmation, which rejected his nomination.[177] Rutledge had given a widely publicized intemperate speech opposing the Jay Treaty,[178] which was condemned as heresy from Federalist beliefs, and was accompanied by allegations of mental derangement, extrapolated from severe depression after his wife's death (and then after his Senate rejection).[179] Rutledge also suffered from fighting against insolvency, resulting from property purchases of more than 50,000 acres by 1795 and consequent payments necessary to retain title.[180] He had to be assisted for years by loans and management of his property by his brother and son.[181] He died in mid-1800.[182]

174 John Rutledge to George Washington (5 Mar.1791), 7 WASHINGTON PAPERS-PRESIDENTIAL 515.

175 JOURNALS OF HOUSE-S.C. 257 (1791) (selected 15 Feb.1791); Jacob Reade to George Washington (16 Feb.1791), 7 WASHINGTON PAPERS-PRESIDENTIAL 366. The court was then called the Court of Common Pleas and Sessions. 1 S.C.Eq. (1 Des.) 183.

176 George Washington to John Rutledge (1 July 1795), 34 WASHINGTON PAPERS-PRESIDENTIAL 225; Temporary Commission (1 July 1795), 1 DHSC 96; Nomination (10 Dec.1795), 1 *id.* 98. Rutledge thereupon resigned the chief justiceship of South Carolina. John Rutledge to Governor (29 July 1795) (CCL, Charleston, Ms. 0077–006).

177 1 EXECUTIVE JOURNAL OF THE SENATE, 4TH CONG. 195–96 (15 Dec.1795); 1 DHSC 98–99.

178 NEW YORK ARGUS, 30 July 1795, reprinted in 18 HAMILTON PAPERS 510–11 n.3.

179 Ralph Izard to Jacob Read (17 Nov.1795), 1 DHSC 807; *e.g.*, Camillus [Alexander Hamilton], *Defence No.V* (5 Aug.1795), 19 HAMILTON PAPERS 89, 90; Alexander Hamilton to Rufus King (14 Dec.1795), 19 *id.* 484, 485; William R. Davie to James Iredell (4 Sept.1795), 2 IREDELL CORRESPONDENCE 454; Edmund Randolph to George Washington (29 July 1795), 1 DHSC 773.

180 John Rutledge, Jr. to Rev. Robert Smith (28 Nov.1798), RUTLEDGE JR. PAPERS-UNC; *A Real Republican*, COLUMBIAN CENTINEL (Boston), 26 Aug.1795, reprinted in 1 DHSC 784, 785; Jacob Reade to Ralph Izard (19 Dec.1795), 1 *id.* 81; John Adams to Abigail Adams (21 Dec.1795), 1 *id.* 816. Rutledge had lived beyond his means, like many plantation owners, for some time. In 1788, the French minister complained, "Il tire parti de sa grande influence et de ses co[n]noissances comme avocat pour ne pas payer ses dettes, qui excèdent de beaucoup sa fortune." 3 FARRAND'S RECORDS 238 ("He takes advantage of his great influence and his connections as lawyer not to pay his debts, which greatly exceed his fortune.").

181 Edward Rutledge to John Rutledge, Jr. (24 Apr.1794), RUTLEDGE JR. PAPERS-DUKE; Memorandum of John Rutledge, Jr. (30 Oct.1795), *id.*; The Honorable John Rutledge in Account at Current with John Rutledge Junior (May 1797) (owed $7,120), *id.*; Statement of Accounts between John Rutledge and John Rutledge Jun[']r; (May 1797), *id.*; Edward Rutledge to John Rutledge, Jr. (16 Mar.1798), *id.*; Edward Rutledge Will, 1799 (SCHS, Charleston, Ms.43/0793) (debts from brother). His son "object[ed] to making any more bank negotiations for my father lest I might ultimately be considered as borrowing of the banks for my own use," and the father "insisted upon my continuing & made the above memorandum." Acknowledgment (9 May 1795), RUTLEDGE JR. PAPERS-DUKE. The father took and destroyed the declaration of trust that enabled his brother and son to manage his property. The Honorable John Rutledge in Account at Current with John Rutledge Jun[']r (May 1797), *id.*

182 CLARE JERVEY, INSCRIPTIONS ON THE TABLETS AND GRAVESTONES IN ST. MICHAEL'S CHURCH AND CHURCHYARD, CHARLESTON 240 (State Co., Columbia 1906).

Early in his career, Rutledge did not impress John Adams at the first Continental Congress. "[H]is appearance is not very promising. There is no keenness in his eye, no depth in his countenance; nothing of the profound, sagacious, brilliant, or sparking, in his first appearance,"[183] though he and his brother "are good lawyers."[184] A more generous delegate described the Rutledge brothers as "ingenious, but impetuous in the cause they are engaged in."[185] But by the Constitutional Convention, Jefferson called him "one of the most distinguished characters of the United States for his wealth, talent, and virtues,"[186] and Hamilton ranked him as one of the five "[m]ost distinguished Patriots in and out of Convention."[187] France's minister concurred that he was "L'homme le plus éloquent, mais le plus fier et le plus impérieux des Etats-Unis."[188]

That pointed to a dark side. Rutledge's hauteur led him to support the state legislature's majority in enforcing a colonial legislative privilege against insults, as the legislature jailed a tavernkeeper, William Thompson, for demanding an apology from Rutledge, and five years later, as it required an apology from a satirist, Samuel Beach.[189] Rutledge was no advocate of democracy, fully accepting the political culture's fear of "the dangers of 'democratic despotism.'"[190] He supported the established church, and resolutely defended slavery.

Nevertheless, Rutledge went to great lengths to support freedoms of press and speech at three critical junctures.

South Carolina Assistance to John Wilkes in His Seditious Libel Cases

England's prosecution of John Wilkes for seditious libel in 1763, for criticism of a speech by King George III,[191] and his expulsion from the House of Commons and

[183] Diary (1 Sept.1774), 2 Adams Works 361; *accord* Diary (15 Sept.1775), 2 *id.* 422.

[184] Diary (2 Sept.1774), 2 *id.* 362.

[185] Silas Deane to Elizabeth Deane (7 Sept.1774), 1 Letters of Delegates 34, 35; *accord* Paul Wentworth, Minutes Respecting Political Parties in America and Sketches of the Leading Persons (1778), in 5 Facsimiles of Manuscripts in European Archives 487 at 37 (Benjamin F. Stevens ed., Malby & Sons, London 1889–98).

[186] Thomas Jefferson to D'Aranda (25 Mar.1789), 14 Jefferson Papers 700; *accord* 3 Farrand's Records 96.

[187] Alexander Hamilton, New York Ratifying Convention[—]Notes for Second Speech (17 July 1788), 5 Hamilton Papers 173, 174.

[188] Liste des Membres et Officiers du Congrés (1788), 3 Farrand's Records 232, 238 ("The man most eloquent, but also the most proud and imperious in the United States.").

[189] Journals of House-S.C. 578, 579–83, 583–85 (1783–84); Nathaniel Pendleton to Nathanael Greene (18 Apr.1784), 13 Greene Papers 295; *see* Creation 482–83. However, Rutledge did not claim libel when the Thompson dispute spilled into the newspapers. On Beach, *see* Journals of House-S.C. 138–41, 158–60 (1789–90).

[190] Ideological Origins 283; *accord* Creation 198.

[191] R v Wilkes, (1763) 2 Wils. K.B. 151, 159–60, 95 Eng. Rep. 737, 742 (C.P.).

exclusion despite reelection,[192] reverberated in the colonies. Wilkes was widely viewed in America as a martyr for liberty,[193] for his defense of freedom of press and of parliamentary speech.[194]

South Carolina's lower house, joining with the English crowds shouting "Wilkes and Liberty!,"[195] voted to contribute £10,500 in colonial money for "the support of the just and constitutional rights and liberties of the people of Great Britain and America," in December 1769.[196] The rights and liberties at issue were clearly identified the next day, in a letter signed by seven legislators including Rutledge, to notify Wilkes's committee of the contribution, and those were freedoms of press and speech.[197] The contribution was designated for the British Society of the Gentlemen Supporters of the Bill of Rights (and was addressed to its secretary),[198] an organization formed to fund Wilkes's defense and fines.[199]

[192] Rudé 35; Thomas 47–54, 79–80, 92–98.

[193] *E.g.*, An Authentic Account of the Proceedings against John Wilkes . . . (Boston repr., n.p. 1763); Committee of the Boston Sons of Liberty to John Wilkes (6 June 1768), 1 Adams Papers 214; James Madison to Thomas Martin (10 Aug.1769), 1 Madison Papers 42, 43; 1 Papers of George Mason 1725–1792, at 290 (Robert A. Rutland ed., UNCP, Chapel Hill 1970); 1 The Diary of Colonel Landon Carter of Sabine Hall 404 (Jack P. Greene ed., UPV, Charlottesville 1965); *see* Robert Middlekauff, The Glorious Cause: The American Revolution 183 (rev. ed. OUP, New York 2007).

[194] Arthur H. Cash, John Wilkes: The Scandalous Father of Civil Liberty (YUP, New Haven 2006); Peter D.G. Thomas, John Wilkes: A Friend to Liberty (CP, Oxford 1996).

[195] Rudé 27, 34, 40, 42, 44, 49, 50, 53, 65.

[196] 38 Journals of Assembly-S.C. 215 (8 Dec.1769); *accord* Peter Manigault, Christopher Gadsden, John Rutledge et al. to Robert Morris (9 Dec.1769), 31 Garth Correspondence 132; Additional Instructions (15 Aug.1770), 1 Drayton's Memoirs 91, 92; 1 *id.* 65, 67; Leigh's Considerations 7; Henry Laurens to William Williamson (28 Nov.1771), 8 Laurens Papers 55, 57–58; Henry Laurens to James Habersham (10 Apr.1770), 7 *id.* 272, 273 & n.9. *Drayton's Memoirs* are by John Drayton, one of the expelled council members, whose father was another, William H. Drayton. 5 DAB 448. *Leigh's Considerations* are by Sir Egerton Leigh, the council president, anonymously but with immediate attribution. Henry Laurens to John L. Gervais (24 Jan.1774), 9 Laurens Papers 250, 251; 1 Drayton's Memoirs 64. *Garth Correspondence* is with South Carolina's London agent. *Laurens Papers* and *Gadsden Writings* are by legislators. *See generally* Jack P. Greene, *Bridge to Revolution: The Wilkes Fund Controversy in South Carolina, 1769–1775*, 29 J. Southern History 19 (1963); The Nature of Colony Constitutions: Two Pamphlets on the Wilkes Fund Controversy in South Carolina (Jack P. Greene ed., USCP, Columbia 1970).

[197] Peter Manigault, Christopher Gadsden, John Rutledge et al. to Robert Morris (9 Dec.1769), 31 Garth Correspondence 132.

[198] 31 *id.* 133, 132; *see* Leigh's Considerations 8.

[199] Adams Elected to Membership in Supporters of the Bill of Rights (21 Sept.1773), 1 Adams Papers 353; 31 Garth Correspondence 132 n.2; *see* 2 Edward M. McCrady, History of South Carolina in the Revolution 707 (MacMillan, New York 1901); Robbins 354; Rudé 61.

Another letter the same day transferred the funds to the organization's bankers.[200]

Rutledge was a leading supporter of that Wilkes contribution. He was one of the seven legislators appointed as the committee to arrange for its delivery,[201] and was still joining letters defending the contribution nearly a year later.[202] He and the house were sincerely trying to assist Wilkes and not to provoke a dispute with the royal government or to fight over legislative powers, because the house buried the item in its annual tax bill[203] under the opaque words "To Jacob Motte, Esq. advanced by him, to certain members of the House, by a resolution of the House of the eighth of December last, 10,500 1."[204]

Despite that burial, the acting governor soon questioned the appropriation, by letter to the Crown,[205] and his council refused to approve the tax bill because it found the item "highly affrontive to His Majesty's Government," in April 1770.[206] The house moved toward adopting resolutions condemning royal authority over this and other colonial taxation and spending,[207] and the governor dissolved the house before the resolutions could be adopted.[208] The Crown responded with instructions to the royal governor requiring future tax bills to contain express restrictions preventing similar disbursements.[209] The council and acting governor reiterated their veto.[210]

[200] Peter Manigault, Christopher Gadsden, J. Rutledge et al. to Hankey and Partners (9 Dec.1769), 5 CORRESPONDENCE OF THE LATE JOHN WILKES 42, 43 (John Almon ed., Richard Phillips, London 1805); LEIGH'S CONSIDERATIONS 8; *see* GADSDEN WRITINGS 95n.; 7 LAURENS PAPERS 273 n.9.

[201] 5 *id.* 42–43; 38 JOURNALS OF ASSEMBLY-S.C. 387 (quoted 5 Apr.1770); 31 GARTH CORRESPONDENCE 132, 133; Additional Instructions (15 Aug.1770), 1 DRAYTON'S MEMOIRS 91, 92.

[202] Peter Manigault et al. (including Rutledge) to Charles Garth (6 Sept.1770), in 31 GARTH CORRESPONDENCE 244, 246.

[203] Motte was the state treasurer; it was a relatively common practice for him to expend available funds and restore them from the next year's taxes. LEIGH'S CONSIDERATIONS 26; Committee of Correspondence to Charles Garth (6 Sept.1770), 7 LAURENS PAPERS 338, 338–39, and 31 GARTH CORRESPONDENCE 244, 244, 246–53 (examples).

[204] LEIGH'S CONSIDERATIONS 10; 38 JOURNALS OF ASSEMBLY-S.C. 387.

[205] Lt. Gov. William Bull to Lord Hillsborough (12 Dec.1769), 6 PRIVY COUNCIL-COLONIAL 474.

[206] 38 JOURNALS OF ASSEMBLY-S.C. 386, 387 (message of 5 Apr.1770); *accord* LEIGH'S CONSIDERATIONS 10–11; *see* 1 DRAYTON'S MEMOIRS 61, 65–66; GADSDEN WRITINGS 95n.; 7 LAURENS PAPERS 274n.

[207] 38 JOURNALS OF ASSEMBLY-S.C. 300–02 (10 Apr.1770). The council refused the house's request for reconsideration. LEIGH'S CONSIDERATIONS 11.

[208] 38 *id.* 303, 393 (11 Apr., 4 June 1770); *accord* 1 DRAYTON'S MEMOIRS 66; *see* LEIGH'S CONSIDERATIONS 11.

[209] 1 ROYAL INSTRUCTIONS 203–04; Additional Instructions (15 Aug.1770), in 1 DRAYTON'S MEMOIRS 91, 93–94; 5 PRIVY COUNCIL-COLONIAL 229.

[210] 38 JOURNALS OF ASSEMBLY-S.C. 434–38 (29 Aug.1770) (council); 38 *id.* 443–44 (31 Aug.1770) (lieutenant governor).

The house similarly stood firm on principle.[211] It again approved a tax bill restoring the same amount for the same purpose, in August 1770,[212] which inevitably provoked the council's and lieutenant governor's rejection,[213] rather than passing a tax bill that would gain approval. The dominant issue was still supporting Wilkes, rather than asserting legislative authority.[214]

Rutledge delivered the report of the "Committee to whom His Majesty's Additional Instructions and . . . the Lieutenant Governor's messages relative thereto, were referred,"[215] once those Instructions reached the legislators, and Rutledge "probably wrote" the report.[216] The report attacked with no holds barred, positing that the "House hath an undeniable right . . . to give and grant money . . . for any purposes whatsoever," and that it was an ancient practice for the treasurer to advance funds to be repaid from incoming taxes.[217] Rutledge's report expressly defended the legality of the Wilkes contribution, and defiantly said its purpose was opposing the unjust and unconstitutional measures of an arbitrary and oppressive ministry.[218] He added that the "Instruction . . . is founded upon a false, partial and insidious representation," so that "the House should not submit thereto." Moreover, the Instructions were "an infringement of the privileges of this House," and "whosoever made the false, partial and insidious representation . . . are guilty of high misdemeanors."[219] That report was approved by the house.[220] The council reiterated its rejection of the tax bill and the £10,500 contribution, leading to a house protest to the lieutenant governor, who hewed to the council's position and noted that consequently "there is no prospect of doing any business during this sitting of the General Assembly."[221] The house responded by directing its London

[211] LEIGH'S CONSIDERATIONS 17; Committee of Correspondence to Charles Garth (6 Sept.1770), in 7 LAURENS PAPERS 338, 339; Henry Laurens to John Rose (5 Dec.1771), 8 LAURENS PAPERS 79–80.

[212] 1 DRAYTON'S MEMOIRS 68, 104; LEIGH'S CONSIDERATIONS 12–13; *see* 38 JOURNALS OF ASSEMBLY-S.C. 438 (29 Aug.1770).

[213] 38 JOURNALS OF ASSEMBLY-S.C. 434 (23 Aug.1770) (council); 38 *id.* 443 (31 Aug.1770) (lieutenant governor).

[214] Though the issue certainly spilled into that. Committee of Correspondence to Charles Garth (10 Apr.1772), 33 GARTH CORRESPONDENCE 136.

[215] 38 JOURNALS OF ASSEMBLY-S.C. 430 (29 Aug.1770). The report is reprinted in LEE'S ANSWER 30–36.

[216] RUTLEDGE 53; 38 JOURNALS OF ASSEMBLY-S.C. 434 (29 Aug.1770) (assigned to write message).

[217] 38 JOURNALS OF ASSEMBLY-S.C. 431; LEE'S ANSWER 43.

[218] 38 *id.* 431–32.

[219] 38 *id.* 432, 433; LEE'S ANSWER 35.

[220] 38 *id.* 444 (31 Aug.1770) (resolutions 1–3), 446 (4 Sept.1770) (resolutions 4–10).

[221] 38 JOURNALS OF ASSEMBLY-S.C. 453 (7 Sept.1770) (council), 454 (7 Sept.1770) (house), 455 (7 Sept.1770) (governor).

agent to challenge the Instructions by petition,[222] and the Privy Council predictably rejected the petition.[223]

Rutledge was also a member of the grievance committee that continued to deal with the Wilkes contribution and the legislature's powers,[224] and of the committee of correspondence whose direction he cosigned requiring the London agent to defend the contribution and challenge the restrictions.[225]

Two years after the original contribution, the council still refused to approve an annual tax bill with the £10,500, and the house still refused to approve a tax bill without it.[226] The house called the new co-treasurers to testify about the issue, and jailed them for refusing to approve the £10,500.[227] A year afterward, the new governor in his first speech to the house chided them for leaving the tax bill unapproved, and the grievance committee called for his removal from office for that and other reasons.[228] The house remonstrated against "that most unreasonable and unconstitutional [Instruction] of the Ministry, to direct and control the House of Assembly in framing money bills."[229]

The house's continued refusal to place in tax bills the Crown's language barring similar contributions "set up a constant collision" so that "the tax-bills since August 1770, were rejected by the Council."[230] The house continued to assemble for its quarterly sessions, but was dissolved by the governor each session[231] as it

[222] 38 *id.* 446 (4 Sept.1770, order), 449 (5 Sept.1770, report and order), 451 (6 Sept.1770, report "unanimously agreed"); LEIGH'S CONSIDERATIONS 14.

[223] Petition of Charles Garth (22 Nov.1770), in 33 GARTH CORRESPONDENCE 120; Privy Council (27 Mar.1771), 33 *id.* 130; 5 PRIVY COUNCIL-COLONIAL 235. The legislature later petitioned to remove the governor. Committee of Correspondence to Charles Garth (30 Oct.1772), 33 *id.* 262, 264 (20 Nov.1772), 275, 277.

[224] 39 JOURNALS OF ASSEMBLY-S.C. 11 (10 Oct.1772); *see* 1 DRAYTON'S MEMOIRS 69.

[225] Committee of Correspondence to Charles Garth (6 Sept.1770), in 7 LAURENS PAPERS 338, 340; Committee of Correspondence to Charles Garth (10 Apr.1772), in 33 GARTH CORRESPONDENCE 136; *see* 1 DRAYTON'S MEMOIRS 69.

[226] 38 JOURNALS OF ASSEMBLY-S.C. 577 (4 Nov.1771), 578–79 (4 Nov.1771); LEIGH'S CONSIDERATIONS 14. The treasurer, Motte, had by now died, so the issue became whether that amount should be deducted from amounts his estate owed the colony. 38 JOURNALS OF ASSEMBLY-S.C. 578 (4 Nov.1771).

[227] 38 *id.* 580–81 (5 Nov.1771), 583 (5 Nov.1771).

[228] 39 *id.* 2, 5 (10 Oct.1772) (speech), 20–21 (29 Oct.1772) (committee on grievances report). The report is reprinted in LEE'S ANSWER 71.

[229] 38 JOURNALS OF ASSEMBLY-S.C. 21, 23 (29 Oct.1772).

[230] 1 DRAYTON'S MEMOIRS 69; *see* LEIGH'S CONSIDERATIONS 13, 15.

[231] 38 JOURNALS OF ASSEMBLY-S.C. 456 (8 Sept.1770); 39 *id.* 1 (describing 10 Apr.1772); 1 DRAYTON'S MEMOIRS 66, 68 (Aug.1770); 7 LAURENS PAPERS 432 (Jan.1771); LEIGH'S CONSIDERATIONS 14 (Oct.1771); 33 GARTH CORRESPONDENCE 262, 263 (Aug.1772), 273, 274 (Nov.1772); 1 DRAYTON'S MEMOIRS 136 ("repeatedly" Mar.1773–Apr.1774), 112 (Apr.1774, June 1774), 140 (Aug.1774); GADSDEN WRITINGS 97 (June 1774); Thomas Farr to Ralph Izard (8 Aug.1774), 6 IZARD CORRESPONDENCE 7–8 (Aug.1774 session); 2 DRAYTON'S MEMOIRS 140 (same); JOURNALS OF PROVINCIAL CONGRESS-S.C. 28 (before 1775), 29 (until Jan.1775), 258 (Sept.1776).

"repeatedly persisted" in omitting the language required by the Additional Instructions or in reimbursing the Wilkes contribution.[232] This produced an impasse in colonial government,[233] effectively closing it down, until the Revolution began and the house was replaced by a new assembly.

Support of Thomas Powell in His Seditious Libel Prosecution

The new acting governor, William Bull, and his council retaliated by refusing to approve various other enactments. Two members of the council, John Drayton and William H. Drayton, placed a statement of dissent in the council records,[234] believing that needed legislation was being held hostage, and gave a copy of their protest to a newspaper printer.[235]

This provoked a Wilkes-like battle of the press in South Carolina. When the South Carolina *Gazette* printed the council members' dissent without the council's permission, in August 1773, the majority of the council found it "a high breach of privilege and a contempt"[236] and a seditious libel.[237] Consequently, the "printer and publisher, of . . . the South Carolina Gazette," Thomas Powell,[238] was imprisoned by the council.[239] He was defended by Edward Rutledge (John Rutledge's brother),[240] whose motion for habeas corpus was granted by two friendly justices of the colony's courts.[241] The grounds were that imprisonment of Powell was not justified by the

[232] LEIGH'S CONSIDERATIONS 17.

[233] Committee of Correspondence to Charles Garth (6 Sept.1770), 7 LAURENS PAPERS 338, 339 ("puts a full stop to the payment of public debts, and the necessary provision for the expences of government."); Henry Laurens to John Hopton (29 Jan.1771), 7 *id.* 428, 432; Charles Garth to Committee of Correspondence (3 June 1772), 33 GARTH CORRESPONDENCE 238, 239; *see* LEIGH'S CONSIDERATIONS 15.

[234] Opinion of J. Lowndes, 1 DRAYTON'S MEMOIRS 118, 123; 1 *id.* 101; LEIGH'S CONSIDERATIONS 33; *see* Henry Laurens to John Laurens (19 Nov.1773), 9 LAURENS PAPERS 152, 154.

[235] Three Councillors Removed (1 June 1775), 6 PRIVY COUNCIL-COLONIAL 564; LEE'S ANSWER 85–86.

[236] 39 JOURNALS OF ASSEMBLY-S.C. 80 (8 Sept.1773, reprinting warrant 31 Aug.1773); Opinion of J. Lowndes, 1 DRAYTON'S MEMOIRS 118, 118; *see id.* 101; LEIGH'S CONSIDERATIONS 33; 6 PRIVY COUNCIL-COLONIAL 564.

[237] 1 DRAYTON'S MEMOIRS 101; *see* LEIGH'S CONSIDERATIONS 33, 82.

[238] 39 JOURNALS OF ASSEMBLY-S.C. 82 (8 Sept.1773, reprinting habeas corpus 1 Sept.1773); Opinion of J. Lowndes, 1 DRAYTON'S MEMOIRS 118, 118.

[239] 6 PRIVY COUNCIL-COLONIAL 389; Henry Laurens to James Laurens (5 Feb.1774), 9 LAURENS PAPERS 264, 267; 9 *id.* 111 n.1; LEIGH'S CONSIDERATIONS 33; 1 DRAYTON'S MEMOIRS 101, 103; 9 LAURENS PAPERS 111 n.1; 39 JOURNALS OF ASSEMBLY-S.C. 80 (8 Sept.1773, reprinting warrant 31 Aug.1773).

[240] 19 ANB 131, 131–32.

[241] Opinion, 39 JOURNALS OF ASSEMBLY-S.C 82 (reprinting 8 Sept.1773); Opinion of J. Lowndes, 1 DRAYTON'S MEMOIRS 118, 124; LEIGH'S CONSIDERATIONS 33; *see* 6 PRIVY COUNCIL-COLONIAL 564, 565.

law of the land, and that the council was not an upper house of the legislature whose acts could claim any legislative privilege at all.[242] In rebuke of the council's request for the assembly to take action against the justices who approved habeas corpus,[243] the house passed resolutions sardonically agreeing with the justices, thanking them, and asking the governor to suspend the other members of the council.[244]

John Rutledge continued to support the cause of the press, leading the committee that asked the governor to suspend the council members who cited Powell, while the London representative petitioned to have them removed.[245] Powell published commentary calling his prosecution "the most violent attempt that ever had been made in this province upon . . . the liberty of the press."[246] Edward Rutledge brought suit for Powell against the council president who had spearheaded the attack on Powell.[247] In response to complaints by both the council and the Draytons,[248] the Privy Council surprised no one and found in favor of the Crown.[249]

In a repeat performance a year later, the council postponed action on a bill to punish counterfeiting, and William H. Drayton protested it in February 1775.[250] The protest was similarly published in the South Carolina *Gazette*.[251] The council president accused Drayton of libeling the King and stirring up sedition,[252] by disseminating his protest and by anonymously publishing a pamphlet.[253] As the house supported Drayton,[254] the council again suspended him[255] and sued Powell, who Edward Rutledge again defended.[256]

242 39 *id.* 83–86; Opinion of J. Lowndes, 1 Drayton's Memoirs 118, 121–23; 1 *id.* 101; Leigh's Considerations 34; Lee's Answer 86; 6 Privy Council-Colonial 564, 566.

243 39 Journals of Assembly-S.C. 77 (7 Sept.1773); Leigh's Considerations 34.

244 39 *id.* 88 (8 Sept.1773); 1 Drayton's Memoirs 101–02; Leigh's Considerations 34.

245 39 *id.* 88, 93, 96 (8, 11, 13 Sept.1773).

246 Leigh's Considerations 79–80. Levy concedes that Powell's defense "invoke[d] freedom of the press." Levy 84.

247 Henry Laurens to John Laurens (19 Nov.1773), 9 Laurens Papers 152, 154; Leigh's Considerations 77–78 (on 12 Oct.1773 after motion 18 Sept.1773); Lee's Answer 124; 6 Privy Council-Colonial 564, 566–67.

248 6 Privy Council-Colonial 564, 566; Henry Laurens to James Laurens (5 Feb.1774), 9 Laurens Papers 264, 266; *see* Leigh's Considerations 14, 34.

249 6 Privy Council-Colonial 564 (1 June 1775); *see* 2 Drayton's Memoirs 69.

250 Dissentient of William H. Drayton (8 Feb.1775), 1 Drayton's Memoirs 233–35; 1 *id.* 209–10; *see* Lee's Answer 128.

251 South-Carolina Gazette (Charleston), 13 Feb.1775, reprinted in 1 *id.* 235; 1 *id.* 211.

252 Address of Council (11 Feb.1775), 1 *id.* 235–36; 1 *id.* 211–12; 5 Privy Council-Colonial 409.

253 Dissentient, 1 *id.* 240, 242.

254 1 *id.* 214–15; *see* Dissentients of William H. Drayton (Feb.1775), 1 *id.* 237–40, 240–42; Prelude 162–63.

255 William Bull to William H. Drayton (1 Mar.1775), 1 *id.* 243; 5 Privy Council-Colonial 409, 410; 6 *id.* 564–67.

256 19 ANB 131, 131–32.

Was this all a fight merely over legislative prerogative, and not over freedom of press? The selection of Wilkes to receive a contribution did not involve a dispute over colonial legislative powers but over freedom particularly of the press and speech. The appropriation of the contribution was obscured to avoid a fight over legislative authority. The Powell incident did not extend legislative powers but instead reduced them, asserting Powell's freedom of press and Drayton's freedom of speech as superior to the council's power to determine whether its records were released or printed.[257] While legislative rights ultimately were caught up in the controversy, the beginning and the end of these incidents was the press and its freedom.

A decade later, it was Rutledge along with Madison who proposed the provision at the Constitutional Convention that Congress must publish journals of its proceedings.[258] They led the vanguard; only recently had a third and fourth state authorized reporting on and observation of legislative proceedings.[259]

Proposed Resolution on Treason by Words

Rutledge prepared a draft of the Declaration and Resolves in 1774, though it was not adopted by the Continental Congress,[260] apparently because Congress sought a list of rights and violations, which became the core of the final document.[261] Nevertheless, what appears to be Rutledge's draft[262] tells much about his view of freedoms of speech and press.

Rutledge took an approach very different from listing rights and grievances. He instead defined what English law did and did not apply to the colonies, extending the resolution of the Stamp Act Congress about taxation to a broad range of subjects.[263] Others had done the same, such as the new chief justice of Rhode Island, when he proclaimed that "the King and Parliament had no more right to pass any Acts of Parliament and govern us than the Mohawks" had.[264] Rutledge's draft flatly stated that Parliament did not have power to legislate regarding "taxation and internal policy" for the colonies, and that much of English law did not

[257] Drayton neatly placed the council in a dilemma: either it was not an upper legislative house, in which case it could not claim breach of legislative privilege, or it was an upper house, in which case his statements were protected as legislative speech. 6 PRIVY COUNCIL-COLONIAL 564, 566.

[258] 2 FARRAND'S RECORDS 259 (11 Aug.1787); *see* U.S.CONST. art.I, §5.

[259] WILLI P. ADAMS, THE FIRST AMERICAN CONSTITUTIONS: REPUBLICAN IDEOLOGY AND THE MAKING OF THE STATE CONSTITUTIONS 249–51 (UNCP, Chapel Hill 1980).

[260] Thomas Jefferson's Autobiography, in 1 LETTERS OF MEMBERS 157 n.2.

[261] 1 JCC 63; 9 EHD 805; John Adams to Edward Biddle (12 Dec.1774), 2 ADAMS PAPERS 199, 201.

[262] John Rutledge's[?] Proposed Resolutions to the Committee on Rights (7–22 Sept.1774), 1 LETTERS OF DELEGATES 44 & n.1.

[263] Declaration of Rights § 5 (19 Oct.1765), 9 EHD 672.

[264] Opposition to the Jurisdiction of the Privy Council (22 Nov.1771), 6 PRIVY COUNCIL-COLONIAL 505, 506 (Stephen Hopkins); *see* IDEOLOGICAL ORIGINS 209–13.

apply to the colonies. It identified the English law that *did* apply to the colonies: royal charters with privileges and immunities, which included colonial legislative powers over taxation and internal policy, and selected "parts of the common civil & maritime law and of the statutes" of Great Britain.[265] The draft also specified the English law that *did not* apply: besides any legislation on taxation and internal policy, statutes enacted after "the settlement of the colonies," statutes enacted before that which were inapplicable to the colonies, some of "the common civil & maritime law," and, most interestingly, two statutes that were singled out:

> We do not however admit into this collection but absolutely reject the statutes of Henry the 8 and Edward 6 respecting treasons and misprisions of treasons.[266]

The great emphasis placed on two specific statutes on treason invites inquiry. The statutes were the High Treason Act of 1534 (or the Treason Act of 1543 that amended it),[267] and the Repeal of Statutes as to Treasons, Felonies, Etc. of 1547 (which was only a partial repeal).[268] The common element of those statutes was criminalization as treason of speech and writing, changing the law established by the Treason Act of Edward III that proscribed acts but not words.[269] Enacted after Henry VIII's break with Rome, the 1534 statute made it high treason to harm the royal family or to "slanderously and maliciously publish and pronounce, by express writing or words, that the King our sovereign lord should be heretick, schismatick, tyrant, infidel or usurper of the Crown."[270] The 1547 statute, though repealing some treason statutes,[271] made it high treason "by writing, printing, overt-deed or act" to affirm that the King is not the "Supream Head in Earth of the Church of England and Ireland," that the Bishop of Rome instead is, that the King is not king of England, France, or Ireland, or that anyone else ought to be King.[272] Its speech provision criminalized the "open preaching, express words or sayings"

[265] John Rutledge's[?] Proposed Resolutions, *supra* note 262.

[266] *Id.*

[267] 26 Hen 8 c13; 35 Hen 8 c2; *accord* ORR 18–19; BROOKS 48.

[268] 1 Edw 6 c12; *see* ORR 20.

[269] Statute of Treason 1350, 25 Edw 3 stat 5, c2; SOURCE BOOK 376; *see* BROOKS 55–56.

[270] 26 H 8 c13 s II. It also provided, when treason was committed out of the realm, for presentment in a shire appointed by the Crown and trial before King's Bench, *id.* s IV, which the 1543 statute expanded to allow trial before commissioners in a shire assigned by the Crown. 35 H 8 c2.

[271] *Id.* s II. While worded broadly, De Lolme could only claim this "repeal[ed] many of the treason laws introduced under Henry VIII." JEAN LOUIS DE LOLME, THE CONSTITUTION OF ENGLAND; OR, AN ACCOUNT OF THE ENGLISH GOVERNMENT 69n. (David Lieberman ed. Liberty Fund, Indianapolis 2007); though Blackstone asserted it repealed all. 4 BLACKSTONE'S COMMENTARIES 86–87, 89–90.

[272] *Id.* s VII.

that affirmed the same things.[273] Though procedural safeguards had been added, dissent by certain words could still cost one's life.[274]

One other issue of colonial concern[275] was raised by the 1534 statute and its amendment, but not by the 1547 statute: that anyone "outside the Realm" committing treason or misprision would be presented and tried in England.[276] However, that was not Rutledge's objection because it was not a common element of both statutes, whereas criminalizing criticism of the King was a common element. Treason by words remained a threat to nonbelligerent but vocal colonial leaders, as James Wilson recognized by reprobating the same statute of Henry VIII.[277] Rutledge, a lawyer trained in England, doubtless knew that both treason statutes were commonly understood to be repealed,[278] but also knew that repeal left "a heritage of procedural confusion" with "treasonable words also continu[ing] to play a part in early Stuart treason law"[279] and in threatened prosecution of constructive treason during colonial disputes.

Two other considerations showed that Rutledge's objection was aimed at the restriction on speech and press. The controversy in South Carolina, which was still ongoing, involved criminal words by Wilkes, but did not involve transporting a colonist to England. Further, earlier in the year of Rutledge's draft,[280] he had been threatened by the president of South Carolina's royal council with prosecution for his words—for "high contempts and misprisions against the King's person and government, by doing any thing that has an immediate and direct tendency to weaken his government, or to raise jealousies between him and his

[273] *Id.* s VI.

[274] Trials for Treason Act (1696), 7 & 8 Wm 3 c3; 8 EHD 89.

[275] *E.g.*, Declaration and Resolves (14 Oct.1774), 9 EHD 805, 808; Benjamin Franklin to William Strahan (29 Nov.1769), 16 FRANKLIN PAPERS 243, 248; William Bollan to Council of Massachusetts (1 Sept.1773), *Bowdoin and Temple Papers*, 9 COLLECTIONS OF THE MASSACHUSETTS HISTORICAL SOCIETY 308 (6th series MHS, Boston 1897); John Adams, Heads of Grievances and Rights (ante 9 Sept.1774), 2 ADAMS PAPERS 152, 154; Franklin's "Hints" or Terms for a Durable Union (4 Dec.1774), 21 FRANKLIN PAPERS 365, 368; James Wilson, Speech Delivered in the Convention (Jan.1775), 1 WILSON WORKS 32, 35; James Iredell, The Principles of an American Whig (c.1775), 1 IREDELL PAPERS 328, 337.

[276] 26 Hen 8 c13 s4; 35 Hen 8 c2 s1. The House of Lords called for enforcement, in December 1768, and the House of Commons followed suit, a couple of months after. 16 FRANKLIN PAPERS 248 n.7; *accord* 16 PARLIAMENTARY HISTORY 1005 (Edmund Burke in 1770: Parliament took "up the menace of Henry the 8th's Act"). Besides the obvious prejudice to a colonist that witnesses and attorney would not be available in England, this violated the common law right of trial by a jury from the vicinage. Michael Macnair, *Vicinage and the Antecedents of the Jury*, 17 LAW & HIST. REV. 537 (1999).

[277] James Wilson, *Lectures on Law*, 2 WILSON WORKS 1151.

[278] Case of John Williams, Cro. Car. 126, 79 Eng. Rep. 711 (K.B.); 4 BLACKSTONE'S COMMENTARIES 86.

[279] ORR 21, 27, leaving it "unclear which statutes and which particular provisions . . . were actually in force," *id.* 11; ASHCRAFT 340.

[280] On January 20, 1774. THE NATURE OF COLONY CONSTITUTIONS: TWO PAMPHLETS ON THE WILKES FUND CONTROVERSY IN SOUTH CAROLINA 38 (Jack P. Greene ed., USCP, Columbia 1970).

people."[281] That threat was directed at "six eminent gentlemen of the bar, all members of the house," including Rutledge.[282] It followed a warning from the provincial agent that parliamentary debate about forcing American acknowledgment of its authority mentioned "the terrors of an old act of Henry 8th."[283]

Wartime Powers and Freedom of Press During the Revolutionary War

At the start of Rutledge's wartime presidency of South Carolina,[284] as he was made commander in chief of the state's troops,[285] he was given authority approaching dictatorial powers[286] when the state legislature was out of session.[287] The legislature also passed a sedition act early in the war in 1776[288] (as did Virginia and other states), which Rutledge signed.[289]

There is no instance of Governor Rutledge using those unlimited powers to restrict speech or press, or enforcing that sedition act, among the large number of his directives preserved from the Revolution.[290] Though the state had wartime restrictions on loyalists typical of all the new states, and suffered similar restrictions on patriots when British troops controlled the state, Rutledge did the opposite of prosecuting sedition and made an offer of amnesty[291] that was lenient enough to contribute to anti-loyalist riots.[292] He also exercised his pardon power in individual cases, such as pardoning some people for violation of the state

[281] LEIGH'S CONSIDERATIONS 82, which immediately followed Leigh's discussion of an English prosecution and conviction for seditious libel. *Id.* 81–82.

[282] *Id.* 80.

[283] Charles Garth to Capt. Ball (12 Jan.1770), 31 GARTH CORRESPONDENCE 139 (copy provided to South Carolina Committee of Correspondence).

[284] JOURNALS OF PROVINCIAL CONGRESS-S.C. 265, 267.

[285] *Id.* 265, 267.

[286] John Rutledge to Nn. (18 Sept.1781), 18 RUTLEDGE LETTERS 155, 159; 2 LIFE AND CORRESPONDENCE OF JOSEPH REED 74 (William B. Reed ed., Lindsay & Blakiston, Philadelphia 1847); *see* Robert W. Barnwell, *Rutledge, "The Dictator,"* 7 J. SOUTHERN HISTORY 215, 216, 217, 221–22 (1941).

[287] JOURNALS OF GENERAL ASSEMBLY-S.C. 229 (Bill 19), 184–85 (Ordinance 16), 209–10 (Resolution 91), 272–73 (Ordinance 28).

[288] Act to Prevent Sedition and Punish Insurgents (4 Apr.1776), *id.* 29.

[289] JOURNALS OF GENERAL ASSEMBLY-S.C. 52.

[290] DOCUMENTARY HISTORY-S.C. 12–223 (37 letters); *id.* 165, 175, 233 (3 proclamations or messages); 3 AMERICAN ARCHIVES 4–79 (22 letters); JOURNALS OF GENERAL ASSEMBLY-S.C. 52, 63; 17 RUTLEDGE LETTERS 131; 18 *id.* 42, 59, 131, 155; 2 LEE PAPERS 53, 57, 236 (Henry Bunbury ed., NYHS, New York 1872–75); 11 GREENE PAPERS 11, 384, 674; 12 *id.* 395 *et seq.*; *John Rutledge to Benjamin Lincoln*, 25 S.C. HISTORICAL & GENEALOGICAL MAG. 133 (1924). After Rutledge left the governorship, the William Thompson incident provided an ugly exception.

[291] Proclamation (27 Sept.1781), DOCUMENTARY HISTORY-S.C. 175, 237; Thomas Sumter Papers, 1734–1832 v.2, at 1458 (LC, Washington, MMC2064).

[292] Nathaniel Pendleton to Nathanael Greene (10 July 1784), 13 GREENE PAPERS 349, 350; John Lewis Gervais to Henry Laurens (15 Apr.1784), 16 LAURENS PAPERS 429, 430–31; John Lewis Gervais to Henry Laurens (12 Feb.1784), 16 *id.* 387, 391.

sedition law.[293] He saw one of the objectives of his administration as "to restore every encroachment on the liberties of the people."[294]

Rutledge appreciated the importance of publishing and disseminating newspapers and information, during the war. He and his beleaguered state government went to some effort to set up a press[295] that was "of great use in printing proclamations, commissions, & hand bills," and Rutledge asked the state's delegates in Congress to help procure smaller type so that a newspaper could be produced, "which wd. be of great service."[296] He effectively was the editor. Fourteen years later, Rutledge and the press again intersected, as his speech on the Jay Treaty of 1795 caused him to be defended as well as attacked in the press.

Rutledge's appreciation for civil rights had grown over two and a half decades, from satisfaction with the rights of British citizens to assertions of broader rights, and from contribution to John Wilkes's defense against seditious libel to becoming an editor himself while avoiding interference with press and speech. His evident opposition to the Sedition Act, and his brother's express opposition, are discussed in Chapter 8.

Justice William Cushing

Figure 4.3 Justice William Cushing (on Supreme Court 1789–1810). Drawing by unknown artist. (Courtesy of New York Public Library/Art Resource.)

[293] 2 DRAYTON'S MEMOIRS 386.

[294] John Rutledge to Gen. Francis Marion (10 Oct.1781), DOCUMENTARY HISTORY-S.C. 185, 186.

[295] John Rutledge to Francis Marion (13 Aug.1781), William G. Simms, *A Sketch of the Life and Public Services of John Rutledge of South Carolina*, 6 AM. REV. 277, 281 (1847).

[296] John Rutledge to Delegates (c. Nov.1781), 18 RUTLEDGE LETTERS 162–63; John Rutledge to Nn. (22 Nov.1781), *id.* 163, 166.

William Cushing (Figure 4.3) entered government by birth—his father and grandfather served on the governor's council and on Massachusetts' highest court—but entered the major controversies of the time by stumbling repeatedly into them: independence, slavery, Shays' Rebellion, and freedom of press.[297]

He took his father's place on the superior court in 1772,[298] and within a year found himself in the middle of the prerevolutionary disputes between the governor and the legislature. The governor sought to pay part of the judges' salaries with royal funds, to secure their loyalty, in June 1773, and the legislature demanded that the judges be paid only with legislative grants, for the same purpose.[299] The judges failing to make a clearcut choice, the legislature warned of impeachment of any judge who did not forswear royal grants, in February 1774.[300] Cushing responded three days later that he would comply and accept only legislative grants,[301] thereby falling onto the patriot side,[302] while the less fortunate chief justice responded that he would accept royal grants and was promptly impeached.[303] As the Revolution began, Cushing was selected as a judge of the new state's superior court in 1776,[304] and upon John Adams's decision not to serve as chief justice,[305] became chief justice the following year.[306] He was continued in that position when the supreme judicial court was reconstituted in 1781.[307] As a

[297] *See generally* John D. Cushing, A Revolutionary Conservative: The Public Life of William Cushing, 1732–1810 (1959) (unpublished Ph.D. dissertation, Clark University); Arthur P. Rugg, *William Cushing*, 30 Yale L. J. 128 (1920); OCSC 213; 1 Justices 57.

[298] Robert Treat Paine Diary (Feb.1772), in 2 Papers of Robert Treat Paine 497, 491 n.1 (Stephen T. Riley & Edward W. Hanson eds., MHS, Boston 1992).

[299] 50 Journals of House-Mass. 87–88 (25 June 1773); 3 Thomas Hutchinson, History of the Colony of Massachusetts 386–90, 412–14 (John Murray, London 1828); *see* 50 Journals of House-Mass. 76, 86; James Bowdoin to Thomas Pownall (24 Oct.1772), *Bowdoin and Temple Papers*, in 9 Collections of the Massachusetts Historical Society (6th ser.) 297, 298–99 (MHS, Boston 1897); *accord* Ideological Origins 107–08.

[300] 50 *id.* 117 (2 Feb.1774); 3 Thomas Hutchinson, History of the Colony of Massachusetts 443 (John Murray, London 1828).

[301] 50 *id.* 139 (5 Feb.1774); William Cushing to Thomas Cushing (5 Feb.1774), Cushing Papers (obverse).

[302] Even if reluctant in early 1774, he soon became a committed revolutionary. Convention of Plymouth County (26–27 Sept.1774), in William Lincoln, Journals of Each Provincial Congress of Massachusetts in 1774 and 1775, at 621, 622 (Dutton, Boston 1838).

[303] 50 Journals of House-Mass. 212–17 (1 Mar.1774); 3 Thomas Hutchinson, History of the Colony of Massachusetts 443–52 (John Murray, London 1828).

[304] John Noble, *Records and Files of the Superiour Court*, in 5 Publications of The Colonial Society of Massachusetts 5, 12n. (MHS, Boston 1902); 51 Journals of House-Mass. 70; 52 *id.* 111; 3 Adams Works 24.

[305] John Adams to John Avery (21 Mar.1777), 5 Adams Papers 116, 117.

[306] 53 Journals of House-Mass. 159; 54 *id.* 106.

[307] Noble, *supra* note 304, at 10n.; Perpetual Laws, of the Commonwealth of Massachusetts 1 (Isaiah Thomas, Worcester 1788). He and the other justices revised the state's laws, *id.*, at the direction of the legislature. Acts and Laws of the Commonwealth of Massachusetts 187 (ch.98) (30 Nov.1780) (Benjamin Eades, Boston 1890).

delegate to Massachusetts' constitutional convention of 1779,[308] he sat on the committee that approved its declaration of rights and constitution.[309]

Cushing stumbled into three particularly significant cases during his service as Massachusetts' chief justice from 1777 through 1789. In the early 1780s, he gave the grand jury charge in the *Quock Walker Case*,[310] which, with some controversy, is credited with abolishing or at least curtailing slavery in Massachusetts[311] and with being America's version of the *Somerset* decision.[312] Also in the late 1780s, the court's sessions were disrupted and sometimes blocked by Shays' Rebellion, and Cushing led in trying and sentencing the rebels.[313] The rebellion was a catalyst and a reason for a stronger general government and a new federal Constitution.[314] In 1789, Cushing faced cases of first impression involving freedom of the press,[315] though he resigned from the state court[316] before they were decided. The first and third of these cases showed a side of Cushing not visible in most histories, supporting liberty, but the second displayed the more familiar side, as a future Federalist concerned both that there be "such a national government as shall effectually secure the union," and equally that the "world seems turning round again . . . perhaps to be overturned by the spirit of democracy."[317]

Cushing was appointed to the United States Supreme Court in 1789.[318] He administered President Washington's second oath of office in 1793,[319] in the absence of Chief Justice Jay. After Rutledge was denied confirmation, Cushing was

[308] JOURNAL OF CONVENTION-MASS. 15.

[309] *Id.* 30.

[310] Indictment v. Jennison, CUSHING NOTES 55 (Mass. S. Judicial Ct.1783); William Cushing Judicial Notebook 95–98 (1783), CUSHING PAPERS (microfilm P-406).

[311] John D. Cushing, *The Cushing Court and the Abolition of Slavery in Massachusetts*, 5 AM. J. LEGAL HISTORY 118 (1961).

[312] Case of James Sommersett, (1771–72) 20 State Trials 1 (K.B.); *see* ROBBINS 288; George van Cleve, *Mansfield's Decision: Toward Human Freedom*, 24 LAW & HIST. REV. 665, 666, 670 (2006).

[313] GEORGE R. MINOT, HISTORY OF THE INSURRECTION IN MASSACHUSETTS IN THE YEAR MDCCLXXXVI (Isaiah Thomas, Worcester 1788).

[314] *E.g.*, George Washington to James Madison (5 Nov.1786), 4 WASHINGTON PAPERS-CONFEDERATION 331; George Washington to Lafayette (25 Mar.1787), 5 *id.* 105, 106; James Madison to George Muter (7 Jan.1787), 9 MADISON PAPERS 230; James Madison to Edmund Pendleton (24 Feb.1787), 9 *id.* 294–95.

[315] William Cushing to John Adams (18 Feb.1789), CUSHING PAPERS (Box 1).

[316] William Cushing to John Hancock (17 Nov.1789), 1 DHSC 678.

[317] William Cushing to George Washington (17 Nov.1789), 41 PROCEEDINGS OF MASSACHUSETTS HISTORICAL SOCIETY 69 (1928); William Cushing to Increase Sum[n]er (15 Jan.1798), 41 *id.* 70.

[318] Nomination (24 Sept.1789), 1 DHSC 9, 2 DHFFC 44; Confirmation (26 Sept.1789), 1 DHSC 9, 2 DHFFC 45.

[319] Cabinet Opinion on the Administration of the Presidential Oath (28 Feb.1793, 1 Mar.1793), 12 WASHINGTON PAPERS-PRESIDENTIAL 231, 242; To the Secretaries of the Treasury, and War (27 Feb.1793), 32 WASHINGTON WRITINGS 361–62 n.41.

appointed and confirmed as chief justice,[320] but he declined the elevation after a week of consideration and never acted in that role.[321] He continued serving as an associate justice until his death in 1810,[322] the longest of the initial justices. He served too long; by the mid-1790s, his health had deteriorated,[323] and "time, the enemy of man, ha[d] much impaired his mental faculties."[324] His reason for hanging onto the office may have been political, "lest a Republican should succeed him," coupled with financial need for the salary.[325]

Cushing's lot in history was to be condemned by faint praise. A contemporary, William Bentley, described his Supreme Court role without intending levity: "He was in high reputation as a judge when he left the bench of Massachusetts, yet but little has been said of him since."[326] Mercy Otis Warren, while noting "his professional abilities and general integrity," found Cushing only worthy of mention in one passage in her three-volume history though he was a family friend.[327] John Adams esteemed him a "very worthy gentleman,"[328] but said little else about Cushing despite their decades of acquaintance. Secretary of the Treasury Oliver Wolcott, without even faint praise, found him "a good and respectable character."[329]

The only thesis written on Cushing (the closest thing to a full-length biography) devotes only seven pages to his Supreme Court role and only a quarter sentence in a footnote to his view on the Alien and Sedition Acts.[330] Yet his view on those Acts

[320] Nomination (26 Jan.1796), 1 DHSC 101; Confirmation (27 Jan.1796), *id.* He also was commissioned, 1 *id.* 102, and the Court's minutes imply that he took the required oath, which has led to the argument that he should be counted as the third chief justice, for a week. Ross E. Davies, *William Cushing, Chief Justice of the United States*, 37 U. Toledo L. Rev. 597 (2006).

[321] *See* William Cushing to George Washington (2 Feb.1796), 1 *id.* 103 (not delivered).

[322] 3 William Bentley, Diary of William Bentley 540 (Essex Institute, Salem 1905–14).

[323] John Adams to Abigail Adams (2 Feb.1796), 1 DHSC 834 ("declining health"); James Iredell to Hannah Iredell (20 Feb.1796), 2 Iredell Correspondence 460 ("infirm state of health").

[324] William Plumer to Jeremiah Smith (19 Feb.1796), 1 DHSC 838; *accord* John Marshall to Charles Cotesworth Pinckney (18 Dec.1800), 6 Marshall Papers 41; Thomas B. Adams to Abigail Adams (20 Dec.1800), 1 DHSC 904; 3 William Bentley, Diary of William Bentley 540 (Essex Institute, Salem 1905–14).

[325] David Howell to James Madison, 3 Madison Papers-Presidential 27; 3 Bentley, *supra* note 324, at 540.

[326] 3 Bentley, *supra* note 324, at 540. Bentley did speak well of his prior state judicial service. *Id.*

[327] 1 Mercy Otis Warren, History of the Rise, Progress and Termination of the American Revolution 118 (repr. AMS Press, New York 1970, original 1805).

[328] John Adams to John Avery (21 Mar.1777), 5 Adams Papers 116, 117. However, John Quincy Adams, as a young man hearing Cushing give a grand jury charge to a Massachusetts court, thought "[h]e spoke with much dignity." 1 Diary of John Quincy Adams 316 (30 Aug.1785 entry) (Robert J. Taylor et al. eds., BP-HUP, Cambridge 1981).

[329] Oliver Wolcott to Nn. (15 Feb.1796), 1 Wolcott Papers 299, 300.

[330] John D. Cushing, A Revolutionary Conservative: The Public Life of William Cushing, 1732–1810, at 334 (1959) (unpublished Ph.D. dissertation, Clark University) (single footnote).

and press and speech warrants more than a footnote, and contrasts sharply with his prior wrestling over the state declaration of rights on press freedom.

Freedom of Press and Limitation of Seditious Libel in Interpreting the Massachusetts Declaration of Rights

Cushing, toward the end of his service as chief judge of Massachusetts' highest court in 1789, confronted two cases that involved prosecutions of the press for seditious libels.[331] The Massachusetts Declaration of Rights of 1780 protected freedom of the press broadly, saying "[t]he liberty of the press is essential to the security of freedom in a state[;] it ought not, therefore, to be restricted in this commonwealth."[332] Cushing pondered the implications of that provision and of the state constitution for the crime of seditious libel. His deliberation did not involve the First Amendment, since it was not approved by Congress until later in 1789 and was not ratified by the requisite number of states until two years after. However, the state and federal freedom of press provisions are similar in their breadth and unqualified language.

Cushing wrote a seven-page letter to his old colleague,[333] John Adams, who drafted that Massachusetts provision[334] (before its rewording in the state convention[335]), outlining his own thinking and inviting Adams's thoughts, in February 1789.[336] Adams's works are not yet published for that year.[337] The John Adams who Cushing consulted was not the embattled Adams who signed the Sedition Act nearly ten years later, but, rather, the postrevolutionary Adams who said ten years earlier, after framing that state declaration of rights, "I think there ought to be an article in the declaration of rights of every state, securing freedom of speech, impartiality, and independence at the bar. There is nothing on which the rights of every member of society more depend."[338] It was the Adams who had condemned

[331] PRESS-MASS. 142 n.1. The cases arose out of publications in 1786, but never reached trial because the publishers were pardoned. *Id.*

[332] Mass. Declaration of Rights art. XVI, 3 FEDERAL-STATE CONSTITUTIONS 1888, 1892.

[333] From years of cases together. *E.g.*, William Cushing to John Adams (20 May 1776), 4 ADAMS PAPERS 199; William Cushing to John Adams (14 Jan. 1777), 5 *id.* 71.

[334] EMPIRE 82; FEDERALISM 532; PRESS-MASS. 133.

[335] 8 ADAMS PAPERS 279, 379; JOURNAL OF CONVENTION-MASS. 41.

[336] William Cushing to John Adams (18 Feb. 1789), Microfilms of the Adams Papers (MHS, Boston, reel 372). The letter is briefly discussed in John D. Cushing, A Revolutionary Conservative: The Public Life of William Cushing, 1732–1810, at 232–37 (1959) (unpublished Ph.D. dissertation, Clark University), LEVY 198–201, PRINTERS 67–68, 88–89, REPRESSIVE JURISPRUDENCE 67–68, in a very brief reference in 3 DHSC 314 n.19, and with a similar reading to mine, in LUCAS A. POWE, JR., THE FOURTH ESTATE AND THE CONSTITUTION 41–42 (UCalP, Berkeley 1991).

[337] It can also be found, paginated differently as the retained copy, in CUSHING PAPERS (MHS, Boston, Box 1).

[338] John Adams to Benjamin Rush (4 Nov. 1779), 9 ADAMS WORKS 507.

British threats of prosecuting "slander and sedition" and had warned that "the jaws of power are always stretched out . . . to destroy the freedom of thinking, speaking, and writing."[339] It was the Adams who had proclaimed, "A free press maintains the majesty of the people."[340]

The Massachusetts chief justice construed freedom of the press to be quite broad, providing "a liberty to treat all subjects and characters freely" so long as it was done truthfully:

> But when the article says—"The liberty of the press is essential to the security of freedom," and, "it ought not to be restrained" does it not comprehend a liberty to treat all subjects and characters freely within the bounds of truth?
>
> . . . .
>
> . . . . Without this liberty of the press, could we have supported our liberties against British Administration? Or could our revolution have taken place? Pretty certain, it could not at the time it did. Under a sense and impression of this sort I conceive this article was adopted.[341]

His focus was on the targets of the common law of seditious libel—"all subjects" including criticism of government, and all "characters" including criticism of officials. He rejected that and other features of the Blackstone-Mansfield view of seditious libel, saying that "this article was adopted" to protect the liberty of the press that had criticized government.

Cushing criticized English common law that treated true statements as potentially seditious libels, and that even treated true statements as more libelous than false ones. He asked "whether it is consistent with this article" to punish a publication supported by truth "that may arraign the conduct of persons in office"?[342] Cushing noted that English law, while requiring a civil action for libel to show the publication was "false as well as scandalous," treated truth or falsity as "immaterial" in a criminal indictment for libel, and in some cases treated a true charge as a greater provocation than a false charge.[343] He found it incongruous "that a man ought to be punished more for declaring truth than for telling lies."[344] However incongruous, English law did not permit truth to be pled as a defense in a criminal indictment for libel,

[339] John Adams, *A Dissertation on the Canon and Feudal Law* (1765), in 3 Adams Works 445, 457; 1 Adams Papers 103, 121.

[340] Press-Mass. 143–44.

[341] William Cushing to John Adams 3, 5 (18 Feb.1789), *supra* note 336; Cushing Papers 8, 11.

[342] *Id.* 1; Cushing Papers 1–2.

[343] *Id.* 1; Cushing Papers 2–3 (citing Blackstone and Coke).

[344] *Id.* 2; Cushing Papers 3.

only in a civil action.[345] Cushing's inquiry was not limited to the English rule excluding a defense of truth.

Cushing next addressed whether English law on criminal libels was applicable in Massachusetts. The state constitution, like many others, adopted colonial law and English common law unless repealed by the legislature or "repugnant to the rights and liberties contained in this constitution."[346] The case was one of first impression, so far as Cushing knew, so there was no precedent to bind him.[347] His belief was that the declaration of rights' wording of freedom of press was "very general and unlimited," though some "guard or limitation" should be placed on the press rather than making the provision absolute.[348] Cushing suggested two limitations: that private libel actions should be allowed so the press was "restrainable from injuring characters" of people, and that criminal libel actions might be allowed so the press was "restrained from injuring the public or individuals, by propagating fals[e]hoods," so long as the latter cause of action departed from English law by being limited to false statements.[349] He recognized that the same rules would apply to speech as to press.[350]

Thus, Cushing concluded that Massachusetts' freedom of the press overrode the English law of libel in at least three aspects. The first, as just mentioned, was that only false statements could be libelous, and truth may be pled as a defense. But he went beyond this *Zenger* amelioration.

He also found that Massachusetts had jettisoned the Blackstone-Mansfield definition of freedom of press as merely freedom from prior restraint, noting that a subsequent punishment could as effectively destroy freedom of press, and must be treated as equally prohibited by the state's declaration of rights:

> Judge Black. says, (4 vol. p.151) the liberty of the press consists—"in laying no previous restraint upon publications," and not in freedom from censure for criminal matter when published. Wherein he refers to a public licenser or inspector of the press. *That* is, no doubt, the liberty of the press as allowed by the law of England.
>
> But the words of our article, understood according to plain English and common sense—make no such distinction, and must exclude *subsequent* restraints—as much as *previous restraints*. In other words, if all men are restrained, by the fear of jails, scourges and loss of ears, from examining the conduct of persons in administration, *and*, where their conduct is

[345] *Id.* 2; CUSHING PAPERS 5–6.

[346] Mass. Const. ch.VI, art.6, 3 FEDERAL-STATE CONSTITUTIONS 1888, 1910.

[347] William Cushing to John Adams 3 (18 Feb.1789), *supra* note 336; CUSHING PAPERS 7.

[348] *Id.* 3; CUSHING PAPERS 7.

[349] *Id.* 3; CUSHING PAPERS 8.

[350] *Id.* 3; CUSHING PAPERS 8 ("by word, writing or printing"), at least as to criminal libel.

> illegal, tyrannical and tending to overthrow the constitution and introduce slavery, *are so* restrained from declaring it to the public; *that* will be as effectual a restraint, as any *previous* restraint whatever.[351]

This was the part of Cushing's analysis that most rejected the English common law of seditious libel. If the Blackstone-Mansfield definition was wrong that liberty of press meant only freedom from prior restraint, a meaningless freedom in a land without licensors, then liberty of press prohibited subsequent restraints, a far-reaching freedom against real-world regulation. Even when Cushing shifted position (or followed other justices) in 1798, he did not adopt the Blackstone-Mansfield definition or framework for seditious libel.

Finally, Cushing repudiated the rule that freedom of press did not include criticism of government, finding it potentially the most important type of expression, so long as it was truthful.

> The propagating literature and knowledge by printing or otherwise, tends to illuminate men[']s minds and to establish them in principles of liberty. But it cannot be denied also—that a free scanning the conduct of administration, and shewing the tendency of it, and, where truth will warrant, making it manifest, that it is subversive of all law, liberty and the constitution, it cannot be denied, I think, that this liberty tends "*to the security of freedom in a state*"; even more directly and essentially, than the liberty of printing upon literary and speculative subjects in general. . . . This liberty of publishing truth can never effectually injure a good government, or honest administration; but it may save a state and prevent the necessity of a revolution, as well as bring one about, when it is necessary. . . .
>
> But the liberty of the press, when it had truth for its basis, who can stand before it? Besides it may facilitate a legal prosecution that is well-founded, which might not otherwise have been dared to be attempted. When the press is made the vehicle of fals[e]hood and scandal, let the authors be punished with becoming rigour. But why need any honest man be afraid of truth? The guilty only fear it—and I cannot but be inclined to think with Gordon (in his letter upon libels vol.3 no.28 of Cato's Letters) that truth sacredly adhered to, in all cases without exception, can never upon the whole prejudice, right religion, equal government, or a government founded upon proper bal[] ances and checks, or the happiness of society in any respect; but must promote them all.

[351] *Id.* 4; CUSHING PAPERS 9–10.

> Suppressing this liberty I am speaking for by penal laws; will it not carry greater danger to freedom, than it will do good to governments? The weight of government is sufficient to prevent any very dangerous consequences occasioned by *provocations* resulting from charges founded in truth, whether such charges are made in a legal cause, or otherwise.[352]

In this, Cushing acknowledged a major rationale for liberties of press and speech—freedom to criticize government as a fundamental means to protect liberty and to arrest tyranny, and as a check on bad government and officials. He reversed the seditious libel concern over a bad tendency, when he found that "this liberty tends to the security of freedom." He cited Cato by book and page. He echoed the words of *Areopagitica* about truth vanquishing error, and turned the burden of proof on those who would hide from truth. And he applied the same rule to the English doctrine of blasphemous libel, finding that "truth . . . can never upon the whole prejudice, right religion."

Cushing has been criticized for pedestrian judicial analysis elsewhere, more because several of his earlier Supreme Court opinions were brief and to the point than because they were undiscerning, and probably because his abilities declined and left him "superannuated & contemptible" in his later years.[353] The Adams letter is an example of the opposite, addressing a question that most were not raising, following instead of avoiding the broad language of the constitutional protection of press and speech, and nicely stating a rationale for the facial meaning of that broad language. John Adams aptly noted, a half year later and apparently in reference to this and another letter, that Cushing's letters "contain profound and careful enquiries."[354]

Adams replied briefly to the letter, not disagreeing with any part of the analysis, but focusing on Cushing's points of departure from English law. Adams was "very clear" that the state constitution required a right to present the defense of truth in a criminal case, where if truth were shown, "they would readily acquit."[355] He agreed that publishing information about government officials was

[352] *Id.* 4–6; CUSHING PAPERS 10–14. The last quoted sentence responds to the objection, *id.* 5, "that a public prosecution is the regular course–in case of mal[]feasance," rather than public criticism.

[353] Jeremiah Smith to William Plumer (24 Feb.1795), 1 DHSC 753. For criticism, *e.g.*, 1 DAVID P. CURRIE, THE CONSTITUTION IN THE SUPREME COURT: THE FIRST HUNDRED YEARS, 1789–1888, at 58 (UChiP, Chicago 1985).

[354] John Adams to William Cushing (8 Sept.1789), 17 DHRC 1485.

[355] John Adams to William Cushing (7 Mar.1789) at 2, CUSHING PAPERS (MHS, Boston, Box 1). Adams did question whether a civil action could be brought for publishing scandalous though true information maliciously, without "just cause for publishing it," which today would amount to invasion of privacy. *Id.* 1.

particularly important in a government "by the people," because "how are their characters and conduct to be known to their constituents but by the press? If the press is to be stopped, and the people kept in ignorance, we had much better have the first magistrate and senators hereditary."[356] Though Adams did not go as far as Cushing, Adams in 1789 still believed in the expansive protection of the press that his draft Massachusetts provision had given, along with the equally expansive protection of speech[357] that he had said every state's declaration of rights should secure.[358]

Cushing soon had a chance to address these issues publicly, in a grand jury charge in the aftermath of Shays' Rebellion in his home state. He addressed what he viewed as dangerous—defamation of character—and does not appear to have warned of seditious libel (assuming the reference to licentiousness of the press pointed to defamation of people's "good name" and not to sedition):

> Chief Justice Cushing gave a most excellent charge to the jury. Among other things, his Honour took notice of the evil tendency of libels: He pointed out, in a very clear and concise manner, the distinction between the liberty and licentiousness of the press—the difference between a citizen's publishing his sentiments on publick measures with a spirit becoming a freeman, and his stabbing and wounding private and publick characters, and robbing them of their good name.[359]

The newspaper summary truncated Cushing's actual charge, but a spectator's diary similarly described it.[360]

Freedom of Press in Drafting the Massachusetts Declaration of Rights

Cushing was quite familiar with the Massachusetts Declaration of Rights, because he had been a delegate to the convention to prepare it and the state constitution, in 1779–1780, and had been one of the thirty members of its drafting committee.[361] The legislature's prior attempt at a new constitution in 1778 had been rebuffed, primarily because a special convention had not been elected and a declaration of rights had not been included.[362] The convention in 1779 began with

[356] *Id.*

[357] 8 Adams Papers 236, 240; *accord* Press-Mass. 133.

[358] John Adams to Benjamin Rush (4 Nov.1779), 8 Adams Papers 279.

[359] *Worcester, April 23*, Salem Mercury, 28 Apr.1789, at 3; *Worcester, April 23*, Independent Chronicle (Boston), 30 Apr.1789, at 3.

[360] 1 William Bentley, Diary of William Bentley 122 (Essex Institute, Salem 1905–14).

[361] Journal of Convention-Mass. 15, 30.

[362] *See id.* 255, 264; *accord* Press-Mass. 132.

drafts prepared by John Adams.[363] The drafting committee adopted his declaration of rights without significant change,[364] evidently unanimously.[365]

The drafting committee's provision for the press was slightly reworded by a committee of three, and was then adopted without apparent disagreement,[366] with expansive language:

> XVI. The liberty of the press is essential to the security of freedom in a state[;] it ought not, therefore, to be restricted in this commonwealth.[367]

Cushing's and the full committee's role was limited, but there was no indication of dissent on his part.[368] Similarly, his exchange with Adams ten years later did not give any hint of disagreement with the provision; instead Cushing embraced it and read it broadly in 1789.

Cushing also attended the Massachusetts ratification convention of 1788, serving as its vice president.[369] He wrote his thoughts on a federal bill of rights in a prepared speech,[370] though he did not actually deliver it because he became the acting presiding officer and sought to remain neutral on disputed issues.[371] His speech embraced the usual federalist rationale that a bill of rights was not necessary because the new federal government had only enumerated powers and not unlimited powers that could touch upon the rights at issue.[372] However, he added that he "would not object to any" amendments amounting to a bill of rights.[373] Cushing also sat on the

[363] John Adams to Edmund Genet (29 Feb.1780), 8 ADAMS PAPERS 378, 379; Report of a Constitution, 8 *id.* 236; Editorial Note, 8 *id.* 230–31.

[364] John Adams to Elbridge Gerry (4 Nov.1779), 8 *id.* 276; Editorial Note, 8 *id.* 230–31.

[365] JOURNAL OF CONVENTION-MASS. 35.

[366] *Id.* 41; *see* Caleb Strong to Nn. (31 May 1819), 3 WILLIAM V. WELLS, LIFE AND PUBLIC SERVICES OF SAMUEL ADAMS 88 (Little, Brown, Boston 1865) ("almost unanimous vote"). Adams' protection for speech was deleted by the three, without explanation or debate. PRESS-MASS. 134.

[367] Declaration of Rights art.xvi, 8 ADAMS PAPERS 226; 3 FEDERAL-STATE CONSTITUTIONS 1892; *cf.* Adams draft art.xvii, 8 ADAMS PAPERS 240.

[368] He was aligned with Adams, and one of "the principal members of the convention." Caleb Strong to Nn. (31 May 1819), 3 WILLIAM V. WELLS, THE LIFE AND PUBLIC SERVICES OF SAMUEL ADAMS 84n. (Little, Brown, Boston 1865).

[369] 2 ELLIOT'S DEBATES 2. He voted for ratification. 6 DHRC 1466, 1483. *See* Charles Warren, *Elbridge Gerry . . . and the Ratification of the Federal Constitution in Massachusetts*, 64 PROCEEDINGS OF MASSACHUSETTS HISTORICAL SOCIETY 143 (1932).

[370] William O'Brien, *Justice Cushing's Undelivered Speech on the Federal Constitution*, 15 WM. & MARY Q. 74, 80 (1958); *id.* 77; 6 DHRC 1428 (c. 4 Feb.1788).

[371] *Id.*; Convention to William Cushing (7 Feb.1788), CUSHING PAPERS.

[372] *Id.* 82–83; *accord* Landholder [Oliver Ellsworth], *Landholder VI* (10 Dec.1787), 3 DHRC 478, 489; 4 ELLIOT'S DEBATES 167 (Iredell); James Wilson, State House Yard Speech (6 Oct.1787), 13 DHRC 339, 340; James Madison to Edmund Randolph (10 Apr.1788), 11 MADISON PAPERS 18, 19; James Madison to Thomas Jefferson (10 Aug.1788), 11 *id.* 226, 226.

[373] *Id.* 90–91. He wrote, then deleted, that "a number of those [amendments] proposed by your Excellency are proper." *Id.* 91 n.49.

"Committee of Twenty-Five" to consider proposed amendments, and signed its report.[374] Its "recommendatory amendments," like amendments from many of the states, addressed structural issues and other rights, though they did not include freedoms of press or speech.[375] In view of Cushing's 1789 letter, he clearly had no objection to such rights themselves, but only the general federalist objection to the superfluity of a federal bill of rights, and the latter objection was not strongly held.

Freedoms of Speech and Press and Seditious Libel under the Federal Constitution

Cushing's approach to the state Declaration of Rights and to the First Amendment, once approved, should have been similar. Each provided a very broad protection of freedom of press, and each lacked any limiting language or any other hint of embodying common law restrictions.

In 1794 Cushing continued to express an expansive view of freedoms of speech and press in his grand jury charge, despite the recent Whiskey Rebellion:

> In this enlightened ag[e], we may well suppose a free government best adapted to maintain liberty, security and general happiness. Such governments we now enjoy. As to religious liberty and the rights of conscience, it is difficult to say how they could be enjoyed in greater latitude. The same, I presume, may be said of civil rights[.] Particularly, due allowance is made for liberty of speech, liberty of the press; and a decent freedom in examining and canvassing all public measures; with the reasonable restrictions of not injuring private characters, or not actually attempting to stir up sedition, or forcible opposition to government.[376]

There, he reiterated the freedom to examine public measures, evidently defining "decent" as truthfully, and he limited his only reference to sedition to "actually attempting to stir up sedition" rather than merely "tending" to do so. He further implied a narrow reach for "sedition" by pairing it with "forcible opposition to government." He did not say, or imply, that "liberty of the press" or "liberty of speech" was mere freedom from prior restraint, nor did he otherwise adopt the Blackstone-Mansfield definition or framework in any way.

The grand jury charge of 1794 also praised the goals of the American Revolution and "the rights of man," a topic raising Federalist suspicions though bringing Republican cheers:

> The great end of government, you know, is peace and protection; peace with nations, protection against foreign force:—peace and order within;

[374] 6 DHRC 1412, 1414, 1415 n.9 (4 Feb.1788).

[375] 16 *id.* 64; 6 *id.* 1415 n.9.

[376] William Cushing's Charge (C.C.D. R.I. 7 Nov.1794), 2 DHSC 491, 492.

> protection of individuals, of all classes of men, whether poor or rich, in the undisturbed enjoyment of their just rights, and which are comprehended under a few, but important words—*security of person and property*, or, if you please, *rights of man*. Hence government involves in it a sacred regard to the principles of justice, and to all moral obligations.
>
> ....
>
> Where people are not permitted to enjoy these blessings, *security of person and property*, unmolested, there is tyranny, whether it arises from monarchy, aristocracy, or a mob. Where all men are equally and promptly protected in the free exercise of these rights, there is liberty and equality;—liberty to do whatever just laws made by a free representative allow; equality, that is, as to right of protection respecting the great objects of life, liberty and property, when not forfeited to the state by criminal conduct; respecting property ....[377]

Though he summarized the "great objects" as "life, liberty and property," Cushing's passion appears to have been the rights of property, judging by his initial summary of the rights of man as "security of person and property," and his extended discussion of property after the quoted language.[378] He had shifted from 1789, because in 1794 he no longer described the rights of "life, liberty and property" in the terminology of inalienable rights or natural law, but in terms of governmental grants of rights, defining "liberty" as being able "to do whatever just laws made by a free representative allow."

Four years later, Cushing restated his understanding of freedom of press and seditious libel, in response to some newspapers' objection to the Sedition Act, in his grand jury charge for circuit courts in the latter half of 1798.[379] Again, some of what Cushing was prepared to give in 1789, he took away, by strongly implying that Republican expression fell in the category of "scandalous and malicious falsehoods," as is discussed in Chapter 6. He changed from a comparatively unlimited reading of the expansive constitutional protection for the press to an almost limitless reading of an unstated seditious libel restriction of that freedom.

Alarm about Shays' Rebellion and Seditious Libel

Cushing, badly shaken by Shays' Rebellion,[380] had reacted by enlarging the reach of seditious libel, and his 1798 retrogression may have been a similar response, as he

[377] 2 *id.* 491–92.

[378] 2 *id.* 492.

[379] William Cushing's Charge (C.C.D. Va. 23 Nov.1798), 3 DHSC 305, 314.

[380] The earliest contemporary history was GEORGE R. MINOT, HISTORY OF THE INSURRECTION IN MASSACHUSETTS IN THE YEAR MDCCLXXXVI (Isaiah Thomas, Worcester 1788); *accord* LEONARD L. RICHARDS, SHAYS' REBELLION (UPP, Philadelphia 2002); DAVID P. SZATMARY, SHAYS' REBELLION (UMP, Amherst 1980).

was alarmed by foreign and domestic dangers in the Quasi-War. In Shays' Rebellion in 1786, rebels sought to prohibit the enforcement and collection of debts in Massachusetts during a difficult economic period,[381] and their focus became preventing the courts from meeting and enforcing debts. Cushing, the state's chief justice, encountered the rebels as the justices traveled around their circuit in August through November of 1786. The supreme judicial court was prevented by insurgents from sitting at Northampton in August, as rebels had taken over the courthouse; it was barred by bayonets from entering the courthouse at Worcester, though courageously the "chief justice remonstrated with the rioters"; it met in Springfield only because troops took the courthouse before the insurrectionists arrived; it could not meet in Berkshire because insurrectionists were marching through town;[382] it only sat in Taunton and Cambridge because the militia supported the court with superior numbers.[383] Not backing down, Cushing gave a grand jury charge at Salem in November that warned that it was high treason "to stop the courts of law," and referred to the insurgents at Worchester who "thrust bayonets at the breast of judges . . .—courts of justice stopped with force of arms."[384] The rebellion was widely viewed as a crisis of government "bordering on a civil war,"[385] which was why it was widely cited as reason for a new federal constitution.

The rebellion collapsed in the face of superior numbers of Massachusetts troops and militia, and in the face of pardons offered by Governor James Bowdoin on a case-by-case basis determined by a commission and with disqualifications from some activities.[386]

Trials of the leading rebels dominated the supreme judicial court's circuits in 1787, while the legislature and governor granted pardons without restrictions for lower ranking participants.[387] Cushing sentenced at least fourteen rebels to be

[381] *E.g.*, Address (Dec.1786), *id.* 83; Isaac Backus, An Address to the Inhabitants of New-England, Concerning the Present Bloody Controversy Therein (S. Hall, Boston 1787); Christopher Babbitt, to His Excellency John Hancock, Esquire, Governor (n.p., Boston 1787) (broadside).

[382] Minot, *supra* note 380, at 38–39, 39–40, 47–49; *accord* Elbridge Gerry to Rufus King (25 Dec.1786), 1 King Correspondence 198 (Worcester).

[383] *Id.* 59–60; James Warren to John Adams (22 Oct.1786), 2 Warren-Adams Letters 278, 280 (Worthington C. Ford ed., MHS, Boston 1925) (Taunton); Elbridge Gerry to Rufus King (29 Nov.1786), 1 King Correspondence 197 (Cambridge).

[384] *Substance of the Charge Delivered at Salem*, American Herald (Boston), 27 Nov.1786, at 4.

[385] James Warren to John Adams (22 Oct.1786), 2 Warren-Adams Letters 278 (Worthington C. Ford ed., MHS, Boston 1925).

[386] James Bowdoin, Commonwealth of Massachusetts, By His Excellency James Bowdoin (Adams & Nourse, Boston 12 Jan.1787) (broadside); Commonwealth of Massachusetts, In the Year of Our Lord, One Thousand Seven Hundred and Eighty-Seven, An Act (Adams & Nourse, Boston 16 Feb.1787) (broadside); *accord* Rufus King to John Adams (10 Feb.1787), 1 King Correspondence 213.

[387] John Hancock, Commonwealth of Massachusetts, By His Excellency John Hancock (Adams & Nourse, Boston 15 June 1787) (broadside); *accord* James Sullivan to Rufus King (14 June 1787), 1 King Correspondence 222, 223.

hanged for high treason, and ten to jail for other offenses, beginning in March of that year.[388] Ten of those received reprieves from the death penalty, granted by the commission followed by the governor's pardons, and the other four were later pardoned as well.[389] Cushing was also described as sentencing to jail "large numbers convicted of seditious words and practices" and other offenses, if a contemporaneous account is accurate.[390] Though his surviving grand jury charge did not use the word "sedition," it did condemn "bold inflammatory misrepresentations, and falsehoods," along with treason by force of arms.[391] During his second circuit, Cushing sentenced at least four more insurrectionists to be hanged for treason, and others to jail for other acts, in October 1787, and that time some of them were hanged.[392]

By 1798 Federalist alarm was even greater, and Cushing's change of position on freedom of press and seditious libel may have been part of it, though his support for the Sedition Act was limited and tepid.

Justice James Wilson

James Wilson was one of America's political theorists who blazed original paths, one of only six signers of both the Declaration of Independence and the Constitution, a leader at the Constitutional Convention, and America's third law professor.[393] He also stood out among the framers of the Constitution as the most thoroughgoing advocate of democracy.[394]

[388] MINOT, *supra* note 380, at 171–73.

[389] *Id.* 172, 187, 188.

[390] *Id.* 172; *accord* LEVY 214.

[391] *Charge to the Middlesex Grand-Jury*, AMERICAN HERALD (Boston), 28 May 1787, at 2.

[392] LEONARD L. RICHARDS, SHAYS' REBELLION 41 (UPP, Philadelphia 2002).

[393] *See generally* MARK D. HALL, THE POLITICAL AND LEGAL PHILOSOPHY OF JAMES WILSON, 1742–1798 (UMoP, Columbia 1997) (best biography and philosophy summary); Mark D. Hall, The Political and Legal Philosophy of James Wilson (1742–1798) (1993) (unpublished Ph.D. dissertation, University of Virginia); CHARLES PAGE SMITH, JAMES WILSON: FOUNDING FATHER, 1742–1798 (UNCP, Chapel Hill 1956); Charles Page Smith, James Wilson, 1787–1798 (1951) (unpublished Ph.D. dissertation, Harvard University); Julius Goebel, *Book Review of "James Wilson, Founding Father,"* 105 U. PA. L. REV. 1027, 1030, 1032 (1957) (Smith biography incompetent, "meagerly footnoted," "smothered with so much undocumented, indeed palpably fanciful detail"). Literature is summarized in Nicholas Pedersen, Note, *The Lost Founder: James Wilson in American Memory*, 22 YALE J.L. & HUMAN. 257, 289–332 (2010).

[394] 1 FARRAND'S RECORDS 52 (direct election of senators as well as representatives), 68 (direct election of president), 127 (people's ratification of Constitution), 179 (proportional representation of people in each state); *see* Ralph A. Rossum, The Popular Pyramid and the Federal Republic: The Political Thought of James Wilson (1973) (unpublished Ph.D. dissertation, University of Chicago).

He was one of the three Supreme Court justices of the first decade who were born abroad, in his case in Scotland, emigrating to New York in 1765[395] in the midst of the Stamp Act crisis. After reading the pamphlet by his law teacher, John Dickinson, arguing that Parliament lacked authority to tax the colonies,[396] he wrote what became an influential pamphlet[397] asserting that Parliament lacked jurisdiction over the colonies, in 1768.[398] In it, he anticipated not only the eventual American rationale for independence but also the ultimate structure of the Commonwealth; he published it in 1774 in time to reach the first Continental Congress.[399] He was soon selected as a delegate to the second Continental Congress[400] and to the next year's Congress,[401] where he voted for and supported independence in 1776[402] and signed the Declaration of Independence.[403] Among other duties, Wilson briefly served on the court of appeals established by Congress.[404] By opposing the Pennsylvania Constitution of 1776, he fell out of favor with the

[395] 2 DAVID DOBSON, DIRECTORY OF SCOTTISH SETTLERS IN NORTH AMERICA 1625–1825, at 209 (GPC, Baltimore 1993).

[396] [JOHN DICKINSON], AN ESSAY ON THE CONSTITUTIONAL POWER OF GREAT BRITAIN OVER THE COLONIES IN AMERICA (London Coffee-House, Philadelphia 1774), reprinted 3 PENNSYLVANIA ARCHIVES (2d ser.) 565, 569, 603–05 (John B. Linn & William H. Egle eds., B.F. Meyers, Harrisburg 1875).

[397] IDEOLOGICAL ORIGINS 225.

[398] *Id.;* William White to James Wilson (27 Nov.1768), 2 WILSON WRITINGS 5.

[399] JAMES WILSON, CONSIDERATIONS ON THE NATURE AND THE EXTENT OF THE LEGISLATIVE AUTHORITY OF THE BRITISH PARLIAMENT (Bradford, Philadelphia 1774); 1 WILSON WORKS 3. He incorporated that reasoning in a draft address from Congress to the colonies, but coupled it with a statement that independence was not sought, which caused its rejection. An Address to the Inhabitants of the Colonies (Feb.1776), 1 WILSON WORKS 46, 47, 53. The newest edition of COLLECTED WORKS OF JAMES WILSON is used herein. It replaces the earlier editions by Bird Wilson, James De Witt Andrews, and Robert G. McCloskey.

[400] 2 JCC 18; 3 *id.* 327.

[401] 5 *id.* 596.

[402] Once he received revised instructions from Pennsylvania. Pennsylvania Assembly: Instructions to Its Delegates in Congress (14 June 1776), 22 FRANKLIN PAPERS 479. Wilson's reason for earlier requesting delay was that his initial instructions prevented a vote for independence. Thomas Jefferson, Notes of Debate (10 May and 7 June 1776), 6 JCC 1075–76, 1087; James Wilson, A Personal Explanation: An Address "To the Citizens of Pennsylvania," 1 WILSON WRITINGS 114, 116. Even when Wilson requested delay, he had consistently denied parliamentary authority over America. James Wilson, Speech Delivered in the Convention (Jan.1775), 1 WILSON WORKS 32, 38; James Wilson, An Address to the Inhabitants of the Colonies (13 Feb.1776), 1 *id.* 46, 47, 52.

[403] 5 JCC 515. When Wilson was attacked as opposing independence, he was defended by fourteen members of Congress who said he supported it but his province's instructions prohibited it. A Defense of Wilson (20 June 1776), 2 WILSON WRITINGS 72.

[404] 3 JCC 357–58 (17 Nov.1775); 5 *id.* 747 (9 Sept.1776); 6 *id.* 931–32 (7 Nov.1776), 985–86 (27 Nov.1776); *see* HENRY J. BOURGUIGNON, THE FIRST FEDERAL COURT: THE FEDERAL APPELLATE PRIZE COURT OF THE AMERICAN REVOLUTION 329 (American Philosophical Society, Philadelphia 1977).

state legislature,[405] which removed him from Congress the next year.[406] When political tides changed, Wilson was reappointed to Congress in 1782 and in 1785–1787.[407]

Wilson was, with Madison, arguably the most influential delegate at the Constitutional Convention of 1787.[408] He made more remarks than any delegate except Gouverneur Morris.[409] He, with future Chief Justices Rutledge and Ellsworth, was on the five-member committee of detail, which drafted the federal Constitution after the first round of debates,[410] and that draft is in his handwriting. He, with Rutledge, Blair, and Paterson, signed the Constitution.[411] He then led the ratification effort at the Pennsylvania convention.[412]

He was listed as the third nomination to the Supreme Court in 1789,[413] though he received the fourth commission;[414] he had hoped to be the first as chief justice.[415] Between court terms, Wilson gave highly publicized law lectures[416] as America's third law professor,[417] at what became University of Pennsylvania Law

[405] James Wilson to Arthur St. Clair (3 July 1777), ST. CLAIR PAPERS: LIFE AND PUBLIC SERVICES OF ARTHUR ST. CLAIR 417, 418 (William Henry Smith ed., R. Clarke, Cincinnati 1882); James Wilson to William Atlee & Jasper Yeates (13 Mar.1777), 6 LETTERS OF DELEGATES 502 n.1.

[406] James Wilson to Arthur St. Clair (19 Feb.1777), 6 LETTERS OF DELEGATES 326. He was reappointed for part of 1777. 6 *id.* 393; 2 WILSON WRITINGS 114.

[407] 23 JCC 726; 28 *id.* 303; 29 *id.* 876; 30 *id.* 123.

[408] MAX FARRAND, THE FRAMING OF THE CONSTITUTION OF THE UNITED STATES 197 (YUP, New Haven 1913); *see* Andrew C. McLaughlin, *James Wilson in the Philadelphia Convention*, 12 POLITICAL SCIENCE Q. 1 (1897).

[409] 13 DHRC 337. His remarks are collected in 1 WILSON WORKS 80–170, and discussed in William Ewald, *James Wilson and the Drafting of the Constitution*, 10 U. PA. J. CONST. L. 901, 936–1003 (2008).

[410] 2 FARRAND'S RECORDS 97, 106, 565–80.

[411] 33 JCC 500.

[412] 14 DHRC 206; 2 *id.* 323; *[No Caption]*, INDEPENDENT GAZETTEER (Philadelphia), 5 May 1788, reprinted in 17 DHRC 385; Anthony Wayne to George Washington (20 May 1789), 2 WILSON WRITINGS 374; *see* JOHN B. MCMASTER & FREDERICK D. STONE, PENNSYLVANIA AND THE FEDERAL CONSTITUTION 1787–1788, at 17 (HSP, Philadelphia 1888).

[413] Nomination (24 Sept.1789), 1 DHSC 9, 2 DHFFC 44; Confirmation (26 Sept.1789), 1 DHSC 9, 2 DHFFC 45.

[414] Nominations (24 Sept.1789), 4 WASHINGTON PAPERS-PRESIDENTIAL 75.

[415] James Wilson to George Washington (21 Apr.1789), 2 WASHINGTON PAPERS-PRESIDENTIAL 111; Benjamin Rush to John Adams (22 Apr.1789), 15 DHFFC 323.

[416] James Wilson, An Introductory Lecture to a Course of Law Lectures (T. Dobson, Philadelphia 1791); 1 WILSON WORKS 431.

[417] Tobias Lear to George Washington (24 Oct.1790), 6 WASHINGTON PAPERS-PRESIDENTIAL 573, 575. George Wythe started teaching law at William and Mary ten years earlier, and Judge Tapping Reeve in Litchfield around the same time. 1 CAMBRIDGE HISTORY OF LAW IN AMERICA 289 (Michael Grossberg & Christopher Tomlins eds., CUP, Cambridge 2007–08), 2 *id.* 46; *Early Courses and Professors at William and Mary College*, 14 WM. & MARY COLLEGE Q. (1st ser.) 71, 77–78 (1905).

School, in 1790–1791.[418] He was selected by Pennsylvania to prepare a revision and digest of its laws,[419] though the project died when the legislature failed to fund it.

However, Wilson was distracted by career-long involvement in land speculation,[420] including investment in one company involved in the Yazoo scandal,[421] and he elsewhere made the largest land purchase in American history to that date.[422] By the mid-1790s, speculation left him unable to pay obligations and sank him into financial ruin,[423] as it did others such as the "financier of the American Revolution," Robert Morris.[424] In 1797, Wilson was said to be "absconding from his creditors"[425] as he traveled to New Jersey, and was briefly jailed there for debts,[426] before leaving to ride the southern circuit. There, he remained in North Carolina from late 1797 through most of 1798[427] to avoid further arrest for

[418] EDWARD P. CHEYNEY, HISTORY OF THE UNIVERSITY OF PENNSYLVANIA, 1740–1940, at 158, 159 (UPP, Philadelphia 1940). The introductory lecture was 15 Dec.1790. *Id.* 159.

[419] James Wilson to William Bingham (9 Mar.1791), 2 WILSON WRITINGS 403; James Wilson to William Bingham (c. 24 Aug.1791), 9 WASHINGTON PAPERS-PRESIDENTIAL 351. He also proposed to prepare a federal digest. James Wilson to George Washington (31 Dec.1791), 9 *id.* 347.

[420] John Dickinson to James Wilson (11 Aug.1774), 2 WILSON WRITINGS 42; James Wilson to Silas Deane (1 Jan.1781), 4 THE DEANE PAPERS 269, 272 (Charles Isham ed., NYHS, New York 1887–90); Silas Deane to Barnabas Deane (10 Mar.1784), 5 *id.* 281, 282; 2 WILSON WRITINGS 237a; 20 LETTERS OF DELEGATES 282, 283; 23 *id.* 361; 24 *id.* 142; 3 FARRAND'S RECORDS 232, 236; Benjamin Rush to Timothy Pickering (29 Jan.1788), 1 LETTERS OF BENJAMIN RUSH 449 (L. H. Butterfield ed., PUP, Princeton 1951); Benjamin Rush to John C. Lettsom (8 Apr.1785), 1 *id.* 350.

[421] James Madison to James Monroe (27 Mar.1795), 15 MADISON PAPERS 498, 499. He was free of impropriety in it. M.C. Klingelsmith, *James Wilson and the So-Called Yazoo Frauds*, 56 U. PA. L. REV. 1, 5, 6, 19, 27 (1908).

[422] James Wilson to Theophile Cazenove (24 Jan.1793), 2 WILSON WRITINGS 449, 450.

[423] Alexander Hamilton to Theophile Cazenove (12 Oct.1796), 20 HAMILTON PAPERS 346; AUTOBIOGRAPHY OF BENJAMIN RUSH 237 (George W. Corner ed., PUP, Princeton 1948) (Commonplace Book (Dec.1796)); Clement Paine to Elisha Pitkin (7 Feb.179[7]), 10 SUSQUEHANNA COMPANY PAPERS 405, 406 (Robert J. Taylor ed., CorUP, Ithaca 1970–). His last major creditor was still seeking judgments 42 years later, Paschall Hollingsworth to C. Loeler (26 Feb.1840), though Wilson's son successfully sold land to pay off other debts.

[424] EMPIRE 116–21, 233–34; FEDERALISM 178–79.

[425] James Iredell to Hannah Iredell (11 Aug.1797), 2 IREDELL CORRESPONDENCE 516; *accord* Harrison Gray Otis to Sally Otis (18 Feb.1798), 1 DHSC 858. Wilson consequently missed the Court sessions of August 1797, February 1798, and August 1798. 1 *id.* 290–97, 298–305, 307–09.

[426] James Wilson to Bird Wilson (6 Sept.1797), 3 DHSC 223. He was also arrested for debt in Delaware. Harrison Gray Otis to Sally Otis (18 Feb.1798), 1 *id.* 858. Shortly before his death, he was threatened with jail for debt in North Carolina. Pierce Butler to Samuel Wallis (14 June 1798), 3 *id.* 276, 277.

[427] James Wilson to Bird Wilson (17 Dec.1797), 3 DHSC 230, 231 (Raleigh to Edenton); James Wilson to Joseph Thomas (17 Dec.1797), 3 *id.* 231 (winter in N.C. and Ga.); *accord* 3 *id.* 254, 263 (N.C.); 3 THE JOHN GRAY BLOUNT PAPERS 213 (Alice B. Keith et al. eds., NCDAH, Raleigh 1952–65) (N.C.); 2 IREDELL CORRESPONDENCE 534 (N.C.). To complicate matters, his attorney disappeared with money of Wilson's investors. James Iredell to Hannah Iredell (6 Aug.1798), 2 IREDELL CORRESPONDENCE 533.

debts.[428] That brought severe strain, and Wilson died of malaria (for which he refused medical treatment) and deteriorating health "occasioned by distress of mind owing to his pecuniary difficulties," in August 1798,[429] a month after the Sedition Act was signed.

Wilson was more than one vote of six on the Supreme Court. Lord Bryce called him "one of the deepest thinkers and most exact reasoners among the members of the Convention of 1787," whose works "display an amplitude and profundity of view in matters of constitutional theory which places him in the front rank of the political thinkers of his age."[430] In the Constitutional Convention, Benjamin Rush called him an "eminent lawyer and a great and enlightened statesman," whose mind "was one blaze of light,"[431] and the French minister, noting that he was France's counsel in America, agreed that he was "eloquent" and "profound."[432] Even in Wilson's youthful first appearance in Congress, John Adams saw a person "whose fortitude, rectitude, and abilities too, greatly outshine his masters."[433] By the early 1780s, George Washington entertained such a "high opinion" of Wilson's legal skills that he sent his nephew Bushrod Washington from Virginia to Pennsylvania to study under Wilson at "a much higher fee than was usually paid."[434] Despite Wilson's role in the front rank of the framers, his statue has always stood in the second or third rank in history, probably because Wilson's finances brought "a miserable termination to such distinguished abilities."[435]

[428] James Iredell to Hannah Iredell (11 May 1798), 2 IREDELL CORRESPONDENCE 527; Pierce Butler to Samuel Wallis (14 June 1798), 3 *id.* 276, 277 (jail). Wilson apparently worked out an agreement with Butler, to remain in North Carolina and avoid jail. James Wilson to Joseph Thomas (12 May 1798), 2 WILSON WRITINGS 529.

[429] James Iredell to Miss Gray (25 Aug.1798), 2 IREDELL CORRESPONDENCE 534 (died 21 Aug.1798); *accord* Jacob Blount to John Gray Blount (8 Mar.1798), 2 BLOUNT PAPERS, *supra* note 427, at 213–14; James Wilson to Joseph Thomas (12 May 1798), 3 DHSC 265, 266 ("hunted–like a wild beast"); Hannah Wilson to Bird Wilson (1 Sept.1798), 3 DHSC 288, 289. Wilson's son believed the creditors "are to receive the whole benefit" of the estate, Bird Wilson to James Iredell (22 Oct.1798), IREDELL-JOHNSON COLLECTION (PC.67.8, Box 8), and evidently paid them ultimately.

[430] 1 JAMES BRYCE, THE AMERICAN COMMONWEALTH 279n., 715n. (2d ed. rev. Commonwealth Publishing, New York 1908).

[431] THE AUTOBIOGRAPHY OF BENJAMIN RUSH 150 (George W. Corner ed., PUP, Princeton 1948); *accord* Francis Hopkinson to Thomas Jefferson (14 Dec.1787), 12 JEFFERSON PAPERS 423; Frederick Muhlenberg to Benjamin Rush (21 Mar.1789), 15 DHFFC 88, 89.

[432] "Liste des Membres et Officiers du Congrés" (1788), 3 FARRAND'S RECORDS 232, 236 ("C'est lui qui fut désigné par M.Gerard comme avocat de la nation françoise" and "éloquent, profond"); *see* James Wilson to French Minister (8 Nov.1783), 2 WILSON WRITINGS 274.

[433] John Adams to Abigail Adams (23 July 1775), 1 LETTERS OF DELEGATES 648, 649; *accord* 3 FARRAND'S RECORDS 91–92.

[434] Bushrod Washington to Bird Wilson (26 Oct.1822), 2 WILSON WRITINGS 594; *accord* George Washington to Robert Morris (2 June 1784), 9 THE PAPERS OF ROBERT MORRIS 374 (E. James Ferguson et al. eds., UPitP, Pittsburgh 1973–).

[435] Jacob Rush to Benjamin Rush (8 Sept.1798), 1 DHSC 862.

Wilson's views of natural law and political theory have been widely studied, more than any other justice of the first decade, but his views of speech and press have never been the subject of study. The little that has been written generally confuses his earlier views with his later views. Wilson's fully evolved views appeared in his 1790–1791 law lectures.

The Law Lectures and the Meaning of the First Amendment Freedoms of Speech and Press

Wilson's law lectures began a year after congressional approval of the Bill of Rights in September 1789, during the ratification process which ended in December 1791.[436] They were viewed as sufficiently important that the audience for the first lecture included President Washington, Vice President Adams, and a number of members of Congress.[437]

Wilson described a very broad First Amendment in the law lectures, without the qualifications that had appeared in his 1787 speeches (which are summarized below):

> The citizen under a free government has a right to think, to speak, to write, to print, and to publish freely, but with decency and truth, concerning publick men, publick bodies, and publick measures.[438]

He saw a central part of freedoms of speech and press as commenting on public officials and government. The reason Wilson emphasized that part was an oppressive English history of prosecuting critics of "publick men, publick bodies, and publick measures," as we will see in Chapter 8. He gave no limitation on those rights but "decency and truth." Shortly before in the lectures, he observed that patriots "disseminate knowledge"; depots "extinguish it."[439]

The critical question is what he meant by "decency and truth"—whether he referred to the common law of seditious libel or to libel and slander of character.

[436] Tobias Lear to George Washington (24 Oct.1790), 6 WASHINGTON PAPERS-PRESIDENTIAL 573, 575 (beginning December 1790). Some were actually delivered, including at least the first 37 lectures (some of Justice Iredell's notes survive). Mr. Wilson's Lectures, IREDELL-JOHNSON COLLECTION (Box 26, item 4). Others were written but not taught. The final sections were never written. *See* JAMES WILSON, *Lectures on Law,* 1 WILSON WORKS 427, 461 (listing additional topics not in published editions or manuscripts).

[437] 1 WILSON WORKS 403; STEPHEN DECATUR, PRIVATE AFFAIRS OF GEORGE WASHINGTON, FROM THE RECORDS AND ACCOUNTS OF TOBIAS LEAR, ESQUIRE, HIS SECRETARY 185 (Houghton Mifflin, Boston 1933); *see* EDWARD P. CHEYNEY, HISTORY OF THE UNIVERSITY OF PENNSYLVANIA, 1740–1940, at 159 (UPP, Philadelphia 1940).

[438] 2 *id.* 1046; *see* 1 *id.* 172, 206–08; 2 *id.* 952.

[439] 2 *id.* 907.

Two things show that Wilson was referring to defamation of private character. First, he addressed the next lecture to "the natural rights of individuals,"[440] where he discussed character as one of four natural rights: "a natural right to his property, to his character, to liberty, and to safety" (life).[441] That natural right to character allowed others to express opinions, though "[o]pinions, upon this as upon every other subject, ought to be founded in truth," so that justice "requires, concerning characters, accuracy and impartiality of opinion."[442] This filled in Wilson's meaning of "decency and truth." He made that clear three pages later, when he stated that "[t]he subject of reputation will again come under your view, when I treat concerning prosecutions for libels and actions of slander: both of which suppose an unjustifiable aggression of character."[443] With that, Wilson proceeded to discuss "liberty and life," the "gifts of heaven."[444]

Further, just four lectures later he addressed libel law and rejected English common law on libel of government and its ministers as an "unwarranted attempt made in the star chamber . . . to wrest the law of libels to the purpose of ministers," warning that "the reasonings on this crime are inaccurate."[445] By inaccurate reasoning, he particularly meant Blackstone, whose *Commentaries* stated that seditious libel was a crime, and who Wilson reprehended on virtually the entire English law of libel. Thus, Wilson disagreed with Blackstone on whether libel of ministers is any different from libel of individuals, whether libel is a breach of the peace that threatens the state instead of just an injury to reputation, whether there must be proof of actual injury instead of an assumed tendency to breach the peace, whether there is any injury if a statement is true (whether truth is a defense), and whether the determination if a libel is "a crime against the right of reputation" must be by jury rather than judge.[446] In effect, Wilson repudiated the crime of seditious libel, and claimed to go back to earlier English law,[447] treating the only crime or civil offense as a false statement injuring reputation. Later lectures dealt with treason, and while he agreed that government may prosecute actual treason,[448] he defined that to require warlike acts and to require far more than just words.[449]

Most importantly, Wilson omitted a crime of seditious libel from his lengthy sections on criminal law,[450] just as he omitted the concept from his section on libel

440 2 *id.* 1053.

441 2 *id.* 1062.

442 2 *id.* 1062, 1063.

443 2 *id.* 1066.

444 *Id.* That discussion of liberty, that "man is naturally free," was in the prior chapter at 2 *id.* 1043–46, and in the introductory lecture, 1 *id.* 432–35.

445 2 *id.* 1134–35.

446 2 *id.* 1134–36.

447 2 *id.* 1133.

448 2 *id.* 1152, 1096.

449 2 *id.* 1153–54.

450 2 *id.* 1085–204.

actions and from his description of freedoms of speech and press. His omission was intentional, as is evident when comparison is made to Blackstone and his framing of discussion of freedom of press around seditious libel.

It would be surprising if Wilson did not disagree with Blackstone on seditious libel, because his law lectures regularly departed from Blackstone on issues of government and individual rights, just as his longest Supreme Court decision did.[451] In those lectures, Wilson disagreed with Blackstone that individuals surrender liberty to government in order for it to provide or secure civil rights, that liberty derives from government instead of from natural law, that Parliament may "do everything that is not naturally impossible," and that people must obey government when it violates their rights.[452] Wilson instead cautioned that Blackstone defined law on "dangerous" principles, that he misstated the "first principles of government" and was not "a zealous friend of republicanism," that on public law Blackstone must be "consulted with a cautious prudence," and that on common law Blackstone was simply wrong that none of its protections applied to America.[453] While Wilson frequently cited Blackstone, he did so for summaries of complex doctrines, not on individual liberties and citizen-state relations. He rejected Blackstone on seditious libel—and on freedom of press.

The Misunderstanding in Scholarly Writing of Wilson's Views of Freedoms of Speech and Press

Two things are remarkable about scholarly writing on James Wilson and seditious libel. First, references to his views on seditious libel almost always cite his pre-First Amendment statements, while his post-First Amendment statements are generally unmentioned. For example, Jenkins wrote that "Wilson apparently had no reservations about the constitutionality of federal seditious libel prosecutions," and that his "statements to the Pennsylvania convention [in 1787] are among the clearest expressions of a possible intent of the framers to permit federal seditious libel prosecutions."[454] Second, the few references to Wilson's views on freedoms of press and speech utterly misinterpret his post-First Amendment

[451] He criticized Blackstone for saying "the individuals of England . . . surrendered the supreme power to the state of government, and reserved nothing to themselves . . . ." Chisholm v. Georgia, 2 U.S. (2 Dall.) 419, 457–58 (1793). "As described by him . . ., the British is a despotic government." *Id.* at 462.

[452] 2 Wilson Works 1054, 1056–57; 1 *id.* 160–61, 151; *accord* 1 *id.* 190–91; 2 DHRC 348.

[453] 1 *id.* 473, 443, 444; 2 *id.* 1049.

[454] David Jenkins, *The Sedition Act of 1798 and the Incorporation of Seditious Libel into First Amendment Jurisprudence*, 45 Am. J. Legal History 154, 168–69 (2001); *e.g.*, Anderson 504–05 n.285; Levy-Liberty 29 & n.30; Leonard W. Levy, Legacy of Suppression 201 (BP-HUP, Cambridge 1960); others cited in the next note; and the otherwise excellent Hamburger 746 n.261.

understanding, pinning on him a "Blackstonian view,"[455] with three exceptions in the 1980s.[456]

More broadly, scholarly writing on the initial justices has widely cited the statements of some justices about freedoms of speech and press during the political crisis of the late 1790s, while ignoring their statements closer to the time of the First Amendment, as discussed in Chapters 6 and 8. Thus, Cushing's support for the Sedition Act is widely cited, but his analysis in 1789 about the state's revolutionary constitution overriding most of the common law of seditious libel is generally overlooked. Jay's, Rutledge's, and Johnson's, as well as Wilson's, support of freedom of press in the constitutional period are overlooked.

Wilson's 1787 Speeches on Freedom of Press, and the Redundancy of a Bill of Rights

Wilson addressed freedom of press in speeches in 1787, though those were not his final word on the issue. They were superseded by his law lectures of 1790–91, as well as his draft of the Pennsylvania Constitution in 1789–90. The speeches only reflected his evolving understanding before two Pennsylvania events occurred and before the First Amendment was adopted.

After the federal Constitutional Convention in 1787, Wilson gave the first public speech by a delegate in support of ratification,[457] a speech that was widely reprinted in newspapers and pamphlets[458] and was equally widely read.[459] That

[455] Open Press 111, 113; *e.g.*, Jerome L. Merin, *Libel and the Supreme Court*, 11 Wm. & Mary L. Rev. 371, 377 (1969); Leonard W. Levy, *The Legacy Reexamined*, 37 Stanford L. Rev. 767, 787 (1985); Kurland 235–36; Andrew Lenner, *A Tale of Two Constitutions: Nationalism in the Federalist Era*, 40 Am. J. Legal History 72, 77 (1996); Jenkins, *supra* note 454, at 168–69; Arthur E. Wilmarth, *Elusive Foundation: John Marshall, James Wilson, and the Problem of Reconciling Popular Sovereignty and Natural Law Jurisprudence in the New Federal Republic*, 72 Geo. Wash. L. Rev. 113, 160 & n.273 (2003); Rodney A. Smolla, *Content and Context: The Contributions of William Van Alstyne to First Amendment Interpretation*, 54 Duke L.J. 1623, 1635 (2005).

[456] William T. Mayton, *Seditious Libel and the Lost Guarantee of a Freedom of Expression*, 84 Colum. L. Rev. 91, 103, 113 n.122, 125 n.180 (1984); Norman L. Rosenberg, Protecting the Best Men: An Interpretive History of the Law of Libel 66 (UNCP, Chapel Hill 1986); Randy E. Barnett, *Reconceiving the Ninth Amendment*, 74 Cornell L. Rev. 1, 11 & n.38 (1988).

[457] James Wilson, State House Yard Speech (6 Oct.1787), 13 DHRC 339, 340; *see* 13 *id.* 337; 1 Wilson Works 171.

[458] 13 DHRC 337; James Iredell, Answers to Mr. Mason's Objections to the New Constitution (Feb.1788), 16 DHRC 163, 168. Washington was sufficiently impressed that he asked to have Wilson's speech published, and quoted it. George Washington to David Stuart (17 Oct.1787), 5 Washington Papers-Confederation 379; George Washington to Lafayette (28 Apr.1788), 6 *id.* 242, 244.

[459] *E.g.*, James Madison to Thomas Jefferson (17 Oct.1788), 11 Madison Papers 295, 297; Thomas Jefferson to James Madison (20 Dec.1787), 10 *id.* 335, 336.

"State House Yard" speech in October 1787 discussed freedom of the press in the context of the usual pro-constitutional argument why a bill of rights was unnecessary, two years before the Bill of Rights was drafted and four years before it was ratified. Wilson asserted that "the leading d[i]scrimination between the state constitutions, and the constitution of the United States," was that state constitutions "invested their representatives with every right and authority which they did not in explicit terms reserve," while the federal Constitution gave powers only "from the positive grant." Thus, "in the former case every thing which is not reserved is given, but in the latter the reverse of the proposition prevails, and every thing which is not given, is reserved."[460]

That was Wilson's basis for stating that a bill of rights was unnecessary, and that the "sacred palladium of national freedom" of the press was fully protected from the federal government:

> This distinction being recognized, will furnish an answer to those who think the omission of a bill of rights, a defect in the proposed constitution: for it would have been superfluous and absurd to have stipulated with a foederal body of our own creation, that we should enjoy those privileges, of which we are not divested either by the intention or the act, that has brought that body into existence. For instance, the liberty of the press, which has been a copious source of declamation and opposition, what controul can proceed from the foederal government to shackle or destroy that sacred palladium of national freedom? If indeed, a power similar to that which has been granted for the regulation of commerce, had been granted to regulate literary publications, it would have been as necessary to stipulate that the liberty of the press should be preserved inviolate, as that the impost should be general in its operation.... But this could not be an object with the convention, for it must naturally depend upon a future compact, to which the citizens immediately interested will, and ought to be parties; and there is no reason to suspect that so popular a privilege will in that case be neglected. In truth then, the proposed system possesses no influence whatever upon the press, and it would have been merely nugatory to have introduced a formal declaration upon the subject—nay, that very declaration might have been construed to imply that some degree of power was given, since we undertook to define its extent.[461]

His reference to what "could not be an object with the convention" referred to a power to regulate literary publications and a needed protection from that power

[460] 13 DHRC 339; 1 Wilson Works 171–72.

[461] 13 *id.* 340; 1 Wilson Works 172.

for liberty of the press. Thus, the federal government was simply not empowered to legislate in regard to the press—"the proposed system possesses no influence whatever upon the press." This speech did not affirm any state power to forbid seditious libel, but the next did, though not a *federal* power.

That "sacred palladium" of freedom of the press, though free from federal control, was not safe from states retaining the common law of seditious libel, as Wilson said two months later, before changing his view.

In the Pennsylvania ratification convention in late 1787,[462] where Wilson was the leader of forces favoring the federal Constitution,[463] he gave another speech which also addressed freedom of the press. He reiterated that the *federal* Constitution gave "no power whatsoever concerning [the press]," but said some *states'* provisions for freedom of press were limited by common law restrictions on libel including seditious libel:

> on the subject of the press, I beg leave to make an observation; it is very true, sir, that this Constitution says nothing with regard to that subject, nor was it necessary, because it will be found that there is given to the general government no power whatsoever concerning it; and no law in pursuance of the Constitution can possibly be enacted to destroy that liberty.
>
> . . . It has been asked, if a law should be made to punish libels, and the judges should proceed under that law, what chance would the printer have of an acquittal? And it has been said he would drop into a den of devouring monsters.
>
> I presume it was not in the view of the honorable gentleman to say there is no such thing as a libel or that the writers of such ought not to be punished. The idea of the liberty of the press is not carried so far as this in any country—what is meant by the liberty of the press is, that there should be no antecedent restraint upon it; but that every author is responsible when he attacks the security or welfare of the government or the safety, character, and property of the individual.[464]

Wilson was not addressing the meaning of the First Amendment, because the Bill of Rights had not been drafted and would not be until mid-1789. Nor was he addressing federal government powers when he discussed libels, because he had just

[462] It met 20 Nov.1789 – 15 Dec.1789, 2 DHRC 322–25, simultaneously with the Pennsylvania convention to amend the state constitution, which attained a quorum on 2 Nov.1789. 1 WILSON WRITINGS 593.

[463] MEMOIRS OF HIS OWN TIME, BY ALEXANDER GRAYDON 344, 352 (John S. Littell ed., rev. ed. Lindsay & Blakiston, Philadelphia 1846); *see* 13 DHRC 337.

[464] 2 DHRC 454–55 (1 Dec.1787); 2 ELLIOT'S DEBATES 443, 449–50; 1 WILSON WORKS 201, 206–07.

said that "no law, in pursuance of the Constitution, can possibly be enacted to destroy that liberty."[465] That is made clear by his very next prepared speech, three days later, when he said he would not further address freedom of press "until it is shown that Congress have any power whatsoever to interfere with it, by licensing it, or declaring what shall be a libel."[466] There was no *federal* power to enact a law punishing seditious libel. Yet this is the passage generally cited as stating Wilson's view of the meaning of the First Amendment and as showing a lifelong acceptance of the Blackstone-Mansfield definition.

This 1787 viewpoint about state libel laws was indeed different from the one Wilson later expressed in his law lectures in 1790–91—and in his draft Pennsylvania constitution in 1789. The 1787 viewpoint flatly contradicts the later viewpoints. Wilson's views simply changed after his second 1787 speech, both as part of his continuing evolution, and in response to intervening events—Congress' approval of the First Amendment in September 1789, its ratification over the next two years until December 1791, his further thought in his Pennsylvania provision for the press in November 1789, and a landmark Pennsylvania case and an influential essay. Wilson's view of freedoms of speech and press in his law lectures changed and superseded his earlier view of 1787, just as his vote and his signature on the Declaration of Independence superseded his earlier hesitancy over independence.[467]

Wilson's 1789 Pennsylvania Declaration of Rights and Freedoms of Press and Speech

That evolution after the 1787 speeches can be seen in Wilson's 1789 draft of the Pennsylvania Declaration of Rights, where his position diverged greatly from the second 1787 speech and was well on the way to his 1790–1791 law lectures.

Wilson is generally credited with drafting the Pennsylvania Constitution of 1790,[468] which replaced the state Constitution of 1776 and included the new Pennsylvania Declaration of Rights.[469] He led the delegates seeking complete

[465] And in the next paragraph, he asked "even if it [the federal government] had the power to make laws on this subject," whether the person would be in a worse position, with the federal right of jury trial, "than he is at present under the state government?" 2 *id.* 454; 1 WILSON WORKS 207. He obviously spoke hypothetically. ANDERSON 504; PALMER 291 n.152.

[466] 2 DHRC 482 (4 Dec.1787), which is punctuated differently than 2 ELLIOT'S DEBATES 453, 468; 1 WILSON WORKS 210, 225–26. He may have been describing current practice instead of his own views. PRINTERS 69; IRVING BRANT, THE BILL OF RIGHTS: ITS ORIGIN AND MEANING 229 (Bobbs-Merrill, Indianapolis 1965).

[467] Other examples are given in Aaron T. Knapp, *Law's Revolutionary: James Wilson and the Birth of American Independence*, 29 J. LAW & POLITICS 189, 194, 197, 239–42 (2013).

[468] 1 JUSTICES 90; PALMER 296; 20 DAB 326, 329; *see* Introduction, 1 WORKS OF JAMES WILSON 5 (Robert G. McCloskey ed., HUP, Cambridge 1967) ("his personal handiwork"); MINUTES-PA. 9.

[469] PA.CONST. art.9, sec.7, 5 FEDERAL-STATE CONSTITUTIONS 3092, 3099–101.

amendment,[470] and worked out a ceasefire with the leader of opposing delegates,[471] so that Wilson could begin the convention with three successful motions to alter the legislative, executive, and judicial sections of the 1776 constitution.[472] He dominated the convention, making and seconding more motions than anyone, and being listed first in all vote tallies.[473] He chaired the resulting committee "to revise the instrument."[474] The revision "was reported out" by him.[475]

The protection for freedoms of press and speech in his draft was expansive:

> [Sec.7.] The printing presses shall be free to every person who undertakes to examine the proceedings of the legislature or any branch of government, and no law shall ever be made restraining the right thereof. The free communication of thoughts and opinions is one of the *most* invaluable rights of man, and every citizen may freely speak, write and print, being responsible for the abuse of that liberty.[476]

That protection was worded to prohibit not just prior restraints, which Wilson knew Blackstone described as the extent of freedom of press under English law,[477] but subsequent restraints as well. The provision secured freedom to discuss the subjects that suffered most prosecution (criticism of "the legislature or any branch of government"), and then repeated the rights to "speak, write and print" on all subjects as stated in the 1776 constitution.[478] The draft included a boundary ("abuse of that liberty"), but did not equate that boundary with seditious libel. In

[470] HOWARD M. JENKINS, PENNSYLVANIA COLONIAL AND FEDERAL 247, 249 (Pennsylvania Historical Publishing, Philadelphia 1903–04); *see* BURTON A. KONKLE, GEORGE BRYAN AND THE CONSTITUTION OF PENNSYLVANIA 1731–1791, at 353 (William J. Campbell, Philadelphia 1922). Wilson's first speech noted that he was "the only member of [the Constitutional Convention] who have the honour to be also a member of this." Remarks of James Wilson in the Pennsylvania Convention (26 Nov.1787), 1 WILSON WORKS 178, 178.

[471] William Findley to William Plummer (27 Feb.1812), 2 WILSON WRITINGS 387–88; *see* JENKINS, *supra* note 470, at 247; Robert L. Brunhouse, The Counter-Revolution in Pennsylvania, 1776–1790, at 225 (1942) (unpublished Ph.D. dissertation, University of Pennsylvania).

[472] MINUTES-PA. 4–5, 6.

[473] *E.g., id.* 5, 7, 10, 11, 13, 14, 17, 19, 22, 24, except of course when he was away on Supreme Court duties. His speeches are collected in 1 WILSON WORKS 178–284.

[474] 1 WILSON WRITINGS 612, 617, 601.

[475] 1 *id.* 13.

[476] MINUTES-PA. 85.

[477] 2 DHRC 455 (1 Dec.1787); 2 ELLIOT'S DEBATES 449; 4 BLACKSTONE'S COMMENTARIES 151.

[478] Pa. Declaration of Rights art.12, 5 FEDERAL-STATE CONSTITUTIONS 3081, 3083, which read: "XII. That the people have a right to freedom of speech, and of writing, and publishing their sentiments; therefore the freedom of the press ought not to be restrained."

light of Wilson's law lectures a year later, the boundary was private defamation of individuals' character.[479] Benjamin Franklin so understood it.[480]

That draft was amended by other delegates to add language that did presuppose a state cause of action for seditious libel and that expressly restricted it by a truth defense and a broad jury right (the *Zenger* protections):

> In prosecutions for the publication of papers investigating the official conduct of officers or men in a public capacity, or where the matter published is proper for public information, the truth thereof may be given in evidence; and in all indictments for libels the jury shall have a right to determine the law and the facts, under the direction of the court, as in other cases.[481]

This was not a casual amendment; "the regulation of the press was the ground of most acrimony in the convention" except for the debate on adding a second legislative chamber.[482] However, Wilson did not sponsor or support the amendment, and did not have the chance to oppose it, because he was serving that week in the first session of the United States Supreme Court in New York City,[483] as the delegates in Philadelphia debated and adopted the amendment and the full state constitution and adjourned,[484] all before his return. This amendment was the most controversial one in the article on rights, which caused it to be postponed for further discussion and alternative proposals, and was the last provision approved before the full constitution was adopted.[485] The convention reassembled in August 1790, with Wilson present, and the press provision was only materially modified by two changes, which Wilson then supported: reaffirming the *Zenger* protections, and expanding cases in which they applied, very broadly, to "where the matter published is proper for public information."[486]

That amendment did not reflect a groundswell of support by the delegates to create a limitation of freedoms of press and speech by the common law of seditious libel, but was instead a response to the Pennsylvania Supreme Court's adoption of

[479] PRINTERS 154–55.

[480] Benjamin Franklin, An Account of the Supremest Court of Judicature in Pennsylvania, Viz. the Court of the Press (12 Sept.1789), 10 FRANKLIN WRITINGS 36, 38.

[481] MINUTES-PA. 86 (3 Feb.1790), 91–92 (5 Feb.1790), 93. Delegate statements in debate were not recorded. Delegates also deleted the word "most" and added the words "on any subject" to the original draft. *Id.* 86.

[482] MEMOIRS OF HIS OWN TIME, BY ALEXANDER GRAYDON 349 (John S. Littell ed., rev. ed. Lindsay & Blakiston, Philadelphia 1846).

[483] 1 DHSC 171, 175, 176; *accord* MINUTES-PA. 79–80, 82–83, 84–85, 88, 90–91, 92–93. Levy incorrectly attributes the amendment to Wilson. LEVY 212.

[484] MINUTES-PA. 85–86, 91–93.

[485] *Id.* 86, 92, 93.

[486] MINUTES-PA. (2ND) 178, 180, 182–83, 219 (24 Aug.1790).

such a limitation in 1788.[487] That response was to add the *Zenger* protections (which were argued for but rejected by the judges there), allowing truth as a defense[488] and allowing jury determination of law as well as fact.[489] Whatever the other delegates believed, Wilson had not proposed in his draft either to embrace the state court's adoption of English common law of seditious libel, or to modify it with protections, evidently thinking along the lines of his law lectures the following winter and not criminalizing seditious libel at all. A year later in his law lectures, Wilson stated the reason why he accepted the amendment to be because it protected the right of jury determination of all issues in prosecutions for defamation of character[490]—immediately after he rejected prosecutions for seditious libel (by attacking "the foundation of the law on this subject," *Case de Libellis Famosis*, as "unwarranted" and wrongly reasoned, and by rejecting its concept that "a libel against a magistrate or other publick person, is a greater offence than one against a private man"[491]), and shortly before he excluded seditious libel from his catalogue of appropriate crimes.[492]

Why did Wilson oppose the state's 1776 constitution?[493] The reason was not any objection to its broad protections for freedoms of speech, press, or

[487] Respublica v. Oswald, 1 U.S. (1 Dall.) 319 (Pa.S.Ct. 1788). The court adopted the Blackstone-Mansfield definition of freedom of press, and limited the jury with the Blackstone-Mansfield framework. *Id.* at 322, 326. After losing, the accused, Oswald, delivered a memorial to the legislature in 1788, asking not only for review of his case but for impeachment of the full state supreme court. *Id.* at 329n. (5 Sept.1788); DEBATES OF THE GENERAL ASSEMBLY OF PENNSYLVANIA . . . VOLUME THE FOURTH 8 (Thomas Lloyd, Philadelphia 1788). Pennsylvania's legislature devoted most of four days to hearing witnesses and argument, DEBATES OF THE GENERAL ASSEMBLY 8, 134–79, 190–206, 207–15, 216–31, 335–44, before voting by a 34–23 margin against impeachment of the judges. THE CASE OF THE COMMONWEALTH AGAINST ELEAZER OSWALD 11, 15–16 (William Spotswood, Philadelphia 1788).

[488] 2 HOWARD M. JENKINS, PENNSYLVANIA COLONIAL AND FEDERAL 249 (Pennsylvania Historical Publishing, Philadelphia 1903–04).

[489] The final provision read:

> Sec.7. That the printing-presses shall be free to every person who undertakes to examine the proceedings of the legislature, or any branch of government, and no law shall ever be made to restrain the right thereof. The free communication of thoughts and opinions is one of the invaluable rights of man; and every citizen may freely speak, write, and print on any subject, being responsible for the abuse of that liberty. In prosecutions for the publication of papers investigating the official conduct of officers or men in a public capacity, or where the matter published is proper for public information, the truth thereof may be given in evidence; and in all indictments for libels the jury shall have a right to determine the law and the facts, under the direction of the court, as in other cases.

PA. CONST. art.9, sec.7, 5 FEDERAL-STATE CONSTITUTIONS 3092, 3100; MINUTES-PA. 100; MINUTES-PA. (2nd) 219.

[490] 2 WILSON WORKS 1136.

[491] 2 *id.* 1134–35 & note k.

[492] 2 *id.* 1085–204.

[493] James Wilson, Objections to the Pennsylvania Constitution (1776): An Address by the Republican Society to the Citizens of Pennsylvania (24 Mar.1779), 3 WILSON WRITINGS 76 (not in his Works); James Wilson to Jasper Yeates & John Montgomery (10 Aug.1776), Wilson, James

religion,[494] because he retained them in different words. His opposition instead was based on three major factors, along with others: the adoption of the earlier constitution by the legislature rather than a specially elected convention,[495] the dangerous concentration of power in a unicameral legislature,[496] and the "arbitrary and unreasonable oath"[497] requiring voters, before casting their ballots for or against the new constitution, to swear or affirm that they would not "do any act or thing prejudicial or injurious to the [new] constitution or government thereof, as established by the convention."[498]

The defenders of the 1776 Pennsylvania constitution had attacked Wilson and his "republican" party as opposing its protections of liberty,[499] and Wilson had responded with his views on freedom and on the threat the 1776 constitution posed to speech. Wilson and his allies issued a broadside during the debate over the 1776 constitution that affirmed full support for freedom of press, as well as for freedom of conscience, as "fundamental principles of a free government":[500]

> we wish for no alterations to be made in the Constitution which shall affect the great and fundamental principles of a free government, such as, Liberty of Conscience—Trial by Juries—Freedom of the Press—Annual Elections—and the Division and Rotation of Offices.—But while we acknowledge these parts of the Constitution to be perfectly just, and highly agreeable to us, we think ourselves bound to declare, that it contains flaws which in a little while will render those inestimable blessings of no efficacy.[501]

Wilson's affirmation of those liberties was sincere, since he did not diminish them in his 1789 draft or in the convention, when he had the votes to change them. (The

---

Papers (HC, Haverford); James Wilson to William Atlee & Jasper Yeates (13 Mar.1777), *id.* His continual opposition from 1776 to 1790 was courageous, because the 1776 constitution had been adopted unanimously with the support of Franklin. THE PROCEEDINGS RELATIVE TO CALLING THE CONVENTIONS OF 1776 AND 1790, at 54, 66 (John S. Wiestling, Harrisburg 1825).

494 5 FEDERAL-STATE CONSTITUTIONS 3081, 3082, 3083.

495 James Wilson to Horatio Gates (c. June 1776), 36 PA. MAGAZINE 473, 474–75 (1912); James Wilson to Arthur St. Clair (3 July 1777), THE ST. CLAIR PAPERS: THE LIFE AND PUBLIC SERVICES OF ARTHUR ST. CLAIR 417, 418 (William Henry Smith ed., R. Clarke, Cincinnati 1882).

496 James Wilson to Jasper Yeates & John Montgomery (10 Aug.1776), Wilson, James Papers (HC, Haverford); BURTON A. KONKLE, GEORGE BRYAN AND THE CONSTITUTION OF PENNSYLVANIA 1731–1791, at 139, 120–21, 123 (William J. Campbell, Philadelphia 1922) (quoting letter from Wilson).

497 Robert L. Brunhouse, The Counter-Revolution in Pennsylvania, 1776–1790, at 28 (1942) (unpublished Ph.D. dissertation, University of Pennsylvania).

498 JOURNAL OF HOUSE-PA. 88 (26 Sept.1776); *accord* EXTRACTS FROM THE DIARY OF CHRISTOPHER MARSHALL 98–99 (William Duane ed., Munsell, Albany 1877).

499 James Wilson, A Personal Explanation: An Address "To the Citizens of Pennsylvania," 1 WILSON WRITINGS 114 (not in WILSON WORKS).

500 At a Meeting of a Number of Citizens of Philadelphia, at the Philosophical Society's Hall (2 Nov.1776) (broadside).

501 *Id.* (original in capitals).

flaws referred to were not liberties, but instead "evils in our new frame of government," such as "the political inquisition, called the Counsel of Censors."[502])

Before Wilson wrote in 1789 and 1790–1791, he had imbibed a liberal view of freedom of press for over two decades, since studying law under John Dickinson, who formulated the first clear statement of that freedom in an official governmental document, his[503] "Address to the Inhabitants of Quebec."[504] There, Dickinson listed "freedom of the press" as the last of five "invaluable rights, that form a considerable part of our mild system of government." "These are the rights, without which a people cannot be free and happy;" "[t]hese are the rights, you are entitled to and ought at this moment" exercise but for the Crown "striving, by force of arms, to ravish from us."[505] Wilson's law lectures were consistent with that.

Intervening Freedom of Press Events and the Pennsylvania Constitution of 1790

This interpretation is supported by two additional events involving the press, both occurring after Wilson's speeches in 1787, and before his draft press clause for the Pennsylvania Constitution in 1789 and his law lectures on individual rights and libel actions in 1790–1791.

A highly publicized case in the Pennsylvania Supreme Court, *Respublica v. Oswald*,[506] was tried and decided in 1788. It was a seditious libel and criminal contempt action brought by the state against Oswald, a newspaper editor, because of Oswald's printed statement that the justices were biased in a pending criminal libel suit against him.[507] The court followed the Blackstone-Mansfield definition that freedom of the press under the state constitution only meant freedom from prior restraint, not from subsequent punishment, and did not bar either the seditious libel prosecution by the state for publishing criticism of future "judgments of the court... to biass [*sic*] and intimidate with respect to matters still in suspense," or the criminal libel action by a teacher for "imput[ing] crimes to another."[508] The court fully adopted the Blackstone-Mansfield framework for seditious libel. Criminal libel actions could "enquire into the motives of such publications, and to distinguish between those which are meant for use and reformation, and with an eye

[502] *Id.* (original in capitals).

[503] John Jay to Richard Henry Lee (12 Feb.1823), 4 Jay Correspondence 468, 470–71; John Dickinson's Draft Letter to Quebec (24–26 Oct.1774), 1 Letters of Delegates 236, 239; 1 *id.* 243n. (in Dickinson's handwriting).

[504] 1 JCC 117.

[505] 1 JCC 122–23.

[506] 1 U.S. (1 Dall.) 319 (Pa.S.Ct. 1788) (some editions at 343). A good summary is in Saul Cornell, The Other Founders: Anti-Federalism and the Dissenting Tradition in America, 1788–1828, at 128–36 (UNCP, Chapel Hill 1999).

[507] *Id.* 324.

[508] *Id.* 325.

solely to the public good, and those which are intended merely to delude and defame" for which there was no "protection and impunity."[509] Moreover, it was a criminal contempt (in the case, seditious libel) if a publication had "the tendency . . . of prejudicing the public . . . and of corrupting the administration of justice," a "tendency" that could be determined by the court both as to fact and law without a jury and without any defense of truth. That is what the court summarily proceeded to do in finding Oswald guilty and sentencing him to a month in prison.[510]

In light of that decision, Wilson's subsequent statements make sense. Pennsylvania's freedom of press under the 1776 constitution had been deracinated by the *Oswald* decision, and Wilson's draft in late 1789 sought to restore a broad liberty by his expansive language protecting criticism of "the official conduct of officers or men in a public capacity," with only the qualification that individuals were "responsible for the abuse of that liberty" (by defamation of character). With Wilson absent and not able to argue that his language overrode *Oswald* entirely, the convention added its amendment to override *Oswald* partially with the *Zenger* protections of truth and jury determination of fact and law.[511] Meanwhile, the new First Amendment was approved by Congress in September 1789, and soon Wilson's summary in his law lectures in 1790–1791 described freedoms of press and speech even more expansively without any qualification except defamation of character, and described libel with specific disagreement toward Blackstone (whose definition and framework had been expressly followed by *Oswald*) and with no provision for a crime of seditious libel.

A satire on the press was published by Benjamin Franklin, whose first vocation had been as a printer and writer, just before Congress approved the First Amendment in September 1789. The satire was of the press as a court, which, because it was unreachable under the broad protection of "liberty of the press," should be subject to "a good drubbing" by a private citizen when it "attacks your reputation."[512] Franklin stated that liberty of the press was so extensive that for checks against its "abuse of power" "there are none," and he was "at a loss to imagine any that could avoid being construed an infringement of the sacred liberty of the press."[513] His concern was that the press could calumniate and defame a person, "tearing your private character to flitters," which he clearly thought required an effective tort

[509] *Id.*

[510] *Id.* 326, 329.

[511] Hamburger is one of the few to recognize that the amendment provision was an attempted reversal of the *Oswald* decision. Philip A. Hamburger, *Natural Rights, Natural Law, and American Constitutions,* 102 Yale L.J. 907, 950 (1993). A number of states added similar *Zenger* provisions over the next decades. *Id.* at 936 n.83.

[512] Benjamin Franklin, An Account of the Supremest Court of Judicature in Pennsylvania, Viz. the Court of the Press (12 Sept.1789), 10 Franklin Writings 36.

[513] *Id.* 39. Levy, however, misdescribed this as "recommend[ing] harsh treatment for anyone calumniating the government," Levy 249, and others regularly have misinterpreted the essay, *e.g.*, Kurland 254–55.

remedy against private libel.[514] He did not identify as a check, or otherwise support, public prosecution for seditious libel,[515] nor did he in an unpublished essay six years before.[516] Just one year prior, Franklin had encouraged a Philadelphia paper to print another satirical article to make the point that "nothing is more likely to endanger the liberty of the press, than the abuse of that liberty, by employing it in personal accusation, detraction, and calumny."[517] Wilson was likely aware of both, because they appeared in newspapers in his and Franklin's hometown,[518] and he was a friend and colleague of Franklin in Pennsylvania's delegations to Congress and the Constitutional Convention and in various organizations.[519]

These Franklin satires, and Wilson's own detraction in the press, illuminate his addition of character to the triad of rights, and his concern that writing and speech be nondefamatory.

Wilson's Other Remarks on Freedoms of Press and Speech

Wilson's other remarks on that freedom and speech, which have gone unnoticed, are consistent with his broad view of freedom of press as the First Amendment was ratified.

Wilson's opposition to the oath requirement of the 1776 state constitution was based on its restriction of dissent. While a biographer attributes that opposition to the oath preventing citizens from voting who opposed the new state constitution,[520] that biographer also concludes that Wilson wrote the "Addison" essays calling for amendment of the constitution.[521] Those essays emphasize the right of dissent as the central objection:

> I will take the liberty of asking a few plain questions concerning this oath—the most extraordinary, perhaps, that was ever heard of.

[514] *Id.* 38. Franklin similarly was "concern'd in the pieces of personal abuse, so scandalously common in our newspapers." Benjamin Franklin to Francis Hopkinson (24 Dec.1782), 8 FRANKLIN WRITINGS 647.

[515] PRINTERS 11, 152–54; FREEDOM'S FETTERS 137.

[516] Where he said, similarly, that liberty of press was jeopardized by the "abuse" of "personal accusation, detraction, and calumny." 16 DHRC 218n.

[517] Benjamin Franklin to the Editors of the Pennsylvania Gazette (30 Mar.1788), 9 FRANKLIN WRITINGS 639.

[518] In the FEDERAL GAZETTE (12 Sept.1789) and the PENNSYLVANIA GAZETTE (Mar.1788). 10 FRANKLIN WRITINGS 36; 9 *id.* 639.

[519] They were fellow founding members of the Society for Political Enquiries, which met regularly in town. RULES AND REGULATIONS OF THE SOCIETY FOR POLITICAL ENQUIRIES, ESTABLISHED AT PHILADELPHIA, 9TH FEBRUARY, 1787, at 5, 17 (Robert Aitken, Philadelphia 1787). Additionally, Franklin was president and Wilson a vice president of the American Philosophical Society. From the American Philosophical Society (7 Feb.1781), 4 JEFFERSON PAPERS 544.

[520] CHARLES PAGE SMITH, JAMES WILSON: FOUNDING FATHER, 1742–1798, at 114 (UNCP, Chapel Hill 1956).

[521] *Id.*

> The convention, it will be said, were elected, for the express purpose of framing a constitution; and consequently had authority to frame one. But does it follow from this, that the people did not reserve to themselves the power of approving or disapproving of the constitution, after it was framed? Does it follow that the people were bound by it, notwithstanding any subsequent dissent?. . . For if the people, by electing the Convention, did not part with the power of approving or dissenting from what the Convention did, *on what pretence* could the right of voting for representatives be taken away from those, who exercised that power in one way, while it was left open to those, who exercised the same power in *another* way?[522]

A week before, he signed, and probably drafted, an address from forty-one political leaders objecting that the majority of citizens "have not had a fair opportunity of expressing their sentiments upon this very important point" of a new convention to amend the constitution, because of the oath.[523]

Also, Wilson anticipated the modern concept of a right to know during the Constitutional Convention of 1787, when he objected to part of a proposal by Madison and Rutledge that the federal House and Senate should "keep a journal of its proceeding, & shall publish the same from time to time except such part of the proceedings of the Senate . . . as may be judged by that house to require secrecy."

> Mr[.] Wilson thought the expunging of the clause would be very improper. The people have a right to know what their agents are doing or have done, and it should not be in the option of the legislature to conceal their proceedings.[524]

He similarly advocated disclosure of the secret article of the Treaty of Paris.[525]

Wilson ended his speech in the Pennsylvania State House Yard in October 1787 by noting that everyone has an equal right to express opinions, a fact which necessitated compromise in the federal Constitution, though he like others would prefer some changes:

> But, when I reflect how widely men differ in their opinions, and that every man (and the observation applies likewise to every state) has an equal pretension to assert his own [opinion], I am satisfied that any thing

[522] Addison, *For the Pennsylvania Journal*, Pennsylvania Journal & Weekly Advertiser (Philadelphia), 14 May 1777, at 2.

[523] *An Address*, Pennsylvania Journal & Weekly Advertiser (Philadelphia), 21 May 1777, at 2.

[524] 2 Farrand's Records 260; 1 Wilson Works 144, except "where public safety would not allow open." Madison's Notes of Debates (18 Feb.1783), 19 Letters of Delegates 702, 704.

[525] Madison's Notes of Debates (19 Mar.1783, 24 Mar.1783), 20 Letters of Delegates 56, 61, 83, 84.

> nearer to perfection could not have been accomplished.... I am bold to assert, that it is the best form of government which has ever been offered to the world.[526]

One reason he gave for this freedom of speech was that it was central to the Revolution and to republicanism. Local forums, provincial conventions, and the Continental Congress met "[t]hat the sentiments of every individual concerning that important object, his liberty, might be known and regarded."[527] Ratification conventions likewise "produced a proportioned diversity of sentiment."[528]

Wilson's law lectures based rights of opinion on "the inherent and inalienable right of judging for themselves"—"a natural and an unquestionable right" to "mental... freedom."[529] He based freedom of conscience on a similar broad right, saying that government has the obligation "to preserve the rights of conscience inviolate," because the "right of private judgment is one of the greatest advantages of mankind," whose deprivation "is insufferable."[530]

Wilson's 1790 and 1791 view of these freedoms made almost unavoidable an opposition to the Sedition Act, as discussed in Chapter 8.

Justice John Blair

Figure 4.4 Justice John Blair (on Supreme Court 1789–1795). Portrait by Charles Willson Peale. (Courtesy of Library of Congress.)

[526] James Wilson, State House Yard Speech (6 Oct.1787), 13 DHRC 339, 343; 1 WILSON WORKS 171, 176.

[527] James Wilson, Speech Delivered in the Convention for the Province of Pennsylvania (Jan.1775), 1 WILSON WORKS 32, 36.

[528] 2 DHRC 351 (24 Nov.1787) (Pa. ratification convention).

[529] James Wilson, *Law Lectures*, 2 WILSON WORKS 952, 1131.

[530] 1 *id.* 539.

John Blair (Figure 4.4)[531] was another of the six justices in the first decade of the Supreme Court who attended the Constitutional Convention, and of the four who signed the Constitution (along with Rutledge, Wilson, and Paterson).[532]

He, like Rutledge, went to England for his legal studies at Middle Temple.[533] Blair, too, came from a privileged upbringing; his father had been a member of the governor's council from 1745–1770,[534] and its president 1768–1770,[535] and was acting governor in 1758 and 1768.[536] His great-uncle,[537] James Blair, had been the founder and first president of America's second college, William and Mary,[538] and also was a member and president of the council.[539] The future justice sat in the Virginia House of Burgesses from 1766–1770,[540] resigning to become clerk of the governor's council during the stormy years of 1770–1776,[541] but that position did not stop him from signing the colonists' associations for nonimportation of British goods in 1770 and 1774.[542] He attended the Virginia convention to establish a new government in May 1776, and his role as member of the committee to prepare the groundbreaking Virginia Declaration of Rights and the state constitution is discussed below.[543] He was a member of the state's governing council in 1776–1778.[544]

Blair's judicial career began with his selection as one of the initial three judges of the new state's general court[545] in 1778,[546] becoming chief justice in

[531] No biography has been written of him except encyclopedia pages. *See generally* OCSC 77; 1 JUSTICES 109.

[532] 33 JCC 500.

[533] E. ALFRED JONES, AMERICAN MEMBERS OF THE INNS OF COURT 21 (Saint Catherine Press, London 1924); C. E. A. Bedwell, *American Middle Templars*, 25 AM. HISTORICAL REV. 680 (1920).

[534] 5 EXECUTIVE JOURNALS OF THE COUNCIL OF COLONIAL VIRGINIA 185 (H. R. McIlwaine et al. eds., Superintendent of Public Printing, Richmond 1925–66); 6 *id.* 1; COLONIAL VIRGINIA REGISTER 47 (1743–1770).

[535] 6 *id.* 286, 366, 589, 609.

[536] 6 *id.* 78; COLONIAL VIRGINIA REGISTER 19, 20.

[537] Daphne Gentry & Brent Tarter, *The Blair Family of Colonial Williamsburg*, 32 VA. MAG. OF GENEALOGY 103, 107, 109 (1994).

[538] *Papers Concerning the College*, 2 WM. & MARY Q. (1st ser.) 36 (1893); Herbert L. Ganter, *Documents Relating to the Early History of the College of William and Mary*, 19 WM. & MARY Q. (2d ser.) 347, 351 (1939); *Edmund Randolph's Essay on the Revolutionary History of Virginia*, 44 VA. MAG. OF HISTORY & BIOGRAPHY 223, 227 (1936).

[539] 3 EXECUTIVE JOURNALS, *supra* note 534, at 23, 4 *id.* 20, 5 *id.* 1 (member); 5 *id.* 24–26, 37–38, 40–41, 43–44, 48, 53, 55, 61 (president); COLONIAL VIRGINIA REGISTER 42 (1689–1743).

[540] COLONIAL VIRGINIA REGISTER 175, 177, 179, 182, 184.

[541] 6 *id.* 367, 380, 427, 504, 602; COLONIAL VIRGINIA REGISTER 189.

[542] The Association Entered into Last Friday (22 June 1770) (broadside); 1 JEFFERSON PAPERS 43, 46 (22 June 1770).

[543] PROCEEDINGS OF CONVENTION-VA. 33, 91, 100.

[544] 1 JOURNALS OF THE COUNCIL OF THE STATE OF VIRGINIA 68 (H. R. McIlwaine et al. eds., Division of Purchase and Printing, Richmond 1931–52), 2 *id.* 1; 2 MADISON PAPERS 216, 224, 226, 227, 230.

[545] 9 HENING'S STATUTES-VA. 401 (Oct.1777); John Parke Custis to George Washington (12 Feb.1778), 13 WASHINGTON PAPERS-REVOLUTION 512, 513.

[546] 2 JOURNALS OF COUNCIL, *supra* note 544, at 95, 117.

1779.[547] He became a member of the high court of chancery in 1780,[548] which meant he also sat on Virginia's first court of appeals,[549] and he and his two colleagues prepared the first compilation of Virginia laws.[550] He was named one of the five initial judges of the state's supreme court in 1788.[551] After participating in the Constitutional Convention,[552] he signed the Constitution and supported it at Virginia's ratification convention.[553] After President Washington nominated him as an initial justice of the Supreme Court,[554] he served until 1795 when "a rattling, distracting noise in my head"[555] compelled his resignation. After suffering strokes,[556] he died in 1800.[557]

His epitaph could have been James Monroe's description of him at the Constitutional Convention, where he gave not one speech: "Blair said nothing, but was for it."[558] A fellow delegate, William Pierce, said Blair, while being "no orator," had "a very extensive knowledge of the laws," and "his good sense, and most excellent principles, compensate for other deficiencies."[559] William Plumer described Blair as "not indeed a Jay," but a "man of firmness, strict integrity, and of great candour."[560] Blair is sometimes given credit for speaking once, on the Establishment Clause in a letter to James Madison calling state aid to a religious denomination a

547 8 Va. (4 Call) xvii.

548 *Id.*; Edmund Pendleton to James Madison (4 Dec.1780), 2 MADISON PAPERS 222; *accord* Pendleton's Account of "The Case of the Prisoners" (29 Oct.1782), 2 LETTERS AND PAPERS OF EDMUND PENDLETON 1734–1803, at 416, 426 (David J. Mays ed., UPV, Charlottesville 1967); Edmund Randolph to William Livingston (6 Dec.1786), 5 LIVINGSTON PAPERS 264.

549 *Id.*; James Monroe to James Madison (22 Nov.1788), 11 MADISON PAPERS 360, 361.

550 Judges of the High Court of Chancery, A COLLECTION OF ALL SUCH PUBLIC ACTS OF THE GENERAL ASSEMBLY (Thomas Nicholson, Richmond 1785).

551 12 HENING'S STATUTES-VA. 765 (22 Dec.1788).

552 3 FARRAND'S RECORDS 558, 587; 1 *id.* 1, 3, 5; 2 *id.* 121, 280, 363, 587.

553 9 DHRC 909; 10 *id.* 1538, 1540.

554 Nomination (24 Sept.1789), 1 DHSC 9, 2 DHFFC 44; Confirmation (26 Sept.1789), 1 DHSC 9, 2 DHFFC 45.

555 John Blair to William Cushing (12 June 1795), 1 DHSC 756; *accord* John Blair to James Iredell (14 Sept.1795), 2 IREDELL CORRESPONDENCE 454, 455; John Blair to James Iredell (10 Oct.1795), 2 *id.* 455.

556 John Blair to Sister (5 July 1799), FREDERICK HORNER, HISTORY OF THE BLAIR, BANISTER, AND BRAXTON FAMILIES 72–73 (Lippincott, Philadelphia 1898).

557 Bernard M. Caperton, Wills of Rev. James Henderson, John Blair Jr., and Mary Blair Andrews (John D. Rockefeller Jr. Library, Williamsburg, Research Query File) (will dated 4 June 1799, probated 1 Oct.1800).

558 James Monroe to Thomas Jefferson (12 July 1788), 13 JEFFERSON PAPERS 351, 352; 10 DHRC 1704.

559 3 FARRAND'S RECORDS 95.

560 William Plumer to Jeremiah Smith (19 Feb.1796), 1 DHSC 838.

"dangerous" and "illicit connexion";[561] but the letter was actually written by John Blair Smith.[562]

He did ponder freedoms of press and speech, though the scholarly literature largely ignores his views.

His Grand Jury Charge of 1794 and Freedoms of Speech and Press

Blair's grand jury charge for 1794 came after the Neutrality Proclamation and the "convulsions of some of the western counties of the state of Pennsylvania,"[563] which became known as the Whiskey Rebellion. He stated that even if "the law ought to be repealed," that "will not justify a forceable resistance," and that there was no basis for "a violent opposition to the Constitution."[564] Then he changed topics from violence to peaceful dissent, and acknowledged the right to petition for redress of grievances (another First Amendment right):

> [All] men have a right in a decent manner to lay open their grievances before the whole legislature, and expose the ground of their complaint. All these modes of redress . . . may be also used, where the evil complained of is an unconstitutional exercise of legislative authority, or an extension of the legislative powers beyond their prescribed limits.[565]

He moved from there to freedom of speech, prefacing the discussion with mention of the national debate about France, and noting that pro-French "sentiments themselves deserve no reproof."[566] He then stated his understanding of freedom of speech, and government's disability to require correct thinking:

> Government . . . could have no pretensions to the character of free, if it should aim at a correction of the minds as well as the actions of the citizens; while men pay an external obedience to the laws, they have a right to think of them as they please, and even beyond this, to express their opinion decently, yet strongly, as a means of obtaining an alteration; but one step farther is culpable: actual disobedience, or prompting others to disobey, can never be justified; for the evil of such behavior must ever outweigh infinitely the evil—whatever it may be—of the law itself.[567]

[561] *E.g.*, 5 THE FOUNDERS' CONSTITUTION 80, 81 (Philip B. Kurland & Ralph Lerner eds., UChiP, Chicago 1987).

[562] John Blair Smith to James Madison (21 June 1784), 8 MADISON PAPERS 80.

[563] John Blair's Charge (C.C.D. Del. 27 Oct.1794), 2 DHSC 485, 485.

[564] 2 DHSC 486, 487; *accord* John Blair's Charge (C.C.D. Ga. 27 Apr.1795), 3 *id.* 31, 33–34.

[565] 2 *id.* 487; *accord* 3 *id.* 34.

[566] 2 *id.* 488; *accord* 3 *id.* 34.

[567] 2 *id.* 489; *accord* 3 *id.* 35–36.

First Amendment freedom was not limited to a "right to think," but included a right "to express their opinion decently," and Blair's decency caveat was not very limiting, because expression could be made "strongly." The dividing line between what the federal government may not touch, and may punish, was "actual disobedience." Blair's next paragraph acknowledged that expression is an "unalienable right[]," and gave a paean to liberty that would have warmed Jeffersonian hearts:

> Can chains be necessary to preserve order? If the sacred and unalienable rights of man must bend at the shrine of power and be sacrificed to protection, what will remain worth protecting?[568]

Blair ended with recognition that the price of freedom is some excesses, in the context of speech:

> And if some few excrescences, the natural price of freedom, must still remain unlopped, let us be consoled by the reflection, that the good order of government is substantially effected, and as far as is practicable without bearing its reigns [*sic*] so tight as to frustrate the most valuable object of the social compact.[569]

Freedom, including speech, was the "most valuable object" of the social compact.

His Grand Jury Charge of 1795 and the Right to Express Dissent

Blair's grand jury charge for 1795 was given soon after the end of the Whiskey Rebellion and, while retaining most of the language from the prior year's charge, he added a sharp condemnation of insurrection:

> it will be salutary to keep in perpetual memory, that a scene of convulsive disorder, exhibited in some of the western counties in the state of Pennsylvania, threatening a calamity no less dreadful than the eversion of our happy government, stood forth lately a melancholy exception to such a pleasing state of things. To those who wish the general prosperity of our nation, it will afford a useful lesson, how dangerous it is to indulge too freely discontent with respect to the measures of government, to oppose with pertinacious petulance private to public opinion, and to urge the removal of grievances, imaginary or real, without the line of constitutional redress. And to those who though they have not undergone so diabolical a perversion as to feast on distress, and delight in disturbing the

[568] 2 *id.*; *accord* 3 *id.* 36.
[569] 2 *id.*; *accord* 3 *id.* 36.

> orderly course of things, though they love not evil for its own sake, can yet consent to introduce it for the sake of advancing their own ill understood, their own distorted good, . . . it will be happy for the public if by fear they may be restrained from annoying the general peace.[570]

Standing alone, his words could be misread to extend to discontented speech about the measures of government, and to contradict directly the First Amendment protection for the right to assemble and "to petition the government for a redress of grievances." However, he allowed for "constitutional redress," and his subsequent words made clear that the prohibited discontent was "forcible resistance," "an appeal to arms," and "insurrection."[571] Blair then mentioned the right of petition, and repeated that "all men have a right in a decent manner to lay open their grievances before the whole legislature."[572]

Blair reiterated his 1794 language acknowledging the right to express dissent from the laws, and to do so strongly. He repeated the 1794 verbiage on freedom of speech that was quoted above.[573] He kept the 1794 language warning of chains on freedom, lauding "sacred and unalienable rights," and conceding that "excrescences" are "the natural price of freedom."[574] The great danger remained that the reins of government might become "so tight as to frustrate the most valuable object," freedom.

Notably absent from either of Blair's grand jury charges was any hint of seditious libel—any restriction on criticizing government, officials, or measures, any criminalization of separating citizens from support of government, any hint of common law crimes or federal prosecution. For the reason, his earlier involvement in declarations of rights must be examined.

The Virginia Declaration of Rights, and the First Freedom of Press Clause in Revolutionary Constitutions

Blair had been a member of the committee in Virginia responsible for producing its constitution and its declaration of rights in 1776.[575] Although George Mason drafted most of Virginia's declaration of rights,[576] the committee and not Mason

570 John Blair's Charge (C.C.D. Ga. 27 Apr.1795), 3 DHSC 31, 32.

571 3 *id.* 33, 34, 36; *see* 3 *id.* 35.

572 3 *id.* 34; *accord* 2 *id.* 487.

573 3 *id.* 35–36. Changes, which may be attributable to newspaper editing rather than Blair, were replacing "correction of the minds" with "coercion of the minds"; and italicizing that citizens have a right to "*express* their opinion decently, yet strongly." *Id.* 36.

574 3 *id.* 36.

575 Proceedings of Convention-Va. 32–33.

576 1 Mason Papers 274–89 (versions); George Mason to Nn. (2 Oct.1778), 1 *id.* 433, 434; *Edmund Randolph's Essay on the Revolutionary History of Virginia*, 44 Va. Mag. of History & Biography 35, 44 (1936).

drafted the "freedom of the press" paragraph.[577] Blair clearly agreed with that press paragraph, because it was he who reported the final version of the declaration of rights from the committee of the whole house,[578] without change[579] in the drafting committee version of the press paragraph.[580] That declaration of rights was the earliest and the most philosophically groundbreaking of the colonies' provisions for rights at the time of the Revolution, with far-reaching freedoms of press and conscience (though it lacked a speech provision, like most of the revolutionary constitutions).

Virginia's freedom of press provision, the first in a fundamental law in history, stated:

> That the freedom of the press is one of the great bulwarks of liberty, and can never be restrained but by despotic governments.[581]

Blair's continued support of that provision is evident from the unanimous approval of Virginia's declaration of rights in June 1776.[582]

Virginia's Proposed Amendments, the Federal Bill of Rights, and Jefferson's Confidence in Blair

Twelve years later, Blair voted with Madison in favor of ratification of the federal Constitution without amendments.[583] When that motion lost, Blair was considered friendly enough to a bill of rights to be appointed to Virginia's committee "to prepare and report such amendments as shall by them be deemed necessary."[584]

[577] First Draft of the Virginia Declaration of Rights (c. 20–26 May 1776), 1 MASON PAPERS 278 (The last paragraph of the draft was the following note: "The above clauses . . . have already been agreed to in the Committee appointed to prepare a declaration of rights," under which was the signature "T. L. Lee."); *id.* 278n. (press paragraph, and the foregoing note, are "in Thomas Ludwell Lee's hand," with the committee making "their additions on G[eorge] M[ason]'s own Ms."); *id.* 284 (press provision remained with only stylistic change in the committee draft); *see* 1 IRVING BRANT, JAMES MADISON 237 (Bobbs-Merrill, Indianapolis 1941–61).

[578] PROCEEDINGS OF CONVENTION-VA. 91 (10 June 1776). Also, the Declaration "was passed unanimously." HUGH B. GRIGSBY, THE VIRGINIA CONVENTION OF 1776, at 19 (1855, repr. DaCapo Press, New York 1969).

[579] Final Draft of the Virginia Declaration of Rights (12 June 1776), 1 MASON PAPERS 287, 288; *cf. id.* 282, 284.

[580] Committee Draft of the Virginia Declaration of Rights (27 May 1776), 1 MASON PAPERS 282, 284.

[581] Va. Declaration of Rights §12, 7 FEDERAL-STATE CONSTITUTIONS 3812, 3814; PROCEEDINGS OF CONVENTION-VA. 102; 1 MASON PAPERS 288.

[582] PROCEEDINGS OF CONVENTION-VA. 100 ("nem. con.," or nemine contradicente); 9 HENING'S STATUTES-VA. 109 ("Unanimously adopted").

[583] 10 DHRC 1538, 1540.

[584] 10 *id.* 1541; 3 ELLIOT'S DEBATES 656 (25 June 1788).

The committee's proposals included an amendment saying that "the people have a right to freedom of speech, and of writing and publishing their sentiments; that the freedom of the press is one of the greatest bulwarks of liberty, and ought not to be violated."[585] The second half obviously came from Virginia's Declaration of Rights, which Blair had approved; the first half added liberty of speech. That and other proposed amendments were approved by the Virginia assembly to accompany its ratification of the Constitution.[586] Blair must have voted for the proposed amendments, in order for Jefferson and Madison soon after to attest to his political orthodoxy.

Jefferson, in his principal letter to Madison about a federal Bill of Rights,[587] urged Madison to introduce amendments, just days before Madison began discussion of the Bill of Rights in Congress in March 1789.[588] Jefferson wrote that an argument with "great weight" in favor of a Bill of Rights was "the legal check which it puts into the hands of the judiciary," so long as the judiciary is independent. He then added,

> In fact, what degree of confidence would be too much for a body composed of such men as Wythe, Blair, and Pendleton? On characters like these the "civium ardor prava jubentium" would make no impression.[589]

For his part, Madison offered no objection, either in his response or later that year when he was notified by Washington of the plan to nominate Blair to the Supreme Court.[590]

Jefferson knew Blair well. Before the Revolution, Blair had retained Jefferson as a lawyer in some of his cases,[591] and when Blair became clerk of the governor's council, he transferred at least a significant part of his law practice to Jefferson.[592] Though over the next twenty years there was only one letter between them, in which Jefferson stated his view of appropriate federal-state relations as the Constitutional Convention was in process,[593] they lived in the same state, albeit at different ends, and traveled in the same circles.

[585] 3 Elliot's Debates 659 (27 June 1788).

[586] 3 *id.* 661, 662 (27 June 1788).

[587] Creating Bill of Rights 218.

[588] Thomas Jefferson to James Madison (15 Mar.1789), 14 Jefferson Papers 659.

[589] *Id.* The internal quotation, from Horace, *Odes* 3:3, means "the frenzy of his fellow citizens bidding what is wrong." Creating Bill of Rights 218 n.2.

[590] George Washington to James Madison (c. 23 Sept.1789), 4 Washington Papers-Presidential 67.

[591] 1 Jefferson's Memorandum Books 101, 275 (James A. Bear & Lucia C. Stanton eds., PUP, Princeton 1997).

[592] 1 *id.* 196, 199, 215, 216, 225; Frank L. Dewey, *The Waterson-Madison Episode;... Jefferson's Law Practice*, 90 Va. Mag. History & Biography 165, 176 (1982).

[593] Thomas Jefferson to John Blair (13 Aug.1787), 12 Jefferson Papers 27, 28.

Madison also knew Blair well, particularly during that twenty-year period. Beginning in 1784, they were founding members of the Constitutional Society of Virginia, along with Patrick Henry, John Marshall, Monroe, Randolph, and other leading lawyers.[594] Evidently with Madison present, Blair "was unanimously elected by a voice vote" to its presidency.[595] Two weeks later with Blair presiding and signing the document, the society's statement of purpose was adopted with what would come to be Republican emphases: to preserve the "sacred principles of liberty," to give "free and frequent information to the mass of people," which is "the surest mode to secure republican systems of government from lapsing into tyranny," and "to keep a watchful eye over the great fundamental rights of the people."[596] In 1786, Madison reported to Jefferson that, among the several Virginia judges serving as a committee to revise state laws, "Mr. Blair is the only remaining character in which full confidence could be placed,"[597] to complete the project and to do so properly. In 1787, they served together at the Constitutional Convention.[598] By March 1789, as Jefferson's correspondence with Madison continued on the Bill of Rights, Madison had come around to Jefferson's position that a Bill of Rights was essential; the two appeared to believe that Blair agreed. Even after 1795 when Blair resigned, Madison exclaimed, "Chase in the place of Blair!!!... Through what official interstice can a ray of republican truth now penetrate to the P[resident],"[599] clearly viewing Blair as a window through which republican verities could shine.

Yet in 1797, Jefferson and Madison found their judgment wrong,[600] when Blair supported a grand jury presentment against a member of Congress, Samuel Jordan Cabell, for what amounted to seditious libel.[601] Blair had abandoned his belief that citizens have "a right to think of [laws] as they please, and even beyond this, to express their opinion decently, yet strongly, as a means of obtaining an alteration." His change of position in 1797 will be discussed in Chapter 8.

[594] Virginia Constitutional Society Subscription Paper (23 Apr.1785), 1 MARSHALL PAPERS 140, 142; Rules of the Constitutional Society of Virginia (c. 14 June 1784), 8 MADISON PAPERS 71, 72.

[595] MEMOIRS OF THE LIFE AND PEREGRINATIONS OF THE FLORENTINE, PHILIP MAZZEI 285 n.6 (Howard R. Marraro trans., ColUP, New York 1942). Early meetings were at "the president's home in Williamsburg." *Id.*

[596] Minutes of the Constitutional Society (29 June 1784), 2 MONROE PAPERS 110.

[597] James Madison to Thomas Jefferson (4 Dec.1786), 9 MADISON PAPERS 189, 190.

[598] 3 FARRAND'S RECORDS 558, 587–89.

[599] James Madison to Thomas Jefferson (7 Feb.1796), 28 JEFFERSON PAPERS 606, 607.

[600] Petition to the Virginia House of Delegates (draft 3 Aug.1797), 29 JEFFERSON PAPERS 493, 498–99 (draft initially listed Blair but then removed names); Thomas Jefferson to Peregrine Fitzhugh (4 June 1797), 29 *id.* 415, 417.

[601] 3 DHSC 181.

Justice James Iredell

James Iredell, added to the Court four and a half months after the other initial justices,[602] replaced Robert Harrison, who declined the seat after being confirmed.[603] Iredell is best known for his opinion in *Calder v. Bull*[604] disagreeing with Justice Chase on judicial use of natural law, finding it not a "fixed standard" for voiding otherwise valid laws.[605] History has generally treated him well.[606]

Iredell's initial occupation was acting comptroller of customs in Edenton, from his arrival from England in 1768[607] until 1774,[608] through the assistance of an uncle and cousin[609] who were members of the governor's council[610] and large landowners.[611] Iredell studied law under the leading citizen of his town, Samuel Johnston, and soon married his instructor's sister;[612] Johnston later became the state's governor and, after ratification of the Constitution, its first senator.[613] Iredell became a king's attorney[614] and collector of the port from 1774 until early 1776,[615] when he resigned[616] because of his support for the colonists. He was warned by a wealthy relative to remain neutral, as "a King's officer," because the

[602] 1 *id.* 64 (8 Feb. 1790), 65 (10 Feb. 1790).

[603] 1 *id.* 34, 36, 37, 42; 4 DHFFC 99, 102.

[604] 3 U.S. (3 Dall.) 386 (1798).

[605] *Id.* 399. Iredell did not reject natural law, however. James Iredell's Charge (C.C.D. Ga. 26 Apr.1792), 2 DHSC 263, 267; Causes of the American Revolution (June 1776), 1 IREDELL PAPERS 370, 386; To the Inhabitants of Great Britain (Sept.1774), 1 *id.* 251, 264.

[606] *See generally* WILLIS P. WHICHARD, JUSTICE JAMES IREDELL (CAP, Durham 2000) (the best biography); Willis P. Whichard, The Sixth Justice: A Life of James Iredell (1994) (unpublished S.J.D. dissertation, University of Virginia); Nettie S. Herndon, James Iredell (1944) (unpublished Ph.D. dissertation, Duke University); OCSC 440; 1 JUSTICES 121.

[607] Henry E. McCulloh to James Iredell (5 Sept.1768), 1 IREDELL PAPERS 15, 16.

[608] Henry E. McCulloh to James Iredell (11 Sept.1767), 1 IREDELL PAPERS 6. He essentially fulfilled his cousin's duties for a cut. 2 CORRESPONDENCE OF WILLIAM TRYON AND OTHER SELECTED PAPERS 109 n.1 (William S. Powell ed., NCDAH, Raleigh 1980–81).

[609] *Id.*; Henry E. McCulloh to Francis Iredell (3 Mar.1768), 1 *id.* 12.

[610] 8 EXECUTIVE COUNCIL-N.C. 491; 9 *id.* 88, 94, 116, 129–35, 141, 145, 168–69, 173–75, 177, 179, 191, 193, 399, 501.

[611] 9 *id.* 481–84, 572–77; *see* 485–90.

[612] James Iredell to Hannah Johnston (c. 1 Apr.1772), 1 IREDELL PAPERS 94; James Iredell to Samuel Munckley (24 July 1773), 1 *id.* 159.

[613] 21 STATE RECORDS-N.C. 628, 666; 1 DHFFC 231.

[614] Commissions as Deputy King's Attorney (16 Aug.1774, 3 Oct.1774), 1 IREDELL PAPERS 248, 268.

[615] Commission (5 May 1774), 1 IREDELL PAPERS 235; An Account of the Exports from the Port of Roanoke (quarter ending 5 July 1774), James Iredell Papers, 1771–1799, IREDELL PAPERS-UNC (v.5); Henry E. McCulloh to James Iredell (28 Feb.1774), 1 IREDELL PAPERS 226.

[616] His last customs book entry was 8 April 1776. IREDELL PAPERS-UNC (ms. box 1, oversize v.5).

"people of America are certainly mad";[617] and paid for his support of the colonists by being disinherited as well as losing his collector's salary.[618]

Though his uncle had assured him that "life may be passed there [in America] very happily, without too great [an] exercise of philosophy,"[619] Iredell began writing anonymous essays supporting the colonies' rights in 1773.[620] The royal governor complained that Iredell "has taken an open and eager part in rebellion."[621] After the governor fled and the new state was formed, Iredell was named a superior court judge in 1777,[622] the highest judicial position in North Carolina at the time; he resigned a half year later.[623] He became the state's second attorney general in 1779,[624] serving a little over two years,[625] and was elected to the council of state in 1787.[626] He was selected to revise the North Carolina laws,[627] and published his compilation in 1791.[628]

Iredell actively supported ratification of the Constitution, and published a widely circulated essay[629] responding to George Mason's anti-federalist objections, in January 1788.[630] He was a leader of federalist forces at North Carolina's first convention,[631] only to see the Constitution rejected.[632] With a colleague he

[617] Thomas Iredell to James Iredell (8 Jan.1775), 1 IREDELL PAPERS 279, 280; *accord* Thomas Iredell to James Iredell (c. 1770), 1 *id.* 54.

[618] Samuel Johnston to James Iredell (3 May 1797), 2 IREDELL CORRESPONDENCE 503; Arthur Iredell to James Iredell (29 Jan.17[86]), 3 IREDELL PAPERS 191.

[619] Henry E. McCulloh to James Iredell (11 Sept.1767), 1 IREDELL PAPERS 6.

[620] Essay on the Court Law Controversy (10 Sept.1773), 1 *id.* 163; To the Inhabitants of Great Britain (Sept.1774), 1 *id.* 261; The Principles of an American Whig (c. 1775–76), 1 *id.* 328; Causes of the American Revolution (June 1776), 1 *id.* 370; To His Majesty George the Third (Feb.1777), 1 *id.* 427.

[621] Josiah Martin to Lord George Germain (15 Sept.1777), 11 STATE RECORDS-N.C. 765, 766.

[622] 12 *id.* 234, 415 (20 Dec.1777); 11 *id.* 825; William Hooper to James Iredell (23 Dec.1777), 1 IREDELL PAPERS 468.

[623] Gov. Richard Caswell to James Iredell (16 June 1778), 13 *id.* 164; 12 *id.* 783, 786; James Iredell to Richard Caswell (13 June 1778), 2 IREDELL PAPERS 32.

[624] 13 STATE RECORDS-N.C. 855, 948 (25–26 Oct.1779); Temporary Commission (8 July 1779), 2 IREDELL PAPERS 98; Commission (20 Nov.1779), 2 *id.* 127.

[625] James Iredell to John Williams (14 Dec.1781), 2 IREDELL PAPERS 319; Pierce Butler to James Iredell (5 Apr.1782), 2 *id.* 333.

[626] 20 STATE RECORDS-N.C. 500 (11 Nov.1788).

[627] 21 *id.* 375–76, 404, 415.

[628] JAMES IREDELL, LAWS OF THE STATE OF NORTH-CAROLINA (Hodge & Wills, Edenton 1791); 23 STATE RECORDS-N.C. 1–1000; 24 *id.* 1–994.

[629] Hugh Williamson to James Iredell (12 Aug.1789), 16 DHFFC 1303; James Iredell to De-Poclinet (25 July 1789), IREDELL PAPERS-DUKE (box 2).

[630] Answers to Mr. Mason's Objections to the New Constitution (8 Jan.1788), 3 IREDELL PAPERS 341; 16 DHRC 162, 242, 322, 379, 427; PAMPHLETS ON CONSTITUTION 14:§5. The author, "Marcus," was Iredell. 16 DHRC 161.

[631] *Journal of the Convention of North Carolina, 1788*, 22 STATE RECORDS-N.C. 1, 4, 23 (he made motion to ratify); 4 ELLIOT'S DEBATES 248 (same); John Steele to James Iredell (26 Sept.1789), 3 IREDELL PAPERS 526.

[632] *Id.* 24–26 (rejected 184–84).

paid to have the convention debates printed in order to encourage ratification,[633] and while he did not attend the second North Carolina convention that succeeded in ratification,[634] no person "contributed more to bring about the amazing change."[635]

His appointment to the Supreme Court in February 1790[636] was based on "the reputation he sustains for abilities, legal knowledge and respectability of character," and the need for representation of North Carolina.[637] The youngest initial justice, Iredell diligently carried out circuit duties, riding horse and stage annually over the 1,900 miles of the southern circuit, and also around another circuit until circuit duties were reduced by a 1793 act; he also traveled semiannually the roughly 800-mile round trip to Philadelphia.[638] The rigors of this travel on often "execrable" roads[639] likely hastened his early death,[640] at the age of forty-eight, in October 1799.[641]

Chief Justice John Marshall tepidly, without elaboration, called Iredell "a man of real talent."[642] Representative Hugh Williamson more enthusiastically said Iredell was "measured as the standard of integrity."[643] Like most of the other early justices, Iredell was by no means a democrat.[644]

He expressed a commitment to liberty generally[645] and to freedom of press specifically, before his position changed in 1797–1798 with the conflict between Federalists and Republicans.

[633] James Iredell to Hugh Williamson (22 Jan.1789), 3 IREDELL PAPERS 471, 472; William R. Davie to James Iredell (21 Dec.1789), 3 *id.* 551.

[634] *Journal of the Convention of North Carolina, 1789*, 22 STATE RECORDS-N.C. 36, 48–49 (ratified 195–77), 51–52 (with recommendation and requirement for subsequent amendments).

[635] Charles Johnson to James Iredell (23 Nov.1789), 3 IREDELL PAPERS 541.

[636] Nomination (9 Feb.1790), 5 WASHINGTON PAPERS-PRESIDENTIAL 121, 122, 2 DHFFC 59; confirmed 2 *id.* 61 (10 Feb.1790).

[637] 6 WASHINGTON DIARIES 29 (6 Feb.1790); *accord* Benjamin Hawkins to George Washington (4 Nov.1790), 6 WASHINGTON PAPERS-PRESIDENTIAL 620.

[638] James Iredell to John Jay and Justices (11 Feb.1791), 2 IREDELL CORRESPONDENCE 322, 323. He averaged an annual trip over that southern circuit, James Iredell to James Wilson (5 Aug.1794), 2 *id.* 427, while sometimes exchanging his second circuit with other justices.

[639] James Iredell to Hannah Iredell (23 Sept.1792), 2 *id.* 359, 360; *accord* James Iredell to Hannah Iredell (8 May 1798), 2 *id.* 523.

[640] James Iredell to Hannah Iredell (11 Mar.1796), 2 *id.* 463, 464; Nathaniel Pendleton to James Iredell (19 Mar.1792), 2 *id.* 344.

[641] CARRIE L. BROUGHTON, MARRIAGE AND DEATH NOTICES FROM RALEIGH REGISTER AND NORTH CAROLINA STATE GAZETTE 1799–1825, at 124 (GPC, Baltimore 1966); NEWPORT MERCURY, 28 Oct.1799, reprinted in 1 DHSC 877.

[642] John Marshall to Archibald D. Murphey (6 Oct.1827), 1 PAPERS OF ARCHIBALD D. MURPHEY 365, 366 (William H. Hoyt ed., Uzzell, Raleigh 1914).

[643] Hugh Williamson to George Washington (19 Sept.1789), 4 WASHINGTON PAPERS-PRESIDENTIAL 58.

[644] To the Public (c. Aug.1786), 3 IREDELL PAPERS 227, 228.

[645] *E.g.*, James Iredell to Richard D. Spaight (26 Aug.1787), 3 IREDELL PAPERS 307.

Pre-First Amendment Position on Freedoms of Press and Speech

Iredell drafted resolutions in 1783, which asserted that "it is the undoubted right of the people at all times, either collectively or individually, to express their sentiments on the situation of public affairs," with "zeal" as well as anxiety.[646] His newspaper essays before and after that date depended on that right.

He published "Answers to Mr. Mason's Objections to the New Constitution" in early 1788, and began by responding to Mason's opening point that "[t]here is no Declaration of Rights."[647] Iredell recited the standard federalist argument that a declaration was unnecessary when the general government only had enumerated powers, and, beyond that, was hazardous "as implying that without such a reservation the Congress would have authority" to invade individual rights.[648] He gave the same argument later that year in the first ratification convention held by North Carolina.[649]

Iredell then responded to Mason's separate point that "[t]here is no declaration [of rights] of any kind for preserving the Liberty of the Press."[650] He dismissed the point on the basis that the Constitution gave Congress no power over the press except to protect authors with a copyright law, assuring his readers that if Congress asserted any other power "they will do it without any warrant from this Constitution" and would instead commit an "act of tyranny":

> The Liberty of the Press is always a grant topic for declamation; but the future Congress will have no other authority over this than to secure to authors for a limited time the exclusive privilege of publishing their works. This authority has long been exercised in England, where the press is as free as among ourselves, or in any country in the world, and surely such an encouragement to genius is no restraint on the liberty of the press, since men are allowed to publish what they please of their own. . . . If the Congress should exercise any other power over the press than this, they will do it without any warrant from this Constitution, and must answer for it as for any other act of tyranny.[651]

His assurance was absolute. Moreover, Iredell had just denied any congressional power to create new crimes, in the immediately preceding paragraph, responding

[646] [James Iredell], Resolutions of the Citizens of Edenton (1 Aug.1783), 2 IREDELL PAPERS 430, 430.

[647] George Mason, *Mason's Objections to the Constitution of Government Formed by the Convention* (17 Nov.1787), 13 DHRC 348, 348; PAMPHLETS ON CONSTITUTION 14:§8.

[648] 16 DHRC 163, 163, 168n.; 3 IREDELL PAPERS 341, 341, 367 n.4 (8 Jan.1788).

[649] 4 ELLIOT'S DEBATES 167; *accord id.* 144–49, 165–67.

[650] 13 DHRC 350; 16 *id.* 163, 379; 3 IREDELL PAPERS 341, 356 (8 Jan.1788).

[651] 16 DHRC 382; 3 IREDELL PAPERS 359–60.

to Mason's charge that the Necessary and Proper Clause might authorize Congress to "constitute new crimes."[652] Iredell instead found Congress' power limited to crimes enumerated in the Constitution (treason, counterfeiting, piracies and felonies on the high seas), and to crimes "to enforce their acts of legislation in the cases where express authority is delegated to them."[653]

Iredell said much the same at the North Carolina ratification convention in 1788:

> A gentleman who spoke some time ago (Mr. Lenoir) observed, that the government might make it treason to write against the most arbitrary proceedings. He corrected himself afterwards, by saying he meant *misprision of treason*. But in the correction he committed as great a mistake as he did at first. Where is the power given to them to do this? They have power to define and punish piracies and felonies committed on the high seas, and offences against the law of nations. They have no power to define any other crime whatever.[654]

His restatement was again absolute. His concluding sentence reaffirmed that Congress could not create any new crime, such as treason by words, or seditious libel. His absoluteness excluded any federal common law crimes, as he later expressly acknowledged.

Initial Disavowal of a Federal Common Law of Such Crimes as Seditious Libel

Eleven years later, Iredell acknowledged that that ratification speech, in saying Congress had "no power to define any other crime whatever," meant he believed "Congress could not provide for the punishment of any crimes but such as are specifically designated in the particular powers enumerated."[655] He admitted his reversal of position, when in 1799 he held that Congress could provide for the punishment of criticism of government in the Sedition Act.

Iredell still held to his earlier position in 1791, when his grand jury charge said that crimes should be specified "by fixed and general laws," and defined federal crimes as simply those specified in the Crimes Act.[656] His position was unchanged

[652] 16 *id.* 381, 379; 3 IREDELL PAPERS 358–59, 356.

[653] 16 *id.* 381; 3 IREDELL PAPERS 358.

[654] 4 ELLIOT'S DEBATES 219 (30 July 1788).

[655] James Iredell's Charge (C.C.D. Pa. 11 Apr.1799), 3 DHSC 332, 341.

[656] James Iredell's Charge (C.C.D. Ga. 17 Oct.1791), 2 DHSC 216, 219, 220; *see* James Iredell's Charge (C.C.D. Ga. 26 Apr.1792), 2 *id.* 263, 264, 265; James Iredell's Charge (C.C.D. Mass. 12 Oct.1792), 2 *id.* 308, 314–15.

in 1792, when his grand jury charge reiterated his implicit denial of federal court jurisdiction over common law crimes.[657] That grand jury charge addressed what the federal criminal law was, and found it carefully "defined . . . in certain Acts of Congress."[658] Criminal law must "be careful" to "prevent an abuse of authority" that would violate "personal liberty and safety," and "ought to be passed with the most trembling solicitude, lest any unfortunate individual should become the object of injustice or oppression."[659] That standard could not be met by filling a federal criminal code automatically with the 160 capital crimes (Blackstone's count[660]) and innumerable other crimes that populated the common law. As Iredell said, the presumption in criminal law must be in favor of liberty.[661]

Drift on Freedoms of Press and Speech in the Mid-1790s

Iredell was drifting by late 1795, as his charges evinced when touching on freedom of speech. In similar charges for fall 1795 and spring 1796, after noting that citizens "who love their country may be expected to obey its laws," he found obedience to include "a deference of private sentiment to that of the public constitutionally expressed."[662] In context, he seemed to refer to sentiments amounting to insurrection like the recent Whiskey Rebellion or violating the Neutrality Act (both of which he described later in the charge[663]), because his sentence continued that "men of morality will in all instances abstain from any criminal conduct which may injure any individual, or community, or mankind at large."[664] However, limiting the point to "criminal conduct" gave little comfort, because Iredell deemed some undefined set of "sentiments" to amount to criminal conduct. The grand jury showed the same confusion, agreeing "that the opinions, passions and interests of individuals, or of any particular part of the community, should be subordinate to the *general will,* and that a deviation from this principle . . . produced that most daring and dangerous insurrection which you have described."[665]

[657] James Iredell's Charge (C.C.D. Mass. 12 Oct.1792), 2 DHSC 308, 314; *see* 2 *id.* 216, 219.

[658] 2 *id.* 314; *see* 2 *id.* 216, 219.

[659] 2 *id.* 312.

[660] 4 Blackstone's Commentaries 18, including many petty offenses, 238, 56, 93, 97, 99, 124, 131–32, 143.

[661] 2 DHSC 312.

[662] James Iredell's Charge (C.C.D. Va. 23 Nov.1795), 3 DHSC 74; *accord* James Iredell's Charge (C.C.D. Pa. 12 Apr.1796), 3 *id.* 106.

[663] 3 *id.* 77, 80 & n.13; *accord* 3 *id.* 108, 110–11 & n.6.

[664] 3 *id.* 74; *accord* 3 *id.* 106.

[665] Reply of the Grand Jury (C.C.D. N.J. 2 Apr.1796), 3 *id.* 102. This followed the same charge, since Iredell typically "deliver[ed] the same [charge] substantially at other courts." James Iredell to Simeon Baldwin (15 July 1795), 3 *id.* 67.

Iredell expanded that charge in his May 1796 circuit, adding both the concept upon which others grounded criminalization of seditious libel and, inconsistently, an acknowledgment of the legitimacy of difference of sentiments:

> All governments depend more or less upon the confidence and support of the people . . . .[H]is individual interest, when it comes into competition, must yield to that of the state in which he resides; and that the interest of the state itself, when it stands in competition with that of the United States, must yield . . . . At the same time that he exercises with zeal, and maintains with firmness, the right of each individual to express his sentiments on all public concerns, he should endeavour as well as his opportunities will admit to understand them thoroughly, that he may neither be unwaringly misled himself nor unwaringly mislead others. . . .[V]arious opinions will be entertained upon the subject of political regulations. They embrace a variety of interests all of which cannot equally be promoted, though all ought to be consulted and as much as possible to be reconciled. . . . The ablest men will often differ about the proper means of obtaining the same common object. . . .[T]here will be always ill-disposed men ready to take advantage of opportunities to do mischief.[666]

Having allowed for various opinions, he quickly limited the bounds of legitimate divergence of opinion, by saying that "ill grounded discontent" led to "actua[l] disobedience," which would be punished.[667] Continuing his dialectic, Iredell ended by saying he had not heard of local crimes connected with political dissent—but strongly implying that crimes could include political dissent. "I have heard, gentlemen, of no offences likely to come before you but such as are unquestionably of a very immoral & dangerous nature, & altogether unconnected with political dissentions."[668] But by 1797 he was hearing of such crimes.

Reversing His Stance on Freedoms of Press and Speech in the Late 1790s

In 1797 Iredell's grand jury charge shifted into more intolerance of dissent, and used language that could be, and was, interpreted as outlining limitations on freedom of speech.[669] "If after all, any individual disapproves of the voice of his country, what does duty and common modesty require of him? To be perfectly confident he is right in his opinion, and those intrusted, to decide are wrong! Who

[666] James Iredell's Charge (C.C.D. Va. 23 May 1796), 3 DHSC 124, 126.

[667] 3 *id.* 127.

[668] 3 *id.* 128 (DHSC also shows draft language that Iredell struck out).

[669] James Iredell's Charge (C.C.D. Va. 22 May 1797), 3 DHSC 181, 173, 173n.

is the man entitled to so arrogant an estimation of his own abilities?" With poorly veiled reference to Republican newspapers, Iredell condemned aspersion of motives of officials and calumny toward them, and called for the opposition to submit quietly to all actions of elected representatives, if they loved their country:

> The part surely for every man who loves his country, but who disapproves of any public authoritative decision, is to submit to it with diffidence and respect, considering the many chances there are that his own opinion may be really wrong . . .; and that the very basis of all republican governments in particular, is, the submission of a minority to the majority, where a majority are constitutionally authorised to decide.[670]

That left no room for dissenting speech against officials and their actions, once a majority elected them, which had ominous overtones for criminal treatment of dissent. Iredell's charge was so interpreted by the grand jury as it presented a member of Congress for seditious libel (described in Chapter 6).

When examined closely, Iredell's words may not have addressed dissenting speech, just disobedience to laws. A paragraph later, his charge expressly allowed for differences of opinion and identified the danger as "if we disunite, if we suffer differences of opinion to corrode into enmity," which would produce a ruinous fate. He concluded by saying that "every man should sacredly obey the laws of the country actually in being,"[671] without any demand for subordinating individual sentiments to government. As Iredell drafted a new grand jury charge for 1798, he restated the point in a way that did not seem to prohibit or even address speech disagreeing with government.[672]

However, when Iredell prepared his charge for 1799, it came full-circle and criminalized speech in exactly the way his critics objected in 1797.[673] The press became a dangerous weapon, as the pen might "inflam[e] the passions of weak minds, delude many into opinions the most dangerous, and conduct them to actions the most criminal."[674] The First Amendment was defanged, because the meaning of liberty of press was "no where more happily or justly expressed than by . . . the Commentaries," and consisted in "laying no *previous* restraints upon publications, and not in freedom from censure for criminal matter when published." Thus, "Congress may make a law *respecting* the press, provided the law be

[670] 3 *id.* 175–76.

[671] 3 *id.* 177, 178.

[672] James Iredell's Charge (C.C.D. S.C. 7 May 1798), 3 DHSC 258, 259.

[673] Scaevola, *To James Iredell*, DAILY ADVERTISER (Richmond), 11 June 1797, reprinted in 3 DHSC 192; Marius, *To Jugurtha*, VIRGINIA GAZETTE, AND GENERAL ADVERTISER (Richmond), 24 June 1797, reprinted in 3 *id.* 203–04.

[674] James Iredell's Charge (C.C.D. Pa. 11 Apr. 1799), 3 DHSC 332, 345.

[675] 3 *id.* 347.

such as not to *abridge its freedom*."[675] The young Iredell had read Blackstone with "infinite pleasure & improvement,"[676] and when his position changed in 1799 he had revived that infinite pleasure.

Iredell did give periodic clues before his changes of position that, when the administration clashed with critics, he might hold governmental powers to prevail and individual liberties to yield. During the Revolution, he was a prosecutor and the crimes he prosecuted included political dissent.[677] In his 1788 response to Mason, his statement that in England "the press is as free as among ourselves,"[678] while not expressly addressing the English law of seditious libel, showed him not to be very concerned with whether it was consistent with freedom of press and speech, as he finally found it to be in 1799. In his 1792 grand jury charge, he warned that "liberty itself, in order to be truly enjoyed, must submit to reasonable and considerate restraints." Indeed, "[t]rue liberty certainly consists in such restraints, and no greater, on the actions of each particular individual as the common good of the whole requires."[679] A restraint the judge liked, of course, would always be found "reasonable." By late 1795, he found obedience to include "a deference of private sentiment to that of the public constitutionally expressed." In 1798 decisions, he readily subordinated private rights to public interests and restraints.[680]

In 1799, these shifts made it no surprise that Iredell supported the constitutionality of the Sedition Act, as described in Chapter 6.

Thus, five of the six initial justices of the Supreme Court failed to live up to their common portrayals as having nothing to say about freedoms of press and speech, before the time of the Sedition Act. They, excepting Iredell, participated in and supported the framing of state constitutions during the Revolutionary War, most with broad protections of the press and sometimes of speech. All the initial justices, except Iredell, addressed the extent of protection of speech and press, and concluded that it was expansive in terms congenial to the later Jeffersonians, though all but Wilson joined in the framers' mistrust of unlimited democracy. Jay proclaimed the "right to think and speak[] our sentiments on these subject[s]," however controversial. Rutledge supported a legislative contribution to a symbol of freedoms of press and speech, and did it so resolutely that he and others shut down the colonial government in South Carolina; later at the Constitutional Convention he appears to have supported a provision for freedom of press. Cushing pondered whether the revolutionary constitution's unqualified language

[676] Diary (13 Dec.1772), 3 *id.* 169,194.

[677] John C. Waldrup, James Iredell and the Practice of Law in Revolutionary Era North Carolina 40–90 (1985) (unpublished Ph.D. dissertation, University of North Carolina).

[678] 16 DHRC 382; 3 Iredell Papers 359.

[679] James Iredell's Charge (C.C.D. Mass. 12 Oct.1792), 2 DHSC 308, 310.

[680] Calder v. Bull, 3 U.S. (3 Dall.) 386, 400 (1798); Minge v. Gilmour, 17 F.Cas. 440, 445 (C.C.D. N.C. 1798).

meant that freedoms of press and speech could not be limited to freedom from prior restraint and had to include freedom from subsequent restraint. The provision's "words . . . being very general and unlimited," he noted that they "make no such distinction" as the Blackstone definition, and "must exclude *subsequent* restraints—as much as *previous restraints.*" Wilson ultimately found the First Amendment to protect press and speech without the qualification of seditious libel and with only narrowly defined limitations against defaming private reputation, reversing his earlier position that defended that qualification of expressive freedom in state legislation but not federal legislation. Blair believed that men "have a right to think of them as they please, and even beyond this, to express their opinion decently, yet strongly," and that "some few excrescences, the natural price of freedom, must still remain unlopped." Even Iredell initially proclaimed that the "liberty of the press is indeed valuable," and when appointed to the Supreme Court he believed that there was no federal common law of crimes such as seditious libel nor could be unless expressly authorized by the Constitution and expressly adopted by statute. However, Iredell retreated from his position, as the crisis of the Quasi-War enveloped the Court in 1798, and the doddering Cushing, time having "impaired his mental faculties," followed him and most successor justices. Most successor justices similarly affirmed expansive understandings of freedoms of speech and press, but retreated from them during 1798–1801.

If the Blackstone-Mansfield definition and framework had been embraced by the initial justices, they should have appeared explicitly, or at least implicitly, in their pre-1798 statements about freedom of press or speech. Instead, they were not embraced by any initial justice before 1798, and were expressly rejected by Wilson and partially rejected by Cushing. The Blackstone-Mansfield definition of freedoms of press and speech and their framework for seditious libel were only adopted during 1798–1801, when motives were suspect, by one or two initial justices and three successor justices who enforced the Sedition Act, and by another successor justice who supported the Act, in a reversal of position traced in Chapter 6. Even then, it was not embraced by three other initial justices, or by two successor justices, whose stories are told in Chapter 8.

In being first adopted by American Supreme Court justices for the first time in 1798–1801, the Blackstone-Mansfield definition and framework replicated their English history, where that definition was embraced by Crown judges for the first time in 1770, not before, in the middle of controversy over the colonists' seditious libels and seditious speeches. In neither case was the Blackstone-Mansfield definition or framework an ancient or even longstanding view of liberties of press and speech. In both cases there were those who disagreed fully, like Bentham in England and Wilson in America, and who disagreed substantially, like Camden in England and Cushing in America, both before and after their late judicial adoption.

5

The Successor Supreme Court Justices and Their Views on Freedoms of Press and Speech

[A] licentious press is the bane of freedom, and the peril of society....
—Supreme Court Justice Samuel Chase[1]

With the second group of six successor justices, President Washington completed his record of appointing the entire Supreme Court and then four successors, and President Adams had opportunities for two appointments. The successor justices were Thomas Johnson (serving 1791–1793), William Paterson (1793–1806), Samuel Chase (1796–1811), Oliver Ellsworth (1796–1800), Bushrod Washington (1798–1829), and Alfred Moore (1799–1804).

The stature and experience of the successors was, in most cases, markedly inferior to the initial justices. Though the successor justices also included two leaders at the Constitutional Convention and two former governors, they differed from the initial justices in lacking any leaders in creating state governments or the continental government during the American Revolution (except Johnson), as well as any chief justices of state supreme courts. In contrast, most initial justices were leaders in forming the state governments and the Philadelphia government to replace royal colonial governments, and most had been chief justices of their states; three were drafters of their state constitutions.[2] Two successor justices had not participated at all in revolutionary government, and two held secondary offices in their states, while only two were prominent during the war—one

[1] Samuel Chase to James McHenry (4 Dec.1796), McHenry Correspondence 203. A list of abbreviated titles is at the end of this book.

[2] Chief Justices Jay and Rutledge, and Justice Wilson.

of those becoming distinguished mostly for scandal and being recalled from Congress.[3]

The dominant assumption is that the six successor justices, three of whom presided over the recognized Sedition Act trials,[4] said nothing about the First Amendment before 1798 or else were robed Vandals toward that Amendment. However, their pre–Sedition Act views generally were friendly views of liberties of press and speech, and not one had embraced the narrow Blackstone-Mansfield definition or framework for those liberties. (The newness of that definition was discussed in Chapter 2.) When the Quasi-War thundered and the Sedition Act passed in 1798, there was a change of position by the three justices who presided over recognized Sedition Act trials (Paterson, Chase, and Washington), as well as by Ellsworth, Iredell, and Cushing. At that point, the first five of those justices embraced for the first time the Blackstone-Mansfield definition of freedoms of press and speech, and defended the Sedition Act and its constitutionality, while adopting the Blackstone-Mansfield framework for seditious libel. In doing so, they differed from most other initial justices (Jay, Rutledge, and Wilson) and from two successor justices (Johnson and Moore) on that narrow Blackstone-Mansfield definition of liberties of press and speech or a broad view of those liberties, and on consistency or inconsistency between seditious libel and the First Amendment.

This chapter presents each successor justice's pre-1798 view of freedoms of press and speech, which is something absent from existing judicial biographies, histories, and legal studies, and challenges the prevailing assumption that the successor justices devalued those freedoms before 1798. For example, Johnson's proclamation has not been included in discussions of press and speech, and his departure from other federalists to give early support to a bill of rights has barely received notice. Paterson's and Ellsworth's leadership in Senate action on the First Amendment has not been noted in discussions of press and speech, nor have Paterson's essays or Ellsworth's speech on freedom of opinion. Chase, though the most discussed early justice, has not had his rise attributed to his use of newspaper essays, nor has his fight for a bill of rights in the Maryland ratification convention and after been developed. Neither has his opposition to a federal common law been characterized as disingenuous for the purpose of assisting enactment of a sedition law. Washington has not been considered in terms of pre–Sedition Act views on press and speech. The successor justices' later views during the Sedition Act storm of 1798–1801 are discussed in Chapters 6–8.

[3] Washington and Moore did not participate in revolutionary government, while Paterson and Ellsworth held secondary offices. Johnson and Chase were prominent during the war, and Chase was dogged by scandal.

[4] William Paterson, most notoriously Samuel Chase, and Bushrod Washington. In unrecognized trials discussed in Chapter 7, James Iredell also presided, and William Cushing also oversaw indictments and pleas.

The mid-1790s[5] were a turbulent period, as these successor justices were appointed.[6] War with England had been averted by the Neutrality Proclamation of 1793, though British seizures of American ships engaging in commerce with France and its colonies led to John Jay's mission to London in 1794 and to the Jay Treaty that was ratified in mid-1795.[7] The Whiskey Rebellion protested the Hamiltonian taxes, and as it came to a head in 1794, it raised Federalist concerns about internal attacks on the new government, until a federal army arrived and the federal courts held treason trials.[8] Meanwhile, most Federalists cast worried eyes at France, while Republicans continued to cheer its revolution as imitating the American Revolution,[9] though their unanimity evaporated with the Reign of Terror. The French minister, Edmond Charles Genet, began to commission American privateers and confirm prizes in 1793, and though he was recalled the next year, relations deteriorated with the Jay Treaty's effective limitations on French privateers and the new French minister's efforts to tip the election of 1796.[10] In that election, John Adams narrowly won the presidency over Thomas Jefferson, keeping the general government in Federalist hands.[11] Even before Adams took office in March 1797, France refused to receive the new American ambassador (Charles Cotesworth Pinckney), and French ships confiscated over

[5] *See generally* GORDON S. WOOD, EMPIRE OF LIBERTY: A HISTORY OF THE EARLY REPUBLIC, 1789–1815, at 174–241 (OUP, New York 2009); STANLEY ELKINS & ERIC MCKITRICK, THE AGE OF FEDERALISM 303–549 (OUP, New York 1993); JAMES R. SHARP, AMERICAN POLITICS IN THE EARLY REPUBLIC 69–171 (YUP, New Haven 1993).

[6] By the mid-1790s, the first successor, Thomas Johnson, had already joined and left the Supreme Court (serving 1791–1793).

[7] TODD ESTES, THE JAY TREATY DEBATE 106, 75–76 (UMP, Amherst 2006); JERALD A. COMBS, THE JAY TREATY: POLITICAL BATTLEGROUND OF THE FOUNDING FATHERS 107–15, 137–70 (UCP, Berkeley 1970); *see* AMERICAN POLITICS 115–23; EMPIRE 194–98.

[8] WILLIAM HOGELAND, THE WHISKEY REBELLION 27–49, 207–44 (Scribner, New York 2006); THOMAS P. SLAUGHTER, THE WHISKEY REBELLION 158–204 (OUP, New York 1986); *United States v. Insurgents*, 26 F.Cas. 499 (C.C.D. Pa. 1795); *see* AMERICAN POLITICS 93–98; EMPIRE 134–38.

[9] JOYCE O. APPLEBY, CAPITALISM AND A NEW SOCIAL ORDER: THE REPUBLICAN VISION OF THE 1790s, at 54–58 (NYUP, New York 1984); *see* AMERICAN POLITICS 69–78; EMPIRE 176, 177, 180–81, 183, 187–88, 205–06.

[10] Aaron N. Coleman, *"A Second Bounaparty?" A Reexamination of Alexander Hamilton During the Franco-American Crisis, 1796–1801*, 28 J. EARLY REPUB. 183, 189–90 (2008); JAY WINIK, THE GREAT UPHEAVAL: AMERICA AND THE BIRTH OF THE MODERN WORLD, 1788–1800, at 465–68 (Harper, New York 2007); HARRY AMMON, THE GENET MISSION 32–155 (Norton, New York 1973); *see* AMERICAN POLITICS 78–83, 151; EMPIRE 185–87, 239.

[11] JEFFREY L. PASLEY, THE FIRST PRESIDENTIAL CONTEST: 1796 AND THE FOUNDING OF AMERICAN DEMOCRACY (UPKan, Lawrence 2013); JAMES GRANT, JOHN ADAMS: PARTY OF ONE 375–79 (Farrar Straus, New York 2005); JOHN PATRICK DIGGINS, JOHN ADAMS 88–89 (Times Books, New York 2003); JOSEPH J. ELLIS, PASSIONATE SAGE: THE CHARACTER AND LEGACY OF JOHN ADAMS 27–28 (Norton, New York 1993); *see* AMERICAN POLITICS 138–62.

three hundred American vessels, as war "seemed imminent."[12] Adams made another effort at negotiation by sending three envoys in July 1797.[13] As 1798 dawned, war hysteria swept over the United States, and in that atmosphere, the Alien and Sedition Acts passed in 1798, as the next chapter discusses.

Justice Thomas Johnson

Figure 5.1 Justice Thomas Johnson (on Supreme Court 1791–1793). Portrait (detail) by Raymond Chard 1926. (Courtesy of Collection of Maryland State Archives.)

Thomas Johnson (Figure 5.1), the first successor to an initial Supreme Court justice (unless Iredell is given that title), participated in the prerevolutionary debates and presided over the formation of Maryland's new government as its first governor. Later, he was chief judge of the state's general court.[14]

Though he had only entered the Maryland assembly in 1762, he was selected as a delegate to the Stamp Act Congress, and to the initial Continental Congresses.[15]

[12] Nathan Perl-Rosenthal, *Private Letters and Public Diplomacy: The Adams Network and the Quasi-War, 1797–1798*, 31 J. Early Repub. 283, 283 (2011); Michael A. Palmer, Stoddert's War: Naval Operations During the Quasi-War with France, 1798–1801, at 5 (USCP, Columbia 1987); *see* William R. Casto, The Supreme Court in the Early Republic: The Chief Justiceships of John Jay and Oliver Ellsworth 105–17 (USCP, Columbia 1995).

[13] *Id.* at 303–08; Frederick C. Leiner, Millions for Defense: The Subscription Warships of 1798, at 13–15 (Naval Inst. Press, Annapolis 2000); *see* American Politics 171–73.

[14] *See generally* OCSC 448; 1 Justices 149; Edward S. Delaplaine, The Life of Thomas Johnson (Hitchcock, New York 1927). He was chief judge of the state's general court, but not of its supreme court.

[15] 1 JCC 22, 27 (5–6 Sept. 1774), 2 *id.* 12, 19 (10–11 May 1775), 245 (13 Sept. 1775); 5 *id.* 574 (18 July 1776), 6 *id.* 962 (19 Nov. 1776); 11 Maryland Archives 34 (14 Aug. 1775).

Johnson was the delegate who nominated his friend George Washington as commander in chief in June 1775.[16] He became one of the initial supporters of the colonists' association in Maryland of July 1775,[17] which took the first steps toward establishing a new state government,[18] and he soon after was placed on the council of safety.[19] Though Johnson was not the earliest to support independence,[20] he voted for it in the Maryland convention on the sixth of July 1776, which along with raising an army kept him away from Congress when the Declaration of Independence was signed.

Johnson was soon chosen as Maryland's commanding general,[21] and personally led its initial force as it joined Washington's army.[22] He was swiftly elected by the legislature as Maryland's first governor in February 1777,[23] and was reelected the maximum number of consecutive annual terms permitted by the state constitution, serving until November 1779.[24] He served the following two years in the state legislature, and returned there in 1786 and 1787, but declined to serve other years. Johnson was an initial director of the Potomac Company, to develop navigation of the river,[25] and later succeeded Washington as its president.[26]

He was selected as a delegate but declined to attend the Constitutional Convention,[27] though he supported the Constitution,[28] as he showed at Maryland's ratification convention.[29] His service as chief judge of his state's general

[16] 2 JCC 91n. (15 June 1775); 2 ADAMS WORKS 418.

[17] 11 MARYLAND ARCHIVES 66–67 (26 July 1775).

[18] He also attended the state convention of 1774. Thomas Johnson to George Washington (28 June 1774), 10 WASHINGTON PAPERS-COLONIAL 102.

[19] 11 MARYLAND ARCHIVES 31 (14 Aug.1775).

[20] John Adams's Notes of Debates (6 Oct.1775), 2 LETTERS OF DELEGATES 124, 125.

[21] Council to Thomas Johnson (10 Jan.1777), 16 MARYLAND ARCHIVES 33–34; John P. Custis to George Washington (8 Aug.1776), 5 WASHINGTON PAPERS-REVOLUTION 619, 620.

[22] Nathanael Greene to George Washington (20 Feb.1777), 8 WASHINGTON PAPERS-REVOLUTION 379; George Washington to Continental Congress Executive Committee (27 Feb.1777), 8 *id.* 451, 452.

[23] Council of State (20 Mar.1777), 16 MARYLAND ARCHIVES 187; John Hancock to Thomas Johnson (2 Apr.1777), 16 *id.* 196.

[24] Reelection (2 Nov.1777), 16 *id.* 417; Journal and Correspondence of the Council (8 Nov.1779), 43 *id.* 10.

[25] Thomas Johnson to Beverley Randolph (16 Jan.1790), WILLIAM P. PALMER ET AL., 5 CALENDAR OF VIRGINIA STATE PAPERS 99 (R.F. Walker, Richmond 1875–93); *accord* Douglas R. Littlefield, *The Potomac Company*, 58 BUSINESS HISTORY REV. 562 (1984).

[26] 4 WASHINGTON DIARIES 207 (17 Oct.1785); Thomas Johnson et al. to Beverly Randolph (16 Jan.1790), 6 DHFFC 1784, 1785.

[27] James Madison to Thomas Jefferson (6 June 1787), 11 JEFFERSON PAPERS 400, 401; J. B. Cutting to Thomas Jefferson (11 July 1788), 3 FARRAND'S RECORDS 339 (11 July 1788).

[28] Thomas Johnson to George Washington (11 Dec.1787), 5 WASHINGTON PAPERS-CONFEDERATION 482, 484; James Madison to Thomas Jefferson (9 Dec.1787), 12 JEFFERSON PAPERS 408, 409.

[29] 2 ELLIOT'S DEBATES 549, 554, 555.

court stretched from April 1790 until shortly after his next judicial appointment in 1791.[30]

Washington appointed him to the Supreme Court in November 1791, to replace Rutledge.[31] Johnson initially declined the appointment out of concern about the burden of circuit duties,[32] until assured by Washington that he would be initially exempted until the law could be amended.[33] When the amendment failed to materialize, he resigned[34] because of the rigors of circuit travel.[35] However, he continued as the senior commissioner of the federal city,[36] where he selected and implemented L'Enfant's design.

That resignation from the Supreme Court capped a virtual career of declining or resigning from office, besides missing the opportunities to sign the Declaration of Independence and to frame the Constitution. He declined the governorship in 1789, a district court judgeship in 1789,[37] consideration as secretary of state in 1793 and nomination in 1795,[38] a commission as circuit judge during the midnight appointments of 1801,[39] and various positions in state government. One writer half-seriously suggested that Johnson's failure to participate in many important national events, and to leave more than one judicial opinion,[40] resulted from consciously avoiding fame or repeatedly missing it.[41] The actual reasons appear to be Johnson's wish to remain close to his businesses—the Potomac Company, his plantation, and his ironworks[42]—and his recognition of the

[30] 2 Md. vii, viii (1790); 6 Washington Diaries 103 (28 Mar.1791); George Washington to Alexander Hamilton (13 June 1791), 8 Hamilton Papers 470, 471.

[31] Temporary Commission (5 Aug.1791), 1 DHSC 74; Nomination (31 Oct.1791), 1 *id.* 77; Confirmation by Senate (7 Nov.1791), *id.*; Commission (7 Nov.1791), 1 *id.* 78.

[32] Thomas Johnson to George Washington (27 July 1791), 1 DHSC 73; Thomas Johnson to George Washington (30 July 1791), *id.*

[33] George Washington to Thomas Johnson (7 Aug.1791), 1 *id.* 76; Thomas Johnson to George Washington (13 Aug.1791), 8 Washington Papers-Presidential 422, 423.

[34] Thomas Johnson to George Washington (16 Jan.1793), 1 *id.* 80, 2 *id.* 344.

[35] *Id.*; Thomas Johnson to James Wilson (1 Mar.1792), 1 *id.* 733, 734.

[36] Commission (22 Jan.1791), 7 Washington Papers-Presidential 258.

[37] Appointment (24 Sept.1789), 2 DHFFC 44; resignation (ante 9 Feb.1790), 2 *id.* 59.

[38] Thomas Jefferson to James Madison (2 Nov.1793), 27 Jefferson Papers 297, 298; George Washington to Thomas Johnson (24 Aug.1795), Washington Papers-LOC; Thomas Johnson to George Washington (29 Aug.1795), Thomas Johnson Collection (LC, Washington).

[39] 1 Journal of Executive Proceedings-Senate 386–87 (28 Feb.1801); Thomas Jefferson to Gabriel Duvall (13 Mar.1801), 33 Jefferson Papers 267. He was appointed during the two and a half weeks between the act and Jefferson's inauguration, not literally during Adams's last midnight in office.

[40] Georgia v. Brailsford, 2 U.S. (2 Dall.) 402, 405 (1792) (Johnson, J., dissenting).

[41] 1 Justices 151.

[42] Thomas Johnson to Council (22 July 1776), 12 Maryland Archives 92. He also had extensive investments in western lands and land companies. *E.g.*, Johnson v. McIntosh, 21 U.S. (8 Wheat.) 550 (1823).

limitations of his literary abilities (which his letters evidence,[43] showing equal animosity to punctuation, grammar, and spelling).

John Adams noted Johnson's business background in describing him at the Continental Congress as having "an extensive knowledge of trade, as well as law," and as "a deliberating man, but not a shining orator."[44] Years later, the mayor of New York called him "an eminent lawyer."[45] Johnson held moderate Federalist views of democracy.[46]

His commitment to freedoms of press and speech was evident in two episodes of his life.

First Proclamation in Maryland History on Freedom of Press

Johnson found himself at the center of a fight over freedom of press in 1777, as he took office as Maryland's governor. When credible evidence arrived that the British general would convey a peace proposal to end both taxation and independence, Samuel Chase of Annapolis wrote a satire and also a critique.[47] Chase[48] published them in the same newspaper issue, with the satire under the signature "Tom Tell-Truth," urging acceptance of Britain's peace proposal "with gratitude to the patriotic virtuous King, and august incorruptible Parliament, and wise disinterested Ministry," assuming even the village idiot would immediately see his dripping irony. His critique warned of nothing but fraud "from the hands of the tyrant of Britain."[49]

Unfortunately, Baltimore was overrun by village idiots, who gathered at the local Whig Club to identify the traitor they must ferret out. The club sent a deputation to demand that the publisher disclose the name of the perfidious "Tom Tell-Truth."[50] When the publisher, William Goddard, refused, the club summoned him to appear the next evening because the article "has given great offense."[51] After Goddard declined, the club's posse dragged him there, while refusing to give their own names, and the club again demanded the traitor's name.[52] As he again refused, the Whig Club passed a resolution banishing Goddard, requiring that he "leave this town by twelve o'clock to-morrow morning, and the county within three days."[53]

43 *E.g., id.*; Thomas Johnson to Council (19 Dec.1776), 12 *id.* 540.

44 John Adams's Diary (10 Oct.1774), 1 Letters of Delegates 168.

45 James Duane to Robert Livingston (6 Jan.1785), 8 Letters of Members 10.

46 Thomas Johnson to Nn. (n.d., letter 2), Johnson Correspondence; Thomas Johnson to Samuel Purviance (23 Jan.1775), 1 Letters of Delegates 298, 300; Thomas Johnson to John Jay (24 Feb.1777), Jay-Revolutionary 374.

47 [William Goddard], The Prowess of the Whig Club, and the Manoeuvres of Legion app.2 (William Goddard, Baltimore 1777) (Tom Tell-Truth); *id.* app.3 (Caveto), reprinting *Maryland Journal and Baltimore Advertiser* (Baltimore), 25 Feb.1777.

48 *Id.* app.4.

49 *Id.* (published 25 Feb.1777).

50 *Id.* 4–5.

51 *Id.* 5–6.

52 *Id.* 6–8.

53 Copy of the Vote of Expulsion in Whig Club (4 Mar.1777), *id.* 11; *id.* 9.

Goddard left, but only to go straight to the Maryland legislature, where he delivered a memorial that, in case village idiots abounded in Annapolis as well, disclosed that the satire was "written by a member of the honourable Congress."[54] A legislative committee quickly concluded that the Whig Club's proceedings were "a manifest violation of the constitution" and that it, not Tell-Truth, threatened "the overthrow of all regular government."[55] The club, deciding to twist the facts rather than admit error, responded that it knew all the time that Tell-Truth meant "ironically to sneer" at the British proposal, and recast its objection as a literary critique, thinking "the author rather unfortunate in framing his piece" so that "the ignorant and uninformed might mistake his intention." Goddard's escort to the club was only because of his "mulish obstinacy" and "brutal impoliteness," and banishment merely "recommended it to him to leave."[56]

However, still more idiots sailed on Baltimore's harbor. Two weeks after the initial incident, Commodore Nicholson marched to the printing press, ordered Goddard to accompany him to the Whig Club, and when Goddard declined, carried him there by force, without blaming it on his impoliteness.[57] The Club resentenced the publisher with the original terms of banishment, conspicuously without the word "recommend."

Governor Thomas Johnson received the new petition Goddard sent. Johnson was sufficiently shocked to forward it immediately to the legislature,[58] which adopted resolutions, drafted by none other than Tom Tell-Truth himself. The resolutions again found the Whig Club's proceedings "a most daring infringement, and manifest violation of the Constitution of this state, directly contrary to the Declaration of Rights."[59]

Johnson promptly issued a proclamation condemning the Whig Club's actions for "presuming to exercise any power over the persons or property of any subject of this state."[60] That proclamation was later called "the first vindication of the liberty of the press in Maryland" history, implementing the new provision in the state's declaration of rights.[61] Goddard reissued his pamphlet on the affray crowned by the governor's proclamation and the legislature's resolution.[62]

[54] The Memorial of William Goddard, Late of Baltimore, Printer (6 Mar.1777), *id.* 10.

[55] By the Committee of Aggrievances and Courts of Justice (Mar.1777), *id.* 12–13.

[56] Whig Club, A Late Affair Between The Whig Club and Mr. William Goddard (11 Mar.1777), *id.* app.1–2 ("rather unfortunate," "mulish obstinancy," and "brutal impoliteness" in italics).

[57] *Id.* 8 (the commodore was president of the Club).

[58] *Id.* app.2.

[59] Resolves (17 Apr.1777), *id.* in Postscript 2; MARYLAND GAZETTE (Annapolis), 17 Apr.1777.

[60] Thomas Johnson, A Proclamation (17 Apr.1777), *id.* in Postscript 3; MARYLAND GAZETTE (Annapolis), 17 Apr.1777.

[61] J. THOMAS SCHARF, CHRONICLES OF BALTIMORE 161 (Turnbull, Baltimore 1874).

[62] *Id.; accord* W. Bird Terwilliger, *William Goddard's Victory for the Freedom of the Press*, 36 MARYLAND HISTORICAL MAG. 139 (1941).

Johnson, a new governor, was not obligated to become involved, to forward the petition, or to issue a proclamation. He evidently felt strongly about the attack on the press, an institution that two and a half years earlier he had relied on to disseminate his jointly written essay shutting off the royal governor's revenue.[63]

First Influential Federalist Support of a Bill of Rights

Johnson's support for declarations of rights was first manifested the year before, in 1776, when he was added to the committee to draft a declaration of rights and constitution for the new state of Maryland.[64] The declaration, which he supported, stated that "the liberty of the press ought to be inviolably preserved."[65]

Johnson similarly supported a federal bill of rights, and was the only pre-Marshall justice to do so during the 1787–1788 ratification debates, except Jay by mid-1788 and except the lone justice who opposed the Constitution.[66] (When a ratification compromise proved necessary, most federalists supported a post-ratification bill of rights.) Johnson's position was expressed, and pressed, in his first letter to his friend George Washington after the Constitutional Convention:

> any necessary guards for personal liberty is [*sic*] the common interest of all the citizens of America. And if it is imagined that a defined power which does not comprehend the interference with personal rights needs negative declarations I presume such may be added by the foederal legislature with equal efficacy & more propriety than might have been done by the Convention—Strongly and long impressed with an idea that no governm[en]t can make a people happy unless they very generally entertain an opinion that it is good in form and well administered I am much disposed to give up a good deal in the [form] the least essential part.[67]

[63] Thomas Johnson, Samuel Chase and William Paca, *To John Hammond*, MARYLAND GAZETTE (Annapolis), 9 Sept.1773, at 1, 1.

[64] Proceedings of the Convention of the Province of Maryland (14 Aug.1776-), 3 AMERICAN ARCHIVES 97; PROCEEDINGS OF THE CONVENTION OF THE PROVINCE OF MARYLAND . . . THE FOURTEENTH OF AUGUST, 1776, at 14 (Frederick Green, Annapolis 1776).

[65] 3 AMERICAN ARCHIVES 143, 147, 145–46 (3 Nov.1776); Maryland Declaration of Rights art.xxxviii, 3 FEDERAL-STATE CONSTITUTIONS 1686, 1690, 1689.

[66] Chase, discussed below.

[67] Thomas Johnson to George Washington (11 Dec.1787), 5 WASHINGTON PAPERS-CONFEDERATION 482, 484.

The letter clearly called for a bill of rights—"negative declarations" about "personal rights"—even though the federalist argument had been laid down by Hamilton and Madison and, recently, Wilson and others that "defined power[s]" did not comprehend "interference with personal rights." Johnson was "much disposed to give up a good deal" on this point. He may have been the first influential federalist to support a federal bill of rights, after Charles Pinckney's motions at the Constitutional Convention.

Johnson continued his support for a bill of rights at the Maryland ratification convention. He did not do so to obtain ratification, because the convention had an obvious preponderance of supporters of the Constitution,[68] making no tactical compromise necessary. When William Paca, an anti-federalist, requested a day's delay in order to formulate amendments, Johnson surprised his fellow federalists by making a motion to grant the requested adjournment.[69] Then, as a member of the committee on amendments,[70] Johnson supported the twelve amendments, including one on freedom of press.[71] When tempers flared among the committee over further amendments and the federalists withdrew support for any, Johnson departed from his fellow federalists and joined the anti-federalist supporters of amendments in unsuccessful votes to recommend the twelve amendments and three additional ones, and to delay adjournment to allow a vote on the amendments, including the one securing freedom of press.[72] The minority that Johnson supported gave as its reason for the press provision that he backed, that if there were prosecutions in the federal courts for libels (something apparently illegal but feared), then "this great and fundamental right may prove invaluable."[73]

Five months later, Johnson again wrote to President Washington, responding in part to rumors that he abandoned his fellow federalists. While assuring Washington that he had engaged in no active conduct "to bring about any amendments" as a condition to ratification, he stuck to his guns on his preference for them: he "should be better pleased with the Constitution with some alterations."[74]

[68] The ratification margin was 63–11. 17 DHRC 242; 2 ELLIOT'S DEBATES 547, 549.

[69] A. C. Hanson to James Madison (2 June 1788), 4 DHC 645, 652 (24 Apr.1788); James McHenry to George Washington (18 May 1788), 4 *id.* 618; CHESAPEAKE POLITICS 291.

[70] 2 *id.* 549; John B. Cutting to Thomas Jefferson (11 July 1788), 13 JEFFERSON PAPERS 331, 333.

[71] 17 DHRC 242; 2 ELLIOT'S DEBATES 549, 555; John B. Cutting to Thomas Jefferson (11 July 1788), 13 JEFFERSON PAPERS 331, 336.

[72] MARYLAND 92–93; CHESAPEAKE POLITICS 292–93.

[73] 17 DHRC 244 (May 1788); 2 ELLIOT'S DEBATES 552 (incorrect date).

[74] Thomas Johnson to George Washington (10 Oct.1788), 1 WASHINGTON PAPERS-PRESIDENTIAL 42.

Justice William Paterson

Figure 5.2 Justice William Paterson (on Supreme Court 1793–1806). Portrait by James Sharples ante 1811. (Courtesy of Princeton University Art Museum/Art Resource.)

William Paterson (Figure 5.2) was New Jersey's governor when he was appointed to the Supreme Court, though during the Revolution he had not participated in congresses and had not stood in the front rank of state leaders.[75] With his appointment, the Court entered a unique period when half its justices were born abroad.[76]

His public career, and his support of the American cause, began as a delegate to New Jersey's provincial congress in 1775,[77] and continued at the state constitutional

[75] *See generally* JOHN E. O'CONNOR, WILLIAM PATERSON: LAWYER AND STATESMAN, 1745–1806 (RUP, New Brunswick 1979); John E. O'Connor, William Paterson and the American Revolution, 1763–1787 (1974) (Ph.D. dissertation, City University of New York); Richard C. Haskett, William Paterson, Councillor at Law (1952) (unpublished Ph.D. dissertation, Princeton University); OCSC 624; 1 JUSTICES 163.

[76] Paterson in Ireland of Scottish ancestry, Wilson in Scotland, and Iredell in England. William Paterson to John Macpherson (12 Nov. 1771), GLIMPSES OF COLONIAL SOCIETY AND THE LIFE AT PRINCETON COLLEGE, 1766–1773 (W. Jay Mills ed., Lippincott, Philadelphia 1903). While this book purports to be Paterson's essays and letters, it must be used with caution because it is "consistently inaccurate." Richard C. Haskett, *Princeton Before the Revolution: Notes on a Source*, 6 WM. & MARY Q. (3d ser.) 90, 91 (1949).

[77] MINUTES OF THE PROVINCIAL CONGRESS AND THE COUNCIL OF SAFETY OF THE STATE OF NEW JERSEY 169, 170 (Naar, Day & Naar, Trenton 1879).

convention in 1776, serving both as secretary.[78] Though in the minority that preferred to defer the new state constitution that marked independence,[79] Paterson joined in the unanimous vote of state delegates approving the Continental Congress's resolution for independence.[80] Soon, he became New Jersey's first attorney general, serving from 1776 into 1783,[81] and was added to the state's legislative council[82] and council of safety.[83] He was elected to the Continental Congress in late 1778 and 1780, but declined the position because of his duties as attorney general.[84] He also served on the state's court of chancery.[85]

Paterson played a more major role at the Constitutional Convention of 1787, and was best known for formulating the New Jersey Plan, or small state plan, as an alternative to the Virginia Plan.[86] With Rutledge, Wilson, and Blair, he was a signer of the Constitution,[87] though unlike them, he did not attend his state ratification convention. He was soon chosen as one of New Jersey's first two senators,[88] but served only briefly until his election as governor of New Jersey in 1790, when he resigned from Congress.[89] While in the Senate, he participated in the

[78] In Provincial Congress, at Trenton, New-Jersey, June 3, 1775 (John Holt, New York 1775) (broadside); JOURNAL OF THE VOTES AND PROCEEDINGS, AS WELL OF THE COMMITTEE OF SAFETY, AT A SITTING IN JANUARY, 1776, AS THE PROVINCIAL CONGRESS OF NEW-JERSEY, AT A SITTING AT NEW-BRUNSWICK, BEGAN JANUARY 31, at 23 (John Anderson, New York 1776); JOURNAL OF THE VOTES AND PROCEEDINGS OF THE CONVENTION OF NEW-JERSEY, BEGUN AT BURLINGTON THE 10TH OF JUNE 1776, at 5 (Isaac Collins, Burlington 1776); Resolves of New-Jersey Convention (3 Aug.1776), 1 AMERICAN ARCHIVES 743–44. He initially was assistant secretary.

[79] CHARLES R. ERDMAN, THE NEW JERSEY CONSTITUTION OF 1776, at 35, 32 n.36 (PUP, Princeton 1929).

[80] JOURNAL OF THE VOTES AND PROCEEDINGS OF THE CONVENTION OF NEW-JERSEY, BEGUN AT BURLINGTON THE 10TH OF JUNE 1776, at 49–50, 75–76 (Isaac Collins, Burlington 1776); *see* Order from New Jersey Convention (16 July 1776), 1 AMERICAN ARCHIVES 369.

[81] NEW JERSEY GAZETTE (Burlington), 17 Oct.1781, reprinted in 5 DOCUMENTS RELATING TO THE REVOLUTIONARY HISTORY OF THE STATE OF NEW JERSEY 305 (William S. Stryker et al. eds., Murphy Publishing, Trenton 1901–17); William Paterson to William Coxe (17 Mar.1783) (resignation), PATERSON CORRESPONDENCE.

[82] Proclamation (25 Sept.1776), 1 LIVINGSTON PAPERS 152.

[83] MINUTES OF THE COUNCIL OF SAFETY OF THE STATE OF NEW JERSEY 7 (John H. Lyon, Jersey City 1872).

[84] 10 JCC 238 (6 Mar.1778); NEW JERSEY GAZETTE (Burlington), 29 Nov.1780, reprinted in 5 DOCUMENTS RELATING TO THE REVOLUTIONARY HISTORY OF THE STATE OF NEW JERSEY 128 (William S. Stryker et al. eds., Murphy Publishing, Trenton 1901–17); William Houston and John Witherspoon to Joint Meeting (19 May 1781), 17 LETTERS OF DELEGATES 266 n.1. His sense of duty is impressive, since he found the circuit riding as attorney general "drudgery." J. Lawrence Boggs, *The Cornelia (Bell) Paterson Letters*, 16 PROCEEDINGS OF N.J. HISTORICAL SOC. 56, 57 (1931).

[85] 4 LIVINGSTON PAPERS 433 (Carl E. Prince ed., NJHC, Trenton 1979–).

[86] The New Jersey Plan (15 June 1787), 5 WASHINGTON PAPERS-CONFEDERATION 230; 1 FARRAND'S RECORDS 242 (15 June 1787).

[87] 33 JCC 500.

[88] 1 DHFFC 5 (19 Mar.1789); 1 ANNALS 16.

[89] 1 DHFFC 495, 8 *id.* 537 (6 Dec.1790).

legislation establishing the national government, most importantly in the Judiciary Act[90] and the Bill of Rights.[91]

His appointment to the Supreme Court in 1793[92] was to fill the seat left vacant by Thomas Johnson's resignation. As he left the governorship for the Court,[93] Paterson was so popular in New Jersey that he was "escorted by the B[r]unswick company of light infantry, and a large number of respectable citizens," accompanied by the poem "On the Departure of Judge Paterson" ("See the once father, ruler of our State, Throng'd by the rich, the poor, the great. . . .").[94] He soon found popularity elusive, as he presided over the main trials of Whiskey Rebellion leaders.[95] However, he impressed President Washington, who made Paterson his first choice as a successor secretary of state.[96] Declining, Paterson continued on the Court and, on the side, completed his compilation of the laws of New Jersey,[97] which he had undertaken while governor.[98] After the Republican victory in 1800, he trimmed his partisan sails to uphold the law abolishing the midnight judgeships,[99] and continued serving on the Supreme Court until his death in 1806.

John Marshall, when he became secretary of state, recommended Paterson to President Adams as chief justice.[100] When Adams instead appointed Marshall, because Paterson was perceived as aligned with Hamilton,[101] Paterson responded

[90] Notes of a Speech Probably Delivered by Paterson in United States Senate (July 1789), PATERSON CORRESPONDENCE 347.

[91] 4 DHFFC 8, 1 ANNALS 182 (21 Sept.1789).

[92] Nomination (4 Mar.1793), 12 WASHINGTON PAPERS-PRESIDENTIAL 266; George Washington to William Paterson (20 Feb.1793), 12 *id.* 194; Commission (4 Mar.1793), 27 JEFFERSON PAPERS 857.

[93] William Paterson to New Jersey Legislative Council (30 Mar.1793), 1 DHSC 740.

[94] DUNLAP'S AMERICAN DAILY ADVERTISER (Philadelphia), 3 Apr.1793, reprinted in 1 DHSC 740, 742.

[95] United States v. Insurgents of Pa., 2 U.S. (2 Dall.) 335, 341 (C.C.D. Pa. 1795); United States v. Vigol, 2 U.S. (2 Dall.) 346, 346 (C.C.D. Pa. 1795); United States v. Mitchell, 2 U.S. (2 Dall.) 348, 355 (C.C.D. Pa. 1795); *accord* PATERSON PAPERS-RUTGERS (folder 158, *Vigol*; folder 119, *Miller*; folder 120, *Philson and Husbands*).

[96] George Washington to Alexander Hamilton (29 Oct.1795), 19 HAMILTON PAPERS 355, 356; Timothy Pickering to Alexander Hamilton (17 Nov.1795), 19 *id.* 435; *see* Tench Coxe to William Paterson (27 Aug.1795), PATERSON PAPERS-NYPL 607.

[97] WILLIAM PATERSON ED., LAWS OF THE STATE OF NEW-JERSEY (Matthias Day, Newark 1800); William Paterson, Draft of The Laws of the State of New Jersey (1792–1800), Along with Some Other Documents (RU, Brunswick, ac.2929).

[98] VOTES AND PROCEEDINGS OF THE SEVENTEENTH GENERAL ASSEMBLY OF THE STATE OF NEW-JERSEY 83 (Isaac Collins, Trenton 1793) (House 23 Nov.1792, Senate 24 Nov.1792).

[99] Stuart v. Laird, 5 U.S. (1 Cranch) 299, 309 (1803).

[100] John Marshall to Joseph Story (25 July 1827), 11 MARSHALL PAPERS 35, 46; Jonathan Dayton to William Paterson (28 Jan.1801), PATERSON PAPERS-NYPL 623, 625.

[101] *See* Jonathan Dayton to William Paterson (28 Jan.1801), PATERSON PAPERS-NYPL 623, 625 (Adams "declared that he would never nominate you"); Diary of William Maclay (11 Mar.1790, 8 Apr.1790), 9 DHFFC 217, 239 (Hamilton's "Gladiatorial band").

graciously that Marshall's "talents have at once the lustre and solidity of gold."[102] A half decade before, as Paterson joined the Court, New Hampshire's leading lawyer called him "unquestionably the ablest Judge."[103] A decade before at the Constitutional Convention, a fellow delegate described him as "one of those kind of men whose powers break in upon you, and create wonder and astonishment."[104] However, not all were so overcome by wonder and astonishment, such as fellow Senator William Maclay, who described a Paterson speech as "warm[ing] himself with his own discourse, as the Indians do with their war song," and who found him "a most despicable character."[105] The Republicans began to agree with Maclay as Paterson upheld and enforced the Sedition Act (as discussed in the next chapter). By the late 1790s, Paterson, no friend of democracy, saw seditious libel as part of the "raging of the people," that "drives with the impetuosity of a hurricane, and upturns everything in its course," unless suppressed.[106]

Though Paterson presided over Sedition Act trials, like Justices Chase and Washington, he had not always seen speech and press as dangerously tempestuous.

Involvement in Congressional Passage of the Bill of Rights

Several critical states, including New York and ultimately Virginia, only ratified the Constitution with a recommendation or promise of a bill of rights.[107] North Carolina initially voted against ratification, and Rhode Island refused even to call a convention, while Virginia delayed its decisive vote. Madison shifted from his earlier position that a bill of rights was superfluous, to support "safeguards to liberty." After ratification, President Washington added his weight to the compromise by indirectly calling for approval of a bill of rights in his inaugural address and in a letter for Madison to show around.

Early in the ensuing first Congress, Madison guided the adoption of the Bill of Rights, first by making a motion to debate amendments in May 1789, and then by proposing a Bill of Rights in early June 1789[108] containing the provisions recommended most by the states. Federalists had been concerned that amendments with rights could lead to further amendments disempowering the new government, but

[102] William Paterson to Jonathan Dayton (25 Jan.1801), 1 DHSC 920, 921. This was evidently sincere. Jonathan Dayton to William Paterson (1 Feb.1801), PATERSON PAPERS-NYPL 627. Sen. Dayton and others were not so gracious, saying all believed Adams's choice showed "debility or derangement of intellect." Jonathan Dayton to William Paterson (20 Jan.1801), PATERSON PAPERS-NYPL 619, 621.

[103] Jeremiah Smith to William Plumer (24 Feb.1795), 1 DHSC 753.

[104] 3 FARRAND'S RECORDS 90.

[105] Diary of William Maclay (16 July 1789, 2 June 1790), 9 DHFFC 114, 283.

[106] PATERSON DRAFT OPINIONS 48 (second opinion).

[107] Amendments Proposed by the Virginia Convention (27 June 1788), 4 DHFFC 15; Amendments Proposed by the New York Convention (26 July 1788), 4 *id.* 19.

[108] 4 DHFFC 9 (8 June 1789). He envisioned inserting amendments throughout the Constitution, until a motion by Roger Sherman provided that they would be added at the end.

through the ratification compromise they generally supported the Bill of Rights.[109] Madison's House committee report approved the Bill of Rights at the end of July,[110] and the House approved it with seventeen provisions and sent it to the Senate in late August.[111]

That is when Paterson, and also Ellsworth, became involved as the Bill of Rights came to them and the other senators by a reading of the House version on August 25, 1789.[112] The House-approved speech and press provisions were as follows: "The freedom of speech, and of the press, . . . shall not be infringed."[113] Initially, amendments to those provisions were rejected on September 3,[114] but then amendments bringing them to their current language were approved on September 9: "Congress shall make no law . . . abridging the freedom of speech, or the press. . . ."[115] The House, rejecting Senate changes to various other provisions, requested a conference committee, and named Madison to head its delegation.[116]

Paterson, Ellsworth, and Charles Carroll were the three senators appointed to the Senate delegation to the conference on September 21.[117] All three supported the conference committee report on September 24, which approved the final language of the First Amendment[118] except for a subsequent minor stylistic change[119]:

> Congress shall make no law respecting an establishment of religion, or prohibiting the free exercise thereof; or abridging the freedom of speech, or of the press, or the right of the people peaceably to assemble, and to petition the government for a redress of grievances.

The House then approved the final Bill of Rights on September 24,[120] and the Senate agreed to the House resolutions on September 25 and 26, 1789.[121] Finally, the Bill of Rights was submitted to the states for ratification,[122] which reached the

[109] *E.g.*, An Address to the Electors of the State of New-York (21 Mar.1801), 25 Hamilton Papers 356.

[110] 4 DHFFC 27 (28 July 1789).

[111] 4 *id.* 35 (24 Aug.1789).

[112] 1 *id.* 135 (25 Aug.1789).

[113] 4 *id.* 36 (24 Aug.1789).

[114] 1 *id.* 152 (3 Sept.1789).

[115] 4 *id.* 43, 44, 1 *id.* 166 (9 Sept.1789), 4 *id.* 45, 46 (14 Sept.1789); *see* 1 *id.* 153 (4 Sept.1789).

[116] 1 *id.* 181 (21 Sept.1789).

[117] 4 *id.* 8, 1 *id.* 182 (21 Sept.1789).

[118] 4 *id.* 47, 1 *id.* 186 (24 Sept.1789). It then was the third of twelve amendments, but the first two were rejected by the states; the phrase "First Amendment" is used for simplicity.

[119] The next day, the Senate changed "peaceably to assemble and petition" to "peaceably to assemble, and to petition."

[120] 4 *id.* 48, 1 *id.* 189 (24 Sept.1789).

[121] 1 *id.* 192 (25 Sept.1789); 1 *id.* 198 (26 Sept.1789).

[122] 4 *id.* 1 (28 Sept.1789). The amendments approved by Congress were entitled "Amendments to the Constitution," rather than "Bill of Rights," and numbered twelve, only the last ten of which were ratified in 1789–1791. *Id.*

required three-fourths on December 15, 1791. Unfortunately, the ratification process was not extensively documented.[123]

Paterson supported the Bill of Rights as it reached the Senate. Neither he nor Ellsworth initiated any Senate consideration of rights, or drafted any version before receiving the House version; they simply responded to and edited the House version. Their involvement was limited, though critical, and was hard to distinguish from other committee assignments, where their task was to get the job done, with enthusiasm being optional. Paterson's concern can perhaps be measured by his waiting nearly a half year to write to New Jersey's governor to remind him that "Congress have not received the ratification of the Amendments to the Constitution by the State of New Jersey,"[124] despite approval. With equal ennui, New Jersey waited two more months before sending its confirmation.[125]

Essays on Politics and Dissent Before and After the Bill of Rights

Paterson wrote essays, some of which were published in local newspapers under the pseudonyms "Aurelius," "Horatius," and "Hortensius."[126] His opening essay (which has not been published or quoted) began with acknowledgment of the legitimacy of "diversity of sentiments" about public officials and measures:

> In free governments, where men enjoy the right of judging for themselves, diversity of sentiments respecting public men and measures must be expected, and is, indeed, unavoidable. This diversity, however, is attended with good or bad effects according to the principle from which it flows. If the agent be an honest and candid inquirer, if his object be truth and information, he will be ever open to conviction, and, when convinced, will think it no dishonor to retract, and acknowledge his error. But, on the contrary, if his mind be darkened by prejudice, be guided by selfish view, or actuated by party spirits, his opinions, however erroneously formed, no course of reasoning nor invocation of facts can induce him to forego. He may be refuted, but will never be convinced; truth may

[123] 2 DHC 321–90.

[124] William Paterson to William Livingston (29 May 1790), William Livingston Family Papers (MHS, Boston, Ms. N-1579.2, Box 3).

[125] An Act to Ratify (19 Nov. 1789), 2 DHC 326–29; Elisha Lawrence to George Washington (4 Aug. 1790), 2 *id.* 325.

[126] PATERSON ESSAYS 2, 6, 10, 12 etc. (Aurelius), 54, 56, 58, 60 etc. (Horatius), 78, 80, 82, 83 etc. (Hortensius).

> dazzle him by its brightness, but will never irradiate or cheer. To attempt conviction under such circumstances would be labor unprofitably betra[y]ed.[127]

Though acknowledging other viewpoints, Paterson attributed sentiments different from his own to contumacy, and darkly ascribed much of that contumacy to the demons of "party spirits." Such dark thoughts began to predominate, as the next essay recited a recurrent maxim in his thinking, that "Party is the madness of many for the gain of a few," in effect treating his own view as objective and the anti-federalists as partisans,[128] foreshadowing his future approach to the Republican opposition[129] and to Sedition Act violators. Both essays preceded ratification of the Constitution in 1788 and his joining the Supreme Court in 1793.[130]

He took a more tolerant tack toward "diversity of sentiment" in a third essay, sometime after his appointment but when he still saw some positive aspects to the French Revolution, as he discussed the difficulty of "fix[ing] upon a constitution and frame of government."

> Our notions with respect to government are extremely mutable and various. On this point, men of the soundest heads and purest hearts entertain very different sentiments; and, in all probability, will continue to do so till the end of time. Nor is this to be wondered at when we consider, that, in matters of opinion, the same person, in his various stages of progression through life, scarcely differs from others more than he does from himself. This diversity of sentiment arises from a thousand sources[].[131]

Here, Paterson did not reprobate opposing views or attribute them to prejudice, selfishness, or party spirits. Instead, he spoke of freedom of speech in much the way he spoke of freedom of assembly, a couple of essays later. "The people have a right to assemble in town-meetings about politics, and to talk them over, and argue pro and con, and resolve and re-resolve upon them. It is the right of man and the birth-right of Americans. True, very true."[132]

The first and second essays and the third could have been written by two different people, one intolerant and the other open to dissenting expression. The First Amendment was approved and ratified in between, but if it made a difference, it was not a permanent difference. Instead, Paterson shifted back in 1798 to the dark

[127] *Id.* 1–2.

[128] *Id.* 7.

[129] *Id.* 54, 56.

[130] *Id.* 13 (ratification), 16 (appointment).

[131] *Id.* 48.

[132] *Id.* 58.

thoughts of the first two essays, the crisis of that year appearing to have resolved the tug of war in his thinking.

Paterson added another maxim that could justify anything: the new government's right of self-preservation. In 1789 he offered it as a justification for the new criminal law.[133] It was essentially the ancient reason of state argument, dressed in more attractive clothing. Not only could it justify anything, but it did. A decade later, Paterson used it to justify the Sedition Act.[134]

What was absent from his essays, and from his grand jury charges before his 1798 change, was any hint that he embraced the Blackstone-Mansfield definition of freedom of press or their framework for seditious libel.

Justice Samuel Chase

Samuel Chase's career, from the Continental Congress onward, left in its wake contention,[135] scandal,[136] or both.[137] His role in the Sedition Act trials brought more protests than other justices' roles. Largely as a result, he became the first Supreme Court justice to be impeached, though he was not convicted because the Senate vote fell short of the required two-thirds majority.[138]

Chase's public life began with strong opposition to the Stamp Act,[139] and service in the Maryland Assembly during most of the years 1765–1784.[140] He was a member of Congress during 1774–1776,[141] and advocated independence by

[133] Notes of William Paterson (22–23 June 1789), 9 DHFFC 474, 475, 476, 479.

[134] PATERSON DRAFT OPINIONS 45; William Paterson's Charge (C.C.D. Vt. 3 Oct.1798), 3 DHSC 292, 293.

[135] *E.g.*, Samuel Chase, MARYLAND GAZETTE (Annapolis), 23 Aug.1781, reprinted in 3 CARROLL PAPERS 1474 (with Charles Carroll); Daniel of St. Thomas Jenifer to Charles Carroll (2 Aug.1779), 3 *id.* 1251, 1260 (with Samuel Wilson); altercations with Walter Dulaney and John J. Zubly; and examples in this section; *accord* Neil Strawser, *Samuel Chase and the Annapolis Paper War*, 57 MD. HISTORICAL MAG. 177 (1962) (1766 controversy over city expenditures).

[136] 5 MEMOIRS OF JOHN QUINCY ADAMS 213 (Charles F. Adams ed., Lippincott, Philadelphia 1874–77).

[137] *See generally* STEPHEN B. PRESSER, THE ORIGINAL MISUNDERSTANDING: THE ENGLISH, THE AMERICANS AND THE DIALECTIC OF FEDERALIST JURISPRUDENCE (CAP, Durham 1991); Jane S. Elsmere, The Impeachment Trial of Justice Samuel Chase (1962) (unpublished Ph.D. dissertation, Indiana University); OCSC 137; 1 JUSTICES 185.

[138] CHASE TRIAL 268.

[139] Remonstrance to Gov. Horatio Sharpe (approved 13 Dec.1765), 59 MARYLAND ARCHIVES 230–31; 59 *id.* 172 (Chase on drafting committee).

[140] 59 MARYLAND ARCHIVES 16, 131 (23 Sept.1765, 1 Nov.1765), after election November 1764.

[141] 1 JCC 14, 22 (5 Sept.1774), 2 *id.* 12, 19 (10 May 1775), 5 *id.* 574, 596 (18 July 1776); 11 MARYLAND ARCHIVES 34 (14 Aug.1775).

mid-1775.[142] He was an organizer of the colony's association for nonimportation,[143] which also sought "to arm a free people in defence of their liberty" and to offer "opposition by arms to the British troops,"[144] and was placed on the colony's council of safety when it was formed in 1775.[145] He joined Benjamin Franklin and Charles Carroll as commissioners to seek union with Canada, in 1776,[146] though the effort failed.[147] Chase is romantically credited with leading the charge in Maryland's provincial congress to rescind the instructions requiring its delegates in Congress to support conciliation,[148] gaining authorization to support independence,[149] and then riding 150 miles in just two days to deliver the news to Congress of the deciding state's vote for independence, just before the critical vote. However, the truth is that he neither led (though he supported independence[150]) nor rode (he was in his legislative seat when the ride supposedly occurred and the congressional vote was held[151]). He did soon sign the Declaration of Independence,[152] and served in Congress through 1778,[153] until scandal engulfed him.

Chase soon engaged in his first scandal, the use of inside information to invest in flour. As a member of the congressional committee "to enquire into the state of the purchases of wheat and flour for the use of the army,"[154] he learned that the commissary general planned to buy flour.[155] Soon "a number of speculators . . . engaged a

[142] *E.g.*, Samuel Chase to John Adams (24 July 1775), 3 ADAMS PAPERS 93; Samuel Chase to John Adams (16 Nov.1775), 3 *id.* 310.

[143] MARYLAND GAZETTE (Annapolis), 26 May 1774.

[144] Association of the Freemen of Maryland (26 July 1775), 11 MARYLAND ARCHIVES 66–67.

[145] 11 MARYLAND ARCHIVES 31 (14 Aug.1775).

[146] Instructions and Commission from Congress (20 Mar.1776), 22 FRANKLIN PAPERS 380; Commissioners to Canada to Israel Putnam (5 Apr.1776), 3 LETTERS OF DELEGATES 490; Samuel Chase to William Livingston (12 May 1776), CHASE CORRESPONDENCE; JOURNAL OF CHARLES CARROLL OF CARROLLTON, DURING HIS VISIT TO CANADA (Brantz Mayer ed., J. Murphy, Baltimore 1845)

[147] *See* William R. Riddell, *Benjamin Franklin's Mission to Canada and the Causes of Its Failure*, 48 PA. MAG. HISTORY & BIOGRAPHY 111 (1924).

[148] PROCEEDINGS OF THE CONVENTION OF THE PROVINCE OF MARYLAND . . . EIGHTH OF MAY, 1776, at 14 (Frederick Green, Annapolis 1776).

[149] PROCEEDINGS OF THE CONVENTION OF THE PROVINCE OF MARYLAND . . . TWENTY-FIRST OF JUNE, 1776, at 10 (Frederick Green, Annapolis 1776).

[150] *E.g.*, Samuel Ward to Henry Ward (2 Nov.1775), 2 LETTERS OF DELEGATES 290, 291; Samuel Chase to John Adams (8 Dec.1775), 3 ADAMS PAPERS 361; Samuel Chase to John Adams (28 June 1776), 4 *id.* 351.

[151] PROCEEDINGS OF THE CONVENTION OF THE PROVINCE OF MARYLAND . . . TWENTY-FIRST OF JUNE, 1776, at 14 (Frederick Green, Annapolis 1776) (1 July 1776); 5 JCC 504, 507 (28 June 1776, 2 July 1776).

[152] 5 JCC 515.

[153] And again during 1784–1785.

[154] 10 JCC 284 (25 Mar.1778).

[155] 11 JCC 734 (letter of 23 July 1778), 831 (24 Aug.1778).

great part of the wheat and all of the flour" in several states.[156] Chase was one of them, through his business partner John Dorsey,[157] and received much censure.[158] Hamilton attacked their dealings as corrupt in three essays,[159] calling it "criminal" to "turn the knowledge of secrets, to which his office gave him access, to the purposes of private profit," and labeling Chase "a traitor."[160] Consequently, the Maryland assembly did not reappoint him to Congress for the next two years,[161] and prohibited such activities by its delegates to Congress.[162] After the legislature exonerated him on narrower charges, Chase in a broadside trumpeted that he had been found innocent of "breach of his duty, as a member of Congress, by revealing a secret resolve," though the far from vindicatory ground was that what he took advantage of "was not a secret."[163] Chase soon shifted his war profiteering to purchasing war supplies for Maryland and producing iron,[164] and his partnerships were nearly as ruinous as unseemly. Chase's business activities ultimately brought him into insolvency,[165] which

[156] Jeremiah Wadsworth to Henry Laurens (29 Sept.1778), 14 LAURENS PAPERS 368; *accord*, Jeremiah Wadsworth to Henry Laurens (1 Sept.1778), 14 *id.* 260, 261.

[157] House of Delegates (11 Jan.1781) (broadside); *accord* JAMES HAW ET AL., STORMY PATRIOT: THE LIFE OF SAMUEL CHASE 104–10 (MHS, Baltimore 1980); EDWARD C. PAPENFUSE, IN PURSUIT OF PROFIT: THE ANNAPOLIS MERCHANTS IN THE ERA OF THE AMERICAN REVOLUTION, 1763–1805, at 194 (JHUP, Baltimore 1975). The partnership is noted in 48 MARYLAND ARCHIVES 347 (21 Jan.1783) and described in State of Mr. Chase's Case (19 Nov.1789), in Samuel Chase Papers, 1787–1816 (DU, Ms. Collection No.994). Chase's defense is in, *e.g.*, Samuel Chase to Charles Carroll (28 Jan.1782), 3 CARROLL PAPERS 1501, 1504–07.

[158] Daniel of St. Thomas Jenifer to Charles Carroll, Sr. (24 May 1779), 12 LETTERS OF DELEGATES 520; Henry Laurens to George Washington (20 Nov.1778), 14 LAURENS PAPERS 514, 517. It contradicted Chase's statement of the obligations of public officers. Thomas Johnson, Samuel Chase and William Paca, *To John Hammond*, MARYLAND GAZETTE (Annapolis), 9 Sept.1773, at 1, 2.

[159] Publius Letters 1–3 (16 Oct.1778, 26 Oct.1778, 16 Nov.1778), 1 HAMILTON PAPERS 562, 567, 580; Alexander Hamilton to James McHenry (26 Feb.1782), 3 *id.* 2, 3.

[160] 1 *id.* 562, 563. He addressed the third public letter to The Honorable S______ C______e. 1 *id.* 580. Charles Carroll similarly accused Chase. MARYLAND GAZETTE (Annapolis), 21 June 1781, 23 Aug.1781, reprinted in 3 CARROLL PAPERS 1474.

[161] 13 JCC 17–18 (2 Jan.1779), 16 *id.* 2–3 (1 Jan.1780).

[162] An Act to Restrict the Delegates of This State in Congress from Engaging in Any Trade Either Foreign or Domestic ch. 2 (27 July 1779), LAWS OF MARYLAND (Frederick Green, Annapolis 1779); VOTES AND PROCEEDINGS OF THE HOUSE OF DELEGATES OF THE STATE OF MARYLAND. JULY SESSION, 1779, at 127 (Frederick Green, Annapolis 1779) (27 July 1779).

[163] House of Delegates (11 Jan.1781) (broadside). His defense was also given in Censor [Samuel Chase], *Censor IV*, MARYLAND GAZETTE (Annapolis), 21 June 1781, reprinted in 3 CARROLL PAPERS 1449; MISUNDERSTANDING 25.

[164] *E.g.*, 21 MARYLAND ARCHIVES 541 (30 Sept.1779), 485 (2 Aug.1779), 468 (9 July 1779), 461 (24 June 1779); 43 *id.* 35 (11 Dec.1779), 92 (21 Feb.1780); *see* Arthur Lee to Thomas Jefferson (13 Mar.1782), 18 LETTERS OF DELEGATES 394, 395.

[165] In late 1789 Chase was jointly liable for partnership debts of above £37,000, in addition to private debts, after "conveying and mortgaging . . . all his property even to his beds, books &c," of "about £2,000." State of Mr. Chase's Case (19 Nov.1789), in Samuel Chase Papers, 1787–1816 (DU, Durham, ms. collection No.994).

required him to request the assembly to discharge him of obligations to purchase real estate in 1787. Two years later, his finances remained in an "embarras[s]ed situation."[166]

Chase opposed the federal Constitution, after misrepresenting his position to gain reelection to the Maryland legislature,[167] with a short essay[168] and leadership of the unsuccessful anti-federalist forces at the Maryland ratification convention.[169] However, after ratification of both the Constitution and the Bill of Rights, Chase became a federalist,[170] seeing where the jobs were, and, later, became the Federalist Party's greatest liability.

A further scandal followed[171] as Chase, already serving as chief judge of Baltimore's criminal court beginning in 1788,[172] added the position of chief judge of the general court in 1791[173] (which was not Maryland's highest court[174]), a position he held until 1796.[175] Maryland's declaration of rights of 1776, which Chase had supported and helped draft, provided clearly that "no person ought to hold, at the same time, more than one office of profit."[176] A grand jury, which Chase had managed to insult by "censuring the sheriff 'for having summoned so bad a jury,'" returned the compliment by presenting Chase for violating the declaration of rights by holding both judicial positions.[177] An impeachment effort failed despite

166 Matthew Ridley to John Jay (22 Sept.1789), 1 DHSC 664; *accord* Samuel Chase to Richard Henry Lee (16 May 1789), 15 DHFFC 565, 566.

167 MARYLAND JOURNAL (Baltimore), 28 Sept.1787, reprinted in ESSAYS ON CONSTITUTION 325 (contradicting his ambivalent "Letter of Caution" two weeks later); James Madison to Edmund Randolph (30 Sept.1787), 10 MADISON PAPERS 181, 182.

168 [Samuel Chase], *Letter of Caution* (12 Oct.1788), in ESSAYS ON CONSTITUTION 325, 327; Daniel Carroll to James Madison (28 Oct.1787), 10 MADISON PAPERS 226, 227 (Chase wrote).

169 2 ELLIOT'S DEBATES 547, 556; James Madison to Thomas Jefferson (24 Oct.1787), 12 JEFFERSON PAPERS 270, 281.

170 As part of the transition, he shed earlier optimism about democracy. *E.g.*, Samuel Chase to Nn. (6 Mar.1803), CHASE CORRESPONDENCE ("Men without sense, and without property, are to men useless."); Samuel Chase to William Paterson (6 Apr.1802), PATERSON PAPERS-NYPL 755.

171 Petition of Charles Carroll 2 (1 Sept.1790), Samuel Chase Papers, 1787–1816 (DU, Durham, ms. collection No.994).

172 71 MARYLAND ARCHIVES 268 (of Criminal Court for Baltimore County, 12 June 1788), 72 *id.* 51 (of Court of Oyer & Terminer and Gaol Delivery, 5 Oct.1789), 72 *id.* 245, 247 (of same, reappointment 31 Dec.1791, commission 2 Jan.1792).

173 72 MARYLAND ARCHIVES 218, 223 (appointment 30 Aug.1791, commission 7 Oct.1791); 2 Md. viii (1791).

174 1 ARCHIVES OF MARYLAND: NEW SERIES 323 (Edward C. Papenfuse ed., MSA, Annapolis 1990).

175 Samuel Chase to Gov. John Howard (9 Sept.1791), CHASE CORRESPONDENCE; James Iredell to Hannah Iredell (29 Jan.1796), 1 DHSC 832.

176 Maryland Declaration of Rights art.xxxii, 3 FEDERAL-STATE CONSTITUTIONS 1689.

177 Presentment and Response (Aug.1794), in *Samuel Chase and the Grand Jury of Baltimore County*, 6 MARYLAND HISTORICAL MAG. 131, 132, 134 (1911).

his multiple offices and multiple complaints,[178] but a majority later found that he violated the declaration of rights provision.

His appointment to the Supreme Court in January 1796 replaced John Blair,[179] after President Washington concluded Chase had become "a steady friend of the general government"[180] (or of federal employment).

Chase's ultimate scandal was his Sedition Act rulings, and his impeachment that largely resulted from them (both described in the next chapter). Six articles of impeachment arraigned Chase's rulings during a Sedition Act trial involving James Callender and a treason trial involving John Fries, and two articles arraigned bellicose charges to grand juries.[181] The last of those grand jury charges warned of "mobocracy,"[182] highlighting Chase's trajectory from when he *was* the mob opposing the Stamp Act. Though Chase was readily impeached by the House, 73 to 32, in March 1804, the Senate after trial the next year did not achieve the required two-thirds on any articles, though a majority favored impeachment on three charges[183] (despite Republican dominance in the Senate of 25 to 9).

Ominously, objurgatory views of Chase were as ubiquitous as tempest in his life. In the Continental Congress, John Adams described Chase's "temper naturally quick and warm,"[184] and their colleague Benjamin Rush said Chase "possessed more learning than knowledge, and more of both than judgement" in his already "checkered" life.[185] When Chase was nominated to the Supreme Court, Vice President Adams regretted that "his character has a mist about it of suspicion and impurity,"[186] and others saw more than just a mist. Among Federalists, Secretary of Treasury Oliver Wolcott had "an unworthy opinion of him,"[187] Governor

[178] William Vans Murray to George Washington (24 Jan.1796), 1 DHSC 111; *see* IDEOLOGICAL ORIGINS 117; MISUNDERSTANDING 24.

[179] Nomination (26 Jan.1796), 1 DHSC 101; Confirmation by Senate (27 Jan.1796), 1 *id.* 101; Commission (27 Jan.1796), 1 *id.* 113; *The First Judges of the Federal Courts*, 1 AM. J. LEGAL HISTORY 76, 77 (1957).

[180] George Washington to Alexander Hamilton (29 Oct.1795), 34 WASHINGTON WRITINGS 346, 349; 1 DHSC 805.

[181] Articles of Impeachment, CHASE TRIAL app.3–6.

[182] Samuel Chase's Charge (C.C.D. c.1803), CHASE CHARGE BOOK 38, 40–41.

[183] CHASE TRIAL 266.

[184] Diary (14 Oct.1774), 2 ADAMS WORKS 398.

[185] THE AUTOBIOGRAPHY OF BENJAMIN RUSH 150 (George W. Corner ed., PUP, Princeton 1948).

[186] John Adams to Abigail Adams (6 Feb.1796), 1 DHSC 835. Adams also said "Chase is violent and boisterous, asking his pardon; he is tedious upon frivolous points," Diary (15 Sept.1775), 2 ADAMS WORKS 422, though three days later Adams found him "ever social and talkative" and in "better humor." 2 *id.* 425 (18 Sept.1775). He could also call Chase "very active, eloquent, spirited, and capable." John Adams to James Warren (18 Feb.1776), 4 ADAMS PAPERS 27.

[187] Oliver Wolcott, Sr. to Oliver Wolcott, Jr. (15 Feb.1796), 1 *id.* 837.

Samuel Johnston was "not impressed with . . . his moral character, whatever his professional abilities may be,"[188] and Jeremiah Smith's reaction to the Supreme Court appointment was to note that Maryland gentry "are very glad to get rid of him which is a very bad symptom."[189] During the Sedition Act trials, Republican Senator Steven Mason characterized Chase's grand jury charge as having "all the zeal of a well fee'd lawyer and the rancour of a vindictive and implacable enemy."[190] Chase was not an enemy of knife and fork as he was of sedition; even rotund Vice President Adams (whose suggestions for lofty presidential titles drew the recommended vice presidential title "Your Corpulency") found himself chiding Chase's own "corpulency."[191] Fortunately, opposition newspapers did not learn of Chase's near-drowning by breaking through ice that, according to Chase, "had been tried and would bear a wag[]on and horses."[192]

Yet positive views of Chase were common. Justice Joseph Story, a luminary of the early nineteenth-century Court and a Republican, wrote that "the elements of his mind are of the very first excellence" though by 1808 affected by "age and infirmity," and that he "abounds with good humor" though "[h]is manners are coarse, and in appearance harsh." Chase was "the living . . . image of Samuel Johnson" "[i]n person, in manners, in unwieldy strength, in severity of reproof, in real tenderness of heart; and above all in intellect."[193] Story, however, wrote that more from hearsay than personal observation, since he did not overlap Chase on the Court, arriving a half year after Chase's death. One modern scholar, going where even Story feared to tread, published an ingenious book and articles rehabilitating Chase[194] (which others have challenged[195]), though the revivified Chase still clutched his scythe and hood from Sedition Act reaping.

Chase expressed support of freedoms of press and speech, before the Sedition Act crisis.

188 Samuel Johnston to James Iredell (27 Feb.1796), 2 Iredell Correspondence 462.

189 Jeremiah Smith to William Plumer (29 Jan.1796), 1 DHSC 833.

190 Stevens T. Mason to James Madison (23 Apr.1800), 17 Madison Papers 382.

191 John Adams to Abigail Adams (6 Feb.1796), 1 DHSC 835. This was not a matter of just a little corpulency. *E.g.*, Henri J. Stier to Nn. (23 Nov.1797), William D. Hoyt, *The Calvert-Stier Correspondence*, 38 Maryland Historical Mag. 123, 126–27 (1943).

192 Samuel Chase to Hannah Chase (4 Feb.1800), 1 *id.* 888.

193 Matthew Bramble to Samuel P. P. Fay (25 Feb.1808), 1 Life and Letters of Joseph Story 166, 167 (William W. Story ed., Little Brown, Boston 1851) (by Story, *id.* 148).

194 *E.g.*, Misunderstanding 8, 13–14, 174 *passim*; Stephen B. Presser, *The Original Misunderstanding: The English, the Americans, and the Dialectic of Federalist Constitutional Jurisprudence*, 84 Nw. U. L. Rev. 106 (1989); Saving 773–74; Stephen B. Presser, *Tale of Two Judges: Richard Peters, Samuel Chase, and the Broken Promise of Federalist Jurisprudence*, 73 Nw. U. L. Rev. 26 (1978); OCSC 764, 765.

195 Stewart Jay, *The Rehabilitation of Samuel Chase*, 41 Buffalo L. Rev. 273 (1993); *see* the Chase discussion at pages 285–302.

Chase's Rise Through Newspaper Debates

His rise to a leading position in Maryland politics, and consequently to the Continental Congress, resulted in large part from his use of the press. In the opening of one essay, he relied on freedom of speech, calling it a natural right, and condemned those who labeled dissent "sedition":

> Freedom in enquiry and opinion we hold with you a natural right; and therefore the terms . . . "the sowers of sedition and discord"—"state-lawyers who pushed forward this publick resolve for the promotion of their own private gains," applied to those, who differed from you in sentiment, are intemperate.[196]

A quarter century later, Chase's fall in public esteem also resulted primarily from newspapers, over whose prosecutions he zealously presided.

During the Stamp Act debates of 1765, he led[197] demonstrations by predecessors to the Sons of Liberty, who, as the royal governor related, "hang'd or burn't in effigie" the stamp collector in front of the gallows, though Chase may not have been involved in the "mob of three of four hundred people" that then destroyed the collector's house.[198] Opponents soon described Chase as a "restless incendiary, a ringleader of mobs,"[199] and Chase shot back that they were "despicable pimps, and tools of power."[200] The printer of the *Maryland Gazette,* which had published what Chase called "the most inveterate and false reflections" against him, "refused to give [his response] a place in his paper" because Chase's libelous vitriol would "subject him to prosecutions, and the dislike of *many* of *his* friends."[201] Chase responded with a broadside that provided his "vindication," benefiting from the press even while criticizing it.[202]

[196] Thomas Johnson, Samuel Chase & William Paca, *To John Hammond,* MARYLAND GAZETTE (Annapolis), 9 Sept.1773, at 1, 1.

[197] Samuel Chase, *To the Publick,* MARYLAND GAZETTE (Annapolis), 16 July 1766.

[198] Horatio Sharpe to Lord Baltimore (10 Sept.1765), 14 MARYLAND ARCHIVES 222, 223; *accord* Horatio Sharpe to Thomas Gage (23 Sept.1765), 14 *id.* 224; MARYLAND GAZETTE (Annapolis), 6 Mar.1766.

[199] Walter Dulany et al., *Letter,* MARYLAND GAZETTE (Annapolis), 19 July 1766, at 5–6 ("Extraordinary" supplement).

[200] Samuel Chase, *To the Publick,* MARYLAND GAZETTE (Annapolis), 16 July 1766, at 1; *accord* CREATION 253–54.

[201] *Id.* at 1.

[202] *Id.* at 1. He occasionally published other broadsides, more than any other early justice, again presumably because newspapers would not provide free space. *E.g.,* To the Citizens of Baltimore-Town (4 May 1794); To the Voters of Baltimore-Town (3 Oct.1788); To the Voters of Anne-Arundel County (25 Oct.1786).

In 1772–1773, Chase entered another major altercation in print opposing the colonial government and the established church. Compensation for many governmental officials was paid from tobacco inspection fees, and under the same law, compensation for the established church clergy was paid in tobacco or money from a related tax on each head in every parish. The law authorizing these taxes expired in 1770,[203] and the lower legislative house refused to extend it,[204] supported by Chase.[205] The governor tried to reinstate the colony's revenue stream by proclamation,[206] and the Anglican ministers tried by petition, which the lower house rejected.[207] The ministers self-servingly argued that nonextension of the 1747 act[208] revived the higher tax of the original 1702 act,[209] and filed suits for the higher tax.[210] Chase first entered the controversy involuntarily when his private legal opinion to a minister was printed, supporting that claim.[211] Chase stanched criticism by arguing that the original 1702 law was unconstitutional,[212] which had far-ranging implications because that law not only paid the established clergy with the poll tax but established the Anglican Church.[213] Chase, with William Paca and Thomas Johnson, offered free defense to parishioners declining to pay the poll tax.[214]

[203] The most recent reenactments extended the fees until 25 Dec.1769, and then until 1 Oct.1770. An Act Continuing an Act Entit[]led an Act for Amending the Staple of Tobacco for Preventing Frauds in His Majesty[']s Customs and for the Limitation of Officers['] Fees (13 Nov.1766), 51 MARYLAND ARCHIVES 222; similar Act (13 Dec.1769), *id.* 62 *id.* 123.

[204] 62 MARYLAND ARCHIVES 200–01 (31 Oct.1770) (upper house passed), 62 *id.* 411–14 (17 Nov.1770) (lower house rejected).

[205] 62 *id.* 414 (17 Nov.1770).

[206] Proclamation (26 Nov.1770), 63 *id.* 109–10.

[207] Hugh Neill to Daniel Burton (18 July 1771), 4 HISTORICAL COLLECTIONS RELATING TO THE AMERICAN COLONIAL CHURCH 342, 343 (William S. Perry ed., n.p., Hartford 1870–78).

[208] An Act for Amending the Staple of Tobacco, for Preventing Frauds . . . (1747), 44 MARYLAND ARCHIVES 595, 604.

[209] An Act for the Establishm[']t of Religious Worsh[i]p in This Province According to the Church of England: and for the Maintenance of Ministers (16 Mar.1702), 24 MARYLAND ARCHIVES 264.

[210] Samuel Chase & William Paca, *To the Rev. Mr. Jonathan Boucher,* MARYLAND GAZETTE (Annapolis), 14 Jan.1773, at 2, 3; Samuel Chase & William Paca, *To the Reverend Mr. Jonathan Boucher,* MARYLAND GAZETTE (Annapolis), 18 Mar.1773, at 1.

[211] *Id.* This is often misdescribed as an opinion that the 1702 law was unconstitutional.

[212] *Old True-Penny,* MARYLAND GAZETTE (Annapolis), 20 Aug.1772.

[213] An Act for the Establishm[']t of Religious Worsh[i]p in This Province According to the Church of England: and for the Maintenance of Ministers (16 Mar.1702), 24 MARYLAND ARCHIVES 264.

[214] Thomas Johnson, Samuel Chase & William Paca, *To John Hammond,* MARYLAND GAZETTE (Annapolis), 9 Sept.1773, at 1, 2. They defended at least four suits. *See* CHARLES A. BARKER, THE BACKGROUND OF THE REVOLUTION IN MARYLAND 363 (YUP, New Haven 1940).

A leading Anglican minister, goaded by his precipitous drop in income,[215] published an attack on Chase and Paca.[216] Their response began a newspaper war,[217] which quickly became front page material.[218] Other essayists joined in debating the officials' fees.[219] Finally, the lower house almost unanimously resolved that the 1702 law was unconstitutional, with Chase's and Johnson's support, in June 1773,[220] and replaced it with a lower tax for the clergy.[221] Chase and Paca published scathing criticism of the opposition,[222] and their fight vaulted them into the Maryland delegation to the Continental Congress.[223] Their rise was due to the press.

The Maryland Declaration of Rights and Freedom of Press

The Maryland Declaration of Rights of 1776 was drafted by a committee of seven of the delegates.[224] Chase's motion brought about the appointment of that

[215] JONATHAN BOUCHER, REMINISCENCES OF AN AMERICAN LOYALIST, 1738–1789, at 70 (repr. Kennikat Press, Port Washington 1967).

[216] Jonathan Boucher, *To Samuel Chase and William Paca, Esqrs.*, MARYLAND GAZETTE (Annapolis), 31 Dec.1772, at 2.

[217] Samuel Chase & William Paca, *To the Rev. Mr. Jonathan Boucher*, MARYLAND GAZETTE (Annapolis), 14 Jan.1773, at 2, 3; Jonathan Boucher, *To Samuel Chase, and William Paca, Esqrs.*, *id.*, 4 Feb.1773, at 2; William Paca, *To the Rev. Mr. Jonathan Boucher*, *id.*, 25 Feb.1773, at 2.

[218] Jonathan Boucher, *To William Paca, Esq.*, MARYLAND GAZETTE (Annapolis), 4 Mar.1773, at 1; William Paca, *To the Reverend Mr. Jonathan Boucher*, *id.*, 11 Mar.1773, at 5–6; Samuel Chase and William Paca, *To the Reverend Mr. Jonathan Boucher*, *id.*, 18 Mar.1773, at 1–4; Jonathan Boucher, *To William Paca, Esq.*, SUPPLEMENT TO THE MARYLAND GAZETTE (Annapolis), 18 Mar.1773, at 1; Samuel Chase & William Paca, *To the Reverend Mr. Jonathan Boucher*, MARYLAND GAZETTE (Annapolis), 18 Mar.1773, at 1, 1, 3.

[219] Most notably Charles Carroll writing as "First Citizen," MARYLAND GAZETTE (Annapolis), 4 Feb.1773, 11 Mar.1773, 6 May 1773, 1 July 1773; Daniel Dulany writing as "Antilon," *id.*, 7 Jan.1773, 18 Feb.1773, 8 Apr.1773, 3 June 1773; and John Hammond, *To the Printers*, *id.*, 29 July 1773, at 1.

[220] 63 MARYLAND ARCHIVES 347 (19 June 1773); 64 *id.* 130 (14 Dec.1773) (reaffirming illegality). The upper house disagreed. 64 *id.* 254 (21 Dec.1773).

[221] 64 MARYLAND ARCHIVES 254 (21 Dec.1773).

[222] Thomas Johnson, Samuel Chase & William Paca, *To John Hammond*, MARYLAND GAZETTE (Annapolis), 9 Sept.1773, at 1–6.

[223] *See* JONATHAN BOUCHER, REMINISCENCES OF AN AMERICAN LOYALIST, 1738–1789, at 69–71 (repr. Kennikat Press, Port Washington 1967); 64 MARYLAND ARCHIVES xviii–xix; Anne Y. Zimmer, *The "Paper War" in Maryland, 1772–1773: The Paca-Chase Political Philosophy Tested*, 71 MD. HISTORICAL MAG. 177 (1976); Jean H. Vivian, *The Poll Tax Controversy in Maryland, 1770–1776: A Case of Taxation* with *Representation*, 71 MD. HISTORICAL MAG. 151 (1976); ANNE Y. ZIMMER, JONATHAN BOUCHER: LOYALIST IN EXILE 118–31 (Wayne State University Press, Detroit 1978); DAVID C. SKAGGS, ROOTS OF MARYLAND DEMOCRACY, 1753–1776, at 128–30 (Greenwood Press, Westport 1973).

[224] Proceedings of the Convention of the Province of Maryland (14 Aug.1776-), 3 AMERICAN ARCHIVES 83, 91.

committee,[225] and Chase was initially on it[226] but lost his seat when he resigned from the convention (because he disagreed with instructions from constituents).[227] The committee's draft, which included a provision for freedom of press, was prepared before his resignation, though it was not debated until two months later.[228]

Chase voted for the final declaration of rights,[229] which contained strong protection for freedom of press:

> XXXVIII. That the liberty of the press ought to be inviolably preserved.[230]

Beyond his motion and vote, two things corroborate Chase's commitment to that liberty, or at least to his own enjoyment of that liberty. A month before his motion to form the committee, he asked John Adams to obtain a book on "Civil Liberties" written by a prominent advocate of press and conscience, Dr. Richard Price.[231] As soon as the committee draft was printed, he sent a copy for comment to John Dickinson,[232] the recent author of the Continental Congress address that first recognized freedom of press and specified other rights.

Twelve years later, in April 1788, Chase again expressed commitment to the state declaration of rights, or at least his own enjoyment of it. His published essay began by affirming that he was "a friend to our present state government because it is wisely calculated to secure all the civil and *religious* rights of the people and fully adequate for all internal state purposes. . . ." He then listed ten provisions of the state declaration of rights, evidently those he found most fundamental, such as trial by jury and freedom of press.[233] Similarly, the day the proposed federal Constitution arrived in Maryland, Chase expressed concern that it "will alter, and

[225] 3 *id.* 90 (17 Aug.1776).

[226] 3 *id.* 91. Additional members were added, including Thomas Johnson, when Chase and two others resigned. 3 *id.* 97.

[227] Proceedings of the Convention of the Province of Maryland . . . Fourteenth of August, 1776, at 12 (Frederick Green, Annapolis 1776) (on 27 Aug.1776).

[228] Reported 10 Aug.1776, and debated 31 Oct.1776. 3 American Archives 135, 138.

[229] 3 *id.* 143–47 (3 Nov.1776); Proceedings of the Convention of the Province of Maryland 53 (Frederick Green, Annapolis 1776).

[230] 3 *id.* 143, 147 (3 Nov.1776); Maryland Declaration of Rights art.xxxviii, 3 Federal-State Constitutions 1686, 1690.

[231] Samuel Chase to John Adams (9 July 1776), 4 Letters of Delegates 415 n.1, referring to Richard Price, Observations on the Nature of Civil Liberty (repr. John Dunlap, Philadelphia 1776).

[232] Samuel Chase to John Dickinson (29 Sept.1776), 5 Letters of Delegates 261; *see* Samuel Chase to John Dickinson (4 & 19 Oct.1776), 5 *id.* 262 n.2.

[233] Objections to the Federal Government, in Samuel Chase Papers 61 (NYPL, Bancroft Collection v.168).

in some instances, abolish our [Maryland] Bill of Rights."[234] That concern, or as some have argued instead Chase's self-interest and hypocritical posturing,[235] flowered into insistence on a federal bill of rights.

The Necessity of a Federal Bill of Rights and of Freedom of Press

Chase was the only early justice who had opposed the Constitution in 1787–1788, and part of his reason was its omission of a bill of rights. After the Maryland ratification convention, he summarized his reasons for opposition as the lack of amendments "to declare & secure the great and essential rights of the people" and to limit some of the new government's powers.[236]

At the Maryland ratification convention, Chase's speeches, according to his notes, addressed five topics, and the fourth was his concern that the proposed Constitution threatened freedom of press and of conscience. His notes for his speech on that fourth topic were:

> Old Whig No. 5–4 Brutus No. 2
> Liberty of Conscience
> Bill or Declaration of Rights
> Liberty of Press[237]

Chase's references to three recent essays fill in many of the gaps, and indicate that he used their reasoning. Old Whig No.5 discussed "some of those liberties" that should be included in a bill of rights.[238] The essay listed five freedoms, beginning with liberty of conscience, followed by "freedom of speech and of writing and publishing their thoughts on public matters."[239] The sequence in the essay matches Chase's sequence of conscience and press in his notes. Old Whig No.4 gave reasons why "we ought carefully to guard ourselves by a bill of rights against the invasion of those liberties which it is essential for us to retain."[240] Without such a bill of rights, it warned, "government is always in danger of degenerating into tyranny."[241] Brutus No.2 similarly insisted that the foundation of a new government

[234] MARYLAND JOURNAL, 28 Sept.1787, reprinted in ESSAYS ON CONSTITUTION 325

[235] Philip A. Crowl, *Anti-Federalism in Maryland, 1787–1788*, 4 WM. & MARY Q. (3d ser.) 446, 463–65 (1947).

[236] Samuel Chase to John Lamb (13 June 1788), ISAAC Q. LEAKE, MEMOIR OF THE LIFE AND TIMES OF GENERAL JOHN LAMB 310 (Munsall, Albany 1850); 18 DHRC 47.

[237] Objections to the Federal Government, in Samuel Chase Papers 97 (NYPL, Bancroft Collection v.168).

[238] *An Old Whig V* (Oct.-Nov.1787), in 3 COMPLETE ANTI-FEDERALIST 34, 34 (§3.3.25–.30).

[239] 3 *id.* 37.

[240] *An Old Whig IV* (Oct.-Nov.1787), in 3 *id.* 30, 34 (§3.3.18–.24).

[241] 3 *id.* 33.

must be expressly reserved rights, beginning with criminal law rights, then freedom of conscience and free elections, and then "that the liberty of the press should be held sacred."[242] Chase's notes also listed two common arguments of opponents of a bill of rights, to be refuted.[243]

The vote for ratification at the Maryland convention in May 1788, which was by a heavy federalist majority of 63 to 11,[244] was both preceded and followed by discussion of a bill of rights. When former Governor William Paca proposed amendments, the committee of thirteen appointed to consider them[245] included Chase as well as Johnson.[246] The only plenary record of Maryland's ratification convention, the one reprinted in *Elliot's Debates* and in *Documentary History of Ratification of the Constitution*, is the address written by the minority supporting the amendments,[247] which included Chase.[248] It recited, apparently accurately,[249] that the committee agreed unanimously to twelve amendments including one on freedom of press, but that the federalist majority on the committee made a strategic decision to recommend no amendments at all,[250] evidently out of frustration or fear at Chase's insistence on arguing for at least three additional amendments.

The minority address reprinted not only the freedom of press provision, which the committee had approved but not reported, but also its reason for deeming the provision critical:

> 12. That the freedom of the press be inviolably preserved.
>
> In prosecutions in the federal courts for libels, the constitutional preservation of this great and fundamental right may prove invaluable.[251]

[242] *Brutus II* (1 Nov.1787), in 2 *id.* 372, 373, 375 (§2.9.24–.33).

[243] Objections to the Federal Government, in Samuel Chase Papers 97 (NYPL, Bancroft Collection v.168).

[244] Address to the People of Maryland ([1 May] 1788), 2 Elliot's Debates 547, 548, 549; 17 DHRC 242 (excerpts); *accord* Bernard C. Steiner, *Maryland's Adoption of the Federal Constitution*, 5 Am. Historical Rev. 207 (1900).

[245] 2 *id.* 549; *see* 17 DHRC 237n. Paca's amendments are reprinted in 17 DHRC 240 (29 Apr.1788).

[246] 2 *id.* 549; John B. Cutting to Thomas Jefferson (11 July 1788), 13 Jefferson Papers 331, 333.

[247] 2 *id.* 547; 17 DHRC 242.

[248] 2 *id.* 556.

[249] A. C. Hanson to James Madison (2 June 1788), 4 DHC 645; John B. Cutting to Thomas Jefferson (11 July 1788), 13 Jefferson Papers 331–36; 2 J. Thomas Scharf, History of Maryland 542–46 (J. B. Piet, Baltimore 1879).

[250] 4 *id.* 656–67; 17 DHRC 242; 2 Elliot's Debates 549, 555; John B. Cutting to Thomas Jefferson (11 July 1788), 13 Jefferson Papers 331, 336. The issues in that strategic decision are summarized in Maryland 91–93.

[251] Address to the People of Maryland ([1 May] 1788), 2 Elliot's Debates 552; 17 DHRC 244.

The way that this provision could "prove invaluable" in prosecutions for libels, was in thwarting them by elevating the constitutionally protected freedom of press over the English common law of seditious libel. Only then would freedom of press "be inviolably preserved." The provision did not mean preservation of rights to jury trial, or of jury rights to determine issues, because those were protected by a separate amendment for all criminal cases. The provision did not mean creation of a defense of truth, because it did not even hint at that.

As the new Congress convened the next year, Chase lobbied for amendments to be adopted to check the new government, by contacting a leading supporter of a federal bill of rights, Senator Richard Henry Lee. Chase drowned his request in pessimism about the prospects:

> I observed that a day is appointed to consider amendments to the new Constitution. I am one of the number that expect no essential alterations. I hope I may be mistaken. I fear that no check will be placed on the exercise of any of the powers granted. I am satisfied that, every amendment must flow from grace & favor. Our people will not contend for any, the most important. In this state we are prepared to submit to any government. The hearts of our people are broke, they are bow[ed] down to the earth with their debts.[252]

His reference to only the "grace and favor" of Providence bringing amendments was because in Maryland the "people will not contend for any" due to being broken and laden with debt. He similarly wrote a year earlier that amendments were favored by the people, but "they are depressed and inactive" and "seem ready to submit to any master."[253] Chase continued to lobby for freedom of press by again writing to Lee, two months later, to express opposition to the Senate doors being closed as contrary to "Republican principles" that demanded openness to public viewers and the press.[254]

Later Reversal on Freedom of Press and on Other Issues of Freedom

In 1787, Chase had marched into the debate over the Constitution by urging caution and delay, so fellow citizens could "lay their sentiments and reasons for or against the measure before you," and urging that "you ought to hear *both* sides, as the man who determines on hearing one part only, will almost always be mistaken in his judgment."[255]

[252] Samuel Chase to Richard Henry Lee (16 May 1789), 15 DHFFC 565–66.

[253] Samuel Chase to John Lamb (13 June 1788), 18 DHRC 47, 48.

[254] Samuel Chase to Richard Henry Lee (2 July 1789), 16 DHFFC 916, 917; *see* CHESAPEAKE POLITICS 291–93.

[255] [Samuel Chase], *Letter of Caution* (12 Oct.1787), reprinted in ESSAYS ON CONSTITUTION 327, 328.

By December 1796, during his first year on the Supreme Court, Chase had enough of hearing both sides, and was far more concerned with the recently emerged Republican press than with protections of the Bill of Rights.[256] He sent a letter amounting to an advisory opinion on the French minister's effort to influence the 1796 election, in response to the secretary of war sending a copy of the *Aurora*, the leading Republican newspaper, criticizing the government. Chase's advice was for the government to bring a criminal libel prosecution of the printer[257]:

> I thank you for the *Aurora*, but my absence prevents me from any knowledge of the sentiments of the people here, respecting Mr. Adet's abuse of our *whole administration*, and appeal to the people. I think the printer ought to be indicted for a false & base *libel* on our government. A free press is the support of liberty and a republican gov[']t, but a licentious press is the bane of freedom, and the pest of society, and will do more to destroy real liberty than any other instrument in the hands of knaves & fools. I see no difference between Genet and Adet.[258]

Chase saw no value in an opposition press, and readily identified its reprinting of anti-administration sentiments as criminal libels and licentiousness. He was primed for prosecutions two years before the Sedition Act.

Chase's change was dramatic from the Maryland ratification convention, where he found a bill of rights indispensable to protect liberty, and called for "freedom of the press [to] be inviolably preserved" because it would be invaluable for defense of libel prosecutions, to that 1796 advisory opinion, in which he urged indicting an opposition newspaper for criminal libel. His change became even more stark once he was armed with the Sedition Act in 1798, as he became the most zealous justice in prosecuting those "knaves and fools" of the press. Under it, he charged grand juries that it was a "false patriot" who "without just cause, creates distrust and suspicion of the legislature, or of the executive, or of the principal officers of government," and that a true patriot must "give up his private sentiments to the public will."[259] By the time of his impeachment trial in 1805, Chase had expanded the category of knaves and fools to include all his enemies.[260]

Chase's reversals on opposing the Constitution, on professing strong commitment to freedom of press, and on believing that the freedom of press provision

[256] His partisanship while on the bench was also manifested in his advisory opinion on an official printer, calling for a "trusty or faithful discreet person of unquestionable attachment to the government" ([Apr.] 1800), McHenry Correspondence 431 n.3; and his active campaigning for Adams in 1800, Aurora (Philadelphia), 9 Aug.1800, reprinted in 1 DHSC 895.

[257] Samuel Chase to James McHenry (4 Dec.1796), Chase Papers (James S. Copley Library, La Jolla).

[258] *Id.* "Pest" may be "peril"; the writing is difficult to read.

[259] Samuel Chase's Charge (C.C.D. Pa. 12 Apr.1800), 3 DHSC 408, 413.

[260] Samuel Chase to Joseph Hopkinson (10 Mar.1805), Samuel Chase Papers (LC, Washington).

shielded against federal libel prosecutions, were not his only reversals. He also reversed positions on a federal common law of crime, on criticizing the administration, and on disobeying unconstitutional laws, as discussed in Chapter 3. Likewise, he reversed positions on freedom of press, never embracing the Blackstone-Mansfield definition or framework until 1798.

Chief Justice Oliver Ellsworth

Figure 5.3 Chief Justice Oliver Ellsworth (on Supreme Court 1796–1800). Print c.1891. (Courtesy of Library of Congress.)

Oliver Ellsworth (Figure 5.3), the third chief justice, held that position as the Sedition Act was passed and as trials under it occurred, though he did not preside over any trials and was away in France on a diplomatic mission during most of them.[261]

He served in the Connecticut assembly during 1773–1776,[262] supporting the patriot cause on the state's committee of finance,[263] and beginning in 1779 on the council of safety,[264] which with the governor directed the state's military in

[261] *See generally* WILLIAM R. CASTO, OLIVER ELLSWORTH AND THE CREATION OF THE FEDERAL REPUBLIC (Second Circuit Committee on History, New York 1997) (the best source); *accord* OCSC 252; 1 JUSTICES 223. No dissertation has been written on Ellsworth, though another book has recently appeared. MICHAEL C. TOTH, FOUNDING FEDERALIST: THE LIFE OF OLIVER ELLSWORTH (ISI Books, Wilmington 2011).

[262] 14 THE PUBLIC RECORDS OF THE COLONY OF CONNECTICUT, 1636–1776, at 159 (14 Oct.1773) (J. Hammond Trumbull & Charles J. Hoadly eds., Case, Lockwood & Brainard Co., Hartford 1850–90); *id.* 214 (12 Jan.1774), 252 (12 May 1774), 325 (13 Oct.1774), 388 (2 Mar.1775), 413 (26 Apr.1775).

[263] 14 *id.* 431.

[264] 2 PUBLIC RECORDS-CONN. 287 (May 1779).

the Revolution. Ellsworth was appointed by the assembly to Congress in 1777,[265] and he continued in Congress until he declined reappointment in 1783.[266] He was added to the governor's council in 1780,[267] serving until 1785, when it became a supreme court of errors. He then became a superior court judge during 1785–1789,[268] and in retirement rejoined the governor's council during 1801–1807.[269]

Ellsworth attended the Constitutional Convention, and was on its important committee of detail with future justices Rutledge and Wilson.[270] He contributed to the Connecticut compromise that resolved the dispute about representation by states or by population by using the first for the Senate and the second for the House of Representatives.[271] He was unable to sign the Constitution, because state judicial duties required his return home,[272] but his support was sufficiently fervent that Madison misremembered him as a signatory.[273] After the Convention, Ellsworth wrote influential essays supporting the Constitution under the nom de plume "Landholder,"[274] and led the federalist forces in the Connecticut ratification convention.[275]

He was chosen as one of Connecticut's first senators in 1789,[276] serving until his appointment to the Supreme Court.[277] He led the Senate delegation in finalizing and adopting many bills, including the Bill of Rights in 1789,[278] though his time devoted to the latter was limited.

[265] A Historical Collection from Official Records, Files, &c., of the Part Sustained by Connecticut, During the War of the Revolution 291 (Royal R. Hinman ed., E. Gleason, Hartford 1842); 6 Letters of Delegates 219 n.1; Connecticut Delegates to Jonathan Trumbull (15 Oct.1778), 11 *id.* 58.

[266] 2 Public Records-Conn. 134 (Oct.1778), 462 (Jan.1780); 4 Connecticut Records 133; 5 *id.* 110, 207.

[267] Oliver Ellsworth to Jeremiah Wadsworth (30 May 1780), 15 Letters of Delegates 215.

[268] 1 Kirby 1 (Conn. 1786); Oliver Ellsworth Family Papers, 1762–1907 (LC, Washington, MM95081076, box 1, folders 9–10).

[269] 11 Connecticut Records 1, 285; 1 Timothy Dwight, Travels in New England and New York 220 (Barbara M. Solomon ed., BP-HUP, Cambridge 1969).

[270] 3 Farrand's Records 557 (delegate); 2 *id.* 97, 106 (24 June 1787).

[271] 1 *id.* 468 (29 June 1787), building on William Samuel Johnson's suggestion, 1 *id.* 461–62 (29 June 1787).

[272] Timothy Pitkin: On Signing the Constitution, 3 Farrand's Records 476.

[273] James Madison to Joseph Wood (27 Feb.1836), 4 Letters and Other Writings of James Madison 427, 428 (Lippincott, Philadelphia 1867).

[274] Essays on Constitution 135–201; *accord* 25 Letters of Delegates 554 n.1.

[275] 15 DHRC 243 (4 Jan.1788, 7 Jan.1788); 2 Elliot's Debates 185, 190; 6 Connecticut Records 553, 559.

[276] 6 Connecticut Records 474; 7 *id.* 178; 8 DHFFC 534, 1 *id.* 3 (4 Mar.1789); Oliver Ellsworth to Gov. Samuel Huntington (29 Dec.1788), A.L.S. Gratz Collection (HSP, Philadelphia, case 1, box 5).

[277] 2 Annals 28 (2nd Cong., 1st Sess.); 3 *id.* 10 (3rd Cong., 1st Sess.); 4 *id.* 10 (4th Cong., 1st Sess.); Resignation (8–9 Mar.1796), 1 DHSC 844; Oliver Ellsworth to Oliver Wolcott (8 Mar.1796), *id.*

[278] 4 DHFFC 8, 1 *id.* 182 (21 Sept.1789).

President Washington appointed him as Chief Justice of the Supreme Court in March 1796, to replace Rutledge.[279] This came as no surprise, because Adams later called Ellsworth "the firmest pillar of his whole administration."[280] However, Ellsworth's talents were much greater as a legislator[281] than as a judge or as a negotiator. After three years on the Court, he was asked by Adams to sail to France as one of three minister plenipotentiaries, seeking to avert formal war following the XYZ Affair.[282] Under Ellsworth's leadership[283] the mission ended in a compromise in the Convention of 1800, though that treaty was unpopular because it failed to require any French reparations for scores of seizures of American ships.[284] While still in France, Ellsworth concluded that his "gravel and gout," whose "pains are constant, and at times excruciating,"[285] precluded further judicial service,[286] and he consequently resigned from the Court in December 1800.[287]

When Ellsworth was appointed, Adams lamented that the Senate lost "the clearest head and the most dil[]igent hand we had,"[288] and Iredell believed he would "fill the office extremely well" and had "an excellent understanding."[289] Federalist

279 Nomination (3 Mar.1796), 1 DHSC 120; Confirmation by Senate (4 Mar.1796), *id.*; Commission (4 Mar.1796), 1 *id.* 121.

280 10 ADAMS WORKS 112; *accord* HENRY CABOT LODGE, A FIGHTING FRIGATE, AND OTHER ESSAYS AND ADDRESSES 106 (Scribner, New York 1902).

281 Fisher Ames to Christopher Gore (5 Oct.1796), 1 WORKS OF FISHER AMES 199, 203 (Seth Ames ed., 2nd ed. Little, Brown, Boston 1854).

282 John Adams to Senate (25 Feb.1799), 2 ADAMS WORKS 205; 1 JOURNAL OF EXECUTIVE PROCEEDINGS-SENATE 317 (25 Feb.1799). Largely because of Hamilton's opposition to the renewed peace mission, MCHENRY CORRESPONDENCE 566, Ellsworth did not sail until late 1799. 2 ASP 307 (3 Nov.1799).

283 Oliver Ellsworth to Alexander Hamilton (16 Oct.1800), 25 HAMILTON PAPERS 160, 161–68; William Vans Murray to John Marshall (1 Oct.1800), 4 MARSHALL PAPERS 310; William Vans Murray to John Quincy Adams (7 Nov.1800), MURRAY LETTERS 658.

284 Convention Between the French Republic, and the United States of America (30 Sept.1800), 1 TREATIES 457; 2 ASP 295; *see* 32 JEFFERSON PAPERS 159n. It was also called the Treaty of Môrtefontaine. Ellsworth believed it to be the best treaty obtainable. Oliver Ellsworth to Alexander Hamilton (16 Oct.1800), 25 HAMILTON PAPERS 160; Oliver Ellsworth to William Paterson (16 Oct.1800), PATERSON PAPERS-NYPL 631. Jefferson disliked the treaty enough that he resubmitted it to the senate. 2 ASP 345 (11 Dec.1801).

285 Oliver Ellsworth to David Ellsworth (10 Oct.1800), 1 DHSC 900; Oliver Ellsworth to Oliver Wolcott (16 Oct.1800), *id.*

286 Oliver Ellsworth to Alexander Hamilton (16 Oct.1800), 25 HAMILTON PAPERS 160, 161; Theodore Sedgwick to Alexander Hamilton (17 Dec.1800), 25 *id.* 262; though ill health is questioned in ELLSWORTH 120.

287 Oliver Ellsworth to Oliver Wolcott (25 Dec.1800), 25 HAMILTON PAPERS 273, 274; John Marshall to Charles Cotesworth Pinckney (18 Dec.1800), 6 MARSHALL PAPERS 41.

288 John Adams to Abigail Adams (5 Mar.1796), 1 DHSC 842; *accord*, John Adams to William Tudor (9 May 1789), 15 DHFFC 489. Abigail Adams was not so impressed, after reading Ellsworth's grand jury charge in 1797: "did the good gentleman never write before? . . . the language is stiffer than his person." Abigail Adams to John Adams (17 Apr.1797), 3 DHSC 169.

289 James Iredell to Hannah Iredell (25 Mar.1796), 2 IREDELL CORRESPONDENCE 465.

senators were equally high in his praises: Tristam Dalton said Ellsworth was "one of the best speakers in the Senate,"[290] Representative Jeremiah Smith regarded him as "a very able lawyer and a very learned man . . . & a very honest man[;] in short he is every thing one would desire."[291] Republican senators saw him differently: the acerbic William Maclay thought he was "the most conceited man in the world" who could be called "the Endless El[l]sworth,"[292] and more seriously believed him "governed by conveniency or cabal" and "not to be trusted."[293] They correctly perceived that Ellsworth held typical Federalist fears of democracy.[294] However, Madison, after the battle fires cooled, wrote that he "always regarded his talents as of a high order" as did others, and that Ellsworth spoke in an "emphatic and impressive" manner.[295] Federalist friends tended to employ superlatives,[296] such as Timothy Dwight, the retired president of Yale College (who said he was "tall, dignified, and commanding," a person who "inspired awe"),[297] and Daniel Webster (who said he left "proofs of the clearest intelligence" and "of the utmost purity and integrity of character").[298]

The only book-length biographies of Ellsworth devoted one sentence and no mention, respectively, to his role in adopting the First Amendment,[299] but his role was as central, though as brief, as Paterson's.

[290] Tristam Dalton to Michael Hodge (4 June 1789), 16 DHFFC 697. Rep. William Smith believed he had "much reputation for legal knowledge," and "remarkable clearness of reasoning." William Smith to Edward Rutledge (10 Aug.1789), 16 *id.* 1283, 1284.

[291] Jeremiah Smith to William Plumer (5 Mar.1796), 1 DHSC 843.

[292] Diary of William Maclay (9 May 1789, 26 Aug.1789), 9 DHFFC 32, 135. Hamilton, after Ellsworth altered his credit plan, labeled him "the great slayer of public faith—the hacknied [*sic*] veteran in the violation of public engagements." Alexander Hamilton to Rufus King (21 Feb.1795), 18 Hamilton Papers 278, 280 n.5.

[293] Diary of William Maclay (5 June 1789, 5 May 1789), 9 DHFFC 69, 24.

[294] Landholder [Oliver Ellsworth], *Landholder XII* (17 Mar.1788), Essays on Constitution 199; *e.g.*, 1 Farrand's Records 335 (no conventions, 20 June 1787), 414 (no direct election of Congress, 25 June 1787).

[295] James Madison to Joseph Wood (27 Feb.1836), 4 Letters and Other Writings of James Madison 427–28 (Lippincott, Philadelphia 1867).

[296] Such as William Pierce at the Constitutional Convention, 3 Farrand's Records 89, or the French counsel, around the same time, who called him "simple in his manners, but wise and infinitely reasonable, . . . wishing only well without considering personal motives." "Liste des Membres et Officiers du Congrés" (1788), 3 Farrand's Records 232, 238 (Ellsworth was "absolument de la même tournure et des mêmes dispositions" as Benjamin Huntington: "simple dans ses manières, mais sage et infiniment raisonnable; . . . sans considérer des motifs personnels.").

[297] 1 Timothy Dwight, Travels in New England and New York 220 (Barbara M. Solomon ed., BP-HUP, Cambridge 1969).

[298] 3 Works of Daniel Webster 485 (9th ed. Little, Brown, Boston 1856).

[299] William G. Brown, Life of Oliver Ellsworth 200 (Macmillan, New York 1905); Michael C. Toth, *supra* note 261, at 133–72.

Revision and Congressional Passage of the Bill of Rights

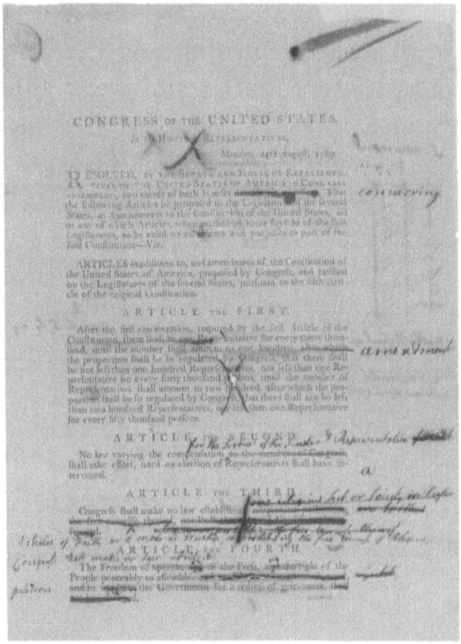
CONGRESS OF THE UNITED STATES.

ARTICLE THE FIRST.

ARTICLE THE SECOND.

ARTICLE THE THIRD.

ARTICLE THE FOURTH.

Figure 5.4 Senate Draft of Bill of Rights edited by Oliver Ellsworth (Sept. 2–9, 1789). (Courtesy of National Archives, R.G.46.)

The Senate amendments of September 9, 1789, which were the final Senate changes to the Bill of Rights, were in Ellsworth's handwriting,[300] though they were doubtless not based mostly on his preferences but on Senate debate. It is significant that the changes did not show hostility toward the House version, but instead mainly improved syntax and renumbered the House amendments. It is equally significant that "he was not particularly enthusiastic about the task."[301] The substantive changes included the final language of the freedoms of speech and press clauses, rewording of the establishment provision to refer to "articles of faith or a mode of worship," the final language of the free exercise clause (deleting freedom of conscience as duplicative),[302] deletion of a conscientious objector

[300] 1 DHFFC 168 n.35, 4 *id.* 45n. (9 Sept.1789).

[301] Ellsworth 77.

[302] Thus, what became the First Amendment was changed from the two provisions in the House version of 24 August 1789 (4 DHFFC 35):

> ARTICLE THE THIRD
>
> Congress shall make no law establishing religion or prohibiting the free exercise thereof, nor shall the rights of Conscience be infringed.
>
> ARTICLE THE FOURTH
>
> The Freedom of Speech, and of the Press, and the right of the People peaceably to assemble, and consult for their common good, and to apply to the Government for a redress of grievances, shall not be infringed.

provision (perhaps also because it was duplicative), and revision of the grand jury and double jeopardy provisions.[303]

Ellsworth led the three senators, joined by Paterson and Carroll, when they were appointed to the conference committee on September 21.[304] He delivered the conference committee report to the Senate on September 24,[305] and it, too, was in his hand.[306] (See Figure 5.4.) He retained, without damage, the final language of the speech and press clauses. In writing these drafts, he did not try to reintroduce the limitation that the Senate had rejected three weeks earlier, which would have reaffirmed the vitality of the English common law of seditious libel by limiting freedoms of press and speech to "as ample a manner as hath at any time been secured by the common law."[307]

Did Ellsworth support the Bill of Rights because he believed in it or because the ratification compromise required it? He at least was not opposed to it, because he had an opportunity to tamper with its wording, and did not when he was the draftsman of at least two Senate versions. However, his time and imprint were miniature compared to his drafting and defending[308] the Judiciary Act of that year,[309] which was intricately crafted to restrict federal court jurisdiction and authority to less than the Constitution's grant in debated areas in order to neutralize objections. The contrast implies strongly that Ellsworth's commitment may have been simply to get a job done in acceptable form,[310] as a skilled negotiator and dutiful implementer,[311] under the ratification compromise. He had, after all, opposed a bill of rights a year and a half before in an influential essay, which is

---

to the Senate version of 9 and 14 September 1789 (4 *id.* 46):

ARTICLE THE THIRD

Congress shall make no law establishing articles of faith, or a mode of worship, or prohibiting the free exercise of religion, or abridging the freedom of speech, or of the press, or the right of the people peaceably to assemble, and to petition to the government for a redress of grievances.

303 4 DHFFC 43–45 (9 Sept.1789), 45–47 (14 Sept.1789).

304 4 *id.* 8, 1 *id.* 182 (21 Sept.1789). Ellsworth was listed first, and presented their report.

305 1 *id.* 185 (24 Sept.1789).

306 1 *id.* 48n.

307 1 *id.* 152 (3 Sept.1789); 4 *id.* 36 n.9.

308 Abraham Baldwin to Joel Barlow (14 June 1789), 16 *id.* 774, 775; Paine Wingate to Nathaniel P. Sargeant (18 July 1789), 16 *id.* 1069, 1070; William Smith to Edward Rutledge (10 Aug.1789), 16 *id.* 1283, 1284; Diary of William Maclay (29 June 1789), 9 *id.* 91; *see* 1 *id.* 11, 14; Charles Warren, *New Light on the History of the Federal Judiciary Act of 1789*, 37 Harv. L. Rev 49, 60, 50 (1923).

309 1 Stat.73 (1789).

310 14 DHFFC 992–97.

311 John Adams to Abigail Adams (5 Mar.1796), 1 DHSC 842; John Adams to William Tudor (9 May 1789), 15 DHFFC 489.

discussed next, and had led the Connecticut convention to ratification without any amendments.[312]

A mixed signal about Ellsworth's fervency about freedoms of speech and press soon came with the issue of making Senate proceedings open to the press and the public. At the Constitutional Convention, he had been willing to delete[313] the constitutional requirement for Congress to publish its journals.[314] As the Senate reconsidered its closed-door policy in 1794, Ellsworth supported opening Senate proceedings to the press and public,[315] and felt strongly enough to vote against the Federalist majority. But nothing indicates that he based that on freedom of speech or press, or a public right to know.

Position During Constitutional Ratification Debates on Freedom of Press

Ellsworth's dutiful attitude to the Bill of Rights in September 1789 was doubtless tied to his opposition a year and a half earlier, in December 1787. When the Constitution was newly written and most federalists opposed a bill of rights, Ellsworth as "Landholder" wrote a series of essays to encourage ratification,[316] the sixth of which responded to demands for a bill of rights. He advocated the federalist position that declarations of rights originated and were necessary when "kings claimed all power" and rights existed only if granted by monarchs, but were unnecessary when "all the power government now has is a grant from the people."[317]

He then cited and responded to the anti-federalist warning that freedom of press was endangered:

> *There is no declaration of any kind to preserve the liberty of the press, etc.* Nor is liberty of conscience, or of matrimony, or of burial of the dead; it is enough that congress have no power to prohibit either, and can have no temptation. This objection is answered in that the states have all the power originally, and congress have only what the states grant them.[318]

Ellsworth's premise that "congress have no power to prohibit" liberty of press set as the standard that only an enumerated power could justify prohibitory regulation. His premise that Congress "can have no temptation" to direct legislation at

[312] 3 DHRC 560–62, 541, 548; *see* 2 Elliot's Debates 196.

[313] 2 Farrand's Records 260 (11 Aug.1787).

[314] U.S.Const. art.I, §5.

[315] James Monroe to Thomas Jefferson (3 Mar.1794), 2 Monroe Papers 690, 691.

[316] Landholder [Oliver Ellsworth], *Landholder I–XIII* (5 Nov.1787–24 Mar.1788), Essays on Constitution 135–202.

[317] Landholder [Oliver Ellsworth], *Landholder VI* (10 Dec.1787), *id.* 160, 163; 3 DHRC 487, 489.

[318] *Id.* 164 (emphasis in original); 3 DHRC 398, 400.

the press implicitly, though unconsciously, approved an opposition press, since the anti-federalist press was precisely what he wrote to refute.

Those assurances clash with the concept that a federal common law authorized Congress or the Supreme Court to provide for prosecution of seditious libel, or that freedoms of press and speech only meant the Blackstone-Mansfield definition and thus did not restrict prosecuting seditious libel. Ellsworth's essays did not even hint at embracing the Blackstone-Mansfield definition of freedoms of press and speech. However, in 1798 his position on that changed dramatically, similar to Iredell, Paterson, Chase, and Washington (as the next chapter discusses).

Advocacy of Freedom of Opinion and Rejection of Libel Against the Church

Ellsworth's next essay addressed freedom of conscience, and the anti-federalist claim that the constitutional prohibition of religious tests made the Constitution "unfavorable to religion." He responded that the provision, far from endangering religious liberty, was "to exclude persecution, and to secure to you the important right of religious liberty." He described freedom of conscience in broad terms, and implicitly repudiated one species of seditious libel, libel against the established church (which Connecticut still had).[319]

He tied this freedom of conscience into a more general freedom of private opinion:

> Civil government has no business to meddle with the private opinions of the people. If I demean myself as a good citizen, I am accountable, not to man, but to God, for the religious opinions which I embrace, and the manner in which I worship the supreme being. If such had been the universal sentiments of mankind, and they had acted accordingly, persecution, the bane of truth and nurse of error, with her bloody axe and flaming hand, would never have turned so great a part of the world into a field of blood.[320]

However, what Ellsworth gave he immediately took away, much as he did a decade later with freedom of press. He criticized mandatory religious oaths as "unjust and tyrannical," but would allow some; he condemned "meddl[ing] with the private opinions of the people," but believed "the civil power has a right, in some cases, to interfere in matters of religion" by prohibiting and punishing "gross immoralities and impieties" and "profane swearing, blasphemy, and professed

[319] Landholder [Oliver Ellsworth], *Landholder VII* (17 Dec.1787), *id.* 167, 168.
[320] *Id.* 170.

atheism."[321] He offered no principle to distinguish permissible from persecutory ones.

Ellsworth, according to his son-in-law's laudatory biography, conceded that "he had no imaginative powers."[322] His approach to these freedoms did not disprove his self-description.

Justice Bushrod Washington

Bushrod Washington, one of the longest serving justices for a total of thirty-one years, now languishes not only in the large shadow of John Marshall, in the company of the other early justices, but in the still larger shadow of his uncle, the commander-in-chief and first president.[323]

Washington, after studying law under James Wilson,[324] attended the Virginia convention and supported ratification of the Constitution in 1788.[325] He hoped for appointment to a position in the new federal government, but was blocked by his uncle, since President Washington sedulously avoided nepotism.[326] By 1795 he was sufficiently skilled as an attorney that Thomas Jefferson commented that because of "equal natural abilities [and] greater reading in the law, he has the reputation of being all attention to business and that of his client,"[327] and hired him in several matters.[328] Washington was also retained by President Washington for

[321] *Id.* 171, 169–70, 171.

[322] Joseph Wood, Draft Biography of Oliver Ellsworth (Mar.1880), ELLSWORTH PAPERS-NYPL 31.

[323] *See generally* David L. Annis, Mr. Bushrod Washington, Supreme Court Justice on the Marshall Court (1974) (unpublished Ph.D. dissertation, Notre Dame University); OCSC 917; 1 JUSTICES 243; Obituary, 28 U.S. (3 Pet.) vii (1832). Washington lacks any published biography, except an inadequate 1858 work.

[324] George Washington to James Wilson (22 Mar.1782), 24 WASHINGTON WRITINGS 88; Bushrod Washington to Bird Wilson (26 Oct.1822), 2 WILSON WRITINGS 594.

[325] 10 DHRC 1538, 1540; James Madison to Thomas Jefferson (22 Apr.1788), 5 MADISON WRITINGS 120, 121; Bushrod Washington to George Washington (7 June 1788), 6 WASHINGTON PAPERS-CONFEDERATION 315–16.

[326] George Washington to Bushrod Washington (27 July 1789), 3 WASHINGTON PAPERS-PRESIDENTIAL 334.

[327] Thomas Jefferson to Thomas M. Randolph (26 Feb.1795), 28 JEFFERSON PAPERS 281, 283. Madison had commended Washington "as a young gentleman of talents." James Madison to Thomas Jefferson (22 Apr.1788), 11 MADISON PAPERS 27, 28.

[328] Thomas Jefferson to James Brown (7 May 1795), 28 JEFFERSON PAPERS 345; Thomas Jefferson to Bushrod Washington (23 Sept.1795), 28 *id.* 479; Thomas Jefferson to Bushrod Washington (1 Oct.1795), 28 *id.* 497; Bushrod Washington to Thomas Jefferson (26 Apr.1796), 29 *id.* 91; Thomas Jefferson to Bushrod Washington (9 Oct.1796), *id.*

personal legal work,[329] and sought to follow his uncle's advice that he should pursue "not the mere study of the law, but to become eminent in the profession of it."[330] He created the earliest published reports of Virginia cases[331] and drafted some of the earliest published reports of circuit court decisions.[332] Upon his uncle's death in 1799, Washington inherited all his papers, along with Mt. Vernon,[333] and worked closely with John Marshall, whom he commissioned as author, on the first president's authorized biography.[334]

President Adams appointed Bushrod Washington to the Supreme Court in the latter part of 1798,[335] to replace Justice Wilson, after Marshall declined the position of associate justice.[336] The appointment was as much a surprise to the first president as it was to the new justice.[337]

Adams noted that the "name, the connections, the character, the merit and abilities of Mr[.] Washington, are greatly respected," though Marshall had been his first choice.[338] Timothy Pickering, the secretary of state, noted that Bushrod Washington was without exception respected "for his talents, virtues and genuine patriotism," because of his "indefatigable pursuit of knowledge and the business of his profession."[339] Republicans soon disagreed, such as a later fellow justice, William Johnson, who privately criticized Justice Washington for so uniformly agreeing with Marshall and joining in his opinions that they "are commonly estimated as a single judge."[340] Their divergence over nearly three decades is often misdescribed as just three opinions,[341] but in fact, Washington differed from five

[329] George Washington to Bushrod Washington (9 Mar.1796), 34 WASHINGTON WRITINGS 488; George Washington to Bushrod Washington (9 Oct.1797), 36 *id.* 43.

[330] George Washington to Bushrod Washington (15 Jan.1783), 26 WASHINGTON WRITINGS 38, 39.

[331] BUSHROD WASHINGTON, REPORTS OF CASES ARGUED AND DETERMINED IN THE COURT OF APPEALS OF VIRGINIA (Thomas Nicholson, Richmond 1798–99) (2 vols).

[332] With editing by Richard Peters, Jr., published as REPORTS OF CASES DETERMINED IN THE CIRCUIT COURT OF THE UNITED STATES FOR THE THIRD CIRCUIT (P. H. Nicklin, Philadelphia 1826–29) (4 vols).

[333] Last Will and Testament (9 July 1799), 37 WASHINGTON WRITINGS 275, 284, 288–89.

[334] John Marshall to Charles Cotesworth Pinckney (21 Nov.1802), 6 MARSHALL PAPERS 124; *e.g.*, John Marshall to Bushrod Washington (25 Mar.1804, 28 Mar.1804, 20 Apr.1804), 6 *id.* 272, 274, 279.

[335] Temporary Commission (29 Sept.1798), 1 DHSC 132; Nomination (19 Dec.1798), 1 *id.* 134; Confirmation by Senate (20 Dec.1798), *id.*; Commission (20 Dec.1798), 1 *id.* 135.

[336] *See* Timothy Pickering to John Marshall (20 Sept.1798), 1 DHSC 129; John Marshall to Timothy Pickering (28 Sept.1798), 1 *id.* 131.

[337] Bushrod Washington to George Washington (19 Oct.1798), WASHINGTON PAPERS-LOC.

[338] John Adams to Timothy Pickering (26 Sept.1798), 1 DHSC 130.

[339] Timothy Pickering to John Adams (20 Sept.1798), 1 *id.* 128.

[340] William Johnson to Thomas Jefferson (10 Dec.1822), 2 HISTORY OF SUPREME COURT 247.

[341] *E.g.*, 2 HISTORY OF SUPREME COURT 99; 1 JUSTICES 251; Lawrence B. Custer, *Bushrod Washington and John Marshall: A Preliminary Inquiry*, 4 AM. J. LEGAL HISTORY 34, 43 (1960). Their convergence was the result of shared philosophy, 2 HISTORY OF SUPREME COURT 381, and of Washington's choice not generally to enter dissents even when he disagreed, Mason v. Haile, 25 U.S. (12 Wheat.) at 379.

Marshall opinions[342] (writing the first dissent from the new chief justice[343]) plus two circuit reversals[344]; and Marshall dissented from seven opinions in which Washington wrote for or joined the majority.[345] Years later, Marshall, commenting on a eulogy, called Washington "one of the worthiest and best," "in professional acquirements and in soundness of intellect."[346] Washington died toward the end of 1829,[347] and in a touching love story, his wife was so grief-stricken that she died on the way home from his funeral in Philadelphia, days after the justice's death.[348]

History has not generally treated Bushrod Washington well; his only published biography was in 1858. Justice Story described his mind, though informally and hastily, as "solid, rather than brilliant; sagacious and searching, rather than quick or eager; slow, but not torpid," and "guided by experience, dwelling little on theory."[349] Story based that on two decades together on the Supreme Court. During his lifetime, Washington was sufficiently respected to receive honorary doctorates from Princeton, University of Pennsylvania, and Harvard, and his intellect was lauded by leading lawyers who practiced before him.[350] However, his

[342] Mason v. Haile, 25 U.S. (12 Wheat.) 370, 379 (1827) (Washington, J., dissenting); Trustees of Dartmouth College v. Woodward, 17 U.S. (4 Wheat.) 518, 654 (1819) (Washington, J., concurring); The Merrimack, 12 U.S. (8 Cranch) 317, 334 (1814) (Washington, J., concurring); Croudson v. Leonard, 8 U.S. (4 Cranch) 434, 442 (1808) (Washington, J., concurring); United States v. Fisher, 6 U.S. (2 Cranch) 358, 397 (1805) (Washington, J., dissenting).

[343] United States v. Fisher, 6 U.S. (2 Cranch) 358, 397 (1805).

[344] Washington reversed a Marshall circuit opinion in Barton v. Petit & Bayard, 11 U.S. (7 Cranch) 194, 200 (1812), and Marshall reversed a Washington circuit opinion in Huidekoper's Lessee v. Douglass, 7 U.S. (3 Cranch) 1 (1805).

[345] Ogden v. Saunders, 25 U.S. (12 Wheat.) 213, 254, 369 (1827) (Marshall, C.J., dissenting from 4–3 majority including Washington, J., on main issue); Bank of the United States v. Dandridge, 25 U.S. (12 Wheat.) 64, 90 (1827) (Marshall, C.J., dissenting); Houston v. Moore, 18 U.S. (5 Wheat.) 1, 12, 32 (1820) (Washington, J., writing majority opinion and referring to two dissenters, apparently including Marshall, C.J.); The Commercen, 14 U.S. (1 Wheat.) 382, 395 (1816) (Marshall, C.J., dissenting); Speake v. United States, 13 U.S. (9 Cranch) 28, 39 (1815); The Venus, 12 U.S. (8 Cranch) 253, 253, 288 (1814) (Washington, J., writing majority opinion with Marshall, C.J., dissenting in part); Hudson & Smith v. Guestier, 10 U.S. (6 Cranch) 281, 285 (1810) (Marshall, C.J., dissenting).

[346] John Marshall to Joseph Hopkinson (17 Dec.1830), 11 MARSHALL PAPERS 395.

[347] John Marshall to George C. Washington (29 Nov.1829), 11 MARSHALL PAPERS 285; Remarks (25 Jan.1830), 11 *id.* 342.

[348] *Bushrod Washington*, NILES' WEEKLY REGISTER (Baltimore), 5 Dec.1829, at 228; *Bushrod Washington*, WATCH-TOWER (Cooperstown), 7 Dec.1829, at 2.

[349] JOSEPH STORY, THE MISCELLANEOUS WRITINGS: LITERARY, CRITICAL, JURIDICAL, AND POLITICAL OF JOSEPH STORY 204, 205 (Munroe, Boston 1835).

[350] HORACE BINNEY, BUSHROD WASHINGTON 11–12, 16–18 (C. Sherman, Philadelphia 1858); 1 DAVID P. BROWN, THE FORUM, OR FORTY YEARS FULL PRACTICE AT THE PHILADELPHIA BAR 356 (R.H. Small, Philadelphia 1856); JOSEPH HOPKINSON, EULOGIUM IN COMMEMORATION OF BUSHROD WASHINGTON 15–16 (Manning, Philadelphia 1830). None of the eulogies mentioned the justice's role in Sedition Act trials.

mind never questioned Federalist doctrine, such as on democracy, as he saw "demagogues" getting into office by "flattering the people,"[351] and warned of "ill consequences" from universal suffrage.[352]

The Patriotic Society and Freedom of Speech

Bushrod Washington, early in his legal career in 1786, joined with other sons of the Virginia aristocracy to form a Patriotic Society. Its purposes, as a debating society, were to discuss "public affairs" and "the conduct of those, who represent us," and "to give them our sentiments upon those laws, which ought to be or are already made."[353] When his advice was sought, George Washington only had time to send hurried "first thoughts" that were overall negative, seeing "as much evil as good result from such societies," particularly when they undertook to instruct representatives on national matters with partial information.[354]

The nephew, in a rare break from his usual deference to his uncle's opinion, defended the society with an emphasis on speech: the "motives which gave birth to the society" were the need of representatives to hear the "sentiments of the people," and the people's "right to instruct their delegates" lest the representatives hear "only the opinion of a few."[355] His uncle remained concerned that constituent instructions to national representatives might prove disunifying.[356]

Bushrod Washington had some positive ties to the press, like other early justices, by publishing his Virginia reports and the George Washington biography. He twice delivered to newspapers essays written anonymously by Marshall defending *McCulloch v. Maryland*,[357] and later delivered his own letter to the editor after newspapers criticized his sale of slaves at Mt. Vernon.

Even as he was using the press to publish his Virginia reports, however, he adopted a Blackstonian definition and framework for freedom of press in 1799 as he presided over his first three Sedition Act trials.

[351] Bushrod Washington to Nn. (18 June 1805), Bushrod Washington (NYPL, New York, Misc. Personal Name File).

[352] Bushrod Washington to Edward S. Burd (7 Jan.1804), H.J. Heaney, *Letters of Bushrod Washington (1762–1829) in the Hampton L. Carson Collection of the Free Library of Philadelphia*, 2 Am. J. Legal History 161, 165 (1958).

[353] Bushrod Washington to George Washington (27 Sept.1786), 4 Washington Papers-Confederation 274.

[354] George Washington to Bushrod Washington (30 Sept.1786), 4 *id.* 278. The uncle later condemned Democratic-Republican societies. American Politics 100.

[355] Bushrod Washington to George Washington (31 Oct.1786), 4 *id.* 322.

[356] George Washington to Bushrod Washington (15 Nov.1786), 4 *id.* 368, 368–70.

[357] John Marshall to Bushrod Washington (17 June 1819), 8 Marshall Papers 316, 317; *accord* Gerald Gunther, John Marshall's Defense of McCulloch v. Maryland (SUP, Stanford 1969).

He seems to have viewed the Federalist-Republican battles as nearly a life or death struggle, after swimming against southern tides to support the Jay Treaty in 1795 and to stand for Congress as a Federalist in 1798.[358] He was concerned before the 1800 election that Hamilton's pamphlet attacking Adams would cause "the election of Mr. J[efferson]—which God forbid."[359] Since it turned out that God did not forbid it, Washington's fears deepened by 1804 to certainty "that the present government could not exist for any considerable length of time."[360] The next year, he confided "what I have always thought of that [Republican] party, that the most violent democrat is, at heart, the greatest tyrant."[361]

The Privileges and Immunities Protected Against State Encroachment

Justice Washington, partway through the Marshall years and his own tenure on the Supreme Court, addressed the meaning of the constitutional provision that he saw as the primary protection against state governments, parallel to the Bill of Rights protection against the federal government. He became the first justice to interpret the Privilege and Immunities Clause,[362] and to rule that it protects a number of specific liberties.[363] He said that his list was not exclusive (a complete list would be "more tedious than difficult to enumerate"), and that under "the general heads" of "the enjoyment of life and liberty" "many others . . . might be mentioned."[364] His relatively broad description of rights was treated by the Supreme Court exactly fifty years later as a statement of the privileges and immunities of state citizenship under Article IV (though not of federal citizenship under the Fourteenth Amendment),[365] and has generated its share of modern-day legal controversy.[366]

His list of privileges and immunities did not expressly include the rights protected in the First Amendment—religion or conscience, speech or press, petition or assembly—among the rights that states must accord to citizens of other states.

[358] Thomas Jefferson to James Monroe (6 Sept.1795), 28 JEFFERSON PAPERS 448, 449.

[359] Bushrod Washington to Oliver Wolcott (1 Nov.1800), 25 HAMILTON PAPERS 249–50 n.7. He supported Adams. *Id.*

[360] Joseph S. Watson to David Watson (17 Feb.[1804]), *Letters from William and Mary College, 1798–1801*, 29 VA. MAG. HISTORY & BIOGRAPHY 129, 169 (1921) (quoting the justice, original underscored).

[361] Bushrod Washington to Nn. (18 June 1805), Bushrod Washington (NYPL, Misc. Personal Name File).

[362] U.S.Const. art.IV, §2, cl.1.

[363] Corfield v. Coryell, 6 F.Cas. 546, 551–52 (C.C.D. Pa. 1823) (No. 3,230) (Washington, J.).

[364] *Id.*

[365] Slaughter-House Cases, 83 U.S. (16 Wall.) 36, 78 (1873).

[366] *E.g.*, Baldwin v. Fish & Game Comm'n, 436 U.S. 371, 394, 395–96 (1978) (Brennan, J., dissenting with White, J. and Marshall, J.); David A. Faber, *Justice Bushrod Washington and the Age of Discovery in American Law*, 102 W. VA. L. REV. 735, 768–69 (2000).

Neither did it exclude them, in view of his statement that "many others . . . might be mentioned," and his identification of mostly fundamental rights. The omission does reflect on the relative value he accorded them.

Justice Alfred Moore

Alfred Moore, though a leading North Carolina attorney, made such little mark on the Supreme Court during his four years there that a modern judge nominated Moore as the most insignificant justice, with the painful sobriquet, "Some men achieve insignificance; others have insignificance thrust upon them."[367] His longest biography is half a pamphlet.[368] Yet that nomination should be challenged, because Moore was the only successor justice between Johnson and Marshall who refused to press federal attorneys and grand jurors for Sedition Act indictments and presentments (as discussed in Chapter 8).

Moore, like Paterson, Ellsworth, and Bushrod Washington, was too young to participate in prerevolutionary debates. However, his father made up for his son's nonparticipation by speaking and publishing in strong opposition to the Stamp Act,[369] and preventing its enforcement, despite his position as a former council member[370] and as one of North Carolina's three colonial justices.[371] His father was also credited with writing an anonymous "Atticus" letter that savaged Governor William Tryon for military overkill and judicial harshness toward dissidents, the Regulators,[372] abandoning earlier support for the royal government's actions that the senior Moore had given in military uniform and in judicial robes.[373]

Moore, Johnson, and Washington were the only pre-Marshall justices to fight in the Revolutionary War. Moore enlisted and fought as a captain in the continental army from September 1775 through March 1777,[374] and then remained

[367] Frank H. Easterbrook, *The Most Insignificant Justice: Further Evidence*, 50 U. Chi. L. Rev. 481, 485 (1983).

[368] *See generally* OCSC 560; 1 Justices 269 (though half is about cases and arguments in which he did *not* participate); Junius Davis, Alfred Moore and James Iredell: Revolutionary Patriots 8–18 (North Carolina Society of the Sons of the Revolution, Raleigh 1899).

[369] Maurice Moore, The Justice and Policy of Taxing the American Colonies, in Great-Britain, Considered (Andrew Steuart, Wilmington 1765).

[370] 9 Executive Council-N.C. 74–85.

[371] 9 *id.* 198 (recommissioned 1 Mar.1768).

[372] Letter from Atticus to Governor Tryon (7 Nov.1771), 8 Colonial Records-N.C. 718; *see* 1 Iredell Papers 247n.

[373] Maurice Moore to William Tryon (13 Mar.1770), 9 Executive Council-N.C. 232.

[374] 10 Colonial Records-N.C. 187 (1 Sept.1775); 13 State Records-N.C. 474 (through 8 Mar.1777); *North Carolina Troops in the Continental Line*, 3 N.C. Historical & Genealogical Register 415 (1900).

involved as a colonel of the militia through the end of the war,[375] being sufficiently effective in troubling the British that they despoiled his plantation in retaliation. He disdained a British offer to return Moore's property, and to cease trying to capture or kill him, if Moore simply left the militia. During the first part of 1782, Moore briefly served in the state senate,[376] where he dissented with a small minority against harsh treatment of loyalists.[377] But he later defended a confiscation law.[378]

Moore was elected as his state's attorney general, and served for nine years until resigning in 1791.[379] He was elected to the state house in 1792, but then was narrowly defeated for a seat in the United States Senate in 1795. Moore also served briefly as a federal commissioner to negotiate a treaty with Native Americans in Tennessee, accurately perceiving and lamenting the "schemes" of Yazoo land companies and other adventurers in thwarting treaties and stirring up war as part of their "avidity for the Indian lands."[380] Eventually, he became a judge of North Carolina's superior court in December 1798.

President Adams appointed him to the United States Supreme Court in December 1799, after Iredell's death.[381] Moore served until his resignation in January 1804, and died in 1810.[382]

One of North Carolina's first pair of senators described Moore as, next to Iredell, "the most respectable and respected law character" in that state.[383] Many years after Moore's death, Marshall said his recollections were "extremely favorable."[384]

Nothing is evident of Moore's views on freedoms of speech and press before he joined the Supreme Court in the midst of Sedition Act prosecutions. He only wrote one Supreme Court opinion (a seriatim opinion),[385] and apparently did not write any circuit court opinions; few of his papers have survived.

[375] 16 STATE RECORDS-N.C. 509 (through at least 13 Feb.1782).

[376] 19 *id.* 2 (15 Apr.1782).

[377] 19 *id.* 89, 90 (8 May 1782).

[378] Bayard v. Singleton, 1 Martin (N.C.) 42 (1787).

[379] 16 STATE RECORDS-N.C. 905 (elected 3 May 1782).

[380] Alfred Moore to James McHenry (30 June 1799), MCHENRY CORRESPONDENCE 445, 448, 446.

[381] Nomination (4 Dec.1799), 1 DHSC 140; Confirmation by Senate (10 Dec.1799), *id.*; Commission (10 Dec.1799), 1 *id.* 141.

[382] CARRIE L. BROUGHTON, MARRIAGE AND DEATH NOTICES FROM RALEIGH REGISTER AND NORTH CAROLINA STATE GAZETTE 140 (GPC, Baltimore 1962).

[383] Benjamin Hawkins to George Washington (4 Nov.1790), 6 WASHINGTON PAPERS-PRESIDENTIAL 620. Later, the state's chief justice lauded Moore's "profound knowledge of the criminal law." State v. Jernigan, 3 Murphey (N.C.) 12 (1799).

[384] John Marshall to Archibald D. Murphey (6 Oct.1827), 1 PAPERS OF ARCHIBALD D. MURPHEY 365 (William H. Hoyt ed., Uzzell, Raleigh 1914).

[385] Bas v. Tingy, 4 U.S. (4 Dall.) 37, 39 (1800); 2 HISTORY OF SUPREME COURT 652.

All these successor justices expressed commitment to freedoms of press and speech before 1789, and supported the Bill of Rights as it was adopted[386] (except that Moore's views at the time have not survived). Paterson and Ellsworth successfully shepherded the First Amendment through the Senate, and did not introduce destructive changes, though they showed more enthusiasm for other topics in their essays of the period. Chase expressed commitment to a bill of rights and to freedoms of press and speech, though his conduct over the years can easily be interpreted as commitment to whatever benefited himself at the time. Only Johnson had shown sufficient commitment to the Bill of Rights to depart from other federalists and support it in late 1787, and Moore later showed similar commitment as he sharply departed from the other sitting justices by not calling for, or even stating legal grounds for, prosecutions under the Sedition Act.

The absence of any mention of the Blackstone-Mansfield definition of freedoms of press and speech or framework for seditious libel in the successor justices' expressions before 1798 is striking. Those concepts only appeared in 1798 in statements by the successor justices, when four of them were rapidly converted to that definition and to most of the framework of six unique English rules for prosecuting seditious libel, soon after enactment of the Sedition Act.

[386] Justice Washington presumably supported the Bill of Rights, since his uncle President Washington did. George Washington, Inaugural Address (30 Apr. 1789), 2 WASHINGTON PAPERS-PRESIDENTIAL 173, 176; George Washington to James Madison (31 May 1789), 2 *id.* at 419.

6

The Sedition Act and the Assault on Freedoms of Press and Speech: The Sitting Supreme Court Justices and the Trials

SECTION 1. *Be it enacted* . . ., That if any persons shall unlawfully combine or conspire together, with intent to oppose any measure or measures of the government of the United States, which are or shall be directed by proper authority,. . . he or they . . . shall be punished by a fine not exceeding five thousand dollars, and by imprisonment during a term not less than six months nor exceeding five years . . . .

SEC. 2. *And be it further enacted,* That if any person shall write, print, utter or publish,. . . or shall knowingly and willingly assist or aid in writing, printing, uttering or publishing[,] any false, scandalous and malicious writing or writings against the government of the United States, or either house of the Congress of the United States, or the President of the United States, with intent to defame the said government, or either house of the said Congress, or the said President, or to bring them, or either of them, into contempt or disrepute; or to excite against them, or either or any of them, the hatred of the good people of the United States, or to stir up sedition within the United States . . . shall be punished by a fine not exceeding two thousand dollars, and by imprisonment not exceeding two years.

—Sedition Act of 1798[1]

Most of the Supreme Court justices on the bench just after passage of the Sedition Act of 1798 upheld its constitutionality, finding that the First Amendment prohibition of any law "abridging the freedom of speech, or of the press" was not violated by a law forbidding any person to "write, print, utter or publish" criticism of

[1] Sedition Act of 1798, 1 Stat.596–97 [ch.74] (expired Mar. 1801 per Act §4).

Congress, the President, or the government. Those Supreme Court justices presided over all of the federal trials, as members of circuit courts, though they did not sit as a group to rule on the Sedition Act. The circuit court trials were sufficiently notorious that one was the primary basis for impeachment of Justice Chase, and other trials brought serious consideration of impeachment of other justices.

The sitting justices at the time the Sedition Act took effect were Chief Justice Ellsworth and Justices Cushing, Iredell, Paterson, Chase, and, momentarily, Wilson. When Wilson died one month later, he was replaced by Justice Bushrod Washington. After Iredell died in 1799, he was replaced by Justice Alfred Moore. Most besides Wilson and Moore vigorously defended the Sedition Act, and Paterson, Chase, and Washington on circuit courts are recognized to have presided over trials and to have sentenced violators—and Iredell did as well. These justices' trials and opinions on the constitutionality of the Sedition Act, in light of the First Amendment, are the subject of this chapter.[2] How did they reconcile a law prohibiting criticism of the president, Congress, or government generally with a First Amendment protecting freedoms of speech and press?

Histories and legal studies are generally silent on that pivotal question. The only book-length histories of the Sedition Act (two of the three were written in the 1950s) do not discuss or evaluate each sitting justice's reasoning about how the Sedition Act could be reconciled with freedoms of press and speech; they only cursorily describe three or four of the six sitting justices on point.[3] The same is true of chapters on the Sedition Act in several legal studies and histories.[4] Articles

[2] Information about cases is based on original court records, which are identified in each section on a trial, and archives. Also cited is *Wharton's State Trials*, the best printed record for some, which was adapted and reprinted in 1885 in *Federal Cases*, which are incompletely included in Westlaw. Information about congressional debates comes in part from *Annals of Congress*, which is dually titled *Debates and Proceedings in the Congress*, the most accurate source for these years. 10 DHFFC xxiii–xxiv, xxvii. A list of abbreviated titles is at the end of this book.

[3] James M. Smith, Freedom's Fetters: the Alien and Sedition Laws and American Civil Liberties 232, 233, 234, 321–22, 326–27, 347–48, 354, 379, 381 (CorUP, Ithaca 1956) (3 justices); John C. Miller, Crisis in Freedom: The Alien and Sedition Acts 129, 218 (LB, Boston 1952) (2 justices); Charles Slack, Liberty's First Crisis: Adams, Jefferson, and the Misfits Who Saved Free Speech 130 (Atlantic Monthly Press, New York 2015) (1 justice on First Amendment).

[4] *E.g.*, Phillip L. Blumberg, Repressive Jurisprudence in the Early American Republic 144–45 (CUP, Cambridge 2010) (about four justices and First Amendment, only mentioning constitutionality "raised in only three of the cases" plus Ellsworth letter); Matthew P. Harrington, Jay and Ellsworth, The First Courts 22, 25–27, 66, 161–65 (ABC-CLIO, Santa Barbara 2008) (textbook, mentioning two justices excluded First Amendment defense in three cases); Stephen M. Feldman, Free Expression and Democracy in America 93 (UChiP, Chicago 2008) (two); Sean Wilentz, The Rise of American Democracy 80–82 (Norton,

about the justices and their cases typically do not mention the Sedition Act at all.[5] All ignore the analysis of Iredell and Cushing,[6] as well as the six remaining early justices. They do not discuss the justices' grand jury charges and unpublished language on the Sedition Act and press and speech. This chapter and the next two describe the justices' positions on the Sedition Act and First Amendment freedoms, and do so principally from hitherto uncited court records, jury charges,

---

New York 2005) (not mentioning any justices); 1 HISTORY OF SUPREME COURT 645, 646 (mentioning four justices and First Amendment, only mentioning defense raised and justices excluded those arguments); AMERICAN POLITICS 218–20; WALTER BERNS, THE FIRST AMENDMENT AND THE FUTURE OF AMERICAN DEMOCRACY 86–119 (Basic Books, New York 1976) (only 138n.); ELLSWORTH 115–17 (only two pages, not on First Amendment); THE KENTUCKY-VIRGINIA RESOLUTIONS AND MR. MADISON'S REPORT OF 1799, at i (Va. Comm'n on Const'l Gov't, Richmond 1960) (three justices); Natalie Wexler, *In the Beginning: The First Three Chief Justices*, 154 U. PA. L. REV. 1373, 1400 (2006) (only one sentence, in otherwise excellent article). One 1950s pamphlet is nonacademic. ELIZABETH LAWSON, THE REIGN OF WITCHES: THE STRUGGLE AGAINST THE ALIEN AND SEDITION LAWS, 1798–1800 (New York, Civil Rights Commission 1952). A good treatment is in GEOFFREY R. STONE, PERILOUS TIMES 33–66 (Norton, New York 2004).

[5] *E.g.*, Herbert A. Johnson, *Bushrod Washington*, 62 VAND. L. REV. 447, 457–58, 486–89 (2009); Daniel A. Degnan, *Justice William Paterson—Founder*, 16 SETON HALL L. REV. 313, 334–35 (1986); Andrew C. Laviano & Charles F. Hickox, *William Paterson: An Irishman's Influence on the American Judicial System*, 41 N. IRE. L. Q. 352, 357 (1990); Lawrence B. Custer, *Bushrod Washington and John Marshall: A Preliminary Inquiry*, 4 AM. J. LEGAL HIST. 34, 42–46 (1960); Francis R. Jones, *Oliver Ellsworth*, 13 GREEN BAG 503, 507 (1901); JUNIUS DAVIS, ALFRED MOORE AND JAMES IREDELL: REVOLUTIONARY PATRIOTS 17–18 (N.C. Society of Sons of the Revolution, Raleigh 1899) (Moore); Bushrod C. Washington, *The Late Mr. Justice Bushrod Washington*, 9 GREEN BAG 329, 330–33 (1897); John B. Uhle, *Oliver Ellsworth*, 2 CURRENT COMMENTARY 65, 74–75 (1890); Henry M. Shepard, *Oliver Ellsworth*, 2 CHICAGO LAW TIMES 109, 123–24 (1888); *Biographical Sketch of Bushrod Washington*, 5 AM. L. MAG. 249, 251–65 (1845); *Biographical Sketch of Chief Justice Ellsworth*, 3 AMERICAN LAW MAGAZINE 249, 264 (1844); JOSEPH HOPKINSON, EULOGIUM IN COMMEMORATION OF BUSHROD WASHINGTON (T. S. Manning, Philadelphia 1830).

[6] *E.g.*, WILLIS P. WHICHARD, JUSTICE JAMES IREDELL 113–15 (CAP, Durham 2000); John D. Cushing, A Revolutionary Conservative 334 (unpublished Ph.D. dissertation, Clark University 1959) (only 6 words in one footnote).

Articles about them generally do not even mention their Sedition Act role. *E.g.*, Michael G. Collins, *Justice Iredell, Choice of Law, and the Constitution—A Neglected Encounter*, 23 CONST. COMMENT. 163 (2006); William R. Casto, *James Iredell and the American Origins of Judicial Review*, 27 CONN. L. REV. 329 (1995); Charles F. Hickox & Andrew C. Laviano, *James Iredell and the English Origins of American Judicial Review*, 23 ANGLO-AMERICAN L. REV. 100, 112 (1994); Martha Dozier, *James Iredell—A Character Sketch*, 1 NORTH CAROLINA L.J. 197, 203 (1900–01); Junius Davis, *James Iredell*, 12 GREEN BAG 165, 171 (1900); DAVIS, *supra* note 5, at 31 (Iredell); W.D. Luckenback, *James Iredell*, 3 CURRENT COMMENT 129, 140–41 (1891) (despite summarizing other grand jury charges); John B. Uhle, *William Cushing*, 2 CURRENT COMMENTARY 1, 7 (1890).

manuscripts, and other primary sources.[7] These chapters also challenge ubiquitous statements about a clean party division on the Act, and pervasive assertions that the Virginia and Kentucky Resolutions failed to attract support from any other states or were opposed by most states.

This story of the storm over the First Amendment brought by the Sedition Act is a story of struggle about a narrow or a broad First Amendment. The stakes were high and the choice was fundamental. The outcome largely determined whether an opposition and political parties would be legitimate or not, at a time when that had not been resolved. The outcome also determined whether opposition newspapers and other challenges to the administration would be permissible or not, at a time when explicitly partisan newspapers were relatively new. It resolved whether the governing administration could prosecute and jail its opponents, at a time when there had not yet been a transition from one party to another. The outcome guided what the First Amendment would mean, at a time when the Supreme Court justices had not yet ruled on it. Passions ran high over the most widely hated law yet passed in America, except perhaps the tax that provoked the Whiskey Rebellion.

The Sedition Act cases and common law seditious libel cases were important in their own right. The seventeen recognized prosecutions included Benjamin Franklin's grandson who edited the leading Republican newspaper, publishers of the other leading Republican newspapers, a member of Congress whose absence narrowed voting margins while he was jailed through most of the winter (initially without heat), a member of the New York legislature whose offense was circulating petitions against the constitutionality of the Sedition Act, and journalists who suffered trials under Chase and other justices. The trials provoked Republican thought and theory about freedom of expression, and stirred the voters, along with other events, to vote out the Federalist administration of John Adams and to vote in the Republican administration of Thomas Jefferson in 1800.

The Sedition Act prosecutions were also important for forcing thought and discussion about the meaning of the First Amendment among Supreme Court justices, as well as among members of Congress and the public. As those prosecutions are summarized, the reasoning of the sitting justices about whether freedoms of press and speech permitted criminalization of publications and words is described in this chapter. The reasoning of the remaining justices is the subject of Chapter 8. While most of the sitting justices after the Sedition Act was passed changed their views to embrace the Blackstone-Mansfield definition of liberties of press and speech, none had adopted that definition beforehand (Chapters 3–4); most of the remaining justices never did.

[7] These include details of each Sedition Act prosecution, analysis of Paterson's ignored draft opinions and overlooked indictments, suggestion of Chase's craftiness in dodging an express constitutional ruling and in rejecting federal common law crimes, identification of probable sources of Washington's thought on seditious libel and freedom of press, and ironies of Iredell's position on the Act, as well as (in the next chapter) the unrecognized prosecutions under the Sedition Act.

The first half of 1798[8] saw many people, both in Congress and across the country, expecting full war with France.[9] An undeclared naval war raged and became the Quasi-War as French privateers confiscated American ships that carried on commerce with Britain.[10] President Adams in 1797 had called on Congress to take defensive measures, and the Federalist Party gained new popularity as French outrages multiplied.[11] War fever swept America as it learned in late spring 1798 that the diplomatic mission to France ended with the XYZ Affair, with French officials demanding a large bribe before negotiating.[12] In that war hysteria, many Federalists viewed sympathy with France as seditious, and saw the nascent Republican Party as not a legitimate opposition but as the Jacobin party,[13] and the small number of Republican newspapers as not legitimate sentiments but as agents of France.[14] Even those not inclined to see Republican newspapers as provocateurs chafed at the personal abuse that more and more characterized journalism.[15] Many Federalists also viewed aliens from France as enemy agents, and

[8] *See generally* Gordon S. Wood, Empire of Liberty: A History of the Early Republic, 1789–1815, at 241–67 (OUP, New York 2009); Stanley Elkins & Eric McKitrick, The Age of Federalism 549–713 (OUP, New York 1993); James R. Sharp, American Politics in the Early Republic 171–84 (YUP, New Haven 1993).

[9] Nathan Perl-Rosenthal, *Private Letters and Public Diplomacy: The Adams Network and the Quasi-War, 1797–1798*, 31 J. Early Repub. 283, 283 (2011); Jay Winik, The Great Upheaval: America and the Birth of the Modern World, 1788–1800, at 534 (Harper, New York 2007); *see* American Politics 171.

[10] Michael A. Palmer, Stoddert's War: Naval Operations During the Quasi-War with France, 1798–1801, at 4–5, 56–229 (USCP, Columbia 1987); Alexander DeConde, The Quasi-War (Scribner, New York 1966); *see* American Politics 163.

[11] James H. Broussard, The Southern Federalists, 1800–1816, at 14–15 (LSUP, Baton Rouge 1978); *see* American Politics 167.

[12] William Stinchcombe, The XYZ Affair, at 3–5, 106–21 (Greenwood Press, Westport 1980); Thomas M. Ray, *"Not One Cent for Tribute": The Public Addresses and American Popular Reaction to the XYZ Affair*, 3 J. Early Repub. 389, 390–92 (1983).

[13] Albrecht Koschnik, "Let a Common Interest Bind Us Together": Associations, Partisanship, and Culture in Philadelphia, 1775–1840, at 22–40 (UVP, Charlottesville 2007); Lance Banning, The Jeffersonian Persuasion 246–70 (CorUP, Ithaca 1978); *see* American Politics 151–52.

[14] Jeffrey L. Pasley, "The Tyranny of Printers": Newspaper Politics in the Early American Republic 105–52, 407–11 (UPV, Charlottesville 2001); Robert W. T. Martin, The Free and Open Press: The Founding of American Democratic Press Liberty, 1640–1800 (NYUP, New York 2001).

[15] *Id.* 22–23; Marcus Daniel, Scandal and Civility: Journalism and the Birth of American Democracy 19–147, 168–86, 187–274 (OUP, Oxford 2009); Joanne B. Freeman, Affairs of Honor: National Politics in the New Republic 124–26 (YUP, New Haven 2001). Despite that asperity, America idealized a polite society and polite publications. David S. Shields, Civil Tongues and Polite Letters in British America 316–19, 322–26 (UNCP, Chapel Hill 1997). The Sedition Act, besides being an effort to suppress the political opposition, was "a concerted effort to shape the way ordinary Americans discussed political matters." Seth Cotlar, *The Federalists' Transatlantic Cultural Offensive of 1798*, in Beyond the Founders: New

aliens from Ireland and other Catholic countries as potential conspirators.[16] In that crisis atmosphere, the fragile new government seemed to many to be easily toppled, and character assassination of its officials seemed to many Federalists to threaten its very foundations.[17]

Congress enacted a score of defense laws in 1798: a Provisional Army was funded, the Navy was revived and expanded, the Marine Corps was established, and harbors were fortified.[18] Congress did not stop there, though: a restrictive Naturalization Act took effect on June 18, the Alien Friends and Alien Enemies Acts were enacted on June 25 and July 6, and the Sedition Act became law on July 14, 1798.[19] We will return to the historical context, after discussing the passage of the Sedition Act and giving an overview of the prosecutions.

The Sedition Act of 1798

Figure 6.1 Sedition Act of 1798. (Courtesy of National Archives.)

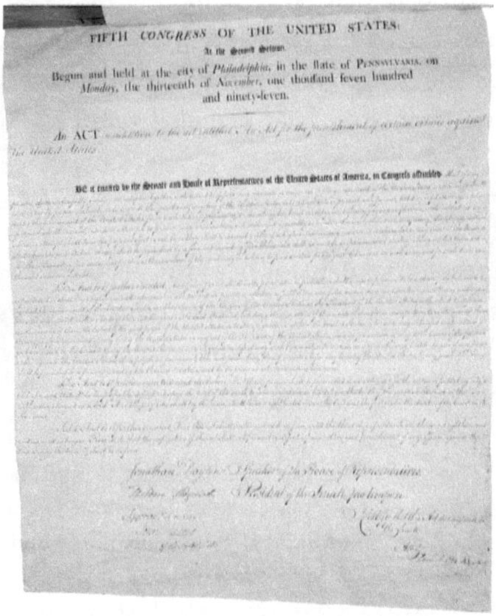
FIFTH CONGRESS OF THE UNITED STATES:

Begun and held at the city of Philadelphia, in the state of Pennsylvania, on Monday, the thirteenth of November, one thousand seven hundred and ninety-seven.

An ACT

APPROACHES TO THE POLITICAL HISTORY OF THE EARLY AMERICAN REPUBLIC 278 (Jeffrey L. Pasley et al. eds., UNCP, Chapel Hill 2004).

16 MARILYN C. BASELER, "ASYLUM FOR MANKIND": AMERICA, 1607–1800, at 270–85 (CorUP, Ithaca 1998); MICHAEL DUREY, TRANSATLANTIC RADICALS AND THE EARLY AMERICAN REPUBLIC 12–133, 221–28 (UPK, Lawrence 1997).

17 Joanne B. Freeman, *Explaining the Unexplainable: The Cultural Context of the Sedition Act*, in THE DEMOCRATIC EXPERIMENT 20, 24–31 (Meg Jacobs et al. eds., PUP, Princeton 2003); Joanne B. Freeman, *The Election of 1800*, 108 YALE L.J. 1959, 1959–60 (1999); *see* JOANNE B. FREEMAN, AFFAIRS OF HONOR: NATIONAL POLITICS IN THE NEW REPUBLIC xvii–xviii (YUP, New Haven 2001).

18 Robert Gough, *Officering the American Army, 1798*, 43 WM. & MARY Q. (3d ser.) 460 (1986); FREDERICK C. LEINER, MILLIONS FOR DEFENSE: THE SUBSCRIPTION WARSHIPS OF 1798, at 20–27, 177–83 (Naval Inst. Press, Annapolis 2000); *see* AMERICAN POLITICS 180–82.

19 EMPIRE 249, 259–60; AMERICAN POLITICS 176–77.

The Sedition Act of 1798 (Figure 6.1), along with the Alien Acts, was enacted when Quasi-War hysteria accompanied possible full war and when Federalists and Republicans were profoundly polarized. When the Sedition Act was signed by President Adams on July 14, 1798, Secretary of State Timothy Pickering wrote of "the impending war with France," and an ailing George Washington was planning to command the Army and was commissioning generals.[20] To the real imminence of war,[21] many Federalists added conspiratorial fears of nefarious Jacobins[22] and of, in their parlance, the Jacobin party.[23] Harper, a House sponsor of the Sedition Act, warned that "there existed a domestic . . . conspiracy, a faction leagued with a foreign power, to effect a revolution or a subjugation of this country, by the arms of that foreign power," which necessitated not only alien legislation but "laws against seditious practices."[24] Hamilton identified the threat as "a decided *French faction*," the Republicans.[25] Though there was an apparent shortage of visible Jacobins, Ames, just leaving his House seat, attributed that to their resting "in their lurking-places, . . . like serpents in winter, the better to concoct their venom."[26] Republicans had their own fears, of creeping tyranny by, as they called them, the Tories and the British party,[27] led by "the quer[u]lous and cankered murmurs of *blind, bald, crippled, toothless* Adams"![28]

Debates over Freedoms of Press and Speech

Congressional debates over the proposed Sedition Act, while raising many issues dividing Federalists and Republicans, focused on whether it violated freedoms of press and speech.[29] As soon as the motion was made to read the bill, a countermotion was made to read the Bill of Rights.[30]

[20] Timothy Pickering to Alexander Hamilton (16 July 1798), 22 HAMILTON PAPERS 22; George Washington to Alexander Hamilton (14 July 1798), 22 *id.* 17, 18, 19; which continued through 1800, John Adams to John Marshall (4 Sept. 1800), 9 ADAMS WORKS 80, 81.

[21] EMPIRE 247, 239–75; MCHENRY CORRESPONDENCE 439–40; 2 ADAMS WRITINGS 360, 362.

[22] *E.g.*, FISHER AMES, WORKS OF FISHER AMES 94, 101 (Wait, Boston 1809); Stephen Higginson to Timothy Pickering (9 June 1798), 1 HIGGINSON LETTERS 806, 808.

[23] *E.g.*, John Adams to John Trumbull (10 Sept. 1800), 9 ADAMS WORKS 83; 1 AMES WORKS 257, 250, 262; 1 HIGGINSON LETTERS 814.

[24] 8 ANNALS 2024, 2025 (21 June 1798); 8 *id.* 2165, 2166.

[25] 5 HAMILTON WORKS 460; *accord* 1 AMES WORKS 250, 262.

[26] Fisher Ames, *Laocoon No. I*, 2 AMES WORKS 109, 113.

[27] *E.g.*, [WILLIAM DUANE], COPY OF AN INDICTMENT 2 ([Duane, Philadelphia 1799]); James Monroe to Thomas Jefferson (4 Jan. 1800), 3 MONROE WRITINGS 169, 170; JACOBIN 119.

[28] *For the Mercury*, MASSACHUSETTS MERCURY (Boston), 8 May 1798, at 2 (quoting *Aurora*); *accord Extract of a Letter*, INDEPENDENT CHRONICLE (Boston), 7 May 1798, at 2.

[29] 3 JEFFERSON 386; *accord* DAVID P. CURRIE, THE CONSTITUTION IN CONGRESS: THE FIRST CONGRESS, 1789–1801, at 260–62, 263–68 (UChiP, Chicago 1994); AMERICAN POLITICS 177–80; CHESAPEAKE POLITICS 532.

[30] 8 ANNALS 2093, 2133.

Supporters of the bill found no abridgment of the First Amendment because that Amendment did not "guarantee, as a sacred principle, the liberty of lying against the Government,"[31] or the liberty to "offend against the laws,"[32] or the liberty of making "false and groundless charges" against magistrates;[33] nor did that Amendment "give the right of . . . exciting sedition, insurrection, and slaughter."[34] Instead, some proponents claimed that the First Amendment meant only what the English common law allowed: "the liberty of the press is merely an exemption from all previous restraints" as described in Blackstone.[35] The bill only criminalized false statements and things already forbidden by common law,[36] and it provided the defense of truth and the protection of a jury's general verdict.[37] Other proponents warned that seditious libel could dissolve loyalty to government,[38] and could bring "revolution and Jacobinic domination" by the "Jacobins of our country"[39] and the party supporting them.[40] Surely government had the right of self-preservation and self-defense,[41] which included proscribing "all means calculated to produce these effects, whether by speaking, writing, or printing,"[42] and included "restrain[ing] abuses of the press" and "licentiousness of the press."[43]

Opponents rejoined that the First Amendment forbade the government "to touch the press,"[44] and "prohibited [government] from adding any restraint, either by previous restrictions, or by subsequent punishment."[45] The bill "abridg[ed] freedom of speech and of the press" by deterring expression "the least offensive to a power which might so greatly harass them" by prosecution,[46] restraining all opinion that "certain measures of government" were unwise or unconstitutional.[47] It struck at "the root of free republican government" by restricting "speaking and writing" necessary to an informed citizenry.[48] Truth could vanquish error, and

[31] 8 *id.* 2112; *accord* 8 *id.* 2097, 2156.

[32] 8 *id.* 2102; *accord* 8 *id.* 2112.

[33] 8 *id.* 2150.

[34] 8 *id.* 2097; *accord* 8 *id.* 2102, 2100, 2101.

[35] 8 *id.* 2148; *accord* 8 *id.* 2149, 2167–68, 2146.

[36] 8 *id.* 2112, 2113, 2141, 2147, 2150.

[37] 8 *id.* 2150, 2149, 2168.

[38] 8 *id.* 2098; *accord* 8 *id.* 2099.

[39] 8 *id.* 2098; *accord* 8 *id.* 2100.

[40] 8 *id.* 2100; *accord* 8 *id.* 2024.

[41] 8 *id.* 2101, 2146, 2167.

[42] 8 *id.* 2146.

[43] 8 *id.* 2112, 2149. *See* Martti J. Rudanko, The Forging of Freedom of Speech 59–130 (UPA, Lanham 2003).

[44] 8 *id.* 2140; *accord* 8 *id.* 2142, 2152, 2160.

[45] 8 *id.* 2160.

[46] 8 *id.* 2140–41; *accord* 8 *id.* 2104, 2105, 2106–07, 2142, 2151, 2153, 2156.

[47] 8 *id.* 2110, 2143, 2144, 2145.

[48] 8 *id.* 2104; *accord* 8 *id.* 2110, 2140, 2144.

newspapers allowed that battle to occur by publishing "on both sides,"[49] though the Federalist majority of newspapers believed government "can do no wrong" and "reject[ed] everything which does not approve of governmental measures."[50] Various opponents also warned that the bill's defense of truth was chimerical, because "how could the truth of opinions be proven by evidence?"[51] and "what writings, what opinions, could escape the severity of the intended law?"[52] They warned that jury general verdicts provided little protection when "juries [were] selected by the marshal" and "judges [were] appointed by the President."[53] Some Republicans disputed whether seditious libel was still a crime, saying the Act "creat[ed] crimes which were never before thought of in this country,"[54] or at least that "the doctrine of libels was very unsettled in this country" and that prosecution "very rarely happened."[55] They disagreed that there was "any such thing as a common law of the United States" giving *federal* courts jurisdiction over libel,[56] whether or not *states* could prosecute seditious libel.[57] Ultimately there was no meaningful line between allowing liberty and forbidding licentiousness, as the shibboleth went, or between restricting the press and utterly censoring newspapers and books.[58]

Enactment of the Sedition Act

The Act was approved by an overwhelming margin of 18–6 in the Senate, but by a close vote of 44–41 in the House.[59] The emerging political parties[60] divided in the vote, though the frequent statement that, besides John Marshall, "[e]very other Federalist who is on record favored the passage of the law," and all Republicans

[49] 8 *id.* 2105, 2106; *accord* 8 *id.* 2109, 2145, 2154, 2164.

[50] 8 *id.* 2143, 2150.

[51] 8 *id.* 2162; *accord* 8 *id.* 2109, 2113, 2141, 2144, 2154.

[52] 8 *id.* 2108; *accord* 8 *id.* 2109, 2113, 2141.

[53] 8 *id.* 2140; *accord* 8 *id.* 2153, 2162, 2163; TRUTH ii.

[54] 8 *id.* 2133; *accord* 8 *id.* 2154, 2164.

[55] 8 *id.* 2135.

[56] 8 *id.* 2137; *accord* 8 *id.* 2113, 2141, 2151, 2156–57.

[57] 8 *id.* 2151, 2152, 2153.

[58] 8 *id.* 2105, 2140, 2141, 2142.

[59] 7 *id.* 599 (4 July 1798), 8 *id.* 2171 (10 July 1798).

[60] Sharp contended that they only formed from protoparties to parties after the deterioration of elite concurrence, and deep division of the political elite during 1792–98, and the "crisis of the union" during 1798–1801, JAMES R. SHARP, AMERICAN POLITICS IN THE EARLY REPUBLIC 50, 187–275 (YUP, New Haven 1993); though Siemers said they emerged in the Third, Fourth, or Fifth Congress, DAVID J. SIEMERS, RATIFYING THE REPUBLIC 138–40, 144, 151, 156–60 (SUP, Palo Alto 2002).

opposed it,[61] is belied by some Federalist opponents and a few Republican supporters inside Congress,[62] as well as outside Congress.[63] Moreover, a steady stream of congressional Federalists became Republicans,[64] some of whom were among the opposing votes.[65]

The Act's central provisions, quoted at the beginning of this chapter, expressly targeted press and speech ("writing, printing, uttering or publishing"), and enacted into statute the common law crime of seditious libel ("with intent to defame" Government, Congress, or the President; "to bring them . . . into contempt or disrepute; or to excite against them . . . the hatred of the good people of the United States"), with two modifications. Those modifications were the *Zenger* ameliorations of that common law crime (though rejected by that court, a truth defense and a jury general verdict). However, those were small comforts to people having to defend themselves against the might of Federalist prosecutors and Federalist judges. Far reaching as the final Sedition Act was, earlier versions went further, in following Blackstone without those ameliorations, declaring France an enemy, imposing capital punishment on giving it aid and comfort, and criminalizing any "unlawful assembly."[66]

The targeting of critical press and speech was for political gain, and not primarily for perceived war necessities, as several features showed.[67] The Act did not

[61] *E.g.*, FREEDOM'S FETTERS 151–52; other examples are given in Chapter 8 at nn.24–31. One article indirectly contradicted the quoted statement, John D. Stevens, *Congressional History of the 1798 Sedition Law*, 43 JOURNALISM Q. 247, 248, 252, 253, 254 (1966); and was noted only by one scholar, PRINTERS 59, who wrote that the "contest over the passage and continuation of the Sedition Act" was waged "almost" exclusively along party lines. *See also* CHESAPEAKE POLITICS 532 ("[t]wo Federalists broke ranks" in the first vote). I appreciate Professor Jeffery Smith bringing Stevens's article to my attention, after this chapter was written.

[62] In the Senate, Federalist John Howard opposed the Act, and Republicans James Lloyd and Alexander Martin supported it. 7 ANNALS 599; ORIGINS-PARTIES 217–18. In the House, Federalists William Matthews, and Stephen Bullock voted against, along with in-transition Abraham Baldwin and George Dent. 8 ANNALS 2171 (votes); ORIGINS-PARTIES 207–09 (party affiliations, summarizing five sources). Republican Thomas Tillinghast voted for. 8 ANNALS 2171; ORIGINS-PARTIES 208.

[63] Federalist opponents are described at the beginning of Chapter 8. Republican supporters included the party's Massachusetts leader, [JAMES SULLIVAN], A DISSERTATION UPON THE CONSTITUTIONAL FREEDOM OF THE PRESS IN THE UNITED STATES OF AMERICA (David Carlisle, Boston 1801), and future Massachusetts Governor Elbridge Gerry, PRESS-MASS. 153–54. Pennsylvania Chief Justice Thomas McKean supported seditious libel prosecution, Trial of William Cobbett, Wharton's State Trials 322, 322–25 (Pa.S.Ct. 1797), but not the Act.

[64] John Jay to Peter A. Jay (17 May 1798), JAY PAPERS doc.90220; DAVID J. SIEMERS, RATIFYING THE REPUBLIC 142 (SUP, Palo Alto 2002).

[65] In-transition, Abraham Baldwin, George Dent, Joseph Hiester, John Trigg, and Abraham Venable voted against, as did others in subsequent votes. 8 ANNALS 2171; ORIGINS-PARTIES 207–09; CHESAPEAKE POLITICS 532. Others are described at the beginning of Chapter 8.

[66] CRISIS 67; SECURING 181; *see* 8 ANNALS 2115–16, 2134. Drafts are in ADAMS FEDERALISTS 343–48.

[67] ANDERSON 520; *accord* 8 ANNALS 2162; FREEDOM'S FETTERS 252 (Thomas Adams); EMPIRE 259.

prohibit libel of the vice president, a Republican, though it did interdict libel of the president, a Federalist. Systematic enforcement did not begin immediately, but instead the year before the federal elections of 1800, with trials scheduled for that election year. Finally, enforcement was against leading Republican newspaper editors—most of them—along with a few Republican politicians, but no federal action was brought against equally scurrilous Federalist editors[68] or officeholders.[69] The Act's expiration date is also sometimes described as partisan,[70] because it was not the end of hostilities but the end of Adams's term; however that date was proposed by an opponent.[71] Jefferson, on hearing that a sedition bill would be proposed, immediately perceived that its "object . . . is the suppression of the whig presses."[72] A Federalist sponsor of the Sedition Act, Allen, publicly admitted that charge: "it is our business to wrest" the engine of the press from the "Jacobins."[73] The Republican newspapers condemned the Act as violative of freedoms of press and speech,[74] christening its supporters as the "Tories."[75]

The Federalist supporters were fighting a rising tide of newspapers, as the total newspapers of all political stripes more than doubled from seventy-nine at the beginning of 1790 to 174 at the end of 1799.[76] They did slow that rise, as newspapers only rose from 172 at the end of 1797 to 174 two years later, but those totals mask the flood of over forty-four new Republican newspapers in those two years.[77] The Federalists' appearance of fighting the Constitution itself, and launching partisan attacks on those holding different opinions, helped turn the elections of 1800 in favor of Republicans and helped destroy the Federalist Party in the process.

America was not quite unique. Great Britain also launched a record number of prosecutions of sedition and treason in the 1790s,[78] and enacted its own Treasonable and Seditious Practices Act and Seditious Meetings and Assemblies Act in 1795.[79] However, scant comfort came to America from that precedent, because it emulated the king whose tyranny had been denounced and fought so recently.[80]

[68] 8 ANNALS 2107; FREEDOM'S FETTERS 14, 15, 25–26, 178–79.

[69] 8 *id.* 2110; FREEDOM'S FETTERS 15, 24, 102, 104; CRISIS 131–33.

[70] *E.g.*, OPEN PRESS 132; FREEDOM'S FETTERS 130.

[71] 8 ANNALS 2138, 2171.

[72] Thomas Jefferson to James Madison (26 Apr. 1798), 30 JEFFERSON PAPERS 299, 300.

[73] 8 ANNALS 2098.

[74] *E.g.*, TRUTH i; [No Caption], TIME PIECE (New York), 20 July 1798, at 3 (quoting *Aurora*).

[75] *E.g.*, *Talleyrand[']s Letter*, AURORA (Philadelphia 21 June 1798), reprinted in TRUTH 2, 6; *From the N. York-Gazette*, AURORA (Philadelphia), 23 June 1798, reprinted in TRUTH 6, 8; *The Plot Unravelled*, GREENLEAF'S NEW YORK JOURNAL, 27 June 1798, at 2.

[76] CHRONOLOGICAL TABLES 22–43.

[77] TYRANNY 408–09; CRISIS 221.

[78] CRESSY-DANGEROUS 244–51; HARLING 109.

[79] 36 Geo 3 c7 & c8.

[80] *E.g.*, *Mr. Editor*, TIME PIECE (New York), 28 Aug. 1798, at 3; FREEDOM'S FETTERS 67; and lifting core wording from the British acts, ADAMS FEDERALISTS 157–58.

The Sedition Act Prosecutions

There were at least fifteen documented federal cases, prosecuting seventeen individuals for seditious libel, whose story was told by Smith and by Miller.[81] Their accounts, based on period newspapers, will be supplemented here with prosecution and trial records[82] that Smith barely used and Miller virtually ignored,[83] grand jury charges that as nonlawyers they rarely noted, and cautious use of additional newspaper accounts that they did not cite.[84] Their accounts told little about the reasoning of the sitting Supreme Court justices about the constitutionality of the Sedition Act and about those seditious libel prosecutions. That is a story that has been overlooked,[85] except in small part in Smith and Miller and various articles,[86] and in smaller part in the justices' leading biographies,[87] when not

[81] James M. Smith, Freedom's Fetters: The Alien and Sedition Laws and American Civil Liberties (CorUP, Ithaca 1956); John C. Miller, Crisis in Freedom: The Alien and Sedition Acts (Little, Brown, Boston 1952). *Freedom's Fetters* incorporated prior essays, which are not cited. These discuss fourteen prosecutions under the Sedition Act and three under common law.

[82] Court records are cited at the beginning of each case discussion, as are any records in Wharton's State Trials and any additional newspaper accounts.

[83] Both rely primarily on newspaper accounts; Wharton was only cited by Miller incidentally, only on the Cooper case, Crisis 207–08; *accord* Frank M. Anderson, *The Enforcement of the Alien and Sedition Acts*, 18 Am. Historical Rev. 113 (1912).

[84] Period newspapers must be and are used with care, because most had strong editorial bias and reprinted undocumented articles, but they are often the best available evidence of details. 2 DHRC 37; Julius Goebel, *Book Review*, 105 U. Pa. L. Rev. 1027, 1029 (1957).

[85] *E.g.*, discussions of the Act and prosecutions without justices' reasoning on constitutionality, in 1 History of Supreme Court 633–51; Susan Dunn, Jefferson's Second Revolution 101–20 (Houghton Mifflin, Boston 2004); David Jenkins, *The Sedition Act of 1798 and the Incorporation of Seditious Libel into First Amendment Jurisprudence*, 45 Am. J. Legal Hist. 154, 164–83, 188–97 (2001); Mark A. Smith, Crisis, Unity, and Partisanship: The Road to the Sedition Act 310–63 (1998) (unpublished Ph.D. dissertation, University of Virginia); Norman L. Rosenberg, Protecting the Best Men: an Interpretive History of the Law of Libel 79–100 (UNCP, Chapel Hill 1986); Daniel N. Hoffman, *Contempt of the United States*, 25 Am. J. Legal Hist. 343, 353–60 (1981); Walter Berns, *Freedom of the Press and the Alien and Sedition Laws: A Reappraisal*, 1970 S. Ct. Rev. 109, 111–35; William L. Richter, Federalism and Civil Liberties: A Reappraisal of the Alien and Sedition Act Controversy of 1798, at 37–82 (1963) (unpublished M.A. thesis, University of Chicago); Thomas F. Carroll, *Freedom of Speech and of the Press in the Federalist Period: The Sedition Act*, 18 Mich. L. Rev. 615, 627–48 (1920).

[86] E.g., David J. Katz, *Grand Jury Charges Delivered by Supreme Court Justices Riding Circuit During the 1790s*, 14 Cardozo L. Rev. 1045, 1079–81 (1993); Jay 1084.

[87] *E.g.*, Willis P. Whichard, Justice James Iredell 113 (CAP, Durham 2000) (half-page); Rutledge 259–78; Wilson 30–31; James Haw et al., Stormy Patriot: The Life of Samuel Chase 194–99, 202–07 (MHS, Baltimore 1980) (in brief Sedition Act discussion, no mention of First Amendment or press-speech); John E. O'Connor, William Paterson: Lawyer and Statesman, 1745–1806, at 245–49 (RUP, Rutgers 1979) (same); David L. Annis, Mr. Bushrod Washington 88–94 (1974) (unpublished Ph.D. dissertation, Notre Dame University) (same); Nettie S. Herndon, James Iredell 291 (1944) (unpublished Ph.D. dissertation, Duke University) (5 sentences, same); John Jay 416–18; Johnson 492–510 (same).

whitewashed.[88] That reasoning about the First Amendment is the focus of this chapter, along with giving an updated full account of the recognized seventeen prosecutions.

Summary of Recognized Federal Prosecutions for Seditious Libel

Those documented federal cases, prosecuting seventeen individuals (fourteen individuals under the Sedition Act and three under common law),[89] and the justices involved, are summarized in Table 6.1. The first two federal cases (involving three defendants) were for common law seditious libel, and did not reach trial. The remaining ones were prosecutions under the Sedition Act, of which eleven cases (twelve defendants) reached trial or a guilty plea. There were also state seditious libel prosecutions, such as the other prosecutions mentioned here of Thomas Adams, William Duane, and David Frothingham.

Even before the Sedition Act, the Adams administration girded its loins for war against critics. Pickering itched to use seditious libel against them, having been personally goaded in January 1798 by allegations of his "shameful breach of the laws" by charging to issue a passport.[90] In the preceding year he had personally authorized and supported a seditious libel prosecution against an editor for criticism of the Spanish minister and of the minister's letter to Pickering.[91] From that 1797 prosecution, Pickering had in hand an opinion from the attorney general that the federal government could prosecute seditious libel under the Blackstone-Mansfield definition

[88] *E.g.*, John D. Cushing, A Revolutionary Conservative: The Public Life of William Cushing, 1732–1810, at 334, 328 (1959) (unpublished Ph.D. dissertation, Clark University) (only 6 word mention of Act; "there is nothing to indicate what, if anything, Cushing contributed . . . as a circuit judge," and "little of significance" in Supreme Court sessions); MICHAEL C. TOTH, FOUNDING FEDERALIST: THE LIFE OF OLIVER ELLSWORTH 193, 190–94 (ISI Books, Wilmington 2011) (characterizing "Ellsworth's measured pronouncements" as a moderate approach); WILLIAM G. BROWN, THE LIFE OF OLIVER ELLSWORTH 265–66 (Macmillan, New York 1905) (denying supported constitutionality); Leonard B. Rosenberg, *William Paterson: New Jersey's Nation-Maker*, 85 N. J. HISTORY 7, 32 (1967) ("never challenged the constitutionality"); W.D. Luckenback, *John Blair*, 3 CURRENT COMMENTARY 65, 75 (1891) (ignoring the Cabell incident, states that Blair's "retirement to private life was so complete that nothing broke that seclusion until his death").

[89] FREEDOM'S FETTERS 185 (14 indictments under Act, 3 under common law, counting James Smith and Brown Clark as separate ones); JOHN C. MILLER, THE FEDERALIST ERA, 1789–1801, at 235 (Harper, New York 1960) (15); 1 HISTORY OF SUPREME COURT 637, 638 n.107 (unspecified 15); *see* 3 DHSC 233 (unspecified 15); AMERICAN POLITICS 218–20 (similar list); *New London, (Bee) Oct.1*, ALEXANDRIA TIMES, 13 Oct.1800, at 2 (listing 7 and Spooner).

[90] Timothy Pickering to John Clarke (26 Jan.1798), PICKERING PAPERS, r.37, fol.265.

[91] Timothy Pickering to William Rawle (29 July 1797), *id.* r.6, fol.480; 3 CHARLES W. UPHAM, THE LIFE OF TIMOTHY PICKERING 309–10, 397–400 (Little Brown, Boston 1873).

Table 6.1 **Sedition Act Cases (The Recognized Half)**

Defendant– **Under Common Law**	*Circuit Court Date and Location*	*Supreme Court Justice Involved*
1 Benjamin Franklin Bache of Philadelphia *Aurora*	Arrested 26 June 1798 (Dismissed after death 10 Sept. 1798) Philadelphia, Pennsylvania	(No Justice Involved) Discussed at page 263
2 John Daly Burk and James Smith of New York *Time Piece*	Arrested 6 July 1798 Smith plea not guilty 5 Sept. 1799 New York, New York	(No Justice Involved) Justice William Paterson Discussed at page 264
Under the Sedition Act		
3 Rep. Matthew Lyon of *The Scourge of Aristocracy* Fair Haven, Vermont	Indicted 5 Oct. 1798 Trial 8 Oct.1798 Rutland, Vermont	Justice William Paterson " Discussed at page 272
4 Thomas Adams of Boston *Independent Chronicle*	Indicted 20 Oct.1798 (Dismissed after death in May 1799) Boston, Massachusetts	Justice William Paterson Discussed at page 276
5 Benjamin Fairbanks Dedham, Massachusetts	Pleaded guilty 7 June 1799 Dedham, Massachusetts	Justice Samuel Chase Discussed at page 287
6 David Brown Originally Bethlehem, Connecticut	Presented 1 June 1799 Pleaded guilty 8 June 1799 Dedham, Massachusetts	Justice Samuel Chase " Discussed at page 288
7 William Duane of Philadelphia *Aurora*	Indicted 4 Aug.1799, 15 Oct. 1799 (two on British infl.), 14 Apr. 1800 (British secret service), 18 Oct. 1800 (Ross bill) Philadelphia, Pennsylvania	 Justice Bushrod Washington Justice Samuel Chase Justice William Paterson Discussed at page 277
8 Ann Greenleaf of New York *Argus*	Indicted Sept.1799 (Suspended without trial Apr.1800) New York, New York	Justice William Paterson Discussed at page 280
9 Rep. Jedidiah Peck Otsego County, New York	Indicted Sept.1799 (Suspended without trial Apr.1800) New York, New York	Justice William Paterson Discussed at page 282
10 Luther Baldwin and Brown Clark Newark, New Jersey	Indicted 3 Oct. 1798 Plea of not guilty 2 Apr. 1799 Trial and guilty plea 3 Oct. 1799 Trenton, New Jersey	Justice William Cushing Justice James Iredell Justice Bushrod Washington Discussed at page 305
11 William Durrell of *Mount Pleasant Register*	Indicted 1–3 Sept. 1798 Trial 3 Apr.1800 New York, New York	Justice William Paterson Justice Bushrod Washington Discussed at page 306
12 Thomas Cooper of Northumberland *Gazette*	Indicted 14 Apr. 1800 Trial 19 Apr.1800 Philadelphia, Pennsylvania	Justice Samuel Chase " Discussed at page 290
13 Charles Holt of New London *Bee*	Indicted 17 Sept. 1799 Trial 14 Apr.1800 New Haven, Connecticut	Chief Justice Oliver Ellsworth Justice Bushrod Washington Discussed at page 308
14 Anthony Haswell of *Vermont Gazette* Bennington, Vermont	Indicted 7 Oct. 1799 Trial 5 May 1800 Windsor, Vermont	Justice William Cushing Justice William Paterson Discussed at page 283
15 James T. Callender of *The Prospect Before Us* Richmond, Virginia (after move)	Presented 24 May 1800 Trial 3 June 1800 Richmond, Virginia	Justice Samuel Chase " Discussed at page 293

and framework under the English common law,[92] which soon after passage of the Sedition Act was supplemented by the attorney general's pamphlet defense, again following the *Commentaries*.[93] Supreme Court Justice Iredell supported the cause, as Jefferson saw it, by charging "the grand juries to become inquisitors on the freedom of speech, of writing and of principle of their fellow citizens."[94]

Figure 6.2 Secretary of State Timothy Pickering. Engraving by T. B. Welsh after Gilbert Stuart. (Courtesy of Library of Congress.)

Even while the Act was under debate in Congress, Secretary of State Timothy Pickering (Figure 6.2), whose responsibilities included directing federal prosecutors,[95] had them indict three editors of leading Republican papers under the common law of seditious libel. After the Act passed, Pickering caused two more prosecutions to be filed immediately, against the leading Republican paper in New England and against a Republican member of Congress, and then five additional prosecutions, of less notable speakers.[96] Pickering's full-scale assault on

[92] Charles Lee, Libellous Publications (27 July 1797), in 1 OFFICIAL OPINIONS OF THE ATTORNEYS GENERAL OF THE UNITED STATES 71, 72 (Benjamin F. Hall et al. eds., GPO, Washington 1852–1919) (on libeling King of Spain); *accord* 1 *id.* 52 (from Thomas Greenleaf prosecution, JAY 1075 n.351).

[93] VIRGINIENSIS [CHARLES LEE], DEFENCE OF THE ALIEN AND SEDITION LAWS 23–31, 25–26 (John Fenno, Philadelphia 1798).

[94] Thomas Jefferson to Peregrine Fitzhugh (4 June 1797), 29 JEFFERSON PAPERS 415, 417; *e.g.*, James Iredell's Charge (C.C.D. Md. 8 May 1797), 3 DHSC 173, 174, 175, 177; William Paterson's Charge (n.d.), 3 *id.* 462, 463.

[95] 1 HISTORY OF SUPREME COURT 633 n.89.

[96] For example, he quickly urged the United States Attorney for Pennsylvania to initiate prosecutions, and promised prompt payment of expenses. Timothy Pickering to William Rawle (28 Aug.1798), PICKERING PAPERS r.37, fol.326. Pickering's other efforts to prosecute Sedition Act violators are described in the next chapter.

Republicans, however, was held back until a half year before elections in 1800 (which occurred from spring onward),[97] when he pressed federal attorneys to prosecute editors of most other leading Republican newspapers,[98] knowing that the cases would reach trial in the first half of 1800 and would best thwart the "Jacobins."[99] As Adams described it two years later, newspaper editors "Callender, Duane, Cooper, and Lyon" were "the most influential men in the country, all foreigners and all degraded characters,"[100] who he agreed should be prosecuted. All had been. Jefferson had a parallel perspective of what was going on: "this onset on the presses is to cripple & suppress the republican efforts during the campaign which is coming on."[101]

Common Law Prosecutions of Bache of the Aurora and Burk of the Time Piece

The first federal prosecution, of Benjamin Franklin Bache,[102] the editor of the Philadelphia *Aurora* (the leading Republican paper[103]) and the namesake of his famous grandfather, began with his arrest for "libelling the President, & the Executive Government in a manner tending to excite sedition,"[104] on June 26, 1798, three weeks before the Sedition Act became law. The alleged libels were Bache's criticisms of those officials, after they made false accusations about him and opened his mail. Bache had printed a letter from French minister Talleyrand to the federal government before the president or Congress knew of it. The administration

97 SECURING 235; FREEDOM'S FETTERS 186.

98 Timothy Pickering to William Rawle (24 July 1799), PICKERING PAPERS r.11, fol.486 (Duane—*Aurora*); Timothy Pickering to John Adams (1 Aug.1799), 9 ADAMS WORKS 5 (Cooper—*Northumberland Gazette*); Timothy Pickering to Charles Hall (1 Aug.1799), PICKERING PAPERS r.11, fol.528 (same); Timothy Pickering to Richard Harison (12 Aug.1799), *id.* r.11, fol.599 (Greenleaf—*Argus*); Timothy Pickering to Thomas Nelson (14 Aug.1799), *id.* r.11, fol.611 (Callender—*Richmond Examiner*).

99 Though the straw that broke the camel's back may have been the *Aurora*'s publication of diplomatic correspondence in July 1799. Kim T. Phillips, William Duane: Revolutionary Editor 77–80 (1968) (unpublished Ph.D. dissertation, University of California-Berkeley).

100 John Adams to Christopher Gadsden (16 Apr.1801), 9 ADAMS WORKS 584; *accord* 9 *id.* 582.

101 Thomas Jefferson to John W. Eppes (21 Apr.1800), 31 JEFFERSON PAPERS 531.

102 *See generally* FREEDOM'S FETTERS 188–204; CRISIS 65–66, 93–97; 1 DAB 462; PRINTERS 156–61; JEFFERY A. SMITH, FRANKLIN AND BACHE 162–63 (OUP, Oxford 1990). Court records for this case do not appear to have survived in U.S. Circuit Court or U.S. District Court records for the Eastern District of Pennsylvania. E-mail from Patrick Connelly (National Archives at Philadelphia) to author (17 June 2015).

103 FREEDOM'S FETTERS 189, 278.

104 JAMES TAGG, BENJAMIN FRANKLIN BACHE AND THE PHILADELPHIA *AURORA* 387 (UPP, Philadelphia 1991); Robert Troup to Rufus King (10 July 1798), 2 KING CORRESPONDENCE 362, 364; *From Saturday's Aurora*, GREENLEAF'S NEW YORK JOURNAL, 7 July 1798, at 2.

investigated allegations that "the French Printer" was a treasonous "agent of the French Directory."[105] The investigation found a letter to Bache from the French Office of Foreign Affairs, which Pickering and Wolcott intercepted and opened only to find innocuous pamphlets.[106] After his arrest, Bache was required to provide security in the princely sum of $4,000, half from himself and half from sureties,[107] and his trial was set for October 1798, when Justice Cushing would be presiding over the federal circuit court in Philadelphia.[108] Believing the best defense to be a strong offense, Bache began printing articles denouncing the Sedition Act as an abridgment of the First Amendment and of the natural rights "to speak or to publish."[109] His death in early September during Philadelphia's epidemic of yellow fever stopped his counterattack, and also ended the prosecution and his quest for review by the full Supreme Court.[110] To the dismay of the Adams administration, Bache's widow arranged for the *Aurora* to continue, with William Duane at its helm.

The other early common law prosecution, of John Daly Burk,[111] editor of the New York *Time Piece* (the fastest growing Republican paper[112]), was launched ten days after Bache's arrest.[113] The *Time Piece* trebly became a federal target, by Philip Freneau having edited it after leaving the *National Gazette*, by Burk fleeing arrest in Ireland for sedition and defending the United Irish once here,[114] and by his being subject to the Alien Act. Pickering instructed the federal attorney to review the *Time Piece*, and though he believed "no man is a fitter object for the operation of the alien act," Pickering decided instead to "punish him for his libels," which he

[105] [BENJAMIN F. BACHE], TRUTH WILL OUT! 1 ([Bache, Philadelphia 1798]) (reprinting *Aurora* articles); *accord* Thomas Jefferson to James Madison (21 June 1798), 30 JEFFERSON PAPERS 416, 417, 419n.

[106] *The Plot Unravelled*, AURORA (Philadelphia), 25 June 1798, reprinted in TRUTH 8, 9; Stephen Higginson to Timothy Pickering (26 June 1798), 1 HIGGINSON LETTERS 813, 814.

[107] *From Saturday's Aurora*, GREENLEAF'S NEW YORK JOURNAL, 7 July 1798, at 2.

[108] 3 DHSC 299 n.1, though some mistakenly expected Paterson. Robert Troup to Rufus King (10 July 1798), 2 KING CORRESPONDENCE 362, 364.

[109] FREEDOM'S FETTERS 203; *accord* PRINTERS 160–61.

[110] United States v. Bache, 1 DHSC 521–22 (8 Aug.1798) (dismissing request for Supreme Court writ of prohibition).

[111] *See generally* FREEDOM'S FETTERS 204–20; CRISIS 97–102; 3 DAB 279; EDWARD A. WYATT, JOHN DALY BURK: PATRIOT-PLAYWRIGHT-HISTORIAN (Historical Publishing, Charlottesville 1936); Joseph I. Shulim, *John Daly Burk: Irish Revolutionist and American Patriot*, 54 TRANS. OF AM. PHILOSOPHICAL SOC. 1 (1964). Court records are in Minutes (1790–1914), U.S. Circuit Court for the District of New York (National Archives at New York City, R.G. 21.34.7).

[112] FREEDOM'S FETTERS 188, 207.

[113] Robert Troup to Rufus King (10 July 1798), 2 KING CORRESPONDENCE 362, 364.

[114] [Masthead], TIME PIECE (New York), 9 Mar.1798, at 1; Robert Troup to Rufus King (10 July 1798), 2 KING CORRESPONDENCE 362, 364; JOHN BURK, HISTORY OF THE LATE WAR IN IRELAND iii–iv, 44–49, 50n. (Francis & Robert Bailey, Philadelphia 1799).

found "the most profuse and attrocious [*sic*] slanders, of the Government, and a ready instrument of sedition," before expelling him.[115] Burk was indicted and arrested for a scandalous "libel of and concerning John Adams," and security was again set at $4,000 (half from him and half from sureties).[116] Burk's utterances were claims of presidential forgery, in a report on Adams forwarding a peace negotiator's letter to Congress: "certain passages in the paper communicated to Congress as a copy of his letter, are a F___ adapted to promote certain ends."[117] Burk, after reporting his arrest, made his next cover story the proposed Sedition Act counterpoised with the First Amendment.[118] He had already reprinted Junius, Erskine, and others on freedom of press. He began to print articles in every issue extolling freedom of press,[119] attacking the Sedition Act ("the Gagging Bill") on that basis,[120] and arguing that seditious libel "ought to pass unpunished."[121] The co-owner of the newspaper, Dr. James Smith, was also charged with libel, and tried to escape further prosecution by leaving the business, appearing but never being tried.[122] Burk predicted that his trial "for libels will determine whether the press is to be the *palladium* and *centinel of liberty*, or . . . the *register* of deaths, births and marriages."[123] However, when he saw a "certainty of fine and imprisonment from the violence of party spirit and the mode of packing juries," and otherwise the certainty of deportation, he entered an agreement for voluntary deportation in exchange for dismissal.[124] Though court had been set for October 1798, Burk's agreement cheated Justice Paterson of a Sedition Act trial. Burk also cheated Pickering out of an Alien Act deportation, by fleeing not to Ireland or French Louisiana but to Virginia, where he used an assumed name until the Act expired.[125]

[115] Timothy Pickering to Richard Harison (7 July 1798), PICKERING PAPERS r.37, fol.315, 315A. Harison had already arrested Burk.

[116] Minutes at 144 (4 Sept.1799); *Monday, July 9*, TIME PIECE (New York), 9 July 1798, at 3.

[117] [No Caption], TIME PIECE (New York), 2 July 1798, at 3; *accord* PICKERING PAPERS r.37, fol.315.

[118] *Congress of the United States* and *Extract*, TIME PIECE (New York), 11 July 1798, at 1; FREEDOM'S FETTERS 212.

[119] *E.g., Mr. Curran in Defence of the Liberty of the Press*, TIME PIECE (New York), 11 July 1798, at 2; *id.*, 13 July 1798, at 2; *id.*, 16 July 1798, at 2; *id.*, 18 July 1798, at 2; *id.*, 20 July 1798, at 1; *Liberty of the Press*, TIME PIECE (New York), 13 July 1798, at 1.

[120] *E.g., Memento*, TIME PIECE (New York), 16 July 1798, at 3; [No Caption], TIME PIECE (New York), 20 July 1798, at 3; [No Caption], TIME PIECE (New York), 8 Aug.1798, at 3.

[121] *Political Justice*, TIME PIECE (New York), 25 July 1798, at 2; *accord Monday, July 23*, TIME PIECE (New York), 23 July 1798, at 3.

[122] *Notice*, TIME PIECE (New York), 20 July 1798, at 3; Minutes at 148 (5 Sept.1799), 167.

[123] [No Caption], TIME PIECE (New York), 13 July 1798, at 2.

[124] John Daly Burk to Thomas Jefferson (ante 19 June 1801), 34 JEFFERSON PAPERS 385, 386–87; Timothy Pickering to Richard Harison (1 Jan.1799), PICKERING PAPERS r.37, fol.381.

[125] 34 *id.* 387; *see* Jacob Wagner (Office of Sec. of State) to Edward Dunscomb (22 May 1799), PICKERING PAPERS r.37, fol.423.

The Historical Context of the Prosecutions of 1798–1800

The congressional sponsors and Pickering miscalculated the political benefits of the Sedition Act and of the prosecutions under it, as the Act was attacked as a violation of freedoms of press and speech in a Republican firestorm[126] that raged in speeches,[127] newspapers and petitions,[128] and pamphlets and books.[129] That firestorm was further fueled by the appearance that the administration's prosecutions of Republican newspapers were a partisan vendetta, and that the Federalist judges were equally partisan. The Virginia and Kentucky Resolutions denounced the Act as a violation of the First Amendment,[130] and will be discussed at the end of this chapter. A House committee report presented the Federalist defense under that Amendment, misquoting the Amendment to omit freedom of speech and to reword "the liberty of the press," and limiting the meaning of that liberty to the Blackstone-Mansfield definition,[131] while denying the claim that the Act "had only halfhearted support."[132] That House report was narrowly adopted.[133] Various defenses of the Sedition Act were also published.[134] Congressional efforts to repeal the Sedition Act, based "chiefly on [its] supposed unconstitutionality," narrowly failed in 1799 and 1800,[135] as did efforts to extend it in 1801.[136]

Meanwhile, the Quasi-War with France continued, though the outbreak of full war looked less imminent after mid-1798, and was finally ended by the Convention

[126] Robert Goodloe Harper Letter (10 Feb.1799), 1 CIRCULAR LETTERS 146,148; *accord* OPEN PRESS 132.

[127] *E.g.*, 8 ANNALS 2104–05, 2105–06, 2106–07, 2107–11, 2134–35, 2136–37, 2151–52; THE AUTOBIOGRAPHY OF MARTIN VAN BUREN 439 (John C. Fitzpatrick ed., GPO, Washington 1920) (John Randolph).

[128] *E.g.*, articles in Bache's *Aurora*, Burk's *Time Piece*, Lyon's *Scourge*, and other prosecuted newspapers described in this chapter.

[129] *E.g.*, besides Madison's Report and George Hay's essays, [ST. GEORGE TUCKER], A LETTER TO A MEMBER OF CONGRESS RESPECTING THE ALIEN AND SEDITION LAWS (n.p., 1799); TUNIS WORTMAN, A TREATISE CONCERNING POLITICAL ENQUIRY AND THE LIBERTY OF THE PRESS 250–62 (George Forman, New York 1800); *accord* ROSENBERG, *supra* note 85, at 89–99; PRINTERS 85.

[130] *Virginia Resolutions* (21–24 Dec.1798), 4 ELLIOT'S DEBATES 528; *Kentucky Resolutions* (10–13 Nov.1798, 14 Nov.1799), 4 *id.* 544.

[131] 9 ANNALS 2985–92, esp. 2988–89 (25 Feb. 1799); 2 WOLCOTT PAPERS 78–85.

[132] OPEN PRESS 131; *accord* FEDERALISM 590.

[133] 9 ANNALS 3016–17 (25 Feb.1799); ADAMS FEDERALISTS 229.

[134] *E.g.*, besides Alexander Addison and Charles Lee, INHABITANT OF NORTH-WESTERN TERRITORY, OBSERVATIONS ON A LETTER FROM GEORGE NICHOLAS (Edmund Freeman, Cincinnati 1799).

[135] Robert Goodloe Harper Letter (20 Mar.1799), 1 CIRCULAR LETTERS 163,167; 9 ANNALS 3017 (25 Feb.1799); Samuel J.Cabell Letter (28 Mar.1800), 1 CIRCULAR LETTERS 177; CRISIS 180.

[136] 10 ANNALS 1047–50 (20 Feb.1801); Robert Williams Letter (26 Feb.1801), 1 CIRCULAR LETTERS 240, 241.

of 1800.[137] Adams's unilateral decision to send new envoys, who negotiated that treaty, left the Federalists "in shock,"[138] and split the party, with the High Federalist wing preferring war and opposing both the mission[139] and Adams's reelection.

The presidential election of 1800[140] was close, with the Federalists' split widening as Hamilton's condemnation of Adams became public[141] in what a leading Republican journalist called "Hamilton's *glorious pamphlet*."[142] Hamilton, a general without an army as it was disbanded that year, quickly also became a party leader without a party as he contributed to its split. Adams was equally unsuccessful in leading his branch of the Federalist Party, and the belief was commonly held that the exasperated secretary of war, James McHenry, voiced: the atrabilious Adams "will destroy himself fast enough without such exposures," since "whether sportful, playful, witty, kind, cold, drunk, sober, angry," he is "almost always in the wrong place to the wrong persons," and that "while he is destroying himself, he will destroy the government also."[143]

After that election, the Federalists, knowing their days to control the presidency and Congress were numbered, sought to lengthen their days to control the judiciary. The Judiciary Act of 1801 enrobed numerous "midnight judges," while making some nonpartisan improvements in the system.[144] Upon taking office in December 1801, the new Republican-dominated Congress repealed that Act (leading to the famous case of *Marbury v. Madison*),[145] and the new President Jefferson ended all federal prosecutions under the Sedition Act.[146]

137 Convention (30 Sept.1800), 1 TREATIES 457; 2 ASP 295.

138 Timothy Pickering to Rufus King (6 Mar.1799), 2 KING CORRESPONDENCE 548, 549; *accord* 2 *id.* 551; AMERICAN REPUBLIC 210.

139 Stephen Higginson to Timothy Pickering (31 Jan.1799), 1 HIGGINSON LETTERS 818, 819; Stephen Higginson to Timothy Pickering (22 Aug.1799), 1 *id.* 822, 823; MCHENRY CORRESPONDENCE 407–08, 416–17; *see* AMERICAN POLITICS 210–13, 229.

140 *See generally* JOHN E. FERLING, ADAMS VS. JEFFERSON: THE TUMULTUOUS ELECTION OF 1800 (OUP, New York 2004); SUSAN DUNN, JEFFERSON'S SECOND REVOLUTION (Houghton Mifflin, Boston 2004).

141 Alexander Hamilton, Letter from Alexander Hamilton, Concerning the Public Conduct and Character of John Adams (24 Oct.1800), 25 HAMILTON PAPERS 186; 25 *id.* 169n.; MCHENRY CORRESPONDENCE 421–22.

142 James T.Callender to Thomas Jefferson (17 Nov.1800), 32 JEFFERSON PAPERS 254.

143 James McHenry to Alexander Hamilton (16 Nov.1800), MCHENRY CORRESPONDENCE 479; *accord* James McHenry to Oliver Wolcott (9 Nov.1800), *id.* 477.

144 2 Stat.89; 4 DHSC 284; Kathryn Turner, *The Midnight Judges*, in BLACKSTONE IN AMERICA 59 (Mary S. Bilder et al. eds., CUP, Cambridge 2009). Others call the midnight judges a myth. *E.g.*, FERLING, *supra* note 140, at 199.

145 2 HISTORY OF SUPREME COURT 163–68; RICHARD E. ELLIS, THE JEFFERSONIAN CRISIS: COURTS AND POLITICS IN THE YOUNG REPUBLIC 36–53 (OUP, New York 1971).

146 Notes on a Cabinet Meeting (9 Mar.1801), 33 JEFFERSON PAPERS 232; 33 *id.* 251, 309.

Justice William Paterson and the First Amendment: The Lyon, Adams, Duane, Greenleaf, Peck, and Haswell Cases

Figure 6.3 Justice William Paterson (on Supreme Court 1793–1806). Portrait by James Sharples ante 1811. (Courtesy of Princeton University Art Museum/Art Resource.)

Robert G. Harper, a House cosponsor of the Sedition Act, crowed to his constituents in February 1801 that "objections to the constitutionality of this law . . . have been fully considered and over-ruled in the only place where they could be properly urged, that is the courts of justice."[147] Justice William Paterson (Figure 6.3) had given a similar summary about a year earlier: "the circuit courts of the U. States have uniformly declared, that congress were authorized to pass the law in question, that it is constl."[148] Both gave an accurate summary of nearly three years of prosecutions.

Paterson spoke of what he knew, because he had presided over the first and one of the last Sedition Act trials, of Matthew Lyon and then of Anthony Haswell, as well as others. Even before the Act, Paterson had been highly exercised over "treasonable and seditious" (which he paired) "language, writings, and actions," and had anathematized sedition in two grand jury charges.[149]

[147] Robert Goodloe Harper Letter (26 Feb.1801), 1 CIRCULAR LETTERS 234, 238; *accord* John Marshall to St. George Tucker (18 Nov.1800), 4 MARSHALL PAPERS 14, 15.

[148] PATERSON DRAFT OPINIONS 544–45.

[149] William Paterson's Charge(n.d.), 3 DHSC 462, 463; William Paterson's Charge (n.d.), 3 *id.* 464, 465. Both are transcribed from originals at Rutgers.

Paterson's Draft Opinions on the Sedition Act and Freedom of Press

Paterson also wrote two opinions[150] upholding the constitutionality of the Sedition Act, over First Amendment challenge, though records and newspaper accounts of his trials do not confirm that he used them. Those opinions began by finding that the Act was justified by implied constitutional powers including an implied power of self-preservation:

> 1. It is a power, which comes under the general clause of the constitution; and besides is necessarily incidental to every government or civil institution. No government can long exist, where libellous publications against its executive and legislative authorities, their acts and measures are suffered to pass with impunity. The power of punishing such offences is a necessary instrument or mean[s] of self-preservation.[151]

Paterson's Hobbesian power of self-preservation, or reasons of state, repeated a lifelong theme, which he had used in 1790 as authority for congressional creation of crimes not mentioned in the Constitution or necessary to express constitutional powers: "an axiom, that every coun'y ought to have within itself & to retain in its own hands the powers of self preservation."[152] His beginning his defense with implied powers, as presumably his strongest point, went a long way toward conceding Madison's and Jefferson's argument in the Virginia and Kentucky Resolutions, that the Sedition Act was not justified by anything in the Constitution. Similarly, his beginning his First Amendment analysis with not its words but implied incorporation of common law went some distance toward conceding the Madison-Jefferson arguments that the Act contradicted that Amendment.

His opinion proceeded to hold the Act warranted by the common law, which Paterson found adopted by the federal government as well as the states, and which he held already proscribed seditious libel:

> And here the question arises, whether the common law extends to the United States in criminal cases. *I have no doubt* of its extension.
>
> . . . .
>
> . . . To calumniate the government or oppose lawful acts is an offence at com. law.[153]

150 The second calls itself an opinion, finding it "necessary for the court to deliver their opinion on it" (the Sedition Act). Paterson Draft Opinions 545.

151 Paterson Draft Opinions 531; *accord id.* 545.

152 William Paterson, Notes, Paterson Papers-NYPL 375; *accord id.* 369, 387.

153 Paterson Draft Opinions 533, 541; *accord id.* 553 (shifted to end of second opinion).

In reaching the conclusions that federal courts had jurisdiction of common law crimes and that seditious libel continued unaltered as part of that American common law, Paterson joined the other sitting justices as they moved to that position, and departed from most of the initial justices who never adopted that stance (as summarized in Chapters 3 and 8).

Paterson then discussed the impact of the First Amendment on federal powers and on the common law of libel:

> [2.] The amendment to the const[']n ordains, that the *liberty of the press* shall not be abridged. The expression is *relative*, and obviously refers to rule or principle then existing, or in other words, to the *common law*. You shall not abridge, that is, narrow or lessen, the liberty of the press. To determine whether this liberty of the press be abridged by any law, we must know in what it consists, or how it stood at the time of making the amendment. This is fully done by the passage, which has been read in Bl. Com. [evidently quoted immediately before, marked by "4 Bl.Com."]. The amendment declares, that Congress shall not abridge the freedom of the press.[154]

He thereby read the First Amendment to grant no right that the common law did not already grant. He also read it to disable no federal power, and exactly as anti-federalists had feared in demanding a bill of rights, Paterson instead interpreted the Constitution to authorize the federal government to regulate press and speech, and the First Amendment to acknowledge that. "The article supposes the power over the press to be in congress, and prohibits them only from abridging the freedom allowed to it by the common law."[155] This conflicted with earlier federalist responses to anti-federalists, as the former argued that a bill of rights was superfluous, asserting that the federal government lacked any enumerated power that could possibly restrain press or speech.

In case the common law of crimes did not govern federal courts, Paterson ended his first opinion by defining freedom of the press by the narrow Blackstone-Mansfield definition:

> But 3dly admitting, that the common law does not extend to the U. States in criminal cases, we are then to inquire, *in what consists the liberty of the press*? Does it consist in a license to publish false, scandalous, and malicious calumnies, or libels agt. the government, its officers, and acts? . . .
>
> . . . .
>
> The *freedom of the press* is to be *determined* by the meaning of these terms in the *common law*.[156]

[154] *Id.* 535, 537; *accord id.* 553.

[155] *Id.* 539; *accord id.* 553.

[156] *Id.* 537, 539; *accord id.* 553; PATERSON PAPERS-NYPL 699, 747.

What he cited from Blackstone, of course, defined "liberty of the press" to "consist[] in laying no *previous* restraints upon publications, and not in freedom from censure for criminal matter when published" or freedom for "licentiousness" of the press.[157]

Paterson's second draft opinion, written after "numerous judl. decisions on this subject," abandoned nothing but fortified much. Implied powers supporting the Sedition Act were expanded to ground the right of self-preservation in "the law of nations" and "the law of nature," and to include from the Constitution's preamble the "com. defence and general welfare" clauses and the necessary and proper provision. The common law prohibition was defended as protecting peace against "[f]alse, scandalous, and malicious writings agt. the president, or congress, or the laws," which have a "direct tendency to bring the government into contempt, to weaken its lawful authority," and to destroy the foundations of republican government; to Paterson, the recent Whiskey Rebellion was "beyond all doubt, from seditious writings."[158] The rationale for that direct tendency test was given as the government's right to "prevent insurrections" and to use "precautionary measures" rather than waiting "to interfere until it actually breaks out." The reason for republican governments' fragility was described as the "raging of the people" that "drives with the impetuosity of a hurricane" and that causes "[l]ife, liberty, property, and governmt." to be "frequently prostrated before popular commotions."[159]

This was nothing less than a different philosophy—of republican government, rights of dissent and opposition activity, treatment of unconstitutional laws, and liberties of press and speech[160]—when compared with the philosophy of Republicans and their radical Whig antecedents. Paterson added an equally different definition of liberty: "Liberty implies the doing of what is right; and must be exercised in such a manner as not to be injurious to others or to the public. This is a necessary restriction. When a person therefore makes the press the vehicle of defamation and abuse, this restriction is disregarded, and he becomes an offender."[161]

Paterson carried this philosophy into court as he presided over two recognized trials and four other indictments under the Sedition Act (more recognized cases than any other justice)—and one other trial and two other indictments discussed in the next chapter—whether or not he formally used the two opinions.

[157] 4 Blackstone's Commentaries 151, 153.

[158] Paterson Draft Opinions 547, 545, 549.

[159] *Id.* 551–53.

[160] E.g., Marc Lendler, *"Equally Proper . . . ": Civility, Bad Tendency, and the Sedition Act*, 24 J. Early Republic 419, 425–44 (2004); Andrew Lenner, *A Tale of Two Constitutions: Nationalism in the Federalist Era*, 40 Am. J. Legal Hist. 72, 90–104 (1996); Andrew Lenner, *Separate Spheres: Republican Constitutionalism in the Federalist Era*, 41 Am. J. Legal Hist. 250, 251–78 (1997); Printers 59.

[161] Paterson Draft Opinions 539.

The Lyon Prosecution and *Lyon's Republican Magazine or Scourge of Aristocracy*

Paterson, as he opened the circuit court in Rutland, Vermont, in October 1798, was on the hunt for violators of the new Sedition Act. His grand jury charge, the first given under the Sedition Act, emphasized "two species of offences, which, under the existing circumstances of the United States, merit your particular attention," one of which was "seditious practices, and false, scandalous, and malicious writings, publications, and libels against the government of the United States."[162] Paterson then read the Sedition Act to the grand jury, and incorporated some of the themes of his first opinion, stressing that the very survival of government and freedom depended on crushing seditious libel. He also incorporated Blackstone's and Mansfield's rationale for criminalizing and prosecuting such alienation of "the affections of the people from their government" that inevitably followed from criticizing its administration or its measures.

> The offences specified in this act are of a serious nature, and, when perpetrated, demand instant and full attention. . . . The man, who is guilty of publishing false, defamatory, and malicious writings or libels against the government of his country, its measures, and its constituted authorities, must, if not callous to the dictates of the moral sense, stand self-condemned. He sins against light; for he must be sensible, that such publications are contrary to clear and known duty. In such case, nothing short of idiocy can operate as an excuse. They destroy confidence, excite distrust, disseminate discord and the elements of disorganization, alienate the affections of the people from their government, disturb the peace of society, and endanger our political union and existence. No government, indeed, can long subsist, where offenders of this kind are suffered to spread their poison with impunity. . . . The truth is, that libellous publications and seditious practices are inconsistent with genuine freedom, and subversive of good government. . . . [163]

Paterson essentially prejudged the only issue he left to the jury in Lyon's case, seditious intent, by including in the charge that "[w]ritten or printed detraction" is a "deliberate act[ ], perpetrated with a view to wound and do injury," and "contrary to clear and known duty." He negated any defense of truth by saying "nothing

[162] William Paterson's Charge (C.C.D. Vt. 3 Oct.1798), 3 DHSC 292, 293, transcribed from the original at Rutgers, Grand Jury Charges (folder 11), in PATERSON CORRESPONDENCE.

[163] 3 *id.* 293, 294.

short of idiocy can operate as an excuse." He portrayed printed criticisms of government as not freedom of press but acts of criminal violence like poisoning, "more to be dreaded than hosts of external foes."[164]

The first person brought to trial under the Sedition Act, Representative Matthew Lyon,[165] incurred treble Federalist fury by being an immigrant from among what xenophobic sponsors of the Alien Act termed the "wild Irishmen,"[166] by responding to a Federalist colleague in Congress' slur on his Revolutionary War record by spitting at him,[167] and by voting against the Alien and Sedition Acts.[168] "[T]he beastly Lyon"[169] further targeted himself by establishing a Republican magazine, *Lyon's Republican Magazine*, which immediately changed its title to "*The Scourge of Aristocracy*"[170] (by aristocrats he meant Federalists), because he found it difficult to get newspapers to publish his responses during his reelection campaign.

The grand jury indicted Lyon under the Sedition Act, and on the same day unwittingly confirmed Lyon's objection that it was packed with Federalists by writing a formal "unanimous" reply to Paterson's "solemn, momentous and invaluable charge," which joined in Paterson's "lament . . . that our liberties, in some instances, are abused to licentiousness," which, the grand jury was quite sure, "more endangers the liberties and independence of a free Government than hosts of invading foes."[171] The grand jury saw exactly such endangerment in Lyon. The first count of the indictment charged that Lyon libeled the president and the executive branch, with intent "to stir up sedition," and "to bring the said government and the President into contempt," by writing a letter printed in a newspaper. The letter charged that Adams caused "every consideration of the public welfare [to be] swallowed up in a continual grasp for power in an unbounded thirst

164 *Id.*

165 *See generally* Trial of Matthew Lyon, Wharton's State Trials 333 (C.C.D. Vt. 1798), reprinted in In re Lyon's Case, 15 F.Cas. 1183 (C.C.D. Vt. 1798) (No.8,646); FREEDOM'S FETTERS 221–46; CRISIS 102–11; 11 DAB 532; EMPIRE 227–30. Court records are partially reprinted in Wharton, and are in Case Files (1792–1869) and Dockets (1792–1811), U.S. Circuit Court for the District of Vermont (National Archives at Waltham, Mass., R.G. 21.48.2, Box 2).

166 1 LIFE AND LETTERS OF HARRISON GRAY OTIS 108 (Samuel E. Morison ed., Houghton Mifflin, Boston 1913); 1 AMES WORKS 259, 247.

167 REPORT OF THE COMMITTEE OF PRIVILEGES . . . RELATIVE TO THE EXPULSION FROM THIS HOUSE, OF MATTHEW LYON 3–4 (n.p., Philadelphia 1798); Wharton's State Trials at 337–39; *cf.* REPORT OF THE COMMITTEE OF PRIVILEGES . . . EXPULSION OF ROGER GRISWOLD AND MATTHEW LYON 5–6 (n.p., Philadelphia 20 Feb.1798) (ensuing fight).

168 8 ANNALS 2171.

169 Stephen Higginson to Timothy Pickering (22 Feb.1798), 1 HIGGINSON LETTERS 801, 802.

170 [No Caption], VERGENNES GAZETTE (Vergennes), 3 Jan.1799, at 3; ALEINE AUSTIN, MATTHEW LYON 169 n.75 (PSUP, Pittsburgh 1981).

171 *Reply of the Grand Jury*, RUTLAND HERALD (Rutland), 5 Oct.1798, reprinted in 3 DHSC 294, 294–95.

for ridiculous pomp[,] foolish adulation or selfish avarice," and caused "men of meanness [to be] preferred for the ease with which they can take up and advocate opinions" required by the executive, in place of "men of real merit."[172] The second and third counts were for libeling Adams and Congress by publicly reading a letter from France denouncing "the bullying speech of your President," who ought to be sent "to a mad house," and the "stupid answer of your Senate"; and for aiding and abetting its publication by having an intermediary hand it to the printer.[173] Complicating matters, Lyon's newspaper letter had been written three weeks before enactment of the Sedition Act, though it was published two weeks after the effective date.[174] Paterson was aware of that complication, and when later challenged by a leading Republican in Congress on ex post facto and First Amendment grounds,[175] stood firm with Blackstone and Mansfield that the "criminality consists chiefly in the publication," and that "he, who procures another to publish a libel, becomes the publisher himself."[176]

At the beginning of the trial, Paterson (sitting with District Judge Samuel Hitchcock) rejected Lyon's argument "that the sedition law was unconstitutional," parrying that it merely restated and relaxed the common law of seditious libel.[177] However, Paterson (according to Lyon's account) allowed him to "appeal to the jury, on the unconstitutionality of the law, the innocence of the passage in my letter, and the innocence of the manner in which I read the letter."[178] Nevertheless Paterson's jury charge began with the instruction that the jury may not question the constitutionality of the Sedition Act:

> You have nothing whatever to do with the constitutionality or unconstitutionality of the sedition law. Congress has said that the author and publisher of seditious libels is to be punished; and until this law is declared null and void by a tribunal competent for the purpose, its validity cannot be disputed.[179]

[172] Indictment at 1, 2 (5 Oct.1798); *Mr. Spooner*, SPOONER'S VERMONT JOURNAL (Windsor), 31 July 1798, at 1, 2; quoted slightly differently in Wharton's State Trials 333 (indictment 5 Oct.1798).

[173] Indictment at 3–4, 5–6; Wharton's State Trials 333–34.

[174] The article was dated 28 June 1798, and published 31 July 1798. Indictment at 1.

[175] William Paterson, "U. States v Mr Lyon Notes," PATERSON PAPERS-NYPL 699, 701; Joseph H. Nicholson to William Paterson (23 June 1801), *id.* 737, 739, 741, 747; William Paterson to Joseph H. Nicholson (23 Feb.1801), *id.* 721, 725–29.

[176] William Paterson to Joseph H. Nicholson (29 June 1801), *id.* 751, 753.

[177] Wharton's State Trials 334, 341. Trial was on 8 Oct.1798, according to the Docket—the Monday after the Friday indictment.

[178] Matthew Lyon, In Jail at Vergennes (14 Oct.1798), reprinted in Wharton's State Trials 339, 340; *accord id.* 335; PATERSON PAPERS-NYPL 711, 715.

[179] *Id.* 336.

His circuit court was clearly not that tribunal for Lyon, though it had been three days earlier in another case (not under the Sedition Act) when Paterson apparently gave the opposite instruction on jury treatment of unconstitutional laws.[180] Paterson instead proceeded to limit the jury to whether Lyon published the writing and, if Paterson was quoted accurately, whether it was done "seditiously?"[181] (In later cases, Paterson instead said the second issue was whether the defendant's "intent was defamatory.") In doing so, Paterson contradicted, or at least ignored, the supposed ameliorative provision of the Sedition Act that the jury "shall have a right to determine the law and the fact, under the direction of the court, as in other cases." He did not inform the jury that conviction required finding the speech or writing false and finding Lyon's intent malicious, or that Lyon's attempted defenses could be full defenses to those requirements. Supplementing his biased grand jury charge on intent, Paterson charged the jury that if they found Lyon's intent was "making odious or contemptible the President and government, and bringing them both into disrepute," they "must render a verdict of guilty"; but he did not charge the converse, or make any reference to the jury's power to render a verdict of not guilty.[182] Though not reported in Wharton, Paterson's own notes show that he followed Blackstone and Mansfield even more sedulously, quoting the analogy that "[p]oison may be kept in a closet, but must not be administered as cordials," and immediately after, conclusively inferring the crime from publication alone: "The malignity consists in the publication. . . . The guilt consists in the public'n."[183]

Despite Lyon's arguments that the law violated the First Amendment, that he lacked seditious intent, that his writing and speech were true, and in an historical epiphany, that his expression was only "a legitimate opposition" to the Federalist administration, the jury found him guilty.[184] After lecturing Lyon and the jury about the "mischiefs which flow from an unlicensed abuse of government," Paterson sentenced him to four months in prison and a $1,000 fine, payable before release.[185] Articles about the trial, fawning over Paterson's handling, appeared in Federalist newspapers across the country.[186] Jefferson spoke for Republicans when he responded to Lyon's trial, "I know not which mortifies me most, that I

[180] 3 DHSC 236 n.24 (law allowing seizure of glebe property); 1 History of Supreme Court 592 n.186, and earlier, *Col. Lyon's Trial*, Alexandria Times, 27 Nov.1798, at 2.

[181] Wharton's State Trials 336; *accord* William Paterson, "U. States v Mr Lyon Notes," Paterson Papers-NYPL 699, 715.

[182] Wharton's State Trials 336. Other bias was alleged in Lyon's letter. *Id.* 340.

[183] William Paterson, "U. States v Mr Lyon Notes," Paterson Papers-NYPL 699, 715.

[184] Wharton's State Trials 335, 336; Mittimus at 1 (9 Oct.1798).

[185] *Id.* 336–37, 337; Sentence (9 Oct.1798). He also had to pay the $61.46 in costs. Bill of Costs (9 Oct.1798).

[186] *E.g., Trial of Matthew Lyon for Sedition*, Albany Centinel, 19 Oct.1798, at 2; *Trial of Matthew Lyon for Sedition*, Vergennes Gazette, 11 Oct.1798, at 3.

should fear to write what I think, or my country bear such a state of things," a fear created by "Lyon's judges."[187] Jefferson had already drafted the Kentucky Resolutions, a month earlier.

Lyon's travails were just beginning, as the federal marshal denied his requests to stop by his home to set affairs in order for his four-month absence, and straightway incarcerated him forty-four miles away in an unheated cell through the Vermont winter (until supporters provided a stove). Detailing his ill treatment, Lyon's letter from jail was printed in Republican newspapers nationally,[188] and his reelection campaign from his cell succeeded with a larger margin of victory than his prior election.[189] Upon his release, Virginians and Vermonters vied to pay his fine, and Lyon stepped out to a "huge crowd" and led "a triumphant procession" as he returned to Congress.[190] The prosecution widened the narrow Federalist margin in the House for a few months, but at a cost of making the "first victim" of the Sedition Act "a martyr" for freedom of press and speech.[191]

The Thomas Adams Prosecution and His Boston *Independent Chronicle*

The first prosecution of a prominent editor under the Sedition Act was directed at Thomas Adams,[192] of Boston's *Independent Chronicle*, the "leading Republican journal in New England, second only to Bache's in the nation,"[193] a paper that excoriated the Sedition Act in nearly every issue. Beginning with its first issue after word reached Boston of the Act, the *Chronicle* announced that "we are now 'abridged the freedom of press'" until citizens could speak in the next election, and the lead article of the next issue dramatically juxtaposed the Sedition Act and the First Amendment,[194] followed by a drumbeat on that theme thereafter.[195]

[187] Thomas Jefferson to John Taylor (26 Nov.1798), 30 JEFFERSON PAPERS 588.

[188] Matthew Lyon, In Jail at Vergennes (14 Oct.1798) (broadside), reprinted in Wharton's State Trials 339, 341–42.

[189] Matthew Lyon, Colonel Lyon's Address to His Constituents (n.p., 10 Jan.1799) (broadside); Wharton's State Trials 339, 343.

[190] FREEDOM'S FETTERS 244; *cf. Vergennes*, WINDHAM HERALD, 7 Mar.1799, at 3.

[191] *Extract of a Letter from Virginia*, INDEPENDENT CHRONICLE (Boston), 10 Dec.1798, at 2; *Gen. Mason to Col. Lyon*, VERMONT GAZETTE (Bennington), 27 Dec.1798, at 1.

[192] *See generally* FREEDOM'S FETTERS 247–57; CRISIS 120–23; PRESS-MASS. 144–45. Court records are in Case Files (1790–1911), U.S. Circuit Court for the District of Massachusetts (National Archives at Waltham, Mass., R.G.21.23.2).

[193] FREEDOM'S FETTERS 247, 178.

[194] *Boston*, INDEPENDENT CHRONICLE (Boston), 19 Jul.1798, at 3; *Sedition Bill*, INDEPENDENT CHRONICLE (Boston), 23 Jul.1798, at 1.

[195] *E.g., Freedom of Opinion and the Liberty of the Press*, INDEPENDENT CHRONICLE (Boston), 30 Jul.1798, at 2, and immediately before Adams's arrest, *At a Meeting of the Citizens*, INDEPENDENT CHRONICLE (Boston), 22 Oct.1798, at 1; *Worcester, id.* 2 (Lyon, Haswell); *Communication, id.* 2; *Centinel, id.* 3.

After Paterson followed his circuit from Rutland to Boston, the grand jury that he charged[196] indicted Adams for publishing articles that "stir up sedition" by libeling the government of the United States—including some articles opposing the Alien and Sedition Acts and favoring the Virginia and Kentucky Resolutions.[197] Brought before Paterson and a district judge for arraignment in late October 1798, Adams pleaded not guilty, and trial was set for June 1799.[198] That was not to happen, however, as he died the month before trial.[199]

In the meantime, a state proceeding for seditious libel was filed against Thomas Adams and his brother Abijah for publishing what "hath a direct and manifest tendency to stir up uneasiness, jealousy, distrust, and sedition," in February 1799. The offending article censured the state assembly for violating their oaths of office in responding to the Virginia Resolutions by disclaiming any right to assess the constitutionality of federal laws—a right the article viewed as an obligation. Though Thomas Adams was too sick to be tried, his brother was tried and convicted the next month of publishing, though not of printing, a libel against the Massachusetts assembly,[200] after the judge insisted freedom of press was limited to Blackstone's definition.[201]

The Sedition Act prosecutions are discussed by justice, rather than chronologically, so other cases occurred before Paterson's remaining cases, as the chronological table (Table 6.1) indicated.

The Duane Prosecutions and His Philadelphia *Aurora*

William Duane,[202] Bache's successor as the *Aurora*'s editor (still the foremost Republican newspaper[203]), was the first target of Pickering's 1799–1800 assault on Republican newspapers. An earlier state court prosecution for riot had been brought in Philadelphia in February 1799, when Duane and compatriots sought

[196] 3 DHSC 300.

[197] Indictment at 2–5 (20 Oct.1798). He was arrested 3 days later. Arrest Warrant (23 Oct.1798). *Accord Boston*, INDEPENDENT CHRONICLE (Boston), 25 Oct.1798, at 3; CONTEMPORARY OPINION 62–63.

[198] Indictment at 13 (20 Oct.1798) (plea not guilty); Memorandum (recognizance bond, 29 Oct.1798) (trial set for 1 June 1799 and bond $4,000); *Boston*, INDEPENDENT CHRONICLE (Boston), 29 Oct.1798, at 3.

[199] *Died*, MASSACHUSETTS MERCURY (Boston), 14 May 1799, at 2.

[200] *Trial of Mr. Abijah Adams*, INDEPENDENT CHRONICLE (Boston), 8, 15, 22, 29 Apr.1799, at 1; PRESS-MASS. 144–45.

[201] CONTEMPORARY OPINION 225, 228; *see id.* 58–63, 225–28.

[202] *See generally* Wharton's State Trials 345; DANIEL, *supra* note 15, at 231–74; FREEDOM'S FETTERS 277–306; CRISIS 194–202; 5 DAB 467. Court records are extracted in Wharton, and are in Criminal Case Files of the U.S. Circuit Court for the Eastern District of Pennsylvania (1791–1840) (National Archives at Philadelphia, R.G.21.40.2, microfilm M986, rolls 1 and 2).

[203] FREEDOM'S FETTERS 278.

after-church "signatures to a memorial for the *repeal* of the *Alien Bill*" from Irish immigrants leaving the service, producing a churchyard scuffle. But to Federalist dismay, they were acquitted.[204]

The first federal prosecution of Duane was brought because of the *Aurora*'s "uninterrupted stream of slander on the American government," and because, even worse, Duane was apparently an alien and "doubtless a United Irishman," who headed volunteers Pickering feverishly believed were "probably formed to oppose the authority of the government; and in case of war and invasion by the French, to join them."[205] President Adams approved the recommendation to prosecute, noting that there was nothing evil "that the Aurora has not suggested of me," and that if the federal prosecutor "does not think this paper libellous, he is not fit for his office."[206] The prosecutor, eager to show his fitness for continued service, indicted Duane in early August 1799, reciting that the *Aurora* libeled the president and the government by claiming "British influence" including the statement that a letter "in the hand-writin[g] of John Adams" showed "that British influence has been employed and with effect in procuring the appointment" of an important officer. The prosecutor soon indicted Duane again.[207] When Duane appeared in court before Justice Washington in October 1799,[208] it turned out Duane indeed had that letter in Adams's handwriting,[209] and later the trial was postponed forever.[210]

Meanwhile, a separate effort to muzzle Duane was made by the Federalist-dominated Senate, after Duane published a pending bill in the *Aurora*, in February 1800, that proposed to resolve disputed electoral college tallies like the 1796

[204] Trial of Duane et al., Wharton's State Trials 345, 345, 348, 388 (Pa. Ct. Oyer & Terminer 1799); Criminal Case Files at 1:I1128, 2:I156 (I refers to unnumbered image, P to numbered image); WILLIAM DUANE, A REPORT OF THE EXTRAORDINARY TRANSACTIONS WHICH TOOK PLACE IN PHILADELPHIA (Aurora, Philadelphia 1799).

[205] Timothy Pickering to John Adams (24 July 1799), 9 ADAMS WORKS 3,4; *accord* Timothy Pickering to William Rawle (24 July 1799), PICKERING PAPERS r.11, fol.486. The volunteers assembled because Duane was attacked several times. JOHN NERONE, VIOLENCE AGAINST THE PRESS 66 (OUP, New York 1994).

[206] John Adams to Timothy Pickering (1 Aug.1799), 9 ADAMS WORKS 5.

[207] Indictment (15 Oct.1799); [WILLIAM DUANE], COPY OF AN INDICTMENT 2 ([Duane, Philadelphia 1799]); *accord* Timothy Pickering to John Adams (1 Aug.1799), 9 ADAMS WORKS 5, 7.

[208] 3 DHSC 389 (12–22 Oct.1799); *Federal Circuit Court*, HERALD OF LIBERTY (Washington, Pa.), 18 Nov.1799, at 1; *Norristown (Penn.) Oct.15*, CITY GAZETTE (Charleston), 5 Nov.1799, at 2.

[209] John Adams to Tench Coxe (May 1792), 2 WOLCOTT PAPERS 424, 425; *A Letter of John Adams*, MARYLAND HERALD (Elizabethtown), 23 Oct.1800, at 1; Worthington C. Ford, *Letters Written by William Duane*, 40 PROC. MASS. HISTORICAL SOC. 257, 260 (1906).

[210] William Cobbett, The Electors of Pennsylvania (1800), LETTERS FROM WILLIAM COBBETT TO EDWARD THORNTON 121, 122 (G.D.H. Cole ed., OUP, Oxford 1937); AMERICAN AURORA 859 (Richard N. Rosenfeld ed., St. Martin's Press, New York 1997) (excerpting AURORA, 3 Oct.1800); FREEDOM'S FETTERS 285–86.

election by an extraconstitutional committee dominated by Federalists.[211] The Senate alleged his criticism to be "false, scandalous, defamatory and malicious" and his publication of secret Senate proceedings to violate its privileges, and summoned him to appear a month later.[212] Because Duane was only allowed to offer "excuse or extenuation" of his publication and not defenses such as freedom of press or truth, his legal counsel refused to represent him and Duane refused to appear,[213] following a carefully orchestrated plan.[214] The Senate ordered Duane's arrest for contempt, but its officer failed to find him, though the *Aurora* continued to appear regularly.[215] Frustrated, the Senate asked for prosecution under the Sedition Act.[216]

President Adams was more than glad to instruct the attorney general and the federal attorney again to prosecute Duane under that Act.[217] After the earlier federal action ended, Duane was indicted by the grand jury for publishing the Senate bill, on the ground it was "libellous against the Senate" under the Sedition Act,[218] after Paterson roused the grand jury with his charge on the perfidiousness of criticism of government, apparently giving the same charge as to Lyon's grand jury and later to Haswell's.[219] With the attorney general agreeing to postpone the trial, Paterson granted a continuance, and the unavailability of witnesses brought further delays. As in Thomas Adams's case, Paterson was shortchanged of a Sedition Act trial of Duane, when delays pushed the trial into Jefferson's term of office, and Jefferson discontinued the Sedition Act prosecution.[220] Not wanting to tread on sensitive Senate toes, Jefferson left the Senate's concerns about Duane's criticisms

[211] Indictment (14 Apr.1800), in Criminal Case Files 2:I156; *Report of the Committee on Privileges*, ORACLE OF DAUPHIN (Harrisburg), 24 Mar.1800, at 2 (citing AURORA, 19 Feb.1800); *Report of the Committee on Privileges*, MASSACHUSETTS SPY (Worcester), 26 Mar.1800, at 2.

[212] REPORT, IN PART, OF THE COMMITTEE OF PRIVILEGES, ON . . . DUANE 3 (Philadelphia, Senate 1800).

[213] *Id.* 4; William Duane to Thomas Jefferson (27 Mar.1800), 31 JEFFERSON PAPERS 466; *accord* Anthony New Letter (8 Apr.1800), 1 CIRCULAR LETTERS 194,195; 31 JEFFERSON PAPERS 454n.

[214] Thomas Cooper to Thomas Jefferson (23 Mar.1800), 31 JEFFERSON PAPERS 451, 451–52.

[215] William Bingham to Rufus King (6 Aug.1800), 3 KING CORRESPONDENCE 284.

[216] 3 *id.* 285; Thomas Jefferson to Littleton Tazewell (10 Apr.1800), 31 JEFFERSON PAPERS 491, 492; FREEDOM'S FETTERS 288–301.

[217] John Adams to Attorney General and District Attorney (16 May 1800), 9 ADAMS WORKS 56.

[218] Indictment (18 Oct.1800), in Criminal Case Files 1:I1136; *Federal Circuit Court*, ALEXANDRIA TIMES, 24 Oct.1800, at 2 (indictment 18 Oct.1800); *Federal Circuit Court*, AMERICAN CITIZEN (New York), 23 Oct.1800, at 3.

[219] He was using the same charge a year after Lyon's grand jury. *Raleigh, December 3*, CONSTITUTIONAL DIARY (Philadelphia), 17 Dec.1799, at 1. *DHSC* found no other charge during mid-1798 through 1800, nor did I in his papers; and the undated Paterson charges at 3 DHSC 457–68 are pre-Sedition Act. Paterson's grand jury charges were rarely in newspapers, because his "invariable rule" was "never to give a copy of any of them for publication." 3 DHSC 295.

[220] Thomas Jefferson to James Madison (19 July 1801), 1 MADISON PAPERS-SECRETARY 442.

to a new prosecution, and as he clearly hoped, the new grand jury refused to indict Duane.[221]

The Greenleaf Prosecution and Her New York *Argus*

Two other Sedition Act prosecutions, of Greenleaf and Peck, have never been identified with Justice Paterson, but the indictments appear to have been obtained after he gave the New York grand jury "an elegant charge ag[ains]t riots, insurrections, & lies against the Government & its officers," while he presided in September 1799, as ex-judge Robert Troup reported.[222]

Ann Greenleaf[223] continued the New York *Argus* upon her husband's death from the yellow fever epidemic of 1798, and it was reviewed for "audacious calumnies against the government,"[224] at Pickering's instigation as part of his July-August 1799 offensive. Objectionable articles were found, with such outrages as raising a "Liberty Pole," calling the Alien and Sedition Acts "tyrannical and unconstitutional," and claiming the federal "government was corrupt and inimical to the preservation of civil liberty."[225] Greenleaf was indicted but the trial was delayed to April 1800, because of her health and another epidemic;[226] Justice Washington was to preside then.[227]

Meanwhile, Greenleaf was publicly charged with defamation by Alexander Hamilton, in a letter to New York's attorney general asking for prosecution. Hamilton's letter described the defamation as charging him "with being at the 'bottom' of an 'effort recently made to suppress the Aurora,'" funded by "'foreign gold'." Hamilton self-servingly claimed he only asked the state to prosecute because "the faction to overturn our government" regularly aimed "to destroy the confidence of the people" in government which would likely bring "very fatal consequences."[228] In a novel twist showing the plasticity of criminal libel, Hamilton also claimed that it was criminal libel to "inspire the belief that the independence and liberty of the press are endangered by the[se] intrigues,"[229] echoing the

[221] Thomas Jefferson to James Madison (22 Aug.1801), 2 *id.* 60, 61, 61–62 n.5.

[222] Robert Troup to Rufus King (2 Sept.1799), 3 DHSC 383; 3 *id.* 381 (session 2–6 September 1799).

[223] *See generally* FREEDOM'S FETTERS 398–417; CRISIS 223. Court records are in Case Files (1790–1915), U.S. Circuit Court for the District of New York (National Archives at New York City, R.G.21.34.7).

[224] Timothy Pickering to Richard Harison (12 Aug.1799), PICKERING PAPERS r.11, fol.599.

[225] Indictment at 1, 2 (undated).

[226] FREEDOM'S FETTERS 400.

[227] 3 DHSC 408.

[228] Alexander Hamilton to Josiah O. Hoffman (6 Nov.1799), 24 HAMILTON PAPERS 5, 6; reprinted, *e.g.*, *New-York, November 6, 1799*, NEW-YORK GAZETTE, 8 Nov.1799, at 3; *New-York, November 6, 1799*, DAILY ADVERTISER (New York), 9 Nov.1799, at 2.

[229] 24 *id.* 6.

sedition charges against Sacheverell, even as Hamilton urged prosecution of the press. The offending article indeed said as much—that Hamilton offered "6,000 dollars down" and a larger balance for the *Aurora,* and the money must either come from "speculation . . . while he was secretary of the treasury" or from "British secret service money"[230]—though the *Argus* merely reprinted what the *Aurora* and a host of earlier newspapers had published.[231] The overlooking of those papers and prosecution of New York City's only remaining Republican newspaper instead[232] did not escape the notice of Republican editors.[233]

New York's attorney general, having scruples Pickering lacked about charging a nonparticipant widow, instead arrested and charged David Frothingham, the journeyman running the *Argus,* in early November 1799. The state court indictment was for a common law libel, rather than a Sedition Act violation, for claiming Hamilton led efforts to buy the *Aurora,* and insinuating corrupt speculation or British funding.[234] At trial just a week later, the court excluded evidence of truth or falsity, holding it irrelevant in a common law prosecution, and ensured a conviction, by giving the jury the judges' unanimous opinion that the article was libelous as charged.[235] New York law also precluded a freedom of press defense, since it was one of the few states not having a constitutional press or speech provision. When the jury pronounced Frothingham guilty, he was sentenced to a $100 fine and four months in prison, only to be released when he posted $2,000 security (half from others).[236] At sentencing, the state judges announced that the case had no implication for freedom of press, citing the Blackstone-Mansfield definition, but had momentous implications for the survival of government.[237]

These two Federalist prosecutions had the desired effect, as Greenleaf was forced to sell the *Argus,* though she limited sale to "republican printers."[238] With Greenleaf "having discontinued her paper," the federal attorney questioned the

[230] 24 *id.* 6–7 n.2.

[231] *E.g., Extract of a Letter, Philadelphia, Sept.20,* CONSTITUTIONAL TELEGRAPH (Boston), 26 Oct.1799, at 3; *Extract of a Letter from Philadelphia,* CITY GAZETTE (Charleston), 2 Nov.1799, at 2.

[232] FREEDOM'S FETTERS 398; OPPOSITION PRESS 881–82.

[233] *E.g.,* [No Caption], ALEXANDRIA TIMES, 18 Nov.1799, at 3; [No Caption], CLAYPOOLE'S AMERICAN DAILY ADVERTISER (Philadelphia), 11 Nov.1799, at 3.

[234] Trial of David Frothingham, Wharton's State Trials 649, 649 (N.Y. Ct. Oyer & Terminer 1799). Wharton questioned the accuracy of the *New-York Gazette* report, *id.* 650n.; *cf. New-York, November 25,* NEW-YORK GAZETTE, 25 Nov.1799, at 2.

[235] *Id.* 650, 651.

[236] *Id.* 651. Wharton mistakenly stated $500, FREEDOM'S FETTERS 414 n.80.

[237] FREEDOM'S FETTERS 413, citing GAZETTE AND GENERAL ADVERTISER (New York), 5 Dec.1799.

[238] *To the Patrons of the Late Argus,* AMERICAN CITIZEN (New York), 12 Mar.1800, at 2; *accord* [No Caption], BEE (New London), 26 Mar.1800, at 4.

need for further prosecution,[239] and Pickering with Adams's approval ordered the federal case discontinued.[240]

The Peck Prosecution for Petitioning Against the Sedition Act

The prosecution of Jedidiah Peck,[241] a New York assembly member, showed how far the Sedition Act could be carried. His primary offense was his petition to repeal the Alien and Sedition Acts as a violation of the Constitution that would "convert freemen into slaves," and to repeal the army's expansion.[242] While most others who were prosecuted had attacked the Sedition Act under the First Amendment before their trials began, and at their trials if not forbidden, Peck's only offense was petitioning to repeal the Act as a violation of the Constitution, along with questioning expansion of the army. Prosecution for an opinion that the Sedition Act was unconstitutional had been presciently predicted by Albert Gallatin in opposing the Act in 1798, as he objected that the truth defense would help little if an opinion was prosecuted and if a packed jury "declar[ed] the opinion ungrounded, or, in other words, false and scandalous, and its publication malicious."[243] The Federalist press, reporting his September 1799 arrest, described Peck as "an influential Jacobin,"[244] though he had publicly condemned Jacobinism and praised Adams before the Sedition Act.[245]

Peck was paraded from his arraignment to prison, and the procession became "the public exhibition of a suffering martyr for the freedom of speech and the press, and the right of petitioning," with the result that a "hundred missionaries in the cause of democracy, stationed between New-York and Cooperstown could not have done so much for the republican cause."[246] On the eve of New York's elections of May 1800, Peck's trial was delayed and his prosecution suspended at the

[239] Richard Harison to Timothy Pickering (10 Apr.1800), PICKERING PAPERS r.26, fol.77, 78.

[240] Timothy Pickering to Richard Harison (22 Apr.1800), PICKERING PAPERS r.13, fol.406.

[241] *See generally* FREEDOM'S FETTERS 390–98; CRISIS 223; EMPIRE 223–27. Court records are in Case Files (1790–1915) and Minutes (1790–1914), U.S. Circuit Court for the District of New York (National Archives at New York City, R.G.21.34.7).

[242] Indictment at 3–4 (undated); Minutes at 144 (4 Sept.1799) (crime on 15 Apr.1799); *see* JOURNAL-N.Y. 123 (16 Feb.1799). That Peck's "writings" were petitions is shown by them being "a bundle of papers at least six inches thick," Affidavit of Nathan Patmer (25 June 1799), "a printed paper" that one deponent signed. Affidavit of Jonathan Brown (27 June 1799).

[243] 8 ANNALS 2162 (July 1798).

[244] *E.g.*, [No Caption], GAZETTE OF THE UNITED STATES (Philadelphia), 9 Oct.1799, at 2; [No Caption], UNIVERSAL GAZETTE (Philadelphia), 17 Oct.1799, at 3.

[245] PLOUGH-JOGGER [JEDIDIAH PECK], POLITICAL WARS OF OTSEGO 95 (E. Phinney, Cooperstown 1796); Jedediah Peck (Chairman), *Address to John Adams*, OTSEGO HERALD (Cooperstown), 31 May 1798, at 3.

[246] 1 POLITICAL PARTIES-N.Y. 132.

same time as Greenleaf's, because "his consequence would be augmented by the measures, which might be taken for his punishment," while "he will be under greater restraint while he remains in his present situation."[247] He was reelected by a strong majority.[248]

The Haswell Prosecution and His *Vermont Gazette*

Paterson finally had two other Sedition Act trials, and other chances to use the reasoning of his draft opinions, as the semiannual circuit brought him back to Vermont in mid-1800.

Anthony Haswell,[249] the editor of the "leading Democratic-Republican newspaper in Vermont,"[250] was another target of Pickering's assault a year before the 1800 election. His sin was to support Lyon, decrying his trial, supporting his reelection,[251] detailing his mistreatment in prison, and printing Lyon's advertisement for his lottery to pay his high fine, which included a strong political statement. Haswell was indicted under the Sedition Act in early October 1799. One count was for printing the advertisement,[252] which described Lyon's incarceration by "the oppressive hand of usurped power . . . in a loathsome prison . . . suffering all the indignities which can be heaped upon him by a hardhearted savage" (the marshal).[253] The second count was for censuring "British Influence" in the Federalist administration by it placing "the confidence of the government" in "Tories, men who had fought against our independence . . . who had shared in the desolation of our towns[,] the abuse of our wives[,] sisters and daughters."[254] After being arrested without being told the charges, taken fifty-five miles by horseback in the rain, and denied bail and kept overnight in a "dungeon" by the same "hard-hearted

[247] Richard Harison to Timothy Pickering (10 Apr.1800), Pickering Papers r.26, fol.77, 78A, 78.

[248] Freedom's Fetters 397.

[249] *See generally* Trial of Anthony Haswell, Wharton's State Trials 684 (C.C.D. Vt. 1800), reprinted in United States v. Haswell, 26 F.Cas.218 (C.C.D. Vt. 1800) (No. 15,324); Freedom's Fetters 359–73; Crisis 123–25; 8 DAB 390. Court records are in Case Files (1792–1911), U.S. Circuit Court for the District of Vermont (National Archives at Waltham, Mass., R.G.21.48.2, Box 4).

[250] Freedom's Fetters 359.

[251] *E.g.*, Constitutional Federalist, *Look at Federalists!*, Vermont Gazette (Bennington), 23 Nov.1798, at 2; *Col. Lyon, in Answer*, Vermont Gazette (Bennington), 12 Oct.1798, at 1.

[252] After the original lottery advertisement without the commentary on 3 Jan.1799, *To the Public*, Vermont Gazette (Bennington), 24 Jan.1799, at 4; *id.*, 31 Jan.1799, at 4; *id.*, 7 Feb.1799, at 4.

[253] Indictment at 2 (7 Oct.1799); Wharton's State Trials at 684.

[254] Indictment at 4–5; *British Influence*, Vermont Gazette (Bennington), 15 Aug.1799, at 2 (from the *Aurora*).

savage,"[255] Haswell was arraigned before Justice Cushing, pleaded not guilty, and had to post $2,000 security until trial in May 1800.[256] While Haswell awaited trial, the zealous federal attorney tried to indict him for an additional publication, but was stopped by an unwilling grand jury.[257]

Paterson presided over the trial (with District Judge Samuel Hitchcock again). Haswell defended the first count, among other things, by pointing out that if anyone was libeled it was the marshal and not, as the Sedition Act required, the President or Congress, and that reference to them should not be inferred.[258] When Haswell sought to defend the second count with the secretary of war's letter stating that he "can see no reason why" former "Tories . . . should not also be considered" for office, Paterson ruled that it "would not be admissible, even if [sender and recipient were] present," unless Haswell proved the specific Tories considered were those that fought against independence, desolated towns, and abused wives and daughters.[259] Haswell's later recollection of the trial had Paterson railing at Matthew Lyon as "a seditious libeller of your government, a convict justly suffering the penalty of a mild law," defending the Sedition Act as preventing "base repetitions of his crime, like that which you now have under consideration," characterizing Haswell's articles as "dangerous and malignant publications" and "base calumny," and refusing to inform him where he would be incarcerated though his son's leg was about to be amputated.[260] Whether or not Haswell's recollection was correct, Wharton's description of the jury charge rings true.

Paterson instructed the jury that for the second count "no attempt at justification has been made," and that if the jury found his "intent was defamatory, and the publication was made, they must convict."[261] Thus, as with Lyon, Paterson restricted the jury to two narrow issues, and told the jury to convict if both were shown while again apparently not using parallel language about acquitting Haswell. After the jury quickly found the hapless printer guilty, Paterson sentenced Haswell to two months imprisonment and a $200 fine plus court costs.[262] Like Lyon, Haswell left prison to a hero's welcome, with marching band and booming cannon.[263]

[255] Wharton's State Trials 687n.

[256] Freedom's Fetters 363–64; *see* 3 DHSC 388; [No Caption], Bee (New London), 20 Nov.1799, at 3.

[257] *Id.* 364; Presentment at 4 (11 Oct.1799); Information (11 Oct.1799).

[258] Wharton's State Trials 686n. The trial was on 5 May 1800. Docket (5 May 1800).

[259] Anthony Haswell, *A Brief Recital*, Green-Mountain Farmer (Bennington), 31 Mar.1813, at 1, cited in Freedom's Fetters 362 n.8; James McHenry to William Darke, 31 Jefferson Papers 493; Wharton's State Trials 685, 686.

[260] *Id.*

[261] Wharton's State Trials 686.

[262] *Id.* 686; Docket (9 May 1800) (case 24); Mittimus at 2 (9 May 1800).

[263] *Id.* 687n.

After Jefferson took office, Justice Chase believed Paterson and himself, and possibly other justices, would be subject to impeachment. He warned Paterson that "a day of severe trial is fast approaching for the friends of the Constitution, and we I fear must be principal actors, and may be sufferers therein." [264]

Justice Samuel Chase and the First Amendment: The Fairbanks, Brown, Cooper, and Callender Cases

Figure 6.4 Justice Samuel Chase (on Supreme Court 1796–1811). Portrait by John Wesley Jarvis 1811. (Courtesy of National Portrait Gallery, Smithsonian Institution/Art Resource.)

Justice Samuel Chase (Figure 6.4) announced his intentions during one of the Sedition Act trials: "I do not want to oppress, but I will restrain, as far as I can, all such licentious attacks on the government."[265] Chase charged grand juries with vehemence, and three did not disappoint him. He presided over the two most controversial Sedition Act trials, those of Cooper and Callender, the latter in a manner that provided the core of impeachment efforts in 1804–1805. He also sentenced a pair of other Sedition Act defendants, Fairbanks and Brown.

Chase's View of the Constitutionality of Restricting the Press and Speech

Chase, in the first of those trials, indirectly addressed the constitutionality of the Sedition Act. He responded to the Federalist-Republican division, in which "one thinks the liberties of our country endangered by the licentiousness, the other, by the restrictions of the press." Chase also responded to the defendant's complaint

[264] Samuel Chase to William Paterson (6 Apr.1802), Paterson Papers-NYPL 755, 759.

[265] Trial of Thomas Cooper, Wharton's State Trials 664, 678 (C.C.D. Pa. 1800).

that "the press is open to those who will praise, while the threats of the law [Sedition Act] hang over those who blame the conduct of men in power."[266] Beginning his jury charge, Chase emphatically supported the law of seditious libel and the Sedition Act, using language that later haunted his impeachment trial:

> All governments which I have ever read of or heard of punish libels against themselves. If a man attempts to destroy the confidence of the people in their officers, their supreme magistrate, and their legislature, he effectually saps the foundation of the government. A republican government can only be destroyed in two ways; the introduction of luxury, or the licentiousness of the press. This latter is the more slow, but most sure and certain, means of bringing about the destruction of the government. The legislature of this country, knowing this maxim, has thought proper to pass a law to check this licentiousness of the press . . . the Sedition Law.[267]

With this ideological framework in mind, Chase painted criticism of officials and the legislature, and "licentiousness" of the press, as not just baneful but uniquely poisonous to America's new form of government, and he prescribed prosecutions of seditious libel as the only antidote. After passage of the Sedition Act, Chase fully accepted the Blackstone-Mansfield rationale for seditious libel, and embellished their canvas.

That left unanswered the degree or kind of criticism that would destroy the confidence of the people in government. However, Chase had provided that answer in his grand jury charge one week earlier, making clear that any criticism whatsoever was prohibited as lethal—"[p]rivate opinion must give way":

> we know that a *party* has since arisen, who wish that the administration of the Government had been entrusted to *other* hands . . . . There can be no Government without subordination, which implies submission; and submission in matters of a *civil* nature implies that the *minority* surrender up their judgement and will to the decision of a *majority*. *Every* citizen in America has engaged to be bound by the acts of the *majority* of his fellow citizens, signified by their representatives in their *national* and *state* legislatures, however repugnant to his own views of *propriety*, or even *justice*. Private opinion must give way to public judgement, or there must be an end of government.[268]

His charge went on to address the claim that some laws were unconstitutional, and treated it as an improper claim for a citizen to make at all; only "those whom

[266] *Id.* 665.
[267] *Id.* 670–71.
[268] Samuel Chase's Charge(C.C.D. Pa. 12 Apr.1800), 3 DHSC 408, 412.

the nation has chosen" as legislators may consider repeal of laws, and only judges may decide their constitutionality.[269] "[U]ntil it is repealed, it is the *duty* of every citizen to submit to it; and to give up his *private sentiments* to the *public will*."[270]

Thus, Chase, like Paterson, believed that, when a majority of representatives acted and passed legislation, or when a majority voted and elected a president, the "*minority* [must] surrender up their judgement" and "give up [their] *private sentiments*," and must not criticize Congress, its legislation, the President, the President's acts, or the government generally. Necessarily, he believed that the First Amendment did not enshrine any right for the minority to dissent, from an election onward. With these conclusions in mind about the constitutionality of the Sedition Act and a restricted scope of freedoms of press and speech, Chase presided over Cooper's and Callender's trials in the spring of 1800. He had similar conclusions in mind as he presided over Fairbanks' and Brown's pleas and sentences in 1799, and as he said much the same thing in 1796 as in 1800 about republics falling from a licentious press, and as he advised even in 1796 that the *Aurora*'s "printer ought to be indicted for a false & base *libel* on our Government."[271]

The Fairbanks Prosecution and the Liberty Pole

Benjamin Fairbanks[272] of Massachusetts was described as a "deluded ringleader" in raising a liberty pole in October 1798.[273] It was topped by a placard saying, "Liberty and Equality—No Stamp Act—No Sedition—No Alien Bills—No Land Tax—Downfall to the Tyrants of America—Peace and Retirement to the President—Long Live the Vice-President and the Minority—May Moral Virtue be the Basis of Civil Government."[274] Liberty poles had a glorious history as part of prerevolution protest,[275] but all were regarded by Pickering and similar Federalists as "sedition poles"[276] or "Jacobin poles,"[277] a position that left Republicans

[269] 3 *id.* 412.

[270] 3 *id.* 413.

[271] Samuel Chase to James McHenry (4 Dec.1796), McHenry Correspondence 203.

[272] *See generally* Jacobin 103–10; Freedom's Fetters 261–62, 265–70; Crisis 119–20. Court records are in Case Files (1790–1911) and Docket (1790–1911), U.S. Circuit Court for the District of Massachusetts (National Archives at Waltham, Mass., R.G.21.23.2).

[273] *The Jacobin Pole*, Gazette of the United States (Philadelphia), 14 Nov.1798, at 3; *The Jacobin Pole*, Oracle of the Day (Portsmouth), 17 Nov.1798, at 3.

[274] Jacobin 105; *Boston, Nov.12*, Bee (New London), 21 Nov.1798, at 2; *Arrest of Mr. Fairbanks*, Independent Chronicle (Boston), 12 Nov.1798, at 3.

[275] Paul A. Gilje, The Road to Mobocracy 52–58 (UNCP, Chapel Hill 1987).

[276] *E.g.*, *Benjamin Fairbanks*, Massachusetts Mercury (Boston), 21 June 1799, at 2 (Ames); *The Centinel*, Albany Centinel, 16 Nov.1798, at 3.

[277] *E.g.*, *The Jacobin Pole*, Gazette of the United States (Philadelphia), 14 Nov.1798, at 3; *The Jacobin Pole*, Oracle of the Day (Portsmouth), 17 Nov.1798, at 3.

incredulous.[278] Though the placard merely advocated legislative change and electoral change, the pole had the misfortune of being raised in the Massachusetts town of a leading Federalist, Fisher Ames, who viewed liberty poles as an "insult on the law,"[279] as he scrutinized the democrats who "abound in Dedham" with constant concern that the "devil of sedition is immortal."[280] The Federalist prosecutor wanted an arrest to stop that abounding, and Fairbanks had the misfortune to be one of the first perpetrators identified. Fairbanks was indicted as "an accessory in erecting this rallying point of insurrection and civil war," and had to post security at $4,000 (double the maximum fine for the offense under the Sedition Act).[281]

Fairbanks's trial was set for June 1799 with Chase presiding (sitting with Judge John Lowell, who reportedly had issued a warrant "to demolish the . . . symbol of sedition"[282]). Abandoning plans to present a defense at trial, Fairbanks pleaded guilty, admitted his presence when the liberty pole was raised, and professed ignorance of "how heinous an offense" it truly was.[283] Ames was moved by such contrition, or at least by Fairbanks being "an opulent farmer,"[284] and urged mercy, leading to Chase's lightest sentence (a mistake he never repeated) of six hours in prison and a $5.00 fine (plus court costs).[285] The defendant in the parallel case was not so fortunate.

The Brown Prosecution as an "Apostle of Sedition"

David Brown,[286] an itinerant Republican speaker and colporteur, also visited Ames's and Fairbanks's town in October 1798. Ames, sure that Jacobins "have sent runners everywhere to blow the trumpet of sedition," quickly identified one of them as "Brown, a vagabond ragged fellow, [who] has lurked around in Dedham, telling everyone the sins and enormities of the government" and whose poison

278 *E.g., Newark, November 20*, Centinel of Freedom (Newark), 20 Nov.1798, at 3.

279 Fisher Ames to Christopher Gore (18 Dec.1798), 1 Ames Works 245, 246.

280 Fisher Ames to Jeremiah Smith (22 Nov.1798), 1 Ames Works 240.

281 Jacobin 106; Docket (June Term 1799) (summarizing indictment). The maximum fine under Section 2 was $2,000, lower than the maximum under Section 1 of $5,000.

282 *Fall of the Dedham Pole*, Massachusetts Mercury (Boston), 9 Nov.1798, at 3.

283 *Benjamin Fairbanks*, Massachusetts Mercury (Boston), 21 June 1799, at 2; *Circuit Court Proceedings*, Connecticut Journal (New Haven), 26 June 1799, at 3; Docket (June Term 1799) (pleaded not guilty, then changed to guilty).

284 Fisher Ames to Timothy Pickering (22 Nov.1798), 1 Ames Works 241, 243.

285 Docket (June Term 1799); *Benjamin Fairbanks*, Massachusetts Mercury (Boston), 21 June 1799, at 2; *Circuit Court Proceedings*, Connecticut Journal (New Haven), 26 June 1799, at 3.

286 *See generally* Jacobin 103–10; Freedom's Fetters 257–61, 262–65; Crisis 114–19. Court records are in the same location as for Fairbanks.

"got them ready to set up a liberty-pole."[287] Finally arrested in March 1799 under state charges of sedition, Brown's federal indictment charged him with "seditious writings" intended to "defame the Government of the United States, and the Congress thereof, and the President," such as "A Dissertation," "A Dagger for Tyrants," and the "Jacobin Pole" itself, in violation of the Sedition Act.[288] Bail at $4,000 was far beyond his means, so he remained in jail until trial.[289] Between indictment and trial, Ames published essays against such emissaries as Brown, imploring the public "to repel the assaults of the jacobins, on law and liberty," and warning that "[e]missaries are sent to every class of men, and even to every individual man," by the wily Jacobins "trained, officered, regimented and formed" more perfectly than the militia.[290]

Brown's trial was set for the day after Fairbanks's trial, with Chase presiding again, and Brown also changed his plea from not guilty to guilty. This time, Ames did not urge mercy, but blamed Brown as the "wandering apostle of sedition" who had deluded Fairbanks,[291] and Brown did not help himself by showing much contrition or divulging names of abettors. Chase's small store of clemency was exhausted, and despite the guilty plea he proceeded to call the government's witnesses to determine "the degree of his guilt," and then imposed the stiffest sentence of any under the Sedition Act, eighteen months' imprisonment in addition to a $400 fine (plus costs) that must be paid before release.[292] Manifesting his zeal against seditious libel, Chase reportedly also lectured Brown on the "malignity and magnitude of his offences, on the vicious industry with which he had circulated and inculcated his disorganizing doctrines, and impudent fals[e]-hoods; and the very alarming and dangerous excesses to which he attempted to incite the uninformed part of the community."[293] Because Brown was unable to pay the fine, he remained imprisoned for a total of two and a half years, until Jefferson pardoned him a week after taking office.[294] The sequel came twelve years

[287] Fisher Ames to Christopher Gore (18 Dec.1798), 1 AMES WORKS 245, 247.

[288] Indictment at 1, 2, 9 (1 June 1799); *Circuit Court*, SALEM GAZETTE, 21 June 1799, at 1, 2; *Circuit Court*, PORCUPINE'S GAZETTE (Philadelphia), 21 June 1799, at 2. The state law arrest is in the federal court files, as is the transfer to federal hands. Complaint at 3 (1 Mar.1799) (arrested 22 Mar.1799); Habeas Corpus (5 June 1799).

[289] Petition (2 June 1800); *Circuit Court*, MASSACHUSETTS MERCURY (Boston), 7 June 1799, at 2; *Circuit Court*, DAILY ADVERTISER (New York), 12 June 1799, at 2.

[290] FISHER AMES, WORKS OF FISHER AMES 94, 95, 101 (Wait, Boston 1809).

[291] Indictment (jacket) (1 June 1799) (not guilty plea changed to guilty); *Circuit Court-Boston*, SALEM GAZETTE, 25 June 1799, at 2; *Benjamin Fairbanks*, AMERICAN MERCURY (Hartford), 27 June 1799, at 2.

[292] Petition (2 June 1800); *Circuit Court*, SALEM GAZETTE, 21 June 1799, at 1, 2; *Circuit Court*, PORCUPINE'S GAZETTE (Philadelphia), 21 June 1799, at 2.

[293] *Id.*

[294] Pardon for David Brown (12 Mar.1801), 33 JEFFERSON PAPERS 251.

later, when the author of the placard on the "Jacobin pole" was finally unmasked as none other than Ames's Republican brother, Dr. Nathaniel Ames![295]

The Cooper Prosecution and His *Northumberland Gazette*

Thomas Cooper[296] came to Pickering's attention[297] by ending his newspaper editorship in rural Pennsylvania with an essay, which the *Aurora* reprinted, describing what he would expect a self-aggrandizing president to do. That included "restrict[ing] by every means in my power the liberty of speech and the liberty of the press," "multiply[ing] laws against libel and sedition," and enforcing "doctrines of *confidence* in the executive."[298] President Adams readily agreed with Pickering that "it is a libel against the whole government, and as such ought to be prosecuted."[299] Cooper was arrested in November 1799, coincidentally the very day he published a handbill defending himself against the charge that his Republican writing was "in revenge" for being denied federal employment.[300] If there was any uncertainty, Cooper ensured that he would be prosecuted at the next circuit court session by publicly denouncing the Senate's "gag" on defense counsel's argument as he (as a lawyer as well as scientist) dramatically refused to defend Duane.[301]

Two weeks after that in April 1800, Cooper was indicted under the Sedition Act for the criticisms of Adams in his handbill defense a half year before.

[295] *Communication*, COLUMBIAN CENTINEL (Boston), 3 Aug. 1811, at 2, cited in JACOBIN 110 n.3.

[296] *See generally* Trial of Thomas Cooper, Wharton's State Trials 659 (C.C.D. Pa. 1800), reprinted in United States v. Cooper, 4 U.S. (4 Dall.) 341, 25 F.Cas.626, 631 (C.C.D. Pa.1800) (No. 14,861, 14,865); DUMAS MALONE, THE PUBLIC LIFE OF THOMAS COOPER, 1783–1839, at 111–49 (YUP, New Haven 1926); Eugene Volokh, *Thomas Cooper, Early American Public Intellectual*, 4 N.Y.U. J. LAW & LIBERTY 372 (2009); FREEDOM'S FETTERS 307–33; CRISIS 202–10; 4 DAB 414. Court records are in Criminal Case Files, *supra* note 202, at 2:I197, 2:pp.268, 261, 242 (C.C.D. Pa. 1800). (I refers to unnumbered images, and p. to numbered images.)

[297] Though one interesting account suggests that Pickering wrote the anonymous attack that spawned Cooper's handbill defense. PETER CHARLES HOFFER, THE FREE PRESS CRISIS OF 1800: THOMAS COOPER'S TRIAL FOR SEDITIOUS LIBEL 74 (UPKan, Lawrence 2011).

[298] Timothy Pickering to John Adams (1 Aug.1799), 9 ADAMS WORKS 5; Thomas Cooper, Mr. Cooper's Address to the Readers of the Sunbury and Northumberland Gazette ([Andrew Kennedy, Northumberland] 29 June 1799) (broadside).

[299] John Adams to Timothy Pickering (13 Aug.1799), 9 *id.* 13, 13–14; *see* Timothy Pickering to Charles Hall (1 Aug.1799), PICKERING PAPERS r.11, fol.528, 529.

[300] THOMAS COOPER, AN ACCOUNT OF THE TRIAL OF THOMAS COOPER 7, 4 (John Bioren, Philadelphia 1800) (a pamphlet Cooper disclaimed compiling); Thomas Cooper, To the Public ([George Schusler, Northumberland] 2 Nov.1799) (broadside), quoted in Wharton's State Trials at 660n.

[301] *Mr. Cooper's Answer*, AMERICAN CITIZEN (New York), 29 Mar.1800, at 2; *Mr. Cooper's Answer*, DAILY ADVERTISER (New York), 29 Mar.1800, at 2.

The indictment charged as criminal libels Cooper's statements that Adams "did sanction the Sedition Law," that when elected Adams was "in the infancy of political mistake," that some "doubted his capacity," that he saddled the country with "the expense of a permanent navy" and "a standing army," that he reduced the nation's credit "so low as to borrow money at eight percent, in time of peace," and that he "interfered . . . to influence the decisions of a court of justice," and wrongly delivered an accused British deserter for a British court martial.[302] The issue was simple but fundamental: whether citizens have a right to criticize government and its officials.

The trial was a cause célèbre, with Pickering sitting with the judges and half the cabinet attending, along with many members of Congress including some Sedition Act sponsors.[303] Pickering was there evidently because, growing up under a father who believed "few if any" of New England's clergy were "sufficiently explicit in showing the people their sins," he wanted to make sure federal judges were not similarly lax toward seditionists and their transgressions. (Though Pickering has been portrayed as an Evangelical Christian, he was at the other end of the theological spectrum as a Unitarian.[304])

Cooper's defenses were that his statements were true, "free from malicious imputation" (intent), and protected by "freedom of the press" which "sedition laws" attack.[305] He questioned "how the people can exercise on rational grounds their elective franchise, if perfect freedom of discussion of public characters be not allowed," if "prosecutions in *terrorem* close all the avenues of information"?[306] Although Chase (sitting with Judge Richard Peters) was generally lenient in relaxing evidentiary rules and allowing continuances,[307] he was adamant in excluding challenge to his refusal to subpoena the president for trial and in insisting that a publisher should already have "proper evidence" in hand "to justify your assertions" before printing any criticism of government.[308] Efforts at impartiality ceased as he charged the jury.

[302] Indictment (9 Apr.1800), Cooper's Account 7–8; Criminal Case Files 2:I197, I208, p.268, p.245.

[303] Thomas Cooper to Judge Chase (1 May 1800), *id.* 58, 64; *Letter from an Anonymous Correspondent*, Aurora (Philadelphia), 7 May 1800, reprinted in 3 DHSC 424, 426.

[304] Timothy Pickering to James McHenry (5 Jan.1811), McHenry Correspondence 561; Timothy Pickering to Charles F. Mercer (20 Feb. 1827), Pickering Papers r.16, fol.203–04.

[305] Wharton's State Trials 664, 665; Cooper's Account 18–19. The free press defense doubtless tracked his essay, Thomas Cooper, *On the Sedition Bill*, Political Essays 13–17 (Andrew Kennedy, Northumberland 1799).

[306] *Id.* 665; Cooper's Account 19.

[307] *Id.* 662, 667; Cooper's Account 41, 8–9, 11, 12, 14, 22, 27, 28, 31; Criminal Case Files 2:I203, p.253.

[308] *Id.* 662, 667; Cooper's Account 10, 13, 21.

Chase's jury charge began with the language quoted above that decried the mortal danger of "the licentiousness of the press" and implicitly upheld the Sedition Act.[309] He then instructed that the prosecution only need prove two things: that Cooper "did publish the matters contained in the indictment," and "did publish with intent to defame" (something he subsequently said was inferred from the publication itself).[310] He thereby deprived the jury of any opportunity to determine if Cooper's statements were libelous at all. Chase then decided both issues for the jury: the "fact of writing and publishing is clearly proved" and "not denied," and his "motives in this publication were to censure the conduct of the President," a point about intent Chase repeated as he went through each alleged libel.[311] Lest the jury mistakenly assume that there was a right to criticize the president, Chase stated in several ways that, "if you believe this, what opinion can you form of the President? Certainly the worst you can form: you would certainly consider him totally unfit for the high station which he has so honourably filled."[312] The "improper motives" were proved not only by intent to criticize the president, but by Cooper's design "to influence the minds against him on the next election," so that his criticisms were "made with intent to bring the President into contempt and disrepute, and excite against him the hatred of the people," just as the indictment charged.[313] Lest the jury fail to be outraged, Chase exclaimed that "I cannot suppress my feelings at this gross attack upon the President," protested that Cooper's publication was "the boldest attempt I have known to poison the minds of the people," and otherwise decried the crime.[314]

To ensure that the Sedition Act defense of truth did not give aid and comfort to such sedition, Chase instructed the jury, in words remembered in his impeachment trial, that Cooper "in his defence must prove every charge he has made to be true; he must prove it to the marrow. If he asserts three things, and proves but one, he fails; if he proves but two, he fails in his defence, for he must prove the whole of his assertions to be true."[315] Whatever proving "to the marrow" meant, it obviously meant the criminal defendant must go far beyond raising a reasonable doubt and instead must carry a heavy burden of proof. Chase appeared to shift the burden of proof to the accused not just for the truth defense but for all issues in the case.[316] His jury charge was described by a Republican senator, who observed it,

[309] *Id.* 670–71; COOPER'S ACCOUNT 42–43.

[310] *Id.* 671, 677; COOPER'S ACCOUNT 43, 50.

[311] *Id.* 671, 672, 672, 673, 673, 674, 675; COOPER'S ACCOUNT 43, 44, 44, 45, 46, 46–47, 48.

[312] *Id.* 672.

[313] *Id.* 674; *accord* 676.

[314] *Id.* 672, 675, 673, 676.

[315] *Id.* 676.

[316] *Id.* 676–77; *accord* MISUNDERSTANDING 122.

as showing "all the zeal of a well fee'd lawyer and the rancour of a vindictive and implacable enemy."[317] Not surprisingly, the jury's verdict was guilty.

Chase sentenced Cooper to a $400 fine and a half year in prison, with release only upon providing $2,000 bond (half himself and half others), though Chase made clear he would not be nearly so charitable if he thought "a party inimical to the government . . . were to pay the fine."[318] That party inimical to government did rise to the challenge and raise money for the fine, with Jefferson supplementing the fund with his personal contribution.[319] Cooper devoted much of his time in prison to a pamphlet containing the trial transcript and his commentary, and to a public letter challenging Chase's rulings, both addressed from the "prison of Philadelphia." After his half year there, Cooper returned home to learn that his wife had died days before.[320] Ironically, soon after Chase's impeachment failed to result in conviction, Cooper's own career as a Pennsylvania judge ended by a successful impeachment,[321] and he began a new career as a college professor and president.

The Callender Prosecution and His *Prospect Before Us*

James T. Callender,[322] a fugitive from seditious libel charges in Britain,[323] fled again from Philadelphia to Richmond, where his newspaper columns produced a Pickering letter asking the federal attorney to prosecute.[324] However, it was Callender's political tract entitled *The Prospect Before Us* that brought him into court, because of its effort to influence the presidential election of 1800 with such

[317] Stevens Thomson Mason to James Madison (23 Apr.1800), 17 Madison Papers 381, 382.

[318] Wharton's State Trials 679, 678 (24 Apr.1800); Sentence (24 Apr.1800); Criminal Case Files 2:I210–11, I221, p.249.

[319] Stevens T. Mason to Thomas Jefferson (11 July 1800), 32 Jefferson Papers 48, 49, 50n., 129n.

[320] Dumas Malone, The Public Life of Thomas Cooper, 1783–1839, at 136–37 (YUP, New Haven 1926); Discharge (8 Oct.1800), in Criminal Case Files 2:p.242.

[321] Wharton's State Trials 680n.; 4 DAB 414. Cooper's subsequent history is in Seymour S. Cohen, *The Correspondence of Thomas Jefferson and Thomas Cooper*, 147 Proc. Am. Philosophical Soc. 39 (2003).

[322] *See generally* Trial of James Thompson Callender, Wharton's State Trials 688 (C.C.D. Va. 1800), reprinted in United States v. Callender, 25 F.Cas. 239 (C.C.D. Va. 1800) (No. 14,709); Michael Durey, "With the Hammer of Truth": James Thompson Callender 129–37 (UPV, Charlottesville 1990); Freedom's Fetters 334–58; Crisis 210–20; 3 DAB 425. Case files are extracted in Wharton and in Chase Trial. Newspaper reports of the trial were later printed as [James T. Callender], Trial of James Thompson Callender, for Sedition (n.p. 1804). Court records are in Ended Cases-Restored (1790–1882), U.S. Circuit Court for the District of Virginia (Library of Virginia, Richmond, Box 17 and microfilm "misc." reel 669).

[323] 23 State Trials 79; 26 Hamilton Papers 36 n.5.

[324] Timothy Pickering to Thomas Nelson (14 Aug.1799), Pickering Papers r.11, fol.611.

charged language as posing the choice "between Adams . . . war and beggary, and Jefferson peace and competency."[325]

Chase, leaving Cooper's trial in Pennsylvania for circuit court in Virginia, was given by Maryland's attorney general a copy of the *Prospect* with the "libellous" passages underlined.[326] According to a lawyer's testimony at Chase's impeachment, Chase said "if a jury of honest men could be found there, he would punish Callender" and "would teach the lawyers in Virginia the difference between the liberty and the licentiousness of the press"; newspapers just before Callender's trial reported Chase's words similarly.[327] Chase clearly chafed to enforce the Sedition Act in the south for the first time, which Virginia's Republican governor branded "an electioneering trick."[328] In response, that governor and Jefferson hoped to bring the Virginia Resolutions and the Sedition Act's unconstitutionality to the nation's attention by the state "employing counsel to defend him" (Callender).[329] Madison, far from bemoaning an electioneering trick, gloated that the Federalist Party "is so industriously co-operating in its own destruction."[330]

Chase gave a riproaring charge to the grand jury in Richmond, the same charge he had given when Cooper was presented in Philadelphia. He quoted "our illustrious patriotic and beloved President" in warning that the United States "are still in jeopardy by the hostile designs, and insidious acts of a foreign nation; as well as by the dissemination among them of those principles, subversive of the foundation of all religious, moral, and social obligations."[331] He instructed the grand jury that once congressional representatives act the minority must "give up . . . private sentiments," in the words quoted earlier.[332] Noting that the constitutionality of the Sedition Act had been questioned, Chase disputed the main arguments of the Virginia and Kentucky Resolutions, and equated private sentiments disagreeing with such laws with openly opposing their execution.[333] He told the grand jury it was their "bounden and indispensable duty to present" or

[325] Indictment at 16 (24–26 May 1800); Wharton's State Trials at 690.

[326] Chase Trial 43, 44; 3 DHSC 438 (*Aurora*).

[327] *Id.* 43; [No Caption], Alexandria Times, 5 June 1800, at 3; 3 DHSC 439 (reprinting *Aurora*).

[328] James Monroe to Thomas Jefferson (4 Jan.1800), 3 Monroe Writings 169, 170.

[329] James Monroe to Thomas Jefferson (25 May 1800), 3 Monroe Writings 179, 180; *accord* Chase Trial 34; Kathryn Preyer, *United States v. Callender: Judge and Jury in a Republican Society*, in Origins of the Federal Judiciary: Essays on the Judiciary Act of 1789, at 173, 180–81 (Maeva Marcus ed., OUP, New York 1992); Misunderstanding 133.

[330] James Madison to James Monroe (23 May 1800), 2 Letters and Other Writings of James Madison 160 (Lippincott, Philadelphia 1865).

[331] The same charge as in Philadelphia, Samuel Chase's Charge (C.C.D. Pa. 12 Apr.1800), 3 DHSC 408, 416; 3 *id.* 435.

[332] 3 *id.* 413, 411.

[333] 3 *id.* 412–13, 413.

indict any violation of the Sedition Act.[334] When later asked whether his charge was "a moral, a political, a religious or a judicial one," Chase said "it was a little of all."[335]

The grand jury did not disappoint him, presenting Callender as a violator of the Act, citing his *Prospect*,[336] and approving an indictment of him. The indictment quoted about twenty passages from the tract, beginning with the claim that the "reign of Mr. Adams" has "been one continued tempest of malignant passions" whose "grand object" has been "to calumniate and destroy every man who differs from his opinions," resulting in "despotism"; and ending with the description of Adams as "[f]oremost in whatever is detestable," an aristocrat, and a "hoary headed incendiary."[337]

The trial was to begin a mere four days after the presentment. Though motions for postponement gave the defense six more days, the trial was held on the third of June 1800 over their repeated objection of being far from prepared. Chase's bias frequently showed in the transcript, as he (supported by Judge Cyrus Griffin) denied further continuances, refused to allow jurors to be asked whether they had formed an opinion about the *Prospect*, refused to strike a juror who "had formed an unequivocal opinion, that such a book . . . came within the sedition law," and allowed only the question whether they had formed "an opinion on this charge"—while refusing to have the indictment read to them so they could know what "this charge" was.[338] Chase declared that "the defence had been conceived and continued in error" and had "all along mistaken the law," and insisted that the defense—but not the prosecution—must make an offer of proof before each witness was called to enable the judges to determine the relevance of the proposed questions.[339]

Chase's rulings were equally tilted. He ruled that wrong opinions were as criminal as false statements of fact and equally must be proved true to provide a defense, and that passages were nonlibellous only if they "contain the truth in all parts" and are "a candid and fair discussion of constitutional subjects, of real grievances, or of political opinions."[340] He ruled that the prosecution must only prove publication

[334] 3 *id.* 414.

[335] Chase Trial 63 (Baltimore iteration).

[336] Presentment (24 May 1800), reprinted in 3 DHSC 435.

[337] Indictment at 1–2, 13–14 (24–26 May 1800); Wharton's State Trials 694, 688, 689; *cf.* Indictment, Chase Trial app.48, 48, 52, citing James T. Callender, The Prospect Before Us: Vol.I, [at 30, 274] (Callender, Richmond 1800); and Extracts, Chase Trial app.55.

[338] Wharton's State Trials 694, 696, 697, 696–97. The motion for postponement (Affidavit (28 May 1800)) is reprinted in Chase Trial app.53.

[339] *Id.* 700, 708, 706. That offer of proof was made by Callender in 6 handwritten pages, Affidavit (28 May 1800), but Chase declined to summon most of the requested witnesses, Summonses (29 May 1800).

[340] *Id.* 695, 698.

and falsity (except for once adding they must also prove libelousness), and most importantly, that the jury had no "right to consider the Constitution" and in effect that no defense of freedoms of press and speech, and no attack on the constitutionality of the Sedition Act, could be offered.[341] The latter ruling was aimed at bigger game than Callender; it was aimed at refuting the Virginia and Kentucky Resolutions, which explains its length and its prior preparation.[342] Another ruling that particularly figured in Chase's impeachment was that no witness could be called or document offered to disprove only part of a charge—no evidence "is admissible that does not go to justify the whole charge," and instead "[y]ou must prove both these points, or you prove nothing," even if the other half of the charge would be addressed by another witness.[343] Not surprisingly, the witness at issue was the former senator who had introduced the Virginia Resolutions.[344] The reality that the case had three prosecutors and no impartial judge caused the defense attorneys to refuse to proceed, leaving the hapless Callender unrepresented.[345] However, the defense had scripted that departure as part of the overall plan to score points for Republicanism, though not for Callender. The defense plan started with futile motions to postpone to generate sympathy,[346] and continued with claims to be "little acquainted with the doctrine of libels" though Hay had written anonymous essays attacking it,[347] ending with the attorneys walking out.

The jury found Callender guilty, and Chase sentenced him to a $200 fine and nine months imprisonment followed by a $1,200 bond.[348] He apparently subjected Callender to a blistering lecture (it did not appear in the transcript and may not be accurately reported in Republican newspapers). Chase reportedly said the verdict was "*pleasing to him*, because it showed that the laws of the U. States could be enforced in Virginia, *the principal object of this prosecution*," and because "he did not think there was so bad a man in the United States" as Callender.[349] Addressing the First Amendment, he repeated much of his jury charge from the *Cooper* trial:

> there was a very great difference between the liberty and the abuse or licen[t]iousness of the press:—that the licentiousness of the press would most certainly destroy any government, and particularly a republican form

[341] *Id.* 708, 695, 697, 712; 710, 709, 711, 712–18; *cf.* Opinion of J. Chase, CHASE TRIAL app.65.

[342] *Id.* 712–18.

[343] *Id.* 706–07; *contra* MISUNDERSTANDING 134–36.

[344] John Taylor, 18 DAB 331, 332.

[345] Wharton's State Trials 712.

[346] *Id.* 690, 691, 692, 694, 709; 3 DHSC 456.

[347] *Id.* 692; HORTENSIUS [GEORGE HAY], AN ESSAY ON THE LIBERTY OF THE PRESS 1–2 (Aurora, Philadelphia 1799).

[348] The court records show that in an uncaptioned sheet. *Accord* Wharton's State Trials 718.

[349] *Richmond (Examiner) June 6*, ALEXANDRIA TIMES, 12 June 1800, at 2; *From the Examiner*, CONSTITUTIONAL TELEGRAPH (Boston), 21 June 1800, at 1.

> of government—that it would corrupt the public opinion, and destroy the morals of the people; . . . that the liberty of the press consisted in the unrestrained but fair discussion of principles and conduct, and would never be said to consist in securing impunity to wilful & malicious slanderers.[350]

To this allusion to the Blackstone-Mansfield definition of freedom of press and rationale for seditious libel, Chase added a reproof of printers who "seemed to mistake the licen[t]iousness for the liberty of the press," and noted that it aggravated Callender's crime that his words were written "avowedly for an electioneering purpose." (Thus, to disagree with officials and the current administration was more seditious if its aim was to urge the electorate to oppose with votes than merely to oppose with opinion.)[351] However, Chase never elucidated for Virginia lawyers, or anyone else, "the difference between the liberty and the licentiousness of the press" as he had promised, unless "liberty" meant praise of officials and government while "licentiousness" meant dissent.

Why did Chase not directly discuss freedoms of press and speech, or quote the Blackstone-Mansfield definition rather than merely alluding to it, or expressly uphold the constitutionality of the Sedition Act, in his trials, other than perhaps after Callender's trial was over? Because he did not want to. He did not want to debate the Virginia Resolutions or the Virginians on their own terms, or to enable defense counsel to respond to a constrictive interpretation of the First Amendment or to reasoning about the Sedition Act. Instead, Chase had cleverly devised a strategy to cut them off at the pass, by denying the jury's authority to consider the constitutionality of an act of Congress, extrapolating that to deny jury capacity to hear a defense based on First Amendment protections, and extrapolating that to handcuff defense lawyers from arguing either to the jury. Furthermore, he would cloak his presuppositions that the Sedition Act was constitutional, and that the First Amendment had only the narrow Blackstone-Mansfield meaning, in unchallengeably vague references to "licentiousness" of the press. It was a devised strategy, because Chase came into court with a lengthy prepared opinion, which was uncharacteristic though not unprecedented (he did the same in the *Fries* trial).[352] Why did Chase not couple his crafty approach with crafty trial management? Because he could not. As an essayist wrote early in his career, Chase's "very existence depends on public convulsion,"[353] drawing him to turbulent controversy as a moth to flame. Callender's counsel successfully provided that flame.

350 *Richmond, June 6*, Federal Gazette (Baltimore), 11 June 1800,at 2; *James Thompson Callender*, Daily Advertiser (New York), 14 June 1800, at 2, 3.

351 *Id.*

352 As he styled it in his impeachment exhibits, Chase Trial app.65–68; Wharton's State Trials 712–18.

353 James Haw et al., Stormy Patriot: The Life of Samuel Chase 48 (MHS, Baltimore 1980).

The sequel to this last Sedition Act trial was that Pickering could only celebrate at a distance, having been dismissed by Adams the prior month,[354] and Callender could not get his wish of "sending Pickering to a *mad house*."[355] Joining Lyon and Cooper in turning a Sedition Act cell into a writer's garret, Callender wrote the other half of his *Prospect* from jail, until Jefferson's pardon released him.[356] A year after Jefferson's election, Callender, long assisted charitably by Jefferson[357] but denied a federal office as postmaster, turned on the Republicans and became an equally vitriolic Federalist writer.[358] Duane later did much the same.[359] Jefferson finally characterized much of Callender's writings as "scurrilities,"[360] after Callender became the journalist who publicized the Sally Hemings account.

The Delaware Circuit Court and the Common Law Crimes Ruling

After the *Callender* trial, Chase held circuit court in Delaware, where he confirmed the Republican charge that he, hooded as grim reaper, was prowling the circuit with scythe aloft to smite any appearance of sedition. Though denied by Federalist newspapers,[361] Delaware's only Republican paper[362] reported that Chase rejected the grand jury's report that it could not find anyone to charge with violating federal law, and told them he was "credibly informed, and [a] report says you have a printer who publishes a *very seditious paper* in this state," which "*must be* taken notice of," because it is "high time, sir, that the *spirit of sedition* which prevails among many of our printers should be checked." Telling the federal attorney that review of newspaper issues "*must be done*," Chase refused to discharge the grand jury, despite their entreaties, and said he was "*determined* to have those seditious printers prosecuted *to the extremity of the law*."[363] Just before the *Callender* trial, Chase had done the same thing in circuit court in Maryland, observing

[354] Gerard H. Clarfield, Timothy Pickering and the American Republic 211–12 (UPitP, Pittsburgh 1980).

[355] Prospect Before Us 4.

[356] James T. Callender to Thomas Jefferson (14 Aug.1800), 32 Jefferson Papers 100; Pardon (16 Mar.1801), 33 *id.* 309.

[357] 32 Jefferson Papers 235, 244–45.

[358] Thomas Jefferson to James Monroe (15 July 1802), 8 Jefferson Writings 164, 166; Thomas Jefferson to Albert Gallatin (7 Oct.1802), 8 *id.* 172, 173.

[359] Thomas Jefferson to James Monroe (19 Oct.1823), 10 Jefferson Writings 275.

[360] Thomas Jefferson to Abigail Adams (22 July 1804), 1 Adams-Jefferson 274, 275.

[361] [No Caption], Daily Advertiser (New York), 9 July 1800, reprinted in 3 DHSC 446.

[362] Which was Chase's quarry, Wilmington's *Mirror of the Times* and its editor James Wilson. 2 Madison Papers-Secretary 398n.; 3 DHSC 443 n.2.

[363] [No Caption], Mirror of the Times (Wilmington), 4 July 1800, reprinted in 3 DHSC 445, 446; *accord Good People of America, Remember Judge Chase*, Carlisle Gazette (Carlisle), 23 July 1800, at 3; *Letter from an Anonymous Correspondent*, Aurora (Philadelphia), 28 June 1800, reprinted in 3 DHSC 442.

to the grand jury that "one of the most *licentious* presses in the United States was supported in Baltimore," and pressing for an indictment, at least according to Republican papers.[364] Chase also gave a glimpse of his motivation, as he took time there to write to the secretary of war to ask "the state of the votes as you expect it will be in each state."[365] As the *Callender* trial was about to begin, Chase also took time to demand that Callender's newspaper release the name of the "false, scandalous, wicked, and malicious *slanderer and calumniator*" who criticized Chase's bias in Cooper's trial, so that Chase could sue him.[366]

This resolute hunt for the demons of sedition raises suspicion about Chase's oft-cited denial of existence of federal common law and federal common law crimes such as seditious libel. That judicial opinion was delivered during April 11–20, 1798.[367] It came at a time when some Federalists were proposing a sedition law, but when most Federalists had not rallied to its support—just a week later, Jefferson wrote to Madison that "one of the war-party, in a fit of unguarded passion declared some time ago they would pass . . . a sedition bill."[368] Federalists were equally aware of that declaration—the same day Abigail Adams wrote of "a Sedition Bill, which I presume they [Congress] will do before they rise."[369] Chase's opinion destroyed the frequent objection that no federal Sedition Act was needed because it would merely duplicate common law, and his opinion was cited against that objection in congressional debates over the proposed bill.[370] Yet Chase had held the opposite view a year and a half earlier, when his advisory opinion said the *Aurora*'s "printer ought to be indicted for a false & base *libel* on our government,"[371] and at sentencing time in the 1798 case; and he is alleged to have "reversed" his 1798 position in a case a mere year later.[372] This suggests that Chase's ruling was disingenuous, a crafty effort to demonstrate a need for a sedition law, a temporary posture rather than a sincere reversal.

The 1804–1805 Impeachment of Justice Chase

Chase was impeached because of his actions in that *Callender* trial, in the ensuing Delaware circuit court, in the *Fries* trial, and in a later Maryland circuit

[364] *Alexandria, June 5*, ALEXANDRIA TIMES, 5 June 1800, at 3; *Baltimore, June 21*, CAROLINA GAZETTE (Charleston), 3 July 1800, at 3; 3 DHSC 439.

[365] Samuel Chase to James McHenry (12 May 1800), MCHENRY CORRESPONDENCE 456–57.

[366] 3 DHSC 437, 440, 443, 424.

[367] United States v. Worrall, 2 U.S. (2 Dall.) 384 (C.C.D. Pa. 1798); 3 DHSC 248.

[368] Thomas Jefferson to James Madison (26 Apr.1798), 30 JEFFERSON PAPERS 299.

[369] Abigail Adams to Mary Cranch (26 Apr.1798), NEW LETTERS OF ABIGAIL ADAMS 164, 165 (Stewart Mitchell ed., Houghton Mifflin, Boston 1947).

[370] 8 ANNALS 2113.

[371] Samuel Chase to James McHenry (4 Dec.1796), MCHENRY CORRESPONDENCE 203.

[372] *E.g.*, SAVING 798–99; MISUNDERSTANDING 95.

court.[373] The impeachment story has been oft told,[374] but its repudiation of Chase's seditious libel trials warrants mention.

A month before the *Callender* trial, Chase presided over the retrial of John Fries, who was charged with treason in the form of levying war by forcibly releasing prisoners and thereby preventing enforcement of a federal tax.[375] In the most attacked ruling, Chase began the trial with a written opinion contradicting the central defense argument, which he handed to the jury, and then announced that Fries's counsel may not argue or cite cases to the contrary.[376] The planned defense argument, as in the original trial of Fries, was that treason (levying war) had been much abused in English history and required more than just resistance to "carrying a particular law or regulation into effect."[377] With their argument gutted, defense counsel abandoned the case, as *Cooper*'s lawyers had done. Fries was tried without counsel,[378] though illiterate and impecunious.[379] Chase told Fries that the judges "will be your counsel," though the guilty verdict and sentence of hanging point to malpractice in that role. His warning to Fries that "whatever you say to your own crimination, is evidence . . .; but if you say anything to your justification, it is not evidence," predictably caused Fries not to testify at all.[380] Further prejudicing the case, Chase told the jury that Fries was convicted in his original trial.[381] Afterward, Adams pardoned Fries and his doomed compatriots, adding to Hamilton's litany of Adams's sins.[382]

Eight articles of impeachment were approved by the House of Representatives in March 1804, and what is most significant is that all but two involved

[373] The Evans transcript is used here, and in relevant part corresponds to the other transcript, which is SAMUEL H. SMITH & THOMAS LLOYD (TRANSCRIPTIONISTS), TRIAL OF SAMUEL CHASE . . . (Samuel H. Smith, Washington 1805, repr. Da Capo Press, New York 1970). Most of Fries' followers were prosecuted under the Sedition Act, as Chapter 7 will demonstrate.

[374] PETER CHARLES HOFFER & N.E.H. HULL, IMPEACHMENT IN AMERICA, 1635–1805, at 228–55 (YUP, New Haven 1984); WILLIAM H. REHNQUIST, GRAND INQUESTS 58–113 (Morrow, New York 1992); Adam A. Perlin, *The Impeachment of Samuel Chase: Redefining Judicial Independence*, 62 RUTGERS L. REV. 725, 742–82 (2010); Richard B. Lillich, *Chase Impeachment*, 4 AM. J. LEGAL HIST. 49 (1960); Robert R. Bair & Robin D. Coblentz, *The Trials of Mr. Justice Samuel Chase*, 27 MD. L. REV. 365, 379–85 (1967).

[375] Second Trial of John Fries, Wharton's State Trials 610, 610–12 (C.C.D. Pa. 1800), reprinted in In re Fries, 9 F.Cas. 924 (C.C.D. Pa. 1800) (No. 5,127); *see generally* Dwight F. Henderson, *Treason, Sedition, and Fries' Rebellion*, 14 AM. J. LEGAL HIST. 308, 309–16 (1970).

[376] *Id.* 615n., 646; William Lewis to Alexander Hamilton (11 Oct. 1800), 25 HAMILTON PAPERS 151, 152–53.

[377] *Id.* 647, rejected in the jury charge, *id.* 634, and written opinion, CHASE TRIAL app.44, 45.

[378] *Id.* 612, 625, 646 (motion for new trial), though he was offered appointed counsel, *id.* 620n.

[379] Oliver Wolcott to John Adams (25 May 1799), 2 WOLCOTT PAPERS 240.

[380] Wharton's State Trials 629, 636, 641.

[381] *Id.* 635.

[382] Proclamation (21 May 1800), *id.* 641; John Adams to Charles Lee (21 May 1800), 9 ADAMS WORKS 60.

Sedition Act trials or allegations; Republican outrage over the Sedition Act had not died with its expiration. The first article alleged Chase was "highly arbitrary, oppressive and unjust" in his opinion and exclusion of argument in the *Fries* trial. The second through sixth articles indicted acts in the *Callender* trial: refusing to exclude the juror who "had formed an unequivocal opinion" that the book "came within the sedition law"; refusing to allow the defense witnesses who would each disprove half of a charge; requiring the defense to write out questions and acting contemptuously and unjustly toward the accused and his counsel; and refusing to follow state procedure which summoned the accused to appear at the next court rather than arresting him and requiring him to stand trial immediately. The seventh article condemned Chase's efforts "to procure the prosecution of the printer" in the Delaware circuit. The eighth censured his later grand jury charge in a Maryland circuit as an "intemperate and inflammatory political harangue"[383] that, the articles of impeachment charged with deliberate irony,[384] amounted to seditious libel against the state and federal governments. (Chase's charge in Maryland had lamented that loss of freedom was "fast approaching" because of the "late alteration of the federal judiciary" and "universal suffrage" in Maryland that would bring "mobocracy, the worst of all possible governments," and that the cause was Jefferson's and the Republican party's delusion of "the natural rights of man . . . in a state of nature" and "under an established government."[385]) Chase immediately fired off a newspaper volley at the attack of "calumniators and party zealots," and then filed a lengthy answer and defense to the charges.[386]

The trial in the Senate was delayed from January to February 1805, as Chase got the postponement he denied to Cooper and Callender, when he argued "it is manifest, that for preparing such an answer as I have a right to make, . . . a considerable time must be necessary."[387] He also got the legal counsel he drove away for others, consisting of leading Federalist lawyers. After a trial lasting throughout February, Chase was acquitted because two-thirds did not vote to convict on any count, though a majority did on the third, fourth, and eighth counts.[388] The result

383 Articles of Impeachment, CHASE TRIAL app.3–6.

384 Deliberate because the articles of impeachment were "solely" drafted by John Randolph of Roanoke, CHASE TRIAL 261, who had long believed that the Sedition Act was "in open contempt of those solemn guarantees that insure the freedom of speech and of the press" and was "odious, tyrannical and unconstitutional." THE AUTOBIOGRAPHY OF MARTIN VAN BUREN 439, 440 (John C. Fitzpatrick ed., GPO, Washington 1920).

385 Samuel Chase's Charge (C.C.D. Md. 2 May 1803), reprinted in CHASE TRIAL app.60, 60–61.

386 *Memorial of Judge Chase*, COMMERCIAL ADVERTISER (New York), 4 Apr.1804, at 2 (widely reprinted); CHASE TRIAL app.7–40.

387 CHASE TRIAL 5.

388 *Id.* 266.

surprised many observers,[389] in a Senate with a Republican-Federalist division of 25–9,[390] and came in large part from superior defense counsel,[391] House prosecutors' ambiguity about impeachable offenses, and concern about setting the impeachment standard too low. Whether the charges amounted to constitutional grounds for impeachment was debated then and remains controversial.[392]

That result put an end to Federalist fears, which had not lacked foundation, that Republicans would also try to "swe[ep] the supreme judicial bench clean at a stroke."[393] Chase gloated that, while it was "cruel persecution I have suffered" and a "wicked prosecution," the outcome showed his "enemies are as great *fools* as *knaves*."[394] While he attracted the prosecution by zealous and overbearing enforcement of the Sedition Act against press and speech, the Republicans were indeed looking for a target in the exclusively Federalist third branch of government. Had Chase not existed they might have found it necessary to invent him.

Justice Bushrod Washington and the First Amendment: The Baldwin and Clark, Durrell, and Holt Cases

Justice Bushrod Washington presided over all or part of three recognized trials or pleas under the Sedition Act: Baldwin and Clark, Durrell of the *Mount Pleasant Register*, and Holt of New London's *Bee*.[395] He also presided over the October 1799 court appearance of Duane, and would have presided over the trials of Greenleaf and Peck had prosecution not been suspended.

Washington, methodical but not innovative, was not the justice who would question Federalist dogma about seditious libel. His mind was described unenthusiastically by Van Buren, the future president, after observing him in court, as "a highly respectable order" but not the "genius of Kent" (New York's chancellor).[396]

[389] Simeon Baldwin to Wife (4 Feb.1805), LIFE AND LETTERS OF SIMEON BALDWIN 348 (Simeon E. Baldwin ed., Tuttle, New Haven 1919); John Davenport to John C. Smith (25 Feb.1805), John Cotton Smith Papers (LC).

[390] *Id.* 349; 2 HISTORY OF SUPREME COURT 244.

[391] *Id.*; Rufus King to Samuel Chase (6 Mar.1805), 4 KING CORRESPONDENCE 444.

[392] John Quincy Adams to John Adams (8 Mar.1805), 3 ADAMS WRITINGS 106, 107–08, 109, 113; 2 HISTORY OF SUPREME COURT 243; RAOUL BERGER, IMPEACHMENT (rev. ed. HUP, Cambridge 1974).

[393] 3 *id.* 108; *accord* Alexander Hamilton to Robert G. Harper (19 Feb.1804), 26 HAMILTON PAPERS 190, 191.

[394] Samuel Chase to Rufus King (13 Mar.1805), 4 KING CORRESPONDENCE 444, 445, 446; Samuel Chase to Joseph Hopkinson (10 Mar.1805), CHASE CORRESPONDENCE; Timothy Pickering to John Marshall (26 Dec.1828), 11 MARSHALL PAPERS 187, 191.

[395] FREEDOM'S FETTERS 271, 285, 379, 388.

[396] *The Autobiography of Martin Van Buren* (pt. 2) 63, in 1918 ANNUAL REPORT OF THE AMERICAN HISTORICAL ASSOCIATION 5 (John C. Fitzpatrick ed., GPO, Washington 1919).

Shaping Washington's Opinion of the Sedition Act and Freedom of Press

Instead, Washington seems to have imbibed the dominant Federalist position unquestioningly. Soon after his nephew's confirmation to the Supreme Court, retired President Washington recommended and sent his nephew a pamphlet discussing the Sedition Act,[397] which he had received from Pickering.[398] The pamphlet, a jury charge and essay by Pennsylvania Judge Alexander Addison,[399] was one of the best Federalist defenses of seditious libel and the Sedition Act. It doubtless was studied by the justice, always deferential to his illustrious uncle's opinion and even more so after being designated his primary heir. As Justice Washington sentenced defendants under the Sedition Act, his actions and words were entirely consistent with Addison's pamphlet.

Addison began by stating that each person's rights extended so far "as not to injure those of others," on the ground that liberty must be restrained "from infringing the rights of others." Applying the principle to reputation, he posited that "[r]eputation, character, good name or opinion is a kind of property or possession," and concluded that reasoning and opinion must "never infringe the right of reputation," and "must not represent . . . exercise of religion, as false or ridiculous," and must not represent an "act or motive of the administration as unlawful, pernicious, or dishonest."[400] Here was a first logical gap in Federalist reasoning; the first conclusion might follow, but the second and third did not. Addison then tried to map the tangled roads where a truth defense was allowed or excluded, and those roads led him to Blackstone; he also stated the rule that "the court will direct . . . whether the matter be libellous or not," and, contradictorily, that a "jury [might] determine that a libel is no libel."[401] The claim that rules applying to other criminal cases should not apply equally to seditious libel cases was a second logical gap in the Federalist case.

Defense of the Sedition Act was the pamphlet's dominant subject. Addison again cited Blackstone for the proposition that seditious libel was already "an offence at common law," so that the new "law does not create any new offence."[402] In doing so, he assumed that seditious libel was part of the English common law received by American states, not part of what was abrogated by the nine state constitutions that safeguarded expansive freedoms of press, and he further assumed that the

397 George Washington to Bushrod Washington (31 Dec.1798), 37 Washington Writings 80, 81; *see* George Washington to John Marshall (30 Dec.1798), 3 Marshall Papers 530, 531.

398 Alexander Addison to Timothy Pickering (22 Nov.1798), Pickering Papers r.23, fol.322.

399 Alexander Addison, Liberty of Speech, and of the Press. A Charge to the Grand Juries (John Colerick, Washington 1798). The longer of two 1798 editions is used; 1799 and 1800 editions ensued.

400 *Id.* 5, 6.

401 *Id.* 7, 8, 9, 10.

402 *Id.* 10, 12.

English common law of seditious libel was adopted by the federal government without being abrogated by the First Amendment. Here was a third logical gap, assuming that English common law narrowly defining freedom of press was not abrogated by constitutional provisions protecting freedom of press and containing no express limitations. Addison then addressed the question whether the passage of the Sedition Act did not disprove that there was an existing common law offense, responding that some laws were "declaratory of the common law," that the Sedition Act resolved the claim that federal courts lacked jurisdiction of offenses not explicitly conferred by legislation, and that the Act benignly limited punishment and benevolently authorized truth as a justification.[403]

Responding to the first constitutional challenge, the absence of a delegated power to pass a Sedition Act, Addison built his case on the Necessary and Proper Clause and asserted, without analysis, "[i]t is evident, that the attempts and writings declared punishable by this law, have a direct tendency . . . to prevent or obstruct the execution of the powers vested by the constitution."[404] The concepts that the direct tendency of actions should be punishable, rather than the actions themselves if criminal, and that direct tendencies could be accurately distinguished from indirect tendencies, were a fourth logical leap in Federalist reasoning. Addison's claim remained unsupported that criminalizing seditious libel was necessary and proper to a delegated federal power.

Moving to the other principal constitutional challenge, the First Amendment, Addison, like Paterson, discussed not what was protected but what was not protected, saying that unless seditious libel was excluded "the most false and malicious libels might be published, against the government, acts, or measures" of government with "absolute impunity," which he found to be "a construction too absurd to be received as true" because it left government "without defence against the most dangerous enemy that can attack it, slander."[405] His reasoning ended at that fifth logical leap, that government could not survive against "false and malicious" criticism, that that was its "most dangerous" foe. He instead returned to the safety of Blackstone, dodging the need to show why government could not survive false criticism, by quoting a full page of Blackstone's definition of what freedom of press did not protect, that "liberty of the press . . . consists in laying no *previous* restraints upon publications, and not in freedom from censure . . . when published."[406]

Addison listed some consequences of his approach, which had long been points of criticism by opponents: "Every man is free to speak, but he speaks at his peril, and is answerable for all he says"; "Every repeater of the tale is, in like manner answerable as the author"; as a general rule "truth is no justification" and true

[403] *Id.* 12–13.
[404] *Id.* 13.
[405] *Id.* 13–14.
[406] *Id.* 14–15, 16.

statements can be criminal; "clubs, societies, and the press" pose identical dangers and implicitly must be equally restrained; and anyone who "attempted to withdraw, from our excellent government, the only effectual support of any government, public opinion," must be subject to criminal prosecution.[407] The last was a sixth logical leap of the Federalists, confounding the government and the administration, positing that depriving the administration of public support is also to "deprive the constitution, the laws" of support and to destroy government.[408] That Federalist argument ultimately relied on self-preservation or reasons of state for suppressing a limitless range of speech and press.

Addison ended by addressing the objection of wishing "to hear both sides" of each issue, responding that "truth has but one side,"[409] with the implied corollary that an opposition party was simply the shameless faction of falsehood and licentiousness or slander against government. Here was a seventh logical break, rejecting a legitimate opposition and assuming impeccability for those in power. Addison's reasoning appeared to brand as seditious any criticism of government measures or officials, and even criticism of the Sedition Act or of those supporting it. He confirmed that interpretation in a letter to Pickering, notifying Pickering of a "seditious address to Mr. Gallatin pointedly censuring as unconstitutional and oppressive the Alien and Sedition Acts," and objecting that a newspaper reprint "contributed not a little to inflame the passions of the people and promote the unfavorable result" in a local election.[410]

Armed with Addison's briefing, Washington rode out to battle the forces of sedition. He later showed his agreement with Addison's arguments in the Charles Holt case, and immediately showed his unflinching determination to apply the law of seditious libel in a case that some found more risible than worrisome.

The Baldwin and Clark Prosecution and Newark's Cannon

Luther Baldwin and Brown Clark[411] of Newark, New Jersey, were indicted for "seditious words,"[412] after a rousing grand jury charge by Justice Cushing on the Sedition Act and its constitutionality.[413] While initial newspaper reports described "a

[407] *Id.* 17, 18, 20.

[408] *Id.* 20, 22.

[409] *Id.* 23.

[410] Alexander Addison to Timothy Pickering (22 Nov.1798), PICKERING PAPERS r.23, fol.322, 323A.

[411] *See generally* FREEDOM'S FETTERS 270–74; CRISIS 112–14. Court records are in Minutes (1790–1911), U.S. Circuit Court for the District of New Jersey (National Archives at New York City, R.G. 21.32.2).

[412] Minutes p.138 (3 Oct.1798).

[413] 3 DHSC 305, 313–14, 314–15 (Cushing's charge preserved in November, probably used in September, 1798).

wish that the President . . . was dead,"[414] later reports gave more detail. As President Adams passed through Newark and was heralded with a cannon salute, an inebriated Baldwin "coming towards John Burnet's dramshop, a person that was there [Brown Clark[415]] says to Luther, there goes the President, and they are firing at his a—: Luther, a little merry, replies, that he did not care if they fired through his a—; then exclaims the dram seller, that is sedition."[416] The case provided not only merriment for modern historians, who solemnly recorded that in this case "enforcement of the Sedition Law hit bottom," but for the early Republican press, which protested that no Republican would be "firing at such a disgusting a target as the a-—of J.A.," and found it laughable that the English crime of threatening the King's head was applied in America to "speaking of the president's a—."[417] While some reports said that the indictment was for common law seditious libel,[418] other reports were probably correct that it was under the Sedition Act,[419] given Cushing's pointed charge.[420]

Justice Washington presided over the scheduled trial (with Judge Robert Morris) in October 1799,[421] and when Baldwin and Clark changed their pleas to guilty, sentenced them to fines of $150 and $50, respectively, without imprisonment.[422] That implied that Washington approved of the constitutionality of the Sedition Act, something he confirmed a half year later in the *Holt* trial. Republican newspapers gave an apt epithet to Baldwin's case: "ludicrous."[423]

The Durrell Prosecution and His *Mount Pleasant Register*

William Durrell,[424] a small-town Republican editor of the *Mount Pleasant Register* in New York, was arrested and charged in late July 1798 "for reprinting a paragraph

[414] *E.g.*, [No Caption], COMMERCIAL ADVERTISER (New York), 9 Nov.1798, at 3; [No Caption], SPECTATOR (New York), 10 Nov.1798, at 3.

[415] Called John Clark in some reports. [No Caption], SALEM GAZETTE, 22 Oct.1799, at 3; [No Caption], DAILY ADVERTISER (New York), 9 Oct.1799, at 3.

[416] *Men May be Conquered, but Principles Cannot*, HERALD OF LIBERTY (Washington, Pa.), 11 Nov.1799, at 4; FREEDOM'S FETTERS 271 (other Republican papers).

[417] FREEDOM'S FETTERS 270, 273, 274 (quoting *Argus* articles).

[418] *E.g., New-Jersey, Trenton April 9*, POLITICAL REPOSITORY (Brookfield), 23 Apr.1799, at 2; [No Caption], DAILY ADVERTISER (New York), 9 Oct.1799, at 3.

[419] *E.g.*, [No Caption], SPECTATOR (New York), 10 Nov.1798, at 3; [No Caption], COMMERCIAL ADVERTISER (New York), 9 Nov.1798, at 3.

[420] 3 DHSC 305, 313–15, 493; 3 *id.* 292 (Paterson's charge); FREEDOM'S FETTERS 271 n.74.

[421] 3 DHSC 388 (1–7 Oct.1799).

[422] Bushrod Washington to James Iredell (20 Oct.1799), 3 DHSC 389; [No Caption], DAILY ADVERTISER (New York), 9 Oct.1799, at 3; [No Caption], ALBANY CENTINEL, 15 Oct.1799, at 3.

[423] *From the* Aurora, *Oct.26*, CONSTITUTIONAL TELEGRAPH (Boston), 6 Nov.1799, at 1.

[424] *See generally* FREEDOM'S FETTERS 385–90; CRISIS 223. Court records are in Case Files (1790–1915) and Minutes, U.S. Circuit Court for the District of New York (National Archives at New York City, R.G.21.34.7). Though court records use Durell, he signed a petition using Durrell.

from a New Windsor Gazette, supposed to be a libel against the President," in what Republicans immediately christened as "The System of Terror."[425] He was the first editor arrested under the new Sedition Act, a mere half-week after its effective date,[426] after Pickering's instruction to the federal attorney to review the article and proceed.[427] Durrell's bail was set at $4,000 (half from sureties), which, coupled with the immediate suspension of the *Register* and his livelihood, left him impecunious and led to a foreclosure sale of his home and furnishings.[428] After delay to September 1799, he was arraigned before Justice Paterson[429] for printing a "false scandalous malicious and defamotry [*sic*] libel of and concerning John Adams." It is not certain that the basis was the Sedition Act rather than common law, but it is likely that the basis was the Act given Pickering's instruction.[430]

Justice Washington presided (joined by Judge John Sloss Hobart),[431] in a trial for sedition delayed, evidently by Pickering's election strategy, until April 1800. Durrell offered no witness testimony and unsurprisingly was found guilty.[432] Again implicitly approving and explicitly enforcing the Sedition Act, Washington sentenced Durrell to four months' imprisonment and a $50 fine, with release only after posting another prohibitive $2,000 bond.[433] After a couple weeks of the sentence was served, President Adams "remit[ted]" Durrell's sentence,[434] in the closest he came to clemency in a Sedition Act case, apparently with Justice Washington's support but apparently more influenced by Durrell having "discontinued his news paper."[435]

[425] *E.g., The System of Terror*, CAREY'S UNITED STATES RECORDER (Philadelphia), 4 Aug.1798, at 2; *accord Mount Pleasant, (N.Y.) July 24*, BEE (New London), 1 Aug.1798, at 3.

[426] Warrant (17 July 1798); Recognizance (bond) (19 July 1798); FREEDOM'S FETTERS 385, 386. His crime was on 19 June 1798. Minutes at 144 (4 Sept. 1799).

[427] Timothy Pickering to Richard Harison (28 June 1798), PICKERING PAPERS r.8, fol.604; *see* Timothy Pickering to Richard Harison (22 Apr.1800), *id.* at r.13, fol.406; Richard Harrison to Timothy Pickering (10 Apr. 1800), *id.* r.26, fol.77.

[428] Recognizance (bond) (19 July 1798); Petition of William Durrell (5 Apr.1800) (discontinued publication and lost all property to sheriff's sale); FREEDOM'S FETTERS 386, 387.

[429] FREEDOM'S FETTERS 387; 3 DHSC 381.

[430] Minutes at 144. The indictment could be on either basis. Indictment at 1–2 (undated).

[431] FREEDOM'S FETTERS 387–88; 3 DHSC 408.

[432] *Id.* 388.

[433] [No Caption], COMMERCIAL ADVERTISER (New York), 17 Apr.1800, at 3; [No Caption], MERCANTILE ADVERTISER (New York), 17 Apr.1800, at 3; FREEDOM'S FETTERS 388.

[434] [No Caption], PRISONER OF HOPE (New York), 3 May 1800, at 2; Timothy Pickering to Richard Harison (22 Apr.1800), PICKERING PAPERS r.13, fol.406.

[435] FREEDOM'S FETTERS 389; Richard Harison to Timothy Pickering (10 Apr.1800), PICKERING PAPERS r.26, fol.77, 77A.

The Holt Prosecution and His New London *Bee*

Charles Holt,[436] another Republican editor, of Connecticut's *Bee,* was indicted for seditious libel based on printing a "false, scandalous and malicious writing of and concerning the government . . . the President . . . and . . . Congress."[437] The offending letter to the editor criticized the "standing army" (not just a provisional army) that was being formed under Hamilton's effective command to repel a French invasion or insurrection, and excoriated "the appointment of Alexander Hamilton to command our army, after the affair" he had recently admitted publicly, asking rhetorically if "our young officers and soldiers . . . like their general are . . . to be found in the bed of adultery?"[438] The indictment followed Chief Justice Ellsworth's charge to the grand jury defending the constitutionality of the Sedition Act, which is quoted below in the discussion of Ellsworth.[439]

Justice Washington, following his circuit from New York to Connecticut, presided at Holt's trial (with Judge Richard Law).[440] Holt's counsel, admitting publication, "rested his defense on two grounds—1st the unconstitutionality of the law to prevent sedition, and 2nd, the tenor of the publication itself" in that facts were true and opinions were nonmalicious. The federal attorney countered with government's "power to defend its measures, from such slanderous attempts," and the lethal effect of criticism, so that "[i]n vain have the people delegated certain powers to the general government, if individuals may with impunity, publish malicious falsehoods respecting it and its officials."[441] The prosecutor argued that the "standing army" opinion was a malicious falsehood, which deterred army recruiting, though he conceded the truth of Hamilton's infidelity. Washington came down squarely on the side of the Sedition Act in his jury charge, as a Connecticut Federalist newspaper fulsomely described it:

> Judge Washington in his charge to the jury (which was given in an unrivalled manner) established the act to be constitutional, by a train of reasoning too powerful to be resisted—he also proved the publication to be libellous, beyond even the possibility of doubt—he explained and pronounced the law in such a mild, clear and masterly manner, as to satisfy

[436] *See generally* FREEDOM'S FETTERS 373–84; CRISIS 126–30. Court records are in Case Files (1790–1911), U.S. Circuit Court for the District of Connecticut (National Archives at Waltham, Mass., R.G. 21.8.2).

[437] Indictment at 3 (17 Sept.1799); *District of Connecticut,* BEE (New London), 21 May 1800, at 1 (reprinting indictment).

[438] *Id.* at 4, 5; *For the Bee,* BEE (New London), 8 May 1799, at 2.

[439] *Id.*; 3 DHSC 385, presumably the charge at 3 *id.* 357.

[440] 3 DHSC 417; [No Caption], COMMERCIAL ADVERTISER (New York), 17 Apr.1800, at 3.

[441] *New-York: Wednesday, April 23, 1800,* COMMERCIAL ADVERTISER (New York), 23 Apr. 1800, at 3.

> all parties, even the prisoner himself, who was thereby prepared for a verdict of *Guilty*.[442]

With such a charge, the prosecutor was superfluous, and the jury convicted Holt.

Washington did not miss the opportunity, in sentencing Holt, to scold him and the public, parroting Addison and the English royal judges from Holt to Mansfield, on the "heinous" circumstances of his seditious libel, as the same Federalist newspaper reported:

> The judge, after pointing out the tendency which libels on a free government have, to discredit and destroy the Government itself;—the heinous and aggravating circumstances which attended the publication of the libel; pronounced sentence . . . in a manner so commanding, and still so dignified, as to make the prisoner blush for his crime, and be satisfied with the punishment inflicted.[443]

At least according to the Federalist press, Holt left for prison singing hosannas to Bushrod Washington and satisfied with his three-month sentence and $200 fine, which had to be paid before release.[444] While in jail Holt's newspaper was suspended,[445] but upon his release he no longer "blush[ed] for his crime" as he regularly attacked the Sedition Act.[446] His lead counsel, David Daggett, later was a founder of Yale Law School.

Justice William Cushing and the First Amendment: Jury Charges

Justice William Cushing, like Paterson, Chase, Washington, Iredell, and Ellsworth from late-1798 through 1800, made the center of his grand jury charge the Sedition Act in late 1798.[447] One author is mistaken that he "presided over some of the trials" under the Sedition Act;[448] the closest Cushing came was to be cheated out of the Bache trial by yellow fever, to preside over Baldwin's and Clark's indictment, and to preside over Haswell's arraignment and over several arrests

[442] *New-Haven, April 24*, CONNECTICUT JOURNAL (New Haven), 24 Apr.1800, at 3.

[443] *Id.*

[444] Indictment (jacket note) (17 Sept.1799); Warrant at 1–2 (17 Apr.1800); *New-York: Wednesday, April 23, 1800*, COMMERCIAL ADVERTISER (New York), 23 Apr.1800, at 3.

[445] *New-London*, BEE (New London), 21 May 1800, at 2; 25 HAMILTON PAPERS 174 n.25.

[446] FREEDOM'S FETTERS 384.

[447] William Cushing's Charge (C.C.D. Va. 23 Nov.1798), 3 DHSC 305, 313–15.

[448] LEVY 202.

and dismissals described in the next chapter. Cushing also was an incidental actor in the aftermath of Brown's trial, hearing a motion for redress after Fisher Ames's Republican brother was arrested for failing to appear as a subpoenaed witness (believing the subpoena invalid), and was without warning "carried to circuit court prisoner & fin'd [$]8." Cushing refused redress for what the outraged Dr. Ames called a shakedown,[449] not realizing that the court had in its grasp the much-sought author of the "seditious" placard on Fairbanks's "sedition pole." Cushing would not condone questioning "the necessity of giving our confidence and support to our own government," and feared "the dangerous tendency of jacobin principles," as he said a year earlier.[450]

Besides these recognized cases, Cushing also presided over three other indictments or presentments under the Sedition Act, which are discussed in the next chapter.

Cushing's grand jury charge, given in the Gallophilic lion's den of Virginia (and typically repeated at each circuit stop[451]), attempted to demonstrate the need for the Alien and Sedition Acts by devoting over half its length to France's "foreign influence and intrigue," its "unprovoked war on property" at sea, its "wild anarchy, terror and cruelty," and its aggression against other nations.[452] The remainder, though focusing more on the Alien Acts than the Sedition Act, began by expressly defending the latter's "full and sufficient guard to innocence" in the forms of jury trial and a truth defense. Cushing briefly denied that the Sedition Act "abridged the liberty of the press," asserting that that liberty did not include the right to publish "scandalous and malicious falsehoods." He then stated that such seditious libels were all the Act prohibited,[453] and defended the Act's constitutionality by asserting that proscription of seditious libel was essential for government:

> But can any reasonable man suppose, that a government, instituted for the protection of all the states and all the citizens, with full powers to do every thing necessary for that important end, has no power to protect itself by laws to prevent crimes which tend directly to its overthrow and destruction?[454]

That was the extent of Cushing's defense of the constitutionality of the Sedition Act, and it consisted, after the unadorned denial of violation of freedom of press,

[449] *The Ames Diary*, 10 DEDHAM HISTORICAL REGISTER 26 (1899).

[450] [No Caption], NEWPORT MERCURY, 19 June 1798, reprinted in 3 DHSC 278.

[451] 3 DHSC 159n.

[452] William Cushing's Charge (C.C.D. Va. 23 Nov. 1798), 3 DHSC 305, 305–06, 306–07, 308–09, 310–11.

[453] 3 *id.* 314

[454] 3 *id.* 314–15.

of three unsupported assertions. Those assertions were that all discourse consists of either truth or malicious falsehoods (ignoring unintentional mistakes and opinions), that "crimes which tend directly to its overthrow and destruction" can be accurately identified and distinguished from falsehoods that do not have such a direct tendency (such crimes could include "misrepresentations [about] public men" and about "every measure taken for the safety of the country"),[455] and that suppression of such falsehoods is essential to prevent "overthrow and destruction" of government (a malleable form of reasons of state or self-preservation).[456] Freedom of press stopped where seditious libel began, and the common law of seditious libel had been enacted in the Sedition Act, ameliorated by truth as a defense.

Cushing's shift on freedom of press from his 1789 letter was not his only reversal of position; he shifted as well on President Adams, despite their long-term friendship. By Jefferson's inauguration in 1801, Cushing echoed Adams's High Federalist opponents, complaining to Paterson that "[t]he lies and lashes of Jacobinism were familiar and unheeded" by Adams.[457]

Justice James Iredell and the First Amendment: Jury Charges

Justice James Iredell, in contrast to Cushing, delivered the most thorough justification for the constitutionality of the Sedition Act, expressly adopting the Blackstone-Mansfield definition of liberty of press and of seditious libel, in a grand jury charge. Chief Justice Ellsworth called the charge "luminous & pointed."[458]

The 1799 Grand Jury Charge Upholding the Sedition Act

Iredell's defense of the constitutionality of the Sedition Act, in his grand jury charge for 1799, was meant to be his "deliberate opinion as a judge," not something less carefully considered.[459] Newspaper reports recognized that it was the justice's "defence of the Alien and Sedition laws."[460]

455 3 *id.* 306.

456 Earlier, he similarly asked, "How is it possible for any free government to stand the shock of such perpetual, inveterate, malicious, hostile attacks," as the "unceasing torrent of calumnies" against Washington and the "same shameless indecencies and abuse towards his able and inflexibly patriotic successor." 3 *id.* 306.

457 William Cushing to William Paterson (18 Mar.1801), PATERSON PAPERS-NYPL 733, 735.

458 Oliver Ellsworth to James Iredell (10 June 1799), IREDELL PAPERS-DUKE; which Republicans criticized, 3 DHSC 366, 370.

459 James Iredell's Charge (C.C.D. Pa. 11 Apr.1799), 3 DHSC 332, 334.

460 3 DHSC 328; *New-Jersey, Trenton April 9*, POLITICAL REPOSITORY (Brookfield), 23 Apr.1799, at 2; [No Caption], FEDERALIST (Trenton), 8 Apr.1799, reprinted in 3 DHSC 328, 330.

Iredell began with the Blackstone-Mansfield premise that seditious libel must be suppressed or government will collapse:

> can it be tolerated in any civilized society that any should be permitted with impunity to tell falsehoods to the people, with an express intention to deceive them, and lead them into discontent, if not into insurrection, which is so apt to follow? It is believed no government in the world ever was without such a power. It is unquestionably possessed by all the state governments, and probably has been exercised in all of them: sure I am it has in some. If necessary and proper for them, why not equally so, at least, for the government of the United States, naturally an object of more jealousy and alarm, because it has greater concerns to provide for?[461]

As a matter of logic, Iredell's justification for his first premise was an inductive fallacy, that all governments claim such a power, or some have fallen because of seditious libel, and therefore government power to suppress seditious libel must be indispensable to government. Yet the power to suppress seditious libel may be necessary only to tyrannical governments, but not to free republican governments. Iredell's retort was that "a republic more is dependent on the good opinion of the people for its support," and without that good opinion "the whole fabric crumbles into dust." There, he equated a particular administration falling with the republican government itself crumbling. Yet an administration might fall without the institution of government itself dissolving, as England's history illustrated throughout the eighteenth century. Iredell undercut his argument for the necessity of suppressing "falsehoods" by acknowledging that they might merely lead to "discontent" and not to "insurrection," which is only "apt" and not certain to follow.[462]

Iredell then discussed whether prohibition of seditious libel violated freedom of press. His next premise was that liberty of press meant what Blackstone defined it as, "laying no *previous* restraints upon publications" rather than "freedom from censure . . . when published." His reasoning was that Blackstone was influential in America, and was known to the framers of the First Amendment, so that Blackstone's definition was presumed to be approved unless the Amendment were "particularly worded, to guard against any possible mistake."[463] Iredell's argument ignored the fact that Blackstone's definitions of the other freedoms addressed by the First Amendment (establishment of religion, free exercise of religion, petition, and assembly), and of many other rights addressed by the Bill of Rights, were clearly not adopted but instead overridden, and yet in no case was the provision "particularly worded" to state that it rejected Blackstone or common

461 3 *id.* 346.
462 3 *id.* 346.
463 3 *id.* 347.

law. Iredell bolstered his point by a generic reference to common law in all the states, without addressing whether the part of common law dealing with freedoms of press and speech was abrogated or modified by the state declarations of rights. He then repeated the Federalist argument that the Sedition Act ameliorated the common law by providing a truth defense and limiting punishments.[464] Further, Iredell's argument assumed that Blackstone accurately summarized the English common law (which was questioned in Chapter 2), that the Blackstone-Mansfield definition was generally accepted instead of disputed, and that it was adopted silently by the Constitution along with a federal common law (which was challenged in Chapter 3), and was unaffected by the First Amendment.

Iredell ended the charge with denunciation of Republicans, implying that his references to prohibiting "malicious falsehood" and "bad sentiments" meant not insurrectionists but the opposition, and showing that he regarded criticism of the administration as criminal. He decried "that ever since the first formation of the present government, every act . . . has been uniformly opposed before its adoption, and every art practi[c]ed to make the people discontented after it," along with efforts "to vilify and undermine the government," accompanied by "the principles of republicanism, the perpetual theme of their declamation." He warned that, if people "suffer this government to be destroyed," the "most dreadful confusion must ensue," anarchy "will ride triumphant, and all lovers of order, decency, truth and justice be trampled."[465]

This was Iredell's defense of the constitutionality of the Sedition Act under the First Amendment.[466] None of its components had appeared in his jury charges, opinions, or extensive correspondence during his prior nine years on the Supreme Court. To find anything like it in Iredell's past, it is necessary to go back to wartime and his Revolutionary War position, when as North Carolina's attorney general he had prosecuted seditious libel or words in at least in three instances. In 1779 and 1780, he prosecuted Theophilus Mann for "seditious and inflammatory words," and James Hobbs for "seditions and disaffected expressions."[467] Also in 1780, Iredell prosecuted Thomas Young for "speaking seditious words," such as that "taking the said oath of allegiance would not avail him any thing" because the "damned rebel's and villain's" [*sic*] would soon lose and the "oath would be of no more service than swallowing a dumpling."[468]

[464] 3 *id.* 348.

[465] 3 *id.* 350.

[466] He also defended it against argument that the Act furthered no enumerated power, construing the Necessary and Proper Clause as expansively as he construed the First Amendment restrictively. 3 *id.* 341–44.

[467] State v. Mann, 2 IREDELL PAPERS 123, 124 (N.C. Super. Ct. 15 Nov.1779).

[468] Indictment, State v. Thomas Young (N.C. Super. Ct., Edenton Dist., May Term 1780), Alfred Moore (1755–1810) Papers (NCSA, PC.774).

Iredell had a deep abiding faith in the precepts of the Federalists, which when compared with his prior faith in Revolutionary War ideas brought unavoidable ironies. The revolutionary Iredell had written eloquently about not being "guilty of any other crime than *an ardent love of liberty,*" and liberty being "dearer than life,"[469] as he challenged the British government and wrote what were seditious libels under existing law. He had found English law so inadequate to protect liberty that "our ancestors . . . left that very country because freedom could not be enjoyed in it."[470] Even as recently as 1795, his Supreme Court opinion on Revolutionary War ship captures similarly found English law "a doubtful and imperfect system of jurisprudence, which has been since happily changed for one so precise and so comprehensive."[471] But Iredell abandoned that disenchantment with English law when he ardently embraced Blackstone's view of seditious libel in the late 1790s, just as he admittedly abandoned his earlier denial of a federal common law (as discussed at the end of Chapter 3). He similarly jettisoned his early insistence on protection of the accused's rights—such as his grand jury charge for 1792 calling for protection of the innocent and warning that criminal laws "ought to be passed with the most trembling solicitude, lest any unfortunate individual should become the object of injustice or oppression,"[472] or his charge for 1795 asking "what precaution can be too great where personal liberty is concerned"[473]—as he supported the Sedition Act's criminalization of a wide swath of expression based merely on its "tendency."

The First Fries Trial in 1799

After hearing Iredell's 1799 charge, a Pennsylvania grand jury indicted John Fries and others for treason, for rescuing opponents of house taxes from prison, with a body of over a hundred armed protesters.[474] Fries's first trial began a fortnight later, on April 30, 1799, with Iredell presiding (joined by Peters).[475] Both judges assumed the constitutionality of the Sedition Act, as they parried defense arguments that combinations, conspiracies, and insurrections under that Act could not themselves constitute treason because they were crimes in their own right, ruling instead that

[469] [James Iredell], Causes of the American Revolution (June 1776), 1 IREDELL PAPERS 370, 371 (emphasis in original); James Iredell to Joseph Hewes (28 June 1775), 1 *id.* 308, 309; 2 *id.* 16, 18.

[470] James Iredell's Charge (N.C. Super. Ct. 2 May 1778), 13 STATE RECORDS-N.C. 431.

[471] Penhallow v. Doane's Administrators, 3 U.S. (3 Dall.) 54, 107 (1795).

[472] James Iredell's Charge (C.C.D. Mass. 12 Oct.1792), 2 DHSC 308, 312; *accord* 2 *id.* 263, 351–52.

[473] James Iredell's Charge (C.C.D. N.Y. 6 Apr.1795), 3 DHSC 14, 16; *accord* 3 *id.* 163, 177.

[474] Indictment (Apr.1799), Trial of the Northampton Insurgents [Fries], Wharton's State Trials 458, 489 (C.C.D. Pa. 1799), reprinted in In re Fries, 9 F.Cas. 826 (C.C.D. Pa. 1799) (No. 5,126), *modified,* 3 U.S. (3 Dall.) 515 (C.C.D. Pa. 1799).

[475] *Id.* 491, 598n.

separately defined crimes still could be overt acts for treason.[476] Iredell included in his trial notes, as evidence significant to treason, that one of the rebels "damned the Alien & Sedition Laws—and finally all the laws of Gov.—*and the laws Congress had made.*"[477] As the trial wound down, Peters ended his jury charge by assuring the jury that "both facts and law . . . are too plain to admit a reasonable doubt," an observation that Iredell did not modify in his own charge, and predictably the jury found Fries guilty.[478] However, when defense attorneys showed that a juror declared before trial that Fries "ought to be hung," Iredell reluctantly granted a new trial,[479] and Peters joined him with still more reluctance.[480]

Most Federalists, including most sitting justices, agreed with Peters that Pennsylvania was now "twice disgraced by infamous insurrection," and that any "weak turn . . . will give strength & spirit to the [Republican] party, forever on the watch for such events."[481] Paterson advised Iredell to stay in Philadelphia "till the criminals are tried,"[482] and Chase had hoped "a body of horse & foot are ordered" to crush the insurgents.[483]

Iredell was no more a foe to partisanship than Peters. He disliked Republicans, "the little barkings of ill-humor which are now perpetually assailing our ears," as much as he liked "a good government-man."[484] A month after the first statement he saw no inconsistency in condemning "all party prejudices," and two months after the second he was thanked by a Federalist candidate for "the interest you are pleased to take in my election."[485]

The Grand Jury Charge and the Samuel Cabell Presentment in 1797, and the "Band of Political Preachers"

The 1799 grand jury charge did not appear out of thin air, but as the end of a process that Iredell began by reversing himself in 1796 to advocate a federal common

[476] *Id.* 585, 588–89.

[477] James Iredell, Charge Book 18–19 (Apr. Term 1799), IREDELL PAPERS-UNC (box 2, v.15); *cf.* Wharton's State Trials 529.

[478] Wharton's State Trials 587, 587–97, 598.

[479] James Iredell to Hannah Iredell (19 May 1799), 3 DHSC 366; though it is often claimed that Iredell was reluctant to sentence Fries because of language in his prior letter, *e.g.*, MISUNDERSTANDING 108.

[480] Wharton's State Trials 601, 605–08, 609; 3 U.S. (3 Dall.) at 519.

[481] Richard Peters to William Paterson (24 Apr.1799), 3 DHSC 352; *see* DOCUMENTS RELATING TO NEW-ENGLAND FEDERALISM 380 (Henry Adams ed., Little, Brown, Boston 1905).

[482] William Paterson to James Iredell (27 Apr.1799), IREDELL PAPERS-DUKE.

[483] Samuel Chase to James Iredell 3 (17 Mar.1799), IREDELL PAPERS-DUKE.

[484] James Iredell to James Wilson (24 Nov.1794), 2 IREDELL CORRESPONDENCE 429; James Iredell to Hannah Iredell (1 May 1798), 2 *id.* 522.

[485] James Iredell to Gov. Henry Lee (26 Dec.1794), 2 *id.* 431, 432; David Stowe to James Iredell (2 July 1798), IREDELL-JOHNSON COLLECTION (PC.67.8, box 8).

law, and that he continued with his 1797 grand jury charge on the illegitimacy of a political opposition—which incited the grand jury to present a member of Congress essentially for seditious libel.[486] Iredell's charge used language that could be, and was, interpreted as outlining limitations on freedom of speech, though on close reading it did not address dissenting speech but civil disobedience (and he corrected that in 1798); but he revised it to apply it to dissenting speech in 1799 (as discussed in Chapter 4).

A Virginia grand jury, later in the day after Iredell's 1797 charge, issued a presentment that censured "as a real evil the circular letters of several members of the late Congress, and particularly letters with the signature of Samuel J. Cabell."[487] Cabell was a Virginia member of Congress. (We return to him in connection with Justice Blair in Chapter 8.) A written debate ensued. Cabell immediately attacked Iredell, in Republican newspapers, for being one of the federal judges who have a "regular practice . . . to make political discourses to the grand jurors," acting as "a band of political preachers," and for giving the Virginia grand jury by his charge "authority for censuring the independence of private opinion."[488] Iredell responded in a handbill that he "never knew that Mr. *Cabell* had written any circular letter at all, until I heard the presentment read in court."[489] Doubt is cast on that explanation, however, by the fact that Iredell had discarded his Pennsylvania charge of just two weeks earlier, which went no further than to say "we must all stand or fall together,"[490] to replace it with his Maryland and Virginia charge proclaiming that if people loved their country they would submit and not slander officials. Further, Iredell clearly approved the seditious libel presentment, telling his wife it came from men with "a temper highly suitable to our present situation."[491] He did nothing to quash it.

Iredell, though generally treated well by historians grateful for his preserving his correspondence, may have been most accurately described by his own assessment soon after joining the Supreme Court: "This high appointment was as much beyond my expectation, as I fear it is above my merit."[492] Not an initial choice but a replacement for an initial justice, he was the only initial justice without any form of higher education except reading law in a law office. He proved unable to think outside the Federalist box, or even to recognize that there was a Federalist box,

486 James Iredell's Charge (C.C.D. Va. 22 May 1797), 3 DHSC 181, 173, 173n.; *accord* American Politics 169–71.

487 Presentment of the Grand Jury (C.C.D. Va. 22 May 1797), 3 DHSC 181; 3 *id.* 173n., 181.

488 *Letter of Samuel Jordan Cabell*, Aurora (Philadelphia), 31 May 1797, reprinted in 3 DHSC 183.

489 James Iredell, *To the Public* (1797), 2 Iredell Correspondence 511; 3 DHSC 201.

490 James Iredell's Charge (C.C.D. Pa. 11 Apr.1797), 3 DHSC 163; *contra* 3 DHSC 198.

491 James Iredell to Hannah Iredell (25 May 1797), 3 DHSC 182.

492 James Iredell to John Rutledge 1 (9 Apr.1790), Iredell Papers-Duke (box 2).

despite progressively confining himself to it by abandoning earlier positions. He jettisoned his revolutionary advocacy of a "right of resistance,"[493] his earlier denial of any federal power affecting press and speech in his 1788 "Marcus" essays, his rejection of federal court jurisdiction over common law crimes, his toleration of difference in sentiments in 1795–1796 charges, and his allowance for dissent short of civil disobedience in 1797. He instead shifted to his ardent 1799 defense of the Sedition Act over freedom of speech and press objections.

He also presided over some unrecognized indictments and trials under the Sedition Act, which the next chapter discusses.

Chief Justice Oliver Ellsworth and the First Amendment: His Opinion and Jury Charges

When Federalist alarm bells rang about newspaper mischaracterization of the Jay Treaty of 1795, Oliver Ellsworth had not advocated seditious libel prosecutions, but instead encouraged reasoned responses. He had said "it is best to let them alone until[] the[y] begin to publish and then answer them."[494] However, his anxiety grew with the Quasi-War and the nascent Republican party. After the Sedition Act became law, he responded to the Adams administration's request with an advisory opinion upholding its constitutionality.

His Advisory Opinion on the Sedition Act and Freedoms of Press and Speech

Five months after the Sedition Act passed, Chief Justice Ellsworth responded to a request from Pickering with an informal advisory opinion[495] upholding the Act. He began by stating that the Act merely codified, and ameliorated, the common law of seditious libel, explicitly following Addison:

> [Judge Addison] is doubtless correct in supposing that the Sedition Act does not create an offence, but rather, by permitting the truth of a libel to be given in justification, causes that, in some cases, not to be an offence which was one before; nor does it devise a new mode of punishment, but restricts the power which previously existed, to fine & imprison.

[493] James Iredell's Charge (N.C. Super. Ct. 2 May 1778), 2 Iredell Papers 16, 18.

[494] Jeremiah Wadsworth to George Washington (11–12 July 1795), 18 Hamilton Papers 459, 460. Wadsworth, a Federalist, was alleging seditious libel by saying newspapers were "slandering the Treaty," and after reciting Ellsworth's advice, he said "I believe otherwise." *Id.*

[495] Ellsworth 116; Repressive Jurisprudence 95, 145; 3 DHSC 90.

He then upheld the Sedition Act over freedom of press challenge—and freedom of speech challenge:

> But, as to the constitutional difficulty, who will say that negating the right to publish slander & sedition, is "*abridging* the freedom of speech & of the press," of a right which ever belonged to it? Or will shew us how Congress, if prohibited to authorise punishment for speaking in *any* case, could authorise it for perjury, of which nobody has yet doubted?[496]

Notably, Ellsworth, like Paterson and Iredell, argued from the worthlessness of a "right to publish slander & sedition" or a right to speak perjury. In this 1798 opinion, he presupposed the Blackstone-Mansfield definition of freedom of press and speech, by denying that punishing sedition "is '*abridging* the freedom of speech & of the press,'" because those freedoms did not include seditious writings or words. He did not choose to address whether the broad language of the First Amendment, and of most state constitutions, abrogated or even modified the common law for those freedoms.

That was a striking change from Ellsworth's 1787 position, when he, like Iredell and Wilson, defended the proposed Constitution against anti-federalist attack with the argument that "Congress have no power to prohibit either" press or speech, or for that matter conscience or other rights. In 1787 he implicitly denied that the federal government had common law power to prohibit seditious speech or words. In 1798 he instead claimed that the Sedition Act "does not create an offense," because the federal offense already existed.

The Grand Jury Charges Supporting Seditious Libel Prosecution and the Sedition Act

In the partisan atmosphere even a year before the Sedition Act, Ellsworth's grand jury charge of 1797 warned of sedition and briefly urged presentment of such offences. He charted the downward regression from the "baleful influence of those elements of disorganization, & tenets of impiety," to an "unhinged" mind that "revolts at every institution which can preserve order or protect right," to a heart "insensible to social & civil obligations," and then from "disaffection" to "a spirit of party" which "poisons the sources of public confidence," and that finally "opens a door to foreign influence." To Ellsworth, the damnable object of this disaffection and this declension could be nothing less than "to sep[a]rate the people from the government; and of course to prepare them by sedition & rebellion, for a new order of things."[497]

[496] Oliver Ellsworth to Timothy Pickering (12 Dec.1798), 3 DHSC 235; Ellsworth Papers-NYPL 47.

[497] Oliver Ellsworth's Charge (C.C.D.N.Y. 1 Apr.1797), 3 DHSC 158, 158–59.

A Republican newspaper, Greenleaf's *Argus*, objected to Ellsworth's charge, saying that "free and manly investigation of public measures is stigmatized by the harsh epithets of 'sedition and rebellion,'" stifling all enquiry, as "a Chief Justice of the United States" joins "the hue and cry of a party against the French nation" and against Thomas Paine's impiety, by which the Chief Justice "wanders most egregiously from the line of his duty."[498] The editor of the *Argus* was soon subjected to a criminal trial, presided over by Ellsworth, for criticism of the British consul, and was convicted.[499] Ellsworth was inching toward his post-Sedition Act position.

After enactment of the Sedition Act, Ellsworth's brief grand jury charge of 1799 began similarly to his advisory opinion, with an affirmation of common law in order to support federal court jurisdiction over seditious libel.[500] It then posited an obligation of obedience, while avoiding a defense of the constitutionality of the Act, apparently, like Chase, not wanting to invite grand jury consideration of "the *policy*" of the law, which was only the purview of "those who *enact* them,"[501] or of the constitutionality of the law. Ellsworth warned that the Constitution and government are "dependent . . . on public confidence" and on "*resistless*" obedience,[502] and peppered his short charge with synonyms for seditious libel and words: "acts manifestly subversive of the national government" and conduct "clearly *destructive* of a government or its powers."[503] Though Ellsworth did not refer to the Sedition Act by name, he listed its essence as central to criminal law—crimes under common law, and acts destructive of government, including reducing public confidence. It was a defense, though a clumsy one, of the Sedition Act.[504] Republican news reports understood what he was doing, and stated that Ellsworth's charge ruled "that the Alien and Sedition Laws are constitutional."[505]

The imprecision of that 1799 defense of the Sedition Act was similar to the imprecision in his 1797 charge that Abigail Adams had lambasted, when she asked "did the good gentleman never write before?. . . the language is stiffer than his person. I find it difficult to pick out his meaning."[506] As Ellsworth "wandered most egregiously" around the First Amendment, he said both that "opposing the existence of the national government, or the efficient exercise of its legitimate

[498] [No Caption], ARGUS (New York), 11 Apr.1797, reprinted in 3 DHSC 161, 161–62.

[499] 1 HISTORY OF SUPREME COURT 629 (in spring 1797).

[500] As Casto points out, ELLSWORTH 116, though it is difficult to see the charge as "another advisory opinion" or a "comprehensive analysis." *Id.*

[501] Oliver Ellsworth's Charge (C.C.D. S.C. 7 May 1799), 3 DHSC 357, 358, 359.

[502] 3 *id.* 359.

[503] 3 *id.* 358.

[504] ELLSWORTH 117; Alan F. Westin, *Out-of-Court Commentary by United States Supreme Court Justices*, 62 COLUM. L. REV. 633, 639–40 (1962).

[505] Hale, *Thoughts on the Judiciary*, ARGUS (New York), 25 Oct.1799, reprinted in 3 DHSC 394; *see* Citizen, *To Oliver El[l]sworth*, VIRGINIA ARGUS (Richmond 9 Aug.1799), 3 DHSC 375, 379.

[506] Abigail Adams to John Adams (17 Apr.1797), 3 DHSC 169.

powers" was an indictable misdemeanor, and three sentences later, that juries should "look, not to the *opinions* of men, but their *actions*."[507] He was equally imprecise about whether there was room for peaceful assembly and petition for repeal of laws: "Till then, the laws they prescribe are *sacred*, and should be *resistless*."[508] Though he was ready, willing, and able, however, Ellsworth did not preside over any Sedition Act trials, because his diplomatic mission to France deprived him of any opportunities.

James Madison and Thomas Jefferson and the First Amendment: The Virginia and Kentucky Resolutions and the Response

The Republican fight against the Sedition Act, after failing to block its passage, shifted to local and state resolutions condemning the Act under the First Amendment,[509] and ended with newly elected President Jefferson "discharg[ing] every person under punishment or prosecution under the sedition law because I considered and now consider that law to be a nullity as absolute and as palpable as if Congress had ordered us to fall down and worship a golden image."[510]

Jefferson's Kentucky Resolutions and Madison's Virginia Resolutions and Report

The Kentucky Resolutions, secretly drafted by Thomas Jefferson[511] and adopted by Kentucky in November 1798, declared the Alien and Sedition Acts unconstitutional[512] in emphatic terms:

> that, no power over the freedom of religion, freedom of speech, or freedom of the press, being delegated to the United States by the

[507] 3 DHSC 358.

[508] 3 DHSC 359.

[509] *See generally* Adrienne Koch & Harry Ammon, *The Virginia and Kentucky Resolutions: An Episode in Jefferson's and Madison's Defense of Civil Liberties*, 5 WM. & MARY Q. (3d ser.) 145 (1948); *see* AMERICAN POLITICS 187–207, 223–24; EMPIRE 270–71; WILLIAM J. WATKINS, RECLAIMING THE AMERICAN REVOLUTION: THE KENTUCKY AND VIRGINIA RESOLUTIONS AND THEIR LEGACY (Palgrave Macmillan, New York 2004).

[510] Thomas Jefferson to Abigail Adams (22 July 1804), 1 ADAMS-JEFFERSON 274, 275; *accord* Notes on a Cabinet Meeting (9 Mar.1801), 33 JEFFERSON PAPERS 232.

[511] Jefferson's Draft (ante-4 Oct.1798), 30 JEFFERSON PAPERS 536, 529n.

[512] Resolutions Adopted by the Kentucky General Assembly (10–13 Nov.1798), 30 JEFFERSON PAPERS 550; 4 ELLIOT'S DEBATES 540; Additional Resolution (14 Nov.1799), 4 *id.* 544.

> Constitution, nor prohibited by it to the states, all lawful powers respecting the same did of right remain, and were reserved to the states, or to the people; . . . that "Congress shall make no laws respecting an establishment of religion, or prohibiting the free exercise thereof, or abridging the freedom of speech, or of the press,". . . . That therefore the [Sedition Act] of the Congress of the United States . . . , which does abridge the freedom of the press, is not law, but is altogether void, and of no force.[513]

While both Kentucky and Virginia went this far, Kentucky's Resolutions went beyond Virginia's, in asserting each state's equal right to judge the constitutionality of federal laws, denying federal power to prescribe crimes beyond the constitutionally enumerated ones, decrying federal arrogation of state "powers of self-government" and of "unlimited powers," and warning that such acts as the Alien and Sedition Acts "may tend to drive these states into revolution and blood."[514] That claim of state power to treat as void and nullify unconstitutional laws[515] would be remembered by South Carolina in 1832 and by all southern states in 1860.

The Virginia Resolutions, secretly drafted by James Madison[516] and adopted by Virginia in December 1798, condemned the Alien and Sedition Acts as "palpable and alarming infractions of the Constitution."[517] Virginia's central resolution found the latter "unconstitutional" under the First Amendment, because the Act

> *exercises, in like manner, a power not delegated by the Constitution, but, on the contrary, expressly and positively forbidden by one of the amendments thereto, . . . the right of freely examining public characters and measures, and of free communication between the people thereon, which has ever been justly deemed the only effectual guardian of every other right.*[518]

Another resolution declared that, if the federal government threatened important rights, states should interpose themselves to protect their citizens.

These states' resolutions merely assumed a meaning of freedom of press, and it was left to Madison a year later forcefully to develop that meaning in his

[513] 4 Elliot's Debates 540–41. This is cited as the most available source to readers.

[514] 4 *id.* 540, 540, 542, 543, 543.

[515] Kentucky's Additional Resolutions (14–22 Nov. 1799), 4 *id.* 544, 545.

[516] James Madison, Resolutions (21 Dec.1798), 6 Madison Writings 326.

[517] Virginia Resolutions (21–24 Dec.1798), 4 Elliot's Debates 528; 6 Madison Writings 341.

[518] 4 *id.* 528–29.

incisive *Report on the Virginia Resolutions.*[519] While earlier historians often treated the *Report* dismissively because of its states' rights facet, appreciation has grown for its broad theory of freedom of press and its equally broad attack on seditious libel.[520] Madison emphatically rejected the Blackstone-Mansfield definition as something abrogated by state and federal bills of rights, and as rendering their protections meaningless if they merely prohibited prior restraints but not punishment after publication. Instead, he asserted that "shall make no law" in the First Amendment "meant a positive denial to Congress of any power whatever on the subject" of the press, which was the only true freedom of press.[521]

The Overstated Opposition by Just Half the States

Upon receiving copies of the Kentucky and Virginia Resolutions, exactly half of the sixteen states opposed them in some manner,[522] when Elliot's list of six state legislatures and New York's senate[523] is supplemented with New York's house (though the two chambers could not agree on a response) and Frank Anderson's addition of the Maryland legislature (finding the "recommendation to repeal . . . unwise and impolitic"[524] though not addressing the constitutional question). That counts Delaware, Maryland, Vermont, and New York, though Delaware and Vermont, too, did not support the Acts' constitutionality but only found state resolutions on federal laws "unjustifiable interference with the general government,"[525] and New York's house only approved a nonconforming resolution that "the right of deciding on the constitutionality . . . appertains to the judiciary."[526] Pennsylvania and New Jersey should not be numbered with the opposition, as we will see

[519] James Madison, *Report on the Virginia Resolutions* (Dec.1799-Jan.1800), in 4 ELLIOT'S DEBATES 546–80; reprinting REPORT OF THE COMMITTEE TO WHOM WAS COMMITTED THE PROCEEDINGS OF SUNDRY OF THE OTHER STATES, IN ANSWER TO THE RESOLUTIONS (General Assembly, Richmond [7 Jan.1800]).

[520] Koch & Ammon, *supra* note 509; LEVY 279–80; FEDERALISM 723.

[521] 4 ELLIOT'S DEBATES 561–67, 571, 572–73; *see generally* RECLAIMING 55–75.

[522] This revisionist approach is developed in Wendell Bird, *Reassessing Responses to the Virginia and Kentucky Resolutions: New Evidence from the Tennessee and Georgia Resolutions and from Other States*, 35 J. EARLY REPUBLIC 519 (2015).

[523] Delaware, Rhode Island, Massachusetts, New York's senate, Connecticut, New Hampshire, Vermont. 4 ELLIOT'S DEBATES 532–39; CONTEMPORARY OPINION 245–49, 229–35; 9 PUBLIC RECORDS-CONN. 357.

[524] CONTEMPORARY OPINION 248 (16, 19 Jan.1799); *id.* 245 (28 Dec.1798) (house); *id.* 46–47 (senate); MARYLAND 200–01; JACOBIN 119.

[525] *Id.* 52, 246–47 (Del.); *accord* 4 ELLIOT'S DEBATES 539 (Vt.).

[526] JOURNAL-N.Y. 122–23 (16 Feb.1799); CONTEMPORARY OPINION 56, 248–49, unlike its senate, *id.* 56–58; 4 ELLIOT'S DEBATES 537.

shortly. (Minority reports should not be counted either—Pennsylvania's and Vermont's for, Virginia's against.[527])

The Overlooked Support by the Tennessee and Georgia Resolutions and the Overlooked Nonopposition

The claim is universally made that the Virginia and Kentucky Resolutions were not supported by any other state,[528] or that "no other states followed" in concluding that "the Alien and Sedition Acts violated the First Amendment."[529] That claim is incorrect—among the other half of the states, two southern states passed resolutions supporting Virginia's and Kentucky's calls for repeal of the Sedition Act, two states' legislatures deadlocked, and two states chose not to take responsive action.

Tennessee's legislature passed resolutions calling for the repeal of the Alien and Sedition Acts as "in several fronts opposed to the Constitution," and as "impolitic, oppressive, and unnecessary."[530] Consequently, the leading Republican newspaper nationally, and others, reported that "the Alien and Sedition laws have met with the same fate in Tennessee, as in Virginia and Kentucky,"[531] and the leading Republican paper in New England, and others, reported that "[t]he legislature of Tennessee have adopted the resolutions of Virginia and Kentucky, respecting the Alien and Sedition Laws."[532] Georgia's legislature passed a resolution that refused "approbation" of the Alien and Sedition Acts, and instead "hope[d]

[527] DISSENT OF THE MINORITY, OF THE HOUSE OF REPRETENTATIVES [*SIC*] OF THE COMMONWEALTH OF PENNSYLVANIA ([Duane], Philadelphia 1799); CONTEMPORARY OPINION 249.

[528] *E.g.*, REPRESSIVE JURISPRUDENCE 88; WATKINS, *supra* note 509, at 75; EMPIRE 270; AMERICAN POLITICS 200; 3 DHSC 238; SECURING 223; OPPOSITION 474; CRISIS 171.

[529] RICHARD LABUNSKI, JAMES MADISON AND THE STRUGGLE FOR THE BILL OF RIGHTS 257 (OUP, New York 2006); *e.g.*, R.B. BERNSTEIN, THOMAS JEFFERSON 126 (OUP, New York 2003); EMPIRE 270; Larry D. Kramer, *Putting the Politics Back into the Political Safeguards of Federalism*, 100 COLUM. L. REV. 215, 275 (2000); FEDERALISM 720; CRISIS 172 n.30; JAY 1089 n.414; CONTEMPORARY OPINION 237 (whose discussion is mistaken); ETHELBERT D. WARFIELD, THE KENTUCKY RESOLUTIONS OF 1798: AN HISTORICAL STUDY 114–15 (Putnam, New York 1894).

[530] Tennessee Senate Journal 1798–1799, at 189 (Tennessee State Library & Archives, Nashville, R.G. no.60) (4 Jan. 1799), cited in Mary L. Gohmann, Political Nativism in Tennessee to 1860, at 50 (1938) (unpublished Ph.D. dissertation, Catholic University), after Gov. John Sevier forwarded the Kentucky Resolutions, "Legislative Message" (7 Dec.1798), 1 MESSAGES OF THE GOVERNORS OF TENNESSEE 72 (Robert H. White ed., THC, Nashville 1952–72). This was consistent with its congressional delegation having voted against the Sedition Act. 7 ANNALS 599, 8 *id.* 2171.

[531] *Norfolk, February 7*, AURORA (Philadelphia), 16 Feb. 1799, at 3; *The Chronicle*, INDEPENDENT CHRONICLE (Boston), 18–21 Feb. 1799, at 3.

[532] *The Chronicle*, INDEPENDENT CHRONICLE (Boston), 2–6 May 1799, at 3; *Newark, April 23*, CENTINEL OF FREEDOM (Newark), 23 Apr. 1799, at 3; [No Caption], UNIVERSAL GAZETTE (Philadelphia), 18 Apr. 1799, at 3.

that they will be repealed without the interposition of the state legislature."[533] The votes were 21–16 in the house and 16–4 in the senate.[534]

Two states did not oppose Virginia and Kentucky because their legislative chambers split. North Carolina's house passed a resolution that the Acts were "a violation of the principles of the Constitution" and should be "repealed without delay," by a 58–21 margin.[535] However, its Federalist-dominated senate[536] rejected it by 31–8.[537] Pennsylvania's house found sister states' resolutions objectionable and the Acts to "contain nothing terrifying,"[538] but it was unable to get its other legislative chamber to condemn the Resolutions in any way despite Federalist control.[539]

Two states chose not to take action. South Carolina's legislature notified Kentucky that its session lacked time for "that attention which the importance of the subject demands."[540] Thus, distant newspapers reported South Carolina's 1799–1800 session was "so short, that they had not time to take up the Kentucky resolutions," though had the legislature done so those resolutions "would certainly have been concurred in."[541] The likely accuracy of that prediction is shown by its legislature having a Republican majority,[542] and its governor believing the Sedition Act unconstitutional.[543] New Jersey similarly did not take a position, instead

[533] JOURNAL OF THE HOUSE OF THE STATE OF GEORGIA 48 (John E. Smith, Augusta, [1800]) (already reflecting deletions called for on page 50).

[534] *Id.* 48 (4 Dec. 1799); JOURNAL OF THE SENATE OF THE STATE OF GEORGIA 19, 35 (John E. Smith, Augusta, [1800]) (22 Nov. 1799, 5 Dec. 1799); GEORGE R. LAMPLUGH, POLITICS ON THE PERIPHERY 156 (UDP, Wilmington 1986); WILLIAM O. FOSTER, JAMES JACKSON 164–65 (UGP, Athens 1960).

[535] JOURNAL OF THE HOUSE OF COMMONS 78 ([Hall, Wilmington 1799]) (24 Dec.1798); *accord* PROLOGUE 299.

[536] Henry M. Wagstaff, *Federalism in North Carolina*, 9 JAMES SPRUNT STUDIES IN HISTORY 5, 30 (1910).

[537] JOURNAL OF THE SENATE. STATE OF NORTH-CAROLINA 77 ([Hall, Wilmington 1799]) (24 Dec.1798); Samuel Johnston to James Iredell (9–30 Dec.1798), 2 IREDELL CORRESPONDENCE 541, 542.

[538] JOURNAL OF THE FIRST SESSION OF THE NINTH HOUSE OF REPRESENTATIVES OF THE COMMONWEALTH OF PENNSYLVANIA 198–200 (Sellers, Philadelphia 1799) (9 Feb. 1799); CONTEMPORARY OPINION 245, 246 (9 Feb.1799); *id.* 248 (11 Mar.1799).

[539] JOURNAL OF THE SENATE OF THE COMMONWEALTH OF PENNSYLVANIA, COMMENCING ON TUESDAY, THE FOURTH DAY OF DECEMBER [1798] 88–89 (Zachariah Poulson, Philadelphia 1798 [actually 1799]) (25 Jan. 1799).

[540] JOURNALS OF SENATE-S.C. 177 (20 Dec.1799) (by 14–11 vote); JOURNALS OF HOUSE-S.C. 164–65 (20 Dec.1799).

[541] *Richmond, January 21*, CONSTITUTIONAL DIARY (Philadelphia), 28 Jan.1800, at 3; *Richmond, Jan. 21*, AURORA (Philadelphia), 30 Jan. 1800, at 2; [No Caption], INDEPENDENT CHRONICLE (Boston), 6 Feb.1800, at 3.

[542] PROLOGUE 229, 236; SOUTH CAROLINA 123.

[543] Edward Rutledge to John Rutledge, Jr. (29 July 1798), RUTLEDGE JR. PAPERS-UNC.

voting for "dismissal of the resolves without explanation,"[544] because its house was so closely divided that the Federalists had only a "majority of only one"; that can be called either a Republican victory or a Federalist triumph.[545]

Thus, only half of the sixteen states responded negatively to the Virginia and Kentucky Resolutions, with a minority of four states basing their opposition on First Amendment grounds, three on non–First Amendment grounds of the Resolutions being "unwise and impolitic" or "unjustifiable interference with the general government," and one state whose legislative chambers chose those different rationales without reconciliation.

The other half of the states did *not* oppose the Resolutions, also varying among four states calling for repeal of the Alien and Sedition Acts (Virginia and Kentucky, and the Tennessee and Georgia Resolutions), two states whose legislative chambers divided (North Carolina and Pennsylvania), and two states that chose not to take action (South Carolina and New Jersey). Besides these legislative votes, there were numerous petitions and speeches against the Sedition Act in most states outside New England.[546]

For Republicans, the resolutions were the opening shots of the elections of 1800. Some Federalists perceived that link to the elections. One ominously disclosed "a plan of the Jacobins . . . to have a majority in our next legislature who will favour . . . the *Virginia* and *Kentucky* resolutions."[547] Other Federalists worried that Republicans "intend to get the state government into their hands," and "to transfer the country, its liberty, and property, at the next election of president and vice-president," as ever-fretful Fisher Ames said.[548]

Epilogue

The impact of the Sedition Act was, as John Quincy Adams observed, an "ineffectual attempt to extinguish the fire of defamation, . . . but it operated like oil upon the flames."[549]

[544] New Jersey 35; *cf.* Votes and Proceedings of the Twenty-Third General Assembly of the State of New-Jersey 10, 11 (18 Jan. 1799); Contemporary Opinion 52–55. The upper chamber did not address the issue, even to vote to dismiss the Resolutions.

[545] Rudolph J. Pasler & Margaret C. Pasler, The New Jersey Federalists 91 n.68 (FDUP, Rutherford, 1974); New Jersey 35.

[546] Douglas Bradburn, *A Clamor in the Public Mind: Opposition to the Alien and Sedition Acts*, 65 Wm. & Mary Q. 565, 567–94 (2008).

[547] *Mr. Cushing*, Salem Gazette, 29 Mar.1799, at 2.

[548] Fisher Ames, *Laocoon I*, Works of Fisher Ames 94, 101, 103, 114 (Wait, Boston 1809).

[549] Worthington C. Ford, *Jefferson and the Newspaper*, 8 Records of the Columbia Historical Soc. 78, 88 (1904).

That oil upon the flames ignited Republican reasoning about the implications of the First Amendment for seditious libel and words, and for press and speech critical of administration, government, and officials. The best product of that developed reasoning was Madison's Report, a powerful response to Addison, Lee, and other Federalist apologias. The oil upon the flames also propelled more leaders and voters across the divide from the Federalist to the Republican Party, and assisted Jefferson in the close presidential election of 1800.[550] The second president's son recognized "there never was a system of measures more completely and irrevocably abandoned and rejected by the popular voice."[551]

Paradoxically, while the Sedition Act was quite effective in assisting the victory of the Republican Party and the demise of the Federalist Party, it was mostly ineffectual on its professed objects. Not a single Jacobin or insurrectionist was apprehended, though the Federalists gave assurances the country teemed with them; and similarly, not a single person was actually deported under the Alien Acts,[552] though not for lack of Pickering's efforts and though many of them voluntarily repatriated.

Instead, the Sedition Act was enforced against newspaper editors, not insurrectionists, with the result that some newspapers closed down permanently (Burk's *Time Piece*,[553] Lyon's *Scourge*, Durrell's *Mount Pleasant Register*[554]), and some suspended publication while the editor was imprisoned (Holt's *Bee*[555]), while others had to be sold (Adams' *Independent Chronicle*, Greenleaf's *Argus*)[556]—but new Republican newspapers more than replaced them. No one would claim that what was termed seditious libel was quelled. Callender's prediction was fulfilled, that "the more persecutions from the Treasury, so much the better. You know the old ecclesiastical observation, that *the blood of the martyrs was the seed of the church*."[557]

The prosecutions under the Sedition Act were partisan, all of Republicans. Not a single Federalist newspaper or speaker was federally prosecuted under the Act, though many railed against Republicans in Congress, and Hamilton with impunity published his "disapprobation" of Adams and his "serious

[550] *E.g.*, NEW JERSEY 251; MARYLAND 206; FEDERALISM 590.

[551] John Quincy Adams to Rufus King (8 Oct.1802), 3 ADAMS WRITINGS 7, 9; *accord* MCHENRY CORRESPONDENCE 452; MARYLAND 206, 208.

[552] 3 DHSC 234; FEDERALISM 592.

[553] CHRONOLOGICAL TABLES 34, which Miller mistakenly says was the only Republican newspaper closed, CRISIS 222.

[554] FREEDOM'S FETTERS 186.

[555] CHRONOLOGICAL TABLES 23; 2 MADISON PAPERS-SECRETARY 292 n.2.

[556] FREEDOM'S FETTERS 255; CRISIS 122.

[557] James Callender to William Duane (27 Apr.1800), Worthington C. Ford, *Thomas Jefferson and James Thomson Callender*, 50 NEW ENG. HIST. & GENEALOGICAL REG. 445, 451, 453 (1896).

errors," which disparaged the president for "undermining the ground which was gained for the government by his predecessor" so that "it might totter, if not fall, under his future auspices."[558] However, various Republicans were prosecuted for criticizing President Adams, and even a drunk Republican was prosecuted for wishing an errant cannonball would lodge itself in the president's ample posterior. Republicans immediately recognized the law "is not equal in its operation but oppressive to one party only," having been "employed against almost every Republican press north of Potomac[]."[559] The Sedition Act and the prosecutions under it amounted to a concerted effort by Pickering and other High Federalists, with the support of President Adams and his administration, to silence opposition newspapers and to defeat the opposition party.[560]

Many sitting Federalist justices were as partisan as the Sedition Act was. Chase openly campaigned in 1800 "mounted on a stump, with a face like a full moon, vociferating in favor of the present President,"[561] and hoped to be chosen a Federalist elector.[562] Bushrod Washington wrote a letter "extremely well calculated to induce a fair & equal vote for Pinckney" and Adams that year, warning that a Federalist split "must end in the election of Mr. J.—which God forbid."[563] That letter was widely circulated, and Washington hosted the Federalist vice presidential candidate at Mt. Vernon "for a few days."[564] Ellsworth had long given political advice,[565] such as his informal advisory opinion supporting the Sedition Act. Paterson had written an essay in the prior election urging voters to support Adams over Jefferson.[566]

[558] Alexander Hamilton, Letter (24 Oct.1800), 25 Hamilton Papers 186, 228, 233.

[559] John Fowler Letter (15 May 1800), 1 Circular Letters 207, 213, 212; *accord* Henry Tazewell to Andrew Jackson (27 Apr.1798), 1 Papers of Andrew Jackson 205, 207 (Sam B. Smith & Harriet C. Owsley eds., UTP, Knoxville 1980-); [No Caption], Centinel of Freedom (Newark), 18 Dec.1798, at 3.

[560] John E. Ferling, Adams vs. Jefferson: The Tumultuous Election of 1800, at 111 (OUP, New York 2004); Tyranny 21; Federalists Reconsidered 5 (Doron Ben-Atar & Barbara B. Oberg eds., UPV, Charlottesville 1998); American Politics 209; Adams Federalists 190, 198–200, 217, 220.

[561] *Aurora* (Philadelphia), 9 Aug.1800, reprinted in 1 DHSC 895; *accord* John Rutledge, Jr. to Alexander Hamilton (17 July 1800), 25 Hamilton Papers 30, 34. He also campaigned in 1798. Chesapeake Politics 549.

[562] James McHenry to Oliver Wolcott (2 Aug.1800), McHenry Correspondence 465.

[563] George Cabot to Alexander Hamilton (29 Nov.1800), 25 Hamilton Papers 247, 248; Bushrod Washington to Oliver Wolcott (1 Nov.1800), 25 *id.* 249–50 n.7; 2 History of Supreme Court 3

[564] Charles C. Pinckney to James McHenry (10 June 1800), McHenry Correspondence 459.

[565] *E.g.*, Oliver Ellsworth to Oliver Wolcott (14 May 1797), 1 Wolcott Papers 523.

[566] William Paterson, The Present Situation 2 (1796), Paterson Papers-LC.

The provisions of the Sedition Act that Federalists trumpeted as ameliorating the common law[567] failed to sound. The defense of truth was never successfully raised, and instead its existence was used perniciously to reverse the presumption of innocence and the prosecution's burden of proof.[568] The jury's decision of all issues by general verdict did not save defendants from the fire breathed by Federalist judges and marshals, with a single exception. Only one Sedition Act prosecution, which the next chapter discusses, resulted in an acquittal. Grand juries in at least some cases were carefully packed[569] as shown by their sycophantic messages commending judge's charges;[570] trial jury panels were chosen by the same presidentially appointed marshal.[571] Emboldened by legal prosecutions, Federalist officers and crowds physically attacked most of the prosecuted Republican editors, at least once.[572]

But even as Pickering and federal prosecutors won Sedition Act battles, they and the Federalist Party lost the war.[573] Yet as the Federalist Party fell, Pickering blamed it not on the Alien and Sedition Acts, or other unpopular actions, but on "intrigues" by Adams in which the country was "sacrificed by Mr. Adams to his ambition and avarice"[574]—which from any other mouth Pickering would have called a seditious libel.

How could Justices Paterson, Chase, Washington, Iredell, Cushing, and Chief Justice Ellsworth seemingly contradict their beliefs of a decade earlier on speech and press in order to support the Sedition Act and, in the case of the first five, to enforce it? They clearly changed their position from their pre-1798 views, when all of them had expressed a broad understanding of freedoms of press and speech, and not one of them had embraced the Blackstone-Mansfield definition. But why? They did so during the threats of a fragile government, internal rebellions, and the

[567] *E.g.*, PATERSON DRAFT OPINIONS 535–37; Wharton's State Trials 341, 686; James Iredell's Charge (C.C.D. Pa. 11 Apr.1799), 3 DHSC 332, 348; Oliver Ellsworth to Timothy Pickering (12 Dec.1798), ELLSWORTH PAPERS-NYPL 47.

[568] Though sometimes elsewhere that defense helped, as with Zenger's acquittal and in Massachusetts libel cases. WILLIAM E. NELSON, AMERICANIZATION OF THE COMMON LAW 95 (HUP, Cambridge 1975).

[569] *E.g.*, 3 DHSC 294, 294–95 (Lyon's grand jury); FREEDOM'S FETTERS 217 (Burk's caused settlement); Brent Tarter & Wythe Holt, *The Apparent Political Selection of Federal Grand Juries in Virginia, 1789–1809*, 49 AM. J. LEGAL HIST. 257 (2007); though not in all cases, 2 DHSC 224, 332; 8 ADAMS WORKS 643, 644.

[570] *E.g.*, 3 DHSC 261, 294, 303, 327, 359, 363, 39, 61, 70, 102, 113, 120, 129, 168.

[571] *E.g.*, FREEDOM'S FETTERS 423 (*Callender*); Thomas Jefferson to Edmund Pendleton (19 Apr.1800), 31 JEFFERSON PAPERS 520, 521 (alleging in *Duane, Cooper, Fries*); 8 ANNALS 2140, 2153, 2162, 2163.

[572] JOHN NERONE, VIOLENCE AGAINST THE PRESS 65–66 (OUP, New York 1994).

[573] 1 WARREN 191; REPRESSIVE JURISPRUDENCE 146–47; CHESAPEAKE POLITICS 533.

[574] Timothy Pickering Notebook (MHS c.1811), PICKERING PAPERS r.46, fol.85, 93; *accord* Timothy Pickering to Rufus King (28 May 1800), 3 KING CORRESPONDENCE 248.

Quasi-War. But a belief in freedom that was disposable under pressure showed a belief in something else that was more important. Their broad view of the importance of forming a strong state trumped their correspondingly narrower view of the right of dissent in its many facets—that the administration could not be opposed, that opponents could not form a party, that citizens could not evaluate laws as unconstitutional, that they could not disobey unconstitutional laws as void, that common law doctrines of seditious libel limited freedoms of press or speech, that those freedoms only meant freedom from prior restraint. Just as the Blackstone-Mansfield definition of liberties of press and speech was a new position for the English judiciary and to English common law in 1770, that definition was a new belief for the American Supreme Court justices in 1798.

By contrast, the majority of the remaining justices differed from the sitting justices in their views of legitimate dissent, of the Sedition Act, and of the Blackstone-Mansfield definition. Before discussing the remaining justices and the Sedition Act, we will look at the unrecognized Sedition Act prosecutions, to complete this chapter's account of the cases and of the early justices' role in them.

7

The Sedition Act and the Assault on Freedoms of Press and Speech: The Missing Half of the Sedition Act Cases

> Federalist enforcement machinery ground out at least seventeen verifiable indictments. Fourteen were found under the Sedition Act, and three were returned under the common law. . . .
>
> —James Morton Smith[1]

The storm that raged over the First Amendment from 1798–1801 brought the fourteen Sedition Act prosecutions, and the three federal common law prosecutions, that were described in Chapter 6. Even before the Sedition Act took effect, the leading Republican newspaper editors in America's two largest cities, Benjamin Franklin Bache of Philadelphia's *Aurora*, and John Daly Burk and James Smith,[2] of New York's *Time Piece*, were arrested and charged with seditious libel under federal common law. Shortly after the Sedition Act was signed by President John Adams,[3] the owners or editors of three more Republican newspapers were prosecuted: Congressman Matthew Lyon, owner of a Vermont newspaper,[4] Thomas

[1] James M. Smith, Freedom's Fetters: The Alien and Sedition Laws and American Civil Liberties 185 (CorUP, Ithaca 1956).

[2] Timothy Pickering to Richard Harison (7 July 1798), Pickering Papers r.37, fol.315, 315A; Timothy Pickering to Richard Harison (1 Jan.1799), *id.* at r.37, fol.381; Jacob Wagner to Edward Dunscomb (22 May 1799), *id.* at r.37, fol.423; John Daly Burk to Thomas Jefferson (ante 19 June 1801), 34 Jefferson Papers 385, 386–87. A list of abbreviated titles is at the end of this book.

[3] This addresses when indictments or presentments were brought. The dates of trials varied: Bache and Adams died before trials could occur; Burk entered a deportation agreement in lieu of trial; Fairbanks and Brown came up for trial and pleaded guilty in June 1799; Duane evaded trial; Greenleaf and Peck were dismissed; Baldwin and Clark reached trial in October 1799; Durrell and Haswell reached trial in April and May 1800; Cooper and Callender were immediately tried in May and June 1800.

[4] Trial of Matthew Lyon, Wharton's State Trials 333 (C.C.D. Vt. 1798), reprinted In re Lyon's Case, 15 F.Cas. 1183 (C.C.D. Vt. 1798) (No.8,646).

Adams, editor of Boston's *Independent Chronicle*, and William Durrell, editor of the *Mount Pleasant Register* in New York.[5] Also prosecuted were supporters of a liberty pole (called a "sedition pole" by most Federalists), Benjamin Fairbanks and David Brown in Dedham, Massachusetts,[6] and tavern critics of President Adams, Luther Baldwin and Brown Clark in Newark.[7] Then a lull in prosecutions occurred until mid-1799, as the deadline approached for filing cases in order to reach trial before the elections of 1800, when four more prosecutions were launched of Republican newspaper editors: William Duane, Bache's successor at the Philadelphia *Aurora*,[8] Ann Greenleaf of the New York *Argus*,[9] Charles Holt of the New London *Bee*, and Anthony Haswell of the *Vermont Gazette*,[10] in addition to prosecution of a state legislator, Jedidiah Peck, for circulating petitions denouncing the Sedition Act as unconstitutional.[11] Finally, in the spring of 1800, Justice Samuel Chase turned his circuit tour into a search and destroy mission for sedition, leading to indictments and trials of two more editors and writers: Thomas Cooper of the Northumberland *Gazette*,[12] and James T. Callender for his book *The Prospect Before Us*.[13]

Those fourteen Sedition Act prosecutions and three common law prosecutions[14] are the canon of cases discussed in the two books,[15] various chapters and

[5] Timothy Pickering to Richard Harison (28 June 1798), Pickering Papers r.8, fol.904; *see* Timothy Pickering to Richard Harison (22 Apr.1800), *id.* at r.13, fol.406; Richard Harison to Timothy Pickering (10 Apr.1800), *id.* at r.26, fol.77.

[6] Jacobin 103–10.

[7] Minutes 137–38 (C.C.D. N.J. Oct. Term 1798) (National Archives at New York City, R.G.21.32.2); *id.* at 140–43, 146–47 (C.C.D. N.J. Apr. Term 1799).

[8] Criminal Case Files of the U.S. Circuit Court for the Eastern District of Pennsylvania, 1791–1840, at 1:I1128–, 1:I147–, 1:I1136–, 2:156– (National Archives at Philadelphia, R.G.21.40.2, microfilm M986, rolls 1 and 2); Timothy Pickering to William Rawle (24 July 1799), Pickering Papers r.11, fol.486; Timothy Pickering to William Rawle (20 Sept.1799), *id.* at r.12, fol.82.

[9] Timothy Pickering to Richard Harison (12 Aug.1799), *id.* at r.11, fol.599; Timothy Pickering to Richard Harison (22 Apr.1800), *id.* at r.13, fol.406.

[10] Trial of Anthony Haswell, Wharton's State Trials 684 (C.C.D. Vt. 1800), reprinted United States v. Haswell, 26 F.Cas. 218 (C.C.D. Vt. 1800) (No. 15,324).

[11] Richard Harison to Timothy Pickering (10 Apr.1800), Pickering Papers r.26, fol.77, 78A, 78; Timothy Pickering to Richard Harison (22 Apr.1800), *id.* at r.13, fol.406.

[12] Trial of Thomas Cooper, Wharton's State Trials 659 (C.C.D. Pa. 1800), reprinted United States v. Cooper, 4 U.S. (4 Dall.) 341, 25 F.Cas. 626, 631 (C.C.D. Pa. 1800) (No. 14,861, 14,865).

[13] Trial of James Thompson Callender, Wharton's State Trials 688 (C.C.D. Va. 1800), reprinted United States v. Callender, 25 F.Cas. 239 (C.C.D. Va. 1800) (No. 14,709).

[14] Some writers refer to fourteen cases under the Sedition Act and common law combined, because three were two-defendant or paired cases: Burk-Smith, Fairbanks-Brown, and Baldwin-Clark.

[15] Freedom's Fetters 185 (14 indictments under Act, 3 under common law); Crisis 65–66, 97–130, 194–223 (15 prosecutions).

articles,[16] and briefer discussions of the Sedition Act.[17] Recent writers generally continue to describe just those prosecutions,[18] and to number fourteen or fifteen Sedition Act prosecutions and three common law ones.[19]

However, there has always been a suspicion that there may have been at least a few additional prosecutions.[20] Republican newspaper articles in late 1799 referred to twenty-two prosecutions (without identifying most).[21] Frank Anderson, in the earliest study of the Sedition Act, after noting between fifteen and seventeen indictments, said that there were "about 24 or 25 persons arrested" (also without identifying the additional ones),[22] an estimate that is periodically quoted (though the additional arrestees are still not identified).[23] James Morton Smith devoted a page to possible cases (mentioned in partisan newspapers or letters) that he was "unable to track down" and confirm, listing those of "Editor Schneider," Benjamin Mayer and Conrad Fahnestock, Judah Spooner, "Dr. Shaw," James Bell, Dr. John Tyler, Dr. John Vaughn, and "a person identified only as Lespenard."[24] Julius Goebel identified Shaw as Dr. Samuel Shaw of Vermont, with a footnote citation to federal court records, though he did not describe the case beyond a sentence.[25]

[16] *E.g.*, Norman L. Rosenberg, Protecting the Best Men: an Interpretive History of the Law of Libel 87 (UNCP, Chapel Hill 1986) (15 prosecutions under Sedition Act, 3 under common law); Anderson 515 (15 indictments under Sedition Act); 4 Jefferson 227 (14 indictments under Act, 3 common law); John C. Miller, The Federalist Era, 1789–1801, at 235 (Harper, New York 1960) (15); Mark A. Smith, Crisis, Unity, and Partisanship: The Road to the Sedition Act 353, 346–63 (1998) (unpublished Ph.D. dissertation, University of Virginia) (7 newspapers); Frank M. Anderson, *The Enforcement of the Alien and Sedition Acts*, 18 Am. Historical Rev. 113, 120 (1912) (15–17 indictments).

[17] *E.g.*, 3 DHSC 233 (15 prosecutions under Sedition Act, including Colie); Federalism 703 (14 cases); American Politics 218–20 (8 mentioned); 1 History of Supreme Court 637–38 & n.107 (15, including Shaw).

[18] *E.g.*, Susan Dunn, Jefferson's Second Revolution 112 (Houghton Mifflin, Boston 2004) (17 prosecutions); Perilous Times 63 (15 indictments); David Jenkins, *The Sedition Act of 1798 and the Incorporation of Seditious Libel into First Amendment Jurisprudence*, 45 Am. J. Legal Hist. 154, 188–97 (2001) (7 of the cases).

[19] *E.g.*, Empire 260 (14 plus 3 indictments); John E. Ferling, Adams vs. Jefferson: The Tumultuous Election of 1800, at 122 (OUP, New York 2004) (17 indictments); Meg Jacobs et al., The Democratic Experiment 32 (PUP, Princeton 2003) (14); Saul Cornell, The Other Founders 233 (UNCP, Chapel Hill 1999) (17 indictments); Marc Lendler, *"Equally Proper at All Times and at All Times Necessary": Civility, Bad Tendency, and the Sedition Act*, 24 J. Early Republic 419, 422 (2004) (17).

[20] *E.g.*, Ferling, *supra* note 19, at 122 ("[a]t least seventeen indictments").

[21] *From the* Aurora, *Oct. 26*, Constitutional Telegraph, 6 Nov.1799, at 1 (22 prosecutions).

[22] Anderson, *supra* note 16, at 120.

[23] *E.g.*, Dunn, *supra* note 18, at 112; Simon Sheppard, American Media, American Bias: The Partisan Press from Broadsheet to Blog 57 (2007) (unpublished Ph.D. thesis, Johns Hopkins University).

[24] Freedom's Fetters 185, 271. Others occasionally cite these without further sources. *E.g.*, Jacobs et al., *supra* note 19, at 45 n.40.

[25] 1 History of Supreme Court 638 n.107.

Maeva Marcus identified Lespenard as Lespenard Colie, citing court records.[26] Phillip Blumberg, noting that all those cases (except Shaw) were still "unconfirmed cases," recently gave a useful five-page summary of what was known about them from Smith's sources and some additional newspaper references.[27]

Surprisingly, no one thoroughly combed through the unpublished papers of Timothy Pickering, the secretary of state during most of the years the Sedition Act was in force, who was the official in charge of its enforcement.[28] Though a dozen of his letters about recognized cases, which appeared in an index to the Pickering papers, were regularly cited, another dozen dealing with recognized cases were never cited, nor were a dozen and a half letters dealing with the additional cases, attempted indictments, and instructions to prosecute that are discussed in this article.

Further, none of those scholars noted that the case reports of the Fries Rebellion[29] trials referred to the nontreason cases as generally being brought under the Sedition Act,[30] or that the unpublished federal court records confirmed that all of the nontreason Fries cases were brought under the Act.[31] Those federal court records show that four of the Fries Rebellion prosecutions were brought under Section 2 of the Sedition Act (criminalizing "writing, printing, uttering or publishing any false, scandalous and malicious writing or writings against the government," Congress, or the president), and the remaining nontreason prosecutions were brought under Section 1 of that Act (criminalizing conspiracies and combinations "to oppose any measure or measures of the government" or, among other things, to "counsel, advise or attempt to procure any . . . unlawful assembly, or combination."). Four Fries Rebellion scholars briefly pointed out that conspiracy charges

[26] 3 DHSC 299 n.2.

[27] REPRESSIVE JURISPRUDENCE 139–44.

[28] The reason is understandable—his papers fill sixty-nine rolls of microfilm and are all handwritten.

[29] This tax protest in 1799, and the prosecutions of the protesters in 1799–1800, is described in the second section of this chapter and in PAUL D. NEWMAN, FRIES'S REBELLION: THE ENDURING STRUGGLE FOR THE AMERICAN REVOLUTION (UPP, Philadelphia 2004).

[30] Second Trial of John Fries, Wharton's State Trials 610, 623n., 624n. (C.C.D. Pa.1800) (prosecutor William Rawle, Justice Samuel Chase), reprinted in In re Fries, 9 F.Cas. 924 (C.C.D. Pa.1800) (No. 5,127); *see* Trial of the Northampton Insurgents [first trial], Wharton's State Trials 458, 585 (C.C.D. Pa.1799) (Judge Richard Peters), reprinted in Case of Fries, 9 F.Cas. 826 (C.C.D. Pa.1799) (No. 5,126), *modified,* 3 U.S. (3 Dall.) 515 (C.C.D. Pa.1799). Wharton essentially reprinted the Thomas Carpenter transcript of the trial, rearranging the location of appended materials. THE TWO TRIALS OF JOHN FRIES (Thomas Carpenter transcriptionist, William W. Woodward, Philadelphia 1800). That transcript included the trial of Jacob Eyerman, where the prosecutor again noted that combination and conspiracy charges were under the Sedition Act. *Id.* at 224.

[31] The exception is Goebel, who without further description said in a footnote that "Smith's count obviously does not include some of the indictments under sec. 1 that were returned against some participants in the Fries rebellion" for conspiracy, and that "[a] number of the indictments under sec. 2 never reached the trial stage because defendants changed their pleas." 1 HISTORY OF SUPREME COURT 638 n.107. Neither Goebel nor any other Sedition Act scholar pursued his suggestion by locating or identifying specific cases.

against Fries rebels used the statutory authority of the Sedition Act,[32] something that "historians previously have overlooked,"[33] but those observations were not picked up in Sedition Act writings. The first of those Fries Rebellion authors, Dwight Henderson, devoted a page of his article to mention Langford Herring, Jacob Eyerman, Morris Llewellyn and codefendants, and Benjamin Mayer and Conrad Fahnestock, without tying their cases to the Sedition Act.[34] The second, Paul Newman, in the leading book on the Fries Rebellion, devoted a page to mention the Benjamin Mayer/Conrad Fahnestock case and the Morris "Schwelein" et al. case as involving sedition, though not the Sedition Act, and the Jacob Eyerman case as involving the Sedition Act, though he did not provide a specific reference.[35] Two other Fries Rebellion authors, Whitman Ridgway and Robert Churchill, while not mentioning any specific Sedition Act cases, noted in single sentences that some prosecutions used Section 1 of that Act, though it was "normally not associated with the Northampton Insurrection" by historians.[36] Apart from those scholars, subsequent discussions of the Fries Rebellion joined earlier ones[37] in silence on any involvement of the Sedition Act.[38]

In fact, over half of Smith's unconfirmed cases, four other prosecutions, and three other Henderson-Newman references, along with eleven other Fries Rebellion cases, should now be deemed confirmed and added to the canon of Sedition Act prosecutions. The test for confirmation is support in federal court records or prosecutor records, and those records have been located to confirm the prosecutions discussed in the first two sections below. The prosecutions in the first section were brought under the Sedition Act's provision criminalizing spoken or printed words, while those in the second section were brought under the Act's provision criminalizing unlawful

[32] FRIES'S REBELLION 174–75; Dwight F. Henderson, *Treason, Sedition, and Fries' Rebellion*, 14 AM. J. LEGAL HIST. 308, 312 (1970); Dwight Henderson, *Book Review of Fries's Rebellion*, 26 J. EARLY REPUB. 341, 342 (2006).

[33] HENDERSON 312.

[34] *Id.* at 315–16

[35] FRIES'S REBELLION 174–75.

[36] Whitman H. Ridgway, *Fries in the Federalist Imagination: A Crisis of Republican Society*, 67 PA. HIST. 141, 147, 145 (2000); *accord* Robert H. Churchill, *Popular Nullification, Fries' Rebellion, and the Waning of Radical Republicanism, 1798–1801*, 67 PA. HIST. 105, 130 (2000). Though their focus on John Fries did not involve discussing this article's cases, Churchill mentioned Greenawalt's outburst without mention that he was prosecuted, *id.* at 118, and Ridgway mentioned a "seditious combination" case without identifying it as Morris Llewellyn et al. 67 PA. HIST. at 156 n.16.

[37] *E.g.*, RICHARD E. ELLIS, THE JEFFERSONIAN CRISIS: COURTS AND POLITICS IN THE YOUNG REPUBLIC 77–78, 97–100 (OUP, New York 1971); PENNSYLVANIA 215–19; W. W. H. DAVIS, THE FRIES REBELLION, 1798–1799 (Doylestown Publishing, Doylestown 1899); Jane Shaffer Elsmere, *The Trials of John Fries*, 103 PA. MAGAZINE OF HIST. & BIOG. 432, 435–37 (1979); Peter Levine, *The Fries Rebellion: Social Violence and the Politics of the New Nation*, 40 PA. HIST. 240, 243, 246 (1973).

[38] E.g., Jeffrey S. Dimmig, *Palatine Liberty: Pennsylvania German Opposition to the Direct Tax of 1798*, 45 AM. J. LEGAL HIST. 371, 384–90 (2001); Terry Bouton, *"No Wonder the Times Were Troublesome:" The Origins of Fries Rebellion*, 67 PA. HIST. 21 (2000); see EMPIRE 260; AMERICAN POLITICS 209–10; FEDERALISM 696–700.

conspiracies and combinations to oppose federal laws or to counsel, advise, or attempt that. All were in federal circuit court, where an individual Supreme Court justice presided with a district court judge, except the de facto case against John C. Ogden. In addition, attempted indictments in at least three other cases, and instructions to prosecute in at least six other cases (involving eight individuals) under the Sedition Act, can be documented, as discussed in the third and fourth sections below.

These cases expand the involvement of U.S. Supreme Court justices, from the three known to have presided over Sedition Act prosecutions (Justices William Paterson, Samuel Chase, and Bushrod Washington) to Justices William Cushing and James Iredell as well. They change the tallies so that Iredell, not Paterson or Chase, presided over the most prosecutions, and Chase, not Paterson, presided over the most sentences. What remains unchanged is the absolute partisanship of the prosecutions (all being against Republicans), and the general harshness of sentences. Most importantly, these additional cases show other victims during the crisis of the First Amendment in 1798–1801, and demonstrate that Sedition Act prosecutions, and accompanying chilling of First Amendment rights, were on over twice the scale previously understood.

Eleven Additional Cases under the Sedition Act for Spoken or Written Words

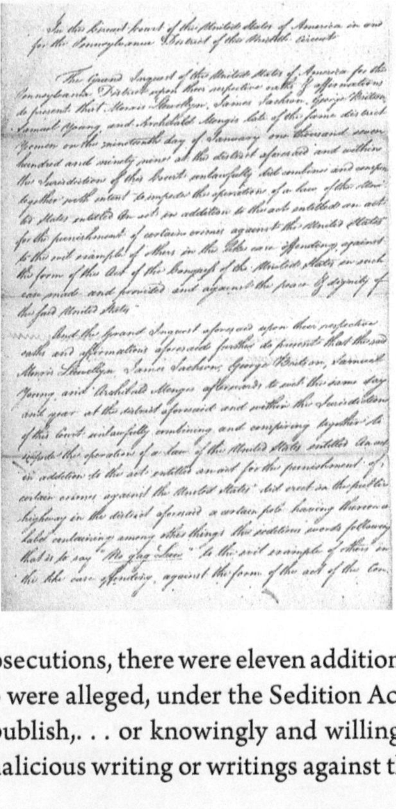
In the Circuit Court of the United States of America in and
for the Pennsylvania District of the Middle Circuit

The Grand Inquest of the United States of America for the
Pennsylvania District upon their respective oaths & affirmations
do present that Morris Llewellyn, James Jackson, George Britton,
Samuel Young, and Archibald Mengis late of the same district
Yeomen on the nineteenth day of January one thousand seven
hundred and ninety nine at the district aforesaid and within
the Jurisdiction of this Court unlawfully did combine and conspire
together with intent to impede the operation of a law of the Uni-
ted States entitled An act in addition to the act entitled an act
for the punishment of certain crimes against the United States
to the evil example of others in the like case offending against
the form of the Act of the Congress of the United States in such
case made and provided and against the peace & dignity of
the said United States

And the Grand Inquest aforesaid upon their respective
oaths and affirmations aforesaid further do present that the said
Morris Llewellyn James Jackson, George Britton, Samuel
Young and Archibald Mengis afterwards to wit the same day
and year at the district aforesaid and within the Jurisdiction
of this Court unlawfully combining and conspiring together to
impede the operation of a law of the United States entitled An act
in addition to the act entitled an act for the punishment of
certain crimes against the United States did erect in the public
highway in the district aforesaid a certain pole having thereon a
label containing among other things the seditious words following
that is to say "The gag Law" to the evil example of others in
the like case offending, against the form of the act of the Con-

Figure 7.1 Indictment of Morris Llewellyn (1799). (Courtesy of National Archives.)

Besides the canon of seventeen familiar prosecutions, there were eleven additional cases prosecuting sixteen defendants, who were alleged, under the Sedition Act's second section, to "write, print, utter or publish,. . . or knowingly and willingly assist or aid . . . any false, scandalous and malicious writing or writings against the

Table 7.1 **Prosecutions For Seditious Words Under Sedition Act § 2 (Unrecognized)**

Defendant and Residence	*Circuit Court Date and Location*	*Supreme Court Justice Involved*
1 Lespenard Colie Springfield, New Jersey	Indicted 3 Oct. 1798 Pleaded guilty 3 Oct. 1798 Trenton, New Jersey	Justice William Cushing "
2 Judah P. Spooner of Matthew Lyon's *Scourge of Aristocracy* Fair Haven, Vermont (now spelled Fairhaven)	Indicted 6 Oct. 1798 Arrested 7 Oct. 1799 Dismissed by nolle prosequi Oct. 1799 Rutland, Vermont	Justice William Paterson Justice William Cushing "
3 Alden Spooner of *Spooner's Vermont Journal* Windsor, Vermont	Indicted 6 Oct. 1798 Dismissed by nolle prosequi Oct. 1799 Rutland, Vermont	Justice William Paterson Justice William Cushing
4 Rev. John Cosens Ogden Troy, New York	Arrested and charged Feb. 1799 in creditor suit (not technically under Sedition Act) Released without trial 10 June 1799 Litchfield, Connecticut	No justice involved (Secretary of Treasury Oliver Wolcott, Jr.)
5 Jacob Greenawalt Greenwich Township, Pennsylvania	Arrested and posted bond to appear in Apr. 1799 [F1:1966] Pleaded guilty, posted bond for good behavior on 22 Apr. 1799 [M289] Philadelphia, Pennsylvania	No justice involved Justice James Iredell
6 Morris Llewellyn, James Jackson, George Britson, Samuel Young, Archibald Mengis Montgomery County, Pennsylvania	Indicted 24 Apr. 1799 [M293, F1:1998] and 7 Oct. 1799 [M342, F1:1997] Pleaded not guilty (first three) and posted bond 29 Apr. 1799 (first two) [M300] & 18 May 1799 (first three) [M326] Reindicted and dropped Jackson 16 Apr. 1800 [M351, F2:278] Philadelphia, Pennsylvania	Justice James Iredell Justice Bushrod Washington Justice Samuel Chase
7 Langford Herring Philadelphia, Pennsylvania	Indicted 27 Apr. 1799 [M299, F1:I1079] Posted appearance bond 17 May 1799 [M322] Prosecution dropped upon payment of costs 7 Oct. 1799 [F1:I1081, 1080] Philadelphia, Pennsylvania	Justice James Iredell No justice involved
8 Rev. Jacob Eyerman Northampton County, Pennsylvania	Indicted for escape 12 Oct. 1799 [M334, 1:I1125], and for conspiracy and "seditious counseling" 15 Oct. 1799 [M335, F1:I1163, 2:I139] Trial 16 Oct. 1799 [M339] Jury found guilty on second indictment 16 Oct. 1799 [M339-40], but conviction thrown out [F1:I1125] Reindicted for escape, conspiracy, and "seditious counseling" 16 Apr. 1800 [M351] Submitted to nonjury trial 1 May 1800 [M380, F1:I1161] Sentenced 1 May 1800 [M386, F2:I145] Philadelphia, Pennsylvania	Justice Bushrod Washington " Justice Samuel Chase " "

Table 7.1 **(continued)**

	Defendant and Residence	*Circuit Court Date and Location*	*Supreme Court Justice Involved*
9	Benjamin Mayer and Conrad Fahnestock of *Harrisburgh Morgenröthe* Harrisburg, Pennsylvania	Indicted 18 Oct. 1799 [M342, F1:I1168] Arraigned 18 Oct. 1799 [F1:I1170] Submitted to nonjury trial 18 Oct. 1799 [M342, F1:I1170] Norristown, Pennsylvania	Justice Bushrod Washington "
10	Matthew Lyon (second prosecution) of *Scourge of Aristocracy* Fair Haven, Vermont	Information filed 7 Oct. 1799 Arrest warrant issued 7 Nov. 1799 for trial 1 May 1800 Rutland, Vermont	Justice William Cushing
11	Dr. Samuel Shaw Castleton, Vermont	Indictment 10 Oct. 1799 Arrest warrant 7 Nov. 1799 for trial 1 May 1800 Trial ca. 6–9 May 1800 Windsor, Vermont	Justice William Cushing Justice William Paterson

Bracketed citations beginning with F refer to Criminal Case Files of the United States Circuit Court for the Eastern District of Pennsylvania, 1791–1840 (National Archives at Philadelphia, R.G.21.40.2, microfilm M986, rolls 1 and 2); 1: or 2: refers to the microfilm roll; the stamped page number is used (indicated by P) for the pages that contained one (2:277–379) and the microfilm image number is used otherwise (indicated by I) as no continuous number appears on those pages.

Bracketed citations beginning with M refer to Original Minutes of the Circuit Court of the United States of America for the Middle Circuit, October Session 1790 to April 1799 (National Archives at Philadelphia, R.G.21.40.2, microfilm M932, roll 1); the stamped page number is used rather than the handwritten page number (which restarts with 1 for every yearly term).

government of the United States, or . . . Congress . . . or the President . . ., with intent to defame" them. Those eleven additional cases are listed in Table 7.1.

Lespenard Colie: Seditious Words "Damning the President" and Supporting the French

When Luther Baldwin was charged under the Sedition Act for wishing that celebratory cannon fire had hit President Adams's posterior, and Brown Clark was charged for joining in that wish, there was a third defendant who Smith said was "identified only as Lespenard." He remained missing from academic writings about the Sedition Act, until he was identified as Lespenard Colie by Maeva Marcus in the *Documentary History of the Supreme Court*, based on court records.[39] Colie's case still remains missing elsewhere.

Hannah Cushing, the wife of Justice William Cushing, accompanied his circuit ride and sat in the New Jersey courtroom when the grand jury found a third indictment "for seditious words," and when that third person pleaded guilty, as

[39] 3 DHSC 299 n.2.

she told Abigail Adams five days later. That defendant, Lespenard Colie, said "some what like this—that if the French came he would join them & fight for a shilling a day, & would deliver up any that were inimical to them—& for D__________g the P__________ &c."[40] Justice Cushing had opened court with a rousing grand jury charge, warning that it is not "possible for any free government to stand the shock of such perpetual, inveterate, malicious, hostile attacks" as unceasing calumnies, and that seditious libel is "a dangerous offence in all societies" and is not allowed by liberty of the press "unless the liberty of the press comprehends a right to print and propagate scandalous and malicious falsehoods, to the injury of the public."[41] Under his charge, free government could not stand if people were "damning the President."

The 1798 court records confirm that Colie initially pleaded not guilty, but immediately withdrew that and pleaded guilty. Cushing imposed a $40 fine, plus court costs, but did not impose a prison sentence, other than leaving him "committed until the fine and costs are paid."[42] That was one of only three Sedition Act sentences that did not require imprisonment (along with Luther Baldwin and Brown Clark, in the same court), and the second-lightest fine behind that of Benjamin Fairbanks, though it was the only Sedition Act prosecution of a French citizen or ex-citizen in an era of widespread Gallophobia.[43] News coverage took two and a half months to appear, when a New Jersey Republican newspaper listed "Mr. Colie of Springfield" among the individuals who had been arrested under the Sedition Act.[44] It said nothing more.

Judah P. Spooner, Printer of the *Scourge of Aristocracy*: Publishing the Barlow Letter Criticizing the Government

The twelve prosecutions of newspaper editors and printers, among the recognized seventeen prosecutions, were not the only ones. Prosecutions can also be confirmed of Judah P. Spooner, printer of the *Scourge of Aristocracy* and of Republican pamphlets, Alden Spooner of *Spooner's Vermont Journal*, Benjamin Mayer and Conrad Fahnestock of *Harrisburgh Morgenröthe*, and Matthew Lyon in an unrecognized second prosecution.

[40] Hannah Cushing to Abigail Adams (8 Oct.1798), 3 DHSC 296.

[41] William Cushing's Charge (C.C.D. Va. 23 Nov. 1798), 3 DHSC 305, 306, 313, 314 (he gave the same charge throughout each circuit).

[42] Minutes at 138 (C.C.D. N.J. 3 Oct.1798) (National Archives at New York City, R.G.21.32.2).

[43] John McNelis O'Keefe, From Legal Rights to Citizens' Rights and Alien Penalties: Migrant Influence, Naturalization, and the Growth of National Power over Foreign Migrants in the Early American Republic 51 (2012) (unpublished Ph.D. dissertation, George Washington University).

[44] *Newark, December 25*, CENTINEL OF FREEDOM (Newark), 25 Dec.1798, at 3. He appears to be the same person as the "Lespnird Colie" of Springfield who placed an advertisement in early 1798. *For Sale*, NEW-JERSEY JOURNAL (Elizabethtown), 6 Feb.1798, at 4.

Judah P. Spooner was a printer who had established the first newspaper in Vermont, the *Vermont Gazette*, in 1778, and in the mid-1790s moved to Fairhaven and printed the *Farmer's Library*, until it ended in April 1798.[45] His print shop also printed almanacs and pamphlets as he had opportunity, though on a very limited basis as compared with his brother, Alden Spooner.[46] In mid-1798 he began printing a new newspaper, Matthew Lyon's colorfully named *Scourge of Aristocracy*.[47]

Period newspapers reported that its printers, Judah P. Spooner[48] and also James Lyon,[49] were arrested and indicted under the Sedition Act. However, the leading historian of the Sedition Act, James Morton Smith, concluded that "there seems to be no basis for these assertions,"[50] and historians have not disagreed. To the contrary, court records establish an indictment and arrest of Spooner.

In fact, Judah P. Spooner was indicted in October 1798,[51] though he was not arrested for trial until a year later, for violating the Sedition Act by printing a "seditious libel entitled *Copy of a letter from an American diplomatic character in France to a member of Congress*." That was the letter from Joel Barlow in Paris that was the second ground for indicting Republican Congressman Matthew Lyon a day earlier. That letter was alleged to "defame the government of the United States, and John Adams, and . . . one house of the Congress" by calling Adams's speech about France's rejection of the new American ambassador a "bullying

[45] 2 Clarence S. Brigham, History and Bibliography of American Newspapers, 1690–1820, at 1096, 1486, 1083 (Am. Antiquarian Soc., Worcester 1947) (co-founding the *Vermont Gazette* with Timothy Green). Biographical information is in Esther L. Woodworth-Barnes, Spooner Saga 343 (Newbury St. Press, Boston 1997); Hamilton Child, Gazetteer and Business Directory of Windham County, Vermont 49 (The Journal, Syracuse 1884).

[46] Marcus A. McCorison, Vermont Imprints, 1778–1820, at 82–122 (Am. Antiquarian Soc., Worcester 1963).

[47] John J. Duffy et al., The Vermont Encyclopedia 276 (Univ. Press of New England, Hanover 2003); J. Kevin Gaffagnino, *"We Have Long Been Wishing for a Good Printer in This Vicinity:" The State of Vermont*, 47 Vermont Hist. 21, 26, 33–35 (1979).

[48] *E.g., Bennington, October 12*, Centinel of Freedom (Newark), 23 Oct.1798, at 2; *From a Boston Paper of October 26*, The Sun (Dover), 31 Oct.1798, at 3.

[49] *E.g., Worcester, (Mass.) Oct. 17*, Independent Chronicle (Boston), 18–22 Oct.1798, at 2; *Newark, December 25*, Centinel of Freedom (Newark), 25 Dec.1798, at 3.

[50] Freedom's Fetters 229 n.22.

[51] Indictment followed a grand jury charge by Justice William Paterson that anyone who publishes "false, defamatory, and malicious writings or libels against the government of his country, its measures, and its constituted authorities, must . . . stand self-condemned" and "sins against light," so that "nothing short of idiocy can operate as an excuse" because "[n]o government, indeed, can long subsist, where offenders of this kind are suffered to spread their poison with impunity." William Paterson's Charge (C.C.D. Vt. 3 Oct. 1798), 3 DHSC 292, 293.

speech,"[52] and the Senate's response to him a "stupid" one with more "servility" than Parliament ever showed to George III. Barlow's letter went on to say that the people of France instead expected the Senate's response to be to send Adams "to a madhouse."[53] Though Benjamin Franklin had once said that Adams was "always an honest man, often a wise one, but sometimes, and in some things, absolutely out of his senses,"[54] such sentiments would have been criminal in the era of the Sedition Act. Spooner's indictment was sparingly reported in October 1798, but then was extensively reported in October 1799 as a new event, when he was arrested.[55] During the week-and-a-half court term in October 1799, the government entered a nolle prosequi of the case, with the consent of Justice Cushing.[56] The reason for the dismissal appears to be an exchange for cooperative testimony against Dr. Samuel Shaw, as is suggested later in the discussion of the Shaw case.

James Lyon was not in fact indicted, but Spooner's brother was, in a separate case for a separate offense.

Alden Spooner: Publishing Matthew Lyon's Letter in *Spooner's Vermont Journal*

Alden Spooner also co-founded a newspaper, the *Vermont Journal*, in 1783, and was its sole editor from 1788 through 1817, until just before he retired.[57] By the late 1790s, it was a strongly Republican voice.

Spooner was indicted the same day as his brother in October 1798 for violation of the Sedition Act, by his separate publication in his separate newspaper (in Windsor, Vermont) of a different article,[58] a prosecution that has never been mentioned in Sedition Act publications but is confirmed in federal court records. What he published in *Spooner's Vermont Journal* was Matthew Lyon's own letter criticizing the president, which was the first ground for indicting the

[52] Indictment at 1 (6 Oct.1798), United States v. Judah P. Spooner, Case Files, 1792–1869, U.S. Circuit Court for the District of Vermont (National Archives at Waltham, Mass., R.G.21.48.2); Warrant for Arrest (4 Oct.1799), *id.*

[53] *Id.* at 2.

[54] Benjamin Franklin to Robert R. Livingston (22 July 1783), BENJAMIN FRANKLIN: WRITINGS 1062, 1065 (J.A. Leo Lemay ed., Library of America, New York 1987).

[55] *E.g., Albany, October 11, 1799*, ALBANY CENTINEL, 11 Oct.1799, at 3; *Boston*, MASSACHUSETTS MERCURY (Boston), 15 Oct.1799, at 2. Others are listed in the appendix.

[56] As recorded on the back of the indictment, noting it was "by consent and advice of the Court," with the date "October Term 1799."

[57] 2 BRIGHAM 1099, 1486 (cofounding the *Vermont Journal* with George Hough).

[58] Indictment at 1–2 (6 Oct.1798), United States v. Alden Spooner, Case Files, 1792–1869, U.S. Circuit Court for the District of Vermont (National Archives at Waltham, Mass., R.G.21.48.2).

congressman the day before (notwithstanding that the letter had been written three weeks before passage of the Sedition Act). That letter lamented that President Adams caused every consideration of public welfare to be "swallowed up in a continual grasp for power, in an unbounded thirst for ridiculous pomp[,] foolish adulation or selfish avarice."[59] That fell within the Sedition Act's prohibition of any writing, printing, uttering, or publishing against the president.

Spooner, like his brother, was arrested a year later, as a few newspaper articles reported in a single sentence.[60] However, his case, too, was dismissed by a decision not to prosecute in October 1799.[61]

Reverend John C. Ogden: Delivering Petitions Supporting Matthew Lyon during His Imprisonment (a Case Tantamount to a Sedition Act Prosecution, but Not Technically under the Act)

Reverend John Cosens Ogden, then of Troy, New York, was an Episcopal minister[62] and ecclesiastical critic of the Federalist clergy of New England, whom he called the "New-England Illuminati,"[63] and of the Federalists generally. Though his arrest was not explicitly under the Sedition Act, we must consider whether the arrest was a de facto Sedition Act arrest because it was ordered by Secretary of the Treasury Oliver Wolcott, Jr. immediately after Ogden delivered petitions to President Adams on behalf of Congressman Matthew Lyon, the first person brought to trial under the Act, asking for Lyon's release and censuring the Act.[64] The arrest for debt avoided the indelicacy of arresting Ogden for "seditious" petitions, in view of the First Amendment freedom of petition, and also avoided the need to wait for the next sitting of the federal circuit court. Ogden had compounded his transgressions, in Federalist eyes, by writing essays on Lyon being subjected to "tyranny" and "dragged . . . as the first victim to the altar of the sedition law," being subjected to barbarity by "an inhuman federal marshal," suffering in an unheated cell with open windows during the frigid Vermont winter, and suffering wrongful conviction

[59] *Id.*, quoting Matthew Lyon, *For Spooner's Vermont Journal*, SPOONER'S VERMONT JOURNAL (Windsor), 31 July 1798, at 1, 2.

[60] *For the Vermont Gazette*, VERMONT GAZETTE (Bennington), 31 Oct. 1799, at 2.

[61] As recorded on the back of the indictment, with the date "October Term 1799."

[62] Alan V. Briceland, *John C. Ogden: Messenger and Propagandist for Matthew Lyon, 1798–1799*, 43 VT. HIST. 103 (1975); 31 JEFFERSON PAPERS 17n.; 4 APPLETON'S CYCLOPEDIA OF AMERICAN BIOGRAPHY 561 (Appleton, New York 1888).

[63] [JOHN C. OGDEN], A VIEW OF THE NEW-ENGLAND ILLUMINATI (James Carey, Philadelphia 1799); *accord* JONATHAN D. SASSI, A REPUBLIC OF RIGHTEOUSNESS: THE PUBLIC CHRISTIANITY OF THE POST-REVOLUTIONARY NEW ENGLAND CLERGY 113–16 (OUP, Oxford 2001).

[64] *The Respectful Petition of the Subscribers, Freemen of the Western District of Vermont*, AURORA (Philadelphia), 14 Jan. 1799, at 3.

through judicial bias.[65] James Morton Smith devoted a page to Ogden's mission and arrest, though he did not treat it as tantamount to a Sedition Act prosecution.[66] But there is much reason to believe it was, when additional facts are considered.

Ogden's own account was that he carried to the president "the petitions of the people of the western district of Vermont in behalf of Colol. Lyon," leaving Adams "offended at my interference," and that in "revenge" for the mission "Oliver Wolcott . . . has cast me into prison for a small sum due honestly to him."[67] Ogden wrote to Jefferson from "Litchfield prison" about "my embassy in support of Colol. Lyon,"[68] and Jefferson had already written to Madison that "a petition has been presented to the President signed by several thousand persons in Vermont, praying a remitment of Lyon's fine," which Adams had rejected.[69]

The *Aurora* published the first Republican account, reporting that "Rev. J. C. Ogden, who some time ago presented a petition from *Matthew Lyon*'s constituents to the President of the United States, upon his return to Litchfield in Connecticut, has been arrested by a Mr. Woolcot, and put into prison for a demand of 200 dollars!"[70] Other Republican newspapers reprinted the article.[71] The *Gazette of the United States* published the first Federalist account, countering that Ogden was "imprisoned in Litchfield for debt," as one of the "martyrs to Jacobinism" and an "idle vicious spendthrift,"[72] and other Federalist newspapers replaced that invective with sarcastic acknowledgments that Ogden was returning from "the pious errand of carrying Lyon's petition to the President."[73] Thus, there was agreement on the petition, the arrest, and the imprisonment.

[65] [John C. Ogden], *To the Enemies of Political Persecution*, AURORA (Philadelphia), 4 Jan.1799, at 2; *accord* [John C. Ogden], *Saturday, January 5, 1798*, AURORA (Philadelphia), 5 Jan.1799, at 3; [John C. Ogden], *Wednesday, January 9, 1798*, AURORA (Philadelphia), 9 Jan.1799, at 3.

[66] FREEDOM'S FETTERS 242–43.

[67] John C. Ogden to George Washington (12 Feb.1799), 3 WASHINGTON PAPERS-RETIREMENT 373. Ogden offered an additional reason, which was to defeat his quest for the position of collector of customs, which was sought by Wolcott's sister's brother-in-law. A published letter, evidently from Ogden, further described the Adams meeting. [John C. Ogden], *For the Bee*, BEE (New London), 20 Mar.1799, at 2.

[68] John C. Ogden to Thomas Jefferson (5 Mar.1799), 31 JEFFERSON PAPERS 72.

[69] Thomas Jefferson to James Madison (3 Jan.1799), 30 *id.* at 610.

[70] *Saturday, February 16, 1799*, AURORA (Philadelphia), 16 Feb.1799, at 3. The actual amount of the debt, with interest, was $180.

[71] *Philadelphia, Feb.18*, BEE (New London), 27 Feb.1799, at 3; *Wednesday, February 20*, NEW YORK JOURNAL & PATRIOTIC REGISTER (New York), 27 Feb.1799, at 3.

[72] *Extract of a Letter from Connecticut*, GAZETTE OF THE UNITED STATES (Philadelphia), 18 Feb.1799, at 3; *accord Extract of a Letter from Connecticut*, DAILY ADVERTISER (New York), 21 Feb.1799, at 2; *Extract of a Letter from Connecticut*, WEEKLY ORACLE (New London), 25 Feb.1799, at 2.

[73] *E.g., Hartford, February 18*, CONNECTICUT COURANT (Hartford), 18 Feb.1799, at 3; *Hartford, Feb. 18*, WINDHAM HERALD, 21 Feb.1799, at 3. Others are listed in the appendix.

Ogden's arrest and four-month imprisonment in Litchfield, Connecticut, are confirmed by court records, which have not been heretofore located, and by Wolcott's own correspondence. Wolcott arranged for his brother, Frederick, a Litchfield attorney and clerk of court, to arrest Ogden and to jail him for nonpayment of the old debt, listing Oliver Wolcott, Jr. in the court filings as plaintiff.[74] Frederick advised his brother to leave the "vile, lying rascal" in prison, and, noting that Ogden may take "the *poor prisoner's oath*," which would avoid having to pay for jail room and board, asked "whether it be your wish that I support him in prison" by paying Ogden's jail charges.[75] The secretary of the treasury obviously approved, because Frederick paid those costs.[76] Ogden entered the jail before the twelfth of February 1799, and remained there until his release on the tenth of June.[77] Ogden devoted his time in jail to flaying the area's Federalist clergy and challenging Connecticut's debtor laws,[78] and to describing the squalor of one of his cells,[79] while remarking ironically about Wolcott paying for his lodging in jail. Federalist papers confirmed the continued imprisonment, as the *Gazette of the United States* stated that "[t]he clerical lunatic, confined in Litchfield jail, for money squandered away, is week after week filling the pages of 'the *Humbug*' with his soporific lucubrations."[80] Not surprisingly, attorney Frederick Wolcott obtained a judgment against Ogden for $187.50, signed by clerk of court Frederick Wolcott (his other vocation), while Ogden was in jail without legal defense.[81] Frederick Wolcott later got Ogden to sign a new demand note for that amount, on June 10, 1799, in order to be released that day, which meant that "unless he, immediately quit this part of the country I will again attach and confine him."[82] The few scholars mentioning it have accepted the

[74] Attachment and Arrest Warrant (4 Feb.1799), Litchfield County Court Files (Conn. Archives, Hartford, file for 1799 Tallmadge-1800 Atwater) (signed by Frederick Wolcott as clerk, instructing sheriff to attach the property or body of John C. Ogden, to pay the 1785 note for 60 pounds plus interest, initially claiming a total of $300).

[75] Frederick Wolcott to Oliver Wolcott, Jr. ([torn] Mar.1799), Oliver Wolcott, Jr. Papers (Conn. Historical Society, Hartford, box 30, folder 9).

[76] Frederick Wolcott to Oliver Wolcott, Jr. at 3 (10 June 1799), Oliver Wolcott, Jr. Papers, *id.*

[77] *Id.* at 3 (released that date); John C. Ogden to George Washington (12 Feb.1799), 3 Washington Papers-Retirement 373 (from "prison in Litchfield"); John C. Ogden to George Washington (13 May 1799), 4 *id.* at 131n. (same). Even when released, Federalist soldiers attempted to force him back to town to be punished, evidently threatening a whipping. *Extract of a Letter from Litchfield,* Greenleaf's New York Journal (New York), 22 June 1799, at 2.

[78] [John C. Ogden], A Short History of Late Ecclesiastical Oppressions in New-England and Vermont (James Lyon, Richmond 1799).

[79] [John C. Ogden], *For the Aurora,* Aurora (Philadelphia), 29 Apr.1799, at 3.

[80] *New-London, May 20,* Gazette of the United States (Philadelphia), 24 May 1799, at 2.

[81] Execution and Arrest Warrant (8 Apr.1799), Litchfield County Court Files, *supra* note 74 (the exchange for a note is on an attached sheet).

[82] Frederick Wolcott to Oliver Wolcott, Jr. at 3 (10 June 1799), *supra* note 76.

substance of this account, that Ogden delivered the Sedition Act petitions, and that Wolcott promptly arranged for his arrest.[83]

The connection between Ogden's mission delivering petitions supporting the notable Sedition Act victim and opposing the Act itself, and his arrest, is strongly supported by circumstantial evidence.[84] The Wolcott debt was fourteen years old,[85] and Wolcott had not taken any action on it until Ogden's mission, though Ogden was periodically in Connecticut because his family continued to live there—but then Wolcott took immediate legal action when Ogden set forth on his return trip from delivering the petitions for Lyon. Moreover, Wolcott was willing to pay $76 and then additional jail costs,[86] to jail Ogden for an obviously uncollectible debt of 60 pounds (in "soldiers notes") plus interest—his brother Frederick confirmed it was uncollectible.[87] Further, reports about Ogden "plotting against his country" were being sent by others to Secretary of State Timothy Pickering.[88] Republican newspapers certainly saw it as a de facto prosecution under the Sedition Act: "This confinement was undoubtedly preconcerted in Philadelphia, on the part of Mr. Secretary" Wolcott, Federalist members of Congress, and "Mr. Pickering," primarily "for delivering the petitions . . . in behalf of Col. Lyon" for pardon from his Sedition Act sentence.[89] It is difficult to see the prosecution for the old debt as anything else, since Ogden had long been a penniless itinerant minister, quite unlikely ever to have funds to pay the debt.

Jacob Greenawalt: Speaking Against the Government by Speaking Against Taxes

The Sedition Act prosecutions for seditious words, as contrasted with seditious publications, were not limited to Matthew Lyon (for reading the Barlow letter in

[83] 30 JEFFERSON PAPERS 586; 31 *id.* at 73n.; 25 HAMILTON PAPERS 23 n.15; ALEINE AUSTIN, MATTHEW LYON, "NEW MAN" OF THE DEMOCRATIC REVOLUTION, 1749–1822, at 124–25 (PSUP, Pittsburgh 1981); Briceland, *supra* note 62, at 108–20.

[84] 10 CONNECTICUT RECORDS vii; Briceland, *supra* note 62, at 116.

[85] Note (10 July 1785), Litchfield County Court Files, *supra* note 74; *accord* Alan V. Briceland, *The Philadelphia Aurora, the New England Illuminati, and the Election of 1800*, 44 PA. MAGAZINE OF HIST. & BIOG. 3, 16 (1976); Pope Joan, *Messrs. Hudson & Goodwin*, CONNECTICUT COURANT (Hartford), 27 May 1799, at 2.

[86] J.C. Ogden to Ephraim Kirby at 2 (7 Mar.1799), Ephraim Kirby Papers (DU, Durham); 31 JEFFERSON PAPERS 73n.; *accord* [John C. Ogden], *For the Aurora*, AURORA (Philadelphia), 9 Apr.1799, at 3.

[87] Frederick Wolcott to Oliver Wolcott, Jr. at 3 (10 June 1799), *supra* note 76 ("I found there was no probability that you would recover any money of him & I thought it was not worth while to be at the expense of supporting in gaol so worthless a fellow.").

[88] Col. Allan McLane to Timothy Pickering (8 Feb.1800), PICKERING PAPERS r.26, fol.26.

[89] *For the Bee*, BEE (New London), 24 Apr.1799, at 2; *accord For the Aurora*, AURORA (Philadelphia), 29 Apr.1799, at 3.

a speech), David Brown (for itinerant speeches), Luther Baldwin and Brown Clark (for wishing a cannon salute had hit the posterior in chief), or liberty poles. They also included cases for seditious words against Lespinard Colie, Jacob Greenawalt, and, as we will see, Langford Herring and Reverend Jacob Eyerman.

When prosecution of Fries Rebellion participants began, Jacob Greenawalt of Greenwich Township, Pennsylvania,[90] was arrested under the Sedition Act and required to appear in federal circuit court in April 1799. The case has not appeared in Sedition Act discussions because his arrest was buried in the recognizance bond book in the federal court records, where his arrest was "to answer" as a defendant.[91] Greenawalt appeared as required, and evidently pled guilty, because his next entry in the court records showed him posting a bond for good behavior, personally of $2,000 and by two friends each of $1,000, to last a year.[92]

His offense was threatening to tie the tax assessor "fast to the liberty pole, and keep him there till he gave an account of the money or duties they had paid on stills," and asserting that the assessor improperly "spent the excise money on drink, or on idle women." Moreover, Greenawalt declaimed that there were "nothing but mean & dirty ragamuffins for officers in government," presumably referring to tax assessors and excise officers.[93] His outburst apparently occurred in January 1799.[94] It was deemed to amount to speaking "against the government of the United States, or either house of the Congress" in violation of the Sedition Act.

[90] Depositions uniformly described him as from Greenwich Township, which was on a road southward to Reading; Newman identified him as from Reading. Newman mentioned the case briefly. Fries's Rebellion 108. Brief biographical information is in 2 Charles R. Roberts et al., History of Lehigh County, Pennsylvania 774 (Lehigh Valley Publishing, Allentown 1914).

[91] Many others in the list were subpoenaed "to testify" as witnesses. Recognizances 4, in Criminal Case Files of the U.S. Circuit Court for the Eastern District of Pennsylvania, 1791–1840, at 1:I966 (National Archives at Philadelphia, R.G.21.40.2, microfilm M986, rolls 1 and 2) [hereinafter Criminal Case Files].

[92] Original Minutes of the Circuit Court of the United States of America for the Middle Circuit, October Session 1790 to April 1799, at 289 (National Archives at Philadelphia, R.G.21.40.2, microfilm M932, roll 1) (22 Apr.1799) [hereinafter Minutes]..

[93] Deposition of Philip Kreamer (13 Feb.1799), in William Rawle Sr. Papers, in Rawle Family Papers 1682–1921 (HSP, Philadelphia, Collection 536, boxes 5–6, folders 8–13); *accord* Deposition of Jacob Bowen (14 Feb.1799), in *id.*; Deposition of Michael Bapst [or Bobst] (10 Apr.1799), in *id.*; Fries's Rebellion 108. I appreciate Dr. Newman directing me to the relevant depositions.

[94] Preceding the date of those depositions, and when the assessors were functioning. *See* Fries's Rebellion 107–08.

Morris Llewellyn, James Jackson, George Britson, Samuel Young, and Archibald Mengis: "Seditious Combinations" in Raising a Liberty Pole and Challenging the Constitutionality of the Sedition Act

The Sedition Act prosecution of Benjamin Fairbanks and David Brown for raising a liberty pole in June 1799 turns out not to be the only one for that "heinous an offense." And the prosecution of Jedidiah Peck for petitioning against the constitutionality of the Sedition Act itself in September 1799 turns out not to be the only one based expressly on questioning its constitutionality.

Morris Llewellyn[95] and four other individuals in Pennsylvania were presented (indicted) by a federal grand jury in late April 1799 for raising a liberty pole, with a "seditious label" on it saying "the constitution sacred, no gag law, liberty or death."[96] That presentment (pictured in Figure 7.1) alleged that erecting that liberty pole, and writing and publishing the "false, scandalous and malicious writing" on it, combined and conspired to stir up sedition and to impede the Sedition Act (the "gag law").[97] The case was widely mentioned in newspapers as one involving "seditious combinations."[98] The first three defendants were arraigned, and pleaded not guilty, a week later, and the first two posted bonds.[99] The presiding judge, who charged the grand jury, was Justice Iredell.[100] During the next court session in October 1799, a new presentment came from the grand jury on the same grounds, after a charge from Bushrod Washington.[101] The main substantive change was to shorten the quotation of "seditious words" to just "no gag law,"[102] showing that challenging the Sedition Act was as grave a crime as raising a liberty pole (though there had been countless numbers of liberty poles during the Revolution). However, it turned out that the federal marshal's commission had expired, which voided all summonses, arrests, and court actions in the October

[95] Newman mentions this briefly, as a Fries Rebellion prosecution that involved sedition, though not expressly as a Sedition Act prosecution. FRIES'S REBELLION 175. Though the name was transcribed from handwritten court papers as "Schwelein," the name was given consistently in court records as "Llewellyn." Minutes 293, 300, 326, 342, 351; Deposition of James Jackson, William Rawle Sr. Papers, *supra* note 93, at 1.

[96] Presentment (24 Apr.1799), Criminal Case Files 1:I999,1001; *see* Minutes 293 (cover described case as "Seditious Combination &c."); *accord* Deposition of James Jackson (23 Oct.1799), William Rawle Sr. Papers, *supra* note 93, at 1–2 (the event was 22 Dec.1798 at Henry Helmbolt's house).

[97] *Id.* at 1:I999, 1001.

[98] *E.g., Philadelphia, Apr.* 23, CLAYPOOLE'S AMERICAN DAILY ADVERTISER (Philadelphia), 23 Apr.1799, at 3; *Tuesday, 23d April, 1799*, PHILADELPHIA GAZETTE, 23 Apr.1799, at 3. Others appear in the appendix.

[99] Criminal Case Files 1:I998; Minutes 300 (29 Apr.1799).

[100] James Iredell's Charge (C.C.D. Pa. 11 Apr.1799), 3 DHSC 332.

[101] 3 DHSC 389 (12 Oct.1799).

[102] Presentment (7 Oct.1799), Criminal Case Files 1:I1185; *see* Minutes 342.

term,[103] though Judge Richard Peters told Pickering that he and Justice Washington did "not say anything about the true reason of our breaking up" and instead gave an ambiguous reason ("an error in the proceedings") and a pretextual reason (a "small number of jurors attending").[104] Consequently, the defendants were re-indicted by the grand jury on the same grounds in April 1800, except for dropping James Jackson.[105]

However, the defendants were not located by the marshal during that April 1800 court term, according to the arrest warrant,[106] doubtless to the chagrin of the presiding judge, Justice Chase.[107] Their case was not brought to trial during the October 1800 session either,[108] evidently for the same reason.

Langford Herring: "Seditious Expressions" Criticizing President Adams and the Federal Tax

The Sedition Act prosecutions against John Daly Burk and James Smith, Anne Greenleaf, and Jedidiah Peck prove not to be the only ones dismissed or suspended permanently. The prosecution of Langford Herring was also dismissed (though he had to pay costs as part of the agreement), as were those of Judah P. Spooner and Alton Spooner. Herring's case paralleled the prosecution of the Fries Rebellion participants charged with forcibly blocking assessors from determining and collecting taxes; his offense was criticizing those taxes and the president who signed them into law.

Langford Herring, of Philadelphia, was indicted for "seditious expressions" in conflict with the prohibition of the Sedition Act, by a federal grand jury in April 1799,[109] after Iredell's charge. The "seditious words" were the following:

> damn the President . . . and all those who take his part. . . . I look upon him . . . to be an enemy to the government . . . .[T] he heavy weight of taxes particularly the stamp act is owing to his influence . . . . The law. . . . laying duties on stamped vellum parchment and paper has been passed and put in force to the great injury of the people . . . . [110]

[103] Bushrod Washington to James Iredell (20 Oct.1799), 3 DHSC 389, 390 ("overwhelmed with mortification and chagrin" at "an end to our further proceedings" because William Nichols' "acts as marshall are void" and "all done here is coram non judice")

[104] Richard Peters to Timothy Pickering (23 Oct.1799), 3 *id.* at 391.

[105] Presentment (16 Apr.1800), Criminal Case Files 2:278; Minutes 351. The likely reason for dropping Jackson is that he gave deposition testimony incriminating himself and the others. Deposition of James Jackson (23 Oct.1799).

[106] *Id.* at 2:281 ("non est inventus").

[107] 3 DHSC 493.

[108] Minutes 400–16; Criminal Case Files 2:379, 382.

[109] Indictment (27 Apr.1799), Criminal Case Files 1:I1079, 1082; Minutes 299.

[110] *Id.* at 1:I1083–84. Herring's statements were dated 1 and 10 Dec.1798.

Tracking the prohibition of the Sedition Act, Herring's words were alleged to "defame the said President of the United States and to bring him into contempt and disrepute[,] to render the laws of the said United States odious to the citizens thereof[,] and to excite opposition and resistance as well to the public acts and measures of the said President. . . ."[111]

The federal attorney agreed to cease prosecuting the case, effective upon Herring's payment of costs.[112] The reasons were not given, but since that did not happen with any Fries Rebellion cases, that lenient disposition casts doubt on Henderson's treatment of the cases as a Fries Rebellion case.[113] In fact, the indictment alleges that Herring's statements were made in December 1798, before resistance peaked or the rescue occurred, though his statements were about the challenged house tax and valuation law. An article in the leading Republican newspaper described Herring as a Philadelphia resident, not a Bucks or Northampton County resident.[114] The day after Herring's second offense that was charged in the indictment, the *Aurora* reported that "Lankford Heron, Brickmaker, a native of Virginia, was taken out of his house in Hickory Lane" and was brought before an alderman, "who committed him to the city gaol for damning the President, all that took his part, and [all] that wore the Black Cockade" (the Federalists).[115] Whatever happened with the city prosecution, the federal attorney's indictment was four months later during the federal circuit court in Philadelphia. Thus, Herring's was a Sedition Act prosecution, but not one of participants in the Fries Rebellion.

Herring was not so fortunate the next year. He was indicted for four larcenies, and found guilty of three, if the report of the most strident Federalist newspaper can be believed.[116] They were probably not his first.[117]

[111] *Id.* at 1:I1084.

[112] *Id.* at 1:I1081, 1080 (5 Oct.1799) ("nol. pros.").

[113] HENDERSON 315.

[114] The article was "Philadelphia" news, and Aldermen's Court and Hickory Lane, which were referred to, were in Philadelphia.

[115] *Philadelphia*, AURORA GENERAL ADVERTISER (Philadelphia), 11 Dec.1798, at 3; *accord Philadelphia Dec.10*, NEW-YORK GAZETTE & GENERAL ADVERTISER, 12 Dec.1798, at 3.

[116] *Saturday Evening, March 8*, GAZETTE OF THE UNITED STATES (Philadelphia), 8 Mar.1800, at 2, 3; *Mr. Fenno*, GAZETTE OF THE UNITED STATES (Philadelphia), 11 Mar.1800, at 2.

[117] He is mentioned as fraudulently conspiring to cause someone to endorse a note, *Respublica v. Ross*, 2 U.S. (2 Dall.) 239, 239 (Pa. S. Ct. 1795), and as fleeing to Maryland to avoid prosecution. Executive Minutes of Gov. Thomas Mifflin (12 Oct.1795, 3 Oct.1796), in 2 PENNSYLVANIA ARCHIVES: NINTH SERIES 1026, 1171 (Gertrude MacKinney ed., Pa. Dept. of Property & Supplies, Harrisburg 1931); *accord Philadelphia, Dec. 31*, COMMERCIAL ADVERTISER (New York), 2 Jan.1799, at 3; *Philadelphia, Dec. 31*, SPECTATOR (New York), 5 Jan.1799, at 2.

Reverend Jacob Eyerman: "Seditious Counseling" and a Combination and Conspiracy Against the House Tax

Reverend Ogden was not alone in using his pulpit to smite the Federalist Philistines and the Sedition Act.

Reverend Jacob Eyerman, a German Lutheran preacher in Pennsylvania, exhorted his congregations and acquaintances to resist the house tax and the assessors, and branded the tax unjust and unconstitutional.[118] Nicknamed "the seditious parson of Northampton" in some press reports,[119] he was one of the tax protesters who were arrested and then escaped in the rescue of March 1799. He fled unsuccessfully to New York, where he was rearrested[120] under instructions from Pickering to arrest "the insurgent German preacher" who "wears a clerical garb to cloak his licentiousness in morals as well as politics."[121] Consequently, he was indicted for escape, and was indicted a second time three days later for escape, conspiracy, and "seditious counseling," in October 1799.[122]

Describing that seditious counseling, the indictment said Eyerman "did counsel, advise and attempt to procure an unlawful assembly and combination" to impede valuation for and collection of the house tax,[123] essentially quoting part of Section 1 of the Sedition Act while not citing it. The prosecutor, in his closing argument, made that explicit by saying that the charge was violation of the Sedition Act.[124] In his trial just one day after the second indictment, Eyerman had no counsel and presented no defense, and Justice Washington told the jury that "the proof is as clear against him as any thing can possibly be" on the combination or conspiracy, noting that many witnesses "proved" that "he was the prime cause" of resistance.[125] Not surprisingly, the jury found Eyerman guilty of all counts in just fifteen minutes,[126] but the conviction had to be thrown out because of the problem of the federal marshal's commission.[127]

[118] Two Trials, *supra* note 30, at 220, 220, 222; Fries's Rebellion 16, 24, 41, 102–03, 170–71, 175–76, 180.

[119] *E.g., Monday, 8th April, 1799*, Philadelphia Gazette, 8 Apr.1799, at 3; *Philadelphia, Apr. 15*, New York Gazette & General Advertiser, 15 Apr.1799, at 2.

[120] Two Trials, *supra* note 30, at 220, 221.

[121] Timothy Pickering to Gov. John Jay (21 May 1799), Pickering Papers r.11, fol.136 and r.37, fol.421; *accord* Timothy Pickering to Judge John Sloss Hobart (21 May 1799), *id.* at r.37, fol.422.

[122] Minutes 334, 335; Criminal Case Files 1:I1125, 1:I1162, 2:I139. Newman mentioned his case as involving the Sedition Act. Fries's Rebellion 175–76.

[123] Criminal Case Files 1:I1165.

[124] Two Trials, *supra* note 30, at 224.

[125] *Id.* at 224, 225.

[126] *Id.* at 225; Minutes 339–40.

[127] Criminal Case Files 1:I1125.

In the next court session, Eyerman was reindicted for escape, conspiracy, and seditious counseling, in April 1800.[128] Having been unsuccessful with the October jury, Eyerman chose to "submit to the court protesting his innocence" at the beginning of May 1800.[129] His bad luck persisted, as the presiding judge was Justice Chase. Chase sentenced him that same day to be "fined fifty dollars and imprisoned one year," and before release to post recognizance bonds "himself in one thousand dollars and two sureties in five hundred dollars each for his good behaviour," plus costs of prosecution.[130]

Benjamin Mayer and Conrad Fahnestock: Publishing an Essay Questioning a Treason Charge

Jacob Greenawalt, Morris Llewellyn and his codefendants, and Jacob Eyerman were not the only ones during the Fries Rebellion who were charged under the Sedition Act with criticizing the government and taxes.

Benjamin Mayer and Conrad Fahnestock[131] were the editors and printers of a German-language newspaper in rural Pennsylvania, the *Harrisburg Morgenröthe*,[132] which for its Republicanism was sometimes called the "Dutch *Aurora*."[133] They founded the paper in March 1799, and edited it together for five months, until Fahnestock left the partnership soon after trouble arrived.[134]

They were arrested in August 1799 for publishing a "'false, scandalous and malicious' libel" and were required to post $4,000 bond each to assure their appearance in federal court in mid-October 1799, according to newspaper reports.[135] Soon after, they were presented by the federal grand jury,[136] presided over by

[128] Minutes 351.

[129] Minutes 380; Criminal Case Files 1:I1161.

[130] Minutes 386–87; Criminal Case Files 2:I145.

[131] Newman mentioned this briefly, as a Fries Rebellion prosecution involving sedition, though not specifically a Sedition Act prosecution. Fries's Rebellion 174–75. The names were occasionally spelled "Meyer" and "Fahnstock," but were spelled in their newspaper as Mayer and Fahnestock.

[132] In 1799 it bore this name, though in some time periods it was *Harrisburger Morgenröthe*.

[133] *E.g., Harrisburg, August 28*, Springer's Weekly Oracle (New London), 16 Sept.1799, at 3; *Philadelphia, September 7*, Eastern Herald & Gazette of Maine (Portland), 23 Sept.1799, at 2.

[134] 2 Brigham 859, 1453; 1 Luther R. Kelker, History of Dauphin County, Pennsylvania 331 (Lewis Pub., New York 1907); Oswald Seidensticker, The First Century of German Printing in America, 1728–1830, at 251 (Schaefer & Koradi, Philadelphia 1893). Mayer sold the newspaper in 1811. *Id.*

[135] *Harrisburg, August 28*, Gazette of the United States (Philadelphia), 6 Sept.1799, at 2; *Harrisburg, P. August 28*, Bee (New London), 18 Sept.1799, at 3. For their bonds, $2,000 each was to be by themselves, and $2,000 each by sureties.

[136] Indictment (18 Oct.1799), Criminal Case Files 1:I1172; Minutes 342; *see* United States v. Meyer, 26 F.Cas. 1242 (C.C.D. Pa.1799) (No. 15,761) (referring to a formbook reprinting excerpts of the indictment).

Justice Washington, for publishing a newspaper essay critical of the government's prosecution of John Fries.[137]

Their offending essay challenged the Fries prosecution, among other grounds, because treason is narrowly defined in the Constitution and by statute to be levying war and aiding the enemy, while Fries's actions, in rescuing people arrested for noncooperation with the valuation law and the house tax, were far short of levying war.[138] Further, English law and an American statute both treated rescue of a person accused of treason as a less serious crime, not as treason, and rescue of the people accused only of obstructing assessors in entering houses and land and collecting taxes was less serious still.[139] Because Fries's actions were far less serious than treason, his prosecution and conviction for high treason "cannot have been according to law," and "must rest on another foundation," perhaps the "expedience" that "produced the sedition and alien bills."[140]

The indictment characterized that newspaper essay as serving "to vilify and defame the Government of the United States and the administration of justice," by claiming they "were actuated by unlawful motives and not by the duty imposed on them by the Constitution," and by weakening their authority and exciting opposition.[141] In other words, the indictment claimed that the essay was a seditious libel, in violation of the Sedition Act; it brought into "contempt" the "United States and the judicial courts . . . to the great scandal and infamy of the judges and jurors."[142] The cover sheet to the indictment, and the court's minutes, described the crime as "libel on the administration of justice."[143]

Mayer and Fahnestock pleaded not guilty.[144] However, the same day they were indicted they agreed to "submit to the Court protesting their innocence," in October 1799.[145] That amounted to waiving a jury trial, and agreeing to a bench trial instead, as regularly occurred in other Fries Rebellion cases.[146] However, Justice Washington did not sentence them because of the problem with the marshal's commission, and the April 1800 session apparently did not bring their case up for

137 *Capt. John Fries*, UNPARTHENISCHE HARRISBURG MORGENRÖTHE, 21 May 1799, at 2.

138 Criminal Case Files 1:I1173–75.

139 *Id.* at 1:I1178, 1180, 1181.

140 *Id.* at 1:I1176.

141 *Id.* at 1:I1172.

142 *Id.* at 1:I1177.

143 *Id.* at 1:I1170; Minutes 342 (18 Oct.1799).

144 *Id.* at 1:I1170.

145 *Id.* at 1:I1170; Minutes 342.

146 "Submitting to the court" was synonymous with "tri[al] without juries." *E.g., Communication*, CENTINEL OF LIBERTY (Georgetown [D.C.]), 29 Oct.1799, at 3; *Philadelphia, October 23*, ALBANY GAZETTE, 31 Oct.1799, at 3. As the next table shows, "submit[ting] to the court protesting their innocence" was routinely followed, often the same day, by sentencing with fine and imprisonment, for example in the Klein, Eberhardt, Yeisley, Stahler, and Marks cases, as well as Eyerman.

sentencing either,[147] perhaps because the available days before Justice Chase had to depart for the next circuit court were consumed by the second Fries trial, the Fries rebel trials and sentencing, and more pressing cases such as the Thomas Cooper trial.

Matthew Lyon (Second Prosecution): Writing His Letter from Prison Criticizing His Trial

Figure 7.2 Matthew Lyon. Portrait by unidentified artist. (Courtesy of Fleming Museum of Art, University of Vermont, Gift of Mr. and Mrs. Robert R. Canfield.)

Matthew Lyon (Figure 7.2), who was the first person tried under the Sedition Act in October 1798, and who was carried from trial to prison for the winter, was subjected to a second prosecution a year later. That second prosecution has been unnoticed in Sedition Act studies,[148] other than Smith's footnote saying that two newspapers "reported that 'two other bills for sedition were cut and dry for Mr. Lyon,'" but that Smith had not found any official corroboration.[149] That corroboration appears in the original federal court records.

Lyon's second prosecution was indeed filed in October 1799 under the Sedition Act (by an information, not an indictment), and was followed by an arrest warrant

[147] Henderson states that they were not "apprehended for trial." HENDERSON 175.

[148] *E.g.*, AUSTIN, *supra* note 83, at 126–30 (no mention of second indictment).

[149] FREEDOM'S FETTERS 244 n.68, 365 n.7, which was cited as unconfirmed in REPRESSIVE JURISPRUDENCE at 140. The second Lyon indictment was also mentioned in all the newspaper articles describing the Shaw indictment, which are cited below.

the next month, in federal circuit court in Vermont.[150] The basis was his letter written from jail and published the preceding January, as part of his campaign for reelection to the House of Representatives, which was characterized in the information as a seditious libel toward the government and the federal courts.[151] It inveighed against Lyons's imprisonment by "the oppressive hand of usurped power," the marshal heaping indignities like "a hard-hearted savage" practicing "barbarity," the "ransom" of a $1,000 fine plus costs that the court required to be paid before Lyon would be released, and his four-month prison sentence until "the measure of federal vengeance is filled up."[152] His other letters from prison doubtless nettled the federal attorney and secretary of state every bit as much, as Lyon insisted that he was not guilty, that he was convicted under "*unconstitutional laws*," and that "patriots of Virginia and Kentucky" were opposing them through their resolutions.[153] A large proportion of the nation's newspapers reported that reindictment in October 1799.[154] However, Lyon was never rearrested or retried, because suspecting another indictment might be afoot, he "took care to elude the pursuit of the marshal, by leaving the state" and proceeding straight to Congress, as a number of newspapers noted.[155]

Dr. Samuel Shaw: Assisting Publication of the Barlow Letter Criticizing Adams and the Senate

All the preceding Sedition Act prosecutions resulted in convictions, except the few that were dismissed because the defendant died, entered a deportation agreement, was uninvolved in the target newspaper, entered a plea bargain, or eluded arrest until Jefferson took office. However, there was a lone acquittal in a Sedition Act trial. The case continues to be generally listed as unconfirmed,[156] but was confirmed by Goebel.[157]

[150] Information at 1–2 (7 Oct.1798), United States v. Matthew Lyon, Case Files, 1792–1869, U.S. Circuit Court for the District of Vermont (National Archives at Waltham, Mass., R.G.21.48.2); Arrest Warrant (7 Nov.1799), *id.*

[151] *Id.* at 1.

[152] *Id.* at 1–2, quoting Lyon's letter, which was printed 12 Jan.1799 and reprinted as *To the Enemies of Political Persecution*, Vermont Gazette (Bennington), 24 Jan.1799, at 4.

[153] *E.g.*, Matthew Lyon, Colonel Lyon's Address to His Constituents (n.p., 10 Jan.1799) (broadside); Matthew Lyon, *To the Freemen of the Western District of Vermont*, Farmer's Register (Chambersburg), 20 Feb.1799, at 182.

[154] *E.g., Albany, October 11, 1799*, Albany Centinel, 11 Oct.1799, at 3; *Worcester, October 16*, Massachusetts Spy (Worcester), 16 Oct.1799, at 3. Others are listed in the appendix.

[155] *New-York: Wednesday, October 23, 1799*, Commercial Advertiser (New York), 23 Oct.1799, at 3; *New-York, October 24*, New-York Gazette, 24 Oct.1799, at 3; *accord Vergennes, (Ver.) Feb.12*, Windham Herald, 7 Mar.1799, at 3 (a strongly Federalist paper).

[156] Freedom's Fetters 185; Robert D. Rachlin, *The Sedition Act of 1798 and the East-West Political Divide in Vermont*, 78 Vermont History 123, 135 (2010); *contra* Repressive Jurisprudence 138.

[157] In a one-sentence reference, saying he had confirmed the case in court records. 1 History of Supreme Court 638 n.107.

Dr. Samuel Shaw was a medical doctor, who moved from Massachusetts to Castleton, Vermont in 1789, and later served in Congress from 1808 to 1813.[158]

He was indicted in October 1799, three days after Lyon's second indictment, for seditious libel against "the Government and . . . President and Congress of the United States," by "writing uttering and publishing" what the indictment identified as *A Copy of a Letter from a Diplomatic Character in France to a Member of Congress in Philadelphia*.[159] That was the letter from Joel Barlow that had been the second ground for indicting Matthew Lyon a year before, and that had been the basis for indicting Judah Spooner at the same time. The same extracts from the Barlow letter were cited, such as the "bullying speech" by the president, the obsequious response of the Senate, and the French surprise that Adams had not instead been sent "to a mad house."[160] The cited version was a pamphlet reprinting the Barlow letter, and though the pamphlet did not indicate that it was published by Lyon's press, no one denied that,[161] and Federalist publications soon spread the allegation that it was,[162] as well as the text of the letter.[163]

The indictment did not specify how Shaw was responsible for the Barlow pamphlet. Shaw was a doctor, not a printer.[164] The strongest clue is that the prosecution of Judah P. Spooner, the printer of Lyon's newspaper, for the same pamphlet was dropped in October 1799 around the time Shaw was indicted, and that Spooner was subpoenaed and actually appeared as a witness in Shaw's case.[165] Under prevailing libel law, a printer was dismissed if he identified the responsible person, whether an anonymous author, an anonymous printer, or an improper

[158] BRUCE A. RAGSDALE, BIOGRAPHICAL DIRECTORY OF THE UNITED STATES CONGRESS, 1774–1989, at 1798 (GPO, Washington 1989); PRENTISS C. DODGE, ENCYCLOPEDIA VERMONT BIOGRAPHY 66 (Ullery Publishing, Burlington 1912).

[159] Indictment at 1 (10 Oct.1799), United States v. Samuel Shaw, Case Files, 1792–1869, U.S. Circuit Court for the District of Vermont (National Archives at Waltham, Mass., R.G.21.48.2).

[160] *Id.* at 2, 3.

[161] [JOEL BARLOW], COPY OF A LETTER FROM AN AMERICAN DIPLOMATIC CHARACTER IN FRANCE, TO A MEMBER OF CONGRESS IN PHILADELPHIA ([probably published by James Lyon], Constitution-Hill 1798); *cf.* 1 MARCUS A. MCCORISON, ADDITIONS AND CORRECTIONS TO VERMONT IMPRINTS, 1778–1820, at 7 (Am. Antiquarian Soc., Worcester 1968).

[162] *E.g., Messrs. Hudson & Goodwin*, CONNECTICUT COURANT (Hartford), 5 Nov.1798, at 1; *From the Connecticut Courant*, MERCANTILE ADVERTISER (New York), 13 Nov.1798, at 2; *Barlow's Letter*, GAZETTE OF THE UNITED STATES (Philadelphia), 17 Jan.1799, at 2.

[163] *E.g.*, [Joel Barlow], *Copy of a Letter from an America Diplomatic Character*, CONNECTICUT COURANT (Hartford), 5 Nov.1798, at 1; [Joel Barlow], *Copy of a Letter from an America Diplomatic Character*, MERCANTILE ADVERTISER (New York), 13 Nov.1798, at 2; *Barlow's Letter*, GAZETTE OF THE UNITED STATES (Philadelphia), 17 Jan.1799, at 2.

[164] He is not mentioned in connection with printing in either the bibliography of newspapers and list of printers, or a brief history of Castleton newspapers. 2 BRIGHAM 1486 *passim*; MARCUS A. MCCORISON, *supra* note 161, at 82–122; Abby M. Hemenway, *Castleton Newspapers*, 3 VERMONT HISTORICAL GAZETTEER 516 (1877).

[165] Summons (21 Apr.1800), United States v. Samuel Shaw, *supra* note 159; Costs Taxed (May 1800), *id.*

discloser. Shaw's role was not to provide the letter to Matthew Lyon, since Lyon had testified that he got the Barlow letter from one senator and heard of it from another. The most likely connection is that Shaw financed or prompted its publication by Judah Spooner and James Lyon (the printer son of Matthew Lyon). Matthew Lyon needed financial help for his press, because at trial he testified that he could not afford a high bail,[166] and three months later wrote in one of his prison epistles that he could not pay his "ransom" (release bond) without arranging a lottery.[167] Another clue is that James Lyon, writing to Jefferson about Shaw two and a half years later, was far too effusive to be describing a mere friend or family doctor.[168]

Shaw was arrested and brought to court for arraignment in November 1799, and after pleading not guilty, was required to post a recognizance bond in February 1800, assuring his appearance at trial in May.[169] The case was extensively mentioned in newspapers, but only as a one-sentence aside to reports of Matthew Lyon being prosecuted anew and Anthony Haswell being "bound over" for trial. That report was that in October 1799 an "[i]nformation was also filed in the same court against Dr. Shaw, of Castleton, for sedition."[170]

Shaw was tried and acquitted in the May 1800 session of the circuit court, with Justice William Paterson presiding (at the time when Haswell was tried and convicted), and the United States was required to pay his attorney fees and other costs of $155.20.[171] Several newspapers reported that "Doctor Shaw of Castleton, was likewise tried for sedition, and acquitted."[172] This was the only acquittal under the Sedition Act.

These eleven cases prosecuting sixteen individuals are not the only ones to be added to the canon of fourteen confirmed prosecutions under the Sedition Act and three under common law, however, because eleven more cases also can be confirmed under its first section.

[166] Trial of Matthew Lyon, Wharton's State Trials 333, 340–41 (C.C.D. Vt. 1798) (reprinting Lyon's account).

[167] *Sandy-Hill, Washington County*, Vermont Gazette (Bennington), 24 Jan.1799, at 4; *To the Enemies of Political Persecution, id.* at 4.

[168] James Lyon to Thomas Jefferson (21 June 1801), 34 Jefferson Papers 404.

[169] Arrest Warrant (7 Nov.1799), United States v. Samuel Shaw, *supra* note 159; Minutes (6 Feb.1800), *id.* The file also contains summons of 11 witnesses including Judah P. Spooner.

[170] *New-York: Wednesday, October 23, 1799*, Commercial Advertiser (New York), 23 Oct.1799, at 3; *New-York, October 24*, New-York Gazette, 24 Oct.1799, at 3. Others are listed in the appendix.

[171] Costs Taxed and Allowed against the United States in a Prosecution of the United States ag[ains]t Saml. Shaw for Sedition in Which He Was Acquitted (May 1800), United States v. Samuel Shaw, *supra* note 159. The federal court file contains two identical cost bills for $155.20, and an apparent draft bill for $91.95, each of which recites Shaw's acquittal.

[172] *Windsor, Tuesday, May 13, 1800*, Spooner's Vermont Journal (Windsor), 13 May 1800, at 3; *Windsor, (Ver.) May 13*, Connecticut Gazette (New London), 21 May 1800, at 3; *Windsor, (Ver.) May 13*, Connecticut Courant (Hartford), 26 May 1800, at 2.

Eleven Additional Cases Under the Sedition Act for Conspiracy to Oppose Government During the Fries Rebellion

The Fries Rebellion began with obstruction of federal assessors seeking to measure houses under the new direct tax that Congress passed in 1798 to finance the military buildup approved that year,[173] and ended with an armed rescue of arrested tax opponents in rural Pennsylvania in early March 1799.[174] John Fries and other leaders were charged with treason for leading between a hundred and four hundred armed men to rescue twenty-two individuals, who had been arrested for resisting and preventing federal assessors from valuing houses, and resisting and preventing the federal marshal from arresting tax opponents.[175] Both the initial trial and the retrial of Fries led to his conviction for treason,[176] as the prior chapter discussed.

The leading work on the Fries Rebellion, by Paul Douglas Newman, paints a very different picture from a treasonous army of tax insurrectionists.[177] He instead portrays the "rebellion" or "insurrection" as the spin of Federalists eager to justify and use the new army weeks after the tax protest ceased, to stamp out a French-inspired plot that did not exist, and to raise a stern warning against future challenges to the new federal government.[178] Instead, Newman points out that the basis of opposition was constitutional, that "not a single assessor or any federal official came to harm," and that there was "absolutely no interpersonal violence, outside of threats."[179] At the time of the rescue, Fries and his armed followers repeatedly sought to bail out the prisoners legally, and only when the federal marshal resolutely refused did they free the prisoners "without gunfire,

[173] An Act To Provide for the Valuation of Lands and Dwelling-Houses (9 July 1798), 1 Stat. 580; An Act To Lay and Collect a Direct Tax (14 July 1798), 1 Stat. 597.

[174] Fries's Rebellion ix; *see generally* Paul D. Newman, The Fries Rebellion of 1799: Pennsylvania Germans, the Federalist Party, and American Political Culture (1996) (unpublished Ph.D. dissertation, University of Kentucky).

[175] Criminal Case Files 1:1937, 2:9; Fries's Rebellion 133–41. The first indictment charged levying war by the armed rescue, while the second indictment expanded the charges to add that the armed rescue also furthered a combination and conspiracy to oppose, resist, and prevent execution of the direct tax and the valuation laws.

[176] Minutes 313 (10 May 1799), 371 (25 Apr.1800); Trial of the Northampton Insurgents [Fries], Wharton's State Trials 458, 598 (C.C.D. Pa. 1799); Second Trial of John Fries, Wharton's State Trials 610, 636, 641 (C.C.D. Pa. 1800); Fries's Rebellion 166–73. The first and second indictments are reprinted in Wharton's State Trials 489, 610. The new trial was ordered because of a tainted juror. Minutes 320.

[177] Fries's Rebellion 160–66.

[178] *Id.* at 145, 152, 163, 164.

[179] *Id.* at 42, 130, 132, 137–41.

fisticuffs, or bloodshed."[180] Newman's position is supported by testimony of various witnesses in the trial record that throughout the day of rescue there was no violence but instead consistent proposals to provide bail, and that after President Adams's proclamation demanding that the "insurgency" end, the protesters met and "unanimously agreed . . . to desist from opposing any public officer . . . and to give due submission to the laws,"[181] weeks before the army arrived and the trials began.

Because John Fries and other ringleaders were not charged under the Sedition Act, writers on the Sedition Act have not examined or identified the charges brought against some Fries Rebellion participants as being under the Sedition Act (though Newman and Henderson did[182]). Period newspapers did not mention the Sedition Act either.[183] Among the non-treason cases, only the Llewellyn indictment expressly stated that the crime was under that Act.[184]

However, the *Fries* trial records and the Chase impeachment transcripts show that the nontreason cases related to the Fries Rebellion were brought under the Sedition Act. In his grand jury charge, Justice Iredell stressed that the Sedition Act prohibited "combinations to defeat the execution of the laws."[185] In the *Eyerman* case, prosecutor William Rawle pointed out that combination and conspiracy charges were under the Sedition Act.[186] In the second *Fries* trial, as it was described in the subsequent impeachment trial, Justice Chase stated that others were "charged with seditious combinations," and Rawle noted the "cases of sedition" such as one morning when "twenty-one persons were brought to the bar for seditious combinations," which were "cases of sedition."[187]

The unpublished court records confirm that all of the nontreason cases in connection with the Fries Rebellion were prosecuted under the Sedition Act. In addition to the four cases that were brought under Section 2 of the Act for

[180] *Id.* at 139–41, 140.

[181] Wharton's State Trials at 550; *accord* FRIES'S REBELLION 144, 145, 163. However, Churchill gives more credence to some claims of a few violent acts. Churchill, *supra* note 36, at 116, 124–25.

[182] FRIES'S REBELLION 174–75; HENDERSON 312; and, briefly, Ridgway and Churchill.

[183] *E.g., Circuit Court of the United States*, PHILADELPHIA GAZETTE, 17 Apr.1800, at 3; *Circuit Court of the United States*, ORACLE OF DAUPHIN (Harrisburg), 28 Apr.1800, at 3.

[184] Criminal Case Files 1:I997, 1185. However, they often referred to sedition or vilifying and defaming the government.

[185] James Iredell's Charge (C.C.D. Pa. 11 Apr.1799), 3 DHSC 332, 350.

[186] TWO TRIALS, *supra* note 30, at 224.

[187] Second Trial of John Fries, Wharton's State Trials 610, 624n., 623n., excerpting REPORT OF THE TRIAL OF THE HON. SAMUEL CHASE, ONE OF THE ASSOCIATE JUSTICES OF THE SUPREME COURT . . . TAKEN IN SHORT HAND, BY CHARLES EVANS 29 (Charles Evans transcriptionist, Samuel Butler & George Keatings, Baltimore 1805).

seditious words or publications (*Greenawalt, Llewellyn* et al., *Eyerman,* and *Mayer-Fahnestock*), the other nontreason cases all were brought under Section 1 of the Sedition Act, though the presentments or indictments for those non-treason cases did not refer specifically to the Act. Those other cases all charged that groups of defendants did "unlawfully combine and conspire together with intent to impede" the valuation and tax laws, or arrests of protesters, and "did counsel advise and attempt to procure an insurrection riot and unlawful assembly."[188] The only federal statute making conspiracy and obstruction criminal at the time[189] was Section 1 of the Sedition Act, which made it a crime to

> unlawfully combine or conspire together, with intent to oppose any measure or measures of the government of the United States, which are or shall be directed by proper authority, or to impede the operation of any law of the United States, or to intimidate or prevent any person holding a place or office in or under the government of the United States, from undertaking, performing or executing his trust or duty; and if any person or persons, with intent as aforesaid, shall counsel, advise or attempt to procure any insurrection, riot, unlawful assembly, or combination, . . . he or they shall be deemed guilty of a high misdemeanor, and on conviction . . . shall be punished by a fine not exceeding five thousand dollars, and by imprisonment during a term not less than six months nor exceeding five years . . . .[190]

The nontreason indictments essentially tracked that statutory language, and occasionally referred to sedition.[191]

The nontreason prosecutions in connection with the Fries Rebellion, besides the four already discussed under Section 2 of the Sedition Act, were ultimately grouped into eleven cases prosecuting eighty-three defendants who were alleged to combine or conspire to oppose government in violation of Section 1 of the Act. Those cases are summarized in Table 7.2.

[188] Henry Ohl et al. (Criminal Case Files 1:I1009, 1010); John Shimer et al. (*id.* 1:I1029, 1030–31); Daniel Klein et al. (*id.* 1:I1039, 1041); John Eberhardt et al. (*id.* 1:I1048, 1050); George Goltner et al. (*id.* 1:I1057); Abraham Samsel et al. (*id.* 1:I1064, 1066); Henry Jarrett et al. (*id.* 1:I1068, 1069); Henry Shiffert et al. (*id.* 1:I1092, 1094); etc.

[189] The valuation act and the house tax act did not, nor did the Crimes Act (30 Apr.1790), 1 Stat. 112 (though §§ 22–23 criminalized obstruction of judicial process and rescues), or its various amendments, *e.g.,* An Act in Addition to the Act for the Punishment of Certain Crimes (5 June 1794), 1 Stat. 381.

[190] Sedition Act § 1, 1 Stat. 596.

[191] The charges against Eyerman centered on "seditious counseling." Criminal Case Files 2:I145; 1:I1162, 1165.

Table 7.2 **Prosecutions For Opposing Government Under Sedition Act § 1**

	Defendants	*Events and Dates*	*Supreme Court Justice Involved*
1	Henry Ohl, Andrew Leutzingen, Adam Laeb, Nicholas Miller, Martin Hester, Michael Best	Indicted for conspiracy 26 Apr. 1799 [M294, 1:1008, 1:1015]	Justice James Iredell
		Dismissed Leutzingen, Laeb, Miller [cf. 1:1008 and 1:1015]	"
		Reindicted Ohl 2 May 1800 [M389]	Justice Samuel Chase
		Dismissed (ignoramus) Hester and Best 2 May 1800 [M389, 1:1008]	
2	John Shimer, John Adam Engelman, Jacob Engelman, John Mumbower, Henry Huber, George Seider, Peter Keefer	Indicted for conspiracy 26 Apr. 1799 [M294, 1:1028], and included George Shaefer, who was named the next day in the Jarrett case (below)	Justice James Iredell
		Not prosecuted Keefer and Shaefer 17 Oct. 1799 [1:1028, 1:934]	Justice Bushrod Washington
3	Daniel Klein, Jacob Klein, Adam Breisch, George Gettman, William Gettman	Indicted for CRO 27 Apr. 1799 [M298, 1:1038, 2:114, 119]	Justice James Iredell
		Submitted to court's judgment and sentence 17 Oct. 1799 [M340, 1:1038], and 22 Apr. 1800 [M363, 2:114]	
		Reindicted for CRO 16 Apr. 1800 [M351]	Justice Samuel Chase
		Sentenced all 1 May 1800 [M381-83, 2:57]	"
4	John Eberhardt, John Huber, Christopher Sax (Sox), John Klein, John Klein Jr., John Fox	Indicted for CRO 27 Apr. 1799 [M298, 1:1047, 2:152, 148], except John Fox and 5 others (who were indicted in later cases) who evidently grand jury declined to indict (ignoramus) [1:1047]	Justice James Iredell
		Not prosecuted J. Klein [1:1047]	Justice Bushrod Washington
		Submitted to court's judgment and sentence 17 Oct. 1799 [M340, 1:1047] (except both Kleins), and 22 Apr. 1800 [M363, 2:147] (except Klein Sr.)	
		Reindicted for CRO 16 Apr. 1800 [M351], and struck the last 6 from indictment [see 2:147, 1:1047]	Justice Samuel Chase
		Sentenced 1 May 1800 [M380, 381] (except Kleins)	"
5	George Goltner, Peter Styerwaldt, John Lechlider, John Smith, William Rex, Charles Styerwaldt, Tobias Shlosser, Jacob Fritz, Laurence Ebner, Andrew Feller, George Hetler, John Kuntz, Peter Rabenholdt	Indicted for conspiracy 27 Apr. 1799 [M47, 1:1056]	Justice James Iredell

continued

Table 7.2 **(continued)**

Defendants	*Events and Dates*	*Supreme Court Justice Involved*
6 Abraham Samsel, Peter Huntsberg, Abraham Shantz, George Mumbower, Henry Mumbower, Peter Hager, Peter Gable, Jacob Gable, Daniel Gable, John Miller, John Marks, Henry Smith, Valentine Kuder	Indicted for conspiracy 27 Apr. 1799 (except Smith and Kuder) [M298, 1:1063]	Justice James Iredell
	Submitted to court's judgment and sentence 17 Oct. 1799 [M341, 1:1063] (all but last four)	
	Reindicted for conspiracy 16 Apr. 1800 (except Smith and Kuder) [M351]	Justice Samuel Chase
	Added Smith and Kuder, and dropped Miller and Marks in this action [2:110]	"
	Submitted to court's judgment and sentence 22 Apr. 1800 [M363, 2:110] (all but Miller and Marks)	
	Sentenced remaining defendants except Samsel 1 May 1800 [M383-86, 2:P364, 2:P299, 2:106, 2:P340]	"
7 Henry Jarrett, Henry Shankweiler, Herman Hartman, Adam Stephan, Daniel Kevely, Jacob Klein, George Shaefer	Indicted for conspiracy 27 Apr. 1799 [1:1068, 2:124–29]	Justice James Iredell
	Convicted Shaefer 15 May 1799 [1:934]	" "
	Sentenced Shaefer 18 May 1799 [1:935]	Justice Samuel Chase "
	Dismissed Stephan, Kevely [2:124]	
	Submitted to court's judgment and sentence 22 Apr. and 2 May 1800 [2:124] (first three)	"
	Sentenced Jarrett and Shankweiler [2:P333, 2:134]	
8 Henry Shiffert, Christian Ruth, Samuel Schwartz, Henry Stahler, Daniel Schwartz, Jr., John Kayser, Daniel Dillinger, George Shaefer, Daniel Schwartz, Adam Stahlnecker	Indicted for CRO 30 Apr. 1799 [M301, 1:1088, 1:1092]	Justice James Iredell
	Dismissed Stahlnecker (ignoramus) [M301, 1:1088]	
	Trial 10 May 1799 [M313]	"
	Convicted Shiffert, Ruth, Stahler, Shaefer, D. Schwartz Sr. 15 May 1799 [M315-16, 1:1096, 1:1088, 2:65–67], and acquitted D. Schwartz Jr. [M316, 1:1096, 1:1088]	
	Sentenced Shiffert, Ruth, Stahler, Shaefer, D. Schwartz 18 May 1799 [M327-28, 2:65–66, 1:933, 1:935]	"

Table 7.2 **(continued)**

	Defendants	*Events and Dates*	*Supreme Court Justice Involved*
9	Michael Yeisley, John Smyer, Michael Smyer, Jacob Smyer, Philip Ruth, Peter Rothenberger, John Huber, Jacob Eisenhardt, George Ehrich, Frederick Hayns, John Stadtler	Indicted for CRO 30 Apr. 1799 [M301, 1:1098, 1103]; amended [2:P375, P372]	Justice James Iredell
		Dismissed (ignoramus) last four 30 Apr. 1799 [M301, 1:1098]	
		Submitted to court's judgment and sentence John Smyer, M. Smyer, Ruth 18 Oct. 1799 [M341, 1:1098]	
		Reindicted all but last four 29 Apr. 1800 [M376, M378]	Justice Samuel Chase
		Dismissed John Smyer 30 Apr. 1800 [2:P371]	
		Submitted to court's judgment and sentence by M. Smyer and Ruth 30 Apr. 1800 [M378, 2:P371]	
		Sentenced M. Smyer, Huber and Ruth 1 May 1800 [M380, M387, 2:P367]	"
10	Anthony Stahler, Jacob Klein, Philip Desh	Indicted for CRO 2 May 1800 [M390, 2:38]	Justice Samuel Chase
		Submitted to court's judgment and sentence 2 May 1800 [M390, 2:46]	
		Sentenced 2 May 1800 [M391-92, 2:46, 2:68]	"
11	Conrad Marks, John Marks	Indicted for conspiracy 29 Apr. 1800 [M376, 2:P347]	Justice Samuel Chase
		Submission by C. Marks to court's judgment and sentence 1 May 1800 [M380, 2:P347]	
		Sentenced C. Marks 1 May 1800 [M387, 2:P351]	"

Abbreviations are the same as in Table 7.1. CRO refers to charges of conspiracy, rescue, and obstruction.

Summary of the Eleven Presentments or Indictments During the Fries Rebellion for Conspiracy and Obstruction Violating the Sedition Act

In each of these nontreason cases, the indictment or presentment contained at least one count of criminal conspiracy, at least one of criminal obstruction, and at least one of counseling, advising, and attempting a riot or unlawful assembly, which were the offenses prohibited by Section 1 of the Sedition Act. Both the conspiracy and the obstruction were alleged to be against the direct tax law and against the valuation law. Five indictments added a count of rescue (*Klein,*

Eberhardt, Shiffert, Yeisley, and *Stahler*). Because the eleven cases were similar, the relevant events, dates, and sources are given in Table 7.2, and the facts are masterfully summarized by Newman.

By Newman's count, forty-four individuals were indicted for conspiracy, thirty-two for conspiracy and rescue, and one for seditious statements, in addition to the treason prosecutions.[192] My Table 7.2 lists eighty-three individuals (excluding the eleven treason indictments), in addition to Table 7.1's list of nine Fries defendants, increasing Newman's total by sixteen. Thirty of the convictions and sentences are usefully summarized by Henderson in a table,[193] and five convictions from 1799 should be added to his tally.[194] The conviction rate was strikingly high, in large part because very few of the defendants had legal counsel, because most agreed to waive a jury trial when pressed by the federal judges, and because the sentencing judge for most was Chase.

The Fries Rebellion Cases under the Sedition Act Presided over by Justice James Iredell

Figure 7.3 Justice James Iredell (on Supreme Court 1790–1799). Engraving by Charles Balthazar Julien Févret de Saint-Mémin 1798. (Courtesy of National Portrait Gallery, Smithsonian Institution/Art Resource.)

Justice Iredell (Figure 7.3) presided over the April 1799 term of the Circuit Court, joined by district judge Richard Peters.[195] The court showed its advance commitment to indict and try a large number of Fries Rebellion participants by taking the

[192] FRIES'S REBELLION 241 n.2. His breakdown does not quite match his total of 91 indictments (11 treason and 80 non-treason indictments), *id.* at 165, unless the difference is failed treason prosecutions that were reindicted for conspiracy etc.

[193] HENDERSON 318.

[194] George Schaefer (Criminal Case Files 1:I934–35); Henry Shiffert, Christian Ruth, Henry Stahler, and Daniel Schwartz Sr. (*id.* 1:I1096, 1:I1088, 2:I65–67; Minutes 315–16, 327–28).

[195] From April 11 through May 18, 1799. 3 DHSC 493; Minutes 275.

unusual step of having fill-in-the-blank indictments for treason printed and ready for the grand jury to use—and they were not wasted.[196] The court also had fill-in-the-blank indictments for criminal conspiracy and obstruction handwritten, though not printed, with blanks for defendants' names[197]—and they were not wasted either. At least nine indictments were approved by the grand jury for groups of defendants ranging from five to thirteen people (in addition to the *Greenawalt* and *Llewellyn* cases). To prepare for mass arraignments and trials and under instructions from Pickering,[198] Peters had issued arrest warrants for at least 142 individuals, requiring them to travel to Philadelphia to provide bonds and sureties for their appearances at the court session.[199] About half of those arrest warrants were for appearances as defendants to answer or be arraigned, and half were for appearances to testify. During the first week of the circuit court, Peters took the unusual step of skipping court in order to issue warrants in the field.

The April 1799 session began with Iredell's grand jury charge, which declared that liberty of the press was limited to liberty from prior restraints (quoting Blackstone that "liberty of the press . . . consists in laying no *previous* restraints upon publications, and not in freedom from censure for criminal matter when published"). After pointing out that the Sedition Act criminalized combinations to defeat execution of the laws, Iredell informed the grand jury that of "the offenders" "many certainly have been guilty of combinations to resist the laws of the United States."[200] The grand jury promptly indicted John Fries, whose trial was set to begin the first of May,[201] and soon indicted nine others for treason and many for combinations and conspiracies under the Sedition Act, along with indictments in three unrelated criminal cases.[202] By the end of the five-week session, Iredell had overseen indictments of the defendants in the first nine conspiracy and obstruction cases listed in the table (as well as of Greenawalt for criticizing a federal official, Llewellyn and others for the "seditious label" on the liberty pole, and Herring for "seditious expressions"[203]), and had tried, convicted, and

[196] *E.g.*, Frederick Heany (Criminal Case Files 1:I953); Anthony Stahler (*id.* 1:I957); Conrad Marks (*id.* 1:I962); Valentine Kuder (*id.* 1:I990); Henry Huber (*id.* 1:I1006); Henry Stahler (*id.* 1:I1025).

[197] Henry Ohl et al. (*id.* 1:I1009); Daniel Klein et al. (*id.* 1:I1039); John Eberhardt et al. (*id.* 1:I1048); George Goeltner et al. (*id.* 1:I1057, 1060); Abraham Samsel et al. (*id.* 1:I1064); Henry Jarrett et al. (*id.* 1:I1068); Henry Shiffert et al. (*id.* 1:I1092); Michael Yeisley et al. (*id.* 1:I1103).

[198] Timothy Pickering to Richard Peters (4 Apr.1799), PICKERING PAPERS r.37, fol.404; Timothy Pickering to Samuel Sitgreaves 3 (1 Apr.1799), *id.* at r.10, fol.544, 545.

[199] Recognizances (Apr.1799), *id.* 1:I964–82 (excluding sureties).

[200] James Iredell's Charge (C.C.D. Pa. 11 Apr.1799), 3 DHSC 332, 347, 350, 349.

[201] Criminal Case Files 1:I938 (after argument on 30 April on the motion to move the trial to his county of residence); Minutes 290, 303 (22 Apr.1799, 1 May 1799).

[202] Minutes 290–93, 293–301.

[203] *Id.* at 342, 299; Criminal Case Files 1:I966, 998, 1079.

sentenced George Shaefer, Henry Shiffert, Christian Ruth, Henry Stahler, and Daniel Schwartz, Sr.[204] Iredell also granted a new trial to Fries because of a prejudiced juror.[205] Though the juror had said before the trial "that Fries ought to be hanged," Pickering decried the grant of a new trial, because "that juror only thought and spoke as every other person did who was equally informed of the facts."[206]

The Fries Rebellion Cases under the Sedition Act Presided over by Justice Bushrod Washington

Figure 7.4 Justice Bushrod Washington (on Supreme Court 1798–1829). Engraving by James Barton Longacre c.1829. (Courtesy of New York Public Library/Art Resource.)

Justice Washington (Figure 7.4) presided over the October 1799 term, joined by Peters.[207] The court oversaw the Sedition Act indictments of Jacob Eyerman for "seditious counseling," of Mayer and Fahnestock for their newspaper's essay, of William Duane for the *Aurora*'s claim of British influence in appointing a high government official (which the court dismissed), and, as a reindictment, of Morris Llewellyn et al.[208] Various defendants "submitted to the Court" for its determination of their case and sentencing,[209] but none of those found guilty was sentenced during the October 1799 term because of the judges' unannounced conclusion that all proceedings

[204] *Id.* at 313–16, 327–28; Criminal Case Files 1:I933–35, 1:I1096, 1:I1088.
[205] *Id.* at 320.
[206] Timothy Pickering to Rufus King at 3 (22 May 1799), PICKERING PAPERS r.11, fol.138, 140.
[207] From 11–22 Oct.1799. 3 DHSC 494; Minutes 332–33.
[208] Criminal Case Files 1:I1125, 1169, 1136, 1185; Minutes 334, 342, 335, 342.
[209] Minutes 340, 341.

were defective because of the marshal acting under an expired commission. Judge Peters lamented over that, describing it to Pickering as "the blowing up of the court."[210]

The Fries Rebellion Cases under the Sedition Act Presided over by Justice Samuel Chase

Justice Chase presided over the April 1800 term, joined by Peters.[211] Chase's grand jury charge similarly limited the scope of freedoms of press and speech (the minority must "surrender up their judgment and will to the decision of a majority," leaving it "the duty of every citizen to submit to it; and to give up his private sentiments"), told the panel that "it is your bounden and indispensable duty to present" any violations of law in the "late insurrection," and urged them to support "our illustrious patriotic and beloved President" and "your federal government, and the present administration thereof" lest it fall.[212] The grand jury did just that, and indicted or reindicted forty-five defendants for either conspiracy or conspiracy-rescue, by the court's tally,[213] reindicting most of the first nine cases (in addition to Llewellyn and Eyerman) and later indicting the last two cases in Table 7.2 as soon as the individuals were acquitted of treason charges.[214] The grand jury issued nine indictments or reindictments for treason,[215] which were encouraged by a supply of new fill-in-the-blank printed indictments,[216] though only Fries and two others ultimately were convicted of that offense.[217] The court also oversaw the second Fries trial and greatly shortened it at the cost of violent objection by the defense attorneys, as Chase announced an opinion excluding testimony and argument about the meaning of treason (which became the first of the eight counts for his impeachment); it was after this that the defense attorneys walked out of the trial and left Fries defenseless.[218] Chase raised mass sentencing to an art form, by in parts of two days sentencing thirty individuals in Sedition Act conspiracy, combination, and sometimes rescue cases to fines ranging from $40 to $1000 and prison terms from six months to two years, suspending none.[219]

210 Richard Peters to Timothy Pickering (23 Oct.1799), PICKERING PAPERS r.25, fol.259.

211 From 11 April through 2 May 1800. 3 DHSC 494; Minutes 344.

212 Samuel Chase's Charge (C.C.D. Pa. 12 Apr.1800), 3 DHSC 408, 411, 413, 414, 416.

213 Affidavit of David Caldwell (21 Jan.1804), Criminal Case Files 2:I6.

214 *E.g.*, Anthony Stahler, *id.* 1:I956, 2:I33, 2:I38; Jacob Klein, *id.* 1:I993, 2:I51, 2:I38; Philip Desh, *id.* 1:I993, 2:I59, 2:I38; John Gettman, *id.* 2:302; Conrad Marks, *id.* 1:I961, 2:342–44, 2:347–50; Valentine Kuder, *id.* 1:I989; Minutes 390 (Anthony Stahler, Jacob Klein, Philip Desh), 376 (Conrad Marks, John Marks).

215 *Id.*; Minutes 350–51, 355.

216 John Fries, *id.* 2:I10; Jacob Engelman, *id.* 2:290.

217 Minutes 371, 378.

218 Wharton's State Trials 615n., 646; REPORT OF THE TRIAL, *supra* note 187, at 29 & App. 65.

219 Some are cited in the above table; 30 are in HENDERSON 318, of which 21 are in Minutes 383–92.

In most of these Sedition Act cases, each defendant "retract[ed] his plea of non cul. [not guilty] and submit[ted] to the Court protesting his innocence,"[220] usually followed by Chase's stiff sentence.[221] Each sentence provided for continued imprisonment, after the end of the specified half-year to two years, until fines were paid and substantial bonds were posted. Those conspiracy sentences paled compared to the treason sentences, however, as Fries and two others were sentenced to death by hanging just three weeks afterward.[222]

Chase's tolerance level for sedition was shown by his overseeing, in the midst of this circuit sitting, the newest indictments of William Duane of the *Aurora*, though he was not found for arrest or trial, and the indictment and trial of Thomas Cooper,[223] where Chase reversed the presumption of innocence to require that a Sedition Act defendant must prove every defense "to the marrow." (Those were summarized in the prior chapter.) When the Pennsylvania circuit court adjourned, Chase rode forth to Maryland, where he pressed the grand jury to indict the editor of "one of the most *licentious* presses in the United States,"[224] and then rode onward to indict and try James Callender in Richmond, where Chase reportedly vowed he "would teach the lawyers in Virginia the difference between the liberty and the licentiousness of the press."[225]

Several weeks after the circuit court ended its session in early May 1800, President Adams issued pardons of Fries and the other two defendants convicted of treason, averting their hangings.[226] Those pardons became a major factor in the High Federalist split from Adams in the election of 1800. The other Fries Rebellion defendants who received sentences had to serve them, except a few pardoned by Adams in early 1801.[227]

[220] Jacob Eyerman, Criminal Case Files 1:I1161; *accord* Daniel Klein et al., *id.* 1:I1038, 2:I114; John Engelhardt et al., *id.* 1:I1047, 2:I147; Abraham Samsel et al., *id.* 1:I1063, 2:I110; Henry Jarrett et al., *id.* 2:I124; Michael Yeisley et al., *id.* 1:I1098, 2:371; Anthony Stahler et al., *id.* 2:I46; Conrad Marks et al., *id.* 2:347; Minutes 363 (Klein and Eberhardt cases), 363 (Samsel case), 378 (Yeisley case), 390 (Stahler case), 380 (C. Marks).

[221] Daniel Klein et al., *id.* 2:I57; Abraham Samsel et al., *id.* 2:364, 2:299, 2:I106, 2:340; Henry Jarrett et al., *id.* 2:333, 2:I134; Michael Yeisley et al., *id.* 2:367; Jacob Eyerman, *id.* 2:I145; Anthony Stahler et al., *id.* 2:I46, 68; Conrad Marks, *id.* 2:351; Minutes 380–83 (Klein and Eberhardt cases); 383–86 (Samsel case), 380, 387 (Yeisley case), 391–92 (Stahler case), 387 (C. Marks).

[222] Criminal Case Files 2:I18, 29; Minutes 395–96 (2 May 1800).

[223] Minutes 347 (Duane, Cooper indictments (14 Apr. 1800)), 359 (Cooper trial (19 Apr. 1800)), 376 (Duane's two indictments (29 Apr. 1800)); Criminal Case Files 2:I176 (Duane arrest warrant (14 Apr. 1800)), 2:I157 (Duane indictment), 2:I196 (Cooper trial).

[224] *Baltimore, June 4*, City Gazette & Daily Advertiser (Charleston), 20 June 1800, at 2.

[225] Report of the Trial, *supra* note 187, at 43.

[226] Minutes 395–96; Fries's Rebellion 183.

[227] *Harrisburgh, Monday, February 2d, 1801*, Oracle of Dauphin (Harrisburg), 2 Feb. 1801, at 2; *Norristown*, National Intelligencer & Washington Advertiser, 26 Jan. 1801, at 2.

These conspiracy and conspiracy-rescue cases under the Sedition Act show several things about the early justices. Justice Iredell presided over the indictments and trials of not only the largest number of Fries Rebellion defendants, but the largest number of Sedition Act defendants when these cases are added in, though he is nearly invisible in books, chapters, and articles on the Sedition Act. Justice Chase, who is far from invisible, presided over the largest number of Sedition Act sentencings, both for Sedition Act cases in the Fries Rebellion (mostly because Justice Washington ended his court session without passing sentences) and for the Sedition Act generally. The number of Sedition Act cases involving Section 1 conspiracy and conspiracy-rescue was only about half the number of Sedition Act cases involving Section 2 words and publications, but the number of defendants, convictions, and sentences was almost twice as many for Section 1 as for Section 2, because most of the former cases involved multiple defendants while most of the latter cases did not. The administration gained temporary partisan points by tying sedition to the Fries Rebellion, but in the process helped lose the crucial state of Pennsylvania to the Republicans in 1800. More broadly, the Adams administration's support of the Sedition Act, as well as its split from the High Federalists, proved fatal for the Federalist Party.

Attempted Indictments for Three Additional Sedition Act Prosecutions

Besides those prosecutions, attempts were made to get indictments to initiate at least three additional Sedition Act prosecutions, which grand juries refused. All three were against Republican newspaper editors, and a possible fourth was against a newspaper's owner as well. Table 7.3 summarizes them.

Table 7.3 **Attempted Indictments Under The Sedition Act**

Potential Defendants	*Events and Dates*	*Justice Involved*
1 John Israel of *Herald of Liberty* Washington, Pennsylvania	Indictment attempted and rejected by grand juries before 22 Nov. 1798 letter Philadelphia, Pennsylvania	Justice Samuel Chase (if 6–7 Aug. 1798)
2 Alexander Martin of Baltimore *American* Baltimore, Maryland	Indictment refused May 1800 Annapolis, Maryland	Justice Samuel Chase
3 James J. Wilson and possibly Dr. John Vaughan of *Mirror of the Times* Wilmington, Delaware	Indictment refused June 1800 Wilmington, Delaware	Justice Samuel Chase

John Israel of the *Herald of Liberty*: Sedition by Printing a Mocking Prayer for the President

One overlooked prosecution is confirmed in Judge Alexander Addison's letter to Timothy Pickering, the chief enforcement officer for the Sedition Act. Addison sent copies of the pamphlet reprinting his jury charge supporting the Sedition Act (the one that influenced Justice Bushrod Washington),[228] and urged new federal efforts to prosecute John Israel, publisher of a Republican newspaper.

Addison's report was that "the predominancy of Jacobinism here" in western Pennsylvania, and the widespread belief "that government is pursuing a systematic plan to deprive them of all their liberties," resulted from "a newspaper printed in this town [Washington, Pennsylvania] by a son of Israel Israel" [John Israel].[229] "It threatens the fall of the federal paper here . . . and the fall of federal principles," Addison wrote. He "had once determined to bind him [Israel] over to the federal court for publishing the Kentucky Resolutions," but found they had already been printed in local newspapers. He also hoped that a grand jury "would have presented him for an impious mocking prayer for the President on the fast day, but two grand juries charged with it refused to find the bill" (a true bill of indictment).[230] The prayer he referred to indeed mocked President Adams, saying that he "threw of[f] the mask, and endeavoured to gull the people," that he used "many artifices . . . to obtain the Presidential chair," and that he prayed for "placing the crown upon the head of thy unworthy servant" or at least on "the head of my son Quincey."[231] Addison found this a clear Sedition Act violation.

Addison added that a county court judge wrote a "seditious address to Mr. Gallatin [the author's representative in Congress] pointedly censuring as unconstitutional and oppressive the Alien and Sedition Acts and . . . the Stamp Act" (the new tax law), and that the address was "triumphantly published in Israel's *Herald of Liberty* just before the election and contributed not a little to inflame the passions of the people and promote the unfavorable result" (something that Addison viewed as aggravating the publication of seditious libel).[232] What Addison found seditious was the statement in the letter that the "Sedition Bill" was "unconstitutional, because it goes to an abridgment of the liberty of speech and of the press—rights expressly guaranteed by the Constitution."[233] The judge ended the letter to Pickering by suggesting another

[228] George Washington to Bushrod Washington (31 Dec.1798), 37 WRITINGS OF GEORGE WASHINGTON 80, 81 (John C. Fitzpatrick ed., GPO, Washington 1931–44).

[229] Alexander Addison to Timothy Pickering 2–3 (22 Nov.1798), PICKERING PAPERS r.23, fol.322, 323 (mistakenly calling it "Herald of Freedom" on p.3 and the correct name on p.4, and stating that two grand juries refused to find true bill of indictment).

[230] *Id.* at 3.

[231] *Prayer of John Adams for the Fast Day*, HERALD OF LIBERTY (Washington [Pa.]), 30 Apr.1798, at 3.

[232] Addison, *supra* note 229, at 4.

[233] Henry Taylor et al., *To Albert Gallatin, Esq.*, HERALD OF LIBERTY (Washington), 1 Oct.1798, at 2.

attempt at federally prosecuting Israel and others by informations, since indictments were not being approved by grand juries: "some measures ought to be taken to prevent the too obvious effects of this slander," and perhaps "the deputy attornies of the United States ought to have express instructions to watch these offences and give information of them or some other method for counteracting detecting and suppressing of them it becomes not me to suggest."[234]

John Israel was the publisher of the *Herald of Liberty* in Washington, Pennsylvania,[235] the most combatively Republican paper in western Pennsylvania,[236] and in August 1800 he also founded and became the editor of the *Tree of Liberty* in Pittsburgh.[237] If challenging the constitutionality of the Sedition Act was sedition, Israel was a prince of sedition as he repeatedly made that challenge. As soon as word arrived of its enactment, he published three items in sequence on a page: the words of the First Amendment (under the caption "Freemen of America Attend!"), the Sedition Act, and an essay that such laws "*in opposition to the Constitution*" are not binding.[238] Israel continued to print criticism of the Act,[239] including the Kentucky Resolutions and then the Virginia Resolutions,[240] along with outraged coverage of Sedition Act cases.[241]

Addison's statement to Pickering that twice a bill of indictment was attempted against Israel, but "two grand juries charged with it refused to find the bill," appears to refer to prosecution in federal courts, not state courts, for several reasons, though they are not conclusive.[242] Addison was writing to the federal chief

[234] Addison, *supra* note 229, at 4.

[235] *Colophon*, HERALD OF LIBERTY (Washington), 18 Nov.1799, at 4 (listing printer and publisher John Israel, and location).

[236] JEFFREY L. PASLEY, "THE TYRANNY OF PRINTERS": NEWSPAPER POLITICS IN THE EARLY AMERICAN REPUBLIC 112–15 (UPV, Charlottesville 2001); DONALD H. STEWART, THE OPPOSITION PRESS OF THE FEDERALIST PERIOD 11, 618, 887 (SUNYP, Albany 1969); RUSSELL J. FERGUSON, EARLY WESTERN PENNSYLVANIA POLITICS 151, 161–62 (UPitP, Pittsburgh 1938).

[237] Sheppard, *supra* note 23, at 72, 74; 2 BRIGHAM 979, 967, 1437; SANFORD W. HIGGINBOTHAM, THE KEYSTONE IN THE DEMOCRATIC ARCH: PENNSYLVANIA POLITICS, 1800–1816, at 73 (PHMC, Harrisburg 1952). Israel closed the *Herald* in February 1802, and sold the *Tree* in December 1805. 2 BRIGHAM 979, 967.

[238] *Freemen of America Attend!*, HERALD OF LIBERTY (Washington), 30 July 1798, at 4; *Sedition Bill, id.; Remarks on the Above from a Boston Paper, id.*

[239] *E.g., To John Clopton*, HERALD OF LIBERTY (Washington), 10 Sept.1798, at 2; *To the Electors of Northumberland County*, HERALD OF LIBERTY (Washington), 7 Oct.1798, at 1; *Frankfort, Sept.18*, HERALD OF LIBERTY (Washington), 15 Oct.1798, at 2.

[240] *Richmond, Dec. 25*, HERALD OF LIBERTY (Washington), 21 Jan.1799, at 1; *Address of the General Assembly*, HERALD OF LIBERTY (Washington), 11 Feb.1799, at 1.

[241] *E.g., Worcester, Oct. 17*, HERALD OF LIBERTY (Washington), 5 Nov.1798, at 3; *Col. Lyon's Tryal [sic]*, HERALD OF LIBERTY (Washington), 26 Nov.1798, at 1.

[242] The case does not appear in federal court records for western Pennsylvania for 1798, though they are sketchy compared to records for eastern Pennsylvania that include the Fries Rebellion, Duane, and Cooper cases.

enforcement officer for the Sedition Act. He complained of publications violating a federal law, the Sedition Act, which prohibited "writing, printing, uttering or publishing against . . . the president . . . to defame the said President, or to bring [him] into contempt."[243] He lamented that the grand juries declined to indict criticism of the president, which violated that Act, in the form of the "impious mocking prayer for the President on the fast day," which Israel had published at the end of April 1798.[244] The reference was preceded by Addison's statement that he "had once determined to bind him [Israel] over to the federal court for publishing the Kentucky Resolutions," and it was followed by his suggestion that "the deputy attornies of the United States" be instructed to prosecute such cases. If Addison meant that one or more federal grand juries refused to indict Israel, that would have occurred at the circuit court session in Philadelphia on August 6–7, 1798, three weeks after the Sedition Act was signed into law, since the court did not have any judges present in its October 11 session because of a yellow fever epidemic.[245] That would help explain why the special session of the court was held in August 1798, which remains a subject of uncertainty (though the sketchy court records do not mention Israel),[246] particularly since Chase was the Supreme Court justice in attendance, who soon became the most zealous justice in prosecuting Republican newspaper editors under the Sedition Act.

Alexander Martin of the Baltimore *American*: "Licentious" Republicanism

Secretary of State Pickering instructed Zebulon Hollingsworth, the United States Attorney for Maryland, to procure a virulent newspaper, the Baltimore *American*, daily, and "to prosecute the publisher, for every libel upon the Government or its officers, which may appear therein either originally or by republication." He asked to be notified of each prosecution, so he could arrange parallel prosecutions "against the original libellers."[247] The publisher of Baltimore's *American and Daily Advertiser* was Alexander Martin.[248] Though his paper was a mouthpiece for Republicanism,[249] Pickering's instructions remained unfulfilled for nine months.

[243] Subsequent enactment of the Sedition Act similarly did not prevent prosecution of Matthew Lyon for material written earlier.

[244] *Prayer of John Adams for the Fast Day*, HERALD OF LIBERTY (Washington), 30 Apr.1798, at 3.

[245] 3 DHSC 284, 299.

[246] 3 *id.* at 284 n.1. The minutes describe nothing but opening and closing court, and the case files are missing or nonexistent. However, cases must have been dealt with, because the court did not adjourn the same day it opened. Minutes at 272.

[247] Timothy Pickering to Zebulon Hollingsworth (12 Aug.1799), PICKERING PAPERS r.11, fol.603.

[248] 1 BRIGHAM 223.

[249] [Alex. Martin], *To the Public*, AMERICAN & DAILY ADVERTISER (Baltimore), 18 May 1799, at 1; TYRANNY 161–62.

Justice Chase, when he held circuit court in Baltimore in May 1800,[250] sought to correct that prosecutorial failure by pressing the grand jury to indict the editor of Baltimore's Republican newspaper. One newspaper in Baltimore reported that Chase, when he informed the grand jury there that "one of the most *licentious* presses in the United States was supported in Baltimore,"[251] was trying to gain approval of "an indictment" that the federal attorney already "had prepared against the Editor of the American" (Alexander Martin of the *American*)—which the grand jury refused to approve.[252] The federal court records do not contain a draft indictment against Martin (and typically would not contain a draft unapproved by the grand jury).[253]

James J. Wilson and Possibly Dr. John Vaughan: The "Seditious" *Mirror of the Times*

Another of the grounds for impeachment of Justice Chase was his insistence that a Delaware federal attorney and grand jury indict "a most seditious printer, unrestrained by any principle of virtue," in Wilmington.[254] The district judge who had sat with Chase (and who had since seen the Republican light) later testified that when the grand jury did not find anyone warranting indictment, Chase refused to discharge them and required them to stay another day, and instructed the federal attorney to collect and investigate copies of the newspaper. Moreover, he recalled Chase telling the grand jury that "you have in this state a seditious printer who is in the constant habit of abusing the government," that "it was high time that these seditious printers should be corrected," and when the federal attorney and grand jury found none, that "it was hard he could not get a single man indicted in Delaware, while he could in every other place."[255] This incident occurred as Chase, having ended the circuit court in Richmond, held court in Wilmington, Delaware, in late June 1800,[256] and it was similarly reported at the time in Republican newspapers.[257]

250 3 DHSC 424 (7–16 May 1800).

251 *Baltimore, June 4*, City Gazette & Daily Advertiser (Charleston), 20 June 1800, at 2.

252 *Id.; accord From the Philadelphia Aurora*, Constitutional Telegraph (Boston), 28 June 1800, at 2.

253 Criminal Case Files [Maryland], *infra* note 332.

254 Report of the Trial app. 5.

255 *Id.* at 97, 98.

256 3 DHSC 494.

257 *Letter from an Anonymous Correspondent*, Aurora (Philadelphia), 1 July 1800, 3 DHSC 442; Mirror of the Times (Wilmington), 4 July 1800, 3 DHSC 445; *Remember Judge Chase*, Centinel of Freedom (Newark), 29 July 1800, at 3.

The person Chase sought to indict has been understood to be James J. Wilson, the printer of the Republican newspaper in Wilmington, the *Mirror of the Times*.[258] Wilson had established the paper at the end of November 1799,[259] as a staunchly Republican voice, publishing "attacks on President Adams, the Sedition Law, and the 'New England Illuminati'" (the term John C. Ogden popularized for that region's Federalist clergy).[260] Two months later, a High Federalist complained to Pickering that he was "almost delirious at seeing our once happy country disordered" by "our little Jacobin paper" and articles in it by Ogden.[261] Contemporaneous newspapers and the impeachment testimony said that Chase, though sparing no effort, failed to get an indictment of the "seditious printer," and the circuit court records do not show any indictment either.[262] Wilson got in the last word, writing that if the "great beast" by which he had "been already *Chased*, should in some future *circuitous* ramble in *search for sedition*, . . . lay his pestiferous paw upon me, and chant in my ear his favorite air, '*two hundred dollars fine, and six months imprisonment*,' no one can imagine what an awkward figure I should make."[263] A decade and a half later, Wilson became the first printer to be elected to the United States Senate.[264]

A letter by Dr. John Vaughan to Thomas Jefferson in early 1801 exulted that Vaughan had passed through "attempted persecutions under the, *ignoble*, sedition law,"[265] but Smith found the report unconfirmed as he did not come across any court record of a prosecution or any further details.[266] Nothing has been added in other Sedition Act discussions. Why would a physician, like Vaughan,[267] face potential prosecution under the Sedition Act? A clue is that he wrote to Jefferson

[258] 3 DHSC at 443 n.2; JOHN A. MUNROE, FEDERALIST DELAWARE, 1775–1815, at 207 (RUP, New Brunswick 1954).

[259] 1 BRIGHAM 84, 2 *id.* at 1505.

[260] JOHN A. MUNROE, *supra* note 258, at 207; OPPOSITION PRESS 871; *e.g.*, *Mr. Wilson*, MIRROR OF THE TIMES (Wilmington), 5 Apr.1800, at 3; *Spirit of the Times*, MIRROR OF THE TIMES (Wilmington), 23 July 1800, at 2.

[261] Col. Allan McLane to Timothy Pickering (8 Feb. 1800), PICKERING PAPERS r.26 fol.26.

[262] Criminal Docket of the Circuit Court of the United States for the Delaware District Commencing. . . . MDCCXCV (National Archives at Philadelphia, R.G.21.9.2, Local Identifier 10-D-11–9.2); Judgment Index, 1790–1912 (C.C.D. Del.) for U-W (same location, Local Identifier 10-D-11–1.5).

[263] [James J. Wilson], *To Correspondents*, REPUBLICAN WATCH TOWER (New York), 30 July 1800, at 1 (reprinting *Mirror*).

[264] His best biography is in TYRANNY 320–29.

[265] Dr. John Vaughan to Thomas Jefferson (10 Jan.1801), 32 JEFFERSON PAPERS 441, 442, cited in FREEDOM'S FETTERS 185 n.87. *See also* Dr. John Vaughan to Thomas Jefferson (10 Oct.1801), 35 JEFFERSON PAPERS 427, 428.

[266] FREEDOM'S FETTERS 185 n.87.

[267] 32 JEFFERSON PAPERS 269n.; HOWARD A. KELLY & WALTER L. BURRAGE, DICTIONARY OF AMERICAN MEDICAL BIOGRAPHY 1247 (Appleton, New York 1928); 1 J. THOMAS SCHARF, HISTORY OF DELAWARE 493 (Kennikat Press, Port Washington 1888); 6 APPLETON'S CYCLOPEDIA OF AMERICAN BIOGRAPHY 268 (Appleton, New York 1888).

from Wilmington, Delaware, and was a dedicated Republican.[268] Though Brigham does not list Vaughan under his description of the *Mirror of the Times*, "Vaughan & Coleman" appeared as owners of the *Delaware Gazette* in its masthead,[269] and Brigham identified its owners as John Vaughan and Daniel Coleman (without suggesting who they were). He also said the *Delaware Gazette* in September 1799 announced that its successor would be the *Delaware Gazette and Mirror of the Times*, and that was just before Wilson started the *Mirror*.[270] The Vaughan who co-owned the *Gazette* and *Mirror* was identified by a leading Delaware historian as one and the same as Dr. John Vaughan.[271] Thus, Dr. Vaughan's brush with possible prosecution under the Sedition Act came from financing and owning the *Mirror of the Times*, and his claimed near prosecution was connected to James J. Wilson's. As with Wilson, the circuit court records show no indictment.

Instructions to Bring Six Additional Sedition Act Cases

Secretary of State Pickering instructed that at least five additional cases be initiated under the Sedition Act, prosecuting seven individuals, and the secretary of war apparently gave instructions for a sixth, though they did not actually progress to indictments or arrests. Those were of a pseudonymous author called Aristides, Virginia Representative John Clopton and a writer describing Clopton's views, newspaper editor Jacob Schneider, Republican writer and activist Dr. Joseph Priestley, and newspaper editor Meriwether Jones, as well as writers. Documentation appears in Pickering's official papers. The instructions to prosecute Schneider, Priestley, and Jones were given in July and August 1799, around the time Pickering sent form letters to the United States Attorneys instructing them to take "measures to correct [printers] by legal process" because of their "audacious calumnies against the Government"[272] (which led to prosecutions of Duane, Greenleaf, Peck, and others), obviously designed to quash or intimidate opposition before the 1800 elections.

In addition, there is some evidence that prosecutions under the Sedition Act were seriously considered, or attempted, in three cases (one involving two people), though they are not confirmed by federal court records or Pickering instructions. On the other hand, several other rumored prosecutions lack confirmation, or were not under the Sedition Act. These instructions to prosecute, and seriously considered cases, are summarized in Table 7.4.

[268] Thomas Jefferson to Dr. John Vaughan (17 July 1801), 34 JEFFERSON PAPERS 587; John Dickinson to Thomas Jefferson (25 May 1801), 34 *id.* at 179.

[269] *E.g.*, DELAWARE GAZETTE (Wilmington), 27 July 1799, at 1.

[270] 1 BRIGHAM 81.

[271] JOHN A. MUNROE, *supra* note 258, at 184.

[272] *E.g.*, Timothy Pickering to Zebulon Hollingsworth (12 Aug. 1799), PICKERING PAPERS r.11, fol.603; Timothy Pickering to Richard Harison (12 Aug. 1799), *id.* at r.11, fol.599; Timothy Pickering to Thomas Nelson (14 Aug. 1799), *id.* at r.11, fol.611.

Table 7.4 **Instructions For Prosecutions And Unconfirmed Prosecutions**

Potential Defendants	*Events and Dates*	*Justice Involved*
Instructions for Prosecutions		
1 Aristides Washington, Kentucky	Consideration of prosecution July 1798	United States Attorney and Secretary of State Timothy Pickering (No Supreme Court justice involved)
2 Rep. John Clopton and Buckskin New Kent County & Richmond, Virginia	Instruction for prosecution Oct. 1798	Secretary of State Timothy Pickering (No Supreme Court justice involved)
3 David Garvin St. Mary's, Georgia	Arrest under Sedition Act 30 Nov. 1798 Related case filed 3 Dec. 1798	Secretary of Navy Benjamin Stoddert (No Supreme Court justice involved)
4 Jacob Schneider of the *Readinger Adler* Reading, Pennsylvania	Instruction for prosecution July 1799	Secretary of State Timothy Pickering (No Supreme Court justice involved)
5 Dr. Joseph Priestley Philadelphia, Pennsylvania	Instruction for prosecution Aug. 1799	Secretary of State Timothy Pickering (No Supreme Court justice involved)
6 Meriwether Jones and writers for Richmond *Examiner* Richmond, Virginia	Instruction for prosecution Aug. 1799 Grand jury charge pressing for indictments June 1800	Secretary of State Timothy Pickering Justice Samuel Chase
Unconfirmed Possibilities		
7 Gov. James Garrard of Kentucky Lexington, Kentucky	Consideration of prosecution Dec. 1798	Secretary of State Timothy Pickering (No Supreme Court justice involved)
8 Charles Webber and Benjamin Brown Portland, Maine	Steps toward indictment Dec. 1798	United States Attorney (No Supreme Court justice involved)
9 Dr. John Tyler Fredericktown, Maryland	Possible effort to indict May 1800 Annapolis, Maryland	Justice Samuel Chase
Excluded Possibilities		
10 James Bell, the Newburgh Printer, and Tristram Jordan	Not federal prosecutions	No Supreme Court justice involved
11 Daniel Dodge and Aaron Pennington of the *Centinel of Freedom* Newark, New Jersey	State prosecution	No Supreme Court justice involved

Thus, instructions for Sedition Act prosecution were given by Pickering or a colleague in (1)–(6). There were unconfirmed steps toward prosecutions in (7)–(9), but the remaining alleged prosecutions in (10)–(11), if they occurred at all, were not Sedition Act prosecutions.

Aristides: A "Seditious" Essay

The ink on the Sedition Act was barely dry, having just been signed a week before, when an essay by Aristides in a Kentucky newspaper was forwarded to Pickering by a federal prosecutor.[273] The letter from William Rawle, the United States Attorney who prosecuted the most Sedition Act cases, attached a letter from Parker Campbell, who he said "prosecutes for the United States under deputation from me." Campbell's letter in turn attached a "seditious" essay by Aristides, published in "a paper printed by Hunter & Beaumont in Washington, Kentucky," which was "in my opinion more highly inflammatory" than any Campbell had yet seen, because it called on westerners in case of open war with France "to separate from the east, and directly to oppose the measures of the administration."[274] The newspaper printed there by Hunter & Beaumont was the very Republican *Mirror*.[275] Rawle was suggesting that Pickering give instructions to prosecute Aristides, the newspaper, or both. However, no evidence has surfaced of an actual prosecution, perhaps because Aristides remained unidentified and Kentucky appeared a difficult venue for prosecution.

Representative John Clopton and Buckskin: Assertedly Calling the President a Traitor Who Bought Congress

Representative John Clopton[276] of Virginia understood his own letters to constituents to be referred to among the "circular letters of several members of the late Congress" that were condemned by a Richmond grand jury in 1797. That grand jury's presentment called them "a real evil" that disseminated "unfounded calumnies against the happy Government of the United States."[277] Clopton responded with a new circular letter that condemned the grand jury's action as "an attack upon the common right of every individual to a *free exercise* of opinion" under "the principles of our constitution" protecting "that valuable right,"

[273] William Rawle to Timothy Pickering (21 July 1798), PICKERING PAPERS r.25, fol.45.

[274] Parker Campbell to William Rawle (12 July 1798), *id.* at r.25, fol.22.

[275] 1 BRIGHAM 179; OPPOSITION PRESS 473.

[276] 3 JOHN T. KNEEBONE ET AL., DICTIONARY OF VIRGINIA BIOGRAPHY 306 (Library of Virginia, Richmond 1998–). Smith briefly mentioned the incident. FREEDOM'S FETTERS 183.

[277] Presentment of the Grand Jury (C.C.D. Va. 22 May 1797), 3 DHSC 181.

turning letter writing into "a species of criminality," and leading "to the exclusion of the great body of the people from knowledge of the measures of their government."[278] That response, in turn, generated a critical article that Pickering read with interest.

Three months after the Sedition Act became law, Pickering found a newspaper article by a pseudonymous Buckskin[279] to warrant examining the printer "with a view to the prosecution of the writer," and ultimately the prosecution of Clopton. Pickering listed what the article said about Clopton that warranted a Sedition Act prosecution: Clopton "wrote not only public circular letters to his constituents but *private* ones 'too violent to be made circular,'" which called "the President of the United States a traitor—says he is grasping at absolute power—that he has bought a majority of the House of Representatives."[280] Pickering also instructed officials to retrieve the original letter from its recipient, Mr. Pollard.[281] Successfully derailing the prosecution, Clopton had already obtained a declaration from Pollard, "supposing myself to be the person alluded to in a piece signed 'Buckskin,'" that he had "no knowledge of any letter having been written by Mr. Clopton" saying those things.[282] However, Clopton was not as successful in fighting to retain his congressional seat, as the Federalists supported John Marshall against him and won the seat.[283]

David Garvin: "Damned the President for an Old Fool"

An arrest under the Sedition Act was seen by Georgia Governor James Jackson, a Republican, as outrageous enough to be mentioned in his annual address to the state legislature. It has not appeared in any Sedition Act discussions. In early January 1799, Jackson described

> a charge against an officer of the United States galley, for landing his men to take a citizen under the sedition act of the United States, as that officer is said to have declared, by order of the secretary of the navy department. Although I cannot believe the secretary ever issued such an order, and forbear to comment on the propriety of the law, I cannot help

[278] Circular letter from John Clopton (19 June 1797), 1 CIRCULAR LETTERS 94, 94–95.

[279] Buckskin, *To the Freeholders of Henrico Congressional District*, VIRGINIA GAZETTE, & GENERAL ADVERTISER (Richmond), 9 Oct.1798, at 2.

[280] Timothy Pickering to Edward Carrington (23 Oct.1798), PICKERING PAPERS r.9, fol.512.

[281] *Id.* The article identified him as "Mr. W.P. of Hanover," holder of "a respectable office."

[282] John Clopton, *Mr. Davis*, VIRGINIA GAZETTE, & GENERAL ADVERTISER (Richmond), 16 Oct.1798, at 2; William Pollard, *Hanover, October 10th, 1798, id.* at 2.

[283] Congressional Election Campaign, 3 MARSHALL PAPERS 494, 497; JOHN T. KNEEBONE, *supra* note 276, at 307.

> observing that an attempt of this nature, by a military or naval officer, in a place where the law is open, and the civil magistrate bound to take cognizance of offences against the union, is not only opposed to the constitution of the United States, but tends to foment jealousies ill suited to our present situation, when unanimity is so necessary; and whilst it impresses the idea of oppression, instead of that protection which I am certain the galley was intended for, operates to awaken apprehensions of an act, supposed by many not to be constitutional [the Sedition Act[284]] . . . .[285]

The galley was one of two naval vessels built in Georgia to protect the Georgia coast and harbors, as the Secretary of the Navy noted in War Department Records.[286] The Secretary, Benjamin Stoddert, became aware of Jackson's complaint, probably through extracts printed in the *Aurora*.[287] In response to Stoddert's letter, Jackson replied that the "commander of a galley" was "Captn. Randolph," that the "person injured" was "David Garwin" of St. Mary's, Georgia (a coastal town), and that Garwin's affidavit and several witnesses' statements were enclosed.[288] The War Department records, which are reproduced online, do not appear to contain those documents, but the nearest newspaper did.

[284] The reference was clearly to the Sedition Act, as the governor's next sentence made clear in transmitting the Kentucky Resolutions "on the subject of that act, and the alien law of the United States."

[285] Gov. James Jackson, *Message of His Excellency Governor Jackson, to Both Houses of the Legislature* (10 Jan. 1799), LOUISVILLE GAZETTE (Louisville, Ga.), 5 Feb. 1799, at 1, 3. The legislature's transcripts are lost for the Jan. –Feb. 1799 session, and this newspaper in the city where the legislature met is the best alternate source. The governor attached "papers marked no. 14," and those too are lost.

[286] Sec. of Navy Benjamin Stoddert to Gov. James Jackson (26 Nov. 1798), Governor's Letter Book of Governor James Jackson (Ga. Dept. of Archives & History, filmed 1940, drawer 202, microfilm 202/58); 7 OFFICE OF NAVAL RECORDS, NAVAL DOCUMENTS RELATED TO THE QUASI-WAR 371 (GPO, Washington 1935).

[287] *Extract from Governor Jackson's Message to the Legislature of Georgia*, AURORA (Philadelphia), 19 Mar. 1799, at 3.

[288] Gov. James Jackson to Sec. of Navy Ben Stoddert (4 May 1799), Governor's Letter Book of Governor James Jackson, *supra* note 286, tr. at 157–58 (drawer 241, microfilm 241/52). This incident appears to be unconnected to Ensign Hugh McCall's complaints about objectionable conduct of Lt. Col. Henry Gaither. Gov. James Jackson to Abraham Baldwin (5 Feb. 1799), *id.* tr. at 32, 33; Gov. James Jackson to Sec. of War James McHenry (9 Mar. 1799), *id.* tr. at 102, 106–07; Gov. James Jackson to Sec. of War James McHenry (2 Dec. 1798),http://wardepartmentpapers.org/document.php?id=29626 (accessed 11 Apr. 2014); Gov. James Jackson to Sec. of War James McHenry (7 July 1799), *id.* id=33386. The only reference to David Garwin in the War Department records appears to be in 1793, *id.* id=8260.

David Garvin (as his name is correctly spelled) and Captain John F. Randolph each wrote statements and published them in the *Columbian Museum & Savannah Advertiser.* Randolph alleged that "Citizen Garvin" was part of "a French faction," and that his infraction was that he "damned the President for an old fool."[289] Garvin submitted an affidavit of seven witnesses, who signed in front of a justice of the peace, claiming the following facts:

> That they were present in the town of St. Mary's, on the 30th day of November 1798, and saw an armed force come from on board the Savannah galley, then lying in the river opposite the town, and attempted to make a prisoner of David Garvin, a citizen of the said State—Captain John F. Randolph, ordered his Lieutenant, Shaw, who appeared intoxicated, to take the said Garvin, and carry him on board the said galley, and confine him in irons . . . . The citizens then present, seeing the impropriety of Capt. Randolph's conduct, disarmed the party, and obliged them to go on board the said galley.[290]

It is easy to confirm that Randolph was captain of a Savannah-based galley as of late November 1798,[291] and that William Moubray, before whom the affidavit was signed, was a justice of the peace.[292]

Garvin also wrote that, the day after his arrest, he caused Randolph and his next in command to be "taken with a states warrant, and carried before three magistrates, who demanded his authority for his conduct." Randolph claimed to have "private orders from the Secretary of the Navy, but shewed none," instead going on the offensive by calling Garvin "a seditious person."[293] Garvin's account was reprinted by a number of Republican newspapers in addition to the *Aurora.*[294]

[289] John F. Randolph, *Messrs. Seymour & Woolhopter,* COLUMBIAN MUSEUM & SAVANNAH ADVERTISER, 4 Jan. 1799, at 3.

[290] David Garvin, *Messrs. Seymour & Woolhopter,* COLUMBIAN MUSEUM & SAVANNAH ADVERTISER, 1 Jan. 1799, at 2. Garvin responded to Randolph late in the month. David Garvin, *To John F. Randolph,* COLUMBIAN MUSEUM & SAVANNAH ADVERTISER, 29 Jan. 1799, at 2.

[291] Recruiting Instructions (11 Sept. 1798), 1 OFFICE OF NAVAL RECORDS, *supra* note 286, at 388; Commission (20 Mar. 1799), 2 *id.* 493; Savannah [Galley], 7 *id.* 371.

[292] James Seagrove's Deposition (9 May 1793), http://wardepartmentpapers.org/document.php?id=8542 (accessed 14 Apr. 2014).

[293] David Garvin, *Messrs. Seymour & Woolhopter,* COLUMBIAN MUSEUM & SAVANNAH ADVERTISER, 1 Jan. 1799, at 2.

[294] *From the Savannah Museum,* THE BEE (New London), 6 Feb. 1799, at 3; *Standing Army,* INDEPENDENT CHRONICLE (Philadelphia), 18–21 Mar. 1799, at 4; *Standing Army,* NEW-JERSEY JOURNAL (Elizabethtown), 26 Mar. 1799, at 3; *Standing Army,* FARMER'S REGISTER (Chambersburg), 27 Mar. 1799, at 203; *Extracts from Governor Jackson's Message,* AMERICAN MERCURY (Hartford), 28 Mar. 1799, at 2; *[No Caption],* EASTERN HERALD (Portland), 15 Apr. 1799, at 3.

The attempted prosecution spurred by Garvin of Randolph can be confirmed in court records for the county where St. Mary's was located (Camden County, Georgia). In the next sitting of the superior court, John F. Randolph and John Shaw (his lieutenant) were indicted for riot[295] on the tenth of March 1799, and a bench warrant was issued to require their appearance at the next superior court session. In the next sitting, the court fined Captain Randolph fifty dollars, on the tenth of October 1799.[296] While the court's minutes do not show whether there was a trial or a plea, an entry in its miscellaneous records shows that there was a trial, because six witnesses are listed, and then Randoph is said to be "guilty of the afs." (the aforesaid riot).[297] That superior court case matches Garvin's account that he caused Randolph and his next in command to be taken with a warrant, and carried before three magistrates.

Continuing attempts by Randolph to prosecute Garvin also can be confirmed in court records. Three days after the arrest, a case was filed in the inferior court under the style "Jn. F. Randolph vs[.] David Garvin," and was carried over to the June 1799 term. The case was dismissed by the four sitting justices in the following court term, on the eighth of January 1800.[298] That inferior court case does not appear to be a Sedition Act prosecution, since it was not in federal court and was not brought by the federal government as plaintiff. However, it corroborates what occurred three days earlier, that Randolph tried to arrest Garvin and have him prosecuted under the Sedition Act. Randolph may have been the plaintiff because he claimed that Garvin slandered him in the altercation, or perhaps because he could not get anyone else to prosecute Garvin. The federal circuit court would not meet until April 1799, the state's indisposition to prosecute was shown by its governor and its legislature opposing the Alien and Sedition Acts,[299] and the county's indisposition to prosecute Garvin was shown by its prosecution of Randolph instead.

It is particularly noteworthy that no mention of the case, or of the Stoddert letters, appears in the quite complete papers of the War Department (or in books on

[295] Georgia had no statutory definition; the common law definition of riot was "an unlawful act of violence" by three or more. 4 BLACKSTONE'S COMMENTARIES 146.

[296] Minutes of Superior Court, Camden County, 1797- (Ga. Dept. of Archives & History, drawer 71, microfilm 71/22) (pages unnumbered).

[297] Miscellaneous Records of Superior Court (March Term 1799), Camden County (Ga. Dept. of Archives & History, drawer 27, microfilm 27/69) (pages unnumbered).

[298] Doquet. Inferior Court[,] Camden County. Commencing November Term 1796 (Ga. Dept. of Archives & History, drawer 32, microfilm 32/26) (pages unnumbered, items dated 3 Dec. 1798, June 1799, and 8 Jan. 1800).

[299] JOURNAL OF THE HOUSE OF THE STATE OF GEORGIA 48 (John E. Smith, Augusta [1800]) (5 Dec. 1799); JOURNAL OF THE SENATE OF THE STATE OF GEORGIA 35 (John E. Smith, Augusta [1800]) (5 Dec. 1799).

the Quasi-War[300]). The Georgia governor responded to a letter from Stoddert, and Randolph claimed to have another one. The letters may have disappeared because of the political implications of this lone case involving the military enforcing the Sedition Act. The Republican press was quick to pick up on the case as an illustration of the danger of a standing army—most of the articles on the case were captioned "Standing Army." This is also the only case involving the Sedition Act south of Richmond, Virginia, where the Callender prosecution occurred.

Jacob Schneider of the *Readinger Adler*: Republican Activism

Jacob Schneider, the editor of the *Readinger Adler* in Pennsylvania,[301] an ardently Republican newspaper in the German language,[302] was also the subject of Pickering instructions to prosecute. Pickering sent the federal attorney an article, "An Address to the Germans in the County of Cumberland," from a "newspaper printed in Reading by one Schneider in the German language." He accompanied it with the instruction that "[i]f any passages in the address in your opinion do make the printer liable to a prosecution, I pray you to direct its being commenced."[303] In Pickering's eyes, Schneider's sins were grave, because the article urged German Americans to vote against High Federalist James Ross, and for Republican Thomas McKean, in the gubernatorial race, among other reasons because Ross had supported the Sedition Act.[304] Schneider only escaped prosecution because the Fries Rebellion cases overwhelmed Rawle for the rest of the year.

However, zealous Federalists did take action, as a detachment of the state militia that had been called up by Adams, upon reaching eastern Pennsylvania to crush the already dissolved "rebellion," demanded that Schneider disclose the author of an article. When he refused, they violently seized him, dragged him from the newspaper office to the public market, and started to administer twenty-five lashes,[305] until another detachment arrived and stopped the extrajudicial

[300] Office of Naval Records, Naval Documents Related to the Quasi-War (GPO, Washington 1935); Alexander DeConde, The Quasi-War (Scribner, New York 1966); Michael A. Palmer, Stoddert's War: Naval Operations During the Quasi-War with France, 1798–1801 (USCP, Columbia 1987); Frederick C. Leiner, Millions for Defense: The Subscription Warships of 1798 (Naval Institute Press, Annapolis 2000).

[301] He and Georg Gerrisch started the paper in January 1797, after a "preliminary sample issue" in late 1796, and edited it until 1804, when Schneider sold out to a recent new partner. 2 Brigham 969, 1478–79.

[302] Fries's Rebellion 80; Opposition Press 887.

[303] Timothy Pickering to William Rawle (5 July 1799), Pickering Papers r.11, fol.390.

[304] *An Address to the Germans of Cumberland County*, Aurora (Philadelphia), 30 July 1799, reprinted in American Aurora 666 (Richard N. Rosenfeld ed., St. Martin's Press, New York 1997).

[305] Jacob Schn[e]ider, *Reading, May 17th, 1799*, Aurora (Philadelphia), 24 May 1799, at 2; *accord Order and Good Government*, Aurora (Philadelphia), 24 Apr.1799, at 3.

proceeding. Interestingly, Robert Goodloe Harper, a House of Representatives sponsor of the Sedition Act, led the first detachment[306] and, while denying much of Schneider's account, admitted that he was taken to the marketplace and given "six lashes."[307]

Dr. Joseph Priestley: "Meddling with Our Government"

Dr. Joseph Priestley, the philosopher-theologian, appears to have been the subject of another Pickering instruction to prosecute. In August 1799 Pickering protested that Priestley's conduct as a Republican activist was "wholly unpardonable," and that "ambition influences him, like the mass of seditious, turbulent democrats." Pickering also suggested that the Alien Act should apply to Priestley (a British citizen), objecting that "[t]he *indecency* of these *strangers* thus meddling with our government" did not need "animadversion." He concluded with his desire for action by the federal attorney: "I hope . . . that Mr. Rawle will prosecute both."[308]

Though Priestley's meddling did not need animadversion generally, it required animadversion to President John Adams. Pickering said Priestley's meddling was intolerable in two areas: his "discontented and turbulent spirit" as shown by attending "the democratic assembly on the 4th of July," and his "indecency in getting Mr. [Thomas] Cooper's address printed," Cooper being an "opposition man"[309] who was later prosecuted under the Sedition Act for that address.[310] However, Adams vetoed deporting Priestley under the Alien Act, and Rawle was still too enmeshed in Fries Rebellion prosecutions to prosecute Priestley under the Sedition Act.

Meriwether Jones and Writers: The "Jacobin" Richmond *Examiner*

While the prosecution of James Callender, a part-time writer for the Richmond *Examiner*, for his independent writing of a book is the best-known case under the

[306] Friederike Baer-Wallis, Joining the Nation: Germans in the Early American Republic 248–49 (2002) (unpublished Ph.D. dissertation, Brown University); *accord* TYRANNY 152; FRIES'S REBELLION 8.

[307] Jonathan Williams & Robert G. Harper, *To the Editor of the Aurora*, AURORA (Philadelphia), 13 May 1790, at 2.

[308] Timothy Pickering to Charles Hall (1 Aug.1799), PICKERING PAPERS r.11, fol.528, 529. Smith describes consideration of prosecuting Priestley. FREEDOM'S FETTERS 173–74, 310–12.

[309] Timothy Pickering to John Adams (1 Aug.1799), PICKERING PAPERS r.11, fol.524, 524.

[310] Thomas Cooper, Mr. Cooper's Address to the Readers of the Sunbury and Northumberland Gazette ([Andrew Kennedy, Northumberland] 29 June 1799) (broadside).

Sedition Act, the planned prosecution of Meriwether Jones, the editor,[311] has escaped notice. However, Pickering gave instructions to the federal attorney for Virginia, in mid-August 1799, that the *Examiner* "be examined as often as it issues from the press, and whenever it contains any libellous [*sic*] matter against the government or its officers, either originally or by republication, that the Editor or Editors may be prosecuted."[312] As in letters to other federal attorneys sent at the same time, Pickering added that prosecutions should be filed against "authors of libels as well as the editor or editors of the paper," and that when prosecutions were of republished libels he should be notified in order to arrange further prosecution "against the original libeller" as well.[313]

Pickering's assault was assisted by Justice Bushrod Washington. Pickering asked him "who at Richmond would undertake *to see this done*, and who he would recommend *to join you as counsel* in this prosecution," and Washington had given recommendations.[314]

The editor who had attracted Pickering's attention was Meriwether Jones, a Richmond attorney and committed Republican. A month later, Pickering wrote to one of Pennsylvania's senators that the *Examiner* was "edited by a Mr. M. Jones" as a "*Jacobin*" newspaper, the mouthpiece of "the violent party in that state," to "vilify the federal government and probably to destroy it."[315] He condemned Jones for publishing letters from Talleyrand and Pinchon, allegedly received "directly from Paris" by "some of our domestic traitors," and he left no doubt of his loathing of France.[316] Pickering soon repeated his condemnation in a letter to an American ambassador, describing the *Examiner* as "a virulent Jacobin paper," and decrying that "the infamous wretch Callender is the *actual* editor."[317] However, Governor James Monroe had foreseen that "an attempt will be made to carry the sedition law into effect here, as an electioneering trick," and continued to "endeavor to keep them [the editors of two Richmond papers] within suitable limits, in their publications,"[318] apparently by private warnings. For that and other reasons, despite Pickering's instructions and wishes, Meriwether Jones was never indicted,

[311] 2 BRIGHAM 1139; 31 JEFFERSON PAPERS 165n., 290n. Printer John Dixon retired before trouble began, at the end of May 1799. *Id.* Smith cites an earlier letter from Pickering to Thomas Nelson in discussing prosecution of Callender, but not the following letters. FREEDOM'S FETTERS 338 & n.19.

[312] Timothy Pickering to Thomas Nelson (14 Aug.1799), PICKERING PAPERS r.11, fol.611.

[313] *Id.*

[314] *Id.*

[315] Timothy Pickering to William Bingham (20 Sept.1799), PICKERING PAPERS r.12, fol.96.

[316] *Id.* at 96–97.

[317] Timothy Pickering to William Vans Murray (4 Oct.1799), PICKERING PAPERS r.12, fol.141, 142A.

[318] James Monroe to Thomas Jefferson (4 Jan.1800), 31 JEFFERSON PAPERS 289, 290.

even when Justice Chase pressed for Virginia prosecutions under the Sedition Act, though Chase snared Callender in his net.

Governor James Garrard: Unconfirmed Serious Consideration of Prosecution for Supporting the Kentucky Resolutions and Questioning the Sedition Act

Governor James Garrard of Kentucky drew Pickering's notice with his support of the Kentucky Resolutions and his November 1798 speech calling the Sedition Act unconstitutional under "that clause which forbids the enacting of any law abridging the freedom of speech or of the press."[319] Pickering wrote to a High Federalist confidant, Rufus King, that "[i]n Kentucky the Governor has made to the General Assembly a very impudent and inflammatory speech" that Pickering found to "misrepresent . . . the *Alien* and *Sedition* Laws." Fortunately, he added, the people of Kentucky "remain uncontaminated."[320] Garrard was skirting disaster, but no evidence has surfaced of instructions being sent to federal prosecutors for his arrest.

Charles Webber and Benjamin Brown: Unconfirmed Steps Toward Prosecution for Raising a Liberty Pole and Burning the Alien and Sedition Acts

Charles Webber and Benjamin Brown, of Vassalborough, Massachusetts (in the part that later became the state of Maine), led the raising of a liberty pole at Webber's house and the burning of the Alien and Sedition Acts at its base, on the middle day of November 1798, bringing serious consideration of a prosecution that discussions of the Sedition Act have never noted. Mirroring the bitter partisan divisions of the period, Republican newspapers reported that "a large majority of the inhabitants of the south parish" assembled to raise "a liberty pole" and to toast the "glorious tree of liberty,"[321] while Federalist newspapers recounted that the "sedition pole" and burning of the Acts[322] were by "a small number of Jacobins"

[319] *Legislature of Kentucky*, Claypoole's American Daily Advertiser (Philadelphia), 10 Dec.1798, at 2; *Lexington, (Ken.) Nov.7*, Herald of Liberty (Washington), 17 Dec.1798, at 2.

[320] Timothy Pickering to Rufus King (14 Dec.1798), 2 Life and Correspondence of Rufus King 493 (Charles R. King ed., Putnam's Sons, New York 1894–1900); *Legislature of Kentucky*, Claypoole's American Daily Advertiser (Philadelphia), 10 Dec.1798, at 2.

[321] *E.g., Boston, Tuesday, December 6, 1798*, Independent Chronicle (Boston), 3–6 Dec.1798, at 3.

[322] *E.g., Firm Support of the Laws*, Federal Gazette & Baltimore Daily Advertiser, 19 Dec.1798, at 3; *Firm Support of the Laws*, New Hampshire Gazette (Portsmouth), 19 Dec.1798, at 2; *Firm Support of the Laws*, Daily Advertiser (New York), 21 Dec.1798, at 2.

at Webber's house.[323] Soon Federalist reports added that the "ringleaders" were Charles Webber and Benjamin Brown, and that the "arm of government ought to punish these Jacobins immediately."[324] The federal attorney for the district, Daniel Davis,[325] heeded that call and promised if evidence warranted prosecution "to cause the principal offenders to be arrested and bound over for trial"; reportedly "[m]easures for this purpose were taken without delay." When Webber and Brown learned of them, they signed a "Recantation" to "publicly declare our unfeigned sorrow for the part we took in those proceedings" that tended to "bring the authority and laws of the [United States] into contempt," in exchange for Davis consenting to "relinquish the prosecution."[326] Davis was true to his word, as no pleadings appear in surviving records of the federal circuit court.[327]

Dr. John Tyler: Unconfirmed Attempt to Prosecute for Republican Essays

Dr. John Tyler, a physician and surgeon in Frederick (then called Fredericktown), Maryland, and one of the first American surgeons to operate on cataracts,[328] found himself close to danger because of his essays published in the newspapers.[329] An acquaintance in Frederick wrote to James Madison, in June 1800, that "Doctr. John Tyler," a Republican, penned a private letter that Federalists "have published . . . with such comments as their *malice* suggested, and forwareded [*sic*] it to the Genl. Government in hopes to have the Docr[.] prosecuted under the Sedition Law. . . ."[330] That likely was Tyler's letter, finally published four days later in Newark, New Jersey, decrying "Federalists" who were "practising every art and every deception, to mislead the judgment, and impose on the candor of the public" for Adams and against

[323] *E.g., Vassalborough, Nov. 30*, GAZETTE (Portland), 10 Dec.1798, at 3; *Vassalborough, Nov. 30*, MASSACHUSETTS MERCURY (Boston), 11 Dec.1798, at 2; *Vassalborough, Nov. 30*, GAZETTE OF THE UNITED STATES (Philadelphia), 17 Dec.1798, at 2.

[324] *E.g., [No Caption]*, COLUMBIAN CENTINEL (Boston), 5 Dec.1798, at 3; *Boston, December 5*, NEW HAMPSHIRE GAZETTE (Portsmouth), 12 Dec.1798, at 2.

[325] Identified in 4 WASHINGTON PAPERS-PRESIDENTIAL 40 n.2; 17 HAMILTON PAPERS 299 n.6.

[326] *E.g., Vassalborough Jacobin Pole*, IMPARTIAL HERALD (Suffield), 15 Jan.1799, at 3 (recantation dated 6 Dec.1798); *Vassalborough Jacobin Pole*, THOMAS'S MASSACHUSETTS SPY (Worcester), 16 Jan.1799, at 3 (Republican paper reprinting); *Augusta, Maine, Dec. 29*, COLUMBIAN COURIER (New Bedford), 19 Jan.1799, at 4.

[327] Email from Jean Nudd, Archivist, National Archives at Waltham, Mass. (20 Sept.2013).

[328] 17 MADISON PAPERS 396 n.3; 1 J. THOMAS SCHARF, HISTORY OF WESTERN MARYLAND 487 (Regional Publishing, Baltimore 1968); KELLY, *supra* note 267, at 1236; 2 T.C. WILLIAMS, HISTORY OF FREDERICK COUNTY, MARYLAND 1398 (Titsworth, Frederick 1910).

[329] 1 J. THOMAS SCHARF, *supra* note 328, at 535.

[330] Charles P. Polk to James Madison (20 June 1800), 17 MADISON PAPERS 394, 395, which was cited in FREEDOM'S FETTERS 185 n.87.

Jefferson.[331] Tyler's enemies were unsuccessful in prosecuting him, as there is no evidence of an indictment in the circuit court records.[332] They were equally unsuccessful in intimidating him, as he soon stood as a presidential elector for Jefferson,[333] and published at least seven more pre-election essays that declared the Sedition Act unconstitutional, opposed Adams, supported Jefferson, and proclaimed the right to investigate and condemn officials.[334] However, the threat of prosecution was very real, because Justice Chase held circuit court in Baltimore in May 1800,[335] and actively sought indictments of Republican newspapers and writers.

James Bell, the Newburgh Printer, and Tristram Jordan: Not Federal Prosecutions

Smith mentioned the case of James Bell as another arrest and prosecution possibly under the Sedition Act,[336] citing a news report in July 1798 that "Mr. James Bell has been apprehended for uttering treasonable expressions, and held in bail for trial."[337] That was not a Sedition Act prosecution, however, because treason was not an offense under the Act, and because Bell's name does not appear in Pennsylvania circuit court records. Further, Bell's expressions occurred on July 3, eleven days before the Act was effective, as the source report shows.[338]

A Republican newspaper in December 1798 printed a list of thirteen arrests under the Sedition Act, including a "printer in Newburgh." Eight were in the standard list of seventeen prosecutions, two are among this article's additions

[331] John Homespun [John Tyler], *For the Centinel [No. I]*, CENTINEL OF FREEDOM (Newark), 24 June 1800, at 2. Stewart attributes the fifth essay of John Homespun to Tyler. OPPOSITION PRESS 547–48 & 835 n.186. Later essays, cited below, bore composition dates 10–11 days before the publication date.

[332] Criminal Case Files of the U.S. Circuit Court for the District of Maryland, 1795–1860 (National Archives at Washington, R.G.21.22.2, microfilm M1010, roll 1).

[333] *E.g., George-Town, June 24*, CENTINEL OF FREEDOM (Newark), 24 June 1800, at 3; *Alexandria, June 26*, TIMES & DISTRICT OF COLUMBIA DAILY ADVERTISER (Alexandria), 26 June 1800, at 3.

[334] John Homespun [John Tyler], *Homespun No. IV*, CENTINEL OF FREEDOM (Newark), 19 Aug.1800, at 2; John Homespun [John Tyler], *Homespun No. V*, CENTINEL OF FREEDOM (Newark), 26 Aug.1800, at 2; John Homespun [John Tyler], *Homespun No. VI*, CENTINEL OF FREEDOM (Newark), 9 Sept.1800, at 3; John Homespun [John Tyler], *Homespun No. VII*, CENTINEL OF FREEDOM (Newark), 16 Sept.1800, at 2.

[335] 3 DHSC 424 (7–16 May 1800).

[336] FREEDOM'S FETTERS 185 n.87.

[337] *[No Caption]*, INDEPENDENT CHRONICLE (Boston), 26–30 July 1798, at 3.

[338] *Carlisle, July 4*, KLINE'S CARLISLE WEEKLY GAZETTE, 4 July 1798, at 3; *Carlisle, July 4*, CAREY'S UNITED STATES RECORDER (Philadelphia), 14 July 1798, at 1. The story was also reprinted in the *Commercial Advertiser, Maryland Herald, Universal Gazette, Albany Centinel*, Litchfield *Monitor*, and *Columbian Museum*.

(Colie and Judah Spooner), and only one was in error ("it is said" Matthew Lyon's son).[339] That "printer in Newburgh" likely meant the publisher of the *Mirror* in Newburgh, New York, who was Philip Van Horne until a November 1798 transition to Joseph W. Barber.[340] Efforts to locate a case have failed.[341]

Tristram Jordan was brought before the Massachusetts legislature in January 1799 for alleged "seditious expressions."[342] The statements at issue were "that John Adams ought to have lost his head a year ago, that he was the cause of all the depredations on our commerce, that he duped President Washington to sign the cursed British treaty, and then persuaded him to resign that he might get his place."[343] However, no legal prosecution was contemplated; instead the issue was whether the legislature would remove Jordan from his position as a justice of the peace. The next month, the issue was resolved by Jordan "formally and solemnly disavow[ing] all knowledge of ever having spoken" those words, and declaring that they were "opinions upon political subjects, which he never embraced." Upon that recantation, he was not removed.[344] That, of course, was a state legislative matter, not a federal prosecution.

Daniel Dodge and Aaron Pennington of *Centinel of Freedom*: State, Not Federal, Prosecution

The prosecution of Daniel Dodge and Aaron Pennington of the *Centinel of Freedom* in Newark, New Jersey,[345] a vocal Republican newspaper,[346] was cited as a Sedition Act case in Prince's study of Federalist New Jersey.[347] Those editors

[339] *Newark, December 25*, CENTINEL OF FREEDOM (Newark), 25 Dec.1798, at 3.

[340] 1 BRIGHAM 707. The reference is not to the very Republican *Rights of Man*, because it was not started until a year later, in November 1799. *Id.* at 709.

[341] The reference is not to the liberty pole in Newburgh, which hit the news but did not generate a prosecution. *New York*, AURORA (Philadelphia), 25 July 1798, in AMERICAN AURORA, *supra* note 304, at 199; *Newburgh, July 9*, HERALD OF LIBERTY (Washington [Pa.]), 30 July 1798, at 3.

[342] *Active Federalism*, PHILADELPHIA GAZETTE, 30 Jan.1799, at 3; *accord Tuesday, January 31, 1799*, AURORA (Philadelphia), 31 Jan.1799, at 3.

[343] *Boston*, RUSSELL'S GAZETTE (Boston), 24 Jan.1799, at 3; *accord Massachusetts Legislature*, ORACLE OF THE DAY (Portsmouth), 26 Jan.1799, at 3.

[344] *Massachusetts Legislature*, MASSACHUSETTS MERCURY (Boston), 22 Feb.1799, at 2; *accord Massachusetts Legislature*, FEDERAL GAZETTE (Baltimore), 6 Mar.1799, at 2.

[345] 1 BRIGHAM 509.

[346] TYRANNY 408; OPPOSITION PRESS 619.

[347] CARL E. PRINCE, NEW JERSEY'S JEFFERSONIAN REPUBLICANS: THE GENESIS OF AN EARLY PARTY MACHINE, 1789–1817, at 38 (UNCP, Chapel Hill 1967), citing GUARDIAN (New Brunswick), 28 Aug.1798. Three issues of the *Centinel of Freedom* that Prince cites do not describe the case, though one of them describes another case, that of William Durrell of the *Mount Pleasant Register*. *Mount-Pleasant, (N.Y.) July 24*, CENTINEL OF FREEDOM (Newark), 7 Aug.1798, at 3. Prince is followed in Douglas Bradburn, *A Clamor in the Public Mind: Opposition to the Alien and Sedition Acts*, 65 WM. & MARY Q. 565, 575 (2008).

printed a letter to the governor of the state laden with invective such as about his "shower of filthy, bilious, and excrementitious matter,"[348] and then refused the governor's demand that they disclose the anonymous author, which led a state court judge to arrest them and require them to post bond.[349] The editors reported that the grand jury refused to indict them in a state court.[350] Federalist young men were not so forgiving, as they tricked Pennington into a tavern and beat him,[351] nor was the Federalist postmaster, who soon sued the editors for libel.[352] Dodge and Pennington tempted the federal government not to be forgiving either, as the *Centinel* heaped unrelenting criticism on the Sedition Act as unconstitutional.[353]

The editors were then summoned for court. The charge was reprinting remarks by Dr. Rogers from the *Time Piece*[354] (whose editor had been prosecuted for seditious libel beginning with an early July 1798 arrest), who had warned of the "impolicy of being engaged in a war" with France because its revolution had fulfilled "ancient prophecies," or of supporting Britain because of "the punishment which awaits her for the multitude of her crimes."[355] The cumulative effect of "the persecution [and] prosecution" of the editors, and the "declining health of Mr. Aaron Pennington," led them to leave the newspaper and transfer control to successors, in early October 1799.[356]

Prince understood the court to be a federal court. He doubtless relied on newspaper reports of a requirement to post recognizance bonds assuring their appearance before a "Justice of the Supreme Court," and to have consideration of an indictment by a "grand jury of the country," for a charge that was similar to some Sedition Act charges. However, the reference to a "Justice of the Supreme Court" was identified in other newspapers as a justice of the state supreme court, Elisha Boudinot.[357] The prosecutor listed in the original article, William Halsey, was not the federal prosecutor. Most importantly, the case does not appear in the minutes

[348] Militia Man, *To Richard Howell, Governor*, Centinel of Freedom (Newark), 14 Aug.1798, at 2.

[349] *Newark, August 21*, Centinel of Freedom (Newark), 21 Aug.1798, at 2.

[350] *Newark, September 25*, Centinel of Freedom (Newark), 25 Sept.1798, at 3.

[351] *Newark, August 28*, Centinel of Freedom (Newark), 28 Aug.1798, at 3; *Newark, April 16*, Centinel of Freedom (Newark), 16 Apr.1799, at 3.

[352] *Newark, April 16*, Centinel of Freedom (Newark), 16 Apr.1799, at 3; *Newark, January 21*, Centinel of Freedom (Newark), 21 Jan.1800, at 3.

[353] *E.g., Newark, July 17*, Centinel of Freedom (Newark), 17 July 1798, at 2; *accord Newark, September 25*, Centinel of Freedom (Newark), 25 Sept.1798, at 3.

[354] *Newark, August 28*, Centinel of Freedom (Newark), 28 Aug.1798, at 3.

[355] *New-York, July 20*, Centinel of Freedom (Newark), 31 July 1798, at 2.

[356] Jabez Parkhurst & Samuel Pennington, *To the Public*, Centinel of Freedom (Newark), 1 Oct.1799, at 3.

[357] *Memorandum*, Commercial Advertiser (New York), 22 Aug.1798, at 3; *Memorandum*, Saratoga Register (Ballston Spa), 5 Sept.1798, at 2.

or surviving records of the federal circuit court for New Jersey. Blumberg appears to be correct in concluding that any actual case was "most likely brought under New Jersey criminal common law."[358]

Conclusion

These additional prosecutions more than double the number of confirmed prosecutions under the Sedition Act, from the recognized prosecutions of fourteen individuals (plus federal common law libel prosecutions of three more) to added prosecution in eleven additional cases of seventeen more individuals plus prosecutions in eleven conspiracy cases of eighty-three individuals. These numbers exclude the three attempted indictments that grand juries refused, and the six instructions to prosecute that, for one reason or another, did not result in indictments. The additional prosecutions show a commensurate increase in the actual scope of the Federalist administration's efforts to suppress dissent, and of the suffering inflicted on citizens for exercising their First Amendment freedoms.

The additional prosecutions show an even broader administration attack against Republican newspapers than the standard seventeen prosecutions show (of which eleven were against newspapers and one was against a newspaper writer's book). Added are prosecutions of Judah P. Spooner who printed Matthew Lyon's *Scourge of Aristocracy* (for a "seditious" pamphlet), Alden Spooner of *Spooner's Vermont Journal*, Benjamin Mayer and Conrad Fahnestock of *Harrisburgh Morgenröthe* (the "Dutch *Aurora*"), and Matthew Lyon in an unrecognized second prosecution (for a "seditious" letter disparaging his trial); as well as attempted indictments of John Israel of *Herald of Liberty*, Alexander Martin of Baltimore's *American*, and James J. Wilson of Wilmington's *Mirror of the Times* (and possibly Dr. John Vaughan, too); and instructions to prosecute Jacob Schneider of the *Readinger Adler*, and Meriwether Jones and one or more authors of the *Richmond Examiner*. Most of those prosecutions of opposition newspaper editors and publishers involved an unexpected arrest that could prevent publication for months, and an unhealthful jail that could bring illness or death, necessitating a strong measure of courage to run a Republican newspaper.

Some things remained the same. The canon of seventeen prosecutions were all against Republicans, and the additional ones were as well, maintaining the strictly partisan use of the Sedition Act. Those recognized cases included not just seditious publications but seditious words (such as Matthew Lyon for reading the

[358] REPRESSIVE JURISPRUDENCE 139.

Barlow letter in a speech, Brown, the "apostle of sedition" for his declamations, and Baldwin and Clark for wishing that celebratory cannon fire had hit the president's posterior), and the additional cases did as well (Colie, Greenawalt, Herring, and Eyerman). Newspaper reports continued to be remarkably accurate, being corroborated by court files, other than the very few reports that James Lyon and perhaps a Newburgh printer were prosecuted.

The Supreme Court justices who actually presided over Sedition Act proceedings, other than brief arraignments, increase from the three who have long been identified as doing so (Justices William Paterson, Bushrod Washington, and Samuel Chase) to two others (Justices James Iredell and William Cushing). Iredell presided over Greenawalt's guilty plea and apparently his sentence, Llewellyn et al.'s indictment, Herring's indictment, and substantial parts of nine of the Sedition Act conspiracy cases. Cushing presided over Colie's indictment and plea, Lyon's second information or indictment, and Shaw's indictment. As the additional cases are considered, Justice Alfred Moore continues to have steered clear of any involvement in Sedition Act prosecutions.

The number of Sedition Act cases presided over by Paterson, Washington, and Chase also is increased. (The following totals exclude the Duane cases, because they involve multiple justices at various stages, since Pickering gave instructions to indict him each time the *Aurora* printed a seditious libel.[359]) Paterson's five cases are increased by the Judah P. Spooner indictment, the Alden Spooner indictment, and the Dr. Samuel Shaw trial. Washington's three cases are expanded by the Morris Llewellyn et al. reindictment, the Jacob Eyerman indictment and trial, and the Benjamin Mayer and Conrad Fahnstock indictment and trial. Chase's four cases are increased by another Llewellyn reindictment, the Eyerman reindictment and trial, and involvement in eight of the Sedition Act conspiracy cases, as well as the attempted indictment of John Israel along with those of Alexander Martin and James J. Wilson, and possibly of Dr. John Vaughan and Dr. John Tyler.

Each of the justices passing sentence on Sedition Act cases in connection with Fries Rebellion showed his comparative animosity toward writing, printing, uttering, or publishing against the government (Section 2) compared with nonverbal opposition to the government (Section 1), by how frequently the maximum or minimum fine or prison sentence was imposed. Many Section 2 sentences reached or approached the maximum of a $2,000 fine and two-year imprisonment, while no Section 1 sentence came anywhere near the maximum sentence of a $5,000 fine and five-year imprisonment (the longest was $1,000 and two years[360]).

[359] Timothy Pickering to William Rawle (20 Sept.1799), PICKERING PAPERS r.12, fol.82.
[360] Minutes 327–28 (18 May 1799), 380–91 (1–2 May 1800); HENDERSON 318.

The assault on the First Amendment by the Sedition Act restrictions and prosecutions was even more serious than has been realized before. In that context, the Republican outrage and eruption of First Amendment theory, the public concern and shift to the Republican party, the Jeffersonian revolution of 1800, and the rapid demise of the Federalist Party, become more intelligible.

Appendix to Chapter 7

Additional References to These Unrecognized Sedition Act Cases

Lespenard Colie

No additional articles

Judah P. Spooner

Arrest—*Portsmouth*, FEDERAL OBSERVER (Portsmouth), 17 Oct. 1799, at 3

[No Caption], NEWBURYPORT HERALD, 18 Oct. 1799, at 3

Bennington, October 15, SPRINGER'S WEEKLY ORACLE (New London), 21 Oct. 1799, at 3

Domestic, EASTERN HERALD & GAZETTE OF MAINE (Portland), 21 Oct. 1799, at 2

Massachu., COLUMBIAN COURIER (New Bedford), 23 Oct. 1799, at 3

Boston, Oct. 21, NEW HAMPSHIRE GAZETTE (Portsmouth), 23 Oct. 1799, at 3

Morris-Town, GENIUS OF LIBERTY (Morristown), 24 Oct. 1799, at 3

Indictment—*From Greenfield, Oct. 20*, AMHERST VILLAGE MESSENGER, 3 Nov. 1799, at 3

The Spooner indictment is also referred to in all articles about the second Lyon indictment (except the *Massachusetts Spy* and *Constitutional Telegraph), infra.*

Dismissal—*From a Late Lansingburgh Paper*, IMPARTIAL JOURNAL (Stonington), 12 Nov. 1799, at 3

New London, (Bee) Oct. 1, TIMES & DISTRICT OF COLUMBIA DAILY ADVERTISER, 13 Oct. 1800, at 2

Worcester, November 6, MASSACHUSETTS SPY (Worcester), 6 Nov. 1799, at 3

AURORA (Philadelphia), 16 Oct. 1800, in AMERICAN AURORA, *supra* note 304, at 869

The Spooner dismissal is also referred to in all articles about the Samuel Shaw indictment (except *Gazette of the United States*, which refers to Spooner's indictment), *infra*.

Alden Spooner

No additional articles found

Rev. John C. Ogden

Federalist newspapers reporting that Ogden was returning from delivering Lyon's petition—

Hartford, February 18, ALBANY CENTINEL, 22 Feb. 1799, at 2

Hartford, Feb. 18, DAILY ADVERTISER (New York), 22 Feb. 1799, at 2

Hartford, Feb. 18, WEEKLY ORACLE (New London), 25 Feb. 1799, at 1

Hartford, Feb. 18, POLITICAL REPOSITORY (Brookfield), 26 Feb. 1799, at 3

Hartford, Feb. 18, OTSEGO HERALD (Cooperstown), 7 Mar. 1799, at 2

Domestic, VERGENNES GAZETTE, 7 Mar. 1799, at 3.

Other—*Tuesday, February 19, 1799*, AURORA (Philadelphia), 19 Feb. 1799, at 3

Wednesday, February 27, NEW YORK JOURNAL & PATRIOTIC REGISTER, 27 Feb. 1799, at 3

Hartford, July 29, CONNECTICUT COURANT (Hartford), 29 July 1799, at 3

For the Monitor, THE MONITOR (Litchfield), 31 July 1799, at 2

New-London, August 12, SPRINGER'S WEEKLY ORACLE (New London), 12 Aug. 1799, at 3

Jacob Greenawalt

Sheriff's Sale, ORACLE OF DAUPHIN, 23 Jan. 1799, at 3 (possibly same person)

Militia Elections, ORACLE OF DAUPHIN, 14 July 1800, at 3 (possibly same person)

Morris Llewellyn et al.

Indictment for "seditious combinations, & c."—

Tuesday Evening, April 23, GAZETTE OF THE UNITED STATES (Philadelphia), 23 Apr. 1799, at 3

Philadelphia, April 23, COMMERCIAL ADVERTISER (New York), 24 Apr. 1799, at 3

Thursday, April 25, 1799, AURORA (Philadelphia), 25 Apr. 1799, at 3

Thursday, April 25, 1799, UNIVERSAL GAZETTE (Philadelphia), 25 Apr. 1799, at 3

[No Caption], NEW YORK GAZETTE & GENERAL ADVERTISER, 25 Apr. 1799, at 3

Philadelphia, April 24, DAILY ADVERTISER (New York), 26 Apr. 1799, at 2

Philadelphia, Apr. 18, THE TIMES AND DISTRICT OF COLUMBIA DAILY ADVERTISER (Alexandria), 27 Apr. 1799, at 3

April 24, JOURNAL OF THE TIMES (Stonington), 30 Apr. 1799, at 3

Philadelphia, April 23, MASSACHUSETTS MERCURY (Boston), 30 Apr. 1799, at 2

Tuesday, April 30, 1799, IMPARTIAL HERALD (Suffield), 30 Apr. 1799, at 3

Philadelphia, April 26, CARLISLE GAZETTE, 1 May 1799, at 3

April 19, UNITED STATES CHRONICLE (Providence), 2 May 1799, at 2

Philadelphia, April 20, NORWICH PACKET, 2 May 1799, at 3

Philadelphia, April 23, FEDERAL OBSERVER (Portsmouth), 2 May 1799, at 3

Insurrection, COURIER OF NEW HAMPSHIRE (Concord), 4 May 1799, at 3

Philadelphia, April 23, NEW HAMPSHIRE GAZETTE (Portsmouth), 7 May 1799, at 2

From Philadelphia, April 24, THE SUN (Dover), 8 May 1799, at 3

Insurrection, HERALD OF LIBERTY (Washington [Pa.]), 13 May 1799, at 2

Philadelphia, April 30, SPOONER'S VERMONT JOURNAL (Windsor), 14 May 1799, at 3

Philadelphia, April 24, GEORGETOWN GAZETTE (Georgetown [S.C.]), 15 May 1799, at 3

Philadelphia, May 3, COLUMBIAN MUSEUM (Savannah), 17 May 1799, at 2

(Other articles mentioned the case without identifying it as involving seditious combinations.)

Langford Herring

Thursday, December 13, 1798, UNIVERSAL GAZETTE (Philadelphia), 13 Dec. 1798, at 3

Alexandria, December 18, ALEXANDRIA TIMES, 18 Dec. 1798, at 2

December 10, ALBANY CENTINEL, 18 Dec. 1798, at 3

Thursday, December 20, 1798, GENIUS OF LIBERTY (Morristown), 20 Dec. 1798, at 3

Philadelphia, Dec. 10, IMPARTIAL HERALD (Suffield), 25 Dec. 1798, at 3

Dec. 11, BEE (New London), 26 Dec. 1798, at 4

Philadelphia, Dec. 13, HAMPSHIRE GAZETTE (Northampton), 26 Dec. 1798, at 2

Rev. Jacob Eyerman

Psarer Eyerman, HARRISBURG MORGENROTHE, 15 Oct. 1799, at 2 (aufruhr, or sedition)

Numerous other articles mentioned the Eyerman case as involving "misdemeanors only," but did not mention sedition

Benjamin Mayer & Conrad Fahnestock

Arrest—*Elizabeth-Town, September 12*, MARYLAND HERALD (Elizabethtown), 12 Sept. 1799, at 3

Harrisburg, August 20, COLUMBIAN MIRROR & ALEXANDRIA GAZETTE, 12 Sept. 1799, at 2

For the Herald of Liberty, HERALD OF LIBERTY (Washington [Pa.]), 16 Sept. 1799, at 3

Harrisburgh, August 28, STEWART'S KENTUCKY HERALD (Lexington), 24 Sept. 1799, at 3

Philadelphia, September 7, GEORGETOWN GAZETTE (Georgetown [S.C.]), 9 Oct. 1799, at 3

Matthew Lyon (Second Prosecution)

Reindictment—*Worcester, October 16*, MASSACHUSETTS SPY (Worcester), 16 Oct. 1799, at 3

New-York, COMMERCIAL ADVERTISER (New York), 16 Oct. 1799, at 3

Wednesday, October 16, MERCANTILE ADVERTISER (New York), 16 Oct. 1799, at 3

Matthew Lyon, PHILADELPHIA GAZETTE, 17 Oct. 1799, at 3

New-York, SPECTATOR (New York), 19 Oct. 1799, at 1

Saturday, October 19, FEDERAL GAZETTE (Baltimore), 19 Oct. 1799, at 3

Providence, October 19, PROVIDENCE GAZETTE, 19 Oct. 1799, at 3

Matthew Lyon, DAILY ADVERTISER (New York), 21 Oct. 1799, at 2

Troy (New York), NEWPORT MERCURY, 22 Oct. 1799, at 3

Alexandria, October 22, COLUMBIAN MIRROR & ALEXANDRIA GAZETTE, 22 Oct. 1799, at 3

George-Town, October 22, CENTINEL OF FREEDOM (Newark), 22 Oct. 1799, at 3

Poughkeepsie, Oct. 15, MONITOR (Litchfield), 23 Oct. 1799, at 3

Troy, Oct. 9, COURIER (Norwich), 23 Oct. 1799, at 3

Norwich, October 24, NORWICH PACKET, 24 Oct. 1799, at 3

Cooperstown, OTSEGO HERALD (Cooperstown), 24 Oct. 1799, at 1

Aurora (Philadelphia), 24 Oct. 1799, in AMERICAN AURORA, *supra* note 304, at 708

Troy, October 9, UNITED STATES CHRONICLE (Providence), 24 Oct. 1799, at 2

Middletown, MIDDLESEX GAZETTE (Middletown), 25 Oct. 1799, at 2

Troy, Oct. 9, NEW-HAMPSHIRE SENTINEL (Keene), 26 Oct. 1799, at 2

Troy, Oct. 9, AMHERST VILLAGE MESSENGER, 26 Oct. 1799, at 3

Windham, October 31, WINDHAM HERALD, 31 Oct. 1799, at 3

Petersburg, October 25, GEORGETOWN GAZETTE (Georgetown [S.C.]), 6 Nov. 1799, at 3

Worcester, November 6, MASSACHUSETTS SPY (Worcester), 6 Nov. 1799, at 3

From a Late Lansingburgh Paper, IMPARTIAL JOURNAL (Stonington), 12 Nov. 1799, at 3

Baltimore, Nov. 4, CONSTITUTIONAL TELEGRAPH (Boston), 23 Nov. 1799, at 4

The second Lyon prosecution is also referred to in all articles about the arrest of Judah P. Spooner, *supra* (saying court officers were seeking Lyon), and about the indictment of Samuel Shaw, *infra* (saying Lyon was reindicted but not arrested).

Dr. Samuel Shaw

Indictment—*Thursday, 24 October 1799*, PHILADELPHIA GAZETTE, 24 Oct. 1799, at 3

Wednesday, October 23, MERCANTILE ADVERTISER (New York), 23 Oct. 1799, at 2

Tuesday Morning, October 24, GAZETTE OF THE UNITED STATES (Philadelphia), 24 Oct. 1799, at 3

Thursday, 24 October 1799, PHILADELPHIA GAZETTE, 24 Oct. 1799, at 3

Aurora (Philadelphia), 24 Oct. 1799, in AMERICAN AURORA, *supra* note 304, at 708

Philadelphia, October 25, CLAYPOOLE'S AMERICAN DAILY ADVERTISER (Philadelphia), 25 Oct. 1799, at 3

New-York: Wednesday, October 23, 1799, SPECTATOR (New York), 26 Oct. 1799, at 2

Alexandria, October 29, TIMES & DISTRICT OF COLUMBIA DAILY ADVERTISER (Alexandria), 29 Oct. 1799, at 3

New-York, Oct. 24, NEWPORT MERCURY, 29 Oct.1799, at 3

New-York, October 29, CENTINEL OF LIBERTY (Georgetown [D.C.]), 29 Oct. 1799, at 2

Troy, October 16, HAMPSHIRE GAZETTE (Northampton), 30 Oct. 1799, at 3

New-York, Oct. 22, CONNECTICUT JOURNAL (New Haven), 31 Oct. 1799, at 1

Middletown, MIDDLESEX GAZETTE (Middletown), 1 Nov. 1799, at 2, 3

Friday, November 1, VIRGINIA ARGUS (Richmond), 1 Nov. 1799, at 3

Domestic Occurrences, POLITICAL REPOSITORY (Brookfield), 5 Nov.1799, at 3

Troy, Oct. 16, NEWBURYPORT HERALD, 5 Nov. 1799, at 2

November 6, 1799, COURIER (Norwich), 6 Nov. 1799, at 3

Extract of a Letter from a Gentleman in Rutland, GAZETTE OF THE UNITED STATES (Philadelphia), 6 Nov. 1799, at 3

Troy, October 16, OTSEGO HERALD (Cooperstown), 7 Nov. 1799, at 2

Thursday, November 7, FEDERAL OBSERVER (Portsmouth), 7 Nov. 1799, at 3

[No Caption], ORACLE OF DAUPHIN (Harrisburg), 11 Nov. 1799, at 1

Troy (N.Y.), COURIER OF NEW HAMPSHIRE (Concord), 16 Nov. 1799, at 1

8

The Sedition Act and the Assault on Freedoms of Press and Speech: The Remaining Supreme Court Justices on the Sedition Act

The citizen under a free government has a right to think, to speak, to write, to print, and to publish freely, but with decency and truth, concerning publick men, publick bodies, and publick measures.

. . . .

Reputation, except that of official characters, seems not, of late times, any more than personal liberty, to have attracted the distinguished regard of our publick law: and even when it deigns a little degree of regard to it, that regard flows from a wrong principle, and is referred to a wrong end. Libels are considered as objects of publick cognizance, not because the character, but because the tranquillity of the citizens[,] is precious to the publick; and therefore, crimes of this nature are classed and prosecuted and punished as breaches of the peace . . . .

A libel may be described–a malicious defamation of any person. . . .

. . . . An unwarrantable attempt made in the star chamber, during the reign of James the first, to wrest the law of libels to the purposes of ministers, and an effort continued ever since to carry that attempt into execution, and even to go beyond some of its worst principles, have, in England, lost to the community the benefits of that law, wise and salutary when administered properly, and by the proper persons. The decision in that case [*Case de Libellis Famosis*] has ever since been considered, in England, as the foundation of the law on this subject. It will be proper, therefore, to examine the parts of that decision with some degree of minuteness.

. . . .

The first resolution is, that a libel against a magistrate, or other publick person, is a greater offence than one against a private man. This, in the unqualified manner here expressed, cannot be rationally admitted. . . .

Another and a more important resolution in that case is–that it is immaterial whether the libel be false or true. This resolution is clearly extra-judicial . . . .

—Supreme Court Justice James Wilson[1]

Did the passage of a mere nine years between the First Amendment and the Sedition Act establish the meaning of the First Amendment by that Act? In other words, did the Sedition Act show that "no law... abridging the freedom of speech, or of the press" was only a narrow prohibition of prior restraints on expression (such as licensing requirements), and not a prohibition against subsequent restraints as well (such as seditious libel prosecutions for criticizing government)? Did that show that the First Amendment provided no meaningful protection of a right of citizens to speak critically of the President, Congress, and other officials, and that Congress could make that sort of criticism a crime? Or was Justice James Wilson right, that the only legitimate libel law was against defamation of character, and that seditious libel law illegitimately "wrest[ed] the law of libels to the purposes of ministers," and that it could not limit the First Amendment right "to speak, to write, to print"?

David Anderson gave an insightful answer:

> the Federalists who passed the Sedition Act in 1798 were a very different group from those who wrote the Constitution and the First Amendment. The men who pushed the Sedition Act through Congress—Harper, Lloyd, Otis, and Allen—were not Framers at all. They were political partisans, none of whom had been members of either the First Congress or the Convention of 1787.[2]

His point about sponsors also turns out to be true of most supporters of the Sedition Act,[3] as congressional records confirm.[4] Only 5 of the 18 senators, and only 3 of the 44 representatives, who voted for the Sedition Act in the Fifth Congress were members of the First Congress, which framed the First Amendment. Moreover, 2 of the 6 senators, and 4 of the 41 representatives, who voted *against* that Act were also members of that Congress that framed the First Amendment.[5] Thus, of those veteran lawmakers, a majority of the senators voted for the Sedition Act, but a majority of the representatives voted *against* the Act. Of those who were also at the Constitutional Convention, only one supported the Sedition Act, and

[1] James Wilson, *Lectures on Law* (1790–1791), 1 COLLECTED WORKS OF JAMES WILSON 427 (Kermit L. Hall & Mark D. Hall eds., LF, Indianapolis 2006), 2 *id.* 1046, 1133–35.

[2] ANDERSON 519 (footnotes omitted). A list of abbreviated titles is at the end of this book.

[3] *Id.* 517.

[4] Based on comparing votes for the Sedition Act, 7 ANNALS 599, 8 *id.* 2171, 9 *id.* 2985, 10 *id.* 423, with membership of the Fifth Congress, ORIGINS-PARTIES 207–09, 217–18, and of the First Congress, 1 DHFFC xxiii–iv, 3 *id.* xxvii–viii.

[5] *Cf.* 7 ANNALS 599 *with* ORIGINS-PARTIES 207–09 *and* 1 DHFFC xxiii–iv (for—Sens. Goodhue, Sedgwick, Livermore, Laurance, Foster; against—Brown, Langdon); *cf.* 8 ANNALS 2171 *with* ORIGINS-PARTIES 217–18 *and* 3 DHFFC xxvii–viii (for—Reps. Thacher, Sinnickson, Hartley; against—Baldwin, Hiester, W. Smith, Sumter); *accord* ANDERSON 517 n.349 (which omits Hiester and W. Smith).

two opposed it.[6] However, the fact that Congress in 1798, or even the veteran members that year, gave majority support to the Sedition Act cannot determine or even indicate that it was constitutional under the First Amendment, or what the meaning of the First Amendment was when written nine years earlier, because partisan battles intervened, war panic prevailed, and nonconstitutional objectives dominated as the Sedition Act was adopted.

The fact that Congress divided over the Sedition Act, and that members' beliefs changed about press and speech as political parties emerged and partisan debates occurred, raises two interesting questions. Could the Supreme Court have had similar divisions over the Sedition Act, and similar changes of some justices' beliefs about freedoms of press and speech? To say it differently, if Congress split, could the early justices also have split over the Sedition Act? Any division of early Supreme Court justices, all of whom were Federalists, was not a Federalist-Republican division but a Federalist Party division. If any Federalists divided over the Sedition Act, could the Federalist Party have undergone a significant division over the Act? If so, conventional views of the early Supreme Court and the Federalist Party would be turned upside down on freedoms of press and speech.

Those conventional views are that the Federalist Party unanimously supported the Sedition Act (with one lone exception, and then not on constitutional grounds),[7] and that the Federalist judiciary as part of that Federalist Party unanimously supported the constitutionality of the Act as well.[8] No further information is given about the individual remaining justices' positions on the Sedition Act in their biographies[9] or in Supreme Court

[6] Martin, Baldwin, and Langdon. ANDERSON 517 n.349. Also, another Convention participant, Richard Spaight, did not participate in the initial vote on the Sedition Act, but later voted for its repeal. 11 ANNALS 976, 1038

[7] Typical sources making this claim are cited in notes 24–26 *infra*.

[8] Typical sources making this claim are cited in notes 27–31 *infra*.

[9] *E.g.*, JOHN JAY 416–18; RUTLEDGE 259–78; WILSON 30–31; JOHNSON 492–510; John D. Cushing, A Revolutionary Conservative: The Public Life of William Cushing, 1732–1810, at 328 (1959) (unpublished Ph.D. dissertation, Clark University) (only 6 word mention of Act; "there is nothing to indicate what, if anything, Cushing contributed . . . as a circuit judge," and "little of significance" in Supreme Court sessions; only seven pages describe his Supreme Court years).

The same is true of biographical articles. *E.g.*, Aaron T. Knapp, *Law's Revolutionary: James Wilson and the Birth of American Independence*, 29 J. LAW & POLITICS 189 (2013); Richard D. Burns & Richard D. Yerby, *John Jay: Political Jurist*, 13 J. PUB. L. 222 (1964); T. Scott Offutt, *Thomas Johnson and Constitutional Government*, 13 CONST. REV. 204 (1929); Randolph C. Adams, *The Legal Theories of James Wilson*, 68 U. PA. L. REV. 337 (1919–20); Lucien H. Alexander, *James Wilson—Nation Builder*, 19 GREEN BAG 98, 137, 265, 272–74 (1907); James B. Scott, *John Jay*, 6 COLUM. L. REV. 289, 321–23 (1906); Henry Flanders, *Chief Justice Rutledge*, 54 AM. L. REG. 203, 213 (1906); James O. Pierce, *James Wilson as a Jurist*, 38 AM. L. REV. 44 (1904); Francis R. Jones, *John Jay*, 13 GREEN BAG 1 (1901); Junius Davis, *Alfred Moore*, 12 GREEN BAG 325, 329 (1900); L.B. Proctor, *John Jay and Other Chief Justices of the Supreme Court of the United States*, 5 MICH. L. REV. 153 (1898); *John Rutledge*, 1 CHI. L. TIMES 305 (1887); *John Jay*, 1 CHI. L. TIMES 215 (1887).

histories,[10] except occasional erroneous assertions that two sitting justices did not support the Act[11] and that two remaining justices supported it or seditious libel prosecutions.[12]

This chapter challenges those conventional views by showing that the Federalist Party did not uniformly support the Sedition Act, and also by showing that the early justices did not either. Instead, there was extensive but unnoticed Federalist opposition to the Sedition Act beyond John Marshall's "unique" nonconstitutional opposition, including some committed Federalists and many transitional Federalists who were provoked into party change. Further, in contrast to most of the sitting justices who supported the Act's constitutionality and adopted the Blackstone-Mansfield definition of freedom of press in 1798 or 1799, most of the remaining justices apparently opposed the Sedition Act[13] and never embraced that definition.[14]

[10] 1 WARREN 191; 1 HISTORY OF SUPREME COURT 637, 645, 656; 1 HENRY FLANDERS, THE LIVES AND TIMES OF THE CHIEF JUSTICES OF THE SUPREME COURT OF THE UNITED STATES (Lippincott, Philadelphia 1859) (vol.1 on Jay and Rutledge); William G. Simms, *A Sketch of the Life and Public Services of John Rutledge of South Carolina, with Extracts from His Unpublished Correspondence*, 6 AMERICAN REVIEW 125, 277 (1847); like JUSTICES and OCSC.

[11] *E.g.*, WILLIAM G. BROWN, THE LIFE OF OLIVER ELLSWORTH 265–66 (Macmillan, New York 1905) (denying supported constitutionality); Leonard B. Rosenberg, *William Paterson: New Jersey's Nation-Maker*, 85 N.J. HISTORY 7, 32 (1967) ("never challenged the constitutionality").

[12] *E.g.*, CHARLES SLACK, LIBERTY'S FIRST CRISIS: ADAMS, JEFFERSON, AND THE MISFITS WHO SAVED FREE SPEECH 267–68 (Atlantic Monthly Press, New York 2015) (Jay "helped lay the intellectual foundation for the Sedition Act," misinterpreting 1788 pamphlet); DEALVA S. ALEXANDER, POLITICAL HISTORY OF THE STATE OF NEW YORK 85, 92 (Friedman, Port Washington 1969) (Jay supported Sedition Act, no citation); MORTON BORDEN, THE FEDERALISM OF JAMES A. BAYARD 38 (ColumUP, New York 1955) (same); David Jenkins, *The Sedition Act of 1798 and the Incorporation of Seditious Libel into First Amendment Jurisprudence*, 45 AM. J. LEGAL HIST. 154, 168–69 (2001) (Wilson, overlooking later position in law lectures while on Supreme Court); ANDERSON 504–05 n.285 (same); LEVY-LIBERTY 29 & n.30 (same); LEONARD W. LEVY, LEGACY OF SUPPRESSION 201 (BP-HUP, Cambridge 1960) (same).

[13] This chapter's facts about the remaining justices generally are not found elsewhere, such as Jay's departures from Federalist orthodoxy, his Republican family, his nonenforcement of the Sedition Act, and his footdragging on the Virginia and Kentucky Resolutions; the Rutledge-Pinckney bloc's disavowal of the Sedition Act, Rutledge's other heterodoxies in Federalist eyes, and his failed confirmation amounting to expulsion from the Federalist party; and Wilson's final position on freedoms of press and speech and its implications for seditious libel, his rejection of most Blackstonian thought about rights and government including seditious libel, his numerous departures from Federalist orthodoxy, and his close friends' rejection of the Sedition Act. Other examples are Johnson's recommendation by Jefferson for cabinet positions in the early 1790s, and his frequent avoidance of identification as a Federalist and his disclaimer of being the instrument of any party in the late 1790s; and Moore's refusal to charge grand juries on the Sedition Act in contrast to all other sitting justices, and his friends' belief that he would emerge "like purged gold" from the crucible of Sedition Act controversy in contrast to Chase and his "indefensible" jury charges.

[14] Their nonembrace of the Blackstone-Mansfield definition was discussed in the sections of Chapters 4 and 5 dealing with Jay, Rutledge, Wilson, Johnson, and Moore, as well as Cushing.

This means that the initial justices and the successor justices not only divided, but divided disproportionately. The sitting justices in 1798–1799 included only two initial justices (and Iredell died in late 1799, while Cushing was as good as dead in terms of independent thought), and four successor justices (Paterson, Chase, Ellsworth, and Washington). The remaining justices besides them were four retired initial justices (Jay, Rutledge, Wilson, and Blair) and two successor justices (Johnson, already off the Court, and Moore, not yet on it).

The commonly noted difference between the sitting justices and the retired justices is their relative stature. The justices who were off the bench by September 1798 were "first characters" in the nation (including Johnson), as Washington described them when selecting them,[15] while the sitting justices were what could be called "second characters" (including one initial justice who remained past 1798, Iredell). A New Hampshire Federalist leader observed that "many of the officers who were first appointed . . . were men of superior talents to those of their successors," speaking of Jay and Blair compared with Cushing and Chase, as well as the initial and later cabinet.[16] With that difference in stature came a difference in independence, in willingness to differ with the Federalist Party, and in ability to see outside a Federalist box. The same was true of the executive branch. The initial cabinet was selected by Washington from "first characters" in the new nation,[17] while among the successors by 1798 "none were 'first characters'" in reputation[18] (and in fact, Pickering was Washington's seventh choice,[19] and Wolcott was his fourth choice, while McHenry was Adams's fourth choice[20]). The initial cabinet members such as Hamilton and Jefferson were independent-minded and diverged sharply on great policy issues, while the dominant three cabinet members during 1798–1800 were High Federalists secretly in league with Hamilton[21] and insistent on conforming beliefs by others.

There is another major, but unrecognized, contrast between sitting justices (except Moore) and initial justices who had left the bench (and Johnson). Those sitting justices went out of their way to support the Sedition Act, defend its constitutionality, stress it in grand jury charges, urge indictments under it, and preside over prosecutions, as we saw in the preceding two chapters. Meanwhile, Jay, Rutledge, and Wilson, like Johnson and Moore, went out of their way to avoid supporting the Act in any way, despite ample opportunity, and despite the Sedition Act being a defining issue of the Federalist Party during 1798–1801. In stark

[15] George Washington to James Madison (23 Sept.1789), 4 Washington Papers-Presidential 67; *accord* 1 DHSC 20, 29, 35, 51, 58, 66; 1 Warren 30–46.

[16] William Plumer to Jeremiah Smith (19 Feb.1796), 1 DHSC 838, 839.

[17] Federalism 627.

[18] *Id.* 631.

[19] 1 Warren 142; Federalism 625; Empire 234.

[20] Federalism 630.

[21] *Id.* 583, 631, 622; Adams Federalists 174.

contrast to the sitting justices, those five justices left no correspondence and no newspaper articles even intimating support of the Act, and instead left a number of largely unnoticed indications of their opposition. To say five early justices probably opposed the Sedition Act is not to say that they repudiated the Federalist Party; John Marshall also opposed the Act on practical grounds while remaining a leading Federalist, though some Federalists did leave the party, in part or whole, over the Sedition Act. However, it is to say that they, like Marshall, were Adams Federalists,[22] in contrast to some of the sitting justices who were High Federalists, such as Paterson and Ellsworth[23]; and that Jay, Rutledge, Wilson, Johnson, and Moore were committed to freedoms of press and speech.

On their road to those positions, the justices finding the Sedition Act consistent with freedoms of press and speech also adopted the Blackstone-Mansfield definition and their framework for seditious libel, while the remaining justices did not. The late adoption by the first group, and the nonadoption by the remaining justices, would be surprising if the Blackstone-Mansfield approach accurately summarized long-standing English common law. However, that late adoption and nonadoption are not at all surprising in the context of the Blackstone-Mansfield definition being no summary at all of ancient common law but only a recent addition to the English common law a year after Blackstone published his summary, when Mansfield inserted it into common law in 1770 (as Chapter 2 discussed). Blackstone's and Mansfield's actions left in their wake great controversy rather than unanimity.

The Overlooked Existence of Federalist Opposition to the Sedition Act

The conventional wisdom is that "not a single Federalist questioned the constitutionality of the Sedition Law," and that "every Federalist favored its subsequent enforcement," except Marshall.[24] That concept has not been challenged except in

[22] As documented below, and as inferred for Moore from Adams' nomination of him.

[23] 1 DHSC 911, 909, 912 (Ellsworth), 902, 923, 928 (Paterson); John Marshall to Joseph Story (25 July 1827), 11 MARSHALL PAPERS 35, 46 (Paterson); Stephen Higginson to Timothy Pickering (12 Jan. 1800), 1 HIGGINSON LETTERS 833, 835 & n.2 (Ellsworth).

[24] FREEDOM'S FETTERS 155; *accord* REPRESSIVE JURISPRUDENCE 92–99; PETER CHARLES HOFFER, THE FREE PRESS CRISIS OF 1800, at 51 (UPKan, Lawrence 2011); PERILOUS TIMES 36, 39, 43; ANDERSON 517; BUSHROD WASHINGTON 88; DONALD H. STEWART, THE OPPOSITION PRESS OF THE FEDERALIST PERIOD 470 (SUNYP, Albany 1969); IRVING BRANT, THE BILL OF RIGHTS 259 (Bobbs-Merrill, Indianapolis 1965); 3 JEFFERSON 389; JOHN C. MILLER, THE FEDERALIST ERA, 1789–1801, at 232–33, 240, 241 (Harper, New York 1960); NOBLE E. CUNNINGHAM, THE JEFFERSONIAN REPUBLICANS 126 (UNCP, Chapel Hill 1957); ADAMS FEDERALISTS 163; CRISIS 182, 22; Stephen B. Presser & Becky B. Hurley, *Saving God's Republic: The Jurisprudence of Samuel Chase*, 1984 U. ILL. L. REV. 771, 778. The converse is also common, that the Sedition Act was "unanimously opposed by the other party." *Id.* 126; *accord* LEVY 280.

an unnoticed article noting a few Federalist opponents.[25] Statements such as Levy's, that "[n]ot a single Federalist in the United States opposed the constitutionality of the Sedition Act,"[26] unavoidably include Federalist Supreme Court justices, both retired and active.[27] The standard portrait of the early justices is that because they were all Federalists, they must all have agreed with the sitting justices of 1798–1801 in supporting the constitutionality of the Sedition Act and in countenancing restriction of press and speech.[28] That portrait aggregates the early justices as a faceless Federalist judiciary.[29] "The entire federal bench joined in the crusade against 'Jacobinism,'" Miller wrote;[30] the "Federalist judges and justices were unanimous in upholding" the Sedition Act, Stone concurred.[31]

That gallery of portraits of the Federalists and of the early justices is marred by the last Federalist appointee, John Marshall, who opposed the Act, though on

[25] John D. Stevens, *Congressional History of the 1798 Sedition Law*, 43 JOURNALISM Q. 247, 248, 252, 253, 254 (1966); *see* PRINTERS 59 ("contest over the passage and continuation of the Sedition Act" was waged "almost" exclusively along party lines). I appreciate Professor Jeffery A. Smith bringing this article to my attention, after this chapter was written. Also, Risjord mentioned, without discussing the implications, that "[t]wo Federalists broke ranks" in the first vote, and Broussard similarly mentioned some Federalists voting against extending the Act. CHESAPEAKE POLITICS 532; JAMES H. BROUSSARD, THE SOUTHERN FEDERALISTS, 1800–1816, at 36–37 (LSUP, Baton Rouge 1978).

[26] LEVY 280; *accord* 3 DUMAS MALONE, JEFFERSON AND HIS TIME 389 (Little Brown, Boston 1962).

[27] *Id.*; *e.g.*, R. Kent Newmyer, *Dusting Off Samuel Chase*, 20 REVIEWS IN AMERICAN HISTORY 486, 487 (1992); JOHN C. MILLER, THE FEDERALIST ERA, 1789–1801, at 240, 241 (Harper, New York 1960).

[28] OPPOSITION 470; H.G. Connor, *James Iredell: Lawyer, Statesman, Judge. 1751–1799*, 60 U. PA. L. REV. 225, 251–52 (1912).

[29] *E.g.*, Michael Kent Curtis, *The Fraying Fabric of Freedom: Crisis and Criminal Law in Struggles for Democracy and Freedom of Expression*, 44 TEX. TECH L. REV. 95, 99 (2011); Jude M. Pfister, Constitutional Development in the United States Supreme Court During the 1790s, at 133, 149, 150–51 (2007) (LL.D. thesis, Drew University); Arthur E. Wilmarth, *Elusive Foundation: John Marshall, James Wilson, and the Problem of Reconciling Popular Sovereignty and Natural Law Jurisprudence in the New Federal Republic*, 72 GEO. WASH. L. REV. 113, 186 n.435 (2003); James P. Martin, *When Repression Is Democratic and Constitutional: The Federalist Theory of Representation and the Sedition Act of 1798*, 66 U. CHI. L. REV. 117, 125 n.14, 175 (1999); Charles F. Hobson, *Book Review*, 40 AM. J. LEGAL HIST. 508, 508–09 (1996); 1 DAVID P. CURRIE, THE CONSTITUTION IN THE SUPREME COURT: THE FIRST HUNDRED YEARS, 1789–1888, at 161, 177, 260 (UChiP, Chicago 1985); Philip D. Kurland, *The Original Understanding of the Freedom of Press Provision of the First Amendment*, 55 MISS. L.J. 225, 239 n.44, 240, 247 (1985); SAVING 778; BRANT, *supra* note 24, at 71 ("all" justices supported), 308; JOHN C. MILLER, THE FEDERALIST ERA, 1789–1801, at 241 (Harper, New York 1960) ("to a man"); Charles Kerr, *The Thirty Years' War on the Supreme Court*, 17 VA. L. REV. 629, 636 (1931); Thomas F. Carroll, *Freedom of Speech and of the Press in the Federalist Period: The Sedition Act*, 18 MICH. L. REV. 615, 634 (1920).

[30] CRISIS 136.

[31] GEOFFREY R. STONE, PERILOUS TIMES: FREE SPEECH IN WARTIME, FROM THE SEDITION ACT OF 1798 TO THE WAR ON TERRORISM 68 (Norton, New York 2004).

grounds of expedience rather than constitutionality, and is marred far more by an overlooked coterie of Federalists who also opposed the Act, typically on grounds of unconstitutionality. If the Federalists could divide in 1800 over reelection of the sitting Federalist president, with the High Federalist wing opposing Adams and the Adams Federalist wing supporting him, it is at least a possibility worth exploring that the Federalists could divide increasingly during the four congressional votes over the Sedition Act in 1798–1801, with the High Federalists sponsoring that Act[32] and many Adams Federalists or transitioning Federalists being concerned over its grave implications for liberty. If Marshall could oppose the Sedition Act on any ground, it is at least a possibility worth exploring that other Federalist justices could oppose the Sedition Act, too, on some ground.

When these possibilities are explored, it becomes clear that a significant minority of Federalists opposed the Sedition Act, both inside and outside Congress, including a significant number of Supreme Court justices as well.

John Marshall and Federalist Opposition to the Expediency of the Sedition Act

Figure 8.1 Chief Justice John Marshall (who, before appointment in 1801, opposed the Sedition Act on practical grounds). Lithograph by Albert Newsam after Henry Inman 1831. (Courtesy of National Portrait Gallery, Smithsonian Institution/Art Resource.)

John Marshall (Figure 8.1), recently returned from the mission to France after the XYZ affair brought it to a halt, was named a candidate for Congress in late 1798, in his words "as a punishment for some unknown sins."[33] In response to questions, Marshall published a newspaper article saying he would have voted against the

[32] 3 Jefferson 390; Federalism 692; Adams Federalists 237.

[33] John Marshall to Timothy Pickering (15 Oct.1798), 3 Marshall Papers 516; *see generally* 2 History of Supreme Court 102.

Alien and Sedition Acts, and planned to vote against their renewal.[34] His reasons were based on those laws being inexpedient because they were useless and divisive, and not on their being unconstitutional because he denied they were "fraught with all those mischiefs which many gentlemen ascribe."[35] Marshall did not hide his departure from Federalist orthodoxy, telling Washington he "regret[ted] the passage of one of the acts" though he condemned the Virginia Resolutions, and telling Pickering that many well-meaning people had concerns about the Sedition Act.[36] Marshall was elected, defeating John Clopton, and did vote for repeal of the Sedition Act.[37] Soon after, he received a letter from a leading Republican, St. George Tucker, who urged the Act's unconstitutionality and asked for release of James Callender, who remained in jail.[38] Marshall responded by acknowledging "doubts some of us may entertain" about the Act, but disagreeing with the suggested release because the "laws are made, & those who violate them are prosecuted." Nine days later, he added his belief that only the Constitution's judicial power and not federal common law gave federal courts jurisdiction over such sedition cases, though he believed state common law applied to federal courts.[39]

There is debate about whether Marshall drafted the Virginia minority's report[40] opposing the Virginia Resolutions. His authorship was generally assumed over the years,[41] but was denied by the editors of his papers,[42] though their conclusion was persuasively disputed by several recent authors.[43] Costa adds that, even if Marshall wrote the minority report, he elsewhere showed some solicitude for freedom of speech and should not be prejudged for it.[44] If Marshall drafted it, he

[34] John Marshall, To a Freeholder (2 Oct.1798), 3 MARSHALL PAPERS 503, 505–06.

[35] *Id.; accord* John Marshall to Timothy Pickering (11 Aug.1798), 3 *id.* 484, 485; CHARLES E. HOBSON, THE GREAT CHIEF JUSTICE: JOHN MARSHALL AND THE RULE OF LAW 50 (UPKan, Lawrence 1996).

[36] John Marshall to George Washington (8 Jan.1799), 4 *id.* 3; John Marshall to Timothy Pickering (11 Aug.1798), 3 *id.* 484, 485.

[37] 10 ANNALS 423 (23 Jan.1800); 3 MARSHALL PAPERS 496n., 4 *id.* 37 n.

[38] St. George Tucker to John Marshall (6 Nov.1800), 6 MARSHALL PAPERS 4, 5.

[39] John Marshall to St. George Tucker (18 Nov.1800), 6 *id.* 14, 15; John Marshall to St. George Tucker (27 Nov.1800), 6 *id.* 23, 24.

[40] ADDRESS OF THE MINORITY OF THE LEGISLATUR[E] OF VIRGINIA (William Prentis, Petersburg 1799).

[41] *E.g.*, Theodore Sedgwick to Rufus King (20 Mar.1799), 2 KING CORRESPONDENCE 579, 581; PALMER 277; JAY 1329–30; FREEDOM'S FETTERS 151; CRISIS 183; CONTEMPORARY OPINION 239.

[42] 3 MARSHALL PAPERS 498–99 & n.1 (not including the report, and suggesting Henry Lee was the author); REPRESSIVE JURISPRUDENCE 97–98; David S. Robarge, John Marshall and His Times, at 295 & n.17 (1995) (unpublished Ph.D. thesis, Columbia University).

[43] Kurt T. Lash & Alicia Harrison, *Minority Report: John Marshall and the Defense of the Alien and Sedition Acts*, 68 OHIO ST. LAW J. 435, 439–516 (2007); Andrew Lenner, *A Tale of Two Constitutions*, 40 AM. J. LEGAL HIST. 72, 79–80 n.26 (1996).

[44] Greg Costa, *John Marshall, the Sedition Act, and Free Speech in the Early Republic*, 77 TEX. L. REV. 1011, 1018, 1019–28, 1031–38, 1040–42 (1999); *accord* John Marshall to Talleyrand (3 Apr.1798), 3 MARSHALL PAPERS 428, 442.

both found the Sedition Act constitutional and embraced the Blackstone-Mansfield approach to seditious libel and the press[45]; that would fit with his opposing the Sedition Act only on practical grounds.

The fury that Marshall encountered from High Federalists and some other Federalists, even though his opposition was based on inexpediency rather than unconstitutionality, is important in explaining the later silence of other Federalist opponents of the Sedition Act. Fisher Ames denounced him: "No correct man,—no incorrect man even,—. . . would give his name to the base opposers of law. . . .—but his character is done for."[46] Cabot joined King "as well as Ames in reprobating the publication of Marshall's sentiments on the Sedition & Alien Acts," though Cabot discouraged public attacks because of Marshall's usefulness and because "the atmosphere of Virginia . . . doubtless makes every one who breathes it visionary."[47] Sedgwick censured Marshall's "foolish declaration, relative to the alien & sedition laws," as did many others.[48]

Even stronger warnings soon came about speaking publicly against the Sedition Act. Pickering considered prosecuting Kentucky's governor for violating the Act by simply calling it unconstitutional,[49] and the federal attorneys indicted Jedidiah Peck and Morris Llewellyn for violating the Act by calling it a First Amendment infringement. All the newspaper editors prosecuted under the Act had done the same.

Alexander Hamilton, oddly, is treated by any number of historians as an opponent of the Sedition Act,[50] based on his call not to "establish a tyranny" by the draconian Senate version.[51] That treatment is mistaken; he clearly supported the law[52] and soon sought to broaden it to criminalize "libels . . . against any officer whatsoever" of the federal government.[53]

However, there were a large number of Federalist opponents of the Sedition Act, though they have escaped notice in the historical and legal literature.[54]

[45] Address of the Minority 13–14.

[46] Fisher Ames to Christopher Gore (18 Dec.1798), 1 Ames Works 245, 246.

[47] George Cabot to Rufus King (26 Apr.1799), 3 King Correspondence 7, 9.

[48] Theodore Sedgwick to Rufus King (11 May 1800), 3 *id.* 236, 237; *accord* Freedom's Fetters 151; Crisis 183–84.

[49] Timothy Pickering to Charles Hall (1 Aug.1799), Pickering Papers r.11, fol.528, 529; Contemporary Opinion 55–56.

[50] *E.g.,* 1 Melvin I. Urofsky & Paul Finkelman, A March of Liberty: A Constitutional History of the United States 202, 210 (3d ed., OUP, New York 2011); Karl-Friedrich Walling, Republican Empire: Alexander Hamilton on War and Free Government 272 (UPKan, Lawrence 1999); Stevens, *supra* note 25, at 249; Freedom's Fetters 153 n.44 (sources); Crisis 71, 73.

[51] Alexander Hamilton to Oliver Wolcott (29 June 1798), 21 Hamilton Papers 522.

[52] Alexander Hamilton to Theodore Sedgwick (2 Feb.1799), 22 *id.* 452, 453; Alexander Hamilton, An Address to the Electors (21 Mar.1801), 25 *id.* 349, 364; Freedom's Fetters 109.

[53] Alexander Hamilton to Jonathan Dayton (Oct.-Nov.1799), 23 *id.* 599, 604; *see* Robert W.T. Martin, *Reforming Republicanism: Alexander Hamilton's Theory of Republican Citizenship and Press Liberty,* 25 J. Early Republic 21, 33 (2005).

[54] Except as mentioned in note 25 *supra.*

Federalist Opponents of the Constitutionality of the Sedition Act

Though Marshall was the most public Federalist opponent of the Sedition Act, he was not the only one. Marshall himself acknowledged that the Sedition Act was "view[e]d by a great many well meaning men, as unwarranted by the Constitution."[55] Most whose reasons were recorded rejected the Act because it abridged freedoms of press and speech, though many opponents' reasons were not captured as they voted against the Act or its extension, or for its repeal or in support of the Virginia and Kentucky Resolutions. Those Federalist opponents were typically what George Cabot derided as "half federalists,"[56] and what Dauer called moderates[57] among the "Adams Federalists."[58]

Federalist opposition to the Sedition Act in Congress merely began with those voting against its passage in July 1798: Senator John Howard (Md.)[59] and four House members, William Matthews (Md.), Stephen Bullock (Mass.), and in-transition George Dent (Md.) and Abraham Baldwin (Ga.).[60] Further Federalist defections came with each new vote on the Act, such as three House members opposing adoption of the report defending the Act in February 1799: Thomas Skinner (Mass.), Josiah Parker (Va.), and Abram Trigg (Va.), along with Baldwin and Dent (Matthews and Bullock reverted to supporting the report).[61]

As the new Sixth Congress was seated, seven more Federalist defections came in the unsuccessful House attempt to repeal the Act in January 1800: James Jones (Ga.), Benjamin Taliaferro (Ga.), Willis Alston (N.C.), Archibald Henderson (N.C.), Thomas Hartley (Pa.), Samuel Goode (Va.), and John Marshall (Va.), along with recent opponents of the Act who still served in Congress (Dent, Trigg, though not Parker).[62] The next year, five additional Federalists broke ranks as the House voted by opposing continuation of the Sedition Act, and by seeking repeal of parts, in early 1801[63]: Benjamin Huger (S.C.), Abraham Nott (S.C.), and Edwin Gray (Va.), along with some already mentioned (Taliaferro, Dent, Alston, Goode, and Parker).[64] Also, Richard Dobbs Spaight (N.C.) and David Stone (N.C.), though elected as Federalists, "influenced by the Republican agitation for repeal of certain obnoxious legislation [Alien and Sedition Acts], soon left the Federalist ranks and

[55] John Marshall to Timothy Pickering (11 Aug.1798), 3 MARSHALL PAPERS 484, 485.

[58] *Id.* 218–37, 255–56.

[56] George Cabot to Rufus King (10 Mar.1799), 2 KING CORRESPONDENCE 551, 552.

[57] ADAMS FEDERALISTS 171; *id.* 316, 321, 326 (10–12 moderates), 220 (Craik, Smith, Dent).

[59] 7 ANNALS 599; ORIGINS-PARTIES 217–18.

[60] 8 *id.* 2171 (10 July 1798); ADAMS FEDERALISTS 306–09; *cf.* CHESAPEAKE POLITICS 532 (Matthews, Bullock); E. MERTON COULTER, ABRAHAM BALDWIN 139, 142 (Vandamere Press, Arlington 1987) (Baldwin earlier a Federalist).

[61] 9 *id.* 3016–17 (25 Feb.1799); ADAMS FEDERALISTS 312–14; *cf. id.* 314 n.1 (Skinner).

[62] 10 *id.* 423–24 (23 Jan.1800); ADAMS FEDERALISTS 318–20; PROLOGUE 187 (Taliaferro-Jones elected as Federalists).

[63] 11 *id.* 975–76 (23 Jan.1801), 1038–39 (19 Feb.1801); *cf.* 11 *id.* 1049 (22 Feb.1801).

[64] 11 *id.* 975–76, 1038–39; ADAMS FEDERALISTS 323–25.

joined the opposition," voting for repeal and against extension.[65] Spaight, like Abraham Baldwin, had attended the Constitutional Convention and signed the Constitution (and Charles Cotesworth Pinckney, who is discussed below, had as well). While most of these are not recorded as giving their reasons for opposition in congressional debates, speakers whose remarks were preserved focused on First Amendment reasons and related concerns,[66] and Trigg was described as finding the Act "in some parts unconstitutional."[67] The magnitude of Federalist opposition is seen in these eighteen House members (not counting Marshall) together being nearly half the size of the forty-four House votes that passed the Sedition Act in the first place, and six times the three-vote margin by which the Act passed.

Because parties and party membership were not clearly defined at this early period, researchers differ as to whether all who ultimately changed parties were still Federalists at the time of their first heterodox vote on the Sedition Act. Dauer's categorization is used here,[68] and alternative studies are also considered.[69] Even if party labels are questioned, a rougher barometer of Federalist opposition is simply that the Sedition Act, like the Alien Friends Act, passed by margins "narrower than was the case with any of the other major legislation enacted in the crisis of 1798."[70]

Figure 8.2 Charles Cotesworth Pinckney (Federalist vice presidential, and presidential, candidate, who opposed the Sedition Act). Portrait by John Trumbull 1791. (Courtesy of National Portrait Gallery, Smithsonian Institution/Art Resource.)

[65] Henry M. Wagstaff, *Federalism in North Carolina*, 9 JAMES SPRUNT STUDIES IN HISTORY 5, 30 (1910); 11 ANNALS 976, 1038.

[66] 3 JEFFERSON 386; CHESAPEAKE POLITICS 532. The debates are described at pages 254–56.

[67] Abram Trigg, Circular Letter (25 Feb.1799), 1 CIRCULAR LETTERS 155, 158.

[68] Except for Baldwin, ORIGINS-PARTIES 202, 204, 207.

[69] Four other sources are tabulated in ORIGINS-PARTIES 192–219; and eight other sources are in KENNETH C. MARTIS, THE HISTORICAL ATLAS OF POLITICAL PARTIES IN THE UNITED STATES CONGRESS 1789–1989, at 261–67 (Macmillan, New York 1989).

[70] FEDERALISM 590.

Some prominent Federalists outside Congress, like those in Congress, opposed the Sedition Act. The most notable was Charles Cotesworth Pinckney (Figure 8.2),[71] the Federalists' 1800 vice presidential candidate and 1804 and 1808 presidential candidate. Others were Edward Rutledge, South Carolina's governor, who found the Act contrary to "liberty of the press, & the freedom of speech,"[72] and Patrick Henry, Virginia's former governor and advocate of liberty.[73] There doubtless were a host of other state-level opponents, but their identification is hindered by limited party affiliation research for state legislatures.

The great majority of opponents of the Sedition Act, among continuing Federalists and transitional Federalists whose reasons for opposition were recorded, stated their basis as its violation of freedoms of press or speech, and few besides Marshall expressed their reasons as only practical. Most voting against the Sedition Act did not have an opportunity to record their reasons, or their speeches were not preserved. Similarly, most transitional Federalists did not record their reasons for leaving the party, but a large number did leave the party in and after the enactment of the Sedition Act, and many of those who did listed opposition to the Alien and Sedition Acts.

Transitional Federalist Opposition Toward the Sedition Act

Ongoing transitions from the Federalist Party to the Republican Party were noted by John Jay in early 1798, as he observed that "[t]hey who from honest motives are in the act of passing, or preparing to pass, from one party to another" should not be "roughly handled."[74] Later, as he looked back, he said that "[a]mong those who had been active Federalists there were individuals who at subsequent points [after the Jay Treaty of 1795] were induced . . . to join the opposing party."[75] Those transitions included Benjamin Rush and, apparently provoked by the Sedition Act, Elbridge Gerry.[76] Transitions only occasionally went in the other direction permanently, such as Patrick Henry[77] and Robert Goodloe Harper.[78]

[71] William Vans Murray to John Quincy Adams (22 Mar.1799), Worthington C. Ford ed., *Letters of William Vans Murray*, 1912 ANNUAL REPORT OF AMERICAN HISTORICAL ASS'N 343, 529, 530 (in Europe with Pinckney); *accord* PINCKNEY 214; Marvin R. Zahniser, The Public Career of Charles Cotesworth Pinckney 281 (1963) (unpublished Ph.D. dissertation, University of California-Santa Barbara).

[72] Edward Rutledge to John Rutledge, Jr. (29 July 1798), RUTLEDGE JR. PAPERS-UNC.

[74] John Jay to Peter A. Jay (17 May 1798), JAY PAPERS doc.90220.

[73] Douglas Bradburn, *A Clamor in the Public Mind: Opposition to the Alien and Sedition Acts*, 65 WM. & MARY Q. 565, 593–94 & n.46 (2008) (citing ms).

[75] John Jay to Richard Peters (12 Mar.1821), JAY PAPERS doc.1166.

[76] ADAMS FEDERALISTS 260, 246; RONALD P. FORMISANO, TRANSFORMATION OF POLITICAL CULTURE: MASSACHUSETTS PARTIES, 1790s-1840s, at 73 (OUP, Oxford 1983); HOFFER, *supra* note 24, at 58–59; 8 ANB 866, 867.

[77] CHESAPEAKE POLITICS 466–67; 10 ANB 615, 618.

[78] ADAMS FEDERALISTS 278; 10 ANB 128.

Some Federalists felt strongly enough to leave the party over the Sedition Act, just as many had over the Jay Treaty; as Beard observed, the Alien and Sedition Acts "no doubt alienated many Federalists."[79] Some others left because of multiple factors including the Act. Not surprisingly, it was Dauer's moderate Federalists who generally made the transition,[80] and they did so in a stream throughout the 1790s.[81]

In Congress, some of those voting against the Sedition Act or its extension were in transition, such as Dent, Baldwin, Skinner, Trigg, Jones, Alston, Goode, and Gray, leading to varying descriptions of their party affiliation at the time.[82] Their transitions, and a number of others such as House member and future governor John Page of Virginia, who similarly condemned the Act,[83] occurred so close in time to the enactment of the Alien and Sedition Acts[84] as to make it probable that the Acts were a major cause at least for some. Edmund Randolph, earlier the Federalist attorney general and secretary of state, had broken with Washington's administration over the Jay Treaty and other matters, but only aligned with the Republicans in 1798[85] at the time he privately condemned the Alien and Sedition Acts as "the two execrable bills"[86]; he soon supported the "close reasoning" of Madison's Report except one part.[87] His basis was likely the First Amendment, since even during ratification debates he spoke strongly in favor of jury trial, habeas corpus, and "liberty of the press."[88]

Many transitions from Federalist to Republican parties had already occurred by 1798, and also swelled the ranks of opponents of the Sedition Act. Examples are Senator Charles Pinckney from South Carolina[89] (cousin of Charles Cotesworth Pinckney), who championed liberty of the press as an expansive right,[90]

[79] Charles A. Beard, Economic Origins of Jeffersonian Democracy 356 (Macmillan, New York 1915) (none identified); *accord* John R. Nelson, Liberty and Property 109 (JHUP, Baltimore 1987).

[80] Adams Federalists 259.

[81] *Id.* 297, 303, 315, 326, 331 ("ex F[ederalist]" columns, though understated).

[82] Origins-Parties 207, 209 (Dent); 207, 218, 219 (Baldwin); 207, 205 (Skinner); 209, 211, 214 (Trigg); 209 (Jones); 210, 213 (Alston); 211 (Goode); 211, 214 (Gray).

[83] John Page to James Madison (7 Apr.1801), 1 Madison Papers-Secretary 73, 74; *see* 14 DHFFC 917, 923 (transition by 1800); 16 ANB 902.

[84] Adams Federalists 234–35.

[85] Chesapeake Politics 535; 30 Jefferson Papers 534n.

[86] Edmund Randolph to St. George Tucker (13 Dec.1798), quoted in John J. Reardon, Edmund Randolph 474 n.32 (Macmillan, New York 1974).

[87] Moncure D. Conway, Omitted Chapters of History Disclosed in the Life and Papers of Edmund Randolph 368 (Putnam's Sons, New York 1888).

[88] 3 Elliot's Debates 203.

[89] Marty D. Matthews, Forgotten Founder, Charles Pinckney 94, 96, 100–01 (UNCP, Columbia 2004); *see* 17 ANB 533, 535.

[90] 10 Annals 69–84 (Mar.1800); Speeches of Charles Pinckney 42, 119–28 ([n.p., Philadelphia] 1800).

and former revenue commissioner Tench Coxe, who believed Adams should be indicted for signing the Alien and Sedition Acts and wrote articles against them.[91] Other transitions were delayed and reflected internal struggle, such as House member Silas Lee, who earlier expressed concern that sentiments could be labeled "*libels against government*" and adversely affect "liberty of the press,"[92] but consistently supported the Sedition Act, at least until he shifted to the Republican Party around 1801,[93] or district judge Cyrus Griffin, who sat quite silently with Chase in the *Callender* trial, but by 1802 was commended by Jefferson for abandoning support of the Sedition Act.[94] Another district judge, Gunning Bedford (a signer of the Constitution), who sat with Chase in Delaware, as Chase unavailingly pressed to prosecute a Republican newspaper, may have expressed his own view in telling Chase, "I believe you do not know where you are[;] the people in this place are not well pleased with the sedition law"; Bedford, too, soon was a Republican.[95]

In state legislatures, similarly, some Federalist transitions to the Republican Party were connected to the Sedition Act. If New York is selected as an example, legislators elected as Federalists but supporting the Virginia and Kentucky Resolutions included Jedidiah Peck, who was prosecuted under the Act for circulating a petition opposing the Sedition Act,[96] and Ambrose Spencer, who just before supporting the Resolutions changed parties in 1798.[97] John Armstrong, the author of Peck's petition,[98] was an "acidulous Federalist who had been converted to Republicanism by the Alien and Sedition Acts,"[99] and attacked the latter as violating the First Amendment, believing a "prohibition more express can scarcely be devised."[100] Others can be found in each state's list of legislators supporting the Resolutions, such as Joseph Bloomfield of New Jersey.[101]

[91] Jacob E. Cooke, Tench Coxe and the Early Republic 349, 344–45 (UNCP, Chapel Hill 1978); *see* 5 ANB 636, 637.

[92] Silas Lee to George Thacher (23 Jan.1788), 5 DHRC 780, 782.

[93] Notes on a Cabinet Meeting (8 Mar.1801), 33 Jefferson Papers 219; 5 DHRC 782 n.1.

[94] 9 ANB 589, 590.

[95] John A. Munroe, Federalist Delaware, 1775–1815, at 207, 206n. (RUP, Rutgers 1954); 2 ANB 455, 456.

[96] Journal-N.Y. 123; Federalism 705.

[97] Journal of the Senate of the State of New-York . . . 1799, at 67 (Loring Andrews, Albany 1799);` 1 Political Parties-N.Y. 125; 20 ANB 441.

[98] 1 Political Parties-N.Y. 131; Freedom's Fetters 393; 1 DAB 356.

[99] Livingston 305; *accord* 25 Hamilton Papers 304 n.3; *see* 1 ANB 617; Robert Troup to Rufus King (9 Aug.1800), 3 King Correspondence 289.

[100] [John Armstrong], To the Senate and Representatives of the United States ([Nicholas Power, Poughkeepsie 1798]).

[101] Carl E. Prince, New Jersey's Jeffersonian Republicans 36 (UNCP, Chapel Hill 1967).

Other Federalists in state government had already made the transition before 1798, such as Chief Justice Edmund Pendleton of Virginia, who assailed the "constitutionality of the sedition bill" under the First Amendment,[102] Governor Thomas McKean of Pennsylvania, who found the Sedition Act clearly unconstitutional (despite his prior support of the Blackstone-Mansfield approach),[103] and Virginia attorney George Hay, one of Callender's trial counsel, who assaulted the Act based on freedoms of press and speech.[104]

Most of this Federalist opposition to the Sedition Act (besides voting) was private, because of the scathing criticism that would ensue like that encountered by Marshall, and the prosecution that could result, like that suffered by Peck and Llewellyn. If opposition by Federalists was generally nonpublic, opposition by early justices of the Supreme Court would be expected to be, too. Before public silence is condemned as cowardly on the presentist assumption that the constitutional infraction was obvious, it is important, and startling, to remember that even in the mid-twentieth century most historians[105] and legal commentators[106] treated the Sedition Act as not violating the First Amendment, and that after that date many persisted in treating the Act as constitutional as a restatement and amelioration of a common law not changed by the Amendment.[107]

If this many Adams Federalists (along with transitional Federalists) could oppose the Sedition Act, it is a possibility worth exploring whether the remaining justices might have opposed the Act as well, particularly since Jay, Rutledge, Wilson, Johnson, and Moore (though perhaps not Blair) were Adams Federalists and had been threatened with seditious libel prosecution in the past.[108] Each will be considered in turn.

[102] Edmund Pendleton, Address to Citizens of Caroline (Nov.1798), 2 PENDLETON PAPERS 650, 653; *accord* DAVID J. MAYS, EDMUND PENDLETON 312, 315 (HUP, Cambridge 1952, repr. 1984); 30 JEFFERSON PAPERS 662n.; *see* 17 DAB 417, 418 (former Federalist).

[103] G. S. ROWE, THOMAS MCKEAN 293, 264 (CAUP, Boulder 1978); SANFORD W. HIGGINBOTHAM, KEYSTONE IN THE DEMOCRATIC ARCH: PENNSYLVANIA POLITICS, 1800–1816, at 16 (PHMC, Harrisburg 1952); PENNSYLVANIA 227.

[104] HORTENSIUS [GEORGE HAY], AN ESSAY ON THE LIBERTY OF THE PRESS 3, 10–16 (Aurora, Philadelphia 1799); LEVY 313; 10 ANB 364.

[105] *E.g.*, JOHN C. MILLER, THE FEDERALIST ERA, 1789–1801, at 232 (Harper, New York 1960); CRISIS 79 n.10; 4 EDWARD CHANNING, A HISTORY OF THE UNITED STATES 231–32 (Macmillan, New York 1923–25).

[106] *E.g.*, Mark D. Howe, *Book Review*, 13 WM. & MARY Q. (3d ser.) 573, 575, 575–76 (1956); *see* Thomas F. Carroll, *Freedom of Speech and of the Press in the Federalist Period: The Sedition Act*, 18 MICH. L. REV. 615, 637, 650 (1920); Mark D. Howe, *Book Review*, 66 HARV. L. REV. 189, 190 (1952); MISUNDERSTANDING 119–20.

[107] LEVY 297; REPRESSIVE JURISPRUDENCE 89, 2; OCSC 764–65.

[108] *E.g.*, HARRY AMMON, THE GENET MISSION 152–53 (Norton, New York 1973) (Jay); James Wilson, An Address to the Inhabitants of the Colonies (1776), 1 WILSON WORKS 46, 51; A Plain Dealing Whig, *For the Pennsylvania Packet*, PENNSYLVANIA PACKET (Philadelphia), 10 Oct.1780, at 2 (Wilson: "your house the public theatre of sedition"); LEIGH'S CONSIDERATIONS 82, 80 (Rutledge). Further threats to Rutledge are discussed later in this chapter and in Chapter 3.

Chief Justice John Jay and the Sedition Act

Chief Justice John Jay, though leaving by far the most complete papers of the dozen early justices (over 13,000), because he meticulously retained correspondence and other papers throughout his life, did not leave a trace of support of the Sedition Act. In his 509 letters from the beginning of 1798 to the end of 1802, there is no hint of support.[109] In his legislative messages as governor of New York (from 1795 until the end of 1800), there is no endorsement of the Sedition Act or call to enforce it or to legislate in its support. In the hundreds of newspaper articles mentioning him or his actions, there is no reference to Jay endorsing or supporting the Act, though New York had the largest number of newspapers of any state during 1798–1800.[110] By contrast, the governors of the seven other states that opposed the Virginia and Kentucky Resolutions emphatically stated their condemnation, and their positions were widely reported and are easily located today, despite their states' comparatively fewer newspapers.[111] Moreover, when New York's house and senate failed to reconcile their responses rejecting the Resolutions, Jay did nothing to get them to agree on a legally effective response (as all other opposing states did) or even to point out their incompatibility, and he only transmitted one of the resolutions to other states (because the state senate required him to) rather than both. This section draws heavily on Jay's unpublished but essentially complete correspondence (cited as *Jay Papers*).

Departures from Federalist Orthodoxy

The French minister Chevalier de la Luzerne privately described Jay to Comte de Vergennes as negotiations began on the Treaty of 1783, saying he "boasts of being independent."[112] Indeed, Jay did,[113] and was repeatedly described as independent-minded.[114]

Jay's independence led to periodic departures from Federalist orthodoxy. Though Federalists generally stressed order strongly over liberty, Jay only believed "a national government, as strong as may be compatible with liberty, is necessary" (as he wrote to John Adams while the Constitutional Convention met),[115] and found

[109] His papers are meticulously gathered by Columbia University at http://www.columbia.edu/cu/lweb/digital/jay/, from which the totals derive.

[110] Judging by the 19 New York papers, and 60 other papers, currently contained in the Early American Newspapers database for 14 July 1798–31 Dec.1800. *E.g., Virginia and Kentucky Resolutions*, OTSEGO HERALD (Cooperstown), 28 Feb.1799, at 2.

[111] *E.g.*, CONTEMPORARY OPINION 232, 247, 231 (Vt., Del., N.H.; others below).

[112] WILLIAM E. O'DONNELL, THE CHEVALIER DE LA LUZERNE: FRENCH MINISTER TO THE UNITED STATES 237 (Bibliotheque de L'Université, Louvain 1938).

[113] John Jay to Samuel Huntingdon (6 Nov.1780), JAY-REVOLUTIONARY 825, 834; JAY-PEACE 8.

[114] *E.g.*, Diary (27 Oct.1782), 3 ADAMS WORKS 299.

[115] John Jay to John Adams (4 July 1787), 3 JAY CORRESPONDENCE 248, 248–49.

liberty as important as order, maintaining that "Government without liberty is a curse; but, on the other hand, liberty without government is far from being a blessing" (as he wrote to Washington during the ratification debates).[116] Though Federalists favored the British and abhorred the French revolutionaries, Jay was suspicious of both,[117] pointed out that he had no British ancestry,[118] initially rejoiced in the French Revolution as "restor[ing] liberty to the people" by overturning an "arbitrary government" and "dreadful" monarchy, before it turned to the guillotine and abolished the constitution, and even in 1796 thanked a congressman for publicly defending him as not "an avowed enemy to France."[119] He had developed close friendships with Lafayette, who called himself Jay's "political aid[e] de camp" at the time of the first treaty, and with other French notables.[120] Whereas Federalists were chary of "the rights of man," Jay wrote in a 1793 opinion that rights are retained by the people, because "the people exercised their own rights" to establish the Constitution, and they were secured in their rights by that government,[121] joining Wilson in proclaiming "the people to be the source of authority."[122] While Federalists narrowed the province of juries, Jay charged a jury in a unique Supreme Court trial that, while it should decide facts and the judges law, "still both objects are lawfully, within your power of decision."[123] While Federalists called for limiting public office to "federal men" and for excluding "jacobins," Jay upon taking office as governor did not dismiss appointees of his Republican predecessor,[124] and while in office "did not wish to hear what were the politics of a candidate for office."[125] Examples of Jay departing from the Federalist Party line can be multiplied.[126]

[116] John Jay to George Washington (21 Sept.1788), 3 *id.* 360; *accord,* An Address to the People of the State of New York (spring 1788), 3 *id.* 294, 303.

[117] JAY-PEACE 519, 549–50; 4 JAY CORRESPONDENCE 202.

[118] John Jay to Robert Goodloe Harper (19 Jan.1796), 4 JAY CORRESPONDENCE 198, 199; *accord* EMPIRE 40.

[119] 4 *id.* 200–01, 199; *accord* JAY PAPERS doc.4787; FEDERALISM 310. The letter was reprinted, evidently with approbation, by Republican newspapers. *E.g., Letter from Governor Jay,* ARGUS (New York), 24 Feb.1796, at 2.

[120] Lafayette to John Jay (15 Feb.1783), JAY-PEACE 517, 518; *id.*12, 455–56; 4 JAY CORRESPONDENCE 472.

[121] Chisholm v. Georgia, 2 U.S. (2 Dall.) 419, 470–71, 479 (1793).

[122] RICHARD B. MORRIS, JOHN JAY, THE NATION, AND THE COURT 70 (BUP, Boston 1967); *accord* 3 JAY CORRESPONDENCE 229; 2 DHSC 390.

[123] Georgia v. Brailsford, 3 U.S. (3 Dall.) 1, 4 (1794).

[124] GEORGE PELLEW, JOHN JAY 298–99 (Houghton Mifflin, Boston 1890); *For the Albany Centinel,* ALBANY CENTINEL, 4 Sept.1801, at 2; *Council of Appointment,* SALEM GAZETTE, 25 Aug.1801, at 1.

[125] *Id.* 299–300; *From the Albany Gazette,* ALBANY CENTINEL, 21 Aug.1801, at 1; *Communication of Thursday Last,* DAILY ADVERTISER (New York), 24 Aug.1801, at 2; JAY PAPERS doc.9967, 3592.

[126] 2 DHSC 27, 363 (rights), 26, 27, 364, 389–90 (differing opinions); 3 JAY CORRESPONDENCE 224, 249 (Native Americans), 414, 443 (rights); 4 *id.* 337 (democracy), 360, 379 (divergent opinions).

Jay remained a Federalist,[127] but was a more moderate "Adams Federalist" rather than a High Federalist,[128] as Adams recognized by renominating him as chief justice in late 1800 after the Hamiltonian split and after the purge of Hamiltonian cabinet members.[129] Though Jay corresponded extensively with various High Federalists, and remained on generally good terms with them,[130] he did the same with people of all stripes, such as Republican governors.[131] For example, he wrote to Pickering four days after the Sedition Act was signed and then a week later—not mentioning the Act—but only to rejoice that Washington accepted command of the new army, and to suggest that the relative rank of generals be clarified.[132] If Jay had supported the Sedition Act, he would have been expected to speak favorably of it, in writing to its chief defender and enforcer, as he wrote favorably of other federal actions. Similarly, Jay was on good terms with Hamilton, his state's dominant Federalist and the leading High Federalist,[133] but was quite willing to disagree with Hamilton, whether about Hamilton's suggestion to denounce the Whiskey Rebellion more strongly in grand jury charges,[134] his requested appointments or pardons,[135] his wish for continued defense spending,[136] his high fee for legal services,[137] his opposition to and criticism of Adams, his preference of Jefferson over his nemesis Burr,[138] or, most importantly, Hamilton's scheme that would have reversed the presidential election of 1800.

Jay demonstrated his independence and fidelity to principle when he faced the opportunity to change the 1800 election results from a narrow triumph of Jefferson to a second term for Adams. That opportunity was raised by Hamilton's Faustian proposal to call the New York legislature into special session and to choose presidential electors while its Federalist majority remained in office, before its new Republican majority took over.[139] Hamilton noted the high stakes, as he

[127] *E.g.*, John Jay to Peter Van Schaack (4 May 1807), JAY PAPERS doc.09435; John Jay to William Coleman (18 June 1807), *id.* doc.12552.

[128] John Adams to John Jay (24 Nov.1800), 9 ADAMS WORKS 90, 91; JAY PAPERS doc.2872, 9007; 1 WARREN 175.

[129] John Adams to John Jay (19 Dec.1800), 9 ADAMS WORKS 91; 1 DHSC 144.

[130] *E.g.*, 2 KING CORRESPONDENCE 428, 474, 475, 489, 578; 3 *id.* 148; 4 JAY CORRESPONDENCE 254, 255, 270, 273.

[131] *E.g.*, John Jay to John Sevier (30 Nov.1798), JAY PAPERS doc.3192; John Jay to John Drayton (28 Dec.1799), *id.* doc.9829; John Jay to James Monroe (14 June 1800), *id.* doc.5145; John Jay to James Monroe (3 June 1800), *id.* doc.9006.

[132] John Jay to Timothy Pickering (18, 26 July 1798), JAY PAPERS doc.4790, 4791.

[133] John Jay to Alexander Hamilton (19 Apr.1798), JAY PAPERS doc.3139, 10775.

[134] Alexander Hamilton to John Jay (3 Sept.1792), 3 JAY CORRESPONDENCE 446; 2 DHSC 294, 237.

[135] 23 HAMILTON PAPERS 62; 22 *id.* 169–70, 163–64.

[136] John Jay to Alexander Hamilton (3 Aug.1799), JAY PAPERS doc.5651.

[137] John Jay to David Jones (8 Aug.1800), JAY PAPERS doc.9009.

[138] 1 POLITICAL CORRESPONDENCE AND PUBLIC PAPERS OF AARON BURR 866–67 (Mary-Jo Kline ed., PUP, Princeton 1983).

[139] Alexander Hamilton to John Jay (7 May 1800), 4 JAY CORRESPONDENCE 270, 271–72; *accord* AMERICAN POLITICS 234–35.

sought to "prevent an *atheist* in religion and a *fanatic* in politics from getting possession of the helm of the state," along with a Republican Party, half of which seeks "the overthrow of the government by depriving it of its due energies" and the other half of which seeks "a revolution after the manner of Buonaparte."[140] Jay was quite aware that the Republicans were likely to win the presidential and congressional elections later that year,[141] unless he acted, and Hamilton was right that it would have changed the presidential outcome.[142] Yet Jay rejected the proposal out of hand, writing on the back of Hamilton's letter, "Proposing a measure for party purposes, which I think it would not become me to adopt."[143] Jay rejected the same proposal from Philip Schuyler (Hamilton's father-in-law), ostensibly supported by John Marshall, though they, too, predicted that by the proposal "Mr. Jefferson's election will be defeated and equally so that Mr. Adams and Mr. Pin[c]kney will be elected."[144]

Such independence drew Federalist criticism of Jay. Even before Jay's refusal to tilt the 1800 election—but after he was notably silent on the Sedition Act and the Virginia and Kentucky Resolutions—Robert Troup wrote, "our influence on a general scale has been considerably diminished by Mr. Jay's administration," despite the best of intentions.[145] When Jay was renominated as chief justice, Wolcott and Pickering were critical of the choice.[146]

By contrast, Jefferson was less negative about the renomination: "We were afraid of something worse."[147] Perhaps the reason was his knowledge of Jay not seeking to have Lewis Littlepage prosecuted for seditious libel, and of Jay having been threatened by Edmond Genet with criminal prosecution for libel, seven years earlier.[148] Jay proved worthy of Jefferson's faint confidence, advising Federalists that the Jefferson administration should be supported in all that was "intelligent and upright."[149]

[140] 4 *id.* 271.

[141] John Jay to Dr. Jedidiah Morse (24 Apr. 1800), 4 *id.* 265, 266.

[142] FEDERALISM 732; JOHN E. FERLING, ADAMS VS. JEFFERSON: THE TUMULTUOUS ELECTION OF 1800, at 168 (OUP, Oxford 2004).

[143] 4 JAY CORRESPONDENCE 272 n.1.

[144] Gen. Philip Schuyler to John Jay (7 May 1800), 4 *id.* 273.

[145] Robert Troup to Rufus King (6 May 1799), 3 KING CORRESPONDENCE 14; *accord* 2 *id.* 431; JAY PAPERS doc.6078.

[146] Timothy Pickering to Rufus King (5 Jan.1801), 3 KING CORRESPONDENCE 365; 1 WARREN 174.

[147] Thomas Jefferson to James Madison (19 Dec.1800), 32 JEFFERSON PAPERS 321, 322.

[148] Thomas Jefferson to Edmund Randolph (18 Dec.1793), 27 JEFFERSON PAPERS 587; *accord* 27 *id.* 527; 3 JEFFERSON 144.

[149] John Jay to Committee of Federal Freeholders (27 Jan.1801), 4 JAY CORRESPONDENCE 288, 289; John Jay, *Answer*, NATIONAL INTELLIGENCER (Washington), 9 Feb.1801, at 3.

Federalist in a Republican Family

Jay was as surrounded by Republicans as by Federalists. His law partner of many years and his wife's cousin, Robert R. Livingston, the chancellor of New York, became the state's leading Republican and an opponent of the Sedition Act.[150] Livingston was later offered a cabinet position and appointed an ambassador by Jefferson.[151] His brother, Edward Livingston, was with Gallatin the leading congressional opponent of the Sedition Act as "an abridgment of the liberty of the press, which the Constitution has said shall not be abridged."[152] He repudiated the concept that there could be slanders against he federal government,[153] and soon defended a seditious libel case.[154] Their brother-in-law was John Armstrong, who had been converted to the Republican Party by the Sedition Act.[155]

The immediate family of Jay's wife,[156] Sarah Livingston Jay, was equally Republican,[157] and generally close.[158] Her brother, Brockholst Livingston, a Republican,[159] represented Frothingham in his seditious libel prosecution,[160] and became Jefferson's second nominee to the Supreme Court.[161] Another brother, William Livingston, soon claimed "reformation" from Republican allegiance.[162] Their sister's husband, James Linn, was "a leader of the Republican movement in New Jersey," and as a Republican in Congress[163] voted for repeal of the Sedition Act and against extension.[164] Sarah's father, William Livingston, though he died in 1790 before parties arose, inspired support for liberty of press, studying law under and befriending two of Zenger's attorneys,[165] editing a newspaper in the

[150] LIVINGSTON 300; 1 POLITICAL CORRESPONDENCE AND PUBLIC PAPERS OF AARON BURR 395 n.1 (Mary-Jo Kline ed., PUP, Princeton 1983); *see* Herbert A. Johnson, *John Jay: Lawyer in a Time of Transition, 1764–1775*, 124 U. PA. L. REV. 1260, 1270, 1274–75 (1976). They diverged over Jay's Treaty and were opponents in the 1798 gubernatorial election.

[151] Thomas Jefferson to Robert R. Livingston (14 Dec.1800), 32 JEFFERSON PAPERS 302, 303.

[152] 8 ANNALS 2105; *accord* FREEDOM'S FETTERS 105, 112, 124.

[153] 8 *id.* 2154, though he was ambiguous on state powers, 2153.

[154] Trial of David Frothingham, Wharton's State Trials 649, 649 (N.Y. Ct. Oyer & Terminer 1799).

[155] LIVINGSTON 305; *see* 1 ANB 617.

[156] 1 THE PAPERS OF WILLIAM LIVINGSTON xxvi–xxix (Carl E. Prince ed., NJHC, Trenton 1979-); JAY-REVOLUTIONARY 123.

[157] RICHARD E. ELLIS, THE JEFFERSONIAN CRISIS 239 (OUP, New York 1971).

[158] *E.g.*, JAY PAPERS doc.13081, 4801; JAY-PEACE 10–11.

[159] Edward Livingston to Thomas Jefferson (11 Apr.1800), 31 JEFFERSON PAPERS 494; LIVINGSTON 259, 262; 13 ANB 764, 765.

[160] Wharton's State Trials 649, 649.

[161] OHSC 507; 1 WARREN 299.

[162] John Jay to Mathew Clarkson (13 Sept.1799), JAY PAPERS doc.2863.

[163] 33 JEFFERSON PAPERS 432n.; 32 *id.* 323n.; ORIGINS-PARTIES 210.

[164] 10 ANNALS 423–24, 975, 1038; ADAMS FEDERALISTS 319, 324.

[165] 20 ANB 303, 304 (on William Smith).

1750s,[166] and writing in 1765 that "the common doctrine of libels is contrary to law" and was "a doctrine invented in the time of the star-chamber."[167] In 1784 he defended the right to censure government and its officials,[168] and argued that year that the precept that a true libel was "more atrocious" than a false one was "ineffable nonsense" and that both true statements and false statements believed to be true should be protected.[169] Republicans were not limited to Jay's in-laws; one of two sons became one.[170]

Aloofness from the Sedition Act

Jay called a special session of New York's legislature for August 1798 to implement recent federal defense legislation. He did so before the Sedition Act passed,[171] and so did not do so with the Sedition Act in mind, but in response to the federal plea for state defense measures. Opening that session with the customary governor's speech, Jay noted that the federal government had "called upon the nation to prepare for defence," and asked the legislature to determine whether "and what measures conducive to that end, should now be adopted by this state," listing as examples militia, arsenals, and funds—but not listing sedition laws or prosecutions.[172] He described "the dangers which demanded immediate attention to their defence and security," because France had rendered "recurrence to arms necessary and justifiable."[173] After discussing other matters and near the speech's end, Jay expressed his concern that "[t]he United States cannot be conquered but by civil discord," which is the cause to which "all fallen republics have owed their destruction," but he did not call for any legislative action about such discord; he instead appealed for unity.[174]

166 Though he is often credited with the protoBlackstonian essay "Of the Use, Abuse, and Liberty of the Press," LEVY 138, it was probably written by his co-editor, William Smith, Jr. Richard D. Brown, *The Shifting Freedoms of the Press in the Eighteenth Century*, in THE COLONIAL BOOK IN THE ATLANTIC WORLD 366, 372 (Hugh Amory & David D. Hall eds., CUP, Cambridge 2000); W.M.S., *Reflections on the Use, Abuse, and Liberty of the Press*, NEW-YORK WEEKLY MUSEUM, 19 Sept.1789, at 1.

167 Sentinel [William Livingston], *Sentinel No. 13* (23 May 1765), reprinted as *Sentinel No. 13*, INDEPENDENT GAZETTEER (Philadelphia), 17 June 1789, at 1 (editor's note attributing to Livingston). His pseudonyms included Sentinel. 1 THE PAPERS OF WILLIAM LIVINGSTON, *supra* note 156, at 4.

168 Scipio [William Livingston], *On the Liberty of the Press (Part IV)*, NEW JERSEY GAZETTE (Burlington), 3 May 1784, at 1; Scipio [William Livingston], *On the Liberty of the Press (Part 1)*, NEW JERSEY GAZETTE (Burlington), 30 Mar.1784, at 2.

169 Scipio [William Livingston], *On the Liberty of the Press (Part 1)*, NEW JERSEY GAZETTE (Burlington), 30 Mar.1784, at 2.

170 CHARLES W. UPHAM, THE LIFE OF TIMOTHY PICKERING 490–91 (Little Brown, Boston 1873); *see* 3 APPLETONS' CYCLOPÆDIA OF AMERICAN BIOGRAPHY 412 (James G. Wilson & John Fiske eds., Appleton, New York 1888–89); JAY PAPERS doc.11634, 6231.

171 Proclamation (2 July 1798), JAY PAPERS doc.3283; JOURNAL OF THE ASSEMBLY OF THE STATE OF NEW-YORK . . . 1798, at 3 (Loring Andrews, Albany 1798).

172 *Id.* 5–6; Speech to the Legislature (9 Aug.1798), 2 MESSAGES-N.Y. 420, 422.

173 2 MESSAGES-N.Y. 420, 421.

174 2 *id.* 423.

Most significantly, Jay did not ask the legislature for sedition legislation, as he asked for defense legislation, though New York had one of the nation's most influential Republican newspapers, which Pickering had recently prosecuted before the Sedition Act,[175] and which Pickering and Hamilton soon prosecuted (Greenleaf and Frothingham of the *Argus*, in addition to prosecuting Durrell of the *Mount Pleasant Register*). Jay's fifty-five letters to Pickering while the latter was in office did not ask for any investigation or prosecution under the Act, or complain about any opposition newspaper or legislator.[176] Similarly, Jay's extensive correspondence with the federal attorney general during "the most furious political barrage of the 1790s," which was over the Jay Treaty in 1795,[177] while acknowledging that the "treaty would be used as a pretext for attacks on the government, and for attempts to diminish the confidence" of the people in it, did not ask for or encourage seditious libel prosecutions; Jay instead trusted that truth would prevail.[178]

The state senate, in its customary "address on the governor's message," did "not hesitate in declaring the measures of defence adopted by the general government . . . indispensably necessary, and entitled to our warmest approbation."[179] It agreed with the governor "that the great source of danger to be apprehended to the United States may be found in the disunion of our citizens under the influence of foreign counsels."[180] This address Jay "receive[d] with great satisfaction," but with no complaint of unfinished business about sedition.[181] The legislature also prepared an address to President Adams, stating that "we unanimously approve of the measures you have taken for that purpose [preserving peace] with respect to France."[182] Because the address was unanimously approved, the measures referred to clearly did not include the Sedition Act, which the Republican minority would ardently oppose,[183] but instead addressed the score of other federal defense laws.[184] Jay's letter transmitting the address to President John Adams assured him

[175] 1 History of Supreme Court 629.

[176] *E.g.*, 4 Jay Correspondence 183, 233, 241, 377.

[177] Opposition 177, a barrage that he found painful but without legitimate remedy, John Jay to Henry Lee (11 July 1795), 4 Jay Correspondence 178; John Jay to George Washington (14 Dec.1795), 4 *id.* 197; *see* Todd Estes, *Shaping the Politics of Public Opinion: Federalists and the Jay Treaty Debate*, 20 J. Early Repub. 393, 399 (2000).

[178] John Jay to Edmund Randolph (20 Aug.1795), 4 Jay Correspondence 186, 187; *accord* John Jay to James Duane (16 Sept.1795), 4 *id.* 191, 192–94; 4 *id.* 197, 214.

[179] Address on the Governor's Message, 2 Messages-N.Y. 442, 442–43 (Aug.1798).

[180] 2 *id.* 443. The state house issued a similar address, but without the reference to the federal "measures of defence," to which Jay replied briefly. 2 *id.* 444, 445.

[181] 2 *id.* 444.

[182] 2 *id.* 445.

[183] Journal-N.Y. 123; Contemporary Opinion 56–57.

[184] Defense legislation in 1798, besides tax laws, appeared at 1 Stat. 547–608.

that the cooperation of the nation could be relied on "in the measures necessary to protect the rights and maintain their honour and independence,"[185] but again did not say anything implying support for the Sedition Act. The resulting state legislation provided for defending the harbor and state, but not for restricting expression. Jay's letter transmitting that legislation to Adams again agreed with it, and suggested that Jay coordinate defense steps with Hamilton, the effective commander of the new army, but suggested nothing about coordinating enforcement of the Sedition Act.[186] Jay, like the legislature's majority, saw danger of French aggression, and like that majority, commended Adams's measures for defense, but again avoided commending the Sedition Act.[187]

Jay thereafter took steps for New York's defense, ordering arms,[188] fortifying the harbor, and other measures.[189] His messages and letters showed calm preparation, but not Federalist hysteria about internal enemies or opposition speech, even as the Republicans won control of the legislature in spring 1800.[190]

After that legislative changeover, Jay's opening speech[191] avoided "any matter respecting national officers or measures," though as he privately assured Adams he was careful to prevent "improper inferences" of opposition to Adams, again in general terms.[192] (His opening speech at the January 1800 session, before the change, similarly had avoided the Sedition Act.[193])

Jay's biographers do not claim that he supported the Sedition Act,[194] nor do period histories[195] or even highly critical articles[196]; the few publications that do

[185] John Jay to John Adams (21 Aug.1798), 4 Jay Correspondence 248.

[186] John Adams to John Jay (17 Oct.1798), 8 Adams Works 607.

[187] John Jay to John Adams (3 Jan.1799), 8 Adams Works 619, 620, 621.

[188] John Jay to Rufus King (30 Sept.1798), 2 King Correspondence 475.

[189] Jay Papers doc.2869, 4368, 3127, 3126, 3130, 3131, 3132, 3138, 3143, 0677, 8981, 3283, 4790, 2615, 10782, 3168, 3169, 0705, 3176, 2873, 10785, 3186, 2867, 3187, 3190 (listed chronologically).

[190] Even in private letters to friends such as Hamilton. 4 Jay Correspondence 249; Jay Papers doc.3169, 9224, 1534.

[191] Opening Speech (4 Nov.1800), 2 Messages-N.Y. 463.

[192] John Jay to John Adams (10 Nov.1800), 9 Adams Works 89, 90.

[193] Speech to the Legislature (28 Jan.1800), 2 Messages-N.Y. 448.

[194] *E.g.*, John Jay 416–18, revising Frank Monaghan, John Jay: Defender of Liberty (1936) (unpublished Ph.D. dissertation, Yale University); James B. Scott, *John Jay, First Chief Justice of the United States*, 6 Colum. L. Rev. 289, 322 (1906); George Pellew, John Jay 292–302 (Houghton Mifflin, Boston 1890); William Whitelock, The Life and Times of John Jay 308–12 (Dodd, Mead, New York 1887); Henry B. Renwick, Lives of John Jay and Alexander Hamilton 119–32 (Harper, New York 1846).

[195] *E.g.*, 1 Political Parties-N.Y. 125–31; Paul A. Gilje, New York in the Age of the Constitution, 1775–1800, at 74, 90–93 (FDUP, Rutherford 1992); 1 Henry Flanders, Lives and Times of the Chief Justices 417–23 (Lippincott, Philadelphia 1858).

[196] *E.g.*, Sandra F. VanBurkleo, *"Honour, Justice, and Interest": John Jay's Republican Politics and Statesmanship on the Federal Bench*, 4 J. Early Republic 239, 244–50, 270–74 (1984).

lack any source.[197] Jay's voluminous messages and letters show no endorsement, and no proposal of legislation or prosecutions, though he had numerous opportunities to do so. Jay is occasionally described as "approv[ing] the Senate's original alien act,"[198] but the cited letter predated revision of the Naturalization Act (and both Alien Acts) and did not support anything but limiting federal offices to citizens.[199] A recent biographer acknowledges that his concern was "considerably less radical than the [alien] law."[200]

Jay's obituaries in Democratic newspapers praised him as an "upright and learned judge," to whom "no reproach can be attached," without any allegation of supporting the Sedition Act,[201] though the Act was still regularly castigated even the month of Jay's death.[202]

Footdragging over Opposition to the Virginia and Kentucky Resolutions

The Virginia and Kentucky Resolutions, after adoption in late 1798,[203] were sent to the other states. Governor Jay transmitted them to the New York legislature, without recommendation,[204] as he transmitted Delaware's response[205] and as he transmitted about half the messages on other subjects from other governments or departments.[206] His approach was the same as for Massachusetts proposals for a constitutional amendment, which he transmitted five months earlier without recommendation,[207] though he clearly supported them, and for Virginia's opposition to those proposals, which he also transmitted without recommendation,[208] though he clearly disapproved.

197 *Supra* note 12.

198 FREEDOM'S FETTERS 55 n.14.

199 John Jay to Timothy Pickering (13 May 1798), JAY PAPERS doc.90219; *see id.* 4793, 0706; 1 CONSTITUTIONAL HISTORY-N.Y. 548.

200 WALTER STAHR, JOHN JAY: FOUNDING FATHER 354 (Hambledon Press, New York 2005).

201 *E.g., Death of the Honorable John Jay*, RICHMOND ENQUIRER, 26 May 1829, at 3; *Death of John Jay*, FARMER'S CABINET (Amherst), 23 May 1829, at 3; [No Caption], AURORA & PENNSYLVANIA GAZETTE (Philadelphia), 21 May 1829, at 1.

202 *E.g., The Union*, SALEM GAZETTE, 12 May 1829, at 1, 2; *The Union*, RICHMOND ENQUIRER, 19 May 1829, at 1, 2; *Extracts from the Speech of Mr. Clay*, NEW-BEDFORD MERCURY, 19 June 1829, at 2, 3.

203 4 ELLIOT'S DEBATES 528, 540.

204 JOURNAL-N.Y. 69 (12 Jan. 1799); JOURNAL OF THE SENATE OF THE STATE OF NEW-YORK ... 1799, at 15 (Loring Andrews, Albany 1799) (12 Jan. 1799).

205 2 MESSAGES-N.Y. 438 (4 Mar. 1799).

206 2 *id.* 402, 403, 404–05, 405, 406, 409, 409, 413, 414–15, 415, 415–16, 416, 416–17, 417, 419, 419 (1798); JOURNAL-N.Y. 7, 11, 69, 143, 193, 220, 251 (1799); while about half were with recommendation, 2 MESSAGES-N.Y. 404, 408, 410, 410, 411, 412, 413, 413–14, 416 (1798); JOURNAL-N.Y. 6, 25, 36, 88, 101, 103, 119, 133–34 (1799).

207 2 *id.* 424 (10 Aug. 1798).

208 2 *id.* 438–39 (16 Mar. 1799).

The state senate responded in March 1799 with a resolve denying that "any unconstitutional powers" were assumed by the general government, and expressing "anxiety and regret" about the "inflammatory and pernicious sentiments and doctrines" in the Resolutions.[209] The resolve went further and endorsed the English common law of seditious libel, finding it essential that government "have authority to defend and preserve its constitutional powers inviolate, inasmuch as every infringement thereof tends to its subversion," and that people have "a reasonable confidence in the constituted authorities and chosen representatives," because "every measure calculated to weaken that confidence, has a tendency to destroy the usefulness of our public functionaries."[210] That was too strong for New York's house, which did not endorse the Sedition Act or seditious libel, but followed an inconsistent and narrower approach of disclaiming state power to decide on the constitutionality of federal enactments.[211] The house vote was a narrow 50–43,[212] and as that would imply, the house never approved the senate's resolve, nor did the senate approve the house's resolve.

Jay made no formal statement in response to the Virginia and Kentucky Resolutions. By contrast, most governors of the seven other states that opposed the Virginia and Kentucky Resolutions publicly opposed the Resolutions.[213] Three governors who supported the Resolutions did as Jay and merely transmitted them.[214] Jay on other occasions did make formal

[209] 2 *id.* 428 n.11; 4 ELLIOT'S DEBATES 537 (5 Mar.1799).

[210] *Id.*; 2 *id.* 428 n.11.

[211] JOURNAL-N.Y. 122–23 (16 Feb.1799); CONTEMPORARY OPINION 248–49.

[212] *Id.*; CONTEMPORARY OPINION 57.

[213] *Speech of His Excellency Governor Tichenor,* CLAYPOOLE'S AMERICAN DAILY ADVERTISER (Philadelphia), 16 Nov.1799, at 2, 3 (Gov. Tichenor-Vt.); *Speech of His Excellency Governor Trumbull,* CLAYPOOLE'S AMERICAN DAILY ADVERTISER (Philadelphia), 18 May 1799, at 2, 3 (Gov. Trumbull-Conn.); 21 ANB 874, 875 (same); CONTEMPORARY OPINION 232 (Gov. Tichenor-Vt.), 247 (Gov. Rogers-Del.), 231 (Gov. Gilman-N.H.); 4 ELLIOT'S DEBATES 539 (Gov. Gilman-N.H.); *The Genuine Spirit of "76,"* ALBANY CENTINEL, 19 June 1798, at 3 (Gov. Sumner-Mass.); Increase Sumner, *Governor's Speech,* RESOLVES, & C. OF THE GENERAL COURT OF MASSACHUSETTS 37, 38 (n.p., 1799) (same); PRESS-MASS. 144 (same); *see* 2 IREDELL CORRESPONDENCE 577 (Gov. Davie-N.C., whose legislature split); 11 ANB 349, 350–51 (Gov. Howell-N.J., which did not oppose the Resolutions). The moderate governor of Pennsylvania did not condemn the Resolutions. Thomas Mifflin, *Opening Address to the Assembly* (7 Dec.1798), 4 PENNSYLVANIA ARCHIVES 405, 422–23 (4th ser., State of Pennsylvania, Harrisburg 1900–1902) (Gov. Mifflin-Pa.).

[214] Gov. John Sevier, "Legislative Message" (7 Dec. 1798), 1 MESSAGES OF THE GOVERNORS OF TENNESSEE 72 (Robert H. White ed., THC, Nashville 1952–72); Gov. James Jackson, *The Governor's Message Concluded,* COLUMBIAN MUSEUM & SAVANNAH ADVERTISER, 29 Jan. 1799, at 1; Resolved, that 150 Copies of the Governor's Message . . . Be Printed (Freneau, Columbia Nov.29, 1799) (broadside) (Gov. Edward Rutledge).

statements opposing legislation that he found problematic.[215] Further, Jay made no effort to get the state senate and house to agree on a common resolve. By contrast, the Virginia legislature and the Kentucky legislature had approved common resolutions, and all opposing states but New York had as well. Nor did Jay transmit the inconsistent house resolution when he transmitted the senate resolution to the sister states; Jay transmitted only the one that required him to disseminate it.[216]

Jay did advert to the Virginia and Kentucky Resolutions and their treatment of the Alien and Sedition Acts in one private letter. He declined to join Federalist apoplexy that the "country is to drink very deep of the cup of tribulation," but agreed with Federalist suspicion that "the Jacobins are still more numerous, more desperate, and more active in this country than is generally supposed," and criticized their leaders' "opposition to their own government, and their devotion to a foreign one." His next sentence asked rhetorically, "Why, and by whom, were the Kentucky and Virginia resolutions contrived, and for what purposes?"[217] That did not signify support of the Sedition Act; many contemporaries who opposed the Act opposed the Resolutions because of their disunifying implications, such as John Marshall, Patrick Henry, and ex-Governor Henry Lee.[218] Jay's concern was directed at foreign influence and the resolutions' treatment of the Alien Acts—Jay had long been concerned with "introduction of foreign influence into our national councils" if noncitizens were allowed to be elected to the presidency or Congress[219]—while not stating or implying agreement with the Sedition Act. (The Virginia and Kentucky Resolutions attacked the Alien Acts as well as the Sedition Act.) Six weeks later and soon after the state senate resolutions were

[215] Message to Assembly (24 Mar.1798) (impact of federal bill governing suits between claimants from different states), 2 MESSAGES-N.Y. 415; Opening Speech (28 Jan.1800) (concern under state constitution's separation of powers about annual legislative allowances to other branches), 2 *id.* 449; Message to Assembly (26 Feb.1801) (ambiguity under state constitution about who nominates lower state officers), 2 *id.* 472, 473–74; Opening Speech (4 Nov.1800) (concern that private acts involving wills and descent may be treated as precedents), 2 *id.* 463, 465–66.

[216] JOURNAL-N.Y. 123; 4 ELLIOT'S DEBATES 538; CONTEMPORARY OPINION 248–49, 56; THE COMMUNICATIONS OF SEVERAL STATES, ON THE RESOLUTIONS OF THE LEGISLATURE OF VIRGINIA, RESPECTING THE ALIEN AND SEDITION LAWS 15 ([Jones & Dixon], Richmond 1799).

[217] John Jay to Jedidiah Morse (30 Jan.1799), 4 JAY CORRESPONDENCE 252, 253; JAY PAPERS doc.1175.

[218] 2 PATRICK HENRY: LIFE, CORRESPONDENCE AND SPEECHES 589 (William W. Henry ed., Scribner, New York 1891); Norman K. Risjord, *The Virginia Federalists*, 33 J. SOUTHERN HISTORY 486, 505 (1967).

[219] JOURNAL-N.Y. 103 (12 Feb.1799); *id.* 6, 103 (proposed constitutional amendment); 4 JAY CORRESPONDENCE 230.

passed, Jay specified the measures that should be taken toward the Jacobins, in private correspondence to a Federalist congressman:

> Union, sedate firmness, and vigorous preparations for war generally afford the best means of counteracting the tendencies of insidious professions, and of too great public confidence in them.[220]

A year later, Jay said much the same thing.[221] Entirely missing was any hint of seditious libel prosecutions or restrictions of speech or press. That single reference by Jay to the Virginia and Kentucky Resolutions, among his extensive preserved correspondence, both private and official, questioning their treatment of the Alien Acts under his long-standing theme of foreign influence but not defending the Sedition Act, contrasts starkly with his Federalist son's pointed constitutional arguments against the Resolutions and for the Sedition Act, among a fifth as much preserved correspondence.[222]

Nonuse of His Ability to Spur Federal or State Seditious Libel Prosecutions

Jay took no official or private action to prosecute seditious libel during his five years as governor of New York, even while wincing at "calumny" by Greenleaf's newspaper in 1797–1800,[223] in contrast to Hamilton who caused prosecution of Greenleaf's printer, Frothingham, in 1799–1800. Yet Jay as governor could easily have caused such prosecution, since Hamilton as an influential private citizen of that state successfully did. Even with Federalist control of all branches of New York's government and the federal government, Jay did not ask for official action or take private action against sometimes scathing criticism in other Republican newspapers and by Republican legislators,[224] instead treating false criticism as "an engine of party in all countries" which "originating in the corruption of human nature, is without remedy, and consequently is to be borne patiently."[225] Just as he did not use his friendship to suggest any prosecution to the eager Pickering, Jay did not use his gubernatorial authority to instruct or hint to the state's attorney general or other officials that any seditious libel prosecution should be brought, though he did order

[220] John Jay to Benjamin Goodhue (29 Mar.1799), 4 JAY CORRESPONDENCE 256, 258.

[221] John Jay to Theophilus Parsons (1 July 1800), 4 *id.* 274, 274.

[222] Peter A. Jay to Augustus Woodward (17 Feb.1799), JAY PAPERS doc.10038.

[223] John Jay to Henry Van Schaack (23 Sept.1800), 4 JAY CORRESPONDENCE 275, 276.

[224] *E.g.*, John Jay to Peter A. Jay (6 Apr.1798), JAY PAPERS doc.90216; *Albany, June 19, 1798*, ALBANY CENTINEL, 19 June 1798, at 3; *Communication*, GREENLEAF'S NEW YORK JOURNAL, 7 July 1798, at 3; *To General Marshall*, GREENLEAF'S NEW YORK JOURNAL, 22 Dec.1798, at 3, 4.

[225] John Jay to Henry Van Schaack (23 Sept.1800), 4 JAY CORRESPONDENCE 275, 276; *e.g.*, 4 *id.* 160, 161; JAY PAPERS doc.90216.

other criminal prosecutions.[226] Instead, Jay's actions and extensive correspondence are consistent with his draft grand jury charge five years before the Sedition Act: "As free citizens we have a right to think and speak[] our sentiments on these subject[s], in terms becoming free men—that is in terms explicit and decorous—As judges and grand jurors the merits of those political questions are without our province"—and those divergent sentiments were different from "seditious practices," which Jay defined as "ende[a]voring to seduce our citizens into acts of hostility" and that he found capable of commission only by "foreigners."[227] Jay was still saying the same thing sixteen years after the Sedition Act, calling for vigilance in "examining the conduct of the administration in all its departments, candidly and openly giving decided approbation or decided censure, according as it may deserve."[228]

What facts should exist if Jay had supported the Sedition Act? His remarkably complete correspondence, including his fifty-five letters to the Act's chief enforcement official, should have shown support, as his Federalist son's letters did. His governor's messages on 1798 crisis legislation should have mentioned it and called for its enforcement, as other governors' messages did. Newspaper articles should have quoted or mentioned his support of the Sedition Act, as they did for the governors of the other seven states that passed resolutions opposing the Virginia and Kentucky Resolutions, even though those states had fewer newspapers. Jay's transmission of the state senate's response to the Virginia and Kentucky Resolutions should have contained positive words for the senate or negative words for the Resolutions. He should have included the state house's response as well, instead of omitting it; and he should have urged the two chambers to agree on a common response. Jay should have requested federal prosecutions and ordered state prosecutions of sedition cases, as Hamilton did and as the successor governor did, since New York had more newspapers and ethnic voices opposing the Adams administration than any other American city except Philadelphia. If Jay supported the Sedition Act, there was no reason for him to be silent, and every reason for him to be as vocal as other supportive governors and officials. Yet none of what would be expected, if Jay supported the Sedition Act, can be found in the quite complete record.

Jay's silence on the Sedition Act was not from cowardice, though he was doubtless aware of Marshall's sufferings. It was his style, rather than public dispute. He had chosen dignified silence over entering the renewed debate about his Treaty of 1783, over challenge of the stolen governorship of 1792, and over entering the fray about his Treaty ratified in 1795.[229] Later, Jay similarly avoided public statements opposing the War of 1812, though he affirmed the right of fellow citizens to speak

[226] John Jay to Josiah Hoffman (3 Jan. 1798), JAY PAPERS doc. 3114; *accord* JAY PAPERS doc. 3033, 3109, 3129, 3195.

[227] John Jay's Charge (Draft) (C.C.D. Va. 22 Apr. 1793), 2 DHSC 359, 364, 363.

[228] John Jay to Timothy Pickering (1 Nov. 1814), 4 JAY CORRESPONDENCE 378, 379.

[229] JAY-PEACE 3; LIVINGSTON 261–63; John Jay to Sarah Jay (18 June 1792), 3 JAY CORRESPONDENCE 434; Jay's Reply (1792), 3 *id.* 442, 444; John Jay to Henry Lee (11 July 1795), 4 *id.* 178; John Jay to Edmund Randolph (20 Aug. 1795), 4 *id.* 186.

on public measures: "there are certain occasions when it is not only their right, but also their duty, to express their sentiments relative to public measures."[230] Moreover, even Republican governors who opposed the Sedition Act remained publicly silent after Kentucky's governor was threatened with prosecution, such as Monroe of Virginia,[231] McKean of Pennsylvania,[232] and Rutledge of South Carolina.

Would the former chief justice have remained silent if he believed a violation of fundamental freedoms was occurring? Jay maintained public silence, until much later in life, about another issue he believed was a violation of even more fundamental rights: slavery.[233] He did not speak publicly as he rejected Hamilton's scheme to manipulate the presidential election results. He did not give public criticism of the Republican administrations for the next twenty-four years, though he certainly disagreed with some actions.[234] Jay was at heart a diplomat, who twice had silently weathered national debate and personal attack over his treaties.

Jay was perhaps the framer most likely to follow his principles, and least likely to act on party wishes. He consistently showed a willingness to take unpopular action required by his principles, such as heading the New York Manumission Association,[235] ruling that states lacked sovereign immunity from suit,[236] and concluding the Jay Treaty, despite certain and thunderous criticism. He similarly showed a willingness to refuse to take action prohibited by his principles, such as doing anything to enforce the Sedition Act, or implementing Hamilton's suggestion that would have thwarted the election of Thomas Jefferson as president.

Is this sufficient evidence to show probable opposition to the constitutionality of the Sedition Act? The best answer is that Jay's words and actions were virtually identical to another governor's words and actions—Edward Rutledge of South Carolina—whose opposition to the Sedition Act is discussed in the next section. Like Jay, he was elected as a Federalist, in a state controlled by Federalists until the 1800 state election. Like Jay, he said nothing publicly about the Sedition Act, cooperated with the federal call for defense measures by fortifying the state's major harbor, forwarded the Virginia and Kentucky Resolutions without a recommendation, and watched silently as the legislature failed to take binding action on the resolutions. Yet there is no question of Rutledge's position that the Sedition Act violated the First Amendment.

230 John Jay to Peter Van Schaack (28 July 1812), Jay Papers doc.9440.

231 James Monroe to James Madison (22 Nov.1799), 3 Monroe Writings 159; James Monroe to Thomas Jefferson (4 Jan.1800), 31 Jefferson Papers 289 (opposition, constitutional grounds); James Monroe to Thomas Jefferson (18 Mar.1800), 31 *id.* 446.

232 G. S. Rowe, Thomas McKean 293 (CAUP, Boulder 1978) (found clearly unconstitutional); The Inagural [*sic*] Address of Thomas M'Kean, Governor of Pennsylvania (Dickson, Lancaster 1800) (silence).

233 3 Jay Correspondence 140, 185, 334, 341, 414.

234 4 *id.* 314, 329.

235 3 *id.* 329n., 344, 356.

236 Chisholm v. Georgia, 2 U.S. (2 Dall.) 419, 471, 473, 479 (1793).

Chief Justice John Rutledge and the Sedition Act

Figure 8.3 Justice John Rutledge (on Supreme Court 1789–1791, also briefly chief justice 1795). Portrait by John Trumbull 1791. (Courtesy of Yale University Art Gallery.)

John Rutledge's brother, Edward Rutledge, opposed the Sedition Act, as did the other leader of the Rutledge-Pinckney faction, Charles Cotesworth Pinckney. Opposition by Edward Rutledge, and apparently by former Chief Justice John Rutledge (Figure 8.3), was a step in the same direction as their earlier support of South Carolina's grant to John Wilkes to defend his freedoms of press and speech, and their support of South Carolina's leading newspaper editor to defend his right to publish. It was a step in the same direction as John Rutledge's and the South Carolinians' support of Charles Pinckney's proposals to add a "liberty of press" clause to the Constitution.[237] Opposition to the Sedition Act was almost predetermined by their opposition to the Jay Treaty of 1795 (which was a test of fidelity to the emerging Federalist Party), by Rutledge's speech being branded as seditious, by his rejection by the Federalist senate as chief justice on that basis and his effective expulsion from the Federalist Party, and by Edward Rutledge's actual break with the Federalists for a period.

Opposition to the Sedition Act by His Alter Ego, Edward Rutledge

Edward Rutledge privately opposed the Sedition Act. He wrote to his nephew in Congress, shortly after learning of its enactment, that

[237] 2 FARRAND'S RECORDS 334, 340–41 (20 Aug.1787), 611, 617–18, 620 (14 Sept.1787); 1 ELLIOT'S DEBATES 249, 310.

> Not that we approve of all measures; among those that I disapprove is the Sedition Bill. The provisions of this bill are carried by much too far, & if I am not mistaken will, from doing so, defeat its own purpose. The Liberty of the Press, & the Freedom of Speech are points so essential to happiness, and on which is much national jealousy, that I may be allowed the election, and easily could [so elect], that I would much rather have left the measures of government to have been defended by the laws as they stood, [illegible word] the rectitude of those measures, than have created a new code of jurisprudence for their protraction.[238]

Rutledge's disapproval centered on the Act's impact on liberties of press and speech, liberties that he praised. The few historians who noted the letter have seen it as a clear condemnation of the Sedition Act.[239] The recipient, nephew John Rutledge, Jr., two weeks later described his uncle as a "political heretic" from Federalist orthodoxy.[240] A half year later, Edward Rutledge wrote to a friend that "I wish our own Government would repeal their Sedition Act, which is a good deal disapproved of, and has been made a handle of to lessen the confidence [in] the Administration."[241]

Edward Rutledge soon became South Carolina's governor, in December 1798, elected as a Federalist and with a Federalist majority in both legislative houses.[242] His inaugural message to the legislature focused on the danger of "hostile invasion" by France, and Rutledge began it by saying "it is incumbent on me to recommend to your consideration, such measures as I shall think the best calculated" for repelling French threats. He then recommended purchase of arms and artillery, ammunition and provisions, and impressment of property if necessary. He stressed the necessity of unity, and acknowledged that the French hoped to divide the nation and "founded their hopes of success on the divisions of our fellow citizens," but he was silent on any enforcement of the Sedition Act or restriction of expression.[243] Yet Charleston had been home to Citizen Genet and "French influence never appeared so open and unmasked" as it recently did there with "French flags, French cockades," and the nation's largest French population.[244] Obviously,

238 Edward Rutledge to John Rutledge, Jr. (29 July 1798), RUTLEDGE JR. PAPERS-UNC.

239 PINCKNEY 205; Richard B. Clow, Edward Rutledge of South Carolina, 1749–1800, at 296 (1976) (unpublished Ph.D. dissertation, University of Georgia); though RUTLEDGE, JR. 134 and PROLOGUE 211 quote only the non-press-and-speech part.

240 John Rutledge, Jr. to Bishop Smith (14 Aug. 1798), RUTLEDGE JR. PAPERS-UNC.

241 Edward Rutledge to Phineas Miller (1 Jan. 1799), quoted in PINCKNEY 206.

242 PINCKNEY 206; PROLOGUE 185.

243 *Governor Rutledge's Speech*, CITY GAZETTE (Charleston), 27 Dec. 1798, at 2; *Governor Rutledge's Speech*, GAZETTE OF THE UNITED STATES (Philadelphia), 15 Jan. 1799, at 3.

244 William Smith to Ralph Izard (8 Nov. 1796), FEDERALIST CORRESPONDENCE 784, 785; *accord* SOUTH CAROLINA 71–72, 76, 78.

Rutledge did not consider prohibition or prosecution of sedition a necessary measure. Like Jay, Rutledge did not publicly oppose the Sedition Act, but took no step to implement it, while sedulously implementing defense measures by seeking cannon and mustering troops,[245] and supporting construction of a new fort to protect the harbor.[246]

Also like Jay, Governor Rutledge forwarded the Virginia and Kentucky Resolutions to the legislature, along with the Maryland response and some unrelated Delaware and Georgia propositions, and did so with a neutral transmittal letter not making any recommendation.[247] He had responded to Virginia's governor and the Virginia Resolutions less guardedly when the Resolutions arrived in January 1799, assuring him that, as soon as the legislature's adjournment ended, he would be "laying the letter before them, with the resolutions contained in it, at their next session."[248] However, South Carolina's legislative session had just ended,[249] and the next one would not occur until November 1799. Though Rutledge then forwarded the Resolutions, it was that session that the newspaper reports said was so short that the Resolutions could not be taken up, though they "would certainly have been concurred in" (as we saw in Chapter 6). The legislature's inaction cannot be attributed to opposition, because it now had a Republican majority,[250] and just a year earlier it had been similarly ineffectual in response to Rutledge's recommendation of defense measures.[251] Like Jay, Rutledge remained silent as the legislature failed to take binding action, and he soon fell ill and died in January 1800,[252] as did his brother in July 1800. Edward Rutledge's stance cannot be attributed to

[245] Edward Rutledge to John Rutledge, Jr. (16 Oct.1798), RUTLEDGE JR. PAPERS-DUKE; *General Orders*, CITY GAZETTE (Charleston), 19 Apr.1799, at 3.

[246] Edward Rutledge to Nn. (8 Mar.1799), Edward Rutledge Papers, 1790–1820 (DU Ms. Section A); Edward Rutledge to Dr. Blythe (12 Apr.1799), Edward Rutledge Papers (SCHS, call no.43/0792).

[247] Resolved, that 150 Copies of the Governor's Message . . . Be Printed (Freneau, Columbia Nov.29, 1799) (broadside); *Legislature of South-Carolina*, CITY GAZETTE & DAILY ADVERTISER (Charleston), 11 Dec.1799, at 2.

[248] Edward Rutledge to Gov. James Wood (11 Jan.1799), Charles Francis Jenkins Collection (HSP) (obverse identifies as Virginia Resolutions). Ratzlaff misconstrues this as a refusal to forward the resolutions. RUTLEDGE, JR. 151 n.85.

[249] *Id.*

[250] JOHN E. FERLING, ADAMS VS. JEFFERSON: THE TUMULTUOUS ELECTION OF 1800, at 159 (OUP, New York 2004).

[251] Message of Governor Rutledge (26 Nov.1799), JOURNALS OF SENATE-S.C. 10, 11 (26 Nov.1799); JOURNALS OF HOUSE-S.C. 90–94 (12 Dec.1799); *see* ACTS AND RESOLUTIONS OF THE GENERAL ASSEMBLY . . . DECEMBER, 1799 (Freneau & Paine, Charleston 1800).

[252] [No Caption], SOUTH-CAROLINA STATE-GAZETTE (Charleston), 25 Jan.1800, at 3; PINCKNEY 212, asking the legislature's consent to leaving even before his stroke, PINCKNEY 212 n.46; JOURNALS OF SENATE-S.C. 99 (13 Dec.1799).

Republicanism; though his earlier flirtation with Jeffersonianism is described below, by 1798 and thereafter, he was an Adams Federalist.[253]

John Rutledge, Sr.'s stance on the Sedition Act is not documented, in either newspapers or his scanty preserved correspondence from 1798–1800.[254] However, a number of considerations indicate that he shared his brother's objection to the constitutionality of the Act.

The Rutledge brothers consistently agreed on major issues, to such an extent that their only published biography is a joint biography. They served together at the Continental Congresses,[255] in the state legislature, and in the state ratification convention.[256] In John Rutledge's stands for freedoms of press and speech that were discussed in Chapter 4, Edward Rutledge joined him, voting for the Wilkes grant and actually representing Powell.[257] (Charles Cotesworth Pinckney joined them as well.[258]) When John Rutledge denounced the Jay Treaty, Edward Rutledge shared his opposition.[259] When Federalists in turn anathematized John Rutledge, Edward Rutledge abandoned them for a time.

John Rutledge's past positions, like his collaboration with his brother, pointed toward opposing the Sedition Act. His leadership of the small group spearheading the South Carolina legislature's grant of £10,500 to the Supporters of the Bill of Rights to assist John Wilkes, even to the point of causing repeated dissolutions of the legislature and stoppage of colonial government, had been fundamentally about freedom of press and speech. His leadership when the state's lower chamber supported the newspaper editor Powell against seditious libel prosecution for printing the Drayton dissents, and against council claims of privilege, was also built upon freedom of press. He supported Charles Pinckney's proposals at the Constitutional Convention to add a "liberty of press" clause to the Constitution (as discussed in Chapter 4).

The argument from family positions can only be taken so far. Unlike Rutledge's brother and their ally Charles Cotesworth Pinckney, his son John Rutledge, Jr. voted for the Sedition Act,[260] and consistently supported it.[261] Though the son became a High Federalist, he was not so before 1797, having befriended Jefferson

[253] Federalism 528; Pinckney 205, 213; Prologue 163, 164.

[254] All extant correspondence from 1798–1800 has been gathered and reviewed.

[255] 1 JCC 252n., 121; 2 *id.* 162. The joint biography is by Haw.

[256] 4 Elliot's Debates 338.

[257] 9 Laurens Papers 111 n.1, 155 n.8.

[258] Committee of Correspondence to Charles Garth (6 Sept.1770), 31 Garth Correspondence 244, 246; 7 Laurens Papers 274 n.2; Pinckney 25; Founding Family 43, 45–46, 57.

[259] William Read to Jacob Read (21 July 1795), Read Family Papers, 1787–1869 (SCHS ms.1088.00); 1 Wolcott Papers 231.

[260] 8 Annals 2171.

[261] 9 *id.* 2985; 10 *id.* 423, 975, 1038.

during a grand tour in the late 1780s,[262] developing strong cases of Francophilia[263] and Anglophobia.[264] The son had opposed the Jay Treaty,[265] and voted for Jefferson as a presidential elector in 1796.[266] The son's party leanings were not certain as he entered Congress in 1796, and he was assumed to be a Republican,[267] before he veered decisively to the Federalists in 1797[268] and into Hamilton's orbit by 1800.[269] Even so, Rutledge Jr. could couple defense of the Act with affirmation that "every man has the privilege of expressing unreservedly whatever he thinks on political subjects."[270] The father was closer to his brother than to his son, as the son spent three years away on his grand tour,[271] and then from the time of his conversion to Federalism, was far away in Philadelphia, at a Rhode Island home, and at a relatively distant South Carolina plantation.[272]

There were many examples of opposite allegiances of father and son, of course. Franklin's son was a loyalist during the Revolution.[273] President Adams's son and namesake became a Republican within a decade.[274] Jay, Wilson, and Johnson had sons who soon became Republicans, as discussed below. Even Chase's son-in-law was "a democrat."[275]

262 12 JEFFERSON PAPERS 340, 349, 492, 556, 605, 631; 13 *id.* 124, 138, 262, 282, 318, 358, 454, 506, 530, 551, 567, 593, 615, 631; 14 *id.* 404, 481, 538, 613, 701; 15 *id.* 24, 63, 72; 16 *id.* 266, 413, 426; 17 *id.* 521; 18 *id.* 52; 19 *id.* 297.

263 SOUTH CAROLINA 71.

264 John Rutledge, Jr. to Thomas Jefferson (20 Nov.1790), 18 JEFFERSON PAPERS 52, 53; John Rutledge, Jr. to Thomas Jefferson (26 Sept.1790), 17 *id.* 521.

265 William Smith to Ralph Izard (23 May 1797), FEDERALIST CORRESPONDENCE 786.

266 SOUTH CAROLINA 98; PROLOGUE 138 n.123.

267 SOUTH CAROLINA 99 n.104, 103 ("leaned toward the Republicans in 1796"); *see* 7 ANNALS 766–67, 8 *id.* 1534; Thomas Jefferson to James Madison (1 June 1797), 29 JEFFERSON PAPERS 411 (evidently counting Jr. among Republicans to call South Carolina "evenly divided").

268 RUTLEDGE, JR. 113, 125–29; PINCKNEY 203.

269 John Rutledge, Jr. to Alexander Hamilton (10 Jan.1801), 25 HAMILTON PAPERS 308; *accord* 25 *id.* 30; PROLOGUE 203 n.62.

270 10 ANNALS 933.

271 James Iredell to Hannah Iredell (23 May 1790), 2 IREDELL CORRESPONDENCE 289; RUTLEDGE, JR. 34.

272 Robert K. Ratzlaff, John Rutledge, Jr., South Carolina Federalist, 1766–1819, at 95, 103, 117, 139, 154, 173, 77 (1975) (unpublished Ph.D. dissertation, University of Kansas); as shown in 1797–1800 correspondence addresses in RUTLEDGE, JR. PAPERS-UNC.

273 SHEILA L. SKEMP, WILLIAM FRANKLIN: SON OF A PATRIOT, SERVANT OF A KING 227–76 (OUP, Oxford 1990); JAY-PEACE 284 n.5.

274 Robert R. Thompson, *John Quincy Adams, Apostate: From "Outrageous Federalist" to "Republican Exile," 1801–1809,* 11 J. EARLY REPUB. 161, 161–62, 177 (1991); *accord* ADAMS FEDERALISTS 260.

275 9 JOHN SANDERSON, BIOGRAPHY OF THE SIGNERS TO THE DECLARATION OF INDEPENDENCE 181, 234 (Pomeroy, Philadelphia 1823–27). *Cf.* Stephen Higginson to Timothy Pickering (25 June 1798), 1 HIGGINSON LETTERS 812, 813.

Departures from Federalist Orthodoxy

John Rutledge, like Jay, was a moderate Federalist rather than a High Federalist, as was his brother and as were Charles Cotesworth Pinckney and his brother Thomas Pinckney.[276]

That "Rutledge-Pinckney faction"[277] was the moderate Federalist bloc in South Carolina. Its prominence and their alliance were reflected in President Washington's joint letter offering the Supreme Court position John Rutledge vacated in 1791 to Edward Rutledge or Charles Cotesworth Pinckney,[278] and in his appointment of Thomas Pinckney to negotiate a treaty with Spain shortly before his recess appointment of John Rutledge as chief justice.[279] The political alliance was undergirded by close friendship and intermarriage,[280] and by a law partnership and plantation partnerships between the younger Rutledge and the elder Pinckney.

Charles Cotesworth Pinckney was reported to oppose the Sedition Act with "his friends."[281] His friends, more than anyone else, were Edward Rutledge, who clearly opposed the Act, and John Rutledge.

Their Rutledge-Pinckney faction had departed from Federalist orthodoxy in a number of ways that lay the groundwork for objecting to the Sedition Act. They disliked Britain,[282] having all studied law at Middle Temple[283] and experienced social marginalization instead of the prominence they enjoyed in South Carolina, followed by Edward Rutledge and Charles Cotesworth Pinckney being British prisoners during the Revolution.[284] All suffered British depredations against their plantations when British troops controlled South Carolina. They all equally liked France, welcomed its revolution and its emissary Genet,[285] and in 1795 remained appreciative of its critical assistance in the American Revolution[286]; their Gallo-

[276] 2 DAVID D. WALLACE, THE HISTORY OF SOUTH CAROLINA 356, 357 (AHS, New York 1934); FOUNDING FAMILY 311; FEDERALISM 544, 559; PINCKNEY 128; SOUTH CAROLINA 101, though Hamilton's schemes to manipulate the Pinckney vote in 1800 can be read to imply otherwise, except that C.C. Pinckney opposed what Hamilton sought.

[277] 17 ANB 536; FOUNDING FAMILY 314; PINCKNEY 202; FEDERALISM 524.

[278] George Washington to Charles Cotesworth Pinckney and Edward Rutledge (24 May 1791), 8 WASHINGTON PAPERS-PRESIDENTIAL 205.

[279] SAMUEL F. BEMIS, PINCKNEY'S TREATY (YUP, New Haven 1960).

[280] PINCKNEY 127, 212–13; FOUNDING FAMILY 172, 332; 17 ANB 536.

[281] William Vans Murray to John Quincy Adams (22 Mar.1799), Worthington C. Ford ed., *Letters of William Vans Murray*, 1912 ANNUAL REPORT OF AM. HISTORICAL ASS'N 343, 529, 530.

[282] PROLOGUE 106–07; FEDERALISM 526 (Rutledges); PINCKNEY 124–25.

[283] E. ALFRED JONES, AMERICAN MEMBERS OF THE INNS OF COURT 171, 173, 187, 189 (SCP, London 1924).

[284] PINCKNEY 66; FEDERALISM 560.

[285] PROLOGUE 108; FEDERALISM 561; PINCKNEY 117–18, 124; SOUTH CAROLINA 82.

[286] Edward Rutledge to Thomas Jefferson (7 Oct.1791), 22 JEFFERSON PAPERS 201, 202–03; Edward Rutledge to Thomas Jefferson (c. 1 Apr.1789), 15 *id.* 11, 12; Robert Troup to Rufus King (14 Sept.1800), 3 KING CORRESPONDENCE 299; PINCKNEY 124, 128.

philia continued into 1797 before cooling.[287] Consequently, the Rutledge-Pinckney bloc rejected Federalist positions on foreign policy.[288]

When the Jay Treaty generated acerbic divisions between Federalists[289] and the emerging Republicans,[290] Edward Rutledge was "violent" in his opposition, which was attributed to his "unconquerable aversion to the British nation,"[291] and he expressed that opposition as he resumed correspondence with Thomas Jefferson.[292] John Rutledge was even more violent, as he gave a scathing speech against the treaty[293] that described it as "a surrender of our rights," and as "prostituting the dearest rights of freemen," such that the elder Rutledge "had rather, the President should die, dearly as he loves him, than he should sign that treaty."[294] The speech was reprinted in newspapers across the country,[295] and though it was probably given before news of Rutledge's nomination reached Charleston,[296] it doomed his confirmation as chief justice.

Denial of Confirmation by Federalists for Seditious Libel, and Expulsion from the Federalist Party

John Rutledge, serving as chief justice by recess appointment in 1795, was denied confirmation by the Senate. The vote was a party-line vote: every one of the fourteen votes against his confirmation was by a Federalist, and every one of the ten

[287] Edward Rutledge to John Rutledge, Jr. (19 May 1797), RUTLEDGE, JR. PAPERS-DUKE; FOUNDING FAMILY 314, 325; PINCKNEY 212; SOUTH CAROLINA 101; *see* Thomas Pinckney to Rufus King (18 July 1798), 2 KING CORRESPONDENCE 369.

[288] Edward Rutledge to Thomas Jefferson (30 Apr.1796), 29 JEFFERSON PAPERS 92; Edward Rutledge to Thomas Jefferson (7 Aug.1791), 22 *id.* 12, 13; *see* Edward Rutledge to Thomas Jefferson (4 May 1797), 29 *id.* 356; PROLOGUE 105.

[289] Charles Cotesworth Pinckney struggled to remain publicly neutral while privately opposing the treaty, and his brother leaving a diplomatic position supported the administration. PINCKNEY 125–26, 126; FEDERALISM 527. Southern Federalists widely opposed the treaty. ADAMS FEDERALISTS 290–92 (col.1–3); PINCKNEY 124.

[290] JERALD A. COMBS, THE JAY TREATY: POLITICAL BATTLEGROUND OF THE FOUNDING FATHERS 152–53, 159–88 (UCP, Berkeley 1970); DAVID J. SIEMERS, RATIFYING THE REPUBLIC 158–59 (SUP, Palo Alto 2002); FEDERALISM 548, 415–31; 1 WARREN 129–34.

[291] William Smith to Oliver Wolcott (8 Sept.1797), 1 WOLCOTT PAPERS 230, 231; *accord* PINCKNEY 124–25.

[292] Edward Rutledge to Thomas Jefferson (12 Oct.1795), 28 JEFFERSON PAPERS 502; Edward Rutledge to Thomas Jefferson (30 Apr.1796), 29 *id.* 92; *accord* Edward Rutledge to John F. Grimke (22 Oct.1798), Grimke Family Papers, 1761–1866 (SCHS Ms.1040.00).

[293] NEW YORK ARGUS, July 30, 1795, reprinted in 18 HAMILTON PAPERS 510–11 n.3; FEDERALISM 526.

[294] SOUTH-CAROLINA STATE-GAZETTE (Charleston), 17 July 1795, reprinted in 1 DHSC 765, 766, 767.

[295] *Id.* 767n.

[296] 1 DHSC 768 n.7.

votes in favor was by a Republican except the lone vote of a Federalist senator from South Carolina in support of a native son.[297] The Jay Treaty had become a test of Federalist loyalty.[298]

Rutledge was not just denied confirmation, but was disavowed by and expelled from the emerging Federalist Party. Hamilton published newspaper essays describing Rutledge's "delirium of rage" that brought Federalists "mortification."[299] Adams branded him seditious.[300] Oliver Wolcott wrote that, "to my astonishment I am told, that John Rutledge has had a tender of the office of Chief-Justice"[301]—a "driveller and fool appointed Chief Justice."[302] Edmund Randolph pressed Washington to withhold a commission.[303] Then-Senator Ellsworth was shocked that "J.R. should act like the devil,"[304] Senator Trumbull called him "dementated,"[305] and Senator Read's brother objected to Rutledge's "mad frollicks."[306] William Davie, who would join Ellsworth as envoy to France, wondered if the "Chief Justice raves on the bench as he does at a town meeting."[307] Rutledge was equally embraced by Republicans, beyond the senators voting for him, such as Chancellor Livingston, who was "sorry for the mortification Rutledge will feel in being made the sport of a party."[308]

Rutledge's worst enemies became the Federalist newspapers,[309] and his best friends were the Republican ones,[310] in the stormy five months between his speech and his Senate rejection. Widely reprinted Federalist articles branded his speech "the silliest expressions that ever fell from human lips," conferred satirical awards from "French Republicans composing the Society of Sans Culottes," condemned

297 1 JOURNAL OF EXECUTIVE PROCEEDINGS-SENATE 195–96 (4th Cong., 1st sess.) (15 Dec.1795).

298 George S. McCowan, *Chief Justice John Rutledge and the Jay Treaty*, 62 S.C. HISTORICAL MAG. 10, 23 (1961).

299 Camillus [Alexander Hamilton], *The Defence No.V*, ARGUS (New York), 5 Aug.1795, at 2–3; 1 DHSC 776.

300 John Adams to Abigail Adams (17 Dec.1795), 1 DHSC 813.

301 Oliver Wolcott to Alexander Hamilton (28 July 1795), 1 WOLCOTT PAPERS 219.

302 Oliver Wolcott to Alexander Hamilton (30 July 1795), 18 HAMILTON PAPERS 526, 531.

303 1 DHSC 772, 773, 776.

304 Oliver Ellsworth to Oliver Wolcott (15 Aug.1795), 1 WOLCOTT PAPERS 225.

305 Jonathan Trumbull to John Trumbull (4 Mar.1796), 1 DHSC 842.

306 William Read to Jacob Read (27 July 1795), Read Family Papers, 1787–1869 (SCHS ms.1088.00).

307 William R. Davie to James Iredell (4 Sept.1795), 2 IREDELL CORRESPONDENCE 454.

308 Robert R. Livingston to Edward Livingston (20 Dec.1795), 1 DHSC 815.

309 *E.g.*, FEDERAL ORRERY (Boston), 6 Aug.1795, reprinted in 1 DHSC 777.

310 *E.g.*, INDEPENDENT CHRONICLE (Boston), 10 Aug.1795, reprinted in 1 DHSC 778; *Society of the Sans-Culottes*, INDEPENDENT GAZETTEER (Philadelphia), 14 Aug.1795, 1 *id.* 781; INDEPENDENT CHRONICLE (Boston), 17 Aug.1795, 1 *id.* 783; INDEPENDENT CHRONICLE (Boston), 20 Aug.1795, 1 *id.* 784; AURORA (Philadelphia), 21 Aug.1795, 1 *id.* 784; My Country's Friend, *Citizens*, INDEPENDENT CHRONICLE (Boston), 27 Aug.1795, 1 *id.* 787; A South Carolinean, *John Rutledge, Vindicated*, COLUMBIAN CENTINEL (Boston), 28 Aug.1795, 1 *id.* 789.

him as "not very far above mediocrity" and immoral, described his past as "fraudulent," and just before the vote, proclaimed him "a Republican,"[311] and after called him "deranged in his mind."[312] Republican newspapers, equally fervent, praised Rutledge as a "sage republican,"[313] lauded him as an "illustrious patriot," and countered the detractors.[314] Edward Rutledge, outraged by the vote,[315] lambasted "that rascal Cobbett,"[316] a leading Federalist editor.

Not surprisingly, the Rutledges moved closer to the Republicans, and Edward Rutledge is sometimes said to have become a Republican for a season.[317] In the election of 1796, Edward Rutledge strongly supported Jefferson over Adams,[318] and in the electoral college, he and John Rutledge, Jr. were electors for Jefferson[319] (for whom all eight electors from South Carolina bestowed their votes in preference to Adams[320]), though a friend perceptively predicted "remorse at having separated from the federalist party."[321] Jefferson was a long-standing friend of both John Rutledge, Sr.[322] and Edward Rutledge.[323] However, Edward Rutledge's flirtation with Jeffersonianism was short lived, and he was again a committed

311 *Vindication of the Treaty*, AMERICAN MINERVA (New York), 5 Aug.1795, at 2; *To Citizens Rutledge and Pinckney*, NEW-JERSEY JOURNAL (Elizabethtown), 19 Aug.1795, at 3; Real Republican, *To His Honor John Rutledge*, AMERICAN MERCURY (Hartford), 31 Aug.1795, at 2; *Mr. Rutledge*, COURIER (Boston), 10 Oct.1795, at 119; *Extract of a Letter*, DUNLAP'S AMERICAN DAILY ADVERTISER (Philadelphia), 11 Dec.1795, at 3; *e.g.*, 1 DHSC 802, 805, 813.

312 *E.g., December 24*, AMERICAN MINERVA (New York), 24 Dec.1795, at 2; *December 24*, HERALD (New York), 26 Dec.1795, at 2; [No Caption], FEDERAL INTELLIGENCER (Baltimore), 30 Dec.1795, at 3.

313 *E.g., Charleston, July 17*, MERCURY (Boston), 7 Aug.1795, at 1; *Charleston July 17*, INDEPENDENT GAZETTEER (Philadelphia), 1 Aug.1795, at 3.

314 [No Caption], INDEPENDENT CHRONICLE (Boston), 10 Aug.1795, reprinted in 1 DHSC 778; *e.g., A Correspondent Observes*, AURORA (Philadelphia), 8 Sept.1795, at 2; 1 DHSC 783, 784, 787, 788, 789, 795, 800, 822, 823, 824, 826.

315 FEDERALISM 527.

316 Edward Rutledge to John Rutledge, Jr. (13 Dec.1797), RUTLEDGE JR. PAPERS-UNC.

317 *E.g.*, JOANNE B. FREEMAN, AFFAIRS OF HONOR 223 (YUP, New Haven 2001); PROLOGUE 111; SOUTH CAROLINA 122, 135.

318 William Smith to Ralph Izard (8 Nov.1796), FEDERALIST CORRESPONDENCE 784, 785; *see* William Smith to Ralph Izard (3 Nov.1796), *id.* 781, 782; JEFFREY L. PASLEY, THE FIRST PRESIDENTIAL CONTEST: 1796, at 401–02 (UPKan, Lawrence 2013); FEDERALISM 525–26.

319 South Carolina Certification (1796 election), Records of the U.S. Senate (National Archives, Washington, Rec. Group 46, SEN4A-H1); Elizabeth Cometti, *John Rutledge, Jr., Federalist*, 13 J. SOUTHERN HISTORY 186, 188 (1947).

320 THE PRESIDENTIAL COUNTS 6 (Appleton, New York 1877).

321 Gabriel Manigault to Nn. 3 (22 Dec.1796), Gabriel Manigault Papers, 1775–1839 (SCHS call no.1068.02.02).

322 3 JEFFERSON PAPERS 179, 415; 7 *id.* 283; 11 *id.* 405; 12 *id.* 287, 461; 13 *id.* 41, 374, 426; 14 *id.* 278, 577; in addition to Jefferson's help to Rutledge's son.

323 10 *id.* 463; 11 *id.* 587; 12 *id.* 225, 263; 13 *id.* 377; 15 *id.* 11, 451; 16 *id.* 600; 22 *id.* 12, 73, 201; 23 *id.* 544; 24 *id.* 373; 27 *id.* 336, 638; 28 *id.* 502, 541; 29 *id.* 92, 231, 356, 386, 455.

Federalist in 1798,[324] even if occasionally heretical. He supported his Federalist nephew's campaign against a Republican challenger,[325] and jettisoned his earlier Francophilia.[326] His brother, John Rutledge, similarly remained a Federalist, or at least Iredell saw nothing amiss when visiting him in 1798,[327] nor did others when they lamented his death two years later.[328]

The underlying issue causing Rutledge's rejection has even greater implications for his position on the Sedition Act than his ostracism from the Federalist Party. The Senate denied confirmation because of Rutledge's criticism of the administration and its measures, and because that amounted to seditious libel. His lone Federalist supporter in that Senate vote wrote, immediately after, that Rutledge "head[ing] a tumultuous assembly which if repeated cou'd not fail to unhinge all order & destroy our Gouvernment [*sic*] was the true & real objection & in this the friends of order were immovable"—Rutledge's actions would "totally destroy all gouvernment" [*sic*].[329] Vice President Adams, who presided over the Senate debates, saw the issue in the same light, writing to his wife that the Senate's basis was that "C. Justices must not go to illegal meetings and become popular orators in favour of sedition, nor inflame the popular discontents which are ill founded"; they must not go to "unlawful assemblies to spout reflections [on government] and excite opposition to the legal acts of constitutional authority."[330] It would have been unimaginable for Rutledge in 1798 to approve of a Sedition Act that his exercise of free speech would have violated, that codified the basis of his rejection and humiliation, and that was sponsored by a party that virtually drummed him out and ridiculed him.

The objurgation suffered by John Rutledge caused most subsequent Federalist opponents of the Jay Treaty to keep public silence and to confine opposition to private correspondence.[331] That also doubtless influenced Federalist opponents of the Sedition Act, three years later, as they avoided public statements and, other than votes, left only private letters disapproving the Act (except Marshall, who had to make a public statement to win his congressional race). The storm of censure in 1795 also made it unlikely that Rutledge himself would again publicly criticize a Federalist measure; his brother certainly kept his criticism of the Sedition Act private.

[324] PROLOGUE 164; PINCKNEY 203; FEDERALISM 528.

[325] Edward Rutledge to Nn. (n.d. 1798), RUTLEDGE JR. PAPERS-UNC.

[326] *Governor Rutledge's Speech*, CITY GAZETTE (Charleston), 27 Dec.1798, at 2; PINCKNEY 204.

[327] James Iredell to Hannah Iredell (11–12 May 1798), 3 DHSC 264; James Iredell to Hannah Iredell (18 May 1798), 3 *id.* 272.

[328] Christopher Gadsden to John Adams (11 Mar.1801), 2 GADSDEN WRITINGS 305, 306.

[329] Jacob Read to Ralph Izard (19 Dec.1795), 1 DHSC 814.

[330] John Adams to Abigail Adams (17 Dec.1795), 1 *id.* 813; John Adams to Abigail Adams (16 Dec.1795), 1 *id.* 812.

[331] *E.g.*, James Habersham, Jr. to Nn. Habersham (30 Mar.1797), Preston Davie Collection (UNC-SHC Series D, Item 224, Collection No.3406).

There is one other theoretical explanation to consider for John Rutledge's public silence on the Sedition Act, besides opposition to it: his declining health in the late 1790s. After his Senate rejection, he suffered depression that fed rumors of insanity[332] and he made two suicide attempts.[333] However, by the summer of 1796 "his health is said to be mended."[334] Two months before the Sedition Act passed, a physician who knew Rutledge's earlier condition,[335] Dr. William Read, told his brother, Senator Jacob Read (who cast the lone Federalist vote for Rutledge) that "I was this day at Mr. Rutledge[']s to visit Master States—the old gentleman was very chatty & communicative."[336] Senator Read surely would not have voted to confirm Rutledge if the latter had continued to be afflicted or had been incapable of serving. Two weeks later, Justice Iredell, who had twice ridden much of the two-thousand-mile circuit with Rutledge and knew him well,[337] visited him as he did several times, and wrote that Rutledge had come out of seclusion and "is perfectly recovered."[338] Two weeks after the Act passed, Thomas Pinckney told Rutledge Jr., who had been in Philadelphia and Newport for months, that "your father has been occasionally less well than his friends wish,"[339] but reported nothing more dire. A few months after the Sedition Act, John Rutledge stood successfully for the state legislature, and participated actively in the late 1798[340] and late 1799 sessions, voting, chairing a committee, and being seen around town.[341] Whatever the nature of Rutledge's breakdown after his December 1795 rejection, he was substantially recovered in and after July 1798, though chastened about publicly speaking against Federalist orthodoxy.

Thus, John Rutledge began a trajectory in 1795, with a vehement speech opposing Federalist orthodoxy in the form of the Jay Treaty, that led to his rejection as chief justice by every Federalist senator but one (and support by every Republican), treating the speech as seditious, and that led to his brother Edward Rutledge evidently becoming a Republican for a time. That trajectory continued with

[332] James Madison to Thomas Jefferson (7 Feb.1796), 28 JEFFERSON PAPERS 606, 607; [Thomas Jefferson], Notes of a Conversation with Edmund Randolph (n.d.), 28 *id.* 568.

[333] William Read to Jacob Read (29 Dec.1795), 1 DHSC 820.

[334] William L. Smith to Herman LeRoy (15 July 1796), William L. Smith Papers (DUL), quoted in GEORGE C. ROGERS, EVOLUTION OF A FEDERALIST: WILLIAM LOUGHTON SMITH 288 (USCP, Columbia 1962).

[335] 1 DHSC 820.

[336] William Read to Jacob Read (27 Apr.1798), Read Family Papers, 1787–1869 (SCHS ms.1088.00).

[337] 2 DHSC 536.

[338] James Iredell to Hannah Iredell (11 May 1798), 2 IREDELL CORRESPONDENCE 527, 528, 527; *accord* 3 DHSC 263, 272; 1 WARREN 135 n.1.

[339] Thomas Pinckney to John Rutledge, Jr. (1 Aug.1798), RUTLEDGE JR. PAPERS-UNC.

[340] *Legislature of South-Carolina*, CITY GAZETTE & DAILY ADVERTISER (Charleston), 4 Jan.1799, at 3; RUTLEDGE 260.

[341] *E.g.*, CHARLES FRASER, REMINISCENCES OF CHARLESTON 87 (John Russell, Charleston 1854).

ostracism from the Federalist Party and in 1798, when the next test for Federalist orthodoxy loomed in the form of the Sedition Act, Edward Rutledge privately opposed it, as did the other leader of the Rutledge-Pinckney faction, Charles Cotesworth Pinckney, in addition to "his friends," and the sizable number of other Federalists, mostly southern, who were described above. The Rutledges cannot have failed to notice that the fateful speech, their opposition to the Jay Treaty, and their amity toward France would have been criminalized by the Sedition Act, if it had been enacted before 1798. John Rutledge is not likely to have had his first policy disagreement with his brother, in their thirty years of political partnership, over the Sedition Act. The earlier fights John Rutledge had led, in favor of a grant to John Wilkes to support freedom of press and speech, and in support of a newspaper editor when prosecuted for publishing a dissent, predisposed his principles to be in conflict with the Act. All indications, except the post-1797 zeal of his son, point toward his intellectual dissonance with the Sedition Act, like his brother, their colleague Pinckney, and many other southern Federalists.

Justice James Wilson and the Sedition Act

Figure 8.4 Justice James Wilson (on Supreme Court 1789–1798). Watercolor on ivory by Jean Pierre Henri Elouis 1792. (Courtesy of Smithsonian American Art Museum/Art Resource.)

Justice James Wilson (Figure 8.4) appears not to have discussed the Sedition Act, though he lived just over a month after its passage, because he was ill from malaria and "too weak to attempt" to write during that month.[342] However, his final and most considered interpretation of the First Amendment and the rest of

[342] Hannah Wilson to Bird Wilson (28 July 1798), 2 WILSON WRITINGS 535. He wrote only one preserved letter in that period, James Wilson to Bird Wilson (4 Aug. 1798), 2 *id.* 537, which like his other 1798 correspondence dealt with his financial problems. 6 James Wilson Papers 1–10 (HSP).

the Constitution, his advocacy of natural rights and anti-Blackstonian views, his numerous other departures from Federalist orthodoxy ranging from democracy to treason, and his mentor's and closest colleagues' positions on the Sedition Act, all dictated rejection of the constitutionality of the Act.

Final Position on Freedoms of Press and Speech and on Seditious Libel

Wilson stated his fully evolved understanding of the First Amendment in 1790–1791, when he wrote in his law lectures that "[t]he citizen under a free government has a right to think, to speak, to write, to print, and to publish freely, but with decency and truth, concerning publick men, publick bodies, and publick measures."[343] That rejected the Blackstone-Mansfield definition of those freedoms. The "decency and truth" limitation meant, in context, avoidance of defamation of character, rather than avoidance of seditious libel, as discussed in Chapter 4.[344]

In a later law lecture that is quoted in part at the beginning of this chapter, Wilson mentioned the English common law of seditious libel, characterizing it as an "unwarranted attempt made in the star chamber . . . to wrest the law of libels to the purpose of ministers," and warned that "the reasonings on this crime are inaccurate."[345] The wrongly reasoned case that he cited as "the foundation of the law on this subject" was *Case de Libellis Famosis*,[346] and he stated that the case "has ever since been considered, *in England*, as the foundation of the law on this subject"—but not in America.[347] Wilson repudiated each of its major holdings described by Coke: "that a libel against a magistrate or other publick person, is a greater offence than one against a private man" (which "cannot be rationally admitted"), "that it is immaterial whether the libel be false or true" (which was "clearly extrajudicial" and senselessly contrary to the rule in civil actions), and that the "provocation and not the falsity . . . is the thing to be punished criminally" (as defended by Blackstone, which "very principle is mistaken," since the defamation of character is the only valid offense).[348]

That first point of disagreement with *Libellis Famosis*, that libel against a government official is a greater offense than against a private person, effectively rejected seditious libel as an offense at all, keeping only the offense of defamation of character. In summary, Wilson stated that "the reasonings on this crime are inaccurate," particularly those of Blackstone, and added a final example, the

343 James Wilson, *Lectures on Law* (1790–91), 2 WILSON WORKS 1046; *accord* 1 *id.* 36, 48, 50, 176, 539; 2 *id.* 907, 952.

344 2 *id.* 1062–63.

345 2 *id.* 1134, 1135.

346 2 *id.* 1134 note k.

347 2 *id.* 1134 (emphasis added).

348 2 *id.* 1134–35.

commentator's dictum that juries may only consider "the making or publishing of the book or writing," while judges determine "whether the matter be criminal" (something that is "remote from a question of law" to be "taken from juries").[349] In essence, Wilson rejected the Blackstone-Mansfield crime of seditious libel, including most of their framework of six unique rules for that crime, and said their approach had never been a legitimate part of the common law. He carried that to its logical conclusion by entirely excluding seditious libel from his lengthy section on crimes.[350] Elsewhere, speaking of constructive treason, he decried "Crimes against the state! and against the officers of the state!," as the subject on which "more wrong" had been done in history than on any other subject.[351]

Wilson's "right to think, to speak, to write, to print, and to publish freely," except for defamation of character, "concerning publick men, publick bodies, and publick measures" demanded rejection of the Sedition Act, which prohibited almost precisely that ("writing, printing, uttering or publishing any false, scandalous and malicious writing or writings against the government of the United States, or . . . Congress . . ., or the President"). Both Wilson and the Act disallowed falsehood, but there the overlap ended, because Wilson only listed as criminal a falsehood against character (defamation), not a falsehood against government officials or measures (seditious libel). That is why he did not list seditious libel as a crime at all. Wilson's approach was not casual or tentative, but was carefully laid out in written versions of lectures, as he obviously aspired to become the American counterpart of Blackstone or Coke or Hale, and there is no evidence of his changing positions on freedom of press or speech or on seditious libel after 1791.

It is true that Wilson's position on seditious libel in the 1790–1791 law lectures, as well as in the 1789 Pennsylvania constitutional convention, diverged sharply from his 1787 speeches after the Constitutional Convention and at Pennsylvania's ratification convention (as addressed in Chapter 4). What intervened was congressional approval of the First Amendment, and Wilson's refinement and formalization of his thinking, perhaps influenced by the 1788 *Oswald* case and the 1789 Franklin satire. His law lectures were his final opinion on expression and libel.

Stances on Natural Rights, Sovereignty, and Blackstone

Wilson's positions on freedoms of press and speech and on seditious libel were not idiosyncratic caprice, but instead were rooted in his beliefs about natural rights and about sovereignty.

He began his lecture on natural rights, after expressing the common belief that such rights were conferred by God or nature,[352] with an assault on Blackstone's

349 2 *id.* 1135–36.

350 2 *id.* 1085–204.

351 2 DHRC 483 (4 Dec.1787).

352 2 Wilson Works 1054, 1055; *accord* 2 *id.* 1066.

"fallacious" concept that natural rights were surrendered to government in trust or were sacrificed in part to obtain governmental protection.[353] Instead, natural rights were based on "the stable foundation of nature" and not the "precarious and fluctuating basis of human institutions,"[354] a point again accompanied by denunciation of Blackstone.[355] The function of government was not to grant but "to secure and to enlarge the exercise of the natural rights," and failing that it "is not a government of the legitimate kind."[356] Such natural rights included rights to life or safety, liberty, property, and character, in Wilson's view,[357] the latter of which was most threatened by falsehood, which Wilson later described as central to libel.[358] Wilson concluded his lecture on natural rights by answering his opening question: "man does not exist for the sake of government, but government is instituted for the sake of man."[359]

Wilson's views on natural rights had strong implications for the future Sedition Act: what Wilson found paramount was natural rights including liberty, which government existed to secure, not government officials or measures to which individuals must surrender rights or serve. Wilson found the right of private character important enough to be a fourth category of natural right, and its violation like violations of life, liberty, and property to be a crime.[360] By contrast, he entirely omitted any right of government not to be reflected upon critically, or not to be divided from the affections of its subjects, or any crime of seditious libel from his lengthy discussion of crimes[361] (his only reference there to seditious libel was to the "unwarranted attempt made in the star chamber").

The frequent references to Blackstone were not coincidental. Wilson regularly cited and excoriated "his *bête noire*"[362] and the *Commentaries* in discussing rights and government,[363] from the first lecture onward. In that first lecture, Wilson warned that he differed from Blackstone on some important principles, that Blackstone was not very friendly to republicanism, and that "he ought not to be implicitly followed."[364] In this context, it is not surprising that Wilson did not

[353] 2 *id.* 1054, 1055; *accord* 2 *id.* 1056, 1057.

[354] 2 *id.* 1056; *accord* 2 *id.* 1061; 1 *id.* 39, 214, 638.

[355] And Burke, 2 *id.* 1056–57.

[356] 2 *id.* 1061; *accord* 2 *id.* 1082.

[357] 2 *id.* 1062; *accord* 2 *id.* 1056–57.

[358] 2 *id.* 1062; *accord* 2 *id.* 1135.

[359] 2 *id.* 1083, 1053; *accord* Chisholm v. Georgia, 2 U.S. (2 Dall.) 419, 461, 455 (1793); 5 DHSC 127.

[360] 2 *id.* 1130–36.

[361] 2 *id.* 1087–204.

[362] *Introduction*, 1 The Works of James Wilson 39, 50 (Robert G. McCloskey ed., HUP, Cambridge 1967).

[363] 1 Wilson Works 471–74, 549, 552–53, 580, 720, 739; 2 *id.* 1049, 1054, 1113; *accord Chisholm*, 2 U.S. at 458, 460, 462.

[364] 1 *id.* 443–44. "Wilson took the lead in warning against the danger of Americans' widespread acceptance" of much of Blackstone. Stephen A. Conrad, *James Wilson's "Assimilation of the Common-Law Mind,"* 84 Nw. U. L. Rev. 186, 197 (1990).

adopt Blackstone's treatment of seditious libel, but citing it, said that the discussion "flows from a wrong principle and is referred to a wrong end."[365]

Wilson focused that first law lecture on "the *vital* principle" of sovereignty, contrasting his belief that "the supreme or sovereign power of the society resides in the citizens" with Blackstone's assumption that it resides in the Crown.[366] That premise not only determined the source of individual liberties, but whether the people have a right to change government including by revolution, which Wilson affirmed while disapproving Blackstone's position.[367] In view of such fundamental differences on sovereignty, Wilson asserted that "many parts of the laws of England can . . . have neither force nor application here," and in later lectures he applied the point to parts of the common law.[368] Similarly, in the next lecture Wilson rejected the definition of law as "prescribed by some superiour," and the concept of superiority of rulers, citing Blackstone as the font of "dangerous" concepts; Wilson offered instead the requirement that human law is valid only with consent of the governed.[369] As with rights, primacy went not to government or rulers, but to the people. Many of these themes reappeared in Wilson's longest Supreme Court opinion in 1793, and are mentioned in the footnotes.

The implications for the future Sedition Act became clear as Wilson ended the law lectures with criminal law, and did not list seditious libel as a proper crime but as a Star Chamber corruption.

Other Departures from Federalist Orthodoxy

Wilson departed from Federalist orthodoxy on a wide range of issues. Aside from his support of some Hamiltonian programs such as a national bank (his judgment biased by financial interests in land speculation), and his use of implied powers to justify them (though limited to carrying out enumerated powers),[370] Wilson was far closer to the radical Whigs[371] and to Jefferson on a number of positions,[372] including the following ones.

[365] 2 *id.* 1133 & n.

[366] 1 *id.* 440–41, 441–42; *accord Chisholm*, 2 U.S. at 454, 458.

[367] 1 *id.* 443, 442, 441–42, 689.

[368] 1 *id.* 446, 35; 2 *id.* 784.

[369] 1 *id.* 471, 473, 496; *accord Chisholm*, 2 U.S. at 458, 456, 458.

[370] James Wilson, Comments on the Bank of North America (1785), 1 Wilson Works 60, 65–66; 2 Farrand's Records 615; *accord Chisholm*, 2 U.S. at 453, 457, 465 (nationalism).

[371] *E.g.*, Chisholm v. Georgia, 2 U.S. at 439, citing Francis Hotoman, Franco-Gallia (Edward Valentine, London 1721) (also reprinted 1775), whose preface by Molesworth was "the liveliest definition of a Real Whig." Robbins 88; *accord* Clark 17; Scott-Commonwealth 192. Similarly, Wilson was among the listed "encouragers" in 3 James Burgh, Political Disquisitions vii (Robert Bell, Philadelphia 1775).

[372] Geoffrey Seed, James Wilson 180–82 (KTO Press, Millwood 1978).

Wilson had been the only thoroughgoing advocate of democracy—of direct election of the president, Senate, and House, and of proportional representation—at the Constitutional Convention.[373] He favored a broad-based electorate, repeatedly using the analogy of a pyramid,[374] and more generally, he welcomed what a recent scholar terms "pluralism as the basis for national identity."[375] That democratic focus carried strong implications for seditious libel. If government was valid only because of consent of the people,[376] their consent if real required a right to refuse consent, which amounted to a right to disagree with government. In a government based on consent of the people, peaceful disagreement could not be a crime.

Wilson denied that an aristocracy of virtue or talent was entitled to rule, allowing its rule only if "*elected* for the exercise of authority" by the consent of the governed,[377] just as he denied that law was "prescribed by some superiour." In his view, "this notion of superiority contains the germ of the divine right . . . of princes, arbitrarily to rule," and being "absurd and ridiculous," conferred no "right of prescribing laws."[378]

His references to sedition equated it with violent conduct, not disagreement with government. In his first reference in preserved essays and letters, in 1776, Wilson exclaimed that "even this peaceful expedient," the nonimportation agreement, was treated "by high authority too, as a seditious and unwarrantable combination."[379] In 1780 he asked in defending his speech that derided Pennsylvania's 1776 constitution, "has anything seditious appeared in my conduct or attempts? Have I endeavored to attain my ends by violence? My only aim has been to accomplish this by the consent and authority of the citizens of the state."[380] Criticism of government was permissible; only sedition amounting to violent actions was proscribable.

Wilson was decidedly pro-French, like Rutledge and like Jay for a time, as the emerging parties divided over England and France. In 1793 Wilson charged a grand jury that "the voice of all France is responsive to the language of our national Constitution," and that "a shout of acclamation" sounded when "the decree

[373] 1 FARRAND'S RECORDS 68, 52, 49, 179; *accord* 1 WILSON WORKS 82, 92, 93, 94, 101–02, 104, 115, 165; *see Notes of the Debate in the Pennsylvania Convention Taken by James Wilson* (Nov.-Dec.1787), 2 PENNSYLVANIA AND THE FEDERAL CONSTITUTION 1787–1788, at 765, 766, 767 (John B. McMaster & Frederick D. Stone eds., HSP, Philadelphia 1888).

[374] 1 WILSON WORKS 82, 299; 2 *id.* 833.

[375] PENNSYLVANIA'S REVOLUTION 258 (William Pencak ed., PSUP, University Park 2010).

[376] 1 WILSON WORKS 47, 92, 191, 201, 235; *accord Chisholm,* 2 U.S. at 455, 456, 462, 463.

[377] 1 *id.* 476, 572; *accord* 1 *id.* 477.

[378] 1 *id.* 472, 477, 501; *accord* 1 *id.* 572–73.

[379] James Wilson, An Address to the Inhabitants of the Colonies (1776), 1 WILSON WORKS 46, 51.

[380] James Wilson, To the Citizens of Pennsylvania (18 Oct.1780), 1 WILSON WRITINGS 114, 118.

was pronounced, that the lives and fortunes of twenty-five millions of men should not be at the disposal of a single individual," Louis XVI.[381] By contrast, most other early justices, except Rutledge and in part Jay (Johnson and Moore being silent), hewed to the Federalist Party line of Gallophobia,[382] such as Cushing's warning against "the dangerous tendency of jacobin principles" that produced an "alarming political situation of the United States."[383]

Wilson similarly departed from Federalist orthodoxy, in 1798–1801, by not accepting a federal common law of crimes. In several grand jury charges, he listed the statutory crimes of the federal government, then identified the role of the common law as providing "definition of those crimes."[384] In another charge, he "enumerated . . . the crimes and offences known to the constitution and laws of the United States," and then contrasted the "few . . . crimes" with the "dismal list" of 160 capital felonies and the nearly innumerable other crimes under common law.[385] His support for federal jurisdiction over treaty offenses and law of nations offenses was not acceptance of a federal common law of crimes, but of constitutional areas of authority.

He also gave broad latitude to juries, as Jay had, instructing them that they were "the ultimate interpreters of the law, with a power to over-rule the directions of the judges." Particularly in criminal cases, "the question of law is so intimately and inseparably blended with the question of fact, that the decision of the one necessarily involves the decision of the other."[386]

Wilson guarded the rights of criminal defendants, calling for "liberty as the principle" governing the system, clear laws drawing unmistakable lines around criminal conduct, moderation of punishment, and avoidance of England's "ensanguined" example.[387] He decried overinclusive treason laws by which "a very great part of their tyranny over the people has arisen."[388]

Finally, with obvious implications for his position on the future Alien Acts that accompanied the Sedition Act, Wilson censured England for its "feudal system" of restricting alien friends, and praised the "very different spirit" that pervaded America, where aliens could become citizens in two years and public officials in seven.[389] He had sought to abolish minimum citizenship periods for holding

[381] James Wilson's Charge (C.C.D. Pa. 22 July 1793), 2 DHSC 414, 423.

[382] 3 DHSC 158 (Ellsworth), 230 (Paterson), 230, 261 (Iredell), 306, 308–09, 310, 312, 313 (Cushing); FEDERALISM 673 (Ellsworth); MCHENRY CORRESPONDENCE 203 (Chase).

[383] 3 DHSC 278 (Cushing).

[384] James Wilson's Charge (C.C.D. Pa. 21 Feb. 1791), 2 DHSC 142, 144–52, 147, 150; *accord* 2 *id.* 42–44, 176.

[385] James Wilson's Charge (C.C.D. Va. 23 May 1791), 2 DHSC 166, 181, 189.

[386] James Wilson's Charge (C.C.D. Pa. 12 Apr. 1790), 2 DHSC 33, 38–39.

[387] James Wilson's Charge (C.C.D. Va. 23 May 1791), 2 DHSC 166, 190, 190–91, 167–68, 167; James Wilson's Charge (C.C.D. Mass. 7 June 1793), 2 *id.* 396, 402.

[388] 2 DHRC 483, 515; *accord* 2 WILSON WORKS 1150–52; 2 DHSC 42, 145, 187.

[389] 2 WILSON WORKS 1052, 1050–51, 1051.

office at the Constitutional Convention,[390] noting that he and half the Pennsylvania delegation were not American-born, and that "inviting meritorious foreigners among us" was beneficial, while "degrading discrimination" drove away talent.[391]

Wilson was criticized by Federalists for many of these positions, whether at the Constitutional Convention on democracy or elsewhere for his attacks on Blackstone.[392] He was bypassed by President Washington in nominating new chief justices in 1795 and 1796,[393] after initial nominations of the most senior justice or former justice, even though he was next in seniority. Yet Wilson remained unshaken in his unorthodoxy. Certainly these departures from Federalist orthodoxy represent only a portion of his thinking, which can best be reviewed in Hall's summary.[394] Still, it is impossible to imagine their exponent upholding the Sedition Act.

Opposition to the Sedition Act by Mentor, Friends, and Family

Wilson's law training occurred under John Dickinson,[395] with whom he remained "lifelong friends."[396] During those studies, Dickinson published his *Address*, stating that rights came "from a higher source" than government—from God and natural law—and "cannot be taken from us by any human power."[397] Just after Wilson's studies ended, Dickinson published his renowned *Letters from a Farmer*, proclaiming the right to freedom and denying Parliament's jurisdiction over many issues, with an argument Wilson adopted and extended in his own essay the next year.[398] It was Dickinson who formulated the first official statement listing "freedom of the press" as one of Americans' "invaluable rights," in 1774.[399] Wilson and Dickinson served together in the Continental Congress, and later at the Constitutional Convention, both being signers of the Constitution.[400] In the 1790s,

[390] 1 FARRAND'S RECORDS 379–80; 2 *id.* 230, 268, 272

[391] 2 *id.* 269, 237.

[392] *E.g.*, MEMOIRS OF HIS OWN TIME, BY ALEXANDER GRAYDON 404 (John S. Littell ed., rev. ed. Lindsay & Blakiston, Philadelphia 1846).

[393] 1 DHSC 837, 838, 840, though Wilson's debts also were factors.

[394] MARK D. HALL, POLITICAL AND LEGAL PHILOSOPHY OF JAMES WILSON, 1742–1798 (UMoP, Columbia 1997); Mark D. Hall, The Political and Legal Philosophy of James Wilson (1742–1798) (1993) (unpublished Ph.D. dissertation, University of Virginia).

[395] 23 ANB 586; WILSON 11.

[396] GEOFFREY SEED, JAMES WILSON 191 n.4 (KTO Press, Millwood 1978); *accord* William Ewald, *James Wilson and the Drafting of the Constitution*, 10 U. PA. J. CONST. L. 901, 904 (2008). Dickinson helped Wilson's advancement. CHARLES P. SMITH, JAMES WILSON: FOUNDING FATHER, 1742–1798, at 37, 170, 195 (UNCP, Chapel Hill 1956).

[397] NORTH-AMERICAN [JOHN DICKINSON], AN ADDRESS TO THE COMMITTEE OF CORRESPONDENCE IN BARBADOS 4 (William Bradford, Philadelphia 1766).

[398] James Wilson, Considerations (1768, 1774), 1 WILSON WORKS 3.

[399] Address to the Inhabitants of Quebec (1774), 1 JCC 117, 122–23, seeing it as a constitutional right, M. EMBICK FLOWER, JOHN DICKINSON, CONSERVATIVE REVOLUTIONARY 176 (UPV, Charlottesville 1983).

[400] 6 ANB 566, 568; 23 *id.* 587; 33 JCC 500.

Dickinson opposed the Jay Treaty,[401] and shared Wilson's pro-French stance, publishing a series of letters and a pamphlet supporting France "with transports of joy."[402] By the late 1790s, Dickinson had become a zealous convert to the Republican party,[403] and wrote to Jefferson in support of the Virginia Resolutions and of personal freedom.[404] "How incredible was it . . . that every measure and every pretence of the stupid and selfish Stuarts, should be adopted by the posterity of those who fled from their madness and tyranny to the distant and dangerous wilds of America?"[405] Dickinson rivaled Wilson in zeal over liberty,[406] including freedom of speech, noting that because of that commitment "Republicans therefore, cannot in any consistency with the principles of their system, proscribe any of their fellow citizens, merely for a difference of political opinion."[407]

Wilson's principal partner in the Pennsylvania ratification convention, Thomas McKean,[408] had also been a colleague at the Continental Congress and a fellow signer of the Declaration of Independence.[409] They and Dickinson denounced Pennsylvania's Constitution of 1776, fought for its replacement in 1790, welcomed the French Revolution, and remained pro-French still in 1798.[410] Even before Dickinson did, McKean left the Federalists around 1796, and equally opposed the Sedition Act as unconstitutional.[411]

Wilson's eldest and only prominent child, Bird Wilson, who published the justice's papers, also was a Republican by 1802, when he was appointed a state court judge[412]

[401] 1 DHSC 834 n.1; 6 ANB 568.

[402] FABIUS [JOHN DICKINSON], THE LETTERS OF FABIUS 86 (Smyth, Wilmington 1797); [JOHN DICKINSON], A CAUTION (Bache, Philadelphia 1798).

[403] CHARLES J. STILLÉ, LIFE AND TIMES OF JOHN DICKINSON 280–96 (HSP, Philadelphia 1891); *e.g.*, John Dickinson to Thomas Jefferson (21 Feb.1801), 33 JEFFERSON PAPERS 31, 32; *accord* 33 *id.* 26, 34 *id.* 590.

[404] John Dickinson to Thomas Jefferson (18 Mar.1800), 31 JEFFERSON PAPERS 445; in response to a pamphlet containing the Resolutions, state responses, and Madison's Report, Thomas Jefferson to John Dickinson (7 Mar.1800), 31 *id.* 417 & n.

[405] *Id.*; *accord* DAVID L. JACOBSON, JOHN DICKINSON 124–25 (UCP, Berkeley 1965).

[406] JANE E. CALVERT, QUAKER CONSTITUTIONALISM AND THE POLITICAL THOUGHT OF JOHN DICKINSON 304 *passim* (CUP, Cambridge 2009), viewing dissent against injustice as a duty, *id.* 201, 212, 216, 219, 287, 289–90, 295.

[407] John Dickinson to Thomas Jefferson (27 June 1801), 34 JEFFERSON PAPERS 464, 465.

[408] PENNSYLVANIA 12; 15 ANB 97, 99. The two leaders' speeches were reprinted as COMMENTARIES ON THE CONSTITUTION OF THE UNITED STATES OF AMERICA (Debrett, London 1792).

[409] 5 JCC 515.

[410] PENNSYLVANIA 225; 15 ANB 97, 98, 99.

[411] G.S. ROWE, THOMAS MCKEAN 241–63, 264–87, 293 (CAUP, Boulder 1978); PENNSYLVANIA 225, 227.

[412] 6 APPLETONS' CYCLOPÆDIA OF AMERICAN BIOGRAPHY 551 (James G. Wilson & John Fiske eds., Appleton, New York 1888–89); *Philadelphia, Saturday Evening, March 1*, UNITED STATES GAZETTE (Philadelphia), 1 Mar.1806, at 2.

soon after Governor McKean limited appointments to the Republican Party faithful.[413]

Thus, Justice Wilson rejected seditious libel as a crime, disparaged the *Case de Libellis Famosis,* and derided Blackstone on rights and sovereignty. Instead, he affirmed natural rights without surrender of any to government, and defended a "right to think, to speak, to write, to print, and to publish freely . . . concerning publick men, publick bodies, and publick measures" that negated the prohibitions of the Sedition Act. He freely departed from the Federalist Party on issues of liberty such as a narrow federal criminal jurisdiction without a federal common law of crimes, democracy and a right of all classes to be elected, a broad province for juries, and freedom of immigration, as well as Francophilia. These and other stances were far more consistent with rejection of the constitutionality of the Sedition Act than with its defense.

Justice John Blair and the Sedition Act

Justice John Blair, another of the initial justices, was not one who questioned the constitutionality of the Sedition Act. His actions in 1797 give reason to believe that he might have supported its constitutionality.

Two years after resigning from the Supreme Court, Blair appeared as foreperson of the Virginia grand jury that brought a presentment against Samuel J. Cabell, a Virginia member of Congress, in May 1797.[414] The wording of the presentment, which Blair likely wrote as the foreperson and a retired judge, and clearly supported, leaves little doubt that by 1797 he believed the common law of seditious libel could be properly enforced by federal courts (though the Sedition Act would not appear until a year later):

> We of the grand jury of the United States for the District of Virginia, present as a real evil the circular letters with the signature of Samuel J: Cabell, endeavoring at a time of real public danger, to disseminate unfounded calumnies against the happy government of the United States, and thereby to separate the people therefrom, and to [i]ncrease or produce a foreign influence ruinous to the peace, happiness and independence of these United States.[415]

The concepts that crimes included calumnies against the government, and efforts to separate the people from the government, were of course ingredients of the common law of seditious libel. What apparently exercised Blair and the grand jury in Cabell's circular letter of January 1797 was the "deep regret" at Adams's election—so that

413 Pennsylvania 263–68; 15 ANB 97, 99.

414 3 DHSC 181 (22 May 1797). That it was the former justice is confirmed by Republican complaints. Scaevola, *To James Iredell,* Daily Advertiser (Richmond), 11 June 1797, reprinted in 3 *id.* 192, 193; [No Caption], Aurora (Philadelphia), 21 June 1797, 3 *id.* 190.

415 3 DHSC 181; *accord* 3 *id.* 197.

"the patriotism of 76 and republicanism must sicken"—instead of electing the "illustrious patriot" Jefferson, along with Cabell's agreement with the French minister that America's policy wrongly threatened war. For over half the letter, Cabell denounced "the unwise, impolitic, nay, ungrateful sound of hostility with France," notwithstanding that "the French *Republic* must be considered as the grand rallying point of the equal rights of man" and the decisive benefactor in the American Revolution.[416]

Though no action was taken by the federal attorney, Cabell and other Republicans were incensed at the threat of criminal action against a member of Congress' freedoms of speech and press.[417] Cabell counterattacked with a public letter protesting violation of "the freedom of opinion which a few years ago we fought and bled for," and protesting Federalist judges' grand jury charges—particularly Iredell's. Especially objectionable in those Federalist judges' charges were "complain[ing] of opinions which they seem to think tend to defeat their system of politics," making "use of their power and influence both personally and officially to control the freedom of individual opinion," and "shew[ing] a political influence over the judges by the executive" which imperils justice.[418] Jefferson went still further, drafting a petition asking Virginia's legislature to take action, and initially suggesting it initiate proceedings to impeach the grand jurors for "the crime committed."[419] His final version (which Virginia's lower house approved[420]) affirmed that "the right of free correspondence between citizen and citizen . . . is a natural right of every individual citizen, not the gift of municipal law."[421] Thus, the issue was quickly broadened to everyone's natural right of writing and speech.

Blair had changed. He was quite different from the John Blair who Jefferson earlier had a high "degree of confidence" would keep liberties safe, and who left the Court "universally beloved."[422] Blair's shift from his own jury charges, and from his commitment to Virginia's Declaration of Rights and proposal for a federal bill of rights, was noted by Virginia's Senator Henry Tazewell as he was "astonished" Blair's name appeared on the presentment.[423] The cause of Blair's shift appears to have been alarm about the Whiskey Rebellion and then the "real public danger" from France.[424]

416 From Samuel J. Cabell (12 Jan.1797), 1 Circular Letters 67, 70, 69; *see* From Samuel J. Cabell (7 Mar.1796), 1 *id.* 39.

417 *E.g.*, Sen. Henry Tazewell to John Page (3 June 1797), 3 DHSC 189; Thomas Jefferson to Peregrine Fitzhugh (4 June 1797), 3 *id.* 190; *accord* 3 *id.* 192, 199–200, 200–01, 203–04.

418 Samuel J. Cabell, *Fellow Citizens*, Aurora (Philadelphia), 31 May 1797, reprinted in 3 DHSC 183.

419 Thomas Jefferson, Petition to the Virginia House of Delegates (ante-3 Aug.1797), 29 Jefferson Papers 493, 497.

420 17 Madison Papers 34n.

421 Thomas Jefferson, Petition to the Virginia House of Delegates (ante-7 Sept.1797), 29 Jefferson Papers 499, 502; *accord* Thomas Jefferson to James Monroe (7 Sept.1797), 29 *id.* 526.

422 Thomas Jefferson to James Madison (15 Mar.1789), 14 *id.* 659; Jeremiah Smith to William Plumer (5 Mar.1796), 1 DHSC 843.

423 Henry Tazewell to John Page (3 June 1797), 3 DHSC 189.

424 3 DHSC 31, 32, 35, 181; *cf.* 2 *id.* 485.

That presentment was not the only place where Blair's name appeared. His last public act was to be listed as a proposed elector in the presidential election of 1800 on the "American Republican Ticket." Its name ostensibly came from being "the most purely republican[s],"[425] though it was really Virginia's Federalist Party fleeing the national name.[426] Blair's loyalty to the Federalists[427] appears to have been undiminished by the Sedition Act, in the years between the grand jury presentment and the electoral ticket, and may have grown.

Justice Thomas Johnson and the Sedition Act

Figure 8.5 Justice Thomas Johnson (on Supreme Court 1791–1793). Portrait by Charles Willson Peale 1824. (Courtesy of Collection of Maryland State Archives.)

Justice Thomas Johnson (Figure 8.5) in prior years showed commitment to freedoms of press and speech. In the prewar years, Johnson was, like Jefferson, highly critical of Mansfield as part of the "corrupt majority" opposing the colonies.[428] During the Revolution, his proclamation curtailing the Whig Club's restraint of a free press was "the first vindication of the liberty of the press in Maryland."[429] In the Maryland ratification convention, Johnson split from the federalist majority to support calls for a bill of rights with protection for freedom of press, and he was the only early justice to do so publicly.

Johnson was not a typical Federalist in the 1790s. As the Jefferson-Hamilton conflict was reaching the boiling point and partisan divisions were deepening, Jefferson recommended Johnson for the positions of secretary of state and secretary of

[425] An Address to the Voters for Electors (n.p., 26 May 1800) (broadside).

[426] CHESAPEAKE 556–57.

[427] John Adams to John Marshall (5 Sept.1800), 4 MARSHALL PAPERS 258.

[428] Thomas Johnson to Horatio Gates (18 Aug.1775), 1 LETTERS OF DELEGATES 702.

[429] J. THOMAS SCHARF, THE CHRONICLES OF BALTIMORE 161 (Turnbull, Baltimore 1874).

the treasury.[430] (Washington actually offered him the former position, twice.[431]) Johnson later showed a similar comfort with Jefferson, by declining Adams's appointment as chief judge of the circuit court for the District of Columbia (one of the "midnight" judicial appointments),[432] and making no effort to deliver his declination before Jefferson took office in March 1801[433] (though his home was less than fifty miles from the White House), which gave Jefferson the opportunity to fill the position. The year before in a eulogy at Washington's death, Johnson carefully avoided the Federalist position on France, condemning both "British pride" and French despotism, and recognizing "the injuries we have received from both sides."[434]

Jefferson's recommendation of Johnson, out of all the potential candidates for those positions, raises the question why. Jefferson recognized that Johnson was a friend of Washington, but that was a reason against instead of a reason for Jefferson's recommendation, since much of the problem with Hamilton was friendship with Washington and his resulting disproportionate influence. Because Jefferson was discussing successors to himself for the first position and to his nemesis for the second, he had particular reason to limit his recommendation to someone compatible with his views. Evidently Jefferson saw that kindred spirit in Johnson.

Johnson disavowed party affiliation from at least late 1800 to 1804, though he was clearly an Adams Federalist earlier.[435] In standing for election to Congress in 1800, he assured voters that "I never was an instrument in the hands of any man or party."[436] As he stood unsuccessfully for selection as a presidential elector in 1804, he gave no party affiliation even though most electors listed a party.[437] Only later did he stand as a Federalist in 1812 for the governor's council—and soon his eldest son stood as a Republican in 1817 for the state legislature.[438] (Johnson's only biographer, unaware of these and other activities, incorrectly stated that after April 1798 "he never emerged from seclusion."[439])

[430] Thomas Jefferson, Notes of a Conversation with George Washington (6 Aug.1793), 26 JEFFERSON PAPERS 627, 629; Thomas Jefferson to James Madison (2 Nov.1793), 27 *id.* 297, 298.

[431] *Id.*; George Washington to Thomas Johnson (24 Aug.1795), WASHINGTON PAPERS-LOC; Thomas Johnson to George Washington (29 Aug.1795), *id.*

[432] Thomas Jefferson to Gabriel Duvall (13 Mar.1801), 33 JEFFERSON PAPERS 267; *accord* 6 MARSHALL PAPERS 90.

[433] 2 HISTORY OF SUPREME COURT 135 & n.133.

[434] Thomas Johnson, *Oration Delivered by Thomas Johnson*, CENTINEL OF LIBERTY (Georgetown), 11 Mar.1800, at 2; JOHNSON 500, 500, 503, 504 (reprinting it).

[435] John Adams to Thomas Johnson (26 Apr.1798), 8 ADAMS WORKS 572; Thomas Johnson to John Adams (8 Apr.1800), 9 *id.* 48, 49; Thomas Johnson to Mr. Thompson (1810), JOHNSON CORRESPONDENCE 2–3.

[436] Thomas Johnson, To the Freemen of the Fourth District (n.p., 1800) (broadside).

[437] American Election Returns 1787–1825 <http://elections.lib.tufts.edu/catalog/tufts:md.presidentialelector3.1804> (accessed 4 Aug.2015). His 1801 candidacy for state senate did list the Federalist Party, though that appears to have been assigned by vote tellers. *Id.*

[438] *Id.*

[439] JOHNSON 506–07.

That decided avoidance of the Federalist label also raises the question why. It is unlikely Johnson foresaw the Federalist congressional rout in 1800, since so few did until the votes were in and since the presidential election was widely expected to be as close as it actually was.[440] The obvious explanation is that Johnson was disenchanted with Federalist policy. His amiable personality led him to remain on courteous terms with everyone including Pickering,[441] but that courtesy was not mutual. Pickering wrote scathingly about Johnson's brother, Joshua Johnson,[442] condemning Adams's nomination of him as commissioner of the stamp office in 1800, and reprehending that "Jefferson gave the casting vote for Mr. Johnson" in the senate.[443]

Though Johnson's position on the Sedition Act has not survived in his limited remaining papers, his record on freedom of press, Jefferson's earlier recommendation, and his later dissociation from the Federalist label, imply discomfort and constitutional concern.

Justice Alfred Moore's Refusal to Follow the Sitting Justices' Sedition Act Charges

Figure 8.6 Justice Alfred Moore (on Supreme Court 1799–1804). Engraving by J. Veagle 1820. (Courtesy of New York Public Library/Art Resource.)

[440] CHESAPEAKE 559, 563 (Md. 5–5); John H. Aldrich, *Election of 1800*, in ESTABLISHING CONGRESS 28–29 (Kenneth R. Bowling & Donald R. Kennon eds., OhUP, Athens 2005).

[441] Thomas Johnson to Timothy Pickering (5 Oct.1808), PICKERING PAPERS r.29, fol.107; Thomas Johnson to Timothy Pickering (9 Apr.1814), *id.* r.15, fol.34.

[442] PAUL C. NAGLE, JOHN QUINCY ADAMS 93 (Knopf, New York 1997); John Quincy Adams to Skelton Jones (17 Apr.1809), SELECT WRITINGS OF JOHN AND JOHN QUINCY ADAMS 261, 266 (Adrienne Koch & William Peden eds., Knopf, New York 1946).

[443] Timothy Pickering to Rufus King (28 May 1800), 3 KING CORRESPONDENCE 248; *accord* Benjamin Goodhue to Timothy Pickering (2 June 1800), 3 *id.* 263, 264.

Justice Alfred Moore (Figure 8.6) did not preside over any Sedition Act trials, after he joined the Supreme Court in early 1800, but the reason was not unavailability or chance. Instead, he avoided provoking cases under the Act, in contrast to Paterson, Chase, Washington, and Iredell, whose grand jury charges focused on the Sedition Act and were immediately followed by presentments of violators. Instead, Moore consciously declined to follow that practice of the other sitting justices, and unlike them, even refused to make reference to the Sedition Act at all. It is true that Cushing, and Ellsworth, did not preside over Sedition Act trials, but it was not for lack of trying. Unlike Moore, Cushing provoked three indictments under the Sedition Act, and Ellsworth focused grand jury charges on the Act, before sailing to France as an envoy in November 1799. Contrasted with the sitting justices, Moore's approach can only be described as an intentional refusal.

His Grand Jury Charge after Joining the Court

Moore's first circuit began with sessions in Savannah and Charleston,[444] followed by sessions in Raleigh in June 1800 that are described in newspaper reports. That was Moore's first federal court session in his home state, two months after the Durrell, Cooper, and Holt trials, a month after the Haswell trial, and two weeks after Callender was arrested. The reports of it began:

> The Hon. Judge Moore arriving here in the afternoon of Tuesday last, the Circuit Court of the United States for this District proceeded to business on that evening[.] The Grand Jury being sworn, Judge Moore charged them with their duty; but, instead of expatiating at length on the several objects cognizable in that Court, and insisting on the necessity of carrying the Sedition Law into effect, in particular (as is usual) he barely reminded them of the oath they had taken to execute the trust reposed in them; said there was no necessity for them to take up their time in explaining the nature of their duty, which had been so often explained in that Court, and which they had doubtless frequently seen in the papers from various parts of the country, which would only tend to divert their minds from their proper business, referring them to the Attorney General of the District for legal information.[445]

Thus, unlike other Supreme Court justices on circuit, whose charges North Carolinians "had doubtless frequently seen in the papers," Moore "barely" spoke of the grand jurors' oath, "instead of . . . insisting on the necessity of carrying the

[444] 3 DHSC 419, 424, 438.

[445] [No Caption], RALEIGH REGISTER, 10 June 1800, at 1, reprinted in 3 DHSC 440; *accord Raleigh, (N.C.) June 10*, CITY-GAZETTE (Charleston), 17 June 1800, at 3.

Sedition Law into effect," and apparently said that such charges or such papers "would only tend to divert their minds from their proper business." In other words, "insisting on the necessity of carrying the Sedition Law into effect" was a diversion, not "their proper business."

The phrase "instead of" referred to insistence on the "Sedition Law," a reading in which others concur,[446] and any uncertainty about that is resolved by the context. The remainder of the article did not deal with any notable words Moore said about the Sedition Act, but with a case of a cabin-boy's death.[447] Any words about the Sedition Act would have been deemed momentous news, because the *Raleigh Register* was a Republican paper,[448] and the circuit court was the first local appearance of the state's son as a Supreme Court justice. The reprint in the *City-Gazette* from Charleston made the point as clearly, because that equally Republican paper (edited by the brother[449] of Jefferson's protégé, Freneau) buried the article between reports of the ship *Iphigenia* arriving after being "treated in the most friendly manner" by a French frigate, and the ship *Eugenia* arriving "to stop a leak."[450] Even an intimation of Moore's endorsement of the Sedition Act would have been major news in North Carolina, where the lower house of assembly a year before opposed the Sedition Act, the senators were both Republicans, and the ten federal representatives included five Republicans and one independent.[451]

Corroboration in Steele-Macon Correspondence and Death Notices

Moore's refusal to follow other justices supporting the Sedition Act is also implied in an 1803 letter from John Steele, Moore's friend (according to the letter), to Nathaniel Macon, a longtime Republican member of Congress from North Carolina and the new Republican speaker of the house,[452] who had been a leading opponent of the Sedition Act.[453] Steele, though a Federalist in 1796 when he was appointed federal comptroller,[454] was a moderate Federalist[455] who had long

[446] Delbert H. Gilpatrick, Jeffersonian Democracy in North Carolina, 1789–1816, at 108 (ColUP, New York 1931).

[447] [No Caption], Raleigh Register, 10 June 1800, at 1; *Raleigh, (N.C.) June 10*, City-Gazette (Charleston), 17 June 1800, at 3.

[448] Opposition 883.

[449] Richard B. Davis, *Peter Freneau, Carolina Republican*, 13 J. Southern History 395 (1947); Tyranny 407.

[450] *Norfolk, June 5*, City-Gazette (Charleston), 17 June 1800, at 3; *Savannah, June 2*, City-Gazette (Charleston), 17 June 1800, at 3.

[451] Origins-Parties 218, 210; William Polk to John Steele (28 Nov. 1800), 1 Steele Papers 190, 192.

[452] 12 DAB 157, 158; 1 Steele Papers 370 n.2; Origins-Parties 201, 203, 206, 208, 209.

[453] 8 Annals 2105–06, 2151–52, 2171; 1 History of Supreme Court 653.

[454] William Smith to Ralph Izard (3 Nov. 1796), Federalist Correspondence 781, 782.

[455] 4 Jefferson 56 n.9; Fischer 390.

opposed Hamiltonian policies[456] and, in the early 1790s, voted with Madison almost as often as against him.[457] The North Carolinian had migrated sufficiently in politics to be invited by Jefferson to remain in office and to be a periodic dinner guest,[458] and to be Macon's partner in extensive correspondence.[459] Steele had taken a number of Republican stances by the time of the letter.[460] Macon's preceding letter asked Steele if he had seen Justice Chase's 1803 charge (which later provided one article of impeachment), adding that he was "dissatisfied with it" and that men like Chase "are a real injury to the country."[461]

Steele, further exhibiting his political migration, responded that the "charge of Judge Chase" was "extra judicial," "extremely indecorous," and "indefensible," and that "[t]he opinions of some of the judges on other subjects are so inaccurate and preposterous that I am not surpri[s]ed at this."[462] However, Steele expressly excepted Moore from his criticism of the Federalist bench:

> my only wish is that friend Moore may prove as I am sure he will, like purged gold, the more bright for being tried in such a crucible.[463]

Steele clearly believed that Moore was different in a positive way from Chase and "some of the judges," and that he thus far was passing his trial in the crucible. The "crucible" did not refer to the Chase impeachment, because that was not initiated for a half year or tried for another year. The "crucible" instead appears to have been the federal judiciary itself and its most severe testing, the Sedition Act prosecutions before and during the first year of Moore's service. While it can be argued that Steele was not referring to Sedition Act positions, because he added that "Mr. Patterson I consider also a man of sterling integrity,"[464] he may simply have

[456] Gilbert L. Lycan, *Alexander Hamilton and the North Carolina Federalists*, 25 N.C. Historical Rev. 442, 453–54 (1948).

[457] Noble E. Cunningham, The Jeffersonian Republicans 272 (UNCP, Chapel Hill 1957). Steele was from North Carolina, and was different from the John Steele from Virginia.

[458] Thomas Jefferson to John Steele (30 June 1802), 1 Steele Papers 285; Thomas Jefferson to John Steele (10 Dec.1802), 1 *id.* 337; *accord* 1 *id.* xxvii; 17 DAB 557; Origins-Parties 198, 201. For Jefferson's invitations, 1 Steele Papers 222, 238, 291; and Madison's, 1 *id.* 241.

[459] Kemp P. Battle, Letters of Nathaniel Macon, John Steele 28 *passim* (UNCP, Chapel Hill 1902).

[460] *E.g.*, John Steele to Nathaniel Macon (11 Apr.1803), 1 Steele Papers 376, 380–82 (disagreeing with *Marbury*); John Steele to Nathaniel Macon (12 Sept.1803), 1 *id.* 407, 409 (objecting to Chase charge); John Steele to Nathaniel Macon (17 Jan.1805), 1 *id.* 444, 444–45 (retained "difft. party name" but Federalist party dead); *accord* 1 *id.* 321; John Taylor to John Steele (3 Dec.1801), 1 *id.* 241, 242 (from sponsor of Virginia Resolutions).

[461] Nathaniel Macon to John Steele (7 Aug.1803), 1 Steele Papers 402, 403.

[462] John Steele to Nathaniel Macon (12 Sept.1803), 1 *id.* 407, 409.

[463] *Id.*

[464] *Id.*

repeated a common accolade for Paterson arising from his sponsorship of the New Jersey Plan and from ignorance of his Sedition Act activities in Vermont, an accolade even the most ardent Republicans sometimes gave.[465]

Even before Moore's appointment, Federalist ex-governor Samuel Johnston of his home state had questioned his Federalist orthodoxy (and Johnston would know, as a lawyer and as Iredell's brother-in-law). Johnston said that "some complain that he pays too little deference to principles founded on respectable decisions, and that he is inclined to eccentricity or novelty." Moore's "strange inconsistency" did not provide "satisfaction" to that ardent Federalist.[466]

The best indication that Moore did not seek to enforce the Sedition Act or defend its constitutionality is that, upon his resignation from the Court, North Carolina's leading Republican newspaper lamented the loss of the "services of so able, independent, and upright a judge,"[467] and Republican South Carolina newspapers edited by Freneau's brother reprinted this.[468] Later, at Moore's death, that leading Republican newspaper praised Moore as "ranked with the highest judicial characters in the American Republic,"[469] and another Republican paper effusively lauded his "powers transcendently acute and ingenious" and his "solid integrity."[470]

Justice William Cushing Revisited on the Sedition Act

The reason for revisiting Justice William Cushing, whose views were summarized in Chapter 6, is to discuss whether his position on the Sedition Act was influenced by the successor justices who surrounded him. Cushing only briefly and tepidly addressed the Sedition Act in his grand jury charges, and though his charges resulted in some presentments or indictments for sedition, his charges and his pressure for cases were not comparable to Justices Paterson, Chase, Washington, Iredell, or before his departure, Chief Justice Ellsworth.

Cushing was prematurely senescent. In 1796 he had turned down Washington's appointment as chief justice, citing "my infirm & declining state of health unequal to" the position.[471] Iredell, after sitting in court with Cushing for a week,

[465] Albert Gallatin to Hannah Gallatin (1 June 1795), 3 DHSC 52, 53; 1 Warren 176 n.1 (*Aurora* similarly praised him); *see* Edward Rutledge to Henry M. Rutledge (1 Nov.1796), 3 DHSC 139.

[466] Samuel Johnston to James Iredell (13–20 Apr.1799), 2 Iredell Correspondence 572.

[467] *Raleigh, Monday, March, 5, 1804*, Raleigh Register, 5 Mar.1804, at 3.

[468] [No Caption], City Gazette (Charleston), 5 Mar.1804, at 3; [No Caption], Carolina Gazette (Charleston), 8 Mar.1804, at 3.

[469] *Died*, Raleigh Register, 1 Nov.1810, at 4.

[470] *Communication*, Star (Raleigh), 1 Nov.1810, at 175.

[471] William Cushing to George Washington (2 Feb.1796), 1 DHSC 103; *accord* John Adams to Abigail Adams (2 Feb.1796), 1 *id.* 834; Jeremiah Smith to William Plumer (29 Jan.1796), 1 *id.* 833.

similarly described his "infirm state of health," and knew his colleague had cancer of the lip the previous year.[472] Others, though professing "love and esteem," said that "time, the enemy of man, has much impaired his mental faculties."[473] By 1800 a family friend from Massachusetts, the president's son, said Cushing was "old__ infirm__unable to travel" and would "not be likely to retain his place much longer" owing to "age & infirmities."[474] (Contrary to that prediction, Cushing continued to cling to his position from sheer financial necessity.[475]) As William Johnson joined the Supreme Court in 1804, he described Cushing as "incompetent."[476] In Cushing's ten years on the Marshall court, he followed other justices and never dissented, and he only wrote four opinions, though he nominally presided and could write the opinion every time the chief justice was absent.[477]

Cushing followed the successor justices, but if the other initial justices had surrounded him instead, he would have found it easier to follow them in the other direction on the Sedition Act. His 1789 views on freedoms of press and speech were at odds with the Sedition Act. He had found the state constitution's press clause to override common law and Blackstone in major ways. Similarly, his slavery opinion found the Massachusetts Constitution (its "free and equal" provision) to override the state's common law in determining that slavery was inconsistent with it.[478] He was an Adams Federalist,[479] unlike some sitting justices such as High Federalists Paterson and Ellsworth. Of the six sitting justices in 1798–1799, Cushing's grand jury charges were the most perfunctory and most timid on the Sedition Act, and may not have been given at most circuit courts. He was the only justice to preside over dismissals (Judah P. Spooner, Alden Spooner) not required by death or presidential order. Overall, Cushing was the most likely to wander in the other direction if most other justices went that direction.

[472] U.S. Supreme Court, Fine Minutes (3–10 Feb.1796), 1 DHSC 255–58; James Iredell to Hannah Iredell (10 Feb.1796), 1 *id.* 836; James Iredell to Hannah Iredell (6 Mar.1795), 2 IREDELL CORRESPONDENCE 441.

[473] William Plumer to Jeremiah Smith (19 Feb.1796), 1 *id.* 838.

[474] Thomas B. Adams to William Cranch (15 Aug.1800), 1 *id.* 897; Thomas B. Adams to Abigail Adams (20 Dec.1800), 1 *id.* 904; *see* David J. Garrow, *Mental Decrepitude on the U.S. Supreme Court: The Historical Case for a 28th Amendment*, 67 U. CHI. L. REV. 995, 1000–01 (2000).

[475] 1 JUSTICES 57, 70.

[476] At least as he recalled in 1822, William Johnson to Thomas Jefferson (10 Dec.1822), 2 HISTORY OF SUPREME COURT 247; *accord* DONALD G. MORGAN, JUSTICE WILLIAM JOHNSON, THE FIRST DISSENTER 182 (USCP, Columbia 1954).

[477] 2 HISTORY OF SUPREME COURT 652; 1 JUSTICES 57, 69; *see* OCSC 214.

[478] Indictment v. Jennison, CUSHING NOTES 55 (Mass. S. Judicial Ct. 1783); William Cushing Judicial Notebook 95–98 (1783), CUSHING PAPERS (microfilm P-406).

[479] Cushing was believed to campaign for Adams in 1800. 1 SAMUEL ELIOT MORISON, LIFE AND LETTERS OF HARRISON GRAY OTIS 192 (Houghton Mifflin, Boston 1913); John Rutledge, Jr. to Alexander Hamilton (17 July 1800), 25 HAMILTON PAPERS 30, 32–33.

Epilogue

Thus, a sizable minority of the Federalist Party opposed the Sedition Act, generally on grounds of unconstitutionality, including the Federalists' vice presidential candidate in 1800 and presidential candidate in 1804 and 1808, the former attorney general and former secretary of state (an ex-Federalist), two Federalist governors and an ex-governor, and other notable Federalists. Eighteen Federalist members of the House of Representatives voted against it at one time or another (not counting Marshall), some leaving the party just before or after. The new chief justice, John Marshall, indisputably opposed the Sedition Act, albeit on nonconstitutional grounds.

Half the initial justices—Jay, Rutledge, and Wilson—apparently viewed the Sedition Act as unconstitutional. The first successor justice and the last successor justice before Marshall—Johnson and Moore—apparently shared that view. Further, none of those remaining justices shifted to embrace the Blackstone-Mansfield definition of freedom of press or their framework for seditious libel, as most sitting justices did in 1798, but instead continued to hold their broader view of freedoms of press and speech, which prohibited abridgment not just by prior restraint (such as licensing) but by subsequent punishment (such as seditious libel). Opposition to the Sedition Act by Federalists generally and by the Federalist remaining justices has been overlooked and generally denied, except for Marshall and single cases in isolated references.

Similarly, a significant minority of the states found the Act unconstitutional, and not just Virginia and Kentucky, but the Tennessee and Georgia Resolutions, and North Carolina's lower chamber (as we saw at the end of Chapter 6). Only half the states rejected the Virginia and Kentucky Resolutions, with the other half spread among opposition, division of the legislative chambers, or failure to reach the issue. That, too, has been overlooked and generally denied, except isolated references to single states.[480]

Is it conceivable that nearly half the early justices viewed the Sedition Act as unconstitutional? The best answer is that a significant minority of their party did, and the next chief justice opposed it on practical grounds. The remaining justices certainly left no trace of public or private support for the Sedition Act, in marked contrast to five of the sitting justices who went out of their way to inflame grand juries to charge violators of the Sedition Act and to defend the constitutionality of that Act. Further, five remaining justices left no trace of changing to adopt the Blackstone-Mansfield definition or framework, again in marked contrast to five sitting justices who expressly adopted that definition and framework during

[480] Wendell Bird, *Reassessing Responses to the Virginia and Kentucky Resolutions: New Evidence from the Tennessee and Georgia Resolutions and from Other States*, 35 J. Early Republic 519 (2015).

1798–1801—though not in the preceding years. Those remaining justices were all moderate or Adams Federalists (except perhaps Blair), like the other Federalists who rejected the Sedition Act (which had been sponsored by the High Federalists). They left a trail of departures from other extreme views of the Federalist Party, and of close relations with others who more visibly challenged the Sedition Act or of other beliefs inconsistent with the Act.

Does it matter that Jay, Rutledge, and Wilson among the initial justices, and Johnson and Moore as the first and last successor justices, apparently found the Sedition Act to violate the First Amendment, and that apparently Cushing simply followed whatever stronger minds surrounded him? (Or that future Chief Justice John Marshall indisputably opposed the Sedition Act on nonconstitutional grounds?) They were, after all, no longer in office during late 1798 through 1801, except Cushing and, in the last two years, Moore (and in early 1801, Marshall). One small and promised change would have left three of them in office (the delay of which was the reason for their departures)—relief from circuit duties. Jay was only age fifty-two, Rutledge fifty-eight, Johnson sixty-five, and Wilson fifty-five.[481] Jay lived three more decades until 1829, Johnson lived two decades until 1819, and Rutledge lived a year after Iredell and could have addressed the constitutionality of the Sedition Act just as Iredell did. Wilson only survived the Sedition Act by a month, but could have avoided his premature and unnecessary death had he not contracted malaria in his circuit riding, or had he not refused medical treatment for it. As Iredell (who was there) described it, "he would not suffer many things to be done for him which were advised, and might possibly have restored him"; newspapers similarly reported.[482] (Alternatively, Wilson's premature death could have been avoided by selling land rather than buying ever more on credit, thereby missing the fugitive year in North Carolina where he contracted malaria, and also missing the financial plight that caused him to decline medical treatment. His final decline was said to be "occasioned by distress of mind owing to his pecuniary difficulties."[483]) As the departures of most of these initial justices and Johnson reflect, Supreme Court tenure in the first decade was shorter than any subsequent decade,[484] and the reason was not high mortality but was primarily the ardor of circuit travel that was, as Jay broadcast widely, "in a degree intolerable."[485]

481 OCSC 446, 750, 932, 448.

482 James Iredell to Sarah Gray (25 Aug.1798), 1 DHSC 861; [No Caption], RUSSELL'S GAZETTE (Boston), 10 Sept.1798, reprinted in 1 DHSC 864.

483 *Id.*; Hannah Wilson to Bird Wilson (1 Sept.1798), 1 *id.* 861.

484 OCSC 965–71, except perhaps the 1940s.

485 Egbert Benson to Rufus King (18 Dec.1793), 1 DHSC 742; 1 WARREN 85–90; Artemus Ward, Deciding To Leave: The Politics of Departure in the U.S. Supreme Court 31–43 (1999) (unpublished Ph.D. dissertation, Syracuse University).

If the initial justices had been relieved of circuit obligations, as was expected[486] and frequently proposed,[487] Jay,[488] Rutledge,[489] and Johnson[490] would not have resigned, since circuit travail was their reason for leaving the bench. (However, Blair would have resigned because his reason was unbearable ringing in the ears.[491]) In fact Rutledge and Johnson resigned before a 1793 law reduced circuit duties by half,[492] and that change was doubtless a factor in Rutledge being willing to rejoin the Court in 1795 (until he was denied reconfirmation) and in Johnson being urged to do so. Rutledge would not have needed reconfirmation if he had remained on the Court instead of resigning in 1791, except to be elevated as chief justice, and would have had strong reason not to imprecate the Jay Treaty, and his depression would not have been triggered by the Senate's rejection and Federalist anathema.

In any event, Rutledge's health was fully recovered in 1796 and he was quite able to serve in the critical years of 1798–1800, because he did serve in the South Carolina legislature.[493] Johnson was also quite able to devote part of his remaining two decades after 1798 to the Court, because he served as judge of a county court in 1799, was deemed fit for appointment as chief justice of a federal circuit court in 1801,[494] and was still practicing law in 1804.[495] Further, he was a candidate for Congress in 1800, organized a monument to Washington that year, along with buying and selling land,[496] sought to be a presidential elector in 1804, and was supported for the governor's council in 1810 and 1812.[497]

486 *E.g.*, 2 DHSC 10, 243, 261, 334, 335n.

487 1 WARREN 88–90, 185–86, beyond the 1793 act, 1 *id.* 89; 2 DHSC 288, 289, 343, 345, 443.

488 John Jay to J.C. Dongan (27 Feb.1792), 3 JAY CORRESPONDENCE 414; William L. Smith to Edward Rutledge (13 Feb.1792), 1 DHSC 732; 2 *id.* 126, 243, 447, 742 (complaining); or may not have declined renomination, John Jay to John Adams (2 Jan.1801), 4 JAY CORRESPONDENCE 284, 286; 1 DHSC 913; 1 WARREN 172–73.

489 John Rutledge to George Washington (5 Mar.1791), 7 WASHINGTON PAPERS-PRESIDENTIAL 515.

490 Thomas Johnson to James Wilson (1 Mar.1792), 1 DHSC 733, 734; Thomas Johnson to George Washington (16 Jan.1793), 2 DHSC 341, 344.

491 John Blair to William Cushing (12 June 1795), 1 DHSC 756; John Blair to James Iredell (14 Sept.1795), 2 IREDELL CORRESPONDENCE 454, 455; *accord* 2 *id.* 455; 1 DHSC 801.

492 1 WARREN 89; 4 DHSC 200.

493 He was placed on the road to financial recovery by his mother's bequest of a third of her estate upon her 1792 death, and the bequest was distributed in 1799. Mabel L. Webber, *Dr. John Rutledge and His Descendants*, 31 S.C. HISTORICAL & GENEALOGICAL MAG. 7, 11 (1930).

494 1 EDWARD C. PAPENFUSE, BIOGRAPHICAL DICTIONARY OF THE MARYLAND LEGISLATURE 495, 496 (JHUP, Baltimore 1977–85).

495 Petition of Thomas Johnson (24 Oct.1804), Baltimore City Register of Wills (MSA, Baltimore, Accession MSA SC4239-14-27) <http://speccol.mdarchives.state.md.us/pages/speccol/unit.aspx?speccol=4239&serno=14&item=27&subitem=-1> (accessed 4 Aug.2015).

496 Thomas Johnson to John Adams (21 Mar.1800), JOHNSON LETTERS; John H. Stone to Thomas Johnson (12 Apr.1800), *id.*

497 Note 437 *supra*; American Election Returns 1787–1825 <http://elections.lib.tufts.edu/catalog/tufts:md.governors.council.1812> and same for 1810 (accessed 4 Aug.2015).

Would these justices have done anything if they viewed the Sedition Act as unconstitutional? After all, the power of judicial review of acts of Congress was not established until 1803, in *Marbury v. Madison*, according to conventional belief. However, the fact is that every one of the initial justices, even before 1789, had acknowledged the power of judicial review[498] (and Johnson did so in 1790[499]), as had Hamilton, Madison, and many others at the Constitutional Convention and in *The Federalist*.[500] Every one of the initial justices in 1792 questioned the constitutionality of the Invalid Pension Act, in circuit court opinions that declined to follow its directive for judges to make judicial determinations subject to congressional review.[501] All but Iredell the next year overturned state statutes as contrary to federal judicial power.[502] All participating justices in 1795 reviewed and upheld federal law over conflicting state statutes and court decisions, expressly or implicitly.[503] The Supreme Court the next year asserted the power of judicial review both of acts of Congress[504] and of acts of states,[505] though it upheld the statutes in those cases and did not actually hold an act of Congress unconstitutional in part until *Marbury*. Most initial justices in circuit court decisions in 1792 held state laws unconstitutional,[506] and most asserted the power to declare that a law "repugnant to the Constitution, is absolutely void."[507] Nearly all the successor

[498] Saikrishna B. Prakash & John C. Yoo, *The Origins of Judicial Review*, 70 U. Chi. L. Rev. 887, 944 n.226 (2003) (Rutledge); John Adams to William Cushing (9 June 1776), 9 Adams Works 390, 390–91 (Cushing's position that judges could instruct juries that acts of Parliament were null); 2 Farrand's Records 73 (Wilson); 2 DHRC 517 (Wilson); James Wilson, *Lectures on Law*, 1 Wilson Works 743, 707; 1 *id*. 203, 204, 246; Commonwealth v. Caton, 8 Va. (4 Call) 5, 20 (Va. Ct. App. 1787) (Blair); James Iredell, To the Public (c. Aug.1786), 3 Iredell Papers 227, 230; James Iredell to Richard D. Spaight (26 Aug.1787), 3 *id*. 307; William R. Casto, *James Iredell and the American Origins of Judicial Review*, 27 Conn. L. Rev. 329 (1995).

[499] State v. Sluby, 2 Md. 480, 481 (Md. Gen. Ct. 1790).

[500] 1 Farrand's Records 97, 98; 2 *id*. 27, 78, 92, 93; Federalist No.78, at 524, No.80, at 535 (Hamilton); 1 Annals 457 (Madison); 1 Warren 14 (same); *see generally* Maeva Marcus, *Judicial Review in the Early Republic*, in Launching the "Extended Republic": The Federalist Era 25 (Ronald Hoffman & Peter J. Albert eds., UPV, Charlottesville 1996).

[501] Hayburn's Case, 2 U.S. (2 Dall.) 409, 410n., 411n., 412n. (1792) (Jay, Cushing, Iredell, Wilson, Blair, and Paterson, JJ.), with Wilson and Blair, JJ. also declining to serve as nonjudicial commissioners, *id*. 411n.; 1 Warren 66–67, 78; 2 ANB 915; 6 DHSC 33.

[502] Chisholm v. Georgia, 2 U.S. (2 Dall.) 419 (1793); 5 DHSC 127.

[503] Penhallow v. Doane's Administrators, 3 U.S. (3 Dall.) 54, 85, 94–95, 113 (1795) (Paterson, Iredell & Blair, JJ.).

[504] Hylton v. United States, 3 U.S. (3 Dall.) 171 (1796); 7 DHSC 358.

[505] Ware v. Hylton, 3 U.S. (3 Dall.) 199 (1796) (though state confiscation act was superseded by treaty); 7 DHSC 203; *accord* Calder v. Bull, 3 U.S. (3 Dall.) 386 (1798).

[506] 1 Warren 66–67 n.1 (Iredell, Paterson, Jay, Cushing, JJ.); Transatlantic 193 (Jay, Cushing, JJ.).

[507] VanHorne's Lessee v. Dorrance, 2 U.S. (2 Dall.) 304, 310, 312 (C.C.D. Pa. 1795) (Paterson, J.); *see* Charles Warren, *Earliest Cases of Judicial Review of State Legislation by Federal Courts*, 32 Yale L.J. 15 (1922).

justices as well supported judicial review well before *Marbury*.[508] These positions were unsurprising, for judicial review had a rich pedigree in English decisions as well as in state rulings.[509] The justices had the tools to overturn a law that violated the First Amendment, and had shown willingness to use them.

If the Blackstone-Mansfield definition was an accurate summary of the English common law, before Mansfield inserted it into the common law in 1770, we would expect all these early justices to embrace it. Yet not one of Jay, Rutledge, Wilson, Johnson, or Moore did, either before or after July 1798, even though Rutledge received his legal education at Middle Temple and Jay and Wilson studied under leading American lawyers. Instead, they expressed broad understandings of freedoms of press and speech before 1798, and gave every indication of rejecting narrower views during the besiegement of 1798–1801. Rutledge had returned from his legal studies in England to support Wilkes. Wilson, though he tolerated state seditious libel concepts in the late 1780s, had abandoned this by the time of his law lectures in 1790–1791, and instead proclaimed that America's republican system repudiated Blackstone on seditious libel and on many other areas of English law. Thus, Wilson wrote that "[t]he citizen under a free government has a right to think, to speak, to write, to print, and to publish freely, but with decency and truth, concerning publick men, publick bodies, and publick measures." He found it an "unwarrantable attempt" to apply defamation law to criticisms of those public men, public bodies, and public measures, rejecting the essence of seditious libel and seditious words. And Wilson found it unjustified throughout the period that began with the case *Case de Libellis Famosis* that introduced the first of six unique rules for seditious libel, not just beginning with formation of the new American republican government.

Independent of all this, an accurate portrayal of Jay, Rutledge, Wilson, Johnson, and Moore is important, and integral parts of that are their affirmations of broad freedoms of press and speech, and the historical facts indicating their opposition to the Sedition Act. The pre-Marshall justices cannot all be painted in the same hues, nor can all Federalists, nor for that matter can all states outside Virginia and Kentucky.

That opposition of many Federalists to the Sedition Act is part of a more complex picture of the Federalists and the Republicans, as we will see in the final chapter.

[508] *Id.* 308–09 (Paterson); William M. Treanor, *Judicial Review before "Marbury,"* 58 STAN. L. REV. 455, 536 (2005) (Johnson); Egan v. Charles County Court, 3 Md. 169, 170 (Md. Gen. Ct. 1793) (Chase); Samuel Chase to John Marshall (24 Apr.1802), 6 MARSHALL PAPERS 109, 112 (same); 3 DHRC 548, 553 (Ellsworth); Cooper v. Telfair, 4 U.S. (4 Dall.) 14, 15, 19, 20 (1800) (Washington, Chase, Cushing); Bayard v. Singleton, 1 N.C. (Martin) 42, 47–48 (1787) (Moore as counsel).

[509] *E.g.*, Dr. Bonham's Case, (1610) 8 Co. Rep. 107a, 77 Eng. Rep. 638 (C.P.); PHILIP HAMBURGER, LAW AND JUDICIAL DUTY 395–503 (HUP, Cambridge 2008); SYLVIA SNOWISS, JUDICIAL REVIEW AND THE LAW OF THE CONSTITUTION 13–44 (YUP, New Haven 1990).

9

The Federalist Justices and the Republican Critics: Historical Misconceptions about Freedom

> Congress shall make no law . . . abridging the freedom of speech, or of the press . . . .
>
> —First Amendment to the United States Constitution

The widely accepted view of First Amendment history[1] is that the Blackstonian definition that was later approved by the authors of the Sedition Act of 1798 was a long-standing part of the common law and was the only concept of freedom of press and speech available in 1789–1791,[2] when the Bill of Rights was written and ratified, and that the opposing concept articulated in the Virginia and Kentucky Resolutions was virtually nonexistent before 1798 and was rejected by all other states. The widely accepted view is also that the earliest twelve justices of the Supreme Court had nothing to say, or at least nothing to say that was positive, about freedoms of press and speech in the years before the Sedition Act.[3] Further, the generally accepted view is that the earliest twelve justices, as Federalists, all supported the constitutionality of the Sedition Act[4] and the Blackstone-Mansfield definition of freedom of press and speech and those jurists' framework for seditious libel, and that the Federalist Party unanimously supported the Act as well (with a single holdout),[5] and that all states did too except Virginia and

[1] *E.g., see supra* pp.82–83 and notes 60–62.

[2] *E.g., see supra* pp.82–83 and notes 60, 63.

[3] *E.g., see supra* p.113 and note 2, pp.249–50 and notes 3–6.

[4] *E.g., see supra* p.400 and notes 27–31, pp.396–97 and notes 9–10, pp.259–60 and notes 85–88, pp.249–50 and notes 3–6.

[5] *E.g., see supra* pp.399–400 and notes 24–26.

Kentucky.[6] More broadly, the Federalists are generally treated monolithically as the consistent opponents of liberty, and the Republicans are treated uniformly as its consistent protectors.

This book undertakes to set the record straight on those issues. The result is a challenge to those views in many histories and legal discussions.

The Inaccuracy of the Narrow Blackstone-Mansfield Summary of Common Law of Liberties of Press and Speech

Blackstone's 1769 summary of freedom of press, as merely "laying no *previous* restraints upon publications, and not . . . freedom from censure for criminal matter when published" (such as seditious libel prosecutions),[7] is widely viewed by scholars as an accurate summary of long-standing common law and consequently as the meaning assumed by Congress and the states in approving and ratifying the First Amendment.[8] Their view is that no "critics had questioned [Mansfield's] narrow definition of a free press," and "[n]o other definition of freedom of the press by anyone anywhere in America before 1798" existed. Thus, "[e]vidence does not exist to contradict the assertion [that freedom of press] was used in its prevailing common law or Blackstonian sense to mean a guarantee against previous restraints and a subjection to subsequent restraints for licentious or seditious abuse."[9]

To the contrary, Blackstone's summary of the English common law of freedoms of press and speech was no summary at all, because it was not present in that common law until a year later, when Mansfield inserted it there in his *Woodfall* and *Almon* decisions. Furthermore, a contrary belief existed and was widespread that criminalizing and prosecuting press and speech critical of government or officials violated freedom of press or speech, during the decade before 1776–1780, when state declarations of rights were adopted, and during the two decades before 1789–1791, when the First Amendment was adopted and ratified.[10] Parallel to that, the Blackstone-Mansfield framework of six unique rules

[6] *E.g., see supra* p.323 and notes 528–29.

[7] 4 Blackstone's Commentaries 151–52 (emphasis in original). A list of abbreviated titles is at the end of this book.

[8] *E.g., see supra* pp.81–83 and notes 55–59, 60–63.

[9] Levy 158; Levy-Liberty 27, 191.

[10] Wendell Bird, *Liberties of Press and Speech: "Evidence Does Not Exist To Contradict the . . . Blackstonian Sense" in Late Eighteenth Century England?*, 36 Oxford J. of Legal Studies ___ (forthcoming 2016).

governing seditious libel and speech prosecutions had only been adopted by English courts over the prior century, with Mansfield being their most outspoken exponent, and faced significant criticism because of their conflict with the rules governing other criminal prosecutions and other jury trials. This first area challenging many existing political and legal histories is the subject of Chapters 2–3.

That opposition to the newly minted English common law of narrow press freedom and broad seditious libel law was embraced by the revolutionist Americans as they adopted freedom of press provisions in new state constitutions, and by the states and Congress as they proposed, adopted, and ratified freedoms of press and speech in the Bill of Rights. They did so by choosing unqualified language to protect those freedoms, and more broadly, by choosing to override English common law by all First Amendment clauses and by many other Bill of Rights provisions. They did not respond by adopting restrictive language specifying that those freedoms meant only the new common law definition as no prior restraint, or by specifying that the common law of seditious libel and seditious speech was not affected by state constitutions or the Bill of Rights. There was no such restrictive language or saving provision in the case of any of the nine states that adopted freedom of press provisions, or in the case of any state's ratification proposal for a constitutional amendment protecting freedom of press or speech, or in the discussions of either house of Congress as each rejected proposed modifications of the freedoms of press and speech provision to limit it to common law freedoms of press and speech ("as ample a manner as hath at any time been secured by the common law").[11]

That opposition to the Blackstone-Mansfield definition and framework was also reflected in the fact that nine of the eleven new states adopting constitutions saw a need to include freedom of press protections at all, and in the source of that need for security in fundamental law. The historical context for the new states' provisions for freedom of press was the revolutionists' essays and speeches being branded as seditious libel and seditious words, and their recognition that the concept of seditious libel was developed to criminalize political opposition and criticism of government. The historical context for the First Amendment's protections for freedoms of press and speech was, besides those uniformly broad state provisions, the demands in the decisive state ratifications of the Constitution for express protection of freedom of press, with language similar to each state's own broad provisions. When the First Amendment was introduced in Congress, Madison announced that it would leave government "disarmed of powers which trench upon those particular rights." This was the context in which the early justices pondered the First Amendment.

[11] *E.g., see supra* pp.75–79.

Figure 9.1 The Pre-Marshall Justices (listed in Introduction). (Courtesy of sources identified earlier, and National Parks Service (Cushing), Library of Congress (Iredell), and U.S. Supreme Court (Washington and Moore).)

The Early Justices' Commitment to Broad Freedoms of Press and Speech, and Nonacceptance of the Narrow Blackstone-Mansfield Definition, Before the Assault of 1798–1801

The earliest twelve justices (shown in Figure 9.1) are all usually portrayed as having nothing to contribute on freedoms of press and speech before 1798, being averse or uncommitted to those freedoms, and embracing the Blackstone-Mansfield definition of freedoms of press and speech. They do not help their portraits by holding many beliefs typical of their age and, to modern eyes, appearing as stiff as their marble statues.

Instead, nearly all the early justices expressed commitment to those freedoms before the assault of 1798, and even more significantly, not one embraced the Blackstone-Mansfield definition as they discussed freedoms of press and speech before that date. If the Blackstone-Mansfield definition had been accepted by all continually before that year, as claimed, it would have been endorsed in the prior statements of the justices on press and speech, rather than being entirely absent, and would not have been repudiated by Wilson or mostly rejected by Cushing. Instead, that definition was only endorsed for the first time in 1798–1799, as most sitting justices changed positions in order to uphold and enforce the Sedition Act, and similarly a federal common law of crimes was only endorsed for the first time in 1798–1799 for the same reason (with the sole exceptions of Iredell moving in that direction in 1796 and Blair the next year).[12] It was not the Blackstone-Mansfield definition that was dominant among the early justices before 1798 but much broader conceptions

[12] This statement treats federal court recognition of the law of nations, which the Constitution supports, as very different from federal court acceptance of a federal common law of crimes.

of freedoms of press and speech, and it was only in 1798–1799 that half the early justices adopted that Blackstone-Mansfield definition and that federal common law of crimes for the first time. This second area in which this book challenges and adds to existing histories and legal discussions is the subject of Chapters 4–5.[13]

Yet the absence before 1798 of the Blackstone-Mansfield definition and framework among the early justices should not be surprising, given the recency of Blackstone's published language about freedoms of press and speech (1769), the equal recency of Mansfield's judicial adoption of it (1770), the intervening adoption of state protections of freedom of press with expansive language and no stated qualifications, the intervening state proposals for a constitutional amendment for liberties of press and speech, and the intervening ratification of the First Amendment with broad language and without express restrictions. Parallel to these developments throughout the 1770s and 1780s was the existence and growth of challenges to the narrow definition and to a seditious libel crime.

Federalists' and Early Justices' Division Over the Sedition Act and the First Amendment

The conventional view is that all the pre-Marshall justices joined in unanimous Federalist support of the Sedition Act (including Marshall on its constitutionality, though he is described as the lone Federalist objecting to its expedience). Put simply, the most common reasoning is that all the early justices were Federalists, and all Federalists supported the Act. It is true that most of the sitting justices supported the constitutionality of the Sedition Act. Even for them, the reasoning about the constitutionality of the Act by the three recognized as presiding over prosecutions, and by the fourth who wrote an informal opinion supporting the Act, has only been cursorily described. The similar opinions of the other two sitting justices, and the views of the six remaining justices, have been virtually ignored, along with one justice's senescent condition.

Instead, the early justices divided over the Sedition Act, with nearly half of the early justices apparently opposing it. Similarly, the Federalist Party as a whole divided over the Sedition Act, with a virtually unrecognized but significant minority opposing its constitutionality, some even to the point of leaving the Federalist Party. The states also divided over the Sedition Act, more than has been recognized, with only half opposing the Virginia and Kentucky Resolutions, and the other half of the states ranging from Virginia's and Kentucky's condemnation of the Sedition Act, to the Tennessee and Georgia Resolutions supporting them, to two states deadlocking their legislatures, and two states choosing not to oppose the Virginia

[13] Delayed acceptance by only half the early justices of a federal common law of crimes, distinct from the law of nations, is discussed at pp. 85–95.

and Kentucky Resolutions. This third area in which this book challenges and supplements existing political and legal histories is the subject of Chapters 6–8.

Why did initial justices and successor justices tend toward different positions in First Amendment commitment, on the Blackstone-Mansfield approach, on the Sedition Act, and ultimately, on the First Amendment?

The most striking difference between most initial justices and most successors, the stature of the former as "first characters" nationally,[14] was accompanied by more independence of thought (prime examples were Wilson and Jay). While all first characters did not depart from Federalist orthodoxy (examples were Adams, to a large degree, and Hamilton), more independent-minded statesmen were increasingly prone to do so.

Another difference, connected to the first, is that the initial justices (except Iredell) appear to have had personal involvement with, and to have thought about, freedoms of press and speech much more than the successors (except Johnson), before the Sedition Act of 1798 forced sitting justices to address those freedoms. Their relative thought about those freedoms can be roughly gauged by the greater number of statements and stances located for Chapter 4 compared to Chapter 5, and by the greater willingness of sitting justices to subordinate the First Amendment to seditious libel as discussed in Chapters 6–7 compared to Chapter 8. This greater personal involvement with those freedoms, in turn, came from the cause of their being "first characters," that they had been major leaders in revolutionary state governments who committed sedition or treason against Great Britain and faced a much greater threat of prosecution for sedition or treason,[15] compared with the successor justices who (except Johnson) were junior officers or officials and who did not face such threats. Thus, when Lord Hillsborough warned colonial governors and legislatures against "any letter or paper that may have the smallest tendency to sedition," Rutledge listened in the South Carolina legislature as the warning was read,[16] and other "first characters" knew Hillsborough meant their own advocacy of colonial rights.[17] No such dangers attended the earlier public service of the successor justices, except Johnson. Further, Rutledge and Johnson, serving as their states' first governors, and Jay and Cushing, serving as their states' first chief justices,[18] had wrestled with reconciling stable government and expressive freedoms, and Wilson, as his state's first law professor, uniquely reasoned about those tensions in constitutional theory.

[14] *E.g., see supra* p.398.

[15] *E.g.,* James Wilson, An Address to the Inhabitants of the Colonies (1776), 1 Wilson Works 46, 51.

[16] Journals of Assembly-S.C. (17 Nov.1768), quoted in Rutledge 47; 5 Privy Council-Colonial 261, 262, 417; as well as from the council president, Leigh's Considerations 82.

[17] *E.g., At the Court at St. James,* Boston Evening Post, 25 Apr.1774, at 4; *By His Excellency Josiah Martin,* Pennsylvania Ledger (Philadelphia), 4 Nov.1775, at 1.

[18] In Cushing's case, after John Adams declined to serve.

A further striking difference between most initial justices and most successors was their divergent positions on seven concepts that sharply limited dissent. Hence, they generally divided on the legitimacy of opposing the administration, and of parties; on the individual's right to evaluate laws as illegal and void, and to disobey illegal laws; and in 1798 on the existence of a federal common law of crimes, as well as on the Blackstone-Mansfield definition of freedoms of press and speech and their framework of unique rules for seditious libel, and the effect of state and federal constitutions on them (as discussed at the end of Chapter 3). To a large extent, the early justices divided along radical Whig and moderate Whig lines, and later along Adams Federalist and High Federalist lines.

Speaking publicly on the unconstitutionality of the Sedition Act appears to have been much more difficult than perceiving it. That doubtless resulted from the Sedition Act prosecutions of Peck and Llewellyn for publicly questioning the constitutionality of the Act, along with the threatened prosecution of Garrard, and the flaying of Marshall for opposing the Act even on nonconstitutional grounds. It also resulted from the earlier excoriation of Rutledge for publicly challenging the Jay Treaty, which led his brother to keep private his challenge to the Sedition Act. The public silence of the remaining justices is less difficult to understand in the context of silence of the Supreme Court on later abridgments of the First Amendment for over a century.[19] Further, it was not just Federalists who failed to make public condemnation of such violations of liberty, though we will not reach that until later in this concluding chapter.

The Unrecognized Half of the Prosecutions under the Sedition Act of 1798

The pervasive descriptions of fourteen or fifteen prosecutions under the Sedition Act, along with three federal prosecutions for common law seditious libel, has remained frozen without confirmation of any additional prosecutions in federal court records or prosecutor records, except two very brief acknowledgments of the prosecution of Dr. Samuel Shaw.[20]

However, a missing other half of the prosecutions under the Sedition Act can now be confirmed: eleven additional cases prosecuting sixteen more defendants for seditious writings and words, and eleven additional cases prosecuting eighty-three defendants for seditious combinations and conspiracies. Additionally, there were at least three attempted indictments that grand juries rejected, and six instructions to bring Sedition Act charges.

[19] *E.g.*, David M. Rabban, *The First Amendment in Its Forgotten Years*, 90 Yale L.J. 514, 531–33, 539–40, 550–51, 582–86 (1981).

[20] 1 History of Supreme Court 638 n.107 (one sentence); Repressive Jurisprudence 139–40 (half page without "any details of the case").

These additional confirmed cases shed more light on the First Amendment views of the sitting justices, adding a fourth justice to those who presided over Sedition Act trials (Iredell, in addition to Paterson, Chase, and Washington), and a fifth justice to those who presided over indictments and sentences (Cushing). These cases also more than double the size of the canvas portraying the Adams administration's attack on the Republican press, and the infringements of liberties of prosecuted individuals. This fourth area in which this book challenges and supplements the history of the Sedition Act is the topic of Chapter 7.

Figure 9.2 President John Adams. Portrait by Gilbert Stuart. (Courtesy of National Gallery of Art.)

Figure 9.3 President Thomas Jefferson. Portrait by Gilbert Stuart. (Courtesy of National Gallery of Art.)

Republican Words and Deeds on Seditious Libel and the First Amendment

Misconceptions are not unique to the Federalists and John Adams (Figure 9.2). They also abound about Republicans, as the party of Jefferson and Madison is often treated as the consistent party of liberty while the Federalists are castigated as the monolithic party opposing liberty.

Thomas Jefferson (Figure 9.3), though courageous in writing the Kentucky Resolutions and coordinating much Sedition Act opposition, did not live up to the common historical claim that "no [seditious libel] charges would be brought, for his administration would not be stained by any such persecutions."[21] Though Jefferson initially told his attorney general that he wished "to see the experiment tried of getting along without public prosecutions for libel,"[22] a year later, becoming frustrated with Federalist hailstorms of excoriation, he incited Governor Thomas McKean of Pennsylvania with the "entirely confidential" words "that a few prosecutions of the most eminent offenders would have a wholesome effect in restoring the integrity of the presses."[23] McKean did not need much incitement, and quickly prosecuted a Federalist editor, Joseph Dennie, under state law in 1803, though the effort failed as the jury ultimately found him not guilty.[24] Jefferson's appointee, the federal attorney in Connecticut, brought seditious libel indictments of three newspaper editors (Hudson and Goodwin, of the *Connecticut Courant*, the largest Federalist paper there, and Thomas Collier, of the Litchfield *Monitor*, also a Federalist paper), in 1807, as well as of an essayist and two ministers (also all Federalists).[25] Nor is Warren's statement true that "Jefferson, who had not known of their existence, ordered their dismissal as soon as he learned of them."[26] Instead, Jefferson's order was quite delayed after learning of the cases (it only followed learning that embarrassing facts would come out at trial),[27] and did not bring dismissal of the first two editors, whose case moved forward until the

[21] OPPOSITION 486; *accord* LEONARD W. LEVY, JEFFERSON AND CIVIL LIBERTIES: THE DARKER SIDE 42–69, 158–76 (BP-HUP, Cambridge 1963, repr. 1989).

[22] Thomas Jefferson to Levi Lincoln (24 Mar.1802), 37 JEFFERSON PAPERS 119. He said much the same about freedom of speech in his inaugural address. PETER S. ONUF, JEFFERSON'S EMPIRE 78 (UPV, Charlottesville 2000).

[23] Thomas Jefferson to Thomas McKean (19 Feb.1803), 39 JEFFERSON PAPERS 552, 553.

[24] 4 JEFFERSON 228–31; *accord* LEVY 341.

[25] LEVY 344–46; REPRESSIVE JURISPRUDENCE 148–86.

[26] 1 WARREN 436; 2 HISTORY OF SUPREME COURT 355.

[27] Veritas [Gideon Granger], *Editors of the National Intelligencer*, NATIONAL INTELLIGENCER (Washington, D.C.), 21 July 1809, at 3; 5 JEFFERSON 371–91; LEVY 344–45; JAY 1014; REPRESSIVE JURISPRUDENCE 160, 165 n.57.

Supreme Court ruled against federal common law crimes.[28] However, those that claim Jefferson otherwise was not Jeffersonian on state laws and prosecutions for seditious libel[29] fail to examine his writings about state power carefully; most are restricted to "punishing slander,"[30] much like his earlier proposed revisions of Virginia laws.

Nor did various other Republicans live up to their pre-1801 opposition to seditious libel prosecution, as they instead prosecuted various Federalists.[31] Blumberg summarized how "at least as many as 30 criminal libel cases—a half dozen federal, the balance state—have been reported during the Jefferson and Madison administrations," many by Republicans and some by Federalists.[32] In federal courts, his half dozen referred to the Connecticut cases,[33] to which he added an attempted prosecution for common law libel of Francis Flourney, a Federalist newspaper editor,[34] and a number of prosecutions under federal common law for nonlibel crimes (despite earlier Republican condemnation of that claimed basis for federal law and federal court jurisdiction).[35]

In state courts, the best-known prosecution was of Harry Croswell, the Federalist editor of *The Wasp*, for seditious libel in maligning Jefferson, a case brought by Jay's Republican successor in New York's governorship, during 1803–1806.[36] In that case, the Federalist-Jeffersonian inversion became complete as Alexander Hamilton entered the case to appeal the editor's seditious libel conviction, arguing that "liberty of the press" meant freedom to "publish with impunity" true information "reflecting on government, magistracy, or individuals."[37] That case and

[28] JAY 1014; United States v. Hudson & Goodwin, 11 U.S. (7 Cranch) 32 (1812).

[29] *E.g.*, ANDERSON 507; REPRESSIVE JURISPRUDENCE 63; LEVY 343.

[30] Thomas Jefferson to Abigail Adams (11 Sept.1804), ADAMS-JEFFERSON 278, 279; Thomas Jefferson to Levi Lincoln (24 Mar.1802), 8 JEFFERSON WRITINGS 139; Thomas Jefferson to Thomas Seymour (11 Feb.1807), 9 *id.* 28, 30; Thomas Jefferson to John Norvell (14 June 1807), 9 *id.* 71, 74. However, Jefferson went through a period of wishing for a state seditious libel prosecution, Thomas Jefferson to Thomas McKean (19 Feb.1803), 8 *id.* 216, 219, as well as a federal one.

[31] *E.g.*, LEVY 341 (Joseph Dennie-Pa., 1803); [No Caption], RALEIGH REGISTER, 5 Mar.1804, at 3 (James Cheetham-N.Y., 1804); 2 HISTORY OF SUPREME COURT 638 n.110 (William Dickinson-Pa., 1806); GEORGE A. BILLIAS, ELBRIDGE GERRY 322–23 (McGraw-Hill, New York 1976) (Federalist editors-Mass.); TYRANNY 258–319.

[32] REPRESSIVE JURISPRUDENCE 150.

[33] *Id.* at 156–66.

[34] *Id.* at 155, citing MARY TACHAU, FEDERAL COURTS IN THE EARLY REPUBLIC 135 (1978).

[35] REPRESSIVE JURISPRUDENCE 152–56, 175, of William Hardin and others for rescue of accused murderers of Indians, of Thomas Passmore for perjury in a bankruptcy action, and of William Smith and others for violation of embargo and nonintercourse laws. *Accord* 2 HISTORY OF SUPREME COURT 638–39 & n.111 (Smith).

[36] TYRANNY 268–69, 271; LEVY 338–39.

[37] People v. Croswell, 3 Johns. Cas. 337, 393–94 (N.Y.1804); *see* 1 LAW PRACTICE OF ALEXANDER HAMILTON 808, 809 (Julius Goebel et al. eds., ColUP, New York 1964–1981).

the *Dennie* case were far from the only Republican prosecutions of Federalist editors, however, as a criminal libel prosecution was aimed at Gardner Tracy of the *Lansingburg Gazette* and civil libel actions were brought against William Dickson of the *Lancaster Intelligencer* in 1805 and 1806, as well as anew against Harry Croswell in 1804.[38] Establishment Republicans also brought seditious libel and civil libel actions against radical Republican editors and factions,[39] and Federalists where they still retained power retaliated with actions against Republicans, in addition to various civil libel actions.[40]

Further, it was principally Republican state legislatures that, throughout the first half of the nineteenth century, adopted provisions for a defense of truth and for jury determination of all issues (the *Zenger* modifications as *Croswell* reformulated them) in seditious libel cases. Often accidentally, they revived or reaffirmed the crime of seditious libel, though their objective was to protect defendants, and doubtless, to assist incumbent officials. The English common law of seditious libel proved very difficult to leave interred or rejected.

Republican Words and Deeds on Slavery and Liberty Generally

Republicans appear much more the party of oppression, and Federalists more the party of liberty, if scrutiny about freedom is broadened from expressive freedom to a still greater issue, slavery.

Five of the twelve early justices (all Federalists) opposed slavery, with varying degrees of consistency, while essentially all of Jefferson's, Madison's, and Monroe's appointees (all Republicans) supported slavery, except one. Among the early justices, Jay, Cushing, Wilson, Paterson, and Ellsworth supported emancipation. The first chief justice, Jay, recognized the inconsistency that

[38] Repressive Jurisprudence 209, 196, 198, 208.

[39] *Id.* at 195 (Alexander Dallas v. Matthew Lawler, 1805), 196, 199, 201–202 (numerous prosecutions of William Duane, 1805–1809), 199 (Commonwealth v. Michael Leib, 1807), 210, 302 (New York Senate v. James Cheetham, and Tillotson v. Cheetham, 1806), 211 (People ex rel. Lewis v. Thomas Farmer, 1807), 212 (People ex rel. Lewis v. William Few, 1807), 212 (Abraham Spencer v. Solomon Southwick, 1814).

[40] *Id.* at 152 (United States v. Samuel Harrison Smith, attempted 1801), 191 (Alexander Dallas v. John Fenno, 1800), 195 (actions of Commonwealth v. Michael Leib, William Duane, Matthew Lawler, Thomas Leiper, Jacob Mitchell, and John Steele, 1805), 215–33 (other Federalist actions); *accord* 1 Warren 195–98 (editor of *National Intelligencer,* 1801); Charles Warren, A History of the American Bar 237 (Little Brown, Boston 1911) (John S. Lillie of *Constitutional Telegraph,* 1801); Press-Mass. 146 (Lillie; William Carleton of Salem *Register,* 1803).

"men should pray and fight for their own freedom, and yet keep others in slavery," saying:

> I wish to see all unjust and all unnecessary discriminations everywhere abolished, and that the time may soon come when all our inhabitants of every colour and denomination shall be free and equal partakers of our political liberty.[41]

He supported gradual abolition on the ground that it was the only feasible approach.[42] Jay served as the first president of New York's manumission society, and he signed into law the state's gradual emancipation law.[43] His gradualism was reflected in purchasing slaves in order to manumit them after being repaid by their work.[44] Cushing was more consistent, besides not owning slaves, as he rendered a major judicial decision on slavery in his jury charge in the *Quock Walker Case* in 1783. There, he noted "the natural rights of mankind," and reasoned from the Massachusetts constitution's provisions ("*that all men are born free and equal*; and that *every subject is entitled to liberty*") that slavery was thereby "abolished" in the state.[45] Even a Cushing enemy noted that the "decision put an end to the idea of slavery in this state,"[46] though historians debate the decision,[47] and Cushing's later decisions retreated from it.[48] Common prejudices about Federalists are betrayed by one author's title on Cushing: "Unlikely Abolitionist."[49] Wilson, in his law lectures written deliberately for posterity, stated that slavery "is unauthorized

[41] John Jay to Richard Price (27 Sept.1785), 3 JAY CORRESPONDENCE 168; John Jay to Benjamin Rush (24 Mar.1785), 3 *id.* 139, 140; *accord* 3 *id.* 341, 4 *id.* 432; 12 LETTERS OF DELEGATES 153.

[42] John Jay to J.C. Dongan (27 Feb.1792), 3 *id.* 413, 414; *accord* 3 *id.* 340, 334, 4 *id.* 431–32; JAY-PEACE 540.

[43] 3 *id.* 185 & n., 329 & n.; JAY-PEACE 14; 3 HAMILTON PAPERS 604 n.4; MESSAGES-N.Y. 553.

[44] John Jay, Rec. of John Jay (Nov.1798), JAY PAPERS doc.9216, p.4; SELECTED LETTERS OF JOHN JAY AND SARAH LIVINGSTON JAY 298–99 (Landa M. Freeman et al. eds., McFarland, Jefferson 2004); JAY-PEACE 705.

[45] John D. Cushing, *The Cushing Court and the Abolition of Slavery in Massachusetts*, 5 AM. J. LEGAL HIST. 118, 133 (1961). Despite controversy about the case, this is entirely consistent with Cushing's draft. William Cushing Judicial Notebook, 1783, CUSHING PAPERS 95–98 (MHS, Boston, microfilm P-406).

[46] James Sullivan to Jeremy Belknap (9 Apr.1795), *Queries Relating to Slavery in Massachusetts*, 3 COLLECTIONS OF THE MASS. HISTORICAL SOC. (5th Ser.) 402, 403 (1877).

[47] William O'Brien, *Did the Jennison Case Outlaw Slavery in Massachusetts?*, 17 WM. & MARY Q. (3rd Ser.) 219 (1960).

[48] Harry Downs, *Unlikely Abolitionist: William Cushing and the Struggle Against Slavery*, 29 J. SUP. CT. HIST. 123, 130–33 (2004); John D. Cushing, *supra* note 45, at 139–43; *e.g.*, William Cushing to John Hancock (20 Dec.1783), William Cushing Papers (LC, Washington, Misc. Manuscript Collection, AC15,966).

[49] *Id.*

by the common law" and "is repugnant to the principles of natural law."[50] At the Pennsylvania ratification convention he looked forward to "banishing slavery out of this country."[51] He was notably less enthusiastic when posterity was not watching, and belatedly freed his one slave three years later, impelled more by his new Quaker bride than by conviction,[52] since he had not freed the slave before.

The third chief justice, Ellsworth, wrote during the ratification debates that "all good men wish the entire abolition of slavery, as soon as it can take place with safety to the public," though he also defended the silence of the Constitution on the issue by saying its "only possible step" was to set a date for nonimportation.[53] Even on the nonimportation provision, his deeds were less ardent than his essay's words, out of worry the provision might prevent agreement on the Constitution.[54] Paterson similarly wrote in a newspaper essay about the irreconcilable claims of southern slaveholders to be "friends to equality and the rights of man," but he then joined them by dismissing objections to the three-fifths compromise on the basis of practical necessity. He also dismissed objections to the treatment of slaves as property, writing in an unpublished essay, "what a frother and deal of fuss do some people make about nothing. Slaves are man, and also a species of property, and therefore of doubtful values in a land of liberty."[55] Later, he provided for a slave to be given basic education and then be manumitted, after five years of service, but did so in the form of a sale to reimburse most of his earlier purchase price.[56]

The remaining early Federalist justices were southerners or Marylanders, owned slaves, and did not criticize slavery—Rutledge,[57] Blair,[58] Iredell,[59]

[50] *Lectures on Law*, 2 Wilson Works 1077.

[51] 2 DHRC 463 (3 Dec.1787).

[52] To Whom It May Concern (2 Jan.1794), 2 Wilson Writings 475; Wilson 30.

[53] Landholder [Oliver Ellsworth], *The Letters of a Landholder* (1787–1788), Essays-Constitution 135, 164.

[54] 2 Farrand's Records 364, 371.

[55] Paterson Essays 15, 14. His convention comments were in the context of opposing the three-fifths compromise. 1 Farrand's Records 561.

[56] William Paterson, Articles of Agreement (9 Mar.1795), William Paterson Papers (NJHS, Trenton, ms. group 14, box 2, folder 40). On Federalists and slavery, *see* Paul Finkelman, *The Problem of Slavery in the Age of Federalism*, in Federalists Reconsidered 135 (Doron Ben-Atar & Barbara B. Oberg eds., UPV, Charlottesville 1998).

[57] Heads of Families at the First Census . . . South Carolina 10 (GPO, Washington 1908) (217 slaves); 2 Farrand's Records 364, though he supported the federal nonimportation provision allowing restriction after 1808, 2 *id.* 559; Journals of House-S.C. 232, 615 (1787–1788); Rutledge 122, 145, 156, 165, 210, 226, 230.

[58] Virginia Tax Records 370 (Gary Parks ed., Baltimore, GPC 1983) (townhouse slaves); Jerome D. Traver, Uncovering the Past at Taskinas Plantation I-42, I-47 (Rockefeller Library, Williamsburg 2003) (sales, will).

[59] 2 DHSC 446 & n.1, 295; 3 *id.* 255–56 (2 slaves); 2 Iredell Papers 24, 326, 354; 3 *id.* 80, 115, 196, 217, 340, 464, 555 (slaves); 1 *id.* 53, 76; 2 *id.* 17, 388 (sales), though he would end the slave trade, 4 Elliot's Debates 100.

Johnson,[60] Chase,[61] Bushrod Washington,[62] and Moore.[63] Apparently oblivious of the irony, these justices used freeman-slavery figures of speech periodically,[64] proving the observation that "those who most denied freedom . . . were the very persons most alive to it."[65] That "irony of slaveholders fighting for the natural rights of man" was not unique to the Supreme Court, of course, and was instead the greatest inconsistency of the framers.[66]

Thus, nearly half the Federalist justices supported emancipation. That was not an overwhelming proportion, but it was much higher than the negligible proportion of subsequent Republican justices on the Marshall Court who supported emancipation, particularly if their deeds rather than words are considered. A similar result comes from comparing the two Federalist presidents with their three Republican successors.[67]

By contrast, the six Republican justices appointed by Jefferson, Madison, and Monroe included three who owned slaves, as did Chief Justice John Marshall.[68] Even two of the three who did not own slaves, and who occasionally decried slavery, still generally ruled in its favor,[69] as is evident in the two most significant decisions about slavery before *Dred Scott*. Marshall's decision in *The Antelope*, that

[60] Thomas Johnson to George Washington (21 Sept.1785), 3 WASHINGTON PAPERS-CONFEDERATION 269, 270; 7 LETTERS OF MEMBERS 376 n.1.

[61] Inv. of Samuel Chase (21 Aug.1811), CHASE CORRESPONDENCE (15 slaves); Samuel Chase, Will (1 May 1795), CHASE CORRESPONDENCE; Samuel Chase to Caesar Rodney (25 July 1777), 7 LETTERS OF MEMBERS 376 n.1. His congressional comments in 1776 addressed which inhabitants were considered for tax quotas. 1 JEFFERSON PAPERS 320; 4 LETTERS OF DELEGATES 568.

[62] Bushrod Washington, *Judge Washington*, NEW-YORK SPECTATOR, 28 Sept.1821, at 2 (arguing, against criticism for selling 54 slaves, his "*legal* right to dispose of this species of property"); Inventory of Bushrod Washington's Estate (28 Jan.1830), Bushrod Washington Papers (MVL, Mt. Vernon); Will (10 July 1826), *id.*; 2 MARSHALL PAPERS 481 n.57. He executed George Washington's will on freeing slaves, and was first president of the society to colonize freed slaves in Liberia. ANNUAL REPORT OF THE AMERICAN SOCIETY FOR COLONIZING THE FREE PEOPLE OF COLOUR 11 (Davis and Force, Washington 1819).

[63] 13 DAB 112; 1 JUSTICES 272; *e.g.*, Cutlar v. Spiller, 3 N.C. (2 Hayw.) 228 (1798).

[64] 2 DHSC 485; 3 *id.* 31; 1 IREDELL PAPERS 264, 399, 408, 432, 435, 438; 2 *id.* 46; IDEOLOGICAL ORIGINS 232.

[65] ORLANDO PATTERSON, SLAVERY AND SOCIAL DEATH ix (HUP, Cambridge 1982).

[66] DAVID B. DAVIS, THE PROBLEM OF SLAVERY IN WESTERN CULTURE 4, 13 (CorUP, Ithaca 1966); *accord* DAVID B. DAVIS, PROBLEM OF SLAVERY IN THE AGE OF REVOLUTION, 1770–1823, at 164–84 (OUP, Oxford 1999); GEORGE W. VAN CLEVE, A SLAVEHOLDER'S UNION: SLAVERY, POLITICS, AND THE CONSTITUTION IN THE EARLY AMERICAN REPUBLIC 182–83, 271, 272 *passim* (UChiP, Chicago 2010).

[67] JOHN C. MILLER, THE WOLF BY THE EARS: THOMAS JEFFERSON AND SLAVERY 104–279 (Free Press, New York 1977); ANNETTE GORDON-REED, THOMAS JEFFERSON AND SALLY HEMINGS (UPV, Charlottesville 1997).

[68] John Marshall, Revoked Will and Codicils (12 Apr.1827–17 Aug.1830), 11 MARSHALL PAPERS 5; 1 ALBERT J. BEVERIDGE, LIFE OF JOHN MARSHALL 167, 180–81 (Houghton Mifflin, Boston 1916).

[69] Donald M. Roper, *In Quest of Judicial Objectivity: The Marshall Court and the Legitimation of Slavery*, 21 STAN. L. REV. 532 (1969).

slave trade vessels could not be lawfully captured,[70] was rendered without any dissent, apparently by appeasing potential dissenters with references to the abhorrence of slave trading and its violation of the law of nature.[71] The five Republican justices who joined in the decision included not only those who held slaves—William Johnson, who saw slavery as "a necessary evil,"[72] Thomas Todd,[73] and Gabriel Duvall[74] (despite the latter in two other cases supporting claims of freedom[75])—but also those who did not—Joseph Story, who condemned slavery but also condemned abolition,[76] and Smith Thompson, who as navy secretary had allowed neutral searches of slave traders but on the Court regularly supported masters' claims of property rights in slave cases.[77] The other member of Story's camp, Brockholst Livingston, had recently left the Court. Later, Story authored the Supreme Court opinion that resoundingly upheld and enforced the first Fugitive Slave Law in *Prigg v. Pennsylvania*,[78] where he took a position that one scholar termed "proslavery nationalism"[79]; Thompson concurred.[80] The Republican judicial record in this period was anything but a pro-freedom record on slavery, just as it was not consistently a pro-expression record.[81]

If the vantage point is moved outside the judiciary, the contrast between Federalists and Republicans on slavery is still more striking. Federalists eliminated

[70] 23 U.S. (10 Wheat.) 66, 120 (1825).

[71] *Id.* 115, 120.

[72] Donald G. Morgan, Justice William Johnson 103, 136 (USCP, Columbia 1954), though on circuit he struck down a law imprisoning free black sailors when ashore, Elkison v. Deliesseline, 8 Fed. Cas. 493 (C.C.D. S.C. 1823) (No. 4,366).

[73] William E. Railey, History of Woodford County, Kentucky 14 (Roberts, Frankfort 1938) (21 slaves in 1810 census).

[74] 1 Edward C. Papenfuse, A Biographical Dictionary of the Maryland Legislature 290, 291 (JHUP, Baltimore 1977–1985) (36 slaves).

[75] Le Grand v. Darnall, 27 U.S. (2 Pet.) 664 (1829); Queen v. Hepburn, 11 U.S. (7 Cranch) 290, 298 (1813).

[76] R. Kent Newmyer, Supreme Court Justice Joseph Story 345, 353–54, 351 (UNCP, Chapel Hill 1985); Robert M. Cover, Justice Accused: Antislavery and the Judicial Process 239, 240 (YUP, New Haven 1975).

[77] 21 ANB 578, 579, 580; 1 Justices 488–90. On the Marshall Court and slavery, *see* Earl M. Maltz, Slavery and the Supreme Court, 1826–1861, at 6–11 (UPKan, Lawrence 2009); on Smith Thompson, *see id.* at 37.

[78] 41 U.S. (16 Peters) 539, 622, 625–26 (1842), which preceded Dred Scott v. Sandford, 60 U.S. (19 How.) 393 (1857). The prior year, Story ruled against slave interests in *The Amistad*, upholding Thompson's circuit opinion. United States v. Schooner Amistad, 40 U.S. (15 Pet.) 518, 597 (1841).

[79] Paul Finkelman, *Prigg v. Pennsylvania: Understanding Justice Story's Proslavery Nationalism*, 22 J. Sup. Ct. Hist. 52 (1997); *cf.* H. Robert Baker, Prigg v. Pennsylvania: Slavery, the Supreme Court, and the Ambivalent Constitution 112–51 (UPKan, Lawrence 2012); Don E. Fehrenbacher, The Slaveholding Republic 219–22 (OUP, New York 2001).

[80] 41 U.S. (16 Peters) at 633; 18 DAB 471–72.

[81] Linda K. Kerber, Federalists in Dissent: Imagery and Ideology in Jeffersonian America 23 (CorUP, Ithaca 1970); Federalists Reconsidered 135–56 (Doron Ben-Atar & Barbara B. Oberg eds., UPV, Charlottesville 1998).

slavery in many northern states, and barred slavery from the Northwest Territory.[82] The intellectual heirs of the Federalists continued the fight.

What of the constitutionality of the Sedition Act? In the author's view, the First Amendment's broadly worded protection of speech and press unavoidably and manifestly conflicted with prohibiting "writing, printing, uttering or publishing any false, scandalous and malicious writing or writings against the government . . . Congress . . . or . . . President." Recognizing the conflict did not require two centuries of hindsight; it was perceived by a significant minority of the Federalist Party as well as by the great majority of the Republican Party during the assault of 1798–1801. The effect of the First Amendment, as Madison commented in guiding it through Congress, was that "[t]he right of freedom of speech is secured; the liberty of the press is expressly declared to be beyond the reach of this government . . . ."[83]

The common understanding of the First Amendment in and around 1789–1791 was not the Blackstone-Mansfield definition of liberties of press and speech, not just because the wording of the First Amendment was as broad as Madison described it to be, but because that definition was not a long-standing common law understanding but, rather, a newly contrived concept entirely absent from the English common law that Blackstone claimed to summarize until it was inserted into that common law by Mansfield the year *after* Blackstone published his summary. The mistaken assumption that the Blackstone-Mansfield definition was a long-standing common law understanding has undergirded First Amendment analysis for far too long, and has wrongly framed the discussion or at least created an assumption of a narrow meaning of liberties of press and speech. Consequently, it should not be surprising that none of the early justices accepted the Blackstone-Mansfield definition or framework before 1798, and that only half of them accepted it during 1798–1801, or that they divided over the constitutionality of the Sedition Act.

Seditious libel and seditious speech proved in the Sedition Act trials to be plastic concepts, easily manipulated by government to include virtually any dissent. The reason was that their elements, a negative "reflection" on government or officials that might "alienate" the affections of the people, and a "tendency" to breach the peace, could reach any expression. By their indeterminacy and their threat to an opposition, seditious libel and seditious speech were inconsistent with rule of law and constitutionalism, as well as with the First Amendment. Seditious libel, seditious words, and the Sedition Act were not struck down under the First Amendment during 1798–1801, or during the next century and a half. However, the eventual decision on their constitutionality had already been made by the First Amendment's use of unrestricted language protecting freedoms of speech and press.

[82] Finkelman, *The Problem of Slavery, supra* note 56, at 135–37, 138–39, 141, 144–49; LINDA K. KERBER, FEDERALISTS IN DISSENT 25–66 (CorUP, Ithaca 1970).

[83] 1 ANNALS 766 (15 Aug.1789).

ABBREVIATED TITLE LIST

Primary Sources

Adams-Jefferson	The Adams-Jefferson Letters (Lester J. Cappon ed., University of North Carolina Press, Chapel Hill 1959) (2 vols.)
Adams Papers	Papers of John Adams (Robert J. Taylor ed., Belknap Press of Harvard University Press, Cambridge 1977–) (14 vols. to date)
Adams Works	The Works of John Adams, Second President of the United States: with a Life of the Author, Notes and Illustrations, by His Grandson Charles Francis Adams (Charles Francis Adams ed., Little, Brown, Boston 1850–56) (10 vols.)
Adams Writings	Writings of John Quincy Adams (Worthington C. Ford ed., Macmillan, New York 1913–17) (7 vols.)
American Archives (5th)	American Archives (5th Series) (Peter Force ed., M. St. Clair & Peter Force, Washington 1848–53) (3 vols.)
Ames Works	Works of Fisher Ames (Seth Ames ed., Little, Brown, Boston 1854) (2 vols.)
Arber	A Transcript of the Registers of the Company of Stationers of London: 1554–1640 (Edward Arber ed., repr. Peter Smith, New York 1950) (5 vols.)
Annals	Debates and Proceedings in the Congress of the United States . . . Annals of the Congress of the United States (Gales & Seaton, Washington 1834–56) (42 vols.)

Army Debates	Puritanism and Liberty, Being the Army Debates (1647–9) from the Clarke Manuscripts with Supplementary Documents (A.S.P. Woodhouse ed., 3d ed. J.M. Dent & Sons, London 1986)
ASP	American State Papers: Documents, Legislative and Executive, of the Congress of the United States (Class I. Foreign Relations) (Gales & Seaton, Washington 1832) (6 vols.)
Bacon	[Matthew Bacon], A New Abridgment of the Law (Catherine Lintot, London 1759) (5 vols.)
Baker	The Reports of Sir John Spelman (J.H. Baker ed., Selden Society, London 1977–78) [Selden Society vols. 93–94, cited as vols. 1–2]
B&M	Sir John Baker, Baker and Milsom Sources of English Legal History: Private Law to 1750 (2d ed. Oxford University Press, Oxford 2010)
Bill of Rights	The Bill of Rights: A Documentary History (Bernard Schwartz ed., Chelsea House, New York 1971) (2 vols.)
Blackstone's Commentaries	Sir William Blackstone, Commentaries on the Laws of England (Clarendon Press, Oxford 1765–69) (4 vols.)
Burgh	James Burgh, Political Disquisitions (Edward & Charles Dilly, London 1774–75) (3 vols.)
Calendar-Anne	Calendar of State Papers, Domestic Series, of the Reign of Anne (Robert P. Mahaffy et al. eds., His Majesty's Stationery Office, Woodbridge 1916-) (4 vols. thus far)
Calendar-William	Calendar of State Papers, Domestic Series, of the Reign of William and Mary (William J. Hardy et al. eds., His Majesty's Stationery Office, London 1895–1937) (11 vols.)
Carroll Papers	Dear Papa, Dear Charley: The Peregrinations of a Revolutionary Aristocrat, as Told by Charles Carroll (Ronald Hoffman et al. eds., University of North Carolina Press, Chapel Hill 2001) (3 vols.)

Cato's Letters	[John Trenchard & Thomas Gordon], Cato's Letters, or, Essays on Liberty, Civil and Religious, and Other Important Subjects (Ronald Hamowy ed., Liberty Fund, Indianapolis 1995)
Chase Charge Book	Samuel Chase Charge Book, ca.1802–1806 (Maryland Historical Society, Baltimore, MS 2565)
Chase Correspondence	Samuel Chase Correspondence (Maryland Historical Society, Baltimore, MS 1234)
Chase Trial	Report of the Trial of the Hon. Samuel Chase, One of the Associate Justices of the Supreme Court . . . Taken in Short Hand, by Charles Evans (Charles Evans transcriptionist, Samuel Butler & George Keatings, Baltimore 1805)
Chronological Tables	Edward C. Lathem, Chronological Tables of American Newspapers, 1690–1820 (American Antiquarian Society, Barre 1972)
Circular Letters	Circular Letters of Congressmen to Their Constituents, 1789–1829 (Noble E. Cunningham ed., University of North Carolina Press, Chapel Hill 1978) (3 vols.)
Colonial Laws-N.Y.	The Colonial Laws of New York from the Year 1664 to the Revolution (Charles Z. Lincoln et al. eds., J.B. Lyon, Albany 1894)
Colonial Records-N.C.	The Colonial Records of North Carolina (W.L. Saunders ed., P.M. Hale et al., Raleigh 1886–90) (10 vols.)
Colonial Virginia Register	Colonial Virginia Register (William G. Stanard & Mary N. Stanard eds., Munsell's Sons, Albany 1902)
Complete Anti-Federalist	The Complete Anti-Federalist (Herbert J. Storing ed., University of Chicago Press, Chicago 1981) (7 vols.)
Complete Bill of Rights-Sources	The Complete Bill of Rights: The Drafts, Debates, Sources, and Origins (Neil H. Cogan ed., Oxford University Press, New York 1997)
Comyns	Sir John Comyns, A Digest of the Laws of England (H. Woodfall, London 1762) (5 vols.)

Connecticut Records	The Public Records of the State of Connecticut (Leonard W. Labaree et al. eds., Case, Lockwood, Hartford 1894–2007) (19 vols.)
Constitutional History-N.Y.	Charles Z. Lincoln, Constitutional History of New York (Lawyers Co-Operative Pub. Co., Rochester 1906)
Cooper's Account	Thomas Cooper, An Account of the Trial of Thomas Cooper, of Northumberland, on a Charge of Libel against the President of the United States; Taken in Short Hand, with a Preface, Notes, and Appendix, by Thomas Cooper (John Bioren, Philadelphia 1800) [Cooper disclaimed compiling the pamphlet]
Creating Bill of Rights	Creating the Bill of Rights: The Documentary Record from the First Federal Congress (Helen E. Veit, Kenneth R. Bowling & Charlene B. Bickford eds., Johns Hopkins University Press, Baltimore 1991)
Criminal Case Files	Criminal Case Files of the U.S. Circuit Court for the Eastern District of Pennsylvania, 1791–1840 (National Archives, at Philadelphia, R.G.21.40.2, microfilm M986, rolls 1 and 2)
Cushing Notes	Notes of Cases Decided in the Superiour and Supreme Judicial Courts of Massachusetts from 1772 to 1789—taken by the Hon'ble William Cushing (John D. Cushing ed., Harvard Law School, Cambridge 1961) (HLS MS 1471)
Cushing Papers	Papers of William Cushing (Massachusetts Historical Society, Boston)
Debate	The Debate on the Constitution: Federalist and Antifederalist Speeches, Articles, and Letters During the Struggle over Ratification (Bernard Bailyn ed., Library of America, New York 1993) (2 vols.)
DHC	U.S. Department of State, Documentary History of the Constitution of the United States of America, 1786–1870 ([Andrew H. Allen ed.], Department of State, Washington 1894–1905) (5 vols.)

DHFFC	Documentary History of the First Federal Congress of the United States (Linda G. DePauw ed., Johns Hopkins University Press, Baltimore 1972–77) (vols. 1–3)
	Documentary History of the First Federal Congress of the United States (Charlene B. Bickford & Helen E. Veit eds., Johns Hopkins University Press, Baltimore 1986) (vols. 4–6)
	Documentary History of the First Federal Congress of the United States (Kenneth R. Bowling et al. eds., Johns Hopkins University Press, Baltimore 1987–88) (vols. 7–8)
	Documentary History of the First Federal Congress of the United States (Kenneth R. Bowling & Helen E. Veit eds., Johns Hopkins University Press, Baltimore 1988) (vol. 9)
	Documentary History of the First Federal Congress of the United States (Charlene B. Bickford, Kenneth R. Bowling & Helen E. Veit eds., Johns Hopkins University Press, Baltimore 1992–2004) (vols. 10–17)
DHRC	The Documentary History of the Ratification of the Constitution (Merrill Jensen et al. eds., State Historical Society of Wisconsin, Madison 1976-) (23 vols. to date)
DHSC	The Documentary History of the Supreme Court of the United States, 1789–1800: Volume 1 (Part 1 & Part 2) (Maeva Marcus & James R. Perry eds., Columbia University Press, New York 1985)
	The Documentary History of the Supreme Court of the United States, 1789–1800: Volumes 2–8 (Maeva Marcus ed., Columbia University Press, New York 1988, 1990, 1992, 1994, 1998, 2003, 2007)
Dickinson's Essay	[John Dickinson], An Essay on the Constitutional Power of Great-Britain over the Colonies in America; with the Resolves of the Committee for the Province of Pennsylvania (Bradford, Philadelphia 1774)

Doctrine of Libels	[James Erskine], The Doctrine of Libels and the Duty of Juries Fairly Stated (M. Cooper, London 1752)
Documentary History-S.C.	R.W. Gibbes, Documentary History of the American Revolution . . . in South Carolina (Banner Steam-Power Press, Columbia 1853)
Drayton's Memoirs	John Drayton, Memoirs of the American Revolution (A.E. Miller, Charleston 1821) (2 vols.)
EHD	English Historical Documents (David C. Douglas ed., Oxford University Press, New York 1953–69) (13 vols.)
Elliot's Debates	The Debates in the Several State Conventions on the Adoption of the Federal Constitution (Jonathan Elliot ed., Lippincott, Philadelphia 1836) (5 vols.)
Ellsworth Papers-NYPL	Oliver Ellsworth Papers (New York Public Library, New York, Bancroft Collection v.178)
Essays-Constitution	Essays on the Constitution of the United States, Published During Its Discussion by the People, 1787–1788 (Paul L. Ford ed., Historical Printing Club, Brooklyn 1892)
Executive Council-N.C.	Records of the Executive Council 1755–1775 (Robert J. Cain ed., North Carolina Division of Archives & History, Raleigh 1984–94) [Colonial Records of North Carolina (2d series) vol. 9]
Farrand's Records	The Records of the Federal Convention of 1787 (Max Farrand ed., rev. ed. Yale University Press, New Haven 1940) (4 vols. including supplement)
	Supplement to Max Farrand's The Records of the Federal Convention of 1787 (James H. Hutson ed., Yale University Press, New Haven 1987)
F.Cas.	The Federal Cases: Comprising Cases Argued and Determined in the Circuit and District Courts of the United States from the Earliest Times to the Beginning of the Federal Reporter (West Pub. Co., St. Paul 1894–97)

Federal-State Constitutions	Federal and State Constitutions, Colonial Charters, and Other Organic Laws (Francis N. Thorpe ed., Government Printing Office, Washington 1909) (7 vols.)
Federal-State Constitutions-Poore	Federal and State Constitutions, Colonial Charters, and Other Organic Laws (Ben P. Poore ed., Government Printing Office, Washington 1878) (2 vols.)
Federalist	The Federalist (Jacob E. Cooke ed., Wesleyan University Press, Middletown 1961)
Federalist Correspondence	Ulrich B. Phillips ed., *Documents* [Part 2 of *South Carolina Federalist Correspondence, 1789–1797)*], 14 American Historical Review 764, 776 (1909)
Franklin Papers	Papers of Benjamin Franklin (Leonard W. Labaree et al. eds., Yale University Press, New Haven 1959–) (39 vols. to date)
Franklin Writings	Writings of Benjamin Franklin (Albert H. Smyth ed., Macmillan, New York 1905–07) (10 vols.)
Gadsden Writings	Writings of Christopher Gadsden, 1746–1805 (Richard Walsh ed., University of South Carolina Press, Columbia 1966)
Garth Correspondence	Joseph W. Barnwell & Theodore D. Gervey eds., *Garth Correspondence*, 28 S. C. Historical & Genealogical Mag. 79, 226 (1927); 29 *id.* 41, 115, 212, 295 (1928); 30 *id.* 27, 105, 168, 215 (1929); 31 *id.* 46, 124, 228, 283 (1930); 33 *id.* 117, 228, 262 (1932)
Greene Papers	Papers of General Nathanael Greene (Robert K. Showman ed., University of North Carolina Press, Chapel Hill 1976-) (13 vols.)
Grotius	Hugo Grotius, The Law of War and Peace (new ed. Johan Bleu, Amsterdam 1646)
Hale	Sir Matthew Hale, Historia Placitorum Coronae. The History of the Pleas of the Crown (E. & R. Nutt, London 1736) (2 vols.)
Hamilton Papers	The Papers of Alexander Hamilton (Harold C. Syrett ed., Columbia University Press, New York 1961–87) (27 vols.)

Hamilton Works	The Works of Alexander Hamilton (Henry Cabot Lodge ed., G.P. Putnam's Sons, New York 1885)
Hawarde	Les Reportes del Cases in Camera Stellata, 1593 to 1609: from the Original Manuscripts of John Hawarde (William P. Baildon ed., Alfred Morrison, London 1894)
Hawkins	William Hawkins, A Treatise of the Pleas of the Crown (Eliz. Nutt, London 1716–21) (2 vols.)
Helmholz-Cases	Select Cases on Defamation to 1600 (R.H. Helmholz ed., Selden Society, London 1985) [Selden Society vol. 101]
Hening's Statutes-Va.	Statutes at Large . . . of Virginia (William W. Hening ed., Barlow, New York 1823)
Higginson Letters	J. Franklin Jameson ed., *Letters of Stephen Higginson, 1783–1804,* in 1896 Annual Report of the American Historical Association (pt. 1) 704 (Government Printing Office, Washington 1897)
Hudson	William Hudson, *A Treatise on the Court of Star Chamber,* in 2 Collectanea Juridica 1–240 (Francis Hargrave ed., E. & R. Brooke, London 1791–92) (2 vols.)
Iredell Correspondence	Life and Correspondence of James Iredell (Griffith J. McRee ed., Appleton, New York 1857–58) (2 vols.)
Iredell-Johnson Collection	Charles E. Johnson Collection (North Carolina State Archives, Raleigh, Manuscript Dept., Ms. PC.67)
Iredell Papers	The Papers of James Iredell, Vols. 1–2 (Don Higginbotham ed., North Carolina Division of Archives and History, Raleigh 1976) The Papers of James Iredell, Vol. 3 (Donna Kelly & Lang Baradell eds., North Carolina Office of Archives and History, Raleigh 2003)
Iredell Papers-UNC	James Iredell Papers, 1771–1799 (University Library of the University of North Carolina, Chapel Hill, Manuscripts Dept., Collection No.365) (14 vols.)

Iredell Papers-Duke	Papers of James Iredell, Sr., and James Iredell, Jr., 1724–1890 (Duke University, Durham, Perkins Library, Special Collections, Ms. 2nd 63:A (Boxes 1–6) and M:M:5355–58)
Izard Correspondence	Correspondence of Mr. Ralph Izard of South Carolina, from the Year 1774 to 1804 (Anne I. Deas ed., Charles S. Francis, New York 1844)
Jacobin	Charles Warren, Jacobin and Junto: or, Early American Politics as Viewed in the Diary of Dr. Nathaniel Ames, 1758–1822 (Harvard University Press, Cambridge 1931)
Jay Correspondence	The Correspondence and Public Papers of John Jay (Henry P. Johnson ed., Putnam's Sons, New York 1890–93) (4 vols.)
Jay Papers	Papers of John Jay <http://www.columbia.edu/cu/lweb/ digital/jay/> (accessed 7 July 2011), Columbia University Libraries [13,000 documents])
Jay-Peace	John Jay, The Winning of the Peace: Unpublished Papers, 1780–1784 (Richard B. Morris ed., Harper & Row, New York 1980)
Jay-Revolutionary	John Jay, The Making of a Revolutionary: Unpublished Papers, 1745–80 (Richard B. Morris ed., Harper & Row, New York 1975)
JCC	Journals of the Continental Congress, 1774–1789 (Worthington C. Ford et al. eds., Government Printing Office, Washington 1904–37) (34 vols.)
Jefferson-Madison Correspondence	The Republic of Letters: The Correspondence between Thomas Jefferson and James Madison 1776–1826 (James Morton Smith ed., Norton, New York 1995) (3 vols.)
Jefferson Papers	The Papers of Thomas Jefferson (Julian P. Boyd et al. eds., Princeton University Press, Princeton 1950–) (41 vols. to date)
Jefferson Papers-Retirement	The Papers of Thomas Jefferson: Retirement Series (J. Jefferson Looney ed., Princeton University Press, Princeton 2004–) (11 vols. to date)

Jefferson Writings	The Writings of Thomas Jefferson (Paul L. Ford ed., Putnam, New York 1892–99) (10 vols.)
JHC	Journals of the House of Commons (n.p., London 1803–52) (101 vols.)
JHL	Journals of the House of Lords (n.p., London 1771–1800) (42 vols.)
Johnson Correspondence	Thomas Johnson Correspondence <http://msa.maryland.gov/megafile/msa/speccol/sc3500/sc3520/ 000700/000743/html/ms1714.html> (Maryland State Archives, Annapolis, transcriptions from Ms.1714) (accessed 11 Aug. 2015)
Johnson Letters	Thomas Johnson Letters <http://collections.digitalmaryland. org/cdm/search/searchterm/%22Thomas%20Johnson%22/order/nosort> (Digital Maryland collection) (accessed 11 Aug.2015)
Journal-N.Y.	Journal of the Assembly of the State of New-York at Their Twenty-Second Session . . . Second Day of January, 1799 (Loring Andrews, Albany 1799)
Journal of Convention-Mass.	Journal of the Convention for Framing a Constitution of Government for the State of Massachusetts Bay (Dutton & Wentworth, Boston 1832)
Journal of House	Journal of the House of Representatives of the United States (Gales & Seaton, Washington 1826)
Journal of Executive Proc.-Senate	Journal of the Executive Proceedings of the Senate of the United States of America (Duff Green, Washington 1828)
Journal of Senate	Journal of the Senate (Gales & Seaton, Washington 1820–21)
Journals of Assembly-S.C.	Journals of the Commons House of Assembly, 1760–1775 (South Carolina Department of Archives and History, Columbia [manuscripts])
Journals of General Assembly-S.C.	Journals of the General Assembly and House of Representatives 1776–1780 (William E. Hemphill, Wylma A. Wates & Nicholas Olsberg eds., University of South Carolina Press, Columbia 1970)

JOURNALS OF HOUSE-MASS.	JOURNALS OF THE HOUSE OF REPRESENTATIVES OF MASSACHUSETTS [1771–1778] (Massachusetts Historical Society, Boston 1979–88) (vols. 48–53)
JOURNALS OF HOUSE-S.C.	JOURNALS OF THE HOUSE OF REPRESENTATIVES 1783–1784 (Theodora J. Thompson ed., University of South Carolina Press, Columbia 1977)
	JOURNALS OF THE HOUSE OF REPRESENTATIVES 1785–1786 (Lark E. Adams ed., University of South Carolina Press, Columbia 1979)
	JOURNALS OF THE HOUSE OF REPRESENTATIVES 1787–1788 (Michael E. Stevens ed., University of South Carolina Press, Columbia 1981)
	JOURNALS OF THE HOUSE OF REPRESENTATIVES 1789–1790 (Michael E. Stevens ed., University of South Carolina Press, Columbia 1984)
	JOURNALS OF THE HOUSE OF REPRESENTATIVES 1791 (Michael E. Stevens ed., University of South Carolina Press, Columbia 1985)
	Journals of the House, 1790–1800 (South Carolina Department of Archives and History, Columbia [manuscripts])
JOURNALS OF HOUSE-PA.	JOURNALS OF THE HOUSE OF REPRESENTATIVES OF THE COMMONWEALTH OF PENNSYLVANIA. BEGINNING THE TWENTY-EIGHTH DAY OF NOVEMBER, 1776, AND ENDING THE SECOND DAY OF OCTOBER, 1781. WITH THE PROCEEDINGS OF THE SEVERAL COMMITTEES AND CONVENTIONS (John Dunlap, Philadelphia 1782)
JOURNALS OF PROVINCIAL CONGRESS-N.Y.	JOURNALS OF THE PROVINCIAL CONGRESS, PROVINCIAL CONVENTION, COMMITTEE OF SAFETY AND COUNCIL OF SAFETY OF THE STATE OF NEW-YORK, 1775–1777 (T. Weed, Albany 1842) (2 vols.)

Journals of Provincial Congress-S.C.	Extracts from the Journals of the Provincial Congress of South Carolina, 1775–1776 (William E. Hemphill ed., South Carolina Archives Department, Columbia 1960)
Journals of Senate-S.C.	Journals of the Senate, 1790–1800 (South Carolina Department of Archives and History, Columbia [manuscripts])
Junius	The Letters of Junius (John Cannon ed., Clarendon Press, Oxford 1978)
Kemp	Censorship and the Press, 1580–1720 (Geoff Kemp and Jason McElligott eds., Pickering & Chatto, London 2009)
King Correspondence	The Life and Correspondence of Rufus King (Charles R. King ed., Putnam's Sons, New York 1894–1900) (6 vols.)
Laurens Papers	Papers of Henry Laurens (Philip M. Hamer et al., University of South Carolina Press, Columbia 1968-) (11 vols. to date)
Lee's Answer	Arthur Lee, Answer to Considerations on Certain Political Transactions of the Province of South Carolina (J. Almon, London 1774), reprinted in The Nature of Colony Constitutions: Two Pamphlets on the Wilkes Fund Controversy in South Carolina 127 (Jack P. Greene ed., University of South Carolina Press, Columbia 1970)
Leigh's Considerations	Sir Egerton Leigh, Considerations on Certain Political Transactions of the Province of South Carolina (Thomas Cadell, London 1774), reprinted in The Nature of Colony Constitutions: Two Pamphlets on the Wilkes Fund Controversy in South Carolina 61 (Jack P. Greene ed., University of South Carolina Press, Columbia 1970)
Letter Concerning Libels	Father of Candor, A Letter Concerning Libels, Warrants, the Seizure of Papers, and Sureties (2d ed. J. Almon, London 1764)
Letters of Delegates	Letters of Delegates to Congress, 1774–1789 (Paul H. Smith ed., Library of Congress, Washington 1976–2000) (25 vols.)

Letters of Members	Letters of Members of the Continental Congress (Edmund C. Burnett ed., Carnegie Institution, Washington 1921) (10 vols.)
Livingston Papers	The Papers of William Livingston (Carl E. Prince ed., New Jersey Historical Commission, Trenton 1979–88) (5 vols.)
Locke	John Locke, Two Treatises of Government (Black Swan, London 1698)
Locke's Works	The Works of John Locke (9th ed. T. Longman, London 1794, repr. Routledge/ Thoemmes Press, London 1997) (9 vols.)
Madison Papers	The Papers of James Madison (William T. Hutchinson et al. eds., repr. University Press of Virginia, Charlottesville 1962-) (17 vols. to date)
Madison Papers-Presidential	The Papers of James Madison-Presidential Series (Robert A. Rutland et al. eds., University Press of Virginia, Charlottesville 1984-) (7 vols. to date)
Madison Papers-Secretary	The Papers of James Madison: Secretary of State Series (Robert Brugger et al. eds., University Press of Virginia, Charlottesville 1987-) (10 vols. to date)
Madison Writings	The Writings of James Madison (Gaillard Hunt ed., Putnam's Sons, New York 1900–1910) (9 vols.)
Mansfield Manuscripts	The Mansfield Manuscripts and the Growth of English Law in the Eighteenth Century (James Oldham ed., University of North Carolina Press, Chapel Hill 1992) (2 vols.)
Marshall Papers	The Papers of John Marshall (Herbert A. Johnson et al. eds., University of North Carolina Press, Chapel Hill 1974–2006) (12 vols.)
Maryland Archives	Archives of Maryland (W.H. Browne et al., Maryland Historical Society, Baltimore 1883–1972, 1990–) (72 vols.)
Mason Papers	The Papers of George Mason 1725–1792 (Robert A. Rutland ed., University of North Carolina Press, Chapel Hill 1970) (3 vols.)
McHenry Correspondence	The Life and Correspondence of James McHenry (Bernard C. Steiner ed., Burrows Brothers, Cleveland 1907)

Messages-N.Y.	Messages from the Governors (Charles Z. Lincoln ed., J.B. Lyon, Albany 1909)
Minutes	Original Minutes of the Circuit Court of the United States of America for the Middle Circuit, October Session 1790 to April 1799 (National Archives at Philadelphia, R.G.21.40.2, microfilm M932, roll 1).
Minutes-Pa.	Minutes of the Grand Committee of the Whole Convention of the Commonwealth of Pennsylvania, Which Commenced at Philadelphia on Tuesday, the Twenty-Fourth Day of November, in the Year of Our Lord One Thousand Seven Hundred and Eighty-Nine (Zachariah Poulson, Philadelphia 1790)
Minutes-Pa. (2nd)	Minutes of the Second Session of the Convention of the Commonwealth of Pennsylvania, Which Commenced at Philadelphia on Monday the Ninth Day of August, in the Year of Our Lord One Thousand Seven Hundred and Ninety (Zachariah Poulson, Philadelphia 1790)
Monroe Papers	The Papers of James Monroe (Daniel Preston ed., Greenwood Press, London 2003–06) (2 vols. to date)
Monroe Writings	The Writings of James Monroe (Stanislaus M. Hamilton ed., Putnam's, New York 1898–1903) (7 vols.)
Murray Letters	Worthington C. Ford ed., *Letters of William Vans Murray to John Quincy Adams, 1797–1803*, 1912 Annual Report of American Historical Association 341 (American Historical Association, Washington 1914)
Pamphlets-Constitution	Pamphlets on the Constitution of the United States, Published During Its Discussion by the People, 1787–1788 (Paul L. Ford ed., n.p., Brooklyn 1888)
Pamphlets-Revolution	Pamphlets of the American Revolution, 1750–1776 (Bernard Bailyn ed., Belknap Press, Cambridge 1965)

PARLIAMENTARY HISTORY	WILLIAM COBBETT ET AL., THE PARLIAMENTARY HISTORY OF ENGLAND, FROM THE EARLIEST PERIOD TO THE YEAR 1803 (R. Bagshaw and other publishers, London 1806–20) (36 vols.)
PATERSON CORRESPONDENCE	William Paterson, Correspondence and Other Papers, 1766–1804 (Rutgers University, New Brunswick, Special Collections, Ac.888)
PATERSON DRAFT OPINIONS	William Paterson, Draft Opinions, in William Paterson Papers 531, 545 (New York Public Library, New York, Bancroft Collection v.300), reprinted in William Hull Hoffer, *William Paterson and the National Jurisprudence: Two Draft Opinions on the Sedition Law of 1789 and the Federal Common Law*, 1997 JOURNAL OF SUPREME COURT HISTORY 36, 45, 47
PATERSON THIRD OPINION	William R. Casto, *The Federal Courts' Protective Jurisdiction Over Torts Committed in Violation of the Law of Nations*, 18 CONNECTICUT LAW REVIEW 467, 526 (1986)
PATERSON ESSAYS	William Paterson, Essays on Politics and Government (1789–93) (Rutgers University, New Brunswick, Special Collections, in Writings and Correspondence, Ac.0.963)
PATERSON PAPERS-LC	William Paterson Papers (Library of Congress, Washington, Misc. folder)
PATERSON LEGAL PAPERS-LC	William Paterson Papers (Library of Congress, Washington, Legal Papers folder 1772–1786)
PATERSON PAPERS-NYPL	William Paterson Papers (New York Public Library, New York, Bancroft Collection v.300)
PENDLETON PAPERS	THE LETTERS AND PAPERS OF EDMUND PENDLETON 1734–1803 (David J. Mays ed., University Press of Virginia, Charlottesville 1967) (2 vols.)
PICKERING PAPERS	Timothy Pickering Papers (Massachusetts Historical Society, Boston, 69 reels)
PRIVY COUNCIL-COLONIAL	ACTS OF THE PRIVY COUNCIL OF ENGLAND (COLONIAL SERIES) (W.L. Grant & James Munro eds., His Majesty's Stationery Office, London 1908–12) (6 vols.)

Proceedings of Convention-Va.	The Proceedings of the Convention of Delegates Held at the Capitol, in the City of Williamsburg, in the Colony of Virginia, on Monday the 6th of May, 1776 (Alexander Purdie, Williamsburg 1776)
Public Records-Conn.	The Public Records of the State of Connecticut, from October 1776 (Charles J. Hoadley ed., Case, Lockwood & Brainard Co., Hartford 1894–95) (2 vols.)
Quincy	Reports of Cases Argued and Adjudged in the Superior Court of Judicature of the Province of Massachusetts (Josiah Quincy ed., Little, Brown, Boston 1865)
Royal Instructions	Royal Instructions to British Colonial Governors, 1670–1776 (Leonard W. Labaree ed., Appleton-Century, New York 1935) (2 vols.)
Rushworth	John Rushworth, *Appendix. Star-Chamber Reports*, in 3 Historical Collections. The Second Volume of the Second Part 3 (D. Browne, London 1721) [appendix pages numbered separately]
Rutledge Letters	Joseph W. Barnwell ed., *Letters of John Rutledge*, 17 South Carolina. Historical & Genealogical Magazine 131 (1916); 18 *id.* 42, 59, 131, 155 (1917)
Rutledge Jr. Papers-Duke	John Rutledge [Jr.] Papers, 1760–1862 (Duke University, Durham, Perkins Library, Special Collections, Ms. 2nd 82:C and Oversize Box 20)
Rutledge Jr. Papers-UNC	John Rutledge [Jr.] Papers (University of North Carolina, Chapel Hill, Southern Historical Collection, Collection No.948)
Select Statutes	Select Statutes and Other Constitutional Documents Illustrative of the Reigns of Elizabeth and James I (G.W. Prothero ed., 2d ed. Clarendon Press, Oxford 1898)
Select Statutes-Cases	Select Statutes, Cases and Documents To Illustrate English Constitutional History, 1660–1832 (C. Grant Robertson ed., Methuen, London 1904)

SHEPPARD	WILLIAM SHEPPARD, ACTION UPON THE CASE FOR SLANDER (Charles Adams, London 1662)
STAMP ACT CONGRESS JOURNAL	C.A. WESLAGER, THE STAMP ACT CONGRESS; WITH AN EXACT COPY OF THE COMPLETE JOURNAL (University of Delaware Press, Newark 1976)
STATE RECORDS-N.C.	THE STATE RECORDS OF NORTH CAROLINA (Walter Clark ed., M.I. & J.C. Stewart Printers, Winston 1895–1906) (15 vols.) [numbered vols. 11–25]
STATE TRIALS	A COMPLETE COLLECTION OF STATE TRIALS AND PROCEEDINGS FOR HIGH TREASON AND OTHER CRIMES AND MISDEMEANORS FROM THE EARLIEST PERIOD TO THE YEAR 1783 (Thomas B. Howell ed., T.C. Hansard, London 1816) (21 vols.)
STAT.	PUBLIC STATUTES AT LARGE OF THE UNITED STATES OF AMERICA (Richard Peters et al. eds., Charles C. Little, Boston 1845–)
STATUTES	THE STATUTES OF THE REALM (Alexander Luders et al. eds., George Eyre & Andrew Strahan, London 1810–28) (12 vols.) [used through reign of Queen Anne]
	THE STATUTES AT LARGE (Danby Pickering ed., J. Bentham, Cambridge 1762–1807) (46 vols.) [used after reign of Queen Anne to 1806]
STEELE PAPERS	THE PAPERS OF JOHN STEELE (H.M. Wagstaff ed., Edwards & Broughton Printing, Raleigh 1924) (2 vols.)
STUART PROCLAMATIONS	STUART ROYAL PROCLAMATIONS (James F. Larkin ed., Clarendon Press, Oxford 1973–83) (2 vols.)
TREATIES	TREATIES AND OTHER INTERNATIONAL ACTS OF THE UNITED STATES OF AMERICA (Hunter Miller ed., Government Printing Office, Washington 1931)
TRUMBULL PAPERS	*The Trumbull Papers*, in TRANSACTIONS OF THE MASSACHUSETTS HISTORICAL SOCIETY (SERIES 5 & 7) (Massachusetts Historical Society, Boston 1885–1902) (4 vols.)

TRUTH	[BENJAMIN F. BACHE], TRUTH WILL OUT! THE FOUL CHARGES OF THE TORIES AGAINST THE EDITOR OF THE AURORA REPELLED BY POSITIVE PROOF AND PLAIN TRUTH AND HIS BASE CALUMNIATORS PUT TO SHAME ([Bache, Philadelphia 1798])
TUDOR-STUART PROCLAMATIONS	A BIBLIOGRAPHY OF ROYAL PROCLAMATIONS OF THE TUDOR AND STUART SOVEREIGNS (Robert Steele ed., Clarendon Press, Oxford 1910) (2 vols.)
WASHINGTON DIARIES	THE DIARIES OF GEORGE WASHINGTON (Donald Jackson et al. eds., University Press of Virginia, Charlottesville 1976–79) (6 vols.)
WASHINGTON PAPERS-COLONIAL	THE PAPERS OF GEORGE WASHINGTON: COLONIAL SERIES (W.W. Abbot ed., University Press of Virginia, Charlottesville 1983–85) (10 vols.)
WASHINGTON PAPERS-REVOLUTION	THE PAPERS OF GEORGE WASHINGTON: REVOLUTIONARY WAR SERIES (W.W. Abbot et al. eds., University Press of Virginia, Charlottesville 1985–2008) (18 vols.)
WASHINGTON PAPERS-CONFEDERATION	THE PAPERS OF GEORGE WASHINGTON: CONFEDERATION SERIES (W. W. Abbot & Dorothy Twohig eds., University Press of Virginia, Charlottesville 1992–97) (6 vols.)
WASHINGTON PAPERS-PRESIDENTIAL	THE PAPERS OF GEORGE WASHINGTON: PRESIDENTIAL SERIES (W.W. Abbot et al. eds., University Press of Virginia, Charlottesville 1987–) (14 vols. to date)
WASHINGTON PAPERS-RETIREMENT	THE PAPERS OF GEORGE WASHINGTON: RETIREMENT SERIES (Dorothy Twohig ed., University Press of Virginia, Charlottesville 1998–)
WASHINGTON PAPERS-LOC	George Washington Papers at the Library of Congress, 1741–99 <http://memory.loc.gov/ammem/gwhtml/gwhome.html> (Library of Congress, Washington, Manuscript Div.) (accessed 15 Oct. 2009)
WASHINGTON WRITINGS	WRITINGS OF GEORGE WASHINGTON (John C. Fitzpatrick ed., Government Printing Office, Washington 1931–44) (39 vols.)

WHARTON'S STATE TRIALS	STATE TRIALS OF THE UNITED STATES DURING THE ADMINISTRATIONS OF WASHINGTON AND ADAMS (Francis Wharton ed., Carey & Hart, Philadelphia 1849)
WILSON WORKS	COLLECTED WORKS OF JAMES WILSON (Kermit L. Hall & Mark D. Hall eds., Liberty Fund, Indianapolis 2006) (2 vols.)
WILSON WRITINGS	Life and Writings of James Wilson (Burton A. Konkle ed., Swarthmore College, Friends Historical Library) (6 vols., unpublished ms.)
WOLCOTT PAPERS	MEMOIRS OF THE ADMINISTRATIONS OF WASHINGTON AND JOHN ADAMS EDITED FROM THE PAPERS OF OLIVER WOLCOTT, SECRETARY OF THE TREASURY (George Gibbs ed., William Van Norden, New York 1846) (2 vols.)

Secondary Sources

ADAMS FEDERALISTS	MANNING J. DAUER, THE ADAMS FEDERALISTS (Johns Hopkins University Press, Baltimore 1953)
AMERICAN POLITICS	JAMES R. SHARP, AMERICAN POLITICS IN THE EARLY REPUBLIC (Yale University Press, New Haven 1993)
ANB	JOHN A. GARRATY ET AL. EDS., AMERICAN NATIONAL BIOGRAPHY (Oxford University Press, New York 1999) (24 vols.)
ANDERSON	David A. Anderson, *The Origins of the Press Clause*, 30 UCLA LAW REVIEW 455 (1983)
ASHCRAFT	RICHARD ASHCRAFT, REVOLUTIONARY POLITICS & LOCKE'S TWO TREATISES OF GOVERNMENT (Princeton University Press, Princeton 1986)
AYLMER	G.E. AYLMER, REBELLION OR REVOLUTION? ENGLAND 1640–1660 (Oxford University Press, Oxford 1986)
BAKER-INTRODUCTION	JOHN H. BAKER, AN INTRODUCTION TO ENGLISH LEGAL HISTORY (4th ed., Oxford University Press, Oxford 2007)

Brant	Irving Brant, *Seditious Libel: Myth and Reality*, 39 New York University Law Review 1 (1964)
Brewer-Party	John Brewer, Party Ideology and Popular Politics at the Accession of George III (Cambridge University Press, Cambridge 1976)
Brigham	Clarence S. Brigham, History and Bibliography of American Newspapers, 1690–1820 (Am. Antiquarian Soc., Worcester 1947)
Brooks	Christopher W. Brooks, Law, Politics and Society in Early Modern England (Cambridge University Press, Cambridge 2008)
Bushrod Washington	David L. Annis, Mr. Bushrod Washington, Supreme Court Justice on the Marshall Court (1974) (unpublished PhD dissertation, Notre Dame University)
CHB	The Cambridge History of the Book in Britain (D.F. McKenzie et al. eds., Cambridge University Press, Cambridge 1999–) (6 vols. to date)
Chesapeake Politics	Norman K. Risjord, Chesapeake Politics *1781–1800* (Columbia University Press, New York 1978)
Clark	J. C. D. Clark, The Language of Liberty, 1660–1832: Political Discourse and Social Dynamics in the Anglo-American World (Cambridge University Press, Cambridge 1994)
Clegg	Cyndia S. Clegg, Press Censorship in Jacobean England (Cambridge University Press, Cambridge 2001)
Clegg-Caroline	Cyndia S. Clegg, Press Censorship in Caroline England (Cambridge University Press, Cambridge 2008)
Colclough	David Colclough, Freedom of Speech in Early Stuart England (Cambridge University Press, Cambridge 2005)
Contemporary Opinion	Frank M. Anderson, *Contemporary Opinion of the Virginia and Kentucky Resolutions*, 5 American Historical Review 45, 225 (1899)

CREATION	GORDON S. WOOD, THE CREATION OF THE AMERICAN REPUBLIC, 1776–1787 (University of North Carolina Press, Chapel Hill 1969)
CRESSY	DAVID CRESSY, DANGEROUS TALK: SCANDALOUS, SEDITIOUS, AND TREASONABLE SPEECH IN PRE-MODERN ENGLAND 16 (Oxford University Press, Oxford 2010)
CRISIS	JOHN C. MILLER, CRISIS IN FREEDOM: THE ALIEN AND SEDITION ACTS (Little, Brown, Boston 1952)
DAB	DICTIONARY OF AMERICAN BIOGRAPHY (Dumas Malone et al. eds., Charles Scribner's Sons, New York 1930–) (20 vols.)
DAVIDSON	PHILIP DAVIDSON, PROPAGANDA AND THE AMERICAN REVOLUTION 1763–1783 (UNCP, Chapel Hill 1941)
DICKINSON	H.T. DICKINSON, LIBERTY AND PROPERTY: POLITICAL IDEOLOGY IN EIGHTEENTH-CENTURY BRITAIN (Weidenfeld & Nicholson, London 1977, repr. 1979)
DICKINSON-POLITICS	H.T. DICKINSON, THE POLITICS OF THE PEOPLE IN EIGHTEENTH-CENTURY BRITAIN (St. Martin's Press, New York 1994)
ELLSWORTH	WILLIAM R. CASTO, OLIVER ELLSWORTH AND THE CREATION OF THE FEDERAL REPUBLIC (Second Circuit Committee on History, New York 1997)
EMPIRE	GORDON S. WOOD, EMPIRE OF LIBERTY: A HISTORY OF THE EARLY REPUBLIC, 1789–1815 (Oxford University Press, New York 2009) (Oxford History of the United States)
ENGLISH SOCIETY	J.C.D. CLARK, ENGLISH SOCIETY 1688–1832: IDEOLOGY, SOCIAL STRUCTURE AND POLITICAL PRACTICE DURING THE ANCIEN REGIME (Cambridge University Press, Cambridge 1985)
FEDERALISM	STANLEY ELKINS & ERIC MCKITRICK, THE AGE OF FEDERALISM (Oxford University Press, New York 1993)
FIFOOT	C.H.S. FIFOOT, HISTORY AND SOURCES OF THE COMMON LAW: TORT AND CONTRACT (Stevens, London 1949)

Fischer	David Hackett Fischer, The Revolution of American Conservatism: The Federalist Party in the Era of Jeffersonian Democracy (Harper & Row, New York 1965)
Founding Family	Frances L. Williams, A Founding Family: The Pinckneys of South Carolina (Harcourt Brace, New York 1978)
Freedom's Fetters	James M. Smith, Freedom's Fetters: The Alien and Sedition Laws and American Civil Liberties (Cornell University Press, Ithaca 1956)
Fries's Rebellion	Paul D. Newman, Fries's Rebellion: The Enduring Struggle for the American Revolution (University of Pennsylvania Press, Philadelphia 2004)
Glorious Cause	Robert Middlekauff, The Glorious Cause: The American Revolution, 1763–1789 (rev. ed. Oxford University Press, New York 2007) (Oxford History of the United States)
Great Rights	Bernard Schwartz, The Great Rights of Mankind: A History of the American Bill of Rights (Oxford University Press, New York 1977)
Greaves	Richard L. Greaves, Deliver Us From Evil: The Radical Underground in Britain, 1660–1663 (Oxford University Press, Oxford 1986)
Green	Thomas A. Green, *The Jury, Seditious Libel, and the Criminal Law,* in R.H. Helmholz & Thomas A. Green, Juries, Libel and Justice 37 (Clark Memorial Library, Los Angeles 1984)
Haller	William Haller, The Rise of Puritanism . . ., 1570–1643 (Harper, New York 1957)
Hamburger	Philip Hamburger, *The Development of the Law of Seditious Libel and the Control of the Press,* 37 Stanford Law Review 661 (1985)
Harling	Philip Harling, *The Law of Libel and the Limits of Repression, 1790–1832,* 44 Historical Journal 107 (2001)

HARRIS-NEWSPAPERS	MICHAEL HARRIS, LONDON NEWSPAPERS IN THE AGE OF WALPOLE: A STUDY OF THE ORIGINS OF THE MODERN ENGLISH PRESS (Fairleigh Dickinson University Press, Rutherford 1987)
HELMHOLZ-CASES	SELECT CASES ON DEFAMATION TO 1600 (R.H. Helmholz ed., Selden Society, London 1985) [Selden Society vol.101]
HELMHOLZ	R.H. HELMHOLZ, ROMAN CANON LAW IN REFORMATION ENGLAND (Cambridge University Press, Cambridge 1990)
HENDERSON	Dwight F. Henderson, *Treason, Sedition, and Fries' Rebellion*, 14 AMERICAN JOURNAL OF LEGAL HISTORY 308 (1970)
HISTORY OF SUPREME COURT	JULIUS GOEBEL, HISTORY OF THE SUPREME COURT OF THE UNITED STATES, VOL.1—ANTECEDENTS AND BEGINNINGS TO 1801 (Macmillan, New York 1971) GEORGE L. HASKINS & HERBERT A. JOHNSON, HISTORY OF THE SUPREME COURT OF THE UNITED STATES, VOL.2—FOUNDATIONS OF POWER: JOHN MARSHALL, 1801–1815 (Macmillan, New York 1981)
IBBETSON	D.J. IBBETSON, A HISTORICAL INTRODUCTION TO THE LAW OF OBLIGATIONS (Oxford University Press, Oxford 1999)
IDEOLOGICAL ORIGINS	BERNARD BAILYN, IDEOLOGICAL ORIGINS OF THE AMERICAN REVOLUTION (enl. ed. Harvard University Press, Cambridge 1992)
JAY	Stewart Jay, *Origins of Federal Common Law: Part One*, 133 UNIVERSITY OF PENNSYLVANIA LAW REVIEW 1003 (1985); Stewart Jay, *Origins of Federal Common Law: Part Two*, 133 *id.* 1231 (1985)
JEFFERSON	DUMAS MALONE, JEFFERSON AND HIS TIME (Little Brown, Boston 1948–81) (6 vols.)
JOHN JAY	FRANK MONAGHAN, JOHN JAY: DEFENDER OF LIBERTY (Bobbs-Merrill, New York 1935)
JOHNSON	EDWARD S. DELAPLAINE, THE LIFE OF THOMAS JOHNSON: MEMBER OF THE CONTINENTAL CONGRESS, FIRST GOVERNOR OF THE STATE OF MARYLAND, AND ASSOCIATE JUSTICE OF THE UNITED STATES SUPREME COURT (Hitchcock, New York 1927)

Justices	The Justices of the United States Supreme Court 1789–1969: Their Lives and Major Opinions (Leon Friedman & Fred L. Israel eds., Chelsea House, New York 1969)
Kenyon	J. P. Kenyon, Revolution Principles: The Politics of Party, 1689–1720 (Cambridge University Press, Cambridge 1977)
Kurland	Philip D. Kurland, *The Original Understanding of the Freedom of the Press Provision of the First Amendment*, 55 Mississippi Law Journal 225 (1985)
Labunski	Richard Labunski, James Madison and the Struggle for the Bill of Rights (Oxford University Press, New York 2006)
Lambert	Sheila Lambert, *State Control of the Press in Theory and Practice*, in Censorship and the Control of Print in England and France, 1600–1910, at 1 (Robin Myers & Michael Harris eds., St Paul's Bibliographies, Winchester 1992)
Lamp	H. Trevor Colbourn, The Lamp of Experience: Whig History and the Intellectual Origins of the American Revolution (University of North Carolina Press, Chapel Hill 1965)
Levy	Leonard W. Levy, Emergence of a Free Press (Oxford University Press, New York 1985)
Levy-Liberty	Leonard W. Levy, *Liberty and the First Amendment: 1790–1800*, 68 American Historical Review 22 (1962)
Livingston	George Dangerfield, Chancellor Robert R. Livingston of New York, 1746–1813 (Harcourt, Brace, New York 1960)
Maryland	L. Marx Renzulli, Maryland: The Federalist Years (Fairleigh Dickinson University Press, Rutherford 1973)
Milsom	S. F. C. Milsom , Historical Foundations of the Common Law (2d ed. Butterworths, London 1981)

MISUNDERSTANDING	STEPHEN B. PRESSER, THE ORIGINAL MISUNDERSTANDING: THE ENGLISH, THE AMERICANS AND THE DIALECTIC OF FEDERALIST JURISPRUDENCE (Carolina Academic Press, Durham 1991)
NEW JERSEY	CARL E. PRINCE, NEW JERSEY'S JEFFERSONIAN REPUBLICANS: THE GENESIS OF AN EARLY PARTY MACHINE, 1789–1817 (University of North Carolina Press, Chapel Hill 1967)
OCSC	THE OXFORD COMPANION TO THE SUPREME COURT OF THE UNITED STATES (Kermit L. Hall ed., Oxford University Press, New York 1992)
ODNB	OXFORD DICTIONARY OF NATIONAL BIOGRAPHY (H.C.G. Matthew & Brian Harrison eds., Oxford University Press, Oxford 2004) (60 vols.)
OHLE	R.H. HELMHOLZ, THE OXFORD HISTORY OF THE LAWS OF ENGLAND: THE CANON LAW AND ECCLESIASTICAL JURISDICTION FROM 597 TO THE 1640S, VOL. I (Oxford University Press, Oxford 2004)
	SIR JOHN H. BAKER, THE OXFORD HISTORY OF THE LAWS OF ENGLAND, VOL. VI, 1483–1558 (Oxford University Press, Oxford 2003)
OPEN PRESS	ROBERT W. T. MARTIN, THE FREE AND OPEN PRESS: THE FOUNDING OF AMERICAN DEMOCRATIC PRESS LIBERTY, 1640–1800 (New York University Press, New York 2001)
OPPOSITION	DONALD H. STEWART, THE OPPOSITION PRESS OF THE FEDERALIST PERIOD (State University of New York Press, Albany 1969)
ORIGINS-PARTIES	JOHN F. HOADLEY, ORIGINS OF AMERICAN POLITICAL PARTIES, 1789–1803 (University Press of Kentucky, Lexington 1986)
ORR	D. ALAN ORR, TREASON AND THE STATE: LAW, POLITICS, AND IDEOLOGY IN THE ENGLISH CIVIL WAR (Cambridge University Press, Cambridge 2002)

Oxford History	Penry Williams, The Later Tudors: England 1547–1603 (Clarendon Press, Oxford 1995) (New Oxford History of England vol.5) Julian Hoppit, A Land of Liberty? England 1689–1727 (Clarendon Press, Oxford 2000) (New Oxford History of England vol.7) Paul Langford, A Polite and Commercial People: England 1727–1783 (Clarendon Press, Oxford 1989) (New Oxford History of England vol.8)
Palmer	Robert C. Palmer, *The Federal Common Law of Crime*, 4 Law & History Review 267 (1986)
Pennsylvania	Harry M. Tinkcom, The Republicans and Federalists in Pennsylvania, 1790–1801: A Study in National Stimulus and Local Response (Harrisburg, Pennsylvania Historical and Museum Commission 1950)
Perilous Times	Geoffrey R. Stone, Perilous Times: Free Speech in Wartime, From the Sedition Act of 1798 to the War on Terrorism (Norton, New York 2004)
Pinckney	Marvin R. Zahniser, Charles Cotesworth Pinckney: Founding Father (University of North Carolina Press, Chapel Hill 1967)
Political Parties-N.Y.	Jabez D. Hammond, The History of Political Parties in the State of New York, from the Ratification of the Federal Constitution to December, 1840 (H. & E. Phinney, Cooperstown 1846) (3 vols.)
Prelude	Arthur M. Schlesinger, Prelude to Independence: The Newspaper War on Britain 1764–1776 (Vintage, New York 1965)
Press-Mass.	Clyde A. Duniway, The Development of Freedom of the Press in Massachusetts (Longmans, Green, New York 1906)
Preyer	Kathryn Preyer, *Jurisdiction To Punish: Federal Authority, Federalism and the Common Law of Crimes in the Early Republic*, 4 Law & History Review 223 (1986)

Printers	Jeffery A. Smith, Printers and Press Freedom: The Ideology of Early American Journalism (Oxford University Press, New York 1988)
Prologue	Lisle A. Rose, Prologue to Democracy: The Federalists in the South, 1789–1800 (University of Kentucky Press, Lexington 1968)
Reclaiming	William J. Watkins, Reclaiming the American Revolution: The Kentucky and Virginia Resolutions and Their Legacy (Palgrave Macmillan, New York 2004)
Repressive Jurisprudence	Phillip L. Blumberg, Repressive Jurisprudence in the Early American Republic: The First Amendment and the Legacy of English Law (Cambridge University Press, New York 2010)
Robbins	Caroline Robbins, The Eighteenth-Century Commonwealthman: Studies in the Transmission, Development, and Circumstance of English Liberal Thought from the Restoration of Charles II until the War with the Thirteen Colonies (rev. ed. Amagi Books, Indianapolis 2004, original Harvard University Press, Cambridge 1959)
Rudé	George Rudé, Wilkes and Liberty: A Social Study of 1763 to 1774 (Clarendon Press, Oxford 1962)
Rutledge	James A. Haw, John and Edward Rutledge of South Carolina (University of Georgia Press, Athens 1997)
Rutledge, Jr.	Robert K. Ratzlaff, John Rutledge, Jr., South Carolina Federalist, 1766–1819 (1975) (unpublished Ph.D. dissertation, University of Kansas)
Saving	Stephen B. Presser & Becky B. Hurley, *Saving God's Republic: The Jurisprudence of Samuel Chase*, 1984 University of Illinois Law Review 771

SECURING	RICHARD BUEL, SECURING THE REVOLUTION: IDEOLOGY IN AMERICAN POLITICS, 1789–1815 (Cornell University Press, Ithaca 1972)
SOUTH CAROLINA	J. HAROLD WOLFE, JEFFERSONIAN DEMOCRACY IN SOUTH CAROLINA (University of North Carolina Press, Chapel Hill 1940)
THOMAS	PETER D.G. THOMAS, JOHN WILKES: A FRIEND TO LIBERTY (Clarendon Press, Oxford 1996)
TRANSATLANTIC	MARY SARAH BILDER, THE TRANSATLANTIC CONSTITUTION: COLONIAL LEGAL CULTURE AND THE EMPIRE (Harvard University Press, Cambridge 2004)
TUCK	RICHARD TUCK, NATURAL RIGHTS THEORIES: THEIR ORIGIN AND DEVELOPMENT (Cambridge University Press, Cambridge 1979)
TYRANNY	JEFFREY L. PASLEY, "THE TYRANNY OF PRINTERS": NEWSPAPER POLITICS IN THE EARLY AMERICAN REPUBLIC (University Press of Virginia, Charlottesville 2001)
VALLANCE	EDWARD VALLANCE, A RADICAL HISTORY OF BRITAIN: VISIONARIES, REBELS AND REVOLUTIONARIES (Little Brown, London 2009)
WARREN	CHARLES WARREN, THE SUPREME COURT IN UNITED STATES HISTORY (rev. ed. Little, Brown, Boston 1926) (2 vols.)
WILSON	MARK D. HALL, THE POLITICAL AND LEGAL PHILOSOPHY OF JAMES WILSON, 1742–1798 (University of Missouri Press, Columbia 1997)
ZUCKERT	MICHAEL P. ZUCKERT, NATURAL RIGHTS AND THE NEW REPUBLICANISM (Princeton University Press, Princeton 1994)

INDEX

www.ingramcontent.com/pod-product-compliance
Lightning Source LLC
Chambersburg PA
CBHW031547021026
52493CB00002B/88
9780190461621